P9-AFP-695

Paradise Found

STEVE NICHOLLS

Paradise Found

Nature in America at the

Time of Discovery

The University of Chicago Press   *Chicago & London*

Steve Nicholls possesses a unique talent for capturing nature, which until now has been used traveling the United States, Canada, and the Caribbean shooting wildlife films for viewers in the United States and Europe, including *Alien Empire* (PBS's award-winning series on insects), *Land of the Eagle,* and *Atlantic Realm.* He has also been a producer for a number of series on PBS's *Nature.* He holds a Ph.D. in entomology from the University of Bristol.

The University of Chicago Press, Chicago 60637
The University of Chicago Press, Ltd., London
© 2009 by Steve Nicholls
All rights reserved. Published 2009
Printed in the United States of America

18 17 16 15 14 13 12 11 10 09   1 2 3 4 5

ISBN-13: 978-0-226-58340-2 (cloth)
ISBN-10: 0-226-58340-6 (cloth)

Library of Congress
Cataloging-in-Publication Data

Nicholls, Steve
   Paradise found : nature in America at the time of
discovery / Steve Nicholls
      p.   cm.
   Includes index.
   ISBN-13: 978-0-226-58340-2 (cloth : alk. paper)
   ISBN-10: 0-226-58340-6 (cloth)
      1. Natural history—North America 2. North
America—Discovery and exploration. 3. Nature—
Effect of human beings on—North America—History.
4. North America—Environmental conditions—History.
I. Title.
   QH102.N53   2009
   508.7—dc22

                                              2008036076

For my parents,
Joan (1922–2008) and Ron:
For never questioning the need
to fill the family home with a
menagerie of wildlife.

Contents

Acknowledgments *ix*

1 A Different World *1*

2 The Discovery of Paradise *8*

3 Abundant Ocean *21*

4 Sea of Whales *45*

5 Living in Paradise *67*

6 Angels from the North *93*

7 Earthly Paradise or Earthly Hades? *106*

8 Poll, Ben, and Martha *143*

9 Souls and Furs *171*

10 Gathering of Waters *192*

11 A Sea of Islands *226*

12 Islands in the Sea *252*

13 La Florida *274*

14 . . . To Shining Sea *298*

15 Blessings Fit for the Use of Man *336*

16 Rivers of Fish *359*

17 Wilderness Cathedral *372*

18 The Great Stillness *396*

19 Devils in Paradise *426*

20 A New World? *450*

Notes *461*

Index *495*

Acknowledgments

This book has drawn on more than twenty years of traveling around North America. In that time I've been privileged to work with a great many experts in so many areas it would be impossible to thank them all individually, but that doesn't lesson my gratitude to all the scientists, park rangers, refuge managers, historians, re-enactors, and anthropologists who have happily shared their work and life experiences.

In particular I would like to thank Steve Burns, then of the Discovery Channel, now at National Geographic Channel, for his insightful comments over a fine lunch in Bethesda, when he told me about some Caribbean pirate manuscripts he had read and that described the enormous numbers of turtles in the seventeenth-century Caribbean. We discussed the possibility of structuring a film around such ideas, and that led me to see the history of North America's wildlife in a new light.

I had been interested in the "history" part of North American natural history for some time, since I worked on a TV series in the late 1980s for the BBC and PBS called *Land of the Eagle*. So I would also like to thank Peter Crawford, the series producer, for giving me the chance to work on that groundbreaking project, which began the journey that ended with this book.

The main consultant on the series, and author of the companion book, was Robert Peck, of the Philadelphia Academy of Natural Sciences, whose expertise combines both history and natural history in equal measure. His perspective on North America's natural world in no small way influenced my own explorations of the continent over the subsequent decades.

I would also like to thank my good friend Stephen Harris, professor of environmental sciences at the University of Bristol, for helping to flesh out the central thesis of this book—that nature was far more abundant in the past than anyone really credits. His extensive knowledge and passion for the subject convinced me that such an idea was worth bringing to wider public attention.

The story of North America's natural history is intimately tied up with that of the continent's original inhabitants, and I am extremely grateful for the time I have spent with Lee Miller, of Kaw descent but also anthropologist, author, TV researcher and writer, and environmentalist. Her knowledge of Indian affairs, current and historical, is unsurpassed and her energy boundless. I always enjoy our discussions, whether on reservations around the United States or back here in the United Kingdom while she was researching her own book on Roanoke. These discussions were invaluable in helping me see a balanced and realistic view of Indian America, past and present.

In all my travels around the continent I rarely traveled alone. As a wildlife film producer, I rely on the skill and expertise of wildlife cameramen, and two in particular have shared many of the moments I describe in the following pages, Kevin Flay and Ian McCarthy. I'm grateful for the good company and friendship of both of these talented people.

And on the subject of friends and good company, I thank Bill Duyck for his unending hospitality and enthusiasm. His knowledge of the plants and birds of the southern Appalachians (as well as of the best places to eat breakfast) is both vast and infectious and in no small measure responsible for the fact that I now see that corner of North Carolina as a second home.

Thanks to Stuart Booth for his initial support of the project and for using his wide knowledge of the international book market to introduce me to Edward Knappman at New England Publishing Associates. I'm extremely grateful to Ed for his enthusiasm over the first few chapters and for representing the project to publishers.

Thanks to Christie Henry at the University of Chicago Press for her unending encouragement and enthusiasm for this project, especially when the light at either end of the tunnel was too far away to be seen.

Thanks also to my colleagues John Capener and Amirah Barri, in our production company, Burning Gold, for their patience and for help with unearthing some of the research materials.

And finally thanks also to my wife Vicky Coules, cofounder of Burning Gold, for unfailing support and for reading and commenting on the manuscripts as well as for knowing when a decent cabernet sauvignon was the only thing to keep the project on course.

CHAPTER 1

A *Different World*

For the last twenty-five years I've been in the happy position of earning my living by making natural history films, traveling the world to search out the rare and intriguing, working closely with local experts, from indigenous people to dedicated scientists, to bring stories from the natural world to as wide an audience as possible. Before that I've always been a naturalist, as far back into my childhood as I can remember, but, despite a lifetime of hands-on experience, nature frequently still surprises me, usually when I least expect it.

One such occasion occurred in Hungary, not long after it first peeked out from behind the iron curtain. Early in the morning I was driving toward the Kiskunsági Nemzeti Park when the urge to drink coffee forced me to pull over just outside a small village in the middle of what looked like undistinguished flat farmland. As I unfolded myself from the small and cramped metal box that passed for a car, I was assaulted by a wall of sound. Well, perhaps most people would find that a slight exaggeration, but my ears are tuned by a lifetime's habit to hear birdsong, and what they heard on that day was truly spectacular.

Back home, in the southwest of England, the dawn choristers can certainly produce a wonderful performance, but I was astounded by the sheer volume and variety of those singers on the edge of the Hungarian Plain, a landscape superficially quite similar to that around my home. Thanks to the poverty of farmers unable to afford trailer loads of insecticides, herbicides, and fertilizers, I had just taken a step backward in time. As I sipped at a cupful of bitter brown liquid, I realized that my own backyard must once have sounded the same. And before I reached the bottom of the cup, my mind had wandered off around the planet, in contemplation of what nature must have been like a century ago, two centuries ago, five centuries ago. But just how different was this world of the past?

Most people are aware of recent extinctions: dodos from Mauritius, thylacines from Tasmania, great auks from the North Atlantic, passenger pigeons from North America. When you add to the tally all those obscure insects, spiders, mollusks, worms, and the rest, it is clear that the actions of humanity are drastically reducing the number of players in the game of life. Yet it is not all these missing species, these "gaps in nature" as Australian scientist Tim Flannery has called them,[1] which make the natural world look so different now. If we really did have a time machine, I'm convinced it would be the sheer abundance of life that would startle any time traveler.

This is a much more elusive concept than extinction. Since extinction is an all or nothing event, you know, quite simply, that you will never see a living, breathing dodo or great auk. Abundance, on the other hand, is more subjective, reflected in something that has been called the "changing baseline syndrome."[2] When, as children, we first become aware of our environment, we assume that what we see around us is the normal state of affairs. From that starting point, judging changes over our individual lifetimes is difficult enough; childhood summers always seemed warmer, butterflies more numerous, with more birds' nests and lizards to find. And maybe that really was the case. However, we are judging any changes against a different baseline from our parents, which is different again from our grandparents, and since we have no direct experience of *their* childhood baselines, our perception of how much has changed, our "gut feeling," must be somewhat incomplete. Over ten or twenty generations, the baseline can drift, unnoticed by most, until we step out of our time machine to stare openmouthed at a world we had no idea ever existed.

In the following chapters, I will paint a picture of what this world looked like in one particular corner of our planet: the North American continent. This is no arbitrary decision. It's a part of the world I know well; over the last twenty-five years, I've worked in nearly all the American states and Canadian provinces. But, more importantly, the changes that have so dramatically altered our world have been played out relatively recently here. It's only a little over five hundred years since European explorers stepped on to the shores of the Americas, and they've left us a vast legacy of documents that described the world they found, records that conjure up images of an extraordinary place, teeming with life.

Such visions of Paradise need to be seen through the filter of their historical context, since some were undoubtedly exaggerated, either for political or commercial reasons or simply for personal aggrandizement. Yet taken together, they do create a coherent picture of a very different world, and modern science points toward a similar conclusion. In the following pages, I will use recent advances in disciplines as varied as archaeology and molecular biology, to flesh out those firsthand historical descriptions. And the picture that all these sources illuminate is a startling one. In comparison to today, nature was vastly, almost unimaginably, more abundant, a perception that is key to understanding our modern relationship with the natural world. From fisheries management to the history of modern societies, the past abundance of nature turns out to be a crucial factor.

Humans, for all our technical ingenuity, are still firmly rooted in the natural world, yet the role that nature has played in shaping our history is often underplayed. In the first half of the twentieth century, ecologist and writer Aldo Leopold, often seen as the father of wildlife management, saw that history needed an ecological interpretation. Yet it is only in the last few decades that the interplay of nature and history has begun to be analyzed in a systematic way, giving birth to the discipline of environmental history.[3] Understanding history is crucial to understanding the present and in planning the future. But, as a biologist, I would contend that all history is environmental. Every person ever born had to eat, and our ever-growing numbers depend on our waste products being recycled. Every action we take has some effect on the rest of nature, so we are as firmly entangled in the web of life as any other life form on the planet, whatever the view from a city apartment might look like.

Environmental historian Donald Worster has echoed Leopold's call but has also pointed out that to write an accurate environmental history means understanding nature not just in the present but in the past.[4] So picturing this different natural world of the past is not just an idle exercise in speculation; it is vital in understanding our interactions with the rest of nature, a relationship on which—whether we like it or not—our ultimate survival depends.

Not that we are the first generation to notice that things have changed, or to try to create an image in our mind's eye of what the past might have looked like. In 1633, English traveler William Wood collected his observations on the landscapes of New England into a book called *New England's Prospect*. Wood described a land full of huge trees; luscious wild strawberries, currants, and gooseberries; vast forests teeming with a large variety of birds and mammals; and rivers so full of fish as to defy imagination. More than two hundred years later, naturalist, writer, and philosopher Henry David Thoreau came to live in these forests, at a place called Walden Pond, not far from his birthplace in Concord, Massachusetts. He had decided to live here alone in order to experience the wilderness firsthand, to learn to live deeply or as Thoreau himself puts it: "I went to the woods because I wished to live deliberately, to front only the essential facts of life, and see if I could not learn what it had to teach, and not, when I came to die, discover that I had not lived."

He so enjoyed the experience that he stayed in his isolated cabin for two years and later gathered his thoughts into what became one of America's great classics of nature writing, *Walden*. During that time he came to know the woods of Massachusetts intimately. But later, when he picked up a copy of *New England's Prospects* he realized that his Walden wilderness was anything but. New England's prospect had changed considerably, and in a plaintive moment of realization, he wrote in his journal: "Is it not a maimed and imperfect nature that I am conversant with?"

One reason for writing this book is simply to evoke an image of a wonderfully different world, before it was "maimed," but that would be to grossly oversimplify the story. Inevitably such a picture raises two related questions that I will also address: why was it like this, and why isn't it now? The answers to these apparently simple questions are often surprising and will overturn some widely held beliefs. They will also take us into the intriguing area of human ecology in its broadest sense, a discipline that must draw on anthropology, social history, economics, and biology in equal measure.

Columbus didn't discover America; he simply ran into a continent already occupied by countless nations as varied in their lives as the ecology of the land they occupied. And, though many people still see the world that Columbus blundered into as pristine wilderness, the native people of the New World had long since wrought great changes in their land. This image of a land untrammeled by humans is such a powerful one that it became enshrined in American law when President Lyndon B. Johnson signed into existence the Wilderness Act, allowing Congress to declare large blocks of land as "wilderness," in which, as well as other restrictions, no motorized vehicles or commercial activities are allowed. The purpose of the Act is, in its own words, "to assure that an increasing population, accompanied by expanding settlement and growing mechanization, does not occupy and modify all areas within the United States and its possessions, leaving no lands designated for preservation and protection in their natural condition, it is hereby declared to be the policy of the Congress to secure for the American people of present and future generations the benefits of an enduring resource of wilderness." But what was the "natural condition" of the land? Certainly not the land that Columbus "discovered." Columbus described the land he saw as "Paradise," but he didn't mean it was a virgin wilderness since he also described it as highly populated. Likewise, many of the areas now declared as wilderness under the Act were heavily managed by Indians and then later transformed again by European settlers. The Wilderness Act is an admirable sentiment, and any law protecting land from rampant development is to be applauded, but it is based on a fundamental misunderstanding of past human ecology in North America, a view that has been termed the "Pristine Myth."[5]

Yet this is still an oversimplification. The North American continent was vast, and population densities varied dramatically across different landscapes. Consequently, the effects of Indian management, intentional or otherwise, varied considerably. It is certainly true that the first explorers found a natural world of overwhelming abundance, but the extent to which this a truly "natural" abundance is another theme of this book.

It is also true that vast tracts of the continent were transformed quickly and dramatically after 1492. The reasons behind the overwhelming impact of the European invasion of the Americas and the subsequent sweeping changes that followed are also, ultimately, to be found in the different ecological relationships of people on the two continents. This intriguing story has been unraveled by Jared Diamond and summarized succinctly in the title of his book *Guns, Germs and Steel*.

In essence, thanks to their living on the largest land mass on the planet, endowed with a particularly suitable collection of plants and animals, humans on Eurasia were able to domesticate a larger variety of plants and animals than those on other continents. Eurasia was also unusual in its predominantly east-west axis, important because domesticates and associated knowledge could easily be transferred along zones of similar latitude and therefore similar ecology to fuel a kind of autocatalysis and a spectacular increase in both population and technology.

In Africa, and even more so in the New World, the essentially north-south orientation of the land masses produced bands of vastly different ecological zones that stopped such a rapid spread of agriculture. Built on the back of expanding agriculture, the more sophisticated technology of Eurasians translated into far superior weapons when they came face to face with the inhabitants of the New World. But the best weapon at their disposal was one they were unaware of—at least at first. Living in close proximity to a large variety of domestic animals, Eurasians became infected with a whole range of diseases that had jumped species and to which they gradually accumulated resistance. With no such long-term exposure, whole nations in the New World were wiped out by devastating epidemics when East met West. These factors set the stage for the inevitable transformation of the New World, but how that transformation actually happened is the final theme I will explore in the following pages.

The expansion of Europe into North America took place at a time when a new way of seeing the world was evolving in Europe, which is broadly encapsulated by the term "capitalism." The origins of capitalism have been much discussed but it's only recently that the role of ecology had begun to be incorporated into such ideas. According to environmentalist Jonathon Porritt, this philosophy of continual economic growth, a need for ever-increasing prosperity, is a relatively new phenomenon.[6] Yet, its roots must run deep into prehistory, since, by definition, capitalism depends on the ability to accumulate capital and that only became possible when agriculture allowed humans to accumulate the most basic form of capital, surplus food, which could be traded for some form of currency.

The path that led to the modern capitalist paradigm of a free market economy seems to have begun sometime in the Middle Ages, though the forces that drove its birth remain unclear.[7] Did medieval peasants laboring under a feudal system for their lords eventually degrade the land, forcing the evolution of a new kind of economy, or did capitalist entrepreneurs slowly force this philosophy on a reluctant society? These questions are beyond the scope of this book. However, the subsequent evolution of capitalism in North America emerges with startling clarity from the wealth of historical documents describing the reactions of Europeans to the different world they encountered on the far side of the Atlantic. The hugely abundant natural world of North America provided the raw capital to fuel the birth of new nations. Those same historical documents that allow us to build up a picture of past natural abundance also provide a stark and sobering illustration of the last five hundred years of our relationship with nature.

Environmental historian Donald Worster considers that one of the key ideas implicit in American history is that America was built in a rediscovered Garden of Eden, a Paradise of plenty.[8] There are certainly plenty of "Edens," "Paradises," and "Gardens" scattered across the states, and such towns and cities continue the tradition of the very first European visitors to the New World who frequently described what they found as Paradise, often embellished to encourage others to follow. Yet in five hundred years, we have, in the words of Joni Mitchell, "paved Paradise, and put up a parking lot."

In the following chapters, I will describe the world that Europeans encountered when they crossed the Atlantic, their reactions to it, and the reasons for their subsequent impact. This long view of humans and nature will raise some important questions. How different were the relationships and attitudes of the original inhabitants of North America from the newcomers? What role did that play in the subsequent history of the continent? What can such a deep perspective bring to our modern environmental crises, and therefore how should an understanding of past abundance affect our approach to conservation?

I have arranged the chapters by environment, though with an eye to the broad sweep of historical exploration. Thus we start on the Atlantic coast and finish on the Great Plains. Each chapter is also structured around the chronology of discovery, exploration and exploitation of that environment though as an *ecological* history I have allowed biology to dictate the detailed structure where appropriate.

I have purposefully included a wealth of detail, partly because the stories are both intriguing and revealing and partly because the interactions of humanity with the rest of nature are varied and complex and only fully understandable at this level. It's always tempting to make sweeping statements and create digestible sound bites; it's the world I live in, working in television. But that would do this story no justice. The devil, as we shall see, is in the detail. However, some underlying themes will emerge, and I will collate these in a final chapter, but if the book has one central message, it is that life—all life—is complicated and therefore, even in limitless abundance, fragile and wonderfully, endlessly fascinating.

CHAPTER 2

The Discovery of Paradise

At first sight, the coasts of Labrador and Newfoundland are bleak, inhospitable places. It's a sobering thought that if not for the Gulf Stream, that great river in the North Atlantic conveying heat from the tropics to the shores of Europe, we Britons would share this climate. But these places aren't that bad. This barren-looking scenery refreshes the soul; here a human can understand his place in the world. Nothing can hide from a searching Newfoundland wind, not even the arrogance of a species that thinks itself master of all it surveys.

Besides, these places are far from barren; you just need to know where to look. All you need to do is smell the wind, laced with the pungent aroma of ammonia. Follow your nose to the cliff tops and a cacophony of grunts and squeals rises to greet you. There below you the rocky stacks are crowded with gannets, perched on every available space. Riding the wind on elegant, ink-dipped wings, returning birds hang motionless in the air over their mates, until they're sure they've found the right spot, a familiar call among the symphony. But, as impressive as the smell and din always is in these colonies, it was once even more impressive. Some of the largest seabird colonies in the world used to exist around the coasts and islands of northeast America. A French explorer in the mid-1500s once declared: "All the ships of France might load a cargo of them without once perceiving that any had been removed."[1]

And there's a good reason for such unimaginable numbers of birds; the seas and shores around these colonies used to be filled with an equally inconceivable abundance of fish. It was these teeming shoals that drew Europeans here in the fifteenth century, but our first glimpse into this crowded ocean didn't come from French or English explorers, nor even from the Spanish who, to most people, were seen as the first to encounter the New World. They're found in two Norse sagas that date to nearly five hundred years before Columbus blundered into the Caribbean. These first recorded encounters don't tell us a great deal about the ecology of the New World, but they do introduce us to the story of the Atlantic salmon, which is a good illustration of the way history interacts with biology and introduces many of the broad themes that will recur throughout the following chapters.

The Vikings were unrivalled in their seamanship and exploration. By the middle of the 800s, they had begun to settle Iceland, though when they first got there, the island was already populated by Irish monks, who promptly left to find peace and quiet elsewhere. For the Vikings, in the long term, Iceland turned out to be a staging post as well as a new homeland. They pushed further west and had established colonies in Greenland by the tenth century, almost on the doorstep of the American continent.

How they made the final step to the New World is recorded in two sagas, *The Saga of the Greenlanders* and *The Saga of Eirik the Red*. The Norse and Icelandic sagas are actually just elaborate family histories, with a touch of adventure for added effect, so they don't always dwell on the natural wonders that these early explorers must have found. And although these two sagas, which describe the same events, disagree in details, they nevertheless provide tantalizing glimpses into the North American continent long before major European contact.

The story begins in the closing years of the first millennium in Norway, from where Eirik had just made a hurried departure to escape punishment for murder. His plan was to settle in the now-thriving colony in Iceland, but it didn't take him long to become unpopular there as well. He gained his name "Red" from the color of his hair, but it might just as well have been from the trail of blood he left behind. When he became involved in a local feud and decided that life in Iceland was also getting just a little too hot, he remembered that a friend called Gunnbiorn had once run into a landmass to the west of Iceland after being blown off course. Eirik decided it would be expedient to go and find it, and to settle there if he could. He did find land and returned to pick up volunteers for his settlement. He decided to call the place Greenland, perhaps an attempt to make it sound more attractive to potential settlers, just as the first colonists in America half a millennium later would send back descriptions of Paradise to encourage expansion of their own settlements in the New World.

Eirik's simple publicity stunt obviously worked. These hardy Norse souls did indeed manage to build several settlements along the southwest coast of Greenland. Among deep fjords that would have reminded them of Norway, they found places where sheltered harbors led up to fertile pastures for their tough little cattle. In addition, the coasts to the north were alive with seals and walrus. Offshore there were great shoals of fish and whales and on land plenty of ducks and caribou, so it didn't take long for a regular trade to build up between Eirik's Greenland, Iceland, and Norway. They traded whale and seal oil or eider duck feathers for such staples of life that they couldn't provide for themselves in their remote colonies on the edge of the known world. The success of these colonies depended on regular communication with Iceland and mainland Europe, and that meant sea traffic through difficult and often dangerous waters. Sooner or later something was bound to go wrong.

It did, and it happened to one of history's unsung heroes, a man by the name of Bjarni Herjolffson. The details of his story are preserved in only one of the sagas, *The Saga of the Greenlanders,* which tells how he was blown off course as he sailed between Iceland and Greenland. He eventually sighted land, which most now agree was somewhere along America's northeast coast. He sailed north along this coast, making his way back toward Greenland, but he never bothered to land. If he had, history might have been kinder in recording him as the first undisputed European discoverer of the New World. As it happens, that honor is usually given to Leif Ericsson, son of Eirik the Red, who decided to follow up on Bjarni's discoveries fifteen years later.

So, in the early years of the second millennium, we get our first glimpse into the nature of North America. Around AD 1000, Leif sailed west from Greenland and encountered land. At first he wasn't impressed. He found a barren land of flat stones, which he called *Helluland*—"slab land." It is now generally agreed that this was Baffin Island, and Leif's description is still a good summary of the place today. Sailing south, things improved. Next he landed at *Mark-land*—"wood land"—covered in fine, large trees. Two days sailing further to the south and west, Leif stopped and built houses ready to overwinter in this strange land. The abundance they found soon impressed them. "There was no lack of salmon in the river or the lake, bigger salmon than they had ever seen. The country seemed to them so kind that no winter fodder would be needed for livestock; there was never any frost all winter and the grass hardly withered at all."[2]

So where were they? The general consensus was that they had landed some-where on the coast of Labrador or Newfoundland, which makes their descriptions of the mild winters sound like a bit more Paradise publicity. However, the reason that the Vikings had been able to colonize Greenland successfully was that they did so during a period of climatic warming, so perhaps the coasts of Labrador and Newfoundland were less bleak than they seem today. Some flesh was put on the bare bones of the sagas in 1960 when, nearly a thousand years after Leif Ericsson, two more Norwegians landed on the coast of Newfoundland. Helge Ingstad and his wife, Anne, were both archaeologists, searching for evidence of their distant ancestors in the New World. What they found was astounding.[3]

A local fisherman told them of an ancient settlement long thought to have been made by Indians. But when the Ingstads visited this site, at l'Anse aux Meadows on the very northern tip of the island of Newfoundland, they saw the unmistakable outlines of Viking long houses, familiar from their work back home in Norway. If that wasn't convincing enough, they returned in successive years to excavate the site and found evidence of iron smelting, something no Indian had even heard of before 1492. Carbon 14 dating from the iron hearths gave figures around AD 900–1070, so it seemed the story was closed. L'Anse aux Meadows was the reality behind the sagas. But the saga isn't finished yet.

The Saga of the Greenlanders describes another discovery that caused some consternation among later scholars. One of the party wandered away from the settlement and, when he returned, reported that he'd found the place festooned with wild grapes. There's nothing too astounding about this. Many later explorers found the trees along the east coast covered in a dense growth of vines sporting wild grapes finer than any in Europe's vineyards. The abundance of wild grapes impressed the Norsemen so much that Leif Ericsson called this area *Vinland* or "Wine-land." But no wild grapes grow in the far north of Newfoundland today. Does this make l'Anse aux Meadows unlikely as Leif's first settlement? Perhaps, though the Vikings were exploring during a period of warmer climate that probably meant that the range of many plants and animals, including wild grapes, extended further north. So did the sagatellers leave any more clues?

Leif thoughtfully measured the day length at the winter solstice, which gives a good indication of latitude. "In this country, night and day were of more even length than in either Greenland or Iceland; on the shortest day of the year the sun was already up by 9 am and did not set until after 3 pm."[4] This should put the general location beyond doubt, but the translation above is deceptively simple. Actually, Leif recorded the sun's position using arcane Viking terminology, and the translation into a specific latitude involves complex calculations and a few assumptions that have led to suggestions for Vinland being as far south as Florida! Other calculations point to a location somewhere to the south of the Gulf of St. Lawrence, and well within the range of *Vitis riparia,* the most widespread of a score of wild grape species that grow across America. *V. riparia* pushes north into New Brunswick and northern Quebec, so perhaps Leif's first settlement was around the Bay of Fundy, along the coasts of Nova Scotia or New Brunswick.

The abundance and size of the fish they recorded doesn't help. We'll see from later descriptions that all the rivers and lakes down the east coast were choked with so many fish that it left those early explorers lost for words. So it seems the exact location of Vinland must remain a mystery, though in a way it doesn't matter. We can still stand with those brave Norsemen, somewhere on the northeast coast of the continent, and see a vitality of nature already gone from most parts of Europe.

We can imagine that small party standing on the banks of a river, staring at water alive with the flashing silver backs of Atlantic salmon. Most of the fish are huge, on average around twenty-five pounds each, but there are plenty that are easily twice this size. They must measure four or five feet from head to tail. It's the height of a late summer run, up river to spawning grounds on exposed gravel beds, and the river is almost solid with fish. It looks as if you could cross without getting your feet wet. These fish were born in this river but have spent the last year or two at sea, feeding and growing. Now they are returning with an almost unerring accuracy to that same river again to lay their own eggs and continue a cycle that began at the end of the last ice age. Many will die after spawning, though a fair proportion will survive to swim to sea again and return to spawn in later years. Atlantic salmon also run up the rivers of Scandinavia, so the sights in Labrador must have been spectacular indeed to have been worthy of recording in the sagas.

Behind the Norsemen, the setting sun is now filtered through arching branches of massive trees, hung with curtains of purple grapes. The vines scramble up every tree, disappearing into the fading light. With the light finally gone, the Norsemen huddle close to their fire, warming themselves against an early fall chill that descends with startling suddenness as soon as the sun disappears behind the unknown land to the west. But none can sleep. The noise coming from the river is almost deafening, like the applause of a vast unseen crowd. The giant salmon are leaping over each other, over cataracts, over and over, falling back into the water with great splashes.

What the Norsemen couldn't have known was that this was being repeated for many hundreds of miles up and down the coast; by one estimate, three thousand such rivers provided hundreds of thousands of spawning beds for an incalculable number of Atlantic salmon.[5] Certainly, Atlantic salmon would have run up the rivers as far south as the Housatonic, which flows into Long Island Sound, not far from New York City. To the north, they ran in numbers all the way up to Ungava Bay, on the Canadian mainland opposite Baffin Island.

And this spectacle would repeat itself year after year. Seven centuries after the Norsemen left these shores, Nicolas Denys also has sleepless nights on the Miramichi River flowing through New Brunswick in Canada:

> So large a quantity of salmon enters the river at night one is unable to sleep, so great is the noise they make in falling upon the water after having thrown or darted themselves into the air passing over the river flats.
>
> I found a little river which I named Riviere au Saulmon. . . . I made a cast of the seine net at its entrance where it took so great a quantity of salmon that ten men could not haul it to land and . . . had it not broken the salmon would have carried it off. We had a boat full of them, the smallest three feet long.[6]

Salmon were still hugely abundant when the New England colony had grown from its beginnings as a handful of starving pilgrims, and it's said that servants along the Connecticut River would only work on the condition that they were *not* fed salmon on more than two occasions each week. As splendid a comment as this is on the abundance of salmon, Robert Behnke, who wrote a definitive work on trout and salmon in North America,[7] can find no basis in fact for what has become an often repeated myth. Nevertheless, it doesn't alter the fact that, from Long Island Sound to Ungava Bay, Atlantic salmon abounded.

In 1770, George Cartwright, recently retired from the army, sailed from England to Labrador to set up trading posts for fur and fish. The sheltered harbor where he started his enterprise still bears his name. The community of Cartwright, population 628, stands on the eastern side of Sandwich Bay, not far from thirty-three miles of pristine sandy beach that was impressive enough for Leif Ericsson to call it *Wonderstrand*. It's still an amazing place a thousand years later. There are large gannet, puffin, and guillemot colonies within a few miles, and Cartwright claims to have the best fly-fishing for Atlantic salmon anywhere in the world. While that claim might be disputed by some, salmon were certainly one of the things that drew George Cartwright here over two hundred years ago. And he kept meticulous records, not just of his salmon operation but of all the wildlife in the area.

For someone trying to earn his living from fish, Labrador must have seemed like Paradise indeed. The salmon runs in the White Bear River were so dense that George reckoned "a ball could not be fired into the water without striking a salmon."[8] Between June 23 and July 20 on one river he and his three companions killed 12,396 salmon, and they felt they could have killed thirty thousand if they had left their nets out.[9] Elsewhere, fishermen only gave up catching salmon when they ran out of salt to preserve the fish. Whatever the modern community of Cartwright boasts about its salmon fishing, I doubt it's anything like it used to be.

But Atlantic salmon, on both sides of the ocean, have had a hard time of it since George's day. They disappeared totally from many rivers in both Europe and America. I remember the fanfares that greeted the first salmon for many years to brave the River Tees in Middlesbrough, in northeast England, the town where I grew up. The lower Tees is hemmed in by industry: a tangle of chemical works, steel foundries, and docks. They all emptied waste into the river, and although the upper reaches, with their bare gravel spawning beds, still flowed cool and clear through the dales of Yorkshire and Durham, the toxic concoction near the river mouth was as effective as any physical barrier in preventing the salmon from running upstream. And, to return to the rivers of their birth, salmon use the unique aroma of their particular river, percolating through salt water, drifting on ocean currents, to find their way. What rivers like the Tees and many others must have smelled like to the salmon's sensitive nose is anyone's guess. I spent many of my weekends watching birds on the Tees Estuary in the early 1970s, and the air there smelled bad enough to my insensitive human nose. To fall into the river around here meant a trip to hospital and an undignified encounter with a stomach pump. So any salmon foolish enough to come too close, even if it could have detected the delicate scent of Teesdale on the water, would soon have gasped its last.

Huge efforts have been made since then to clean up many of these rivers, and salmon have responded. Although most salmon return to the rivers where they hatched, a very small percentage—the Leif Ericssons of the salmon world—explore new territory. These pioneering fish can naturally recolonize rivers, even if all the river's native fish have long since been eliminated. Thus, the first salmon in living memory returned to the Mersey, in northwestern England, in 2001. By then eighty to a hundred salmon per season were being reported in the higher reaches of the Tees, so presumably many more were running the gauntlet of the concrete and steel-fringed estuary. Similarly, salmon began to run once more in the rivers of Newfoundland and New Brunswick, Nova Scotia, and Quebec. But what happened to transform astonishment at limitless abundance into mere delight at the sight of a few hundred? It wasn't entirely the fault of George Cartwright.

The problem is that there are lots of ways to kill salmon. Certainly, George and his fellow commercial fishermen contributed. Before the early 1700s, there wasn't much interest in actually eating the salmon, but they were hauled out of the river to feed hogs or dumped in their thousands on the fields as a substitute for manure. It's often said that the first settlers in New England were shown how to grow crops by the Indians, who taught them to bury a fish as fertilizer in a mound of earth, before planting it with corn. If so, the Indians can have only stared on in disbelief at the profligate enthusiasm with which later settlers adopted this practice.

Then, after about 1700, Europe developed a taste for salted or smoked salmon. This huge market supported men like Cartwright in growing numbers, and by the end of the eighteenth century some estimates put the total salmon exports from North America in excess of 30 million pounds each and every year.[10] Massive seine nets spread across the entrances to rivers mopped up most of the fish trying to enter. Often the numbers were so great that the nets simply burst. But being caught for human or hog consumption or as substitute manure wasn't the only problem facing salmon.

To support the expansion of towns and cities along the east coast, rivers were being dammed and water mills built. Then, later, iron smelters and tanneries began to pollute the pristine waters. Finally, as the human population grew, ever-increasing quantities of sewage flowed into the rivers, so both physical and chemical barriers began to impede any fish that escaped the nets. The Connecticut River lost its salmon to a dam in 1798, presumably a cause for great celebration among the working people there, if they really were trying to avoid overdosing on fish. And still the problems for salmon mounted. Wood was needed for ever-expanding building, so sawmills sprang up to serve each new township. Great rafts of logs were floated down river and destroyed the gravel spawning beds. Any that survived often ended up buried in sawdust from the lumber mills. Salmon can only spawn in clean gravel, so the few that finally made it upstream usually found they'd made a wasted journey.

In the late 1800s, a new market, in tinned salmon, stimulated the fishery, and since most of the rivers near the big population centers in New England had lost their fish, the last wild rivers of the Labrador coast were soon being plundered. The writing was on the wall. A few farsighted people could see what was happening, though, as still happens today, no one took much notice until it was way too late. One of the most eloquent of these observers was an English visitor to Canada around 1870 named John Rowan. "Thirty years ago, the salmon fishing in Nova Scotia was superb. But where nature is so bountiful in her gifts man rarely appreciates them. It would really seem that Nova Scotians hate the salmon. Overfishing is bad enough, but to shut the fish out of the rivers is little better that insanity. . . . By and by, when the forests have been destroyed and the rivers rendered barren, Canadians will spend large sums of money in, perhaps, fruitless efforts to bring back that which they could now so easily retain."[11] How right he was. In Great Britain alone, the cost of cleaning up just the sewage has climbed to over £30 billion. Industry has had to spend billions more to clean up its act.

But there's one final twist in the salmon's tale. Despite well-publicized returns to once-polluted rivers, Atlantic salmon populations have fallen dramatically over the last few decades right around the ocean. In November 2000, Maine, the only U.S. state with any remaining wild salmon runs, listed several of its distinctive genetic stocks as endangered. And not before time. As few as fifty fish may have returned to these rivers the year before. Six months later, in May 2001, the Committee on the State of Endangered Wildlife in Canada met to declare Atlantic salmon in the Bay of Fundy endangered.

Paradoxically, *Salmo salar* is much more common now than it ever was in the days of Leif Ericsson or George Cartwright, and it lives in many more places around the world, but these aren't the powerful fish flashing silver through white water that fill the early accounts of the northeast coast. These are pallid ghosts, penned in the sea cages of salmon farms, fed bulk food and doctored with high-tech medications. These fish have never leapt up a falls in their lives. Yet they may pose a real threat to their wild brethren.

The recent decline in wild salmon stocks has mirrored the exponential rise in fish farms, whose nets often lie just offshore, close to salmon rivers. Salmon farmers around the North Atlantic produced 4,783 metric tons of fish in 1980 and 658,735 metric tons in 2000, well over a hundredfold increase in just twenty years, and since then farmed salmon production has remained around 700,000 metric tons a year.[12] But, as any good statistician will tell you, correlation doesn't imply causality. Those on the side of wild salmon cite pollution from the crowded nets in the form of fish sewage and antibiotics and other drugs used to boost fish growth or increased populations of parasites like fish lice. These claims are just as vehemently denied by the fish farmers. But it now seems that one of the biggest problems is the fish themselves or at least those that escape the cages. Each year so many salmon find their way off the farm that their numbers would have astounded even George Cartwright. In 2002, one estimate suggests 2 million salmon wriggled their way to freedom in the North Atlantic.[13] Friends of the Earth has provided a list of these "great escapes," at least those that have been reported. One of the largest, in Scotland in 2000, involved a breakout of some 395,000 fish, but the single largest was in the Faeroes, involving six hundred thousand fish.[14] Overall, the numbers of escaped farm fish swimming in the Atlantic may be enormous. Some researchers suggest that 40 percent of fish caught in the Atlantic are of farm origin,[15] while researchers in Norway found that up to 80 percent of salmon entering Norway's rivers were nonnative. But does it matter, so long as there are still salmon swimming up river?

Because most wild salmon return to the rivers of their birth, there is very little movement of genes between populations. Over time, each river has therefore developed its own distinct genetic forms of Atlantic salmon. Farmed fish, on the other hand, come from a variety of sources, and through generations in captivity have acquired a very different genetic makeup from wild salmon. Once they've tasted freedom, instinct guides farmed fish into freshwater; and though they might be flabby couch potatoes compared to their wild cousins, they can interbreed with wild fish, introducing foreign genes into the distinctive gene pools of local fish. But why does this matter? After all, they are all Atlantic salmon.

The answer to that depends on how the distinct local genetic forms of wild salmon arose in the first place. The genes of isolated populations can diverge for two reasons. The first is "genetic drift," a process where random changes in genes that have no effect on survival gradually accumulate in the population purely by chance. The smaller a population, such as salmon from one isolated river, the greater the potential for such drift. The other way is through classic Darwinian selection. In this case, the distinct gene pools in each river would represent adaptations to specific local conditions. In the first case, crossbreeding with farmed salmon might not be of much concern; in the second, it could dilute exquisitely honed adaptations and threaten the continued existence of wild salmon. The weight of evidence suggests the latter.[16]

Different populations of salmon differ in many ways, including the timing of their spawning runs and their migration to the sea. Recent work is now suggesting that such differences are under the control of those distinctive local genes. Entering the ocean, for example, requires big physiological changes. Different enzyme systems must be activated in the gills to rid the fish of excess salt as it swims from fresh into saltwater, and these enzymes activate at different times in different genetic strains. These differences correlate very precisely with the timing of the run to sea in different populations.[17]

If more proof were needed, modern DNA analysis, familiar from TV crime thrillers, has also been used to study the genetic makeup of salmon populations in a number of Danish rivers through time. Scales from fish caught between 1913 and 1989 had been stored in collections and can yield enough DNA for modern techniques to show that the local genetic patterns have remained constant over this whole period. This too suggests that the distinct local gene pools are indeed adaptations to local conditions, maintained by natural selection, and not random changes over time.[18]

Although recent studies show that, over their lifetimes, farmed fish are less than a fifth as effective at breeding as wild fish, this is enough to worry scientists.[19] Experiments have shown that the hybrids of farmed and wild fish are much less successful at surviving than purebred wild fish.[20] And a quirk in the salmon's breeding behavior means that such hybrids might be more common than expected from the poor competitiveness of farmed fish.

When salmon eggs hatch, the young fish spend two or more years as juveniles, called parr, living in the river of their birth. After that they turn into silvery smolts and head down to the sea. Once in the ocean they can feed in highly productive waters that allow them to grow to much larger sizes than they could if they simply stayed at home. After a period in these rich ocean feeding grounds, the salmon reach sexual maturity and return to the rivers to spawn. But these fish have a decision to make. Spawning is very competitive for the males, so the bigger they are, the more likely they can battle their way to fatherhood. And for the females, the bigger they are the more eggs they can lay. So in some ways, it pays a salmon to spend a longer time at sea, feeding and growing. On the other hand, not returning to the spawning river delays the arrival of their first offspring, and there's the distinct risk of ending up inside a killer whale or seal before getting a chance to spawn. So some salmon return early, after just one winter at sea, while others spend two years at sea. But for males there's another, much sneakier, alternative. They could mature sexually while still parr.

The production of sperm doesn't take a lot of energy, especially compared to the production of eggs, so males don't need to be big just to produce sperm. These parr simply stay in the relative safety of the rivers where they hatched and wait for fish returning from sea to spawn. They can't compete with the massive, ocean-fed males directly, but their small size means they can use a different strategy. They wait until a female drops her eggs, then sneak in and fertilize a few without her guardian male even noticing. Adult farmed salmon might lose out in competition with wild fish, but it turns out that the story is reversed for parr.[21] Fish farmers, like farmers since the dawn of agriculture, have selected their animals to be fast growing to reach market size as quickly as possible, so escaped farm parr are much faster growing and also much more aggressive than wild ones, and this gives them an edge on the spawning beds. To see what was actually happening on the spawning beds, scientists fitted wild and farmed parr with tiny microchips so they knew who was who and monitored their activity with underwater surveillance cameras. After spawning, the DNA of the eggs was analyzed to check who had fathered what. The results were conclusive: wild parr had managed to father only a quarter of the eggs.

The demand for copious and cheap salmon means that salmon farmers are always looking for new ways to expand their operations and their profits. Genetic engineering offers the technology to make salmon grow much faster to marketable size, but if such genes pass to wild salmon, they could have even more disastrous results. Proponents of aquaculture argue that such farm-produced fish have the capacity to ease pressure on wild fish stocks, though, since it takes around three pounds of wild caught fish to grow each pound of farmed salmon, salmon farming really only shifts the pressure from one set of overtaxed marine resources to another. In a nutshell, salmon farming is a big and expensive business driven by a desire to maximize short-term profits, and that, as we shall see in the following pages, is never good news for natural resources.

The changing fortunes of Atlantic salmon illustrate the close relationship between history and ecology and how complex this relationship is. The details of this history are shaped by the specific biology of salmon and can only be fully appreciated through an intimate understanding of that biology. In the following chapters I will amplify the broad themes of this chapter with a range of other species, as diverse as mammals and mollusks, each with their own distinct biology that has helped fashion each unique history. The other half of such histories is driven by the motives and reactions of people, shaped by historical and cultural circumstances. The social and historical factors that shaped this new dialogue with nature varied with time and place, each a fascinating study in its own right. But, equally fascinating, common themes begin to emerge that throw our own relationship with the world around us into sharp focus.

CHAPTER 3

Abundant Ocean

Leif Ericsson's party wasn't the only one to visit the shores of America. In the years following, many Norsemen crossed the cold, grey Davis Strait to make landfall somewhere in the New World. Some were recorded in the sagas, but probably most were not. And presumably one of those visits left us the outlines of the long houses at l'Anse aux Meadows, proof that the epic voyages recited in sagas around hearth fires in later years were entirely possible. Like Leif Ericsson, these later visitors found the oceans and shores teeming with life—so rich that they thought about establishing permanent settlements in Vinland as they had in Greenland. After Leif Ericsson's voyage, *The Saga of Eirik the Red* introduces us to Thorfinn Karlsefni, an Icelandic merchant who led a large colonizing expedition, around 1020, to the New World. "Karlsefni and his men sailed into an estuary and named the place Hop [tidal lake]. Here they found wild wheat growing in the fields on all the low ground and grapevines on all the higher ground. Every stream was teeming with fish. They dug trenches at the high tide mark, and when the tide went out there were halibut trapped in the trenches."[1] The abundance of life along the shore, both above and below the water, impressed Thorfinn as much as it had Leif: "so many eider duck . . . that a man could hardly take a step for the eggs [and] no shortage of provisions, for there was hunting of animals on the mainland, eggs in the island breeding grounds, and fish from the sea."

L'Anse aux Meadows is tangible proof that some Norsemen spent a lot of time here, but it doesn't answer *how* they made such long ocean voyages. Yes, they had fine oceangoing ships and excellent navigation techniques, but the ships weren't big enough to carry the bulky supplies needed for such long voyages. The solution lay beneath the keels of the Norse boats, in the abundance of marine life in the northwestern Atlantic, and specifically in one superabundant species: *Gadus morhua*—cod.

In fact, this one species of fish did far more than just fuel Viking expeditions; it shaped much of Europe's history and subsequently the early history of Europeans in North America. If ever proof were needed that history needs an ecological interpretation to be fully understood, then *G. morhua* is it.

Cod belong to the family Gadidae, along with similar-looking fish like haddock and pollock. They are demersal fish, associated with the ocean bottom, as opposed to pelagic or open-water species, and they seem to prefer waters between thirty and six hundred feet in depth. They are therefore found mostly on the continental shelf or over offshore banks, originally from Cape Hatteras in North Carolina, north around both sides of Greenland, and then eastward around Iceland and into the Barents Sea north of Norway and Russia. Most importantly, they are top predators. In the northwest Atlantic, they seem to relish capelin, a small and oily baitfish that used to exist in immense shoals,[2] though they also eat many other kinds of small fish—indeed anything they can get their jaws around. In their position at the apex of the ecosystems of the northwest Atlantic, they play a key role in shaping those ecosystems. For these reasons, as well as its role in shaping human history, the cod is the central character in this chapter, the first of two reconstructing the past abundance of the waters off eastern Canada and the northeastern United States.

This impressive ocean predator was drawn into the human story of the North Atlantic in a major way around the same time that Norsemen first saw the shores of North America, at the end of the first millennium. A growing urban population back in Europe had severely depleted its resources of freshwater fish through overharvesting and pollution and was being forced to turn to marine fish in response. This—the very beginnings of intensive marine fishing—is marked in middens in England from this time as a change in frequency of fish bones, from freshwater species to species like cod and herring.[3] This archaeological evidence also points to an increasing trade between England and Norway, since the warm climate at the time, which helped the Viking colonization of Greenland, would also have depleted stocks of herring and cod around English shores but increased them around Norway. By implication, therefore, the fish remains found in middens in England may have been coming from farther afield.

There isn't a better fish for such long-distance trade than cod because, even before the days of freezing and fast transport, they could easily be preserved. By the time they were exploring North America, Norsemen had long since learned the art of air-drying cod, in which state it is light, nutritious, and fairly long lasting. They still use it. Just as the Norse explorers sustained themselves on their long journeys on dried cod, so today it hangs in every gas station convenience shop on the island of Iceland. It *looks* like strips of recycled cardboard, and worse yet, it even *tastes* like recycled cardboard, albeit with a fish flavor. Yet it is strangely addictive. After a few days of filming in Iceland around the summer solstice and finishing at sunset (midnight in the south of the island), it was pretty much all we managed to find to eat. But after that, I began to buy it even though we were now able to return to Reykjavik's cosmopolitan selection of restaurants each evening. I can only hope that after not visiting Iceland for a few years, I am now, like the cod, cured.

The earliest form of preservation was simply to allow the fish to dry through the cold winter months. Later, cod was both salted and dried, which meant it could be kept for much longer. But neither technique can be carried out on board ship; dry land and cold winds are required. In Greenland and North America, the Norsemen had both and could have dried all the cod they needed to sustain their lengthy stays in the New World and their journeys back. Yet the sagas are noticeably quiet on the subject of cod, perhaps because the Norsemen took it for granted. In those days, immense shoals would still have been common around Iceland and Norway. But even after the Norse expeditions, fuller descriptions of the abundant northwest Atlantic were a surprisingly long time in coming.

There is a persistent story around the city of Bristol that local fishermen had known about, and been exploiting, the vast fish resources of the western Atlantic long before Columbus's voyage in 1492. The good folks of Bristol even claim that the man for whom the whole continent of America was named lies buried in St. Mary's Church near the center of the city—a Bristol man called Richard Amerike. Most of the rest of the world believe that America was named for Amerigo Vespucci, but that doesn't seem to dampen the enthusiasm of Bristolians one little bit. Likewise, there's a bit of a problem with Bristol's early discovery of those vast shoals of cod—there's no evidence that Bristol ever had a fishing fleet. What it did have was a large number of merchant vessels whose owners were always on the look out for new trading opportunities and profits. It was the power of profits that drove exploration, putting such merchants at the center of the discovery and exploitation of the New World's natural resources.

Spain and Portugal had discovered a whole series of islands in the Atlantic in the middle of the fifteenth century, and by 1480 Bristol merchant ships were regularly trading with Madeira, the Canaries, the Cape Verdes, and the

Azores.[4] But what other islands and resources, ripe for exploitation, lay in the vast ocean to the west of Bristol? There's some evidence that, in pushing ever westward in search of trade, Bristol vessels might even have touched on the shores of North America.

In 1956, a letter was found in an archive in Spain. Part of it reads: "All along the coast they [the English] found many fish like those which in Iceland are dried in the open and sold in England and other countries, and these fish are called in English 'stockfish.'" The letter was written by John Day, a Bristol merchant, in 1497 or 1498 reporting to the grand admiral—presumably Columbus himself—on a voyage that had just returned to Bristol, and he goes on to suggest that this expedition had found an extensive land mass in the western ocean that was already well known to the Bristol men. "It is considered certain that the cape of the said land was found and discovered in the past by men of Bristol, who found 'Brasil' as your Lordship well knows. It was called the Island of Brasil, and it is assumed and believed to be the mainland that the men from Bristol found."[5]

The ship that had just returned to Bristol was called the *Matthew,* and it was commanded by John Cabot, who, like Columbus, was from Genoa. And like Columbus, Cabot had also been trying to raise backing to take an expedition west in the hopes of finding a sea route to Asia. Columbus beat him to it by getting backing from Queen Isabella of Spain for an expedition in 1492. However, Cabot didn't give up. He reasoned that the route around the globe would be shorter further north, so he might have more success raising money for his own expedition from northern European countries. It worked. In 1497, he persuaded Henry VII of England that whatever Columbus had discovered, he could pioneer a quicker and therefore more profitable route from Bristol. He may well have chosen Bristol because sailors there already knew something of what lay across the western ocean.

Cabot undoubtedly made landfall in northeast America, though no one is exactly sure where. That's because Cabot is frustratingly silent on his discoveries, though he did give us the first impressions of what lay beneath the waves on the far side of the Atlantic thanks to reports of people like John Day. And Day wasn't the only person interested in the comings and goings in Bristol. There was also an Italian agent operating in England at this time. This man, Raimondo de Soncino, was working for the duke of Milan and sent all he could find on Cabot's voyage back to his employer. He wrote: "And they say that it is a very good and temperate country . . . and they affirm that the sea is covered with fishes which are caught not only with a net but with baskets, a stone being tied to them in order that the baskets may sink in the water. And this I heard the said Master John relate. And the aforementioned Englishmen, his comrades, say that they will bring so many fishes that this kingdom will no longer have need of Iceland."[6]

Cabot might not have found a route to the East Indies with their gold and spices, but he had found just as big a prize. He was the first undisputed person to see the great shoals of cod in the western Atlantic, though some scholars suggest that Diego de Tieve, the Portuguese explorer who discovered several islands in the Azores in 1452, may have ventured as far as the cod grounds of Newfoundland decades before Cabot. But, whoever found them, word of these natural riches just a few weeks sailing from Europe had certainly spread by the beginning of the sixteenth century, and in the years that followed, hundreds of boats would make this journey.

In 1997, five hundred years after Cabot sailed from Bristol, a replica of the *Matthew* made the same voyage to Newfoundland. Today, it is berthed on the River Avon next to another famous Bristol ship, Brunel's transatlantic steamship, the *S. S. Great Britain*, and it is completely dwarfed by even this modest vessel. The twentieth-century *Matthew* is open to visitors between sailings, and it's a sobering experience to stand on its decks. The ship is tiny, just over sixty feet from stern to bow at the waterline. It's amazing to think that a modern crew would dare face the Atlantic in such an insubstantial vessel, even though today's "sailing ship" is equipped with an engine and propeller for windless days, a satellite navigation system to pierce the Newfoundland fogs, and a radio to call for help if all else fails. It says a lot for the characters of those early explorers that they had none of this—just cramped conditions, lousy food, hard work, and after a few weeks, if all went well, their world disappeared as they ran into a damp gray wall of fog. Welcome to the Grand Banks.

The Grand Banks are a series of underwater plateaus to the south and east of Newfoundland, where the sea is only 75–350 feet deep. The frequent fogs arise because two great ocean currents collide over the banks, the warm Gulf Stream—a huge river of warm water flowing up from the Gulf of Mexico—and the cold Labrador Current, chilled from its origins near the ice sheets of northern Greenland and Canada. As warm moist air over the Gulf Stream is suddenly cooled, water vapor condenses into the dense fog that makes fishing the banks so dangerous. But it's that same mixing of waters that makes it worth coming here in the first place. The shape of the underwater plateaus together with the turbulent collision of currents churns up nutrients from the sea bed, lifting them into sunlit surface waters and creating perfect conditions for that ancient alchemy of life, photosynthesis. Virtually unlimited food and copious light produces unimaginable numbers of minute plants, the phytoplankton, and, grazing this oceanic pasture, equally unimaginable numbers of zooplankton. In turn these feed larger creatures and, eventually, the vast shoals of cod that Cabot saw.

It's hard to imagine the scale of these three-dimensional pastures, but it might help to envisage that they are big enough to cover the whole continent of North America to a depth of around three feet. That's a lot of fish, which is presumably what Cabot thought if he really did watch his men hauling endless cod from the ocean, merely by lowering weighted baskets into the water. And these were no tiddlers. Later records tell us that some of these fish weighed in at around two hundred pounds and measured four or five feet in length. I suppose they had big baskets. But compare that with an average cod today, which weighs less than a *twentieth* of that, and you begin to get a feel of what the first fishermen encountered on the far side of the Atlantic.

So after anything from two weeks to a month of hard tack and hard work, depending on wind and weather, you would be hanging over the rail, looking for the first signs that you were over the banks. Then, off the bow, the horizon begins to blur. After another hour, the horizon has gone altogether. Ahead of you the sea fades into nothingness, and somewhere higher overhead a gray sky is barely distinguishable from the bank of fog into which you are about to sail. Then, in the space of a few seconds, the world shrinks from an endless ocean to a few feet of damp clinging grayness. It's a good sign that you are approaching the banks.

As tiny as your ship is, the bow is now lost to sight from the stern; just the faint gray outline of rigging, growing ever fainter until gray finally fades into gray. The fog muffles sound, and the world has fallen eerily silent. The sound of one of your shipmates, invisible, calling soundings, is all there is, until out of the mist the first braying calls are heard. Soon it's a cacophony, as the ship is surrounded by rafts of great black-and-white birds the size of geese. The old hands call these big birds "penguins," and they never take to the air. Other smaller ones appear in flight, emerging from the mist on whirring wings, hurtling through the rigging and disappearing again in the space of a few seconds. They fly with supreme confidence and seem to know exactly where they are going. A ship looming out of the fog necessitates a quick change of direction, but otherwise they barely acknowledge you. As their numbers grow, it feels like the ship is under fire from an unseen enemy firing feathered bullets. These birds are the most reliable sign that you are over the banks. They are here for the same reason you are—fish.

One of the things that struck me most forcefully while leaning over the side of the new *Matthew* is how to close to the water I was: barely more than yard. Staring into the murky waters of Bristol's Floating Harbor, where the *Matthew* has its home, I could begin to imagine what those sixteenth-century fishermen and sailors might have seen: gray outlines of giant cod swirling beneath the keel. So dense were these shoals that John Cabot's son, Sebastian, on a later voyage, reported that they halted the progress of his ship. "Cabot himself called those lands Baccallaos because in the adjacent sea he found so great a quantity of a certain kind of great fish like tunnies, called baccallaos [cod] by the inhabitants, that at times they even stayed the passage of his ships."[7] Whether that is literally true or not, Farley Mowat considers that the Banks supported a sheer mass of life unmatched anywhere else on the planet.[8] But it wasn't just the Grand Banks.

As later vessels explored more and more of the northeastern coast, it became clear that the whole area was infested with fish. In 1534, the mouth of the St. Lawrence was described as "the richest in every kind of fish that anyone remembers ever having seen or heard of . . . great numbers of mackerel, mullet, sea bass, tunnies, large eels."[9] In the same year, off Cape Royall, today called Bluff Head, early French explorers found "there is the greatest fishing of Cods that possible may be, for staying for our company, in lesse than an houre we took above an hundreth of them."

In 1719, Pierre de Charlevoix, a French priest visiting Canada, considered the number of cod to equal that of the grains of sand on the beach and later, in 1876, John Rowan found vast shoals of cod in only three fathoms of water so clear he could see right to the bottom. Sebastian Cabot's name for Newfoundland—Baccallaos—derived from a Flemish name for cod, could not have been more appropriate.

To support such immense numbers of large predatory fish, as well as those great flocks of birds, there must have been unimaginable numbers of smaller "bait" fish, like shad, smelt, alewives, and capelin. One of the most evocative descriptions of the sheer abundance of fish in the waters around Newfoundland comes from John Mason. Apart from being the founder of New Hampshire, he also produced one of the earliest maps of Newfoundland and a detailed description of the island, *A Brief Discourse on the New Found Land,* supposedly to promote settlement by Scotsmen. In his *Discourse,* Mason describes a truly astounding place:

> the most admirable is the Sea, so diuersified with seuerall sorts of Fishes abounding therein, the consideration whereof is readie to swallow vp and drowne my senses not being able to comprehend or expresse the riches thereof. For could one acre therof be inclosed with the Creatures therein in the moneths of Iune, Iulie, and August, it would exceed one thousand acres of the best Pasture with the stocke thereon which we haue in England. May hath Herings on equall to 2. of ours, Lants and Cods in good quantity. Iune hath Capline, a fish much resembling Smeltes in forme and eating, and such aboundance dry on Shoare as to lade Carts.[10]

Most of these fish are much reduced in numbers today, although capelin in particular can still put on a spectacular show. Certain beaches in Newfoundland have just the right sized grains of sand to be of interest to these six-inch-long silver darts. In June and July, great shoals assemble in shallow water off these beaches, and on cloudy days they perform a remarkable ritual that is utterly absorbing to watch. Surfing in on a wave, they try to throw themselves as high up the beach as they can. At first, it's just a few fish, often a female with a couple of males in tow. As they hit the sand, the female releases her eggs and the males their sperm, and then the fish try to flip their way back to the sea. Soon the numbers build until the beach is littered with little silvery fish leaping out of the waves.

Many of these beaches have been used for centuries, since capelin are very fussy about finding exactly the right grade of sand in which to bury their eggs. In the fifteenth century, the quantities of fish beaching themselves along this same shoreline must have been truly astounding. You're left imagining a fog-shrouded beach where the surf breaks silver. No sand is visible, just dark, jagged rocks rising from a solid mass of fish, many struggling to reach the waves again, but many more lying dead having achieved their life's aim.

Laying eggs above the high watermark protects them from marine predators, but the mortality among the spawning adults is immense. Although these suicidal missions are obviously worth it in the long run for the capelin, not all populations spawn above the tide. Others spawn in the shallows over the Grand Banks, and some fisheries biologists think they might have been doing this since the last ice age, when, thanks to lower sea levels, their spawning grounds would have been beaches as high and dry as those of their New-foundland kin. You can't help admire a fish for such dogged, if instinctive, determination.

Beaches littered with the corpses of capelin must have been a magnet to seabirds looking for an easy feast. But there were infinitely more fish in the sea. There were so many baitfish swarming in these waters that they supported not only endless shoals of cod but breathtaking numbers of birds. In the years af-ter Cabot's voyage, there were increasing numbers of fishing trips and voyages of exploration, which left us much clearer descriptions of all of these specta-cles, allowing us to build up a more complete picture of the lost ecology of the northwest Atlantic. In 1534, just thirty-seven years after the *Matthew* ploughed through seas thick with cod, two 60-ton ships with 120 men on board sailed out of St. Malo in Brittany. They were commanded by a native son of St. Malo, Jacques Cartier, who was headed west to chart the coastline of Newfoundland and Labrador. By now Basque, Breton, and Portuguese fishermen were regular visitors to Newfoundland in the summer, and when Cartier finally arrived he found several boats already fishing there. But the time was fast arriving when governments wanted to know exactly what resources the New World had to offer, and that, in part, was Cartier's task.

Bad weather and ice forced them to remain at anchor in Newfoundland for more than a week, but as soon as it cleared and a fair wind rose they began their explorations.

> Upon 21 of May the winde being in the West, we hoised sail, and sailed to-ward North and by East from the cape of Buono Vista until we came to the Island of Birds which was environed about with a banke of ice, but broken and crackt: notwithstanding the sayd bank, our two boats went thither to take in some birds, whereof there is such plenty, that unlesse a man did see them, he would think it an incredible thing; for albeit the island (which containeth about a league in circuit) be so full of them, that they seem to have been brought thither and sowed for the nonce [for that express pur-pose], yet are there an hundredfold as many hovering about it as within.[11]

Today, this place is known as Funk Island, and it lies about forty miles off the northeast coast of Newfoundland. Cartier's men may well have already known about the Island of Birds, since it, like many other seabird colonies, was used as a navigation beacon by fishermen. In the frequent Newfoundland fogs, the constant calls of the birds served as a warning of dangerous rocks or nearby coastline, a natural fog horn for which fishermen were extremely grateful in these treacherous waters. They were also grateful for the sustenance provided by these colonies.

Fresh eggs and birds were taken on board whenever a vessel passed close to such a colony. You can still visit Funk today, though thankfully not to collect birds or their eggs. But you'll see neither the spectacle nor one particular bird that Cartier saw: "which are as big as jayes, blacke and white, with beakes like unto crowes: they lie alwayes upon the sea; they cannot flie very high, because there wings are so little, and no bigger than halfe ones hand, yet they do flie as swiftly as any birds of the aire levell to the water; they are also exceeding fat; we named them Aporath."[12]

Aporath, or apponatz as they are sometimes called, existed in huge numbers around Newfoundland and Labrador, as well as Iceland and northern Europe. This was the bird that many sailors called the "penguin." It was, in fact, the original penguin, the name only later transferred to the birds of the southern oceans. Today its common name is "great auk," but that's all it is—just a name. Great auks haven't fished the North Atlantic for well over 150 years. The last two were beaten to death by collectors in June 1844 on the island of Eldey, off Iceland, and their only egg destroyed in the struggle. Although a few scattered and unconfirmed sightings after that sparked some hope that it might yet survive, this was the last definite encounter between man and great auk, and as in every other such encounter since the days of Cartier, the great auks came off worse. All we have now are the dramatic accounts of those lucky enough to see these birds in their heyday.

To land on Funk Island with Cartier's men would have been an extraordinary experience. Funk was probably the great auk's largest breeding colony, and in the breeding season the flat-topped rocks would have been solid with these great black-and-white birds guarding their large eggs. The smell would have been overpowering; "Funk" comes from an old word meaning "stinking," and the place was often referred to as "the stinking island." The only experience that compares to it today is walking through a densely packed colony of king penguins. At thirty inches or so in height, great auks were only a little smaller than king penguins, and, like penguins, their wings were adapted as flippers and so useless for flight. Generally unafraid of human visitors, the great auks must have merely shuffled out of the way as Cartier's men made their landing. They were, however, armed with a very large, flattened beak, quite capable of inflicting a nasty wound even through clothing if they were approached too closely. But they were defenseless against men armed with clubs or guns, which is how they were collected by fishermen.

The local Beothuk Indians also knew about these huge colonies and paddled out here in canoes to harvest the birds, which surprised George Cartwright; "It is a singular and almost incredible fact that these people should visit Funk Islands, which lies forty miles from Cape Freels, and sixty from the Island of Fogo. The island being small and low, they cannot see it from either of those places, nor is it possible to conceive, how they could get information from any other nation. The Indians repair thither once or twice every year, and return with their canoes laden with birds and eggs; for the number of seafowl which resort to this island to breed, are far beyond credibility."[13] Actually the Beothuk had been meeting—and usually fighting with—Europeans since the days of the Norsemen. Other travelers among them said they found many Beothuk who could speak several European languages, so they could have learned about these islands from fishermen. But more likely they had been collecting birds from islands around Newfoundland long before it was "new found." And, at first, neither Indians nor fishermen would have had much impact on these multitudes. After the intruders had left, the birds would just get back to the serious business of incubating their eggs.

Very little is known about the natural history of the great auk, though it is possible to piece together part of the picture from scattered descriptions. It seems from some accounts of a smaller colony on St. Kilda that the chicks were led down to the ocean almost as soon as they hatched. That would have been an amazing time to sit on Funk's rocky shoreline, to watch the adults leaping into the surf and encouraging their gray youngsters to follow—the reluctant chicks waddling to the waterline, then staggering back as a breaking wave soaks them. Torn between wanting to follow their parents and wanting to stay on solid rock, they would have waddled backward and forward, getting ever closer to the water, until a sudden resolve finally grabbed them, and they plunged into the waves. Several observers saw young great auk chicks climb on to their parents backs once at sea, and I can imagine many of the Funk Island chicks doing the same, since the parents were about to head for the Grand Banks, a swim of some forty miles.

As ungainly as the birds were on land, they were now in their element. They seem to have been deep-diving specialists, easily able to reach the seabed of the banks to catch their main prey, bottom-living fish like lumpsuckers and sculpins, together with crabs and other crustaceans. Those big, powerful beaks could crush and slice up even large and heavily protected crabs. They were also fast and maneuverable underwater and able to catch open-water fish like capelin when swimming over deeper water.[14] Today, it's possible to watch their smaller relatives—murres, razorbills, and puffins—flying through the water like miniature torpedoes, but the great auk would have put them all to shame. That's because all these smaller auks have opted, in evolutionary terms, for a compromise.

All auks, including the great auk, use their wings not their feet to swim, or more correctly, fly through the water. Because water and air are so different in density, the optimum wing design for each is rather different. Flying underwater needs smaller wings, but take that too far and you'll never be able to get airborne. The smaller auks, by having fairly short wings, manage to do both, though neither perfectly. Penguins and great auks, on the other hand, have taken the plunge and gone for optimum underwater design.

Watching penguins underwater is simply breathtaking. It's impossible to believe they could move so fast and so easily if the evidence wasn't before your eyes. How sad then that we'll never be able to marvel at the underwater flight of the great auk. Since Jacques Cousteau didn't perfect scuba gear until four hundred years after Jacques Cartier and one hundred years after the last great auk was killed, no one has ever swum with great auks in their world. No respectful and awed David Attenborough commentary will ever accompany stunning slow-motion images of vast flotillas of great auks powering themselves toward the dark depths, streaming trails of silver bubbles behind them as the pressure compresses their feathers. And of course we have no idea how deep they could dive. Perhaps they rivaled the deep-diving champion of the bird world today, the emperor penguin. These birds regularly dive to depths of 350–450 feet, and the current record holder reached a depth of about 1,800 feet! We'll never know whether the northern equivalent of the penguin was really a match for its Antarctic counterparts.

The remaining Atlantic auks have survived, but in nothing like the spectacle that greeted Cartier, as he continued his exploration and entered the Gulf of St. Lawrence:

> [We] came to three Ilands, two of which are as steepe and upright as any wall, so that it was not possible to climbe them: and betweene them there is a little rocke. These Ilands were as full of birds, as any field or medow is of grasse, which there do make their nestes: and in the greatest of them,

there was a great and infinite number of those that wee call Margaulx, that are white, and bigger then any geese, which were severed in one part. In the other were onely Godetz, but toward the shoare there were of those Godetz, and great Apponatz, like to those of that Iland that we above have mentioned: we went downe to the lowest part of the least Iland, where we killed above a thousand of those Godetz, and Apponatz. We put into our boates so many of them as we pleased, for in lesse then one houre we might have filled thirtie such boats of them: we named them The Ilands of Margaulx.

Today, these rocky islets are still known as Bird Rocks. Margaulx are gannets, and godetz either guillemots or razorbills, or both. The apponatz we've already met. Any colony of northern sea birds is still a wonderful place to visit. Such colonies assault every sense—sight and sound combined with a pungent aroma so strong you can both smell and taste it. But according to Farley Mowat, there might have been a hundred times as many birds as this back in the sixteenth century, and it certainly sounds feasible from Cartier's descriptions. The grassy tops of the islets must have looked like sponges, covered in so many puffin burrows. It was probably impossible to walk over them without breaking through. Razorbills and guillemots nest on narrow ledges on vertical cliff faces, as well as more remote, flatter rocky areas, and every available toehold must have been stacked with birds. The air would have been full of feathered bullets whizzing about their business, and the noise overwhelming. And towering above their smaller brethren, the stately great auk, packed almost shoulder to shoulder on each and every part of the island they could reach without the ability to fly. And that inability to fly is the main reason why we can only see great auks today in our imagination.

As the sheer volume of cod in the northwestern Atlantic became more widely known, more and more fishing vessels headed this way. In 1550, eleven English vessels made the crossing. In 1600, 150 came to load up with cod, and by 1620, that had doubled to three hundred.[15] By the eighteenth century, in just one year, 1747, 564 vessels came here from France alone, much larger vessels carrying between them twenty-seven thousand hungry sailors. All these ships loaded just enough salt meat in France to get their crews as far as Newfoundland. After that, they lived on local food, of which great auks were both easy to collect and large and meaty.

Not content with clubbing hundreds of birds on each visit ashore, there are accounts of great flocks being herded across planks or sails onto the ship and then marched into the hold to await their fate. The hungry sailors could hardly believe their luck: "shaping their course thence north-eastwards they came to the island of Penguin, which is very full of rocks and stones, whereon they went and found it full of great fowls white and grey, as big as geese, and they saw infinite numbers of their eggs. They drove a great number of their fowls into their boats upon their sails and took up many of their eggs. The fowls they flayed, and found them to be very good and nourishing meat."[16] As far as everyone was concerned, such an easy and infinite supply of nutritious meat can only have been placed there for hungry sailors by God: "They multiply so infinitely upon a certain flat island that men drive them from hence upon a board, into their boats by the hundreds at a time, as if God had made the innocency of so poor a creature to become such an admirable instrument for the sustenation of man."[17]

This is a telling comment. Although it was the emerging philosophy of capitalism that drove these voyages, that philosophy was embedded in a larger Judeo-Christian worldview, in which God had created the natural world for man, to exploit as he wanted. So there was neither economic nor moral reason to refrain from taking whatever was needed in whatever manner was most profitable, an attitude well illustrated by those early encounters with great auks.

It wasn't just the adult birds that provided sustenance for these ventures; their eggs were also large and tasty. Often, to ensure a supply of fresh eggs, sailors visited an island and systematically destroyed all the eggs they could find. Then they would return a few days later, knowing that any eggs they found must have been laid recently. Some accounts of the great auk suggest that the birds laid only one egg each season, not re-laying if it is destroyed. So the quest for fresh eggs meant wiping out virtually all of each season's breeding effort. And it didn't take long for these people to find a way of turning such vast numbers of auks directly into profit.

These poor birds also had the misfortune to be insulated from the cold Atlantic waters by a thick layer of fat. Combined with their large powerful swimming muscles, it made them delicious to eat, the French comparing them favorably with goose. While the massive populations of great auks might have been able to withstand collection for food, it soon became apparent that their fatty bodies could also be rendered down to produce oil, and oil, then as now, can make fortunes. Mineral oil was unknown in those days; instead most oil, usually called *trayne* or train oil, came from whales or seals or any other creature with a thick enough layer of fat. But producing oil from great auks meant heating the birds in large metal cauldrons, and there was no fuel on the islands. The solution to this dilemma is as breathtaking in its cruelty as it is in its ingenuity. The fatty bodies of great auks burned just as well as wood, so the oil men of the sixteenth century onward simply kindled fires of birds, and then tossed their kin into the pot. And these were the fortunate ones.

Their feathers were also valuable. Sometimes birds were tossed alive into boiling water (heated by their own kind again) to make feather extraction easier, but even that was too much trouble for some: "If you come for their feathers you do not give yourself the trouble of killing them, but lay hold of one and pluck off the best of the Feathers. Then you turn the poor Penguin adrift, with his skin half naked and torn off, to perish at his leisure."[18] This seems inhumane in the extreme, though it might be argued that times change; perhaps it seems more cruel to us now than it did to them. But even at the time, it's clear that many people realized the cruelty of their actions: "While you abide on this Island you are in the constant practize of horrid crueltys for you not only Skin them Alive, but you burn them Alive also, to cook their bodies with."[19]

In the eighteenth century, some voices were finally raised against the slaughter of the auks. The commercial exploitation was depriving local people of a valuable food source and fishermen of valuable navigation aids. Great auks were the most reliable indicators of the Grand Banks, which they rarely left except in the breeding season. But by now it was almost certainly too late. A chilling comment comes from George Cartwright in 1785. While salmon still abounded in his rivers, he noted changes on the great seabird islands:

> Innumerable flocks of sea fowl breed [on Funk Island] every summer, which are of great service to the poor inhabitants who make voyages there to load with birds and eggs . . . but it has been customary in later years for several crews of men to live all summer on that island for the sole purpose of killing the birds for the sake of their feathers; the destruction they have made is incredible. If a stop is not soon put to that practice, the whole breed will be diminished to nothing, particularly the penguins, for this is now the only island they have left to breed upon; all others lying so near the shores of Newfoundland, they are continually robbed.[20]

Cartwright suggests that even by 1785, Funk was the last known breeding colony in the western Atlantic, and not long after that, his words proved prophetic, as their breed did indeed diminish to nothing.

Other seabirds were also hard hit, particularly by commercial egg collecting to supply insatiable markets in the fast-growing cities of Canada and the United States. Some were also victims of the fashion trade, like the delicate arctic tern whose elegant sweeping wings or long tail streamers often graced the hats of the beautiful. But many of these seabirds were facing an even more critical problem: food. The unimaginable was happening: the infinite shoals of fish were rapidly becoming finite.

At first, cod were the main target. In 1747 those twenty-seven thousand Frenchmen, fed on nutritious great auks, hauled £1 million worth of fish back to France, an astounding sum of money at the time. In 1783, 1,500 vessels from many nations were all pulling cod from the sea at an incredible rate. At the turn of the twentieth century, the annual catch of cod (together with haddock) had reached the million ton mark. But the remarkable cod seemed to be holding up in the face of this onslaught.

It *seemed* to be.

For a fish that has made so many people rich, we still don't know a great deal about the life of a cod. Like Atlantic salmon, there are distinct genetic populations of cod seemingly adapted to their local conditions. Although not confined to individual rivers like spawning salmon, complex ocean currents over cod spawning grounds serve to keep the tiny cod larvae segregated enough from neighbors to allow local adaptations to build up.[21] So the vast shoals that amazed sixteenth- and seventeenth-century fishermen weren't one great amorphous mass of fish, just lying there waiting to be caught. They were, like the Atlantic salmon thronging the rivers, discrete populations of animals living complex lives.

Although much of the cod's life is still little understood, the fishermen soon learned any aspects of their quarry's behavior that would make them easier to find or catch. In Nova Scotia, fishermen found that cod preferred areas of reddish gravel, called "cherry bottom." So they used to lower soft tallow candles to the sea bed, which would stick to a sample of gravel, allowing the fishermen to home in on the best cod grounds.

Good local knowledge was rewarded with prodigious catches. In the middle of the seventeenth century, Nicolas Denys described the scene around Cape

Breton. "Scarcely a harbour where there are not fishing vessels . . . taking every day 15,000 [to] 30,000 fish . . . this fish constitutes a kind of inexhaustible manna."[22] Decades passed, and the seas off this northeastern corner of the New World seemed as inexhaustible as Nicolas Denys believed.

Centuries passed, and numbers seemed undiminished. Cod had been fished for two hundred years when the French priest Charlevoix observed: "The number of the cod seems to equal that of the grains of sand."[23] But Charlevoix, with a prescience rarely displayed in this period, thought that, despite appearances, the stocks might not really be infinite. "It might not however be amiss to discontinue this fishery from time to time. These are true mines which are more valuable and require much less expense than those of Peru and Mexico."[24]

Not a hope. That the stocks were inexhaustible was still official policy more than a century later. And now the idea was backed by a new understanding of nature that had emerged from the thinking of Charles Darwin and Alfred Russel Wallace. Life was an indomitable force—constantly changing, constantly adapting through the process of natural selection. Darwin himself was reluctant to defend his theory of evolution in public, but he had a dedicated champion in Thomas Huxley, who became known as "Darwin's bulldog" for his fierce defense of evolution. After he famously won a heated debate with Bishop Wilberforce, evolution was part of the scientific map. And when not savaging opponents of evolution, Huxley also served on three fishing commissions in the middle of the nineteenth century. An address at the 1883 International Fisheries Exhibition clearly shows that he saw the seas as holding infinite supplies of fish. "I still believe the cod fishery . . . and probably all the great fisheries are inexhaustible; that is to say nothing we do seriously affects the number of fish."[25] He also considered that fishing was subject to natural laws, just like any other predator-prey relationship. "Any tendency to overfishing will meet with its natural check in the diminution of the supply. . . . This check will always come into operation long before anything like permanent exhaustion has occurred."[26]

Some recent research has shown that, at least for some inshore fishing communities, Huxley was probably right. Canadian fisheries scientist, Ransom Myers, has looked carefully at the detailed records of settlement for over a century around three bays in Newfoundland and found that fishermen tended to settle in an area when catch rates were above forty quintals of dried salt cod (about ten metric tons of wet fish). Below forty quintals, and the fisher-men moved away, to more profitable areas.[27] A similar pattern can be found in many animals, where it is called "optimal foraging." A small shorebird, prob-ing for food in the sand will continue to feed in an area provided the catch rate is high. As soon as the catch rate falls, the bird moves, sampling other areas until the catch rate rises beyond a certain threshold again.

But any such similarity between humans and nature is masked by a much greater difference. Humans are driven by economics rather than biology, though, in fact, a free market economy and evolution by natural selection work in very similar ways. Both work on the principle of self-interest, and both are blind to anything but their immediate consequences, yet both are extraordinarily powerful forces given their simple basic rules. Huxley's con-fidence in the guiding hand of a totally free market was as great as his confi-dence in natural selection; he was the free market economy's bulldog as well as Darwin's. His commission repealed all laws restricting fishing on the assump-tion that the blind laws of economics would do a better job.[28] But economics is also shaped by human culture, values, and history—an ever-changing con-text that often produces unexpected results, many of which will emerge over the following chapters.

In the case of cod, it is human ingenuity that has shaped the story. Humans have seemingly unlimited abilities to invent new technology, making people unique predators. In nature, when a prey species becomes scarce, the popula-tion of its predator also drops, giving the prey chance to recover and starting the cycle again. If human prey, like cod, gets scarcer, we simply invent more efficient and ingenious ways of catching them, provided there is money to be made in doing so. And since scarce commodities attract high prices, this is more often than not the case. The cod fishery is an excellent example of this technological ratchet at work.

At first, cod were caught with hand lines. Then the French introduced long-lining, lowering thousands of hooks to the sea bed on great lengths of rope. Gill-netting followed: a fine net sunk to the bottom, which traps fish as they try to pass through it. And there were improvements to the ships them-selves. In 1713, near Gloucester, Massachusetts, Andrew Robinson is credited with perfecting the schooner, a fast and maneuverable vessel, named, so it is said, from a New England word. "See how she scoons (skims over the water like a stone)," a bystander is reputed to have said, and the name stuck. Schooners revolutionized both fishing and the trade in salt cod. Then came steam, and a huge leap in the power of fishing vessels. Now great trawl nets could be dragged over the bottom, swallowing the infinite shoals. Later, tickler chains were added to the front, to rake the sea bottom, chasing fish into the gaping mouths of the trawl, and, incidentally, destroying the sea bed.

The history of commercial fishing, exemplified by the cod's tale, is one of continuing technical improvements, but it's also one of lack of understanding and inadequate responses. As time passed in the North Atlantic, some worries were voiced about how long the fish would last. And a few conservation measures were enacted, like limits on the size of mesh, to protect younger fish. But at the same time, standard fishing practices negated any benefits from such protection measures. Many vessels practiced "high grading." To maximize the value of their catch, fisherman would keep only the biggest fish, throwing away great quantities of perfectly edible smaller fish, until their holds were filled with premium-sized specimens.

Another hammer blow fell in the early twentieth century when a certain Mr. Clarence Birdseye ended up in Labrador. Born in Brooklyn, Clarence Birdseye was both a naturalist and business entrepreneur. He traveled to Labrador as a fur trader, where he was fascinated to watch local Inuit using barrels of brine and freezing temperatures to preserve food. He realized that food frozen quickly like this tasted much better than food preserved in ice. The ice crystals in such flash frozen food don't have time to grow very large, which preserves the structure and the taste of the food. Armed with a $7 electric fan, plenty of ice and brine, and a kitchen sink, Clarence Birdseye set about experimenting. By 1923, he had perfected his technique of rapid freezing, and the age of frozen food was born.

Together with the more powerful ships and improved catching techniques, everything was set for the birth of the great factory fleets that could process huge numbers of fish. The first of these new factory freezer stern trawlers appeared over the horizon in 1954. The *Fairtry* was a British ship capable of scooping out of the ocean as many cod in two 30-minute trawls as could be caught in a whole long summer season in the sixteenth century.[29] Soon, the *Fairtry* was joined by similar ships from other nations, many of which were further insulated from the reality of ecology by financial subsidies.

The fishing industry has a long history of subsidies, both for commercial and political reasons. John Adams, second president of the United States, famously pointed out that maintaining a long-distance cod fleet through subsidies was a far cheaper way of supplying experienced sailors than maintaining a standing navy. All of these factors worked together to maintain predator pressure even when the prey should have been no longer viable, economically or ecologically.

In the 1970s, the catch began to fall under the onslaught of factory ships from many nations. Canada reacted by extending its exclusive economic zone out to two hundred miles and closing it to foreign vessels. The Canadian government then set its own quotas and began to build up its own fleet to exploit the stocks under the guidelines of Canadian fisheries scientists. And for a while, surveys showed that cod numbers were slowly building.

But in the 1980s, numbers began to fall again. Fisheries scientists sounded warnings, but cod numbers went into free fall, a precipitous decline unmatched by any other population of animals on land or sea.[30] By the early 1990s, the population had fallen by 99.9 percent from its 1960s level, making it an even more vanishingly small fraction of the population that Cabot and Cartier encountered. In 1992, Canada closed the Grand Banks fishery. Other fisheries too are now closed or restricted as seven separate stocks of cod collapsed. The scale of the collapse is almost beyond belief. One estimate put the mass of fish over the Scotian Shelf, off Nova Scotia, alone at 4 million tons in 1492. Today the estimate is fifty thousand tons. Cod that were dense enough to slow down boats could now be fitted into the holds of sixteen average-sized schooners.

How on Earth could this have happened?

Some were quick to blame other predators, like seals. Ransom Myers and his colleagues have refuted this. They found that, though the three seal species in the area, harp, hooded and gray, do feed on cod, they mainly take fish younger than three years old, and the numbers of this age group had been constant in the population, right up until the collapse in 1992. The verdict: although seals eat cod, they don't seem to have undermined the population and caused the catastrophic collapse.[31]

It is also possible that other natural factors could have played their part. In the Baltic, severe storms have been implicated in fluctuating cod numbers, so perhaps the same happened over the Grand Banks. Perhaps, but it is not considered likely by fisheries scientists. In hindsight, there seems to be several reasons behind the cod collapse, all related to human exploitation. Environmental changes such as habitat destruction by trawls may have played a part, but the main problem seems to have been errors in assessing the cod numbers needed for the computer models that were used to calculate maximum sustainable catches. In particular, a critical time seems to have been the period just after Canada closed the fishery to foreign vessels. The models set up at this time were overoptimistic, predicting much larger populations than actually existed and Canada consequently built its cod fleet to too large a size.[32]

Fish populations are notoriously difficult to estimate, a fact well understood by fisheries scientists but much less appreciated by the politicians who make the laws. They expect science to provide hard and fast answers, and they therefore put more faith in the computer models than is justified. For example, one way of estimating cod numbers is to monitor catch per unit effort, on the principle that the harder fish are to catch the fewer there must be, which would certainly be true for most predators in the natural world. But this doesn't take into account the technological ingenuity of humans. As we've already seen, a free market and more especially a market shaped by subsidies can drive technological advancements to such an extent that catch per unit effort goes down even though the prey population is falling. Fishing companies borrow money to invest in new technology, but then need to increase their profits to pay back loans, which they can only do by investing in yet more technology to increase their catches. And at each stage, increasing technology makes fish easier to find and catch, even though numbers are falling. The economics of fishing drives a feedback loop which irreversibly cranks down the numbers of fish.

Fisheries models also underestimate the complexity of real animal populations, often because not enough is known about the basic biology of even familiar creatures like cod. For example, what part the existence of genetically distinct populations of cod played is still not clear. But what is clear is that the really big fish are the first to go. These are the ones that can lay the most eggs, but what would surprise most people is that these are also the ones that know what they are doing. George Rose of the Canadian Department of Fisheries and Oceans has spent many hours watching cod on sonar screens and has seen these big, old fish lead the shoals from spawning grounds to feeding areas. So targeting the big fish might be the most profitable but could both reduce the number of eggs laid and disrupt the cod's social system.

As our knowledge of ecology grows, it is also becoming clear that the very structure of complex ecosystems can make them prone to sudden and surprising collapses. Ecosystems are made up of different layers, of phytoplankton, zooplankton, plankton-eaters, and predators in many different guises. Elements in each level are linked by complex webs of interactions, and each level is organized into a hierarchy through which all the different levels also interact. Such a structure can be very stable as changes within levels are damped out between levels. In other words, the whole system is buffered against perturbations. But when the perturbations get too large, such a system will reach a tipping point, at which time even the smallest nudge will set in motion a series of radical and dramatic changes. With almost no warning, whole populations can collapse and the hierarchy reform in a new way.

Before the final collapse of the cod, scientists were aware that something was wrong, but by then the economic and political juggernaut was in motion. Calls for drastically reduced quotas were largely ignored in favor of political expediency. In the end such expediency cost Canada dearly. Over forty thousand people were put out of work by the moratorium on cod fishing imposed in 1992, the worst social and economic disaster in Canadian history.[33] With such a cost, surely the lessons from the cod collapse must have been taken to heart. Sadly not. Fish stocks continue to collapse in all the world's oceans, and they still catch both scientists and fishermen alike by surprise. But if even a fraction of human ingenuity for making money could be turned to understanding the nature of the real world, what should we have learnt from the long history of cod?

First, proceed with caution. Many scientists now argue for extreme conservatism in setting quotas for fisheries, since we clearly don't understand enough about fish populations to be any bolder. Such recommendations are never acted upon for the same reasons outlined above for cod. Second, hedge your bets. Set up no-take reserves where, even if our best guesses inadvertently cause another fisheries collapse, there will still be areas left unaffected. As fisheries biologists Carl Walters and Jean-Jacques Maguire so succinctly put it, if you want to insure that no more than 20 percent of a population is caught, make sure that only 20 percent is exposed to the fishing nets.[34]

Part of the reason for writing this book is to illustrate the sheer abundance of nature just a few centuries ago, to give a more realistic baseline against which to judge out current actions. Nowhere is this more critical than in the oceans. Those early reports suggest extraordinary, almost unbelievable numbers of fish, though such numbers are rarely taken into account when assessing what a healthy stock should look like. And even if we use what hard data can be mustered to build up a picture of a pristine ecosystem, we may still be grossly underestimating what nature *should* look like.

In a controversial paper in 2003, Ransom Myers and his colleagues suggested that populations of predators, like cod or tuna, drop within a very few years of the start of exploitation to just 10 percent of their original population. This is well before anyone considers recording or counting the population, so our management targets are inevitably aimed at maintaining depauperate populations. Some animals are hit even harder. Sharks in the North Atlantic could be down to only 0.1–1 percent of their former abundance. And, as we've seen, after five centuries of steadily increasing fishing pressure, cod are in a similar predicament.

If this is true, our picture of the natural state of the oceans seriously underestimates the abundance of these predatory fish. By the time anyone tries to measure the population, it is already only a tenth of what it should be so our estimates of the size of virgin populations could be out by a factor of ten. That's certainly what all those early reports of the northwest Atlantic suggest. I'll return to the implications of this for the future when we've completed the picture of the northwest Atlantic in the next chapter.

The humble cod has helped shape world history. The wealth it represented drew people across the Atlantic as surely as gold and silver did in Central and South America. For the first time, Europe's emerging capitalists met unlimited, unclaimed natural resources, and set in progress a trajectory that led to today's capitalist paradigms.

Often regarded as one of the founding fathers of today's free market capitalism, Adam Smith singled out the New England cod fishery, in which many fishermen worked not for wages but for a share in the profit, in his key work on capitalism, *The Wealth of Nations*. For him the cod fishery was an example of how quickly an economy could grow if given a free hand.[35] Those sentiments were echoed by Congressman James Gallivan of Boston at the end of the nineteenth century. He saw cod as commemorating democracy and the rise of free institutions. So it's appropriate therefore that it was the cod fishers of New England that began some of the first stirrings of what would become the world's greatest experiment in capitalism. Nearly one hundred years before the War of Independence, New Englanders sent a thousand cod to Charles II of England, with a polite note explaining, "We humbly conceive that the laws of England are bounded within 4 seas, and do not reach America."[36]

The wealth of cod and other natural resources of the northwest Atlantic were giving the inhabitants of North America a taste for independence, to pursue their ultimate capitalist venture unconstrained by laws and taxes from a country more than 1,500 miles away. Put more simply, it was this extraordinary past abundance of nature that made America possible.

CHAPTER 4

Sea of Whales

It was a cold, gray spring day, nearly twenty years ago, when I left Provincetown, at the very tip of Cape Cod, on board one of its whale-watching boats. The cold didn't matter though; it was a very well-equipped vessel, with gallons of hot coffee and plenty of snacks for sale in a heated observation lounge. After a few hours, and more than a few cups of coffee, the boat slowed and changed course toward a patch of undistinguishable gray foam, where our eagle-eyed captain had just seen a great tail fluke slide beneath the surface. As a seasoned naturalist, I felt it my duty to brave the cold, to experience this encounter directly, on equal terms with the whale rather than from the cocoon of a warm observation lounge. So I climbed the stairs into a bitter wind and clung, coffee-less, to the side rail. About five minutes later, and about fifty yards from the boat, the waters quietly parted around a dark gray shape. No fuss, no commotion.

As its blowhole cleared the surface, the whale spouted—a deep gentle sigh. In one fluid motion the whale's body continued to arch through the water. Its dorsal fin emerged, then its flukes, barely breaking the surface, and then it was gone—except that it wasn't. It left behind a huge footprint on the surface, a great circle of water that seemed to have been calmed by the quiet presence of the whale. Long after the whale had gone, its footprint gave a real sense of the scale of this animal. The whale's imprint on the water lasted for nearly a minute, but its imprint on my mind will last a lifetime. It left an overall impression of supreme fluid motion; the whale and the water seemed to be one. I've never felt such a sense of power and size anywhere else in the natural world, and yet the whale's presence was barely noticeable. No splashing, no rush and roar of water, just a gentle gush of whale-warm air and a lingering, silent footprint.

This was my first encounter with one of the great whales, and the first of their clan that I met was a humpback. We saw two other whales that day, both humpbacks, and I celebrated those extraordinary meetings with several more cups of coffee as we sailed back to Provincetown. I was both elated and contented by the fact that it was possible to sail out into the Atlantic and see such amazing creatures. Then, a few years later, I read the account of another vessel anchored in Cape Cod Bay, nearly three hundred years ago but only a few miles away from where I met my first whale. It is quite a famous vessel today; it was called the *Mayflower*. "[We] every day saw whales plying hard by us; of which in that place, if we had instruments and means to take them we might make a very rich return."[1]

The early accounts of the waters of the northeast coast of North America are filled with descriptions of the abundance of whales. Many explorers described them as a hazard to shipping, they were so numerous. Fifteen years after the *Mayflower* landed, "multitudes of great whales" were reported in Massachusetts Bay, "spewing up water in the air like the smoke of chimneys and making the sea about them white and hoary . . . which now was grown ordinary and usual to behold."[2] Similar sights were reported in the Gulf of St. Lawrence as well as the seas off Newfoundland and Labrador. And whales were here in great variety as well as great number. Jacques Cartier described the waters of the upper St. Lawrence as teeming with "a certain kind of fish never before of any man seene or knowen. They are of the bigness of a porpoise, yet nothing like them . . . the body and head white as snow."[3] He was describing a beautiful small whale called the beluga. They live in large schools and communicate with calls that are clearly audible above the surface—hence the explorers that followed Cartier called them sea canaries. They are thought of today largely as an Arctic species, but these early accounts show that they were much more widespread as well as much more numerous. They were common as far south as Boston,[4] though there were several periods of colder climate from the sixteenth to the eighteenth century, together often called the Little Ice Age, that would have probably allowed northern species to extend their range further south than today.

It wasn't long before the seas off Labrador and Newfoundland became known as the "Sea of Whales." Yet many early accounts contain such vivid descriptions of huge numbers of whales that it is easy to assume a certain amount of exaggeration— overexcited explorers wanting to impress the folks back home. But, just as we seem to have consistently underestimated the numbers of fish in a virgin ecosystem, so too we might be guilty of the same mistake with whales. There are figures around for historic whale populations, based on the records of whalers and tax returns for whale products, which have generally been accepted as good approximations. But some recent research by two scientists at Harvard University suggests we may need to think again.

They relied for their estimates on tiny structures called mitochondria that lie inside each and every body cell. Their usefulness to the cell is that they provide energy by burning sugar, but their usefulness to population scientists is that they have their own DNA, entirely separate from the DNA that makes up the chromosomes in the cell's nucleus. This is because mitochondria were once free-living bacteria, with their own genomes, but which, very early in evolution, partnered up with another cell to give rise to a more complex, more efficient cell. Mitochondrial DNA is handy stuff, since it isn't involved in all the sexual gymnastics performed by nuclear DNA each time we reproduce. You just get a clone of your mother's mitochondria, more or less. That makes it good for tracking populations through time.

But it has also been discovered that variation in mitochondrial DNA between individuals in a population is related to the size of that population. In other words, the bigger a population, the bigger the total variety in mitochondrial DNA. Or, the other way round, the bigger the variety of mitochondrial DNA in a sample of individuals, the bigger the population those individuals must have come from. The Harvard team looked at the variation of mitochondrial DNA in a sample of humpback whales and amazed themselves with the results. Historical research puts humpback numbers at around twenty thousand in the North Atlantic before whaling. The genetic estimates put the figure at 240,000, a *tenfold* difference. Genetic estimates for fin whales give an even greater historical population of 360,000, and for minke whales 265,000—all much larger than estimates based on historical records. Of course, certain assumptions have to be made about the modern whale populations. For example, there should be little mating with members of another population, like humpbacks in the south Atlantic, because that would increase variation. But even taking all such provisions into account, the historical whale population looks to be much greater than anyone ever imagined.[5]

What a time to have gone whale watching. An encounter with a single whale is a powerful experience. What must it have been like to stand on the shore of the Gulf of St. Lawrence and watch such great flotillas of whales passing so close you could almost touch them? Augustin le Gardeur, Sieur de Courtemanche, did just that in 1704. He was a French military officer who had come to the south coast of Labrador to make his fortune from fish and fur, and he must have been mightily encouraged when he saw whales "in such abundance that they came so close to the land they could be harpooned from the rocks."[6] He knew that whales meant money. Whale oil fueled the civilized world, and the discovery of the Sea of Whales was just like finding a vast new oil field today. In the modern world, there is no way that such a large new reserve wouldn't be exploited, nor was there then.

Whaling was already old by the time the first whalers came to the Sea of Whales. It seems to have begun as early as the eleventh or twelfth century when the Basques first ventured into the Bay of Biscay in pursuit of these ocean giants. And it was the Basques that dominated whaling in the Sea of Whales in the early years, though it didn't take long for other seafaring nations to follow suit. Whalers from all nations soon learned from the Basques which were the best whales to hunt and targeted those first. The right whale has the dubious honor of receiving its name for being at the head of the list, the "right whale" to hunt since it floats after it has been killed and yields a lot of oil and whalebone.

Whales can be divided into two sorts, baleen whales and toothed whales. Most of the great whales are baleen whales that feed by sieving small crustaceans or fish from the water through curtains of baleen (or whalebone) hung from their upper jaws. Whalebone was a kind of Middle Ages plastic, used for skirt hoops, knife handles, bristles for brushes, buggy whips, strapping for beds, and just about anything else. A single large right whale has over one thousand pounds of whalebone hanging in its mouth, enough to pay for a transatlantic voyage, ship, crew, and all. And that still leaves the ninety barrels of oil from each whale as pure profit. Not surprisingly, right whales were pursued with all possible vigor.

Having marveled at the sight of so many whales in the St. Lawrence, Courtemanche leaves us with another more chilling image of just how many of those whales had already been killed by the start of the eighteenth century. "[We found] a quantity of bones cast up on the coast like sticks of wood, one upon the other . . . there must have been in our estimate the remains of more than two or three thousand whales. In one place we counted ninety skulls of prodigious size."[7] The evidence of the slaughter remains to this day. In the 1960s, writer and campaigner for the northwest Atlantic, Farley Mowat, talked to an engineer building a highway up the west coast of Newfoundland. Wherever the engineer's crews dug they found the bleached bones of whales. They were so numerous that the roadbed was, in the words of the engineer "constructed more of bones than stones." Not surprisingly, right whales soon became harder to find.

Their numbers were much reduced by the end of the sixteenth century,[8] which means that even the spectacle described by the Pilgrim Fathers was only a fraction of what it might have been. There was a brief respite for the whales here around this time, as the Basque whalers became embroiled in conflicts back in Europe. Many Basque whaling ships were recalled in 1588 to become part of the Armada sent by Spain to invade England and depose the Protestant Elizabeth I. Despite surviving wind and weather in the hazardous northwest Atlantic, a large part of the Basque whaling fleet was lost as the Armada foundered in storms around the English coast, and the Basques never again returned in large numbers to the Sea of Whales.

The Basques were Europe's master whalers, and some of those that survived the Armada were employed by Dutch and English whalers in the early decades of the seventeenth century to help develop a whale fishery in the virgin seas around Spitsbergen. This also helped shift the European focus from the Sea of Whales. But the whales weren't left in peace. A homegrown whaling industry, based out of New England, was growing quickly.

In fact, there was whaling in New England long before it was New England. In 1605, an English explorer called George Waymouth described the way the Indians along the coast of Maine hunted whales.

> One especiall thing is their maner of killing the Whale, which they call Powdawe; and will describe his forme; how he bloweth up the water; and that he is 12 fathoms long; and that they go in company of their King with a multitude of their boats, and strike him with a bone made in fashion of a harping iron fastened to a rope, which they make great and strong of the barke of trees, which they veare out after him; then all their boats come about him, and as he riseth above water, with their arrowes they shoot him to death; when they have killed him and dragged him to shore, they call all their chiefe lords together, and sing a song of joy.[9]

They could have been taking right whales, which habitually passed close inshore as they migrated from their summer feeding grounds in the Sea of Whales to wintering grounds around the Bahamas and northern Caribbean. But they could also have been hunting a whale that no longer swims in the Atlantic: the Atlantic gray whale.

Pacific gray whales still amaze whale watchers on the coasts of California and Oregon as they pass close to shore on their way to and from calving grounds off Baja California. The gray whale spectacle along North America's Pacific coast is now very familiar, but I'm prepared to bet that virtually all those who've marveled at this sight would be surprised to learn that the gray whale was first described from specimens found in England and Sweden.[10] Admittedly these were subfossil remains, thousands of years old, but there is some evidence that this mysterious whale survived in the North Atlantic until the seventeenth century.

In 1725, a naturalist called Paul Dudley described the whales that New Englanders caught in the early days of whaling: a species they called the scrag whale. Since he was also the chief justice of Massachusetts, we can presume his evidence is reliable. "It is near a-kin to the Fin back [another large baleen whale], but, instead of a Fin upon his Back the ridge of the Afterpart of his back is scragged with half a Dozen Knobs or Knuckles . . . his bone [whalebone] is white but won't split."[11]

This sounds much more like a gray whale than any other species in the northern Atlantic. Although this is one of the few accounts in English, there are dozens of similar descriptions in Icelandic, Danish, and Swedish, recently translated and published by Ole Lindquist,[12] which make it certain that gray whales swam in the Atlantic in historical times though in what kind of numbers it's hard to say. They may have been abundant in the early days of colonization since there are innumerable coves, harbors, and points all along this coast with "scrag" in their name. However, reliable records during the heyday of whaling are few and far between, so it is entirely possible that the population was already much reduced, possibly by Indian hunting, as described by George Waymouth, or by long-term climate change.[13] Whatever the case, the last one seems to have been killed sometime in the early eighteenth century.

Now, just as with the great auk, the only way we can reconstruct the natural history of this species is from historical descriptions and archaeology. It's a great pity that we can't observe it today, since, although Atlantic and Pacific gray whales are now regarded as the same species, the Atlantic population seems to have had some very unusual behavior. In account after account from Iceland and Denmark, these whales are described as resting on sandbars on the shore. This observation was made by Thomas Bartholin: "It is happy to rest on land. If one comes upon it on the sand one cannot get near it because it throws up the surrounding sand and moves vigorously in an extraordinary way."[14]

It was called *sandlaegja* (sand-lier) in Icelandic because "it takes its name from the sand in which it loves to lie, because it is generally seen on the shore." A seventeenth century Icelandic work says of the *sandlaegja:* "It is very tenacious of life and can come to land to lie as a seal to rest the whole day."[15] It seems extraordinary that a whale would beach itself voluntarily in this way. Pacific gray whales enter very shallow water and often lie in lagoons with their backs exposed, but I know of no observations of them hauling out like seals. Nor is it generally a good idea for a whale to behave like this, for several reasons. The blubber of the gray whale, while not as thick as that of the right whale, is still thick enough to yield a good thirty barrels of high-grade oil. Its original purpose though was not to light the lamps of Europe and America but to insulate the whale against the cold Atlantic. It is so efficient a blanket that, out of water, a whale is in danger of overheating. Further, robbed of the support of water, stranded whales have difficulty breathing. Yet the Icelandic and Danish whalers knew the different kinds of whales well and paid close attention to the habits of their quarry. Their reports should not be lightly dismissed.

So one legacy of the whalers is that we'll never really know whether it would have been possible to crawl cautiously through the dunes fringing some remote windswept bay and peer through the grasses to see a flotilla of forty-foot whales hauled up on offshore sandbanks like giant seals. Would a careless movement alert them to your presence and send then off in gargantuan convulsions, raising a great sand storm as Thomas Bartholin described? Maybe. Maybe not. And we'll never know.

Whaling prospered in New England because it provided a valuable export in an area that lacked agricultural alternatives, such as tobacco in the mid-Atlantic states or sugar in the Caribbean. But relentless commercial pressure quickly and dramatically reduced whale numbers. Some reports suggest that the inshore waters were largely fished out by 1740.[16] In the four preceding decades, between two and half and three thousand right whales had been taken from the waters between Maine and Delaware. Nor were these the first signs that the Sea of Whales was a finite resource. Whale populations had already been severely depleted in the Straits of Belle Isle between Newfoundland and Labrador as early as the sixteenth century, after tens of thousands of whales had been taken by Basque whalers alone.

It is generally assumed that the Basques had targeted right whales, for all the reasons that made them "right," together with another impressive species, the bowhead, in more or less equal numbers. But a recent analysis of bones from a Basque whaling station at Red Bay in Labrador suggests that the Basques were taking far more bowheads than rights. Genetic analysis on this admittedly small sample suggests that the reason for this was that the right whale population was already low when the Basques arrived.[17] Like Atlantic gray whales, the cause may have been climate change or Indian hunting. However, not everyone agrees with this interpretation, and many still maintain that the population of right whales remained large until the start of European whaling. Such are the difficulties of reconstructing the details of the past; the natural world is a dynamic and complicated place. It's clear though that, whatever the species composition, the overall population of cetaceans in the Sea of Whales was enormous—and probably far more enormous than we previously imagined—before the advent of commercial whaling.

The second species targeted by the Basques, the bowhead, is a high Arctic species that descends to the Sea of Whales in winter. So it wasn't until the middle of the sixteenth century that whalers finally met the mighty bowhead, and they were overawed by this immense creature. A bowhead sieves small crustaceans from the water with a mouth that is ten feet high, twenty feet deep, and hung with two tons of baleen. To survive in cold Arctic waters, each whale is insulated with enough blubber to produce seven thousand gallons of oil. So the whalers didn't linger long in admiring the bowhead, but set about a relentless pursuit.

Historical estimates put the numbers of bowheads in the northwest Atlantic at about 150,000, although, as we now realize, this could be an underestimate. There must have been considerable numbers, because it took a long time for the combined whaling fleets of many nations to finally reduce the population to almost nothing. There were still bowheads when right whales were a scarce sight and gray whales a mere memory. But the whalers eventually followed the bowheads back to their summer feeding grounds in the high Arctic and found "such sholes of whales and seals, as is no where else to be met with in the known world."[18] The slaughter continued there. "Along the floe edge lay the dead bodies of hundreds of flinched whales, and the air for miles around was tainted with the foetor which arose from such masses of putridity.

Towards evening the numbers we came across were even increasing and the effluvia which assailed our olfactories became almost intolerable."[19]

By 1914, bowheads were so scarce that many thought that they had followed the gray whale into oblivion, and so great was the slaughter of all the "right" kinds of whales that whalers had to turn to some of the wrong ones. Humpbacks don't yield as much oil and, worse still, sink when killed, so the whalers resorted to a strategy, called "blasting," which epitomizes the carelessness with which we treat life when it seems boundless.

The whalers harpooned as many humpbacks as they could and allowed them to swim off and die of their wounds. But as each sunken carcass began to putrefy, gas built up in the body cavity until eventually the whale "blasted" to the surface, where it floated until decomposition had gone far enough to release the gas and send the whale back to its ocean grave. The whalers relied on spotting carcasses that had blasted to the surface. But, because they had no idea where the whales had died or how the currents would carry the floating carcass, they had to rely largely on luck and at best probably only recovered one in three of the whales that they killed.

As the Sea of Whales lost its whales, even the smaller whales and porpoises were hunted. The beautiful white beluga abounded in the St. Lawrence all the way up to Montreal, where they were described as "leaping about in the river." But each beluga could be turned into a barrel of oil, and a good grade of leather could be made from their porcelain white skins. So they were trapped in nets in large numbers at high water, then "as the tide ebbs you have the pleasure of seeing their confusion and fruitless struggles to escape. In other words they are left high and dry and in such numbers that they are sometimes heaped upon one another."[20]

Canada's Department of Fisheries and Oceans put the population of belugas in the St. Lawrence at about ten thousand prior to 1885,[21] and that was after many decades of scenes such as the one above. Today, there are between five hundred and one thousand left, and their bodies are so full of chemical pollutants in this busy industrial waterway that their carcasses are classed as contaminated waste. As if whaling and pollution wasn't enough, belugas have also been blamed for the crash in the salmon population. They had a bounty placed on their heads through the early decades of the twentieth century, and even in the last few decades some people along the shores of the St. Lawrence still take pot shots at any passing beluga.

If anything, the other small whales, porpoises, and dolphins were even more numerous. Several early explorers described passing through schools of thousands every day as they approached the shores of the New World, shores that were themselves often smothered in other kinds of marine mammals. As one French explorer put it, there were "seals and porpoises so numerous they became a nuisance."

Among the hoards of smaller seals were even more magnificent creatures. Called *hvalross,* or whale horse, by Norwegian explorers, their name has become corrupted in English to walrus. Bull walruses from the Atlantic average over ten feet in length, impressive enough on their own, but when hauled up on beaches and sandbars in their thousands, or even hundreds of thousands, the sight of so many of these huge beasts slowly turning pink in the sun (which they do) must have been truly extraordinary. Yet such sights were common to those that explored the northwest Atlantic in the seventeenth and eighteenth centuries.

One of the first places that these great herds were encountered was on tiny Sable Island, no more than a sliver of sand on the edge of the Scotian Shelf, nearly two hundred miles off the coast of Nova Scotia. Even in the mid-eighteenth century, after many years of hunting, there were one hundred thousand walruses here, so the unknown sailors who first found this speck of land would likely have seen many more taking their ease on the sand. As explorers felt their way along the great funnel of the Gulf of St. Lawrence, they encountered yet more herds, the largest probably on the Isles de Madeleine (Magdalen Islands), a string of hilly islands connected by long sandy spits in the center of the Gulf. Some estimates suggest up to a quarter of a million animals lived in this Central Gulf herd.[22] The mud and sand on the floor of the Gulf of St. Lawrence and the Scotian shelf must have been crammed with a large variety of mollusks to support these great herds.

Like the white belugas, walruses are today thought of as creatures of the high Arctic, but, before hunting, they lived in huge numbers much further south. In fact, some of those vast walrus herds were only about four hundred miles from New York City. But each walrus yielded a lot of oil, and its tough hide made strong ropes, much sought after by mariners in the early days. In addition, those great ivory tusks were at one time literally worth their weight in gold. Not surprisingly, the walrus herds diminished along with the great whales, and today they have vanished from all the southern parts of their range. Now they really are creatures of the remote Arctic. A report from the mid-eighteenth century in the Sessional Papers of the Quebec government summarized the end of the whale horse story in the south:

> They used to be found basking in the sun and breathing at their ease on the sandy beaches of the Gulf. But first the French, then the English and Americans waged as bitter a war against them that at the commencement of this century they were almost totally destroyed. . . . Their tusks are often found buried in the sand of the shores of the River and Gulf of St Lawrence. These are the last remains of those animals whose spoils have helped to build up many fortunes. But the indifference and want of foresight of governments, and the cupidity of merchants, have caused their total[23]

For the other seals in this area, the story is far from over. Some of these tales of exploitation of the northwest Atlantic might seem relentless and brutal when viewed in the sharp focus of hindsight, the excesses of less enlightened generations. The saga of the seals, however, belies this notion. It brings our story right up to date and asks some very fundamental questions about how much our relationship with the natural world has really changed.

There are four common seals in the northwest Atlantic. Harbor and gray seals extend right down the northeast coast, while harp and hooded seals are so-called ice seals, northern species that move south in winter with the pack ice and then haul out on the ice in the spring, before it melts, to give birth to their pups.

The gray seal is a large creature—the largest not that much smaller than an Atlantic walrus. They hauled out on beaches and sandbars up and down the northeast coast in such numbers that their braying could be heard several miles away. In 1535, some of Cartier's men, exploring the northwest Gulf of St. Lawrence, found a river in which there were "fish in appearance like unto horses . . . we saw great number of these fishes in this river."[24] These were probably gray seals, rather than walrus; gray seals were often called "horseheads" by both French and English. And horseheads were abundant all the way along the St. Lawrence as far as the site of Quebec City. Later French explorers found islands "completely covered in seals." There still must have been many tens of thousands on the Isles de Madeleine in the seventeenth century, to judge from Nicolas Denys's comment that as many as eight hundred could be killed in a single day. More than a century later, a British naval officer reported being able to see several thousand seals at a time around these same islands. And at the start of the eighteenth century, the Sieur de Courtemanche, exploring the north coast of the Gulf to expand his fur and oil enterprise, was able, on his own, to kill two hundred seals in two days.

But such spectacular numbers of gray seals pale into insignificance when compared to harp seals. As the sea in their summer Arctic feeding grounds begins to congeal, they move south down the coast of Labrador—a great stream of life numbering millions of seals. A French observer in 1760 watched in awe as he described the sea filled from shore to horizon with migrating seals, a procession that took ten whole days to pass. Each winter, part of that great stream swung into the Gulf of St. Lawrence and traveled almost as far as Quebec City. At the end of winter, the seals hauled out on the ice to give birth and, as the ice broke up, dispersed once more around the Arctic to feed.

As the whale and walrus populations were converted into oil and other products, so the attention of hunters switched to the still-abundant seals. Because of its size, the gray seal was an early target. At the beginning of the nineteenth century, each seal produced oil worth an average week's wages, more than enough incentive to hunt them. As gray seals inevitably became harder to find, attention switched to the smaller but far more abundant harp seals. On occasions during the eighteenth century, an early breakup of the ice cast tens of thousands of pups adrift. As ocean currents and wind drove the ice ashore along the Gulf of St. Lawrence, locals reacted to the unexpected bounty with a killing frenzy, taking tens of thousands of pups.

By the beginning of the nineteenth century, the habits of the harp seal were better understood, and their ice-floe nurseries had been discovered. Hunters no longer had to wait for a lucky breakup of the ice or the wind to blow a small fortune their way. The potential harvest on the ice spurred the design of bigger and better ice breakers that, by the start of the third decade of the nineteenth century, could reach into the heart of harp seal territory. It was not a pretty sight. The following was recorded by Professor J. B. Jukes in 1840:

> When piled in a heap together, the young seals looked like so many
> lambs and when out from the bloody and dirty mass of carcasses one
> poor wretch, still alive, would lift up its face and begin to flounder about,
> I could stand it no longer and, arming myself with a handspike, I pro-
> ceeded to knock on the head and put out of their misery all in whom I
> saw signs of life . . . I saw one poor wretch skinned while yet alive . . . the
> vision of [another] writhing its snow-white woolly body with its head

bathed in blood, through which it was vainly endeavouring to see and breathe, really haunted my dreams.[25]

In these early days, the slaughter was driven by market forces: the ever-increasing demand for oil. At the start of the twentieth century, it looked like that same market economy might come to the rescue of the seals with the arrival of technology to process fossil oil buried deep beneath the ground. As demand for marine oil fell, the seals should have had chance to recover, but fate was not that kind. As we've already seen, the once-abundant salmon stocks of the northeast coast were fast disappearing around this time, and seals got the blame.

Gray seals had been much reduced by hunting for oil, but the smaller harbor seals had largely escaped and still existed in good numbers. In 1927, Canada placed a $5.00 bounty on each harbor seal's head, or rather its muzzle, which was the part a hunter had to produce to claim his reward. The Great Depression, already heaping misery on people, wasn't great news for seals either. As folks struggled to scratch a living any way they could, the seal bounty increased pressure on already declining populations. Not content with the rate at which the seal populations were falling and seeing no recovery in salmon or other commercial fish stocks, the Canadian government increased the bounty on several occasions. It never seemed to occur to anyone that seals and salmon had been existing side by side in huge numbers before the arrival of the Europeans. In 1967, in response to a partial recovery in gray seal numbers, government officials, from the somewhat euphemistically named Conservation and Protection Branch, began to kill seals at all Canadian colonies apart from Sable Island, which was too far away for the seals to be realistically accused of salmon predation.

Between 1967 and 1984, Farley Mowat, in his harrowing book *Sea of Slaughter,* estimated that 90 percent of all Canadian gray seal pups were killed outside of Sable Island. In response to an explanation for such slaughter, Mowat received the following "government-speak" reply: "Seals inhibit the maximization of fisheries growth potential, adversely affecting rational harvesting of these natural resources and the maximization of a healthy economy. Such negative flow factors must be dealt with by scientifically validated management programmes such as the one we are engaged in." Unfortunately, science didn't entirely back up this stance. Unpicking the statistics suggests that seals were taking no more than 1.6 percent of the commercial catch. The problems facing the northwest Atlantic fisheries were (and are) far more complicated than a simple competition between predators.

Meanwhile, south of the border, both gray and harbor seals received full protection by the U.S. government in 1972. Increasing concern for populations worldwide led to an attempt in 1981 to list both species on appendix II of CITES (the Convention on International Trade in Endangered Species of Wild Fauna and Flora), to afford some measure of global protection, a move blocked by Canada.

Harp seals still exist in large numbers, though because of their remote range, it is hard to know exactly how many there are. The latest "guesstimates" suggest somewhere from 4–6 million animals living in the northwest Atlantic, which, while impressive, must be substantially less than precommercial hunting populations, if for no other reason than between 1840 and 1860, half a million seals were taken each year.

In the twentieth century, with seal oil no longer a market commodity, human economic ingenuity found another way to make money from the harp seals: the white fur of the young pups. The full potential of this market wasn't realized at first, since the white fur only remained attached to the skin of those pups that were taken from the bodies of their mothers, but in the 1950s Norwegian chemists found ways of treating the pelt of newborn pups so that the hair was not shed. The fashion market then supported a very lucrative trade, initially driven by Norwegians based in Newfoundland but which, by the 1960s, had become something of a free-for-all, with aerial spotters guiding the killing boats to the largest pup concentrations. Comments by one of the pilots suggest that not much had changed out on the ice since the days of Professor Jukes, more than a hundred years earlier. "They weren't even trying to kill their seals. Guys was holding them down with one foot and ripping them up the belly, then trying to peel the skin off. . . . I seen things I won't forget. You ever see a skinned pup trying to wiggle out of the water where some guy had kicked it. . . . I never went back the next year. It was too rough for me."[26]

Then, in 1964, the Quebec tourism department commissioned a film to interest the world in the wonders of the province. In a somewhat misguided reading of the situation, the film included scenes from the harp seal pup harvest, and the world suddenly took more interest in the province than anyone had intended. It's not an understatement to say there was worldwide revulsion at the scenes on the blood-red ice. An activist called Brian Davies took on the Canadian government—and the government fought back. In response,

Davies, founder of the International Fund for Animal Welfare (IFAW), began a highly successful campaign for the hearts and minds of world opinion — though more for the hearts than the mind.[27] Many of the antisealing campaigns were founded as much on the emotional arguments as the practical, and I don't see anything wrong with this. The moral and animal welfare aspects of such "harvests" are as important as any other. But, of course, it's much easier to engage hearts when the victims are cute white seal pups rather than cod or herrings.

At the same time, other newly formed organizations, like the Sea Shepherd Conservation Society and Greenpeace began direct action against the seal hunters, and these varied strategies began to bite home. In 1983, the European Community banned the import of seal products, though with the proviso, negotiated by the sealing nations of Canada and Norway, that this would only last for two years in the first instance. While the politicians traded platitudes, celebrities became the latest weapon in the war when Brigitte Bardot began her high-profile campaign. Canada responded to adverse publicity by banning the taking of whitecoats, though, through some quick redefining of seal pup stages, that ban was never entirely effective. Slowly the market for products of the seal hunt began to wane, reaching a low point in 1995 when only sixty thousand pups were taken. In the mid-1990s, in response to a reduction in hunting pressure, the harp seal population seemed to be recovering,[28] or at least so the computer models of the population suggested. Then a year later, a new market in Asia opened up, and, in 1996, nearly a quarter of a million seals were taken. There's no more clear indication of the power of free market forces to shape ecology.

The increased kills of recent years have also been justified on the grounds that harp seals are preventing the recovery of the collapsed cod stocks. Again, as for gray and harbor seals, the science backing this up is somewhat equivocal, enough that Canadian government statements in 2004 seem to be backing away, at least a little, from this old "seals eat cod" argument. Instead, they now argue that they are managing a sustainable commercial harvest. In the same year, the government announced its Atlantic Seal Hunt Management Plan, for the period 2003–5, which raised the total allowable catch to 325,000 animals per year. The seal hunt is still in full swing, so much so that Brigitte Bardot returned to the campaign trail in 2006, along with Sir Paul McCartney, who was photographed on the ice with the iconic white pup with baleful black eyes. In that year, 335,000 such pups were taken.[29]

The Canadian government feels it has the right to harvest its natural resources in whatever way it chooses. And the seal harvest is worth around C$16 million a year to the people of Canada's Atlantic coast—people hard hit by the collapse of many of the other fisheries. Yet this is not a great sum in federal or international terms, and it's even less if the subsidies were removed. The real issue is an official attitude that results in statements like the following, from John Efford, addressing the Newfoundland House of Assembly in 1998: "I would like to see the six million seals, or whatever number is out there, killed and sold, or destroyed or burned. I do not care what happens to them. The more they kill, the better I will love it." In 2003, he was named minister for national resources.

Harp seals are undeniably still abundant—but so were cod. The lessons of history, despite being so graphic, are slow to be learned. The Canadian government says that the models they use to calculate how many pups can be taken are based on a precautionary approach. But in reality, the estimates are far from cautious. On the contrary, running these models for different ranges of realistic assumptions shows that there is a real danger that the current hunt could drive the seal population to critically low levels.[30] In addition, a significant percentage of animals are struck and lost, so never reported, which means that the number of seals killed each year could well exceed even the government's own targets. Since the cod collapse was the result of similar circumstances and caused so much hardship, it's almost impossible to believe that anyone could have their heads so deeply buried in the sand.

And now, harp seals face another danger, one that, in the face of continuing culls, threatens to wipe out this species over much of its range. Over the last decade, it has become almost universally accepted that our planet is warming as the oil that replaced whale and seal oil is burned and releases greenhouse gases into the atmosphere. A consequence of this is that the harp seal's sea-ice nurseries are shrinking.

Observers from IFAW, overflying the ice in 2007, reported that they had never seen so little ice, and it's thought that virtually all the seal pups in the southern Gulf of St. Lawrence may have drowned. In response to the impact of climate change, the Canadian government reduced the 2007 quota to 270,000 pups, still far too high according to IFAW scientists, who say the computer models used to calculate the harp seal population, as well as the quotas for the culls, are just too unreliable. For example, the model estimated that there were 5.2 million seals in 2000, and quotas were set at a level to reduce that population. Yet in 2004, the estimated population had risen to 5.9 million animals—more likely a mark of the inaccuracies in the population models than the resilience of the seals. The saga of the cod has shown that the unthinkable can happen; the saga of the seals, that such a lesson has yet to be taken to heart.

It's not just the lack of astounding spectacles, of endless shoals of fish, of great flocks of birds, vast herds of seals and walrus, or flotillas of mighty whales, that make today's experience of the northwest Atlantic so different from those of Cabot and Cartier. You can't remove so much from an ecosystem and not change it fundamentally. As predatory species disappear, others multiply, which in turn causes changes further down the food chain. Ecologists call this a "trophic cascade."[31]

In some places, the virtual disappearance of so many predatory fish led to a rise in the populations of zooplankton. These in turn caused a crash in the tiny planktonic plants (the phytoplankton) on which they fed. But there are other, more noticeable, effects. In the absence of vast shoals of bottom-feeders like cod, there are many more open water or pelagic fish. The northwest Atlantic has shifted from a demersal to a pelagic system, a transformation helped by the destruction of the sea bottom by trawls. And on the sea floor these days there are many, many more crabs. Snow crab populations exploded on the Grand Banks after the cod crash, and, ironically, snow crabs, a luxury food, are far more valuable than cod. So a lucrative snow crab fishery has emerged to take the place of the cod fishery. The 1995 season in Newfoundland made more money than any cod fishing season in history.

A critical reader might observe that the fact that fishermen can now make more money from crabs than cod is surely a good thing. How resilient and adaptable nature is that we can continue to make money from it, even after such long exploitation. But the crab fishery, however long that might last, is a symptom of an insidious change happening in all the world's oceans. As we deplete the stocks of favored prey—big, top predators—we move on to the next ecological layer below and then to the layer below that, in a process that Daniel Pauly has called "fishing down the marine food web."[32] But marine food webs are finite. We can only go so far and after that, as economist Herman Daly points out, we can't eat recipes.[33]

The degree of transformation of the northwest Atlantic ecosystem cannot be overstated. Our understanding of marine ecology—even our textbook picture of a pyramid-shaped stack of many producers at the base through to an apex of few predators—is based on studies of modern oceans. It is now clear that the original ocean was teeming with top predators like cod and whales, sharks and tuna. Marine biologist Jeremy Jackson has gone as far as suggesting that our actions over the past five centuries have turned the ocean food pyramid upside down.[34] And even if not completely inverted, the pyramid should really have an un-pyramid-like bulge at the top, so perhaps we should stop referring to species like cod as "apex" predators.

The removal of cod seems to have allowed their prey to flourish, but, curiously, the removal of the great whales from the Sea of Whales seems to have had no effect on the baitfish populations, even though there were marked changes when whale numbers plummeted in the Bering Straits between Alaska and Siberia.[35] But changes in the Atlantic's ecology were only followed over a relatively short time, and relatively recently, so it's likely that major effects had already happened without our noticing.

This vision of a drastically transformed ocean has a bearing on the last and most obvious question to ask. Can we hope to see the abundant ocean in its former glory ever again? Tuna, swordfish, marlin, sharks, and many of the other predators whose populations are so low are still being overfished. One recent mathematical model suggests that for sharks in the northwest Atlantic, a reduction in fishing of 40–80 percent is required to prevent them for sliding into extinction. But for other fish, protection is already at hand. And sometimes they begin to recover quickly. When areas of the Georges Bank, the southernmost of the underwater plateaus in the northwest Atlantic, were closed in 1994, haddock and yellow-tail flounder populations quickly began to rise. However, there was little increase in cod numbers. Cod, it seems, are a different kettle of fish.

Large areas of the cod's former strongholds have been closed to fishing since the collapse, and many other areas, where cod do still occur, though in much reduced numbers, have severe restrictions on catches. At the time of the collapse, the Canadian government optimistically suggested that the stocks would recover in a couple of years and fishing could resume. Cod, after all, can lay millions of eggs, so it shouldn't take them long to repopulate the Grand Banks. In the mid-1990s, a glimmer of recovery prompted a tentative restart of small-scale fishing, but that proved to be a false hope. The fishery was soon reclosed and has stayed that way. In 2003, a report to the Canadian fisheries minister said that there was very little sign of any recovery in the collapsed cod stocks.

The reason for this failure is that many of our presumptions about fish are wrong. We have been seduced by the incomprehensibly vast numbers of the past into believing that it is impossible to overfish them. Huxley believed that in the nineteenth century, and many people still believe this today, despite all the evidence from history. Yet, if each and every fish in those infinite shoals can produce vast numbers of offspring, where's the problem? True, a single big female cod can produce a million eggs, yet, surprisingly, population studies show that the rate of recovery depends on the size of the existing stock, just as it does for much less productive animals. Such a counterintuitive finding shows again how little we really understand the complexity of linkages in these ecosystems.

At the moment, however, several cod stocks don't seem to be recovering at all, and many politicians still seek to transfer the blame to other species. There are still plenty of people that justify the continuing harp seal hunt on the grounds that the seals are preventing recovery of the cod stocks. Yet everything we've learned from what the ocean should look like and how we've changed it shows that, in the words of Jeremy Jackson, "the culling of large predators to increase more desirable fish stocks is bound to fail."[36] Others argue that there is some evidence for a beneficial effect on cod populations by removing seals, but it is based purely on computer models, all of which are only as good as the assumptions they are based on and the quality of data they are fed. It was, after all, unreliable computer models that were in large part responsible for the cod collapse in the first place.

Whales, in their severely depleted numbers, have also been blamed for competing with hard-pressed fishermen though a recent study has shown that, geographically, the main whale feeding areas and human fisheries hardly overlap at all.[37] In the light of such studies, it would be a huge step forward in our stewardship of the oceans if, instead of blaming every other factor, we stood up and accepted responsibility for our actions.

It is quite possible that the changed ecology of the ocean will prevent cod from ever regaining their former numbers. The flow of energy through the system has been fundamentally changed, and cod may not be able to reinsert themselves into the food web. They may not, for example, be able to cope with vastly increased numbers of pelagic fish that eat cod eggs.[38] As we turned the food pyramid upside down, the ecosystem may have flipped from one stable state to another, and the future for cod could be, at best, uncertain.

The same problems facing cod could also affect the chances of recovery of both seabirds and whales. At the end of the nineteenth century, many seabirds were being heavily hunted for the fashion trade as well as for food and for fish bait. Most of these received protection in 1918 under the Migratory Birds Treaty Act, and numbers steadily grew. You could be forgiven for thinking that we were well on our way to restoring the spectacles that greeted Cartier on his voyages around the Gulf of St. Lawrence, except of course for the great auk and the Atlantic gray whale, but the ocean's ecology is more complicated than that.

Machias Seal Island is located about ten miles off the coast of Maine on the U.S.-Canada border, and like many such islands is home to colonies of seabirds. But in 2004, not a single arctic or common tern managed to raise any chicks there. Adult birds were bringing in tiny larval fish instead of larger baitfish, and some were even seen, in desperation, trying to feed their chicks on ants. All the chicks starved, and there are stories like this from right around the Atlantic. It is clear that there is a drastic food shortage, though no one is completely sure of the underlying causes.

Some baitfish populations, like sand eels and herring, are heavily fished, and on top of that, climate change is probably affecting the distribution of many ocean creatures. And fishing pressure might even change the behavior of some fish. Sonar surveys suggest that offshore shoals of capelin in heavily fished areas now seem to live in great sheets over the bottom and don't rise up into the water column as they used to. This puts them out of reach of many surface-feeding seabirds. A higher proportion of seabirds are now listed as endangered than any other group of birds, almost certainly because of centuries of mismanagement of the oceans.

And what about restoring the Sea of Whales? Globally, whales were given protection only as late as 1986, when the International Whaling Commission introduced a moratorium on commercial whaling. There were, however, some glaring loopholes, such as allowing scientific whaling, presumably to increase our understanding of these creatures before they become extinct. But whales are long-lived, slow-growing animals and, for some, the damage has already been done. Estimating current whale stocks is a tricky business, but the best guess is that North Atlantic right whales number only 300–350. Between 1970 and 2001, fifty of these creatures were killed in collisions with boats, or by becoming entangled in fishing gear. Like some of the cod stocks, northern right whales are showing no signs of rebuilding their population, though, under the moratorium, southern right whales have grown at 7 percent a year.[39]

The problems for the whales are probably the same as those facing cod: they simply may not be able to recover in the new Atlantic. If so, there's a good chance that northern right whales will join the Atlantic gray whale. Atlantic bowheads are also down to their last few hundreds, and the same fate could await them. Even for commoner whales the picture is not all that rosy. There is some evidence that young humpbacks are smaller now than they should be, suggesting that, like the seabirds, they may be having difficulty in finding enough food.

One fundamental problem emerges from this broad trawl through five hundred years of European history in the northwest Atlantic, a problem of perception. The ocean is so vast and so full of life that it was seen as both infinite and outside of time—both unchanging and unchangeable. That's how Cartier and Cabot saw it and that's how the majority of people, particularly those with the power to do something about it, see it today. David Henry Thoreau saw this problem back in the nineteenth century: "We do not associate the idea of antiquity with the ocean nor wonder how it looked a thousand years ago for it was equally wild and unfathomable always."[40]

Even Rachel Carson, whose book *The Silent Spring* woke up the world to the dangers of pollution, subscribed to a similar view. In her earlier book, *The Sea around Us,* she argues that the sea is too vast for man to control or damage in the way he had the continents. The ocean has been seen as outside history, yet it is only when we incorporate it into history that we gain a true vision of what it should be.

In a 1995 paper, marine biologist Daniel Pauly coined the phrase "shifting baseline," by which he meant that each generation judges changes in marine ecology over their own generation. Our own personal experience is so much more powerful, especially in the absence of a deeper historical overview, that the true impact of five hundred years of exploitation has not been widely recognized. The shifting baseline problem, however, is more pervasive and more widely applicable than just the oceans. Here then is the true value of exploring North America's past abundance, both at sea and on land.

Recently, a group of ecologists and historians have come together to try and shift our perceptions of the oceans in exactly this manner. In 1999, the History of Marine Animal Populations project began with centers at the University of Hull in the United Kingdom, the University of Southern Denmark, and the University of New Hampshire. A generous indemnity from the Alfred P. Sloan Foundation enabled them to work through the initial culture shock of historians and scientists sitting in the same room and to begin to put our long-term effects on the marine environment into a much clearer perspective. It's only when we know what the oceans should look like that we know the scale of the conservation problems that we face.

Marine ecosystems the world over are in crisis thanks to centuries of over-fishing. Yet in the past, an extraordinary abundance of predators, of fish, seals, and whales, had been harvesting much greater quantities of marine resources than fishermen and had been doing so sustainably for millennia. How was that possible? Unfortunately, we have all but destroyed the very system that could have shown us.

Biologists at the University of British Columbia have begun a series of projects under the heading "Back to the Future" in which they are looking at ways to rebuild past marine ecosystems off both coasts of North America. There are strong economic incentives to do this. Sustainable harvests and therefore profits from rebuilt ecosystems will be much greater, but the problem is that these increased financial returns are long term. Democratic politics are short term, and there are no votes to be gained by taking the drastic measures needed to recreate the extraordinary abundance of the Sea of Whales.

CHAPTER 5

Living in Paradise

There are some things every naturalist should try to do at least once in a lifetime. One is to stand on the shore of Delaware Bay in May or June at high tide when the moon is full or new. You'll be rewarded, not just by one spectacle, but by two of the most wonderful sights nature has to offer. The first is amazing because it's been happening since long before Delaware Bay or even North America existed; the second because it's a demonstration of precision timing in every sense of the word.

The first time I visited Delaware Bay in the right season, the high tide was around dawn, though on that particular day dawn didn't so much break as creep into existence, almost unnoticed under a blanket of fog. The water of the bay was eerily calm, like gray silk, and a banging shutter on one of the deserted beachfront houses added an air of Hitchcock suspense. Then, as in any good horror film, strange dark shapes began to emerge at the water's edge, and creatures that looked a lot like alien robots began to inch themselves ashore. This was it. The first spectacle had begun—a mass spawning of horseshoe crabs.

Actually, horseshoe crabs don't look anything like crabs, for the very good reason that they're not crabs. They have a much more ancient heritage. Creatures almost indistinguishable from modern horseshoe crabs have been preserved in rocks at least 350 million years old, which meant that the drama that I was now watching unfold must have happened somewhere on planet Earth many millions of times before. But that doesn't make it any less special.

In no time at all, so many horseshoe crabs had emerged from the slick waters of the bay that they looked like a continuous heap of flotsam stranded at the high water mark, as far along the beach as I could see in the fog. I've returned several times over the years to different beaches around the bay to film this spectacle, and it doesn't get any less amazing. In fact, on the last trip, we filmed at night, when, if anything, the spectacle is even more amazing. Much bigger numbers of crabs emerge when the high tides fall during the hours of darkness, though at night it's harder to appreciate the scale, even with powerful film lights.

As they emerge, larger females have at least one smaller male in tow, often several. The males have a special pair of pincers with which they hang on to the female's shell, making her efforts to reach a point just above the high tide line all the more difficult. When a female finally reaches the right place on the beach, she digs a nest in the sand and lays her eggs, which her attendant male promptly fertilizes. The crabs usually crawl up the beach on either the new or full moon because these are the highest tides of the month. Their eggs won't be washed out until the next spring tide, by which time they'll be ready to hatch. When horseshoe crabs first began going to all this trouble to spawn, it was an extremely good idea. The oceans were full of creatures that relished horseshoe crab eggs, but above the waves there wasn't, as yet, much going on at all. Dry land was the safest place for their eggs to develop.

How times have changed. Three hundred and fifty million years later, and the crabs barely have time to lay their eggs before squadrons of laughing gulls emerge from the clearing mist, a braying hoard, hopping and fluttering around the heaps of spawning crabs, scooping up beakful after beakful of rich, oily eggs. Yet, the effort must still be worth it, otherwise natural selection would have long since written new spawning instructions into the horseshoe crab's genes.

As I was musing on these thoughts, the fog finally cleared and revealed what looked like tendrils of dark smoke drifting over the bay. Time for the second spectacle—the red knots had arrived. These shorebirds have traveled up from wintering grounds as far away as Tierra del Fuego, in the deep south of Argentina. They're heading on up to the Arctic, making them one of the longest-distance fliers in the natural world. But although Delaware Bay is only a stopover, it's a vital part of their travel plans. They time their arrival here just as the crabs are dumping uncountable millions of highly nutritious eggs into the sand. Each bird will need to double its weight over the next few weeks if it's to reach its Canadian nesting sites in good enough condition to breed, and luckily those oily horseshoe crab eggs are stuffed full of valuable calories. Even so, it's been calculated that each bird will still need to eat 135,000 of them to double their weight and give them the energy they need to fly that last one thousand miles and rear a family.[1]

So with little time to lose, the great flocks sweep over the bay. Hidden among tall dune grasses, I'm almost immersed in a flock that twists and turns over my head as it checks out the spawning beach. It behaves like a single organism with a single purpose. I never tire of the hypnotic dance of huge flocks of birds, even though high-speed photography has shown that there is no telepathy or mysterious forces involved in this performance, just incredible split-second timing. A single bird initiates a move, and other flock members respond so quickly that the whole flock seems to move as one. Yet as far as I'm concerned, even if the mystery has gone, the magic still remains.

Walking back along the beach, the fog descends again. Pleasantly isolated from the rest of the world, all I can hear is the laughing of gulls and the distant twittering of the knot flocks—an audible affirmation of the productivity of the great bays of America's east coast. But I also knew that, as spectacular as my day had been, it was nothing in comparison to the experiences of the first Europeans to stand on these shores. Although the Atlantic horseshoe crab occurs all the way down the east coast of North America, from Maine to the Yucatan Peninsula, today it is most abundant between Virginia and New Jersey, with the largest population centered on Delaware Bay. But when the first explorers and settlers arrived on these Atlantic shores, the sights I had just witnessed would have been common right up and down the coast and magnified many times.

One of the first naturalists to describe in detail the bounty of America's Atlantic coast was Thomas Hariot, who found that this creature, that the local Indians called *seekenauk,* was common in the shallow waters behind the Outer Banks of North Carolina. Hariot was an exceptional man, a graduate of Oxford University, an astronomer, navigator, scientist, and naturalist, and it was because of these talents that he was on the Outer Banks in 1585; he'd been sent by his friend, Sir Walter Raleigh, with a colonizing expedition. Raleigh's plan was to build a settlement at a place called Roanoke, an island protected from the Atlantic by the barrier islands of the Outer Banks. Hariot's mission, along with artist John White, was to document the natural resources of the area and, in so doing, encourage further settlement and the profitable exploitation of those resources. Yet, even taking into account this need to cast the venture in a positive light, Hariot described a wonderful place, rich in fish, turtles, birds, and shellfish, including, of course, the horseshoe crab. Many of these creatures were illustrated in beautiful watercolors by John White—words and pictures that together make it easy to gain a sense of the rich coastal ecology in the sixteenth century.

Hariot's *A Brief and True Report of the New Found Land of Virginia* is one of the most complete early accounts of the natural history of the east coast, but he wasn't the first to experience the riches of these shores. Ever since Columbus had touched on the Bahamas and the Caribbean in 1492, the Spanish had been steadily building settlements (and wealth) in Central and South America. Long before Raleigh's Roanoke venture, they had also been exploring northward from their Caribbean strongholds. Gradually, the outline of the Florida peninsula began to appear on maps, first as an island then joined to a steadily growing coastline to the north. Although no one as yet had any idea of the sheer scale of the North American continent, it was now clear that this was not China or Japan, as Columbus had assumed.

In 1513, Balboa stood on a peak in the Darien Mountains in Panama and saw the vast Pacific Ocean beyond. A few years later, Magellan sailed round the southern tip of South America, through the hazardous straits that now bear his name, and proved beyond doubt that there was a large continent in the south. It could only be hoped that the emerging outline of the northern landmass would prove to be much smaller, perhaps even just a collection of large islands that would allow easy passage to the Pacific. This, and the hope of treasures to equal those of the Incas and the Aztecs, spurred further Spanish exploration to the north.

In 1526, Lucas Vasquez de Allyón, a judge on Hispaniola, set off with the intention of building a settlement somewhere along the coast of what is today Georgia and South Carolina. After searching up and down the coast, he eventually founded San Miguel de la Gualdape, probably at the mouth of the Savannah River in Georgia—a river, he discovered, that held "a great abundance and excellence of fish." He reported that more than six hundred could be taken with a single cast of the nest, and one fish was so big that twelve colonists dined on it and still had some left. He also recorded countless numbers of birds, such as cranes, thrushes, geese, and ducks.[2] Unfortunately, disease wiped out about half of the settlers, including Allyón himself. The remaining settlers soon abandoned San Miguel and returned to the relative civility of Hispaniola. After several more abortive attempts to find gold and establish settlements, the Spanish government decided to stop wasting money on La Florida, as the whole of southeastern North America was now called. But although this vast area was claimed by the Spanish, other European nations didn't necessarily see it that way, and in 1562, the French tried to set up a colony here.

The French felt they had some claim on this coast since nearly forty years before, in 1524, they had sent an Italian navigator, Giovanni da Verrazano, at the head of a French expedition to explore the eastern seaboard of America. He made landfall somewhere around Cape Fear, North Carolina, and then sailed south for about 150 miles along the coast of South Carolina. Eventually, fearing that he would run too deep into Spanish territory, he turned back north. He sailed along the Outer Banks but didn't enter any of the great sounds that lay beyond, though he must have sailed very close to Roanoke Island where Thomas Hariot would stand more than sixty years later, describing the strange creatures he found.

In fact, Verrazano thought that the Pamlico and Albamarle Sounds behind the Outer Banks were the *Mare Orientale,* the Eastern Sea that bathed Japan and China, and that a thin, discontinuous isthmus was all that separated Europe from a lucrative sea route to Asia. Sailing further north still, he must have been too far out to sea to spot the entrance to Chesapeake Bay, the largest estuary in North America. He also missed Delaware Bay, just a little further to the north, but on he went, into New York Harbor through the narrows that now bear his name. He barely paused here, before heading up to Narragansett Bay in today's Rhode Island, where he finally allowed himself the luxury of more than two weeks exploring and taking on supplies. Then on he went again, along the coast of New England and Newfoundland before finally setting his course to the east and back to France.

Verrazano showed that the coastline of North America stretched unbroken from Florida to Cape Breton, and over the next couple of years, both Spanish and English vessels would confirm this. Yet Verrazano's reports from the Outer Banks suggested that a sea route could still be found connecting the Atlantic to the Eastern Sea, and that spurred more expeditions. So too did his reports of a veritable Paradise along these shores. So impressed was he at one point in his journey that he named an area "Arcadia," after the Paradise of the ancient Greeks, Pan's domain of virgin wilderness unspoiled by humanity. Everywhere that he touched the shore he described magnificent forests, and vast meadows and marshes full of game and birds. But it's not really clear from Verrazano's writings just where Arcadia was. Some have placed it as far south as Cape Hatteras on the Outer Banks, others further north. In any event, Arcadia continued to migrate north, until it finally came to rest on the French speaking areas around Nova Scotia, an area still known as Acadie. In the years following, Verrazano's Arcadian landscape, wherever it was, helped transform the European view of the continent from a barrier to the riches of the Orient to a place worth exploring and exploiting in its own right. It's not surprising, therefore, that the French thought it was worth the risk of trying to plant settlements perilously close to the territorial Spanish.

So, in 1562, a Frenchman by the name of Jean Ribault began searching the coast for a suitable place to land a band of hopeful settlers. His reports were like those of Verazzano and made it sound like he was spoiled for choice. He arrived off the mouth of the St. Johns River in today's northern Florida and found a country that was "the fairest fruitfulest and pleasantest in all the world."[3] He found meadows full of herons and ducks and grapes that were of "wonderful greatness." Verrazano's Paradise indeed, but Ribault didn't stay there. He headed north, perhaps because he felt he was just a little too close to the Spanish, here at the top of peninsular Florida. Further north, he explored the rivers and islands along the South Carolina coast and found them just as rich. Here was a land of "havens, rivers and islandes of such frutefulness as cannot with tonge be expressed."[4] The waters were full of fish and the land of deer and turkeys. At the mouth of a river was an island covered in so many egrets that the bushes appeared pure white.

Here, near the present town of Port Royal, he left his band of pioneers to start their settlement. It didn't take long for the Frenchmen to fall out among themselves, and with the local Cusabo Indians, which doomed the colony to an early failure. The settlers tried to sail back to France in a homemade boat and were lucky enough to be picked up by a passing English ship before either starving or drowning. Undeterred, the French sent a larger colonizing party back down to the St. Johns River, where they built Fort Caroline, provocatively close to the Spanish. The members of this second expedition were equally delighted by the prospect of the St. Johns. "I leave you to imagine the joy we all felt, especially since toward the south we saw a very beautiful river [St. John's]."[5]

But by now, the Spanish had realized that they were going to need settlements of their own along this coast, to protect their treasure-laden ships that were riding the Gulf Stream back to Spain. They needn't have worried. The settlement at Fort Caroline was already suffering the same fate as that at Port Royal. Nevertheless, the Spanish sent an armada to extinguish both the colonists and the French claim. Pedro Menéndez de Avilés, governor of Florida, was doubly motivated; he slaughtered the settlers, he later explained, not just as Frenchmen, but as heretics. He then set about establishing his own colonies along the coast.

In 1565, St. Agustín appeared on the map, a little to the south of the recently destroyed French fort, a landmark moment in North American history. Despite repeated attacks by the English, who were now pursuing their own claims on this continent, St. Agustín survived to become today's St. Augustine, and the longest continually settled town in North America. The Europeans were here to stay. Yet, though they were late in realizing the potential of these shores, it would be English settlements that would come to dominate both the middle latitudes of the Atlantic coast and, subsequently, North American history.

And that began in 1585, when Thomas Hariot came to stand on Roanoke Island and wonder at such creatures as seekanauk, the horseshoe crab. It is clear, even from the fairly sparse reports of all those that came before, that the east coast of North America was extraordinarily rich, and Hariot and White helped put some flesh on those bones. "For foure monethes of the yeere, February, March, Aprill, and May, there are plenty of Sturgeons. And also in these same monethes of Herrings, some of the ordinary bignesse as ours in England, but the most part far greater, of eighteene, twentie inches and some two foote in length and better. There are also Troutes, Porpoises, Rayes, Oldwives, Mullets, Plaice, and very many other sortes of excellent good fish."[6] Later observers described porpoises as so numerous they were a danger to canoes and bathers; they even made their way into a freshwater lake in one of North Carolina's sounds.[7] But back on Albemarle Sound, Hariot goes on to describe a wealth of other creatures:

There are also in many places plenty of these kindes which follow.

Sea Crabbes, such as we have in England.

Oystres, some very great and some small, some round and some of a long shape.

There are many tortoyses, both of land and sea kinde, their backes and bellies are shelled very thicke . . . some have been found a yard breadth and better.

And, of course, the horseshoe crab: "Seekanauk, a kinde of crusty shell fishe which is good meat, about a foot in breadth, having a crustie tayle, many legges like a crab; and her eyes in her backe."[8]

How exhilarating it must have been for a sixteenth-century naturalist to stand on Roanoke. The "tortoyses" of a yard in breadth were presumably sea turtles—green, hawksbill, and loggerhead—cruising the shallows of the sounds and hauling up on the sandy beaches to lay their eggs. But the marshes would have teemed with smaller terrapins, particularly the beautiful diamondback terrapin, a salt marsh specialist named for the diamond-shaped etchings on its shell. His sea crabs were likely to have been blue crabs, which would have existed in great numbers in the beds of submerged vegetation. An aggressive species, quick to use its powerful, shellfish-crushing claws, it was nevertheless hauled out of the sounds by the local Indians using nothing but hand nets made of plant fibers. I've worked with blue crabs, and I've nothing but admiration for anyone prepared to put their hands anywhere near even a moderate-sized specimen.

A few years back, we were filming blue crabs mating in aquaria at the Virginia Institute of Marine Sciences field lab on Chesapeake Bay. Since mating only takes place immediately after a female has molted, I had a line of buckets, each containing a prospective film star, which I checked regularly to see if any were approaching a molt. Every time I walked down the row of buckets, each crab in turn erupted from the water, snapping its claws as it tried to attack me. So I'm not at all sure from Hariot's account whether the Indians were catching the crabs or the crabs were catching the Indians.

Looking through John White's evocative paintings of the wildlife and the lives of the Indians it is all too easy to be seduced into thinking, like Verazzano, that this really was Paradise. But looks can be deceptive. Despite this natural abundance, that first Roanoke colony failed. By the summer of 1586, the remaining settlers were only too willing to be picked up by Francis Drake, who called at Roanoke during a lull in pillaging Spanish treasure ships.

Raleigh sent a new colonizing expedition a year later, but by then war with Spain was looming back in Europe, and no relief expedition made it back to Roanoke until 1590, by which time the colony had vanished. All that remained were the letters "CRO" carved into one tree and "CROATOAN" carved into another, a prearranged signal that the colony had moved to join the nearby Croatoan Indians, at least according to John White, who accompanied the relief expedition. For various reasons, the expedition didn't go looking for the colonists, and this second attempt at colonizing Roanoke soon became known as the Lost Colony, a mysterious episode in American history that has attracted much discussion and speculation. The important point, though, in our context is not what happened to the colonists, but that, like almost every other European attempt to date, the colony failed, surrounded by an incredible natural abundance.

It wasn't that these first colonists were entirely unprepared. Raleigh had already sent a scouting mission prior to the main colonizing force. That expedition brought back to England two Indians, called Manteo and Wanchese, and Manteo in particular proved a font of knowledge on the land and its people. Before the colonizing expedition, Hariot spent a lot of time with these Indians, first becoming competent in their particular variant of the Algonquian language, then learning as much about the New World as he could.

At the same time, Richard Hakluyt (actually, just to add confusion to an already complicated history, there were two Richard Hakluyts—uncle and nephew) had pulled together accounts from many of the previous voyages to the New World and written some very sound guidelines on how to establish colonies in the Americas. He advised Raleigh to take blacksmiths, farmers, and doctors. He thought about the best crops to plant and how to relate to the Indians to give the colonists the best chance of surviving in an alien environment. Unfortunately, Raleigh didn't have the financial resources to follow all this advice fully and, even if he had, he couldn't plan for bad luck. The expedition ended up losing most of its supplies when the ships, having run aground while attempting to negotiate the dangerous entrance to the Pamlico Sound, were battered by a fierce storm. Nevertheless, the colonists had prepared as well as they could, so the failure of this and many other early colonies shows just how difficult the New World would prove to be.

One lesson that all the early colonists were slow to learn was that this was not Europe, nor was it Paradise in the sense they would have liked to believe. To survive here, at least in the early years, meant understanding the local ecology, which many that came here were simply not equipped to do, either intellectually or philosophically. But the lure of this abundant continent together with overhyped reports published back in Europe ensured a plentiful supply of settlers.

Around 4:00 a.m. on April 26, 1607, three more English ships sighted the coast of Virginia and passed between two low headlands into a great bay to the north of Roanoke. Explorations by the Roanoke colonists had previously reached this far north, as had Spanish Jesuits, so some details of this huge bay were already known, including the name given to it by local Indians—Chesapeake. There has been much discussion as to the exact origins and meaning of this name. One of the more likely translations, and certainly the most appropriate, is "Great Bay of Shells," though even this name hardly does it justice, as the settlers on board the *Susan Constant, Godspeed,* and *Discovery* were about to find out.

Traveling with this expedition, originally of 144 men and boys (there were no women), were several figures whose writings help paint a picture of the Chesapeake in the seventeenth century. George Percy, a son of the Earl of Northumberland, was a young man of twenty-six when he first saw Chesapeake, and it seems to have made quite a first impression: "we entered into the bay of Chesupioc. . . . There we landed and discovered a fair way, but wee could find nothing worth the speaking of but faire meddowes and goodly tall Trees, with such Fresh-waters running through the woods, as I was almost ravished at the first sight thereof."[9] As the expedition explored, George Percy soon found why this was called the "Great Bay of Shells": "We went further into the Bay, and saw a plaine plot of ground. Upon this plot of ground we got good store of Mussels and Oysters, which lay on the ground as thicke as stones."[10] And as they explored the bay further, Percy describes more huge piles of oysters that had been collected by the local Indians: "We came to a place where they had made a great fire and had beene newly a rosting oysters. When they perceived our coming, they fled away to the mountains and left many of the oysters in the fire. We ate some of the oysters, which were very large and delicate in taste."

In the bay and rivers, these oysters made reefs so large they were a shipping hazard. In 1701, a ship carrying Swiss traveler Francis Louis Michel ran aground on such a reef, so the passengers passed their time, while waiting for the tide to lift them off, by eating the reef they had struck. Michel recorded: "The abundance of oysters in incredible, There are whole banks of them so that ships must avoid them. . . . They surpass those of England by far in size . . . they are four times as large. I often cut them in two, before I could put them in my mouth."

The creature that these settlers and travelers were describing was the eastern oyster, *Crassostrea virginica*. It occurs naturally all along the eastern coast, from the St. Lawrence in Canada to the Atlantic coast of Argentina, and from all the early reports, it was fantastically abundant throughout its range. And not just abundant: oysters of more than a foot in length were frequently described. In Chesapeake Bay, it's been estimated that around 193 square miles of oyster reefs covered the bottom of the open bay and river channels. The single largest bed, off Anne Arundel County, was twenty-eight square miles in extent.[11]

Such vast reefs were a vital part of the ecology of the Atlantic coasts. They provided shelter for all kinds of other creatures, from crabs to fish, and they even purified the water. In Chesapeake, oysters were so numerous they could filter all the water of this entire vast bay in just under three and half days,[12] which explains why the first colonists in the Chesapeake often remarked on the clarity and purity of the water. In those early days, it was possible to see the teeming life of the bay through twenty feet of water, something almost impossible to imagine today.

So those first colonists could easily see the potential of their new home right beneath their boats. Enough was already known about the Chesapeake that the colonists carried instructions from the merchant company that was backing them, suggesting that they settle at least one hundred miles from the mouth of a large river that emptied into the southern part of the bay. Like the rest of the bay, this river, which they called the James River after their king, was teeming with fish, shellfish, and birds. Perhaps the colonists were overwhelmed by this abundance, but they only traveled about thirty miles from the mouth before the president of the council of the colonists, Edward Maria Wingfield, insisted that they stopped. And why not? George Percy later described the abundance of the James: "Wheresoever we landed upon this river, wee saw the goodliest Woods . . . and Vines in great abundance, which hang in great clusters on many Trees . . . and all the Ground bepsred with many sweet and delicate flowers . . . there are many branches of this River, which runne through the Woods with great plenty of fish of all kinds."[13]

But Wingfield had picked a low-lying marshy area, infested with mosquitoes and difficult to defend from the local Indians. Furthermore, none of the hundred or so survivors of the transatlantic crossing who built Jamestown, on the north bank of the James River, were farmers, and few had any inclination to labor to provide food. Backed by companies of merchant venturers looking for profits in the New World, many of the early colonizing expeditions were an ill-suited assortment of characters, mostly people who, like their backers, were here to make money quickly. And no doubt many thought that subsistence in a natural Paradise would be easy. If fruit didn't fall from the trees or fish throw themselves onto the shore, then they could always trade with or steal from the local Indians.

But the Indians of the southern Chesapeake were led by the politically astute Powhatan, who wasn't always willing to fall in with that particular English plan. Worse still, the winter of 1607 was particularly severe and quickly tempered any visions of Paradise. Not only did the settlers underestimate how easy it would be to get food, they also underestimated the climate. Knowing that Chesapeake Bay lay at the same latitude as southern Spain, they arrived expecting mild Mediterranean winters and warm summers. Instead, they had to endure cold worse than any in England followed by summers of killing heat and humidity. Disease, conflicts with the Powhatan Indians, and starvation meant that only thirty-two of the original colonists saw the spring of 1608.

Although the next two winters were milder, it didn't stop the hardships. In fact, this period became known as the "starving time." But at least one of the colonists realized that survival meant learning how to exploit the local resources. His name was Captain John Smith, and he seems to have been a kind of Indiana Jones of his day. Before he began his American adventures, he'd been captured as a slave by the Turks and sold to a Turkish princess, from whom he made a daring escape across Europe. Later in Virginia, he apparently managed a similar daring escape from Powhatan with the help of one of the chief's daughters, Pocahontas.

He became governor of the colony a year after they arrived, but even so, Virginia would remain a death trap for English settlers for some time to come. Of the 7,549 people who came to Virginia between 1607 and 1624, only 1,095 survived[14]—all the more surprising since they were living on the shores of a bay that once produced more seafood per acre than any other body of water on Earth. Such a death toll in the midst of one of the most productive environments on the planet seems extraordinary, but it shows how hard it was to come to terms with this New World Paradise. However, unlike earlier English settlements, Jamestown would struggle through. Roanoke was a private venture, but Jamestown was backed by a joint stock company with the financial fortitude to overcome these initial difficulties and a strong incentive to see a return on their investments.

The creature that helped the colony survive through these early hard times, and become the first permanent English colony on the continent, was the eastern oyster. Unless the river was frozen solid, they were easy to gather in large numbers, since many of the great oyster banks were under just a few feet of water. But oysters were not relished at first. Given its modern reputation as gourmet food, it's hard to believe that oysters used to be spurned as poor people's food. Perhaps its early reputation was tainted by associations with the "starving time" and by the fact that it later became a staple for the plantation slaves. Another reason for its poor reputation was that the eastern oyster was so abundant and so readily available. There was simply nothing special about it. However, that would gradually change and with the oyster's rise to gourmet fame, the great filtration plants and nurseries of the east coast would come under increasing threat.

As oysters began to attract the attention of the upper classes, gourmands began to distinguish between specimens from different parts of the coast; what was once a cheap mass food for slaves became bluepoints and box oysters from Long Island, Wellfleets from Cape Cod, Cotuits from Nantucket, Malpeques from Prince Edward Island in Canada, and, of course, James Rivers from the Chesapeake. All of these were just local populations of the eastern oyster, their distinct texture and taste created by the local growing conditions, which is why most are named for the place they were collected. Each variety's characteristics were extolled with the same kind of impenetrable descriptions usually associated with fine wines, and all of them lay in great beds that were easy to exploit.

As the market in luxury seafood grew, New England oysters were first to become scarce. By the late eighteenth century, Wellfleet oysters were commercially extinct. In the 1830s, New England oyster boats began to clear out the banks around Cape Cod, before moving on to Long Island Sound. Then, in 1836, an oysterman from Connecticut, called Caleb Maltby, moved to Baltimore and began what would become a multimillion-dollar industry based on the great oyster reefs of the Chesapeake. The story of the subsequent Chesapeake oyster industry is perhaps the most dramatic of all, but it also exemplifies the fate of this mollusk right up and down the east coast. In 1850, there were six oyster-packing plants in Baltimore, and by the eve of the Civil War, there were sixty. There was a brief respite for the oysters during the Civil War, after which the oyster rush really got under way.

The town of Crisfield, on the Eastern Shore of Maryland was, both economically and literally, built on oysters. The town began life on a vast mound of oyster shells in 1867, and by 1872, had the largest oyster trade in the world. As similar towns sprang up along the coast, Maryland's Eastern Shore became the "Wild East." Men flocked to this marine gold mine as they had to the real gold mines of California or the Black Hills, and the towns began to fill with bars and brothels to help oystermen spend the money they earned from the high price of oysters. These towns were just as lawless as those of the western frontier, but with the added ingredient of a rank smell of "defunct oysters," as one New York newspaperman described it in 1879.[15]

Those that got rich the quickest were the oyster packers, who thought nothing of improving their profits by cheating their customers with underweight consignments. The oystermen themselves had the hard and often dangerous job of collecting oysters from the waters of an unpredictable Chesapeake Bay. As those first colonists at Jamestown found, the weather on the bay can swing wildly; an unseasonably warm winter's day can turn into a freezing storm in almost no time at all. But the work of the oystermen was made all the more dangerous when a shooting war broke out over the Chesapeake's oysters.

There had been conflicts from the earliest days of the oyster industry on the Eastern Shore, but a real war was sparked by the fact that there were two very different kinds of oystermen fishing the bay. Oyster banks occurred both in the open bay and in the lower reaches of the rivers. In open waters, oysters were scraped off the bottom by dredge boats, which did tremendous damage to the reefs, whereas river oysters were collected by hand, with long-handled tongs, as they had been since the days of Jamestown. Furthermore, the two kinds of oystermen often came from different backgrounds. Forty percent of rivermen were freed slaves. Dredgers were, in theory, banned from the rivers, but by 1868, nearly one thousand dredgers were regularly poaching oysters from the rivermen's banks. The rivermen took armed action, and the dredge boat captains, with more money behind them, escalated the conflict.

As the lower Chesapeake began to look more and more like the Wild West, the oyster packers, worried that fighting was lowering the oyster catch, demanded action from the state authorities. Maryland responded by setting up the State Oyster Police Force, under the command of Captain Hunter S. Davidson. An ex-commander of the Confederate Navy, he now had three armed steamers—an oyster navy—under his command and a remit to enforce law and order on Chesapeake Bay. He did his best, but more often than not, the dredgers were better armed, and despite several dramatic battles, they continued to haul in oysters from wherever they wanted.

To add to this, there were also disputes between Maryland and Virginia over some particularly large beds claimed by both states. This dispute had finally to be settled federally, but when the new boundaries removed some large beds around Smith Island from Maryland, more armed conflicts broke out. The shooting war continued until 1910 and only stopped because there was nothing left to fight over. Those huge beds that sustained Jamestown through the "starving time" were all but gone.

When not dodging bullets and cannon fire from the dredge boats, Captain Davidson got to know the oyster banks of the lower bay very well. As early as 1869, he warned that the beds were being recklessly depleted, but no one wanted to hear of licensing or any other conservation measures. This was big business. By 1890, a quarter of the entire population of Maryland worked in the $5 million a year oyster industry. Nevertheless, a few worrying signs soon began to be noticed. Shortly after Davidson's warnings, oyster landings began to decline. Worried seafood millionaires finally sent a U.S. Navy engineer to survey the beds in 1879. He reported finding an average of just one oyster per three square yards. A second survey four years later found one oyster per four square yards.

Clearly, the eastern oyster was in serious trouble, but the reaction of the oyster industry was not one of immediate concern. Instead oystermen embarked on a mad scramble to dredge up the last of the oysters while some profit remained on the bay floor. This attitude was well summed up by a comment from an oysterman recorded by Captain Davidson: "Them's the Lord's oysters and the Lord put them there so we could get them." Even when the industry was close to collapse, the reaction was the same. An old folk saying from the bay sums up the philosophy: "Get it today! To hell with tamar. Leave it till tamar, and somebody else'll get it."[16]

This "Lord's oyster" philosophy is all too common when people are presented with what looks like an infinite resource, free for the taking and with large profits from its exploitation. The Lord's oyster is a perfect summary of a philosophy I've already alluded to in a previous chapter, something that might be called Christian capitalism—a free market backed by a conviction that the natural world was made for human benefit alone. And of course this was a frequent occurrence during the European settlement of the New World. The northwestern Atlantic cod fishery is another tragic example.

In more purely economic terms, this process has been called the "tragedy of the commons." It was first outlined by Garrett Hardin, an ecologist from Dallas, Texas, in a 1968 essay and says, in simple terms, that any communal, unowned resource exploited for individual gain will inevitably result in the destruction of the resource.[17] It was formulated around the example of the extensive common lands of England in the Middle Ages, where peasants had traditional rights to graze their stock or sometimes cut wood on land they didn't themselves own. Hardin suggests that there was no reason for any individual peasant to use this land sustainably. Why not put as many cattle as you can on this land even if it means it will be overgrazed? If you refrain from overexploitation, there is nothing to stop your neighbor taking advantage of your prudence and feeding more of his own cattle, so the only logical choice is to maximize your own benefit and accept the long-term consequences.

In fact, the title of this idea is somewhat unfortunate, since these traditional commons were usually managed very well through all kinds of complex social and legal mechanisms.[18] Some still exist and are so rich that they are now nature reserves. There have been further criticisms of this theory and other exceptions pointed out, but it's also impossible to deny the reality of the destruction of the oyster banks by such a mechanism, since we have eyewitness testimony to unrestrained and selfish exploitation.

On the other hand, it's also too easy to see this process in simplistic terms of human greed. In both cases, there was a hierarchy of motivations, ranging from the fishermen and oystermen at the bottom to the big packing and processing companies at the top. On the bottom rung, people were often just trying to survive from day to day. At the top, however, the race to maximize profits often blinds big operations to ecological realities.

But despite this frenzy of exploitation, the Lord's oysters are still harvested, though the haul from the Chesapeake is now measured in thousands rather than millions of bushels, reflecting the fact that oysters here have been reduced to about 1 percent of the abundance that greeted George Percy and John Smith. This has had major impacts on the bay. Not only were the oysters the bay's filtration plant and nurseries, but the rugged topography of the reefs caused the bay waters to mix, bringing up nutrients to stimulate productivity in the sunlit surface and sending oxygen-rich water to the bay's floor.

Recently, the realization that oyster bars were such an important ecological feature of Chesapeake, and indeed of the whole of the eastern coast, has spurred efforts to restock oysters. In 2000, a number of organizations, under the umbrella of the Chesapeake Bay Program, committed themselves to a tenfold increase in the numbers of oysters in the bay. But that's easier said than done. If the oyster was hammered by overfishing in the nineteenth and early twentieth centuries, its bane in the late twentieth and twenty-first is disease.

Two diseases, called dermo and MSX, are now the leading causes of mortality of eastern oysters.[19] Research is under way to test whether a resistant Asian species of oyster is suitable as replacement for the native one, but this is meeting with a mixed response. Part of the pressure to restock oysters is coming from the oyster fishery, who don't mind if they harvest the equally tasty suminoe oyster. And perhaps suminoe oysters would form reefs that would be perfectly acceptable to the worms, crabs, and fish that depended on the original eastern oyster reefs. But introducing a nonnative species is a risky game. It is now believed that MSX was introduced to the Chesapeake during a former experiment to introduce another Asian oyster, *Crassostrea gigas*, into the bay.[20]

The long list of ecological tragedies in North America caused by alien species can't be overlooked by the scientists carrying out the tests. But neither can the pressure from the oyster industry, with all that means for the local economy and local jobs. The remnant eastern oysters of the Chesapeake illustrate how difficult it is to restore any ecology to its former glory. And nature doesn't always help.

The population of cow-nosed rays in the bay has recently risen dramatically and the huge crushing teeth of these twenty- to thirty-pound fish can make short work of oysters. Great shoals have been bulldozing their way through the oyster beds, leaving them looking like bomb fields, as one scientists has described it. One school of rays apparently ate around sixty thousand oysters in one night, while another devoured around seven hundred thousand young oysters just days after they had been planted out as part of a reintroduction scheme.[21] They also plow through beds of aquatic vegetation, which are just as important in Chesapeake's ecology as the oyster beds.

In the recent past, cow-nosed rays were frequently trapped by nets set for other fish and that could have kept their numbers artificially low. Now, with increasing regulation of fisheries, their numbers are rebounding to former levels, but today the Great Bay of Shells no longer has its vast beds of shellfish, forcing the rays to concentrate on smaller areas and literally eat themselves out of house and home. One suggestion is to start a fishery for the cow-nosed ray itself, and so keep the population down while the oyster beds recover, but cow-nosed rays don't give themselves up easily. They are difficult fish to handle and process, which would make them expensive. And besides, each one is armed with a vicious poisonous spine at the base of its tail.

Perhaps the first European to find this out was Captain John Smith as he led a small group of Jamestown colonists in an exploration of their new home. Smith, with his flair for the dramatic, tried catching what was presumably a cow-nosed ray by stabbing it with his sword, and the ray, reasonably enough one might think, retaliated by stabbing him in the wrist: "no bloud nor wound was scene, but a little blew spot, but the torment was so instantly extreame, that in four hours had swolen his hand, arme and shoulder, we all with much sorrow concluded his funerall, and prepared his grave in an Island by, as himselfe directed."[22] But the funeral preparations were premature. The redoubtable Smith survived, and later that night ate his less fortunate adversary: "which gave no lesse joy and content to us then ease to himselfe, for which we called the Island Stingray Isle after the name of the fish.""

The place is still called Stingray Point today, a name which should remind us not only of Smith's lucky escape, but also of the fact that these first settlers were in very unfamiliar territory, and very unprepared. Although the rivers and bay abounded in fish wherever they looked, the exploration party had brought no nets. But they seem to have brought plenty of frying pans, perhaps assuming that in Paradise the fish would simply jump into the pans. Since they didn't, the explorers tried using the pans as fishing nets: "but we found it a bad instrument to catch fish with: neither better fish, more plenty, nor more variety of small fish, had any of us ever seen in any place so swimming in the water, but they are not to be caught with frying pans."[23] As amusing as the sight must have been, it underlines how hard life was going to be for all the early settlers until they learned how to exploit the abundance up and down the Atlantic coast of North America.

One thing they could have done much sooner than they did was to learn from the local Indians, who caught fish in all kinds of ways, though never with frying pans. They built large weirs of brushwood to trap vast shoals of smaller fish or used fires in dugout canoes to draw fish close at night so they could be speared.[24] But most spectacularly of all, they caught huge sturgeon. "The Indian way of catching sturgeon, when they came into the narrow part of the rivers, was by a man's clapping a noose over their tails, and by keeping fast his hold. Thus a fish finding itself entangled would flounce, and often pull the man under water, and then that man was counted a cockarouse, or brave fellow, that would not let go; till with swimming, wading and diving, he had tired the sturgeon, and brought it ashore."[25]

It is, perhaps, understandable why the Jamestown settlers didn't leap at the chance to catch sturgeon this way, but they did gradually learn other ways of hauling these mighty fish from the rivers. In a report written in 1612, after the colony had struggled through its first difficult years, Smith was able to report: "In summer no place affords more plenty of sturgeon. . . . There was once taken 52 sturgeon at a drought, at another drought 68. From the later end of May till the end of June are taken few but young sturgeons of 2 foot or a yard long. From thence till the midst of September, them of 2 or three yards long."[26]

Sturgeon are extraordinary creatures. They look like prehistoric monsters—and with good reason. Fish easily recognizable as sturgeon were swimming in the seas and rivers of our planet 200 million years ago. Today, there are two species of sturgeons living along America's east coast. Short-nosed sturgeons are the smaller species, rarely reaching more than three or four feet in length; Atlantic sturgeons, on the other hand, can be real giants. They have occasionally been known to reach fifteen feet in length and weigh in at eight hundred pounds. Try lassoing the tail of one of those!

But sturgeon entering shallow water were easier to catch than most fish, which meant the desperate settlers ended up overdosing on them: "onely of Sturgion wee had great store, whereon our men would so greedily surfet, as it cost manye their lives." The survivors of this lethal feast soon realized that sturgeon might make a better export than a staple, some return on the investments of the colony's backers, and by 1609, the first ship had arrived at Jamestown to take on board pickled sturgeon. Unfortunately, the first few cargoes were not preserved properly and spoiled long before they could be turned into profit for the company back in England. But by 1612, the potential value of this commodity had been recognized, and all sturgeon caught had to be reported to the governor of the colony, or face the loss of both ears. After this, the fishery began to take increasing numbers of sturgeon from the Chesapeake's waters: "in one day within the space of two miles only, some gentlemen in canoes caught above six hundred."[27]

And it wasn't just the Chesapeake. All the rivers, right along the east coast, were thick with sturgeon in season, some perhaps even bigger than modern records suggest: "The sturgeons be all over the country, but the best catching of them is upon the shoals of Cape Cod and in the river of Merrimac, where much is taken, pickled, and brought for England. Some of these be twelve, fourteen, eighteen foot long." This report from New England was written by a young man of twenty-three who settled near Lynn in 1629, in what is today a suburb of Boston. The Pilgrim Fathers had by then survived nine tough years at Plymouth, to the south of modern Boston, and other colonies, like Salem, had already sprung up. This man's name was William Wood, and he had been commissioned by the Puritans to assess the commodities and the character of the land of New England. He left a valuable account of his time in New England in a book called *New England's Prospect.*

Meanwhile, to the south, the Dutch were exploring the area that is now New York and found that here too the rivers were full of sturgeon as well as other fish. "Salmon are plenty in some rivers, and the striped bass are plenty in all the rivers and bays of the sea."[28] Striped bass are also magnificent fish that, like both kinds of sturgeon, swim upstream from salt to freshwater during the summer to spawn. The largest one ever reliably recorded was a six-foot specimen from South Carolina, caught in the late 1800s, but much earlier reports suggest that similar or bigger monsters were very common at the beginning of the colonial period. In visualizing these abundant ecosystems, we also need to remember that it wasn't just big numbers. Without heavy exploitation, many species also grew to much larger sizes.

The spring and summer spawning runs of such huge numbers of great fish must have been truly spectacular. It's still possible to get a flavor of the action at places like Weldon, North Carolina, on the Roanoke River, perhaps the most famous striped bass spawning site today. Here, they thrash the surface of the shallow rapids into a foam as so-called rock fights break out—actually the desperate attempts of several males to fertilize a female's eggs as she releases them. Although sports fishermen still haul plenty of three-foot fish out of the river, what would Thomas Hariot have seen if he'd had time to explore the Roanoke River more than four hundred years ago?

And even more impressive, the spawning frenzies of fifteen-foot Atlantic sturgeon might have created as much of a navigation hazard as the great oyster bars. In New England in the mid-seventeenth century, John Josselyn certainly thought so: "This fish [sturgeon] is here in great plenty, and in some rivers so numerous, that it is hazardous for canoes and the like small vessels to pass to and again, as in Pechipscut River to the Eastward."[29]

Although sturgeon feed by grubbing out creatures buried in the bottom mud, striped bass are voracious predators, and to support such huge numbers, the rivers and bays of the east coast must have been alive with smaller baitfish. And that's exactly what many observers found. "In the winter season, the creeks and backwaters abound with a small kind of fish which comes from the sea, about the size of a smelt. Some call them little mullets. These fish are so tame that many are caught with the hand." At such times, people described wading knee-deep through a solid mass of fish and the stench of dead fish in the aftermath of spawning could be smelled a long way from the river. But it wasn't just one kind of fish that filled the rivers during spawning runs; several species traveled upstream in these unimaginable numbers.

Two of these innumerable fishes are all but indistinguishable except to ichthyologists or fishermen: the alewife and the blueback herring. Certainly there's no way to discern references to these two species in early reports, and they're often just lumped together as "river herrings," though they do differ a little in their biology and habitat preferences. The river herrings are joined by larger species, the American shad and the hickory shad, that occur right down the east coast, and the Atlantic menhaden, which differs from the others in spawning at sea, but feeding in vast shoals in bays and estuaries. All these fish are vital links in the coastal food chain. They swim openmouthed through clouds of plankton, trapping the tiny plants and animals in filters on their gills, so converting the primary productivity of the coastal waters into something that the great shoals of predators, like striped bass, can get their teeth into.

It was these vast shoals that the Indians of Chesapeake were trapping in their brushwood weirs, and once the settlers learned the habits of these fish, they too could haul out prodigious quantities. There are many descriptions of nets filled to bursting and of shoals so dense they can be scooped out with hand nets: "It is an astonishing sight to paddle down the Restigouche [in New Brunswick] and see the farmers 'smelting'—scooping up the little fish in hand nets. The amount they take is incredible and most of their potatoes spring from this fishy manure."[30] Apart from manure, these fish became a valuable commercial catch. On the Connecticut River, great shoals of river herrings were trapped in seine nets and sent to the Caribbean to feed slaves on the sugar plantations. In return, New England received plentiful supplies of molasses, which could be turned into rum. River herrings were also hauled from the rivers in uncounted numbers to be fed to pigs. Later, this seemingly endless resource was converted into pet food or fish oil, and slowly large commercial fisheries built up.

George Washington was in on this act. He had a herring and shad fishery which he used to supply food for slaves on his Mount Vernon plantation and in 1772 shipped more than a million fish to Alexandria for a sum of £184. And even the location of the nation's capital is due in part to these immense shoals. Washington chose the site "at the head of a river plentiful with fish the year round."[31]

These little fish were also put under increasing pressure as farmland spread and dams were built. Such obstructions prevented them from reaching their spawning grounds. However, this broad sweep of relentless habitat destruction, overexploitation and decline is too simple a story. The runs of shad and alewives, along with salmon, were recognized as a valuable common resource. In New England in the mid-eighteenth century, several acts were passed "to Prevent the Destruction of the fish called Alewives." By law, milldams were required to leave their sluice gates open at certain times of the year to allow the fish to pass, both upstream and downstream. Such legislation was designed to give all the towns along the rivers equal access to the fish and to prevent the lowest town from building weirs that could mop up the whole supply—an attempt to prevent a "tragedy of the commons" by legal means. On the Chesapeake, similar legislation was passed to prevent weirs at the river mouths taking all the fish. But in the end, all these attempts at legislation were left behind by accelerating environmental changes.

As farmland spread, silt began to accumulate in once-crystal rivers. Now the only way to catch fish in these murky waters was with weirs. Legislators in Delaware were forced to overturn the laws that controlled fishing with weirs in the rivers that fed Delaware Bay. This in turn resulted in a free for all—a mad scramble to get the last fish, before they were killed by pollution or turned into profit by neighbors.[32] The Lord's oysters again. One after the other, these river fisheries collapsed—at least all but one. Menhaden still swam in vast shoals: "with their heads so close to the surface, packed side by side, and often tier above tier, almost as closely as sardines in a box."[33] Menhaden are too oily to find their way on to the table, but they can be processed into a high-grade oil so large-scale fishing of menhaden began in New England, where they provided an alternative to whales.

After the Civil War, the fishery spread south along the coast and gradually became more industrialized. Today, the fishery uses spotter aircraft to locate the shoals and direct the fishing boats. Two boats work together, surrounding whole shoals with a large seine net stretched between them that can be closed to trap the fish. Processed into animal feed, the chicken industry is the largest user of menhaden, though, in 1997, the Food and Drug Administration approved the use of the oil—a significant source of omega-3 fatty acids—for human consumption. This looks like creating a major new market. Already, a company called the Omega Protein Corporation has become the largest catcher of menhaden—the latest market to exploit the once-extraordinary coastal resources of the Atlantic shore.

That the fisheries have lasted so long is a testament to the fecundity of these little fishes. Menhaden catches peaked in the late 1950s and early 1960s after which they have declined. River herring catches in the Chesapeake declined from the start of the twentieth century through to the 1980s, and although the drop in commercial landings was due in part to a loss of some of the markets, some was undoubtedly due to declining fish numbers. And that left predators like the striped bass in double trouble.

They too were targeted by commercial fisheries, since, from the earliest days of settlement, they were a highly esteemed fish. William Wood described the qualities of the striped bass with mouthwatering prose: "The bass is one of the best fish, and though men are soon wearied of other fish, yet are they never with bass; it is a delicate, fine, fat, fast fish, having a bone in his head which contains a saucerful of marrow, sweet and good, pleasant to the palate and wholesome to the stomach."[34] Those striped bass that escaped the nets and spears found themselves going hungry as the herring shoals shrank. By the 1970s, the striped bass was almost extinct in the Chesapeake.

Both kinds of sturgeons suffered a similar fate. Like the river herrings, they were so prolific (large females can produce 3 million eggs) that the fishery survived exploitation well into the nineteenth century. But the sturgeon is a provider of more than just flesh the quality of beef. In the middle of the nineteenth century, it was realized that American sturgeons' eggs can be converted into caviar to rival that of the Russians and the swim bladder yields isinglass, a kind of gelatin used for clarifying wine and beer. So the spawning runs were assaulted with everything from guns to bombs.[35] In 1890, the Delaware River alone gave up more than 5 million pounds of sturgeon. In earlier days, sturgeon had become the first cash crop of Jamestown and the first profits for the company of merchants that backed the venture, and by the end of the nineteenth century, the annual hauls on the Chesapeake had grown to 7 million pounds of fish. By the 1920s, both species were rare fishes. But there is a glimmer of hope for these fishes whose size and abundance so astonished early settlers, a glimpse of the sheer fecundity of the east coast before commercial exploitation.

In 1976, a fish lift was built around Holyoke Dam, on the Connecticut River in Massachusetts, and a fish counter installed to count the number of river herring passing upstream. Previously, the dam had prevented any fish from reaching the spawning grounds, and at first, just a few thousand herring pushed their way upstream through the fish lift. But five years later, two hundred thousand fish passed the lift, and in ten years, half a million flashing silver bodies were passing Holyoke Dam, giving some sense of the resilience of nature.

Likewise, both American and hickory shad have recovered to some extent in the Susquehanna River at the head of Chesapeake Bay, though elsewhere shad have failed to recolonize spawning rivers despite a moratorium on fishing. But an expensive artificial restocking program undertaken by the Maryland Department of Natural Resources seems to be having some success, as increasing numbers of juvenile shad are being monitored in the stocked rivers, the first young shad to swim in the Patuxent and Choptank rivers for more than three decades.

Striped bass, an important sport fish, has also been the subject of an intensive recovery program and is now held up as a triumph of modern conservation. But as with all the stories we've seen so far, nature is far more complicated than we would like. After a spectacular recovery of numbers starting in the mid-1990s, there seems to be more trouble ahead for the striper. Many of the fish being caught are not the fast, fine, fat fish described by William Wood three and a half centuries ago. These fish look skinny, and worse, nearly half the fish in Chesapeake are infected with a wasting disease called mycobacteriosis. Some scientists think that food is at the heart of the problem.

Menhaden are a major food source for stripers, especially for the larger ones, and there's much debate about the true state of menhaden stocks. Omega Protein say the stocks off Chesapeake are both healthy and self-sustaining, and because the stocks are deemed healthy, there is no regulation of menhaden catches in this area. An astounding 400 million pounds are still landed each year.[36] But Omega Protein have laid off some boats and spotter planes recently, and the 2000 catch was the lowest since records began in 1940. The average landings between 1996 and 1999 were only 40 percent of those in the late 1950s[37]—all of which should sound alarm bells, especially in the aftermath of the spectacular collapses of other fisheries in recent years. And even if menhaden can survive the pressure of new markets, like that for omega-3 fatty acids, some scientists fear that there may not be enough menhaden to provide for the bay's predators as well. Many think that the striped bass numbers are destined to crash once again as disease and starvation hit them.

The sturgeons are not doing so well either. Despite a recent recovery in the Hudson River, the short-nosed sturgeon is still listed as endangered in New York State. It is almost certainly extinct as a breeding species in the Chesapeake Bay. Atlantic sturgeons have also made some recovery in the Hudson River and in some South Carolina rivers, and there's evidence that a few fish are managing to breed in the York and Rappahannock rivers, flowing into the Chesapeake Bay. But we are still a long way from seeing the sturgeon spectacles witnessed by John Smith and others. To add to the complications, sturgeons are now facing another problem.

Both sturgeon species are very sensitive to low oxygen concentrations, a situation that develops all too frequently in summer due to algal blooms. In the past, the great filter beds of oysters and the vast shoals of filter-feeding fish kept the water clear. Now algae grow unhindered, indeed encouraged by fertilizer runoff from farm fields. Such oxygen stress is probably also a factor in the wasting disease of striped bass.

Sturgeon are long-lived fish and so don't breed every year. A female short-nosed sturgeon doesn't mature until she's eight years old and then might only breed every three to five years. Atlantic sturgeon females don't mature until eighteen or nineteen years of age and even when on the spawning beds may reabsorb their eggs if spawning conditions are not suitable. Since they've been recorded as reaching sixty years old, it's not a biological imperative that they breed every year, but that's not a help when it comes to staging a population comeback. Even so, figures from the recovery of the short-nosed sturgeon in the Hudson River suggest that they've been increasing their population at 10 percent per year, which, for a long-lived, late maturing fish, is impressive enough to have surprised many scientists.[38] As with the river herrings, such incipient vitality must be a cause for some small glimmer of hope if conditions in the rivers and bays can be improved.

The plight of the great east coast bays and rivers is a clear illustration of why fisheries policies so often fail. Most fisheries models currently work by considering each individual species separately—something that nature never does. For several decades, many ecologists have argued for an ecosystems-based fisheries policy, one that takes into account the relationships between species. In fact, some now see this approach as the only way forward if we are to have any fisheries left in fifty years time.[39] Catch limits need to consider not just effects on the target species, but on all connected species, otherwise trophic cascades will have unpredictable but dramatic effects on the whole ecosystem. However, single-species policies are hard enough to formulate and even harder to get accepted by fishermen. Ecosystem models are even more complicated; as one marine biologist remarked, it's not rocket science—it's much harder.

Ecosystems-based approaches are also expensive, since we need to know much more about the ecology of all the animals and plants involved to set up predictive models. Yet there is a fifty-year history of failure for our current models. If these were engineering models used to build bridges, they would have been abandoned many years ago, yet the stakes for the fisheries and therefore for people are much higher.

CHAPTER 6

Angels from the North

Today, it's hard to get a real appreciation of the former abundance of the bays and rivers along the east coast since so many of the fish and shellfish spectacles no longer exist. But there are a few places where it's much easier to step back in time. One of those is back on the Delaware Bay, though you'll need to visit six months after the horseshoe crabs have left the beaches. It was a clear, bright November day when I approached the town of Smyrna in Delaware with rising spirits. I'd been filming peregrine falcons in New York City, and although the sight of these falcons soaring around towers of glass and steel as if they were great sea stacks or cliffs was a great testament to nature's adaptability, I'm personally not so well adapted to life in concrete canyons. So after driving through the conurbation of the eastern corridor, from Manhattan past Philadelphia, I was glad to see the country of the Delmarva Peninsula finally opening up.

From Smyrna I turned onto small roads leading across fields of late standing corn and stubble, heading toward Bombay Hook National Wildlife Refuge on the western side of Delaware Bay. As I approached, mesmerizing flocks of redwing blackbirds and cowbirds were feeding on the stubble. These great flocks appear to roll across the fields, as those at the back fly to the front to find unscavenged ground. They are soon leapfrogged by birds behind, and before long they find themselves at the rear again and have to repeat the process.

Driving closer, the whole flock, most of which had actually been hidden by the stubble, erupted, an almost solid black mass filling the air. Through binoculars, tens of thousands of blackbirds flashing their red epaulettes in the late afternoon sun was a spectacular sight. Eventually, and now slightly late, I pulled up outside the refuge headquarters and got out to look for the refuge manager, but I only managed a few steps. Above the restless twittering of the blackbirds, the air was full of wild cries. The sky above me was the intense blue of a fall evening and hung across the heavens like innumerable strings of pearls were skeins of white geese.

I was reminded of some lines from a Lakota healing song:

Behold, a sacred voice is calling you,
All over the sky a sacred voice is calling,
The White Goose Nation is appearing, behold.

This song was given to a Lakota holy man called Hehaka Sapa (Black Elk) in a vision. He died in 1950, but throughout his life he used this song to summon up the cleansing power of the white birds blowing in like a snowstorm from the north. As I stood watching the geese sweep across the darkening sky, I could catch a sense of that power.

These were snow geese, and they were returning from feeding in the stubble fields to roost in the safety of the lakes on the refuge. So next morning, before dawn, I crept to the edge of the marshes to wait for first light. Long before the sun was up, the sky was already graded from orange and pink on the eastern horizon to deep inky blue over my head, a color combination that only nature can get away with. Even now the geese were keeping up their wild braying when, with no warning, the noise changed; it rose several orders of magnitude and, as if this were a prearranged signal, a great section of the flock took off. Now I knew what those early explorers must have felt like, struggling to put into words the spectacles they witnessed. There are simply no words to describe the sound of tens of thousands of snow geese calling as they lift off the marsh or the sight of a web of loose skeins filling your vision across an orange sky. Black Elk had it right. The sky *was* full of sacred voices, but paradoxically, these awe-inspiring sights also present a real problem—the opposite problem to those we've seen so far.

Each fall, snow geese head south from their Arctic breeding grounds. Those in the east belong to a form called the greater snow goose, which head via staging grounds on the St. Lawrence River to the mid-Atlantic coast. These days around two hundred thousand birds assemble at Bombay Hook, though in the 1960s the average was just four to five thousand. The birds that visit the central and western parts of the United States are lesser snow geese, and they have done even better than the greaters over the last few decades.

One of the reasons for their success is all those stubble fields that I drove across the previous day. After they've left the marshes in the early morning, the geese descend on those fields like an early winter storm, a blizzard of snow geese voraciously feeding on spilt grain or unharvested crops. It seems that this access to virtually unlimited winter food has sent their numbers skyrocketing. The population is growing so fast that any census is usually out of date a year later, but a rough estimate at the end of the 1990s put the total breeding population of both forms at around 5 million birds, making it one of the most abundant species of waterfowl on the planet.

The continued explosive rise in population has worried wildlife biologists. Snow geese nest in colonies on the tundra, where they feed by grubbing up sedges and rushes to get at their nutritious roots. The recent increase in numbers has meant that the geese are now stripping the delicate tundra bare. Increased evaporation from the bare surface then pulls up salts from below, turning the tundra into a hypersaline wasteland.[1] As the geese run out of food in one area, they move to another, and recent surveys along the coast of Hudson Bay, where many of the lesser snow geese nest, have revealed that one third of their preferred habitat has been damaged. This now seems to be affecting the numbers of other waterfowl and shorebirds that use these areas to breed. At Bombay Hook and similar staging and wintering refuges, the worry is that they are damaging delicate salt marsh vegetation. Wildlife managers are now putting in place drastic measures, such as relaxing hunting regulations and extending the open season, to reduce snow goose numbers, though the most recent censuses suggest they are not as yet having much effect.

The story seems conclusive, that the spread of agriculture has recently created a new "pest" species. But an appreciation of the past abundance of bird spectacles along the eastern shores suggests that this is too simple a view. There are eighteenth-century descriptions from both the breeding and wintering areas that suggest as large or larger populations of many species in the past. And further back in time, a Dutch explorer called van der Donck saw plenty of snow geese in the Hudson Valley in the early 1600s. "Some of the latter kind [of geese] are almost white, like unto our tame geese. Those kinds, in cold weather, frequent and resort to places near the sea shores in great numbers, where many are killed, often eight or ten at one shot." In South Carolina, naturalist John Lawson also described numerous snow geese: "There is also a white Brant, very plentiful in America. This Bird is all over as white as Snow, except the Tips of his Wings, and those are black. They eat the Roots of Sedge and Grass in the Marshes and Savannas, which they tear up like Hogs."[2]

Of course no accurate censuses exist for that period, so no one can be sure of the historic population of snow geese. But was it really substantially smaller than today? In the past, so the current thinking goes, their migrations took them over forests or grasslands with limited feeding opportunities for the flocks. Having to depend on wetlands for food may have limited their numbers. Now, vast tracts of those woodlands and grasslands have been replaced by fields, full of food for hungry geese. With a much larger area for feeding, the snow goose population has exploded.

But in the past salt and freshwater marshes were far more extensive—enough, it seems from historical accounts, to support impressively large populations of snow geese. So perhaps the current problem on staging and wintering areas is one of too little habitat rather than too many geese. Also, I've found no historical accounts of extensive damage on the nesting grounds. Does this mean that there are as yet unrecognized factors in the equation?

We also need to remember that in the past it wasn't just snow geese that darkened the skies with their numbers. From the St. Lawrence to the St. Johns, there are descriptions from openmouthed observers almost unable to, or perhaps not daring to, report the sheer numbers of waterfowl, particularly on spring and fall passage. William Wood could hardly believe how easy it was to hunt waterfowl in New England. "If I should tell you how some have killed a hundred geese in a week, fifty ducks at a shot, forty teals at another it may be counted impossible though nothing more certain."[3]

Around the same time, but further south in the New Netherlands, van der Donck eloquently describes the volume of noise that so many birds produce.

> Among the other subjects wherewith the New Netherlands is abundantly provided are the fowls that keep to the waters, which we find principally in the spring and fall of the year . . . at those seasons the waters by their movements appears to be alive with water fowls; and the people who reside near the water are frequently disturbed in their rest at night by the noise of the water fowls, particularly by the swans, which in their season are so plenty, that the bays and shores where they resort appear as if they were dressed in white drapery.

The swans he saw were tundra swans, which had nested along the as yet unknown far northern fringes of the continent, from Baffin Island to Alaska. Swans from as far west as Alaska's north slope still make their way down to the mid-Atlantic coast, wintering from southern New Jersey to North Carolina, though Chesapeake Bay is the preferred destination of many. For John Smith and the other Jamestown colonists, the arrival of these great flocks of swans along with other waterfowl must have seemed like manna from heaven during the harsh winter months on the Chesapeake. "In winter, there are great plenty of Swans, Cranes grey and white with black wings, Herons, Geese, Brants, Wigeon, Dotterell, Oxeies, Parrots and Pigeons."[4]

A decade or so later and another description from Virginia's coast tries to give some idea of the size of these flocks: "I saw there an infinite quantity of Buzzards, Swans, Geese and Fowl covering the shores. . . . Swans, Hoopers, Geese, Ducks. Teles [Teal] and other fowls a mile square and seven miles together on the shore." In 1680, two Dutch immigrants visited Maryland and like those that came before them were amazed by the numbers of ducks and geese. "The water was so black with them that it seemed when you looked from the land below upon the water as it were a mass of filth or turf, and when they flew up there was a rushing and vibration of the air like a great storm coming through the trees, even like the rumblings of distant thunder."[5]

Forty years later, the bays and marshes of Virginia still echoed with the wild calls of waterfowl. "As in summer, the rivers and lakes are filled with fish, so in winter they are in many places covered with fowl. There are such a multitude of swans, geese, brants, sheldrakes, ducks of several sorts, mallards, teal, blewings and many other kinds of waterfowl that the plenty of them is incredible. I am but a small sportsman, yet with a fowling piece have killed above twenty of them at a shot."[6] There are countless similar reports right along the eastern seaboard, but the selection above should suffice to make it clear that in the past many kinds of waterfowl provided spectacles to equal or exceed those of snow geese today, though most are now mere ghosts of that former glory.

Tundra swans still turn up each year on Chesapeake, as well as on a number of staging posts, rest areas on their aerial highway from the high Arctic to the east coast. But on Chesapeake today they face an unusual problem—from another swan. In 1962, five mute swans escaped from captivity and began to breed. So what's wrong with more swans gracing the Chesapeake's waters?

Mute swans are not natives; they are from Europe, and unlike those earlier European invaders that built Jamestown, these recent colonists thrived on the bay from the very start. By 1999, five birds had become four thousand, and the spread continues unabated. Wildlife scientists fear they may reach twenty thousand by 2010, and mute swans are large aggressive birds. They drive the smaller tundra swans from the best feeding and roosting areas and have also been seen trampling the nests of least terns and black skimmers. In addition, they keep black ducks from good feeding and roosting areas and are therefore probably contributing to the general decline of this shy species of duck.[7]

And, most importantly, they eat large quantities of submerged vegetation—at the moment more than 10 million pounds a year. One of the most important submerged plants in Chesapeake is wild celery, a plant whose main seed production coincides with the time when migratory waterfowl are absent from the bay. Unfortunately, mute swans don't migrate, so much of each year's seed crop now ends up inside alien mute swans long before it has chance to germinate. These aquatic vegetation beds are of vital importance in the Chesapeake's ecology, so, all in all, these European invaders are not good news for the natives. But the great waterfowl spectacles have been threatened before.

Like the fish and shellfish, these huge bird flocks were a valuable resource, a story that's becoming horribly familiar. But the story doesn't follow quite the same pattern as that of oysters and sturgeon. As the eastern cities began to grow, there was a ready market for birds of all kinds, so market hunters and punt-gunners began to make their appearance in places like Chesapeake. Actually, "punt gun" is a bit of a misnomer. In reality, the punt has something more akin to a small cannon mounted on the front. It was often used at night, when the birds were dazzled by kerosene lamps. As the birds took off in panic, a single punt gun could bring down dozens if not hundreds. At the end of the nineteenth century, each juicy pair of canvasbacks might fetch $3–$4 on the Baltimore markets, and with such easy profits, the future looked bleak for the great waterfowl spectacles of the east coast. But a different kind of hunter was also beginning to brave the freezing winter winds sweeping over the coastal marshes.

These hunters counted presidents among their number, Theodore Roosevelt and Benjamin Harrison. The Chesapeake, in Washington's backyard, began to attract these luxury hunters, who were prepared to pay handsomely for the privilege. This new breed of hunters also stimulated local businesses like outfitters and guides. Today, you only have to walk into one of the big hunting stores scattered right across the United States and Canada to realize the size of the hunting business. It is immense, but it doesn't work without animals to hunt. Unlike market hunting, which usually seems to follow the Lord's oyster philosophy, luxury or sports hunting has been more farsighted, at least since the dying years of the nineteenth century.

Theodore Roosevelt lived at a time when he could witness at firsthand the rapid destruction of wildlife of all kinds right across the continent. In a message to Congress in 1907, he spelled out his worries: "To waste, to destroy our natural resources, to skin and exhaust the land instead of using it so as to increase its usefulness, will result in undermining in the days of our children the very prosperity which we ought by right to hand down to them amplified and developed."

But being Roosevelt, these weren't just idle words. In 1887, he founded the Boone and Crockett Club to promote a voluntary "fair chase" policy of limited bags, closed seasons, and ethical hunting methods, which laid the foundations for later hunting legislation. It may have been founded to encourage the sustainable uses of America's wildlife, but in many ways it was much more than that. It embodied a vital part of the American psyche. Roosevelt named the club after Daniel Boone and Davy Crockett, both of whom were seen to personify an American ideal, a pioneering spirit of people living in intimate contact with nature and using its products with wisdom and thoughtfulness. Actually there are many environmental historians who wouldn't recognize either Boone or Crockett from that description, but a name is just a name—it's what the club stood for and achieved that's more important.

As America opened its doors to the tired and poor, "the huddled masses yearning to breathe free," people from many nations and many backgrounds accepted the invitation. How was a nation made of such disparate parts ever to achieve a sense of national identity? That's a whole separate story, but in as far as it relates to the natural world, one shared experience on which a common identity could be built was the pioneering spirit—living off the continent's natural abundance. One of the reasons for the extraordinary scale of the hunting business in North America is that this ethic is still so much a part of being American or Canadian. The Boone and Crockett Club took this feeling and codified it.

At first, those identifying with that pioneering spirit still saw wildlife as limitless and free for the taking, but the Boone and Crockett Club gradually transformed such people into "sportsmen" with a duty to preserve the wildlife on which a significant part of the American identity depends. The club stood in opposition to free market exploitation—and consequent destruction—of natural resources, though the right to make money is, of course, another integral part of the American Dream. They became a potent force in the conservation of anything that could be hunted, from elk and bear to the diminishing flocks of waterfowl. The club, one of the first conservation organizations in the world, still exists today and is still vigorous in promoting conservation and ethical hunting. In 2000, it hosted a meeting of thirty-five other wildlife and hunting organizations to form a partnership supported by 4.5 million hunting conservationists—a powerful voice for Roosevelt's vision of wise use.

But at the end of the nineteenth century, many of the wildfowl spectacles no longer existed. Population growth had vastly increased the size of the population centers and of the food market. The twin pressures of hunting and habitat destruction pushed some species of waterfowl to the very verge of extinction. But the voices of those in organizations like the Boone and Crockett Club were growing louder.

In 1929, Congress passed the Migratory Bird Conservation Act. Among other things, this act allowed the government to buy up remaining wetland areas and protect them as waterfowl habitats. Unfortunately, it didn't provide for a source of funds to maintain these preserves. It took a stroke of conservation genius, five years later, to solve that problem—the Migratory Bird Hunting Stamp Act.

This act meant that all hunters over sixteen years old had to buy a duck stamp each year, as a kind of license, in order to hunt waterfowl. Ninety-eight cents in every dollar goes straight into the Migratory Bird Conservation Fund, where it is used to buy up wetlands for inclusion in the National Wildlife Refuge System administered by the Fish and Wildlife Service—more than $600 million since the program started in 1934. Now the duck stamp program has spread beyond hunters. Anyone can buy a duck stamp and know that they are making a direct contribution, not only to wildfowl conservation, but to all wildlife that depend on the refuges.

They've also become something of a collectors' item. Each year a big competition is held among professional and amateur artists for the privilege of painting the design for the year's duck stamps. They've become miniature works of art and a long-term investment, which has encouraged more non-hunters to buy them. The end result has been described as one of the most successful conservation stories ever, and it has certainly seen a tremendous turnaround in the fortunes of many, though not all, waterfowl populations.

I've seen refuges stuffed with so many mallards that the flocks looked more like those of redwing blackbirds and lakes that rang with the clarion calls of two thousand tundra swans, enough to keep anyone awake at night. Whatever your opinion of hunting as a sport, it can't be denied that hunters, along with hunting organizations from the Boone and Crockett Club to Ducks Unlimited, have helped recreate some of the spectacles of colonial America. And with all those hunters, you might think that Chesapeake's mute swan problem could be easily solved. After all, more than two thousand tundra swans are shot each year across the United States under license, and mute swans are a bigger target. But rarely are conservation issues so simple.

Different states had different regulations in place concerning waterfowl. Maryland didn't allow the hunting of swans at all, whereas swans were not protected in Virginia, Pennsylvania, or Delaware. A step forward was taken in 2001, when the U.S. Court of Appeals ruled that mute swans were covered under the Migratory Bird Treaty Act, passing responsibility for the problem to the U.S. Fish and Wildlife Service who could now oversee a more coherent plan of attack. Individual states are now looking at the best way to control the alien swans. But even now, it's far from smooth sailing. When the Maryland Department of Natural Resources came up with a plan that combined addling mute swan eggs with shooting adults, animal rights organizations filed a lawsuit in the federal courts to challenge the action. Meanwhile, the mute swan population continues to grow at an astounding 1,200 percent, as it has done since the mid-1980s, undoing some of the good work done by waterfowl and wetland conservation organizations.

But before we get too carried away with the conservation success story of waterfowl in general, we must spare a thought for the Labrador duck. You may never have heard of it, and you certainly won't have seen one. It is beyond any help from the duck stamp program; it has the dubious honor of being one of the first birds to become extinct during the colonial period. The last reliable record was of one shot off Long Island in the fall of 1875. The male in particular was a beautiful duck with a white head and neck, separated by a dark neck band and white wings. The rest of its body was dark. And that's most of what we know for certain about this duck; it was an enigmatic little bird. Its coloration gave it the alternative name of pied duck, but since this name was sometimes applied to other species, it is not always certain what the old accounts are referring to. And even where more certainty exists, accounts don't always agree.

Some suggest the species was abundant on the northeast coast as far south as the Chesapeake. Others suggest it was always a rare species. Some have said that it was a delicious species to eat, others that its flesh was dry and fishy. But even if it wasn't good eating, that didn't prevent it from joining many other kinds of waterfowl hanging in the markets of New York, Philadelphia, Boston, and Baltimore. Yet there are also descriptions of this species left hanging in the markets until its flesh rotted, presumably by those agreeing with the latter opinion of its taste.

It had peculiar soft edges to its bill, which suggested to some that it fed on small mollusks, an idea supported by the fact that there are records of fishermen catching these birds on hooks baited with bits of mussel. But despite such hunting, it is not at all clear what caused its early extinction. It was not hunted with any more vigor than other ducks, perhaps even less. Its peculiar bill might suggest a specialized diet, which may have made it susceptible to even small environmental changes brought about by the rapid rise in population on the east coast, and the equally rapid demise of the great shellfish beds can't have helped. But all this is only guesswork. Its death is likely to remain just as mysterious as its life.

It wasn't just ducks and geese that found their way in large numbers into the city markets. Plovers and other shorebirds also existed in prodigious numbers along the coast, and one of these arrived in such vast flocks that it would have shamed the red knot spectacle that so hypnotized me on Delaware Bay.

This bird was the Eskimo curlew. It bred in vast numbers on the Arctic tundra, where the Inuit described the colonies as making the land look as if it was smoking. At the end of the short Arctic summer, they headed south to winter in Patagonia, as the red knots still do. But their first stopping point was the coast of Labrador and Newfoundland, still a journey of three or four thousand miles for birds from the western Arctic. Here, they assembled on the coastal heaths in incredible numbers from late July through August. John James Audubon witnessed the arrival of these flocks on the Labrador coast, and so impressive were they that they called to mind a more famous bird spectacle. "On the 29th of July, 1833, during a thick fog, the Esquimaux Curlews made their appearance in Labrador, near the harbour of Bras d'Or. They evidently came from the north and arrived in such dense flocks as to remind me of the Passenger Pigeons . . . flock after flock passed close round our vessel and directed their course toward the sterile mountainous tract in the neighbourhood."[8]

In reality, those mountainous tracts were not sterile but covered in a low growth of crowberry bushes, at this time of year black with ripening fruits. This is why the curlews came here. To most of us they might be crowberries, but here they are curlew berries. In 1884, Lucien Turner, a meteorologist working for the U.S. Army who seemed to share my fascination for large bird flocks, described the spectacle of flocks settling on the berry bushes. "The leader plunges downward followed by the remainder of the flock in graceful undulations, becoming a dense mass, then separating into a thin sheet spread wide again . . . reforming into such a variety of shapes that no description would suffice . . . each day adding to their number until the ground seems alive with them. They feed on the ripening berries, becoming wonderfully fat in a few days."[9]

Curlew berries, like the horseshoe crab eggs that refuel the red knots on their spring journey, are very nutritious. The curlews picked and ate these berries at an incredible rate, stripping whole areas bare in no time at all, so that, as Lucien Turner observed, they really did become "wonderfully fat" in just a few days and ready for their onward migration.

It's very hard to gain any real idea of the historical population of Eskimo curlews. Numbers in the millions are often guessed at, but more conservative—and evasive—estimates put their numbers at "not less than hundreds of thousands."[10] Part of the problem is that the birds were mostly observed in the few brief weeks of fall passage, when they were concentrated in areas of curlew berry shrubs. The frequent superlatives in describing these flocks could easily lead to overestimation of the population. But flocks of Eskimo curlews were often accompanied by American golden plovers, a species that might have even outnumbered the Eskimo curlew. So whatever their actual populations, there's no doubt that these shorebirds existed in extraordinary numbers and provided one of the truly great wildlife spectacles of North America.

Within weeks of their arrival, the birds were off again, but they didn't follow the coastline south, which might seem sensible for shorebirds. Instead, they headed out into the Atlantic, swinging south to pass over Bermuda and then on over the eastern edge of the Caribbean to make landfall in South America, probably somewhere in the Guianas. These oceangoing flocks of curlews and plovers must have been immense, although there were virtually no observers out in that vast expanse of Atlantic to marvel at them. It would take extreme luck for a ship and a migrating flock to cross paths, but that's exactly what might have happened on October 7, 1492, to judge from a record in Columbus's log: "Immense flocks of birds, far more than they had seen before, passed overhead all day long, coming always from the north and heading always towards the southwest."[11]

His sailors trapped some of the birds, and they were clearly "field" birds rather than seabirds, which convinced Columbus to alter course and follow their flight, assuming that such birds were probably heading for land. Five days later, Columbus landed on San Salvador in the Bahamas. If these birds really were Eskimo curlews and American golden plovers, which is fairly likely, then Columbus was doubly lucky; he had no idea that these birds were some of the longest distance migrants in the bird world and that they are quite capable of sustained flight of thousands of miles over open ocean. But even these powerful, fast flying flocks didn't always have it their own way.

In some years, storm force nor'easters would drive the flocks ashore in New England. Such "big flight" years were a bonanza to the New Englanders since, as one Massachusetts resident said, they were "considered by epicures the finest eating of any of our birds." According to another nineteenth-century account, "Their arrival was the signal for every sportsman and market hunter to get to work, and nearly all that reached our shores were shot."[12] In one year on Nantucket Island, such numbers sought refuge from autumn storms that the inhabitants ran out of powder and shot well before the whole flock could be killed. And these birds were especially easy to kill. Apart from the density of the flocks, they had the habit of staying around wounded flock members, as one visiting English sportsman records. "I once shot one in a marsh; its companion took a short flight and then re-alighted beside the dead bird, quietly waiting there until I had reloaded my gun and was ready for him."[13]

The birds were also hunted when they first arrived in Labrador and Newfoundland, though probably not as intensively as in New England, where there were more people waiting for them. But at least they didn't descend on New England every year, and certainly not if they could avoid it. There were only five or six such big flight years in Massachusetts between 1808 and 1888. Nevertheless, observers in Labrador noticed dramatic decreases in numbers between 1885 and 1890. By the first half of the twentieth century, sightings were so rare that at times the bird was feared extinct. Since then, there have been a few, a *very* few, reliable sightings that suggest the Eskimo curlew has somehow managed to escape the fate of the Labrador duck. But no one has yet found the breeding site of this handful of birds, a population now estimated at anything from twenty-five to one hundred individuals.

Yet it's unlikely that hunting during the fall migration was responsible for the Eskimo curlew's demise. Hunting was fairly light in Labrador and very intermittent in New England. Also, the curlews' longtime companion, the golden plover is still an abundant bird, even though it followed the same arduous migration route, and was subject to the same hunting pressures. However, both birds followed a different route on the spring return journey, crossing the Gulf of Mexico, to travel north across the Great Plains and on into the Canadian Arctic, and it's here that the answer to the mysterious disappearance of the Eskimo curlew might lie. So I will leave the conclusion to this story until a later chapter.

With the exception of Eskimo curlews and Labrador ducks, the story in this chapter has been a refreshing change from the relentless gloom of ocean and coastal fisheries. Not everything is rosy, as species like black ducks decline while introduced mute swans are far too numerous. And, despite the efforts of many organizations, wetlands continue to decline at the alarming rate of eighty thousand acres a year—or, as Ducks Unlimited translate it, at seven football fields an hour. Yet the relative success of waterfowl conservation is undeniable. In this case, short-term commercial gain was tempered by a longer view, eloquently articulated by Theodore Roosevelt, of handing on natural resources to our children, not diminished but amplified. That view was made more powerful by the fact that it also embraced an iconic self-image of what it means to be an American, but it also shows that when enough people act out of enlightened self-interest, it makes a real difference.

CHAPTER 7

Earthly Paradise or Earthly Hades?

It was some two decades ago when I first visited Asheville, North Carolina. I arrived at its tidy little airport sometime after sunset on a freezing January evening and was met by Bill Duyck, a retired firefighter, a great naturalist and photographer, and now a longtime friend. He's a real mountain man, but in these days of political correctness, he tells me I should refer to him as an Appalachian American. I was there to enlist his help in setting up some filming in the southern Appalachian Mountains later in the spring and to look at some possible locations in an area of America that I had always wanted to visit.

Next morning, Bill dragged me out of bed at a ridiculously early hour to show me some serious southern hospitality in the form of a mountain of pancakes, then bundled me into his car to show me the real thing. We drove up onto the Blue Ridge Parkway, which was closed due to ice and snow, but since Bill was a volunteer for the Forest Service, he was able to produce a key to the barriers, and we were soon climbing the winding road north out of Asheville, just as first light was showing. Standing on an exposed ridge a short time later, we watched a bitter dawn break to reveal the classic scenery of these southern mountains, ridge upon forested ridge stretching off into infinity, like waves in an ocean of trees.

Coming from England, where the trees come in much smaller patches, I was captivated. At that moment I became a lifelong fan of the southern Appalachians and have made countless return visits. But on that first occasion, I had never seen so many trees in one place, a thought that I'm sure must have crossed the minds of the first explorers and colonists when they landed on these shores. Although it would be some time before any of them gazed across the ridges and valleys of the Appalachians, this sea of trees extended right down to the coast to greet the pioneers of sixteenth century. These travelers came from a land perhaps even more denuded of trees than the one that I know, so the prospect of this endless forest would have been all the more amazing. In his epic voyage along the east coast in 1524, Verrazzano found "broad plains, covered with immense forests of trees . . . too delightful and charming to be described."[1] Other explorers too numerous to mention echoed that description, from Florida to Canada. But there are major differences between Verrazano's "delightful and charming" view and mine, separated by a gulf of nearly five centuries, which reveal some of the key reasons for the historic abundance of nature on the North American continent. Unlike the teeming ocean offshore, humans have been an integral part of this ecology for well over ten thousand years. The manner in which different human ecologies and philosophies have shaped the eastern forests is the subject of this chapter.

To understand how both Indians and Europeans fitted into forest ecology, we first need to remember that the eastern forest was not one forest at all. The eastern forests can be divided into a range of different types, and each of those types has been further subdivided many times as ecologists try to fit each and every variation into its own box. The resulting ecological maps are both complicated and colorful, but it is possible to paint a simpler, broader picture of the different kinds of forests that pioneers and settlers would encounter as they began to explore the continent.

To the north, the *boreal forest* stretches unbroken across the continent from the Atlantic to the western mountains. In the far north, the forest consists of stunted trees as it grades into open Arctic tundra. To the south, there is a dense canopy of spruce and fir, and further south still this gradually changes into pine and hemlock, though a few hardwood trees, like quaking and big-tooth aspen, paper birch, and balsam poplar brighten the dark green of the conifers. Many of these conifers were real giants, like the white pines described by John Josselyn, but even the balsam poplar, the northernmost of the hardwoods, could grow to nearly one hundred feet and reach diameters of three feet— still an impressive tree by today's standards.

But these northern forests were not the only great tracts of conifers to confront early explorers. Much of the south and east of the continent was also covered in evergreen forest, though of a very different character to the boreal forest. When the first Spanish conquistadors marched through this hot and humid landscape, the dominant tree was the longleaf pine, a beautiful species that, as its name suggests, is draped in cascades of long flowing needles.

These pine forests exist (or existed) because of fire—both natural and Indian-set—and indeed the endless tracts of longleaf pine stretching across the southeast may only have been so large because of Indian burning.

The longleaf has some exquisite "behavioral" adaptations to turn fire to its advantage. Young seedlings, looking like tufts of grass, just sit for years, slowly storing energy below ground. Then, in a rapid sprint (at least for a plant) they shoot upward, and in just a few years carry their sensitive growing shoots up through the dangerous zone of ground fires, hopefully not encountering any during that time. Once at a safe height, each seedling can begin to turn itself into a proper longleaf pine, with tough bark to resist the ground fires that sweep quickly through forest. Hardwood trees, which could outcompete pines in a straight race, are not so able to survive these fires; so, as long as the forest burns with reasonable frequency and at the right time of year, the pines remain in control.

In between the two major zones of conifer forest, there is a varied landscape of deciduous trees. Moving south through the boreal forest, broad-leafed hardwoods become much more numerous and varied in the so-called *transition* or *northern hardwood* forest. This zone varies both north to south and east to west. In the north, white pines remain common; in the south, trees like sugar maple and American basswood increase in abundance. Toward the west, the eastern hemlock becomes rarer, but other trees like red, white, and bur oaks are commoner. On its southern edge, this forest gradually completes its transition into an even more complicated zone, the *mixed deciduous forest*. There is now a bewildering variety of hardwoods vying for sunlight in the canopy, creating many different types of forest across this vast region. At one extreme, there are forests around the Great Lakes that are almost pure stands of American beech and sugar maple; this is caused by the strange fact that the maple seedlings do best under a beech canopy and the beech seedlings do better under maple, so neither tree ever becomes dominant. At the other extreme, the cove forests of the southern Appalachians are more like tropical rainforests in their diversity. Some 120 species of trees are crowded into these forests.

All of these forests are now very different to those encountered by the first explorers, and the first and most obvious difference is the size of the trees. When I returned to the Appalachians in spring, Bill and I met up with Dan Pitillo, a botanist from the University of North Carolina who was going to show us a real glimpse of the past. He took us to the Joyce Kilmer Memorial Forest, just south of the Great Smoky Mountains National Park, and there guided us along a narrow path that wove its way through great mossy boulders alongside a small stream. There were wildflowers everywhere—trilliums, orchids, Solomon's seals, dwarf crested irises, bluets—a truly captivating display, but when I finally forced myself to look up, I was even more enthralled to find myself in a grove of *the* most enormous trees. They were tulip poplars, at their very best in fresh, bright green leaves. The forest is a memorial to the poet Joyce Kilmer, and although I can't say I'm particularly fond of his lines on trees I do share his sentiments:

> I think that I shall never see
> A poem lovely as a tree

Seeing trees of this size, it's easy to imagine Daniel Boone hollowing a sixty-foot canoe out of a single tulip poplar. Elsewhere in this forest, there are also mighty eastern hemlocks, and scattered across the southern mountains are several other tiny fragments of giant old-growth forest that I've managed to explore over the years. Today, finding such trees usually involves a scramble into inaccessible valleys, but giants like Joyce Kilmer's tulip poplars—and bigger—were commonplace in the days of Verrazzano and those that followed.

Sycamores were often hollow, and large enough to shelter twenty or thirty men during a sudden storm. On the northeast coast there were groves of white pines—each tree one hundred feet in height and five feet in diameter, though some of them might have towered twice that height above the forest floor. The larger ships that arrived off the coast of America had masts made, of necessity, from several smaller timbers spliced together, so it didn't take long for shipwrights and ship's carpenters to realize the value of these tall straight white pines. And some of these trees were so large that John Josselyn, writing in New England, felt they were simply *too* big as masts, even for the largest ships.

In the same area, there were spruce trees measuring twenty feet in circumference, while back in the Carolinas, explorers were frustrated in their attempts to shoot turkeys out of their roosts by the sheer size of the trees: "We saw plenty of Turkies, but perch'd upon such lofty Oaks, that our Guns would not kill them, tho' we shot very often, and our Guns were very good."[2] Magnificent chestnut oaks, which these turkeys had wisely chosen as a roost, often rose sixty feet before there were any branches. So, while it's easy to be impressed by the great tracts of forest carpeting the ridges and valleys of the Appalachians today, we should remember that these forests are nothing like the precolonial forests. Those first explorers found themselves walking through a natural cathedral whose green roof arched fifty or more feet above their heads or, as one early visitor to the Chesapeake region noted, "like the retreat of some Ancient Druids."

These forests must have been truly magnificent; so much so that in the late eighteenth century, the naturalist William Bartram, traveling through the Carolinas, is almost afraid to describe the scenes he encountered: "To keep within the bounds of truth and reality, in describing the magnitude and grandeur of these trees, would, I fear, fail of credibility; yet, I think I can assert, that many of the black oaks measured eight, nine, ten and eleven feet diameter five feet above the ground, as we measured several that were above thirty feet in girth, and from there they ascend perfectly straight with a gradual taper forty or fifty feet to the limbs . . . the tulip tree, liquidamber and beech were equally stately."[3]

Another obvious difference between forests then and now is the abundance of wildlife; the numbers of larger game animals, in particular, were immediately obvious even to the earliest explorers. During his two-week restocking stop in Narragansett Bay in Rhode Island, Verrazzano found that "Animals there are in very great number, stags, deer, lynx and other species."[4] Later, Thomas Hariot's scientific mind recorded more detail of the abundance around Roanoke: "In some places there are a great number of deer. Near the seacoast their size is that of our ordinary English deer, though sometimes they are smaller; but further inland, where there is better feed, they are larger. They differ from our deer in two ways: their tails are longer and the snags of their horns point backwards."[5] Hariot was describing white-tailed deer, which were extremely abundant all through the eastern forests. An indentured servant on the Chesapeake once described them as being commoner than London cuckolds, a telling comment both on the numbers of deer and of life back in merry old England. But can we get a more accurate measure of white-tail abundance in precolonial North America?

The first person to turn to is Ernest Thompson Seton, who at the end of the nineteenth and beginning of the twentieth century wrote a whole library's worth of books on American wildlife and Indian lore as well as being instrumental in founding the Boy Scouts of America. He was born about thirty miles from where I was, in northeastern England, but emigrated to Canada as a young boy, where he immersed himself in the wilderness. Although some of his work was a highly romantic and anthropomorphic view of American wildlife, he did also produce more carefully researched tomes, and in 1909, he published estimates of whitetail numbers in precolonial times, based on his knowledge of the densities deer could reach and the size of their range. He came up with a figure of 20 million animals. Twenty years later he revised that figure to 40 million.

More recent estimates have also been made, using more sophisticated techniques. Apart from better computing techniques, these estimates also used Indian population sizes, as well as the numbers of animals they needed over the course of the year for their survival. On the assumption that their hunting was sustainable (which is a reasonable assumption given how long Indians had been hunting deer), this gives a minimum size for the population. Together with a better understanding of the ecological range of whitetails, these new estimates suggest whitetail populations in the region of 23.6–32.8 million animals.[6] So Seton wasn't far out. But whitetails weren't the only deer in the forests.

Verrazzano's "stags" were elk, a much bigger species than whitetails, though one which was still seen in large numbers by many early explorers. John Lederer, a German explorer, was one of the first people to travel westward from the Chesapeake colonies and see the Appalachians, and in 1670, in the shadow of the then-unknown Blue Ridge, he described a typical scene: "To heighten the beauty of these parts, the first Springs of most of those great Rivers which run into the Atlantick Ocean, or Cheseapeack Bay, do here break out, and in various branches interlace the flowry Meads, whose luxurious herbage invites numerous herds of Red Deer (for their unusual largeness improperly termed Elks by ignorant people) to feed."[7] Apart from evoking a wonderful image, John Lederer also points out one of the early confusions of names between the Old and New Worlds. He tried to explain his point: "The right Elk, though very common in New Scotland, Canada, and those Northern parts, is never seen on this side of the Continent: for that which the Virginians call Elks, does not at all differ from the Red Deer of Europe, but in his dimensions, which are far greater."

Confused? People still are, though Lederer had it right back in 1670. Simply put, the North America elk and the European red deer are usually considered the same species, though some forms in North America grow much larger. However, to add a little more confusion, a few authorities are now suggesting that North American "red deer" be elevated to the status of a full and separate species. And one final point—in case you weren't confused enough—North American elk are often referred to by an Indian name, *Wapiti.* The animal called "elk" in Europe is the same thing as the North American moose, and, as Lederer points out, the moose was very common further north. It was certainly a familiar creature in New England, though not common in the immediate vicinity of the settlements, as William Wood found: "There be not many of these in the Massachusetts Bay, but forty miles to the north-east there be great store of them."[8] But they were common enough for the English to consider turning them into farm animals: "This beast is as big as an ox. . . . The English have some thoughts of keeping them tame and to accustom them to the yoke, which will be a great commodity: first because they are so fruitful . . . secondly because they will live in winter without fodder."[9]

Not a good idea if you believe John Josselyn, another earlier chronicler of New England. The moose, he records in his book, *New England's Rarities Discovered* "is a very goodly Creature, some of them twelve foot high, with exceeding fair Horns with broad Palms, some of them two fathoms [about twelve feet] from the tip of one horn to the other."[10] Although Josselyn was almost certainly exaggerating their size, if you surprise a moose in dense willow scrub, you might well be inclined to believe him. The largest subspecies of moose today live in Alaska. They stand about six and half feet at the shoulder and carry a rack of antlers perhaps six feet across. However, the Irish elk (or should it be the Irish moose?), which occurred across Europe at the end of the last ice age, carried vast palmate antlers, similar to the modern moose but with twice the span, so Josselyn's description is not a physical impossibility. Perhaps there were some bigger moose around in Josselyn's day and his description less exaggerated than we might at first sight think. But in another book, Josselyn also describes porcupines laying eggs, and such passages are reminders to take care in interpreting these early reports. They were written by all kinds of people for all kinds of purposes. We are on the safest ground where there is consensus between different reporters.

Josselyn goes on to describe another large deer in the area, though one a lot less common. "The Maccarib, Caribo, or Pohano a kind of deer as big as a stag. . . . This creature is nowhere to be found, but upon Cape Sable in the French Quarters; and there too very rarely, they being not numerous."[11] He was describing the woodland caribou, a subspecies of caribou that once extended through the northern forests from New England through Michigan and Minnesota to British Columbia.[12] Woodland caribou are generally larger than the more familiar barren grounds form and lived to the south of this sub-species. But their range contracted northward as forest in the south gave way to farms and towns, a new habitat that was far more suitable for white-tailed deer, allowing these adaptable deer to extend their range north and outcompete woodland caribou. Whitetails also carry a disease called "moose sickness," which is lethal to caribou and probably hastened the demise of woodland caribou in the south of their range. Woodland caribou are declining right across their range, largely from the same factors that drove them from their southern homes in historic times.[13] Today, most people think of caribou as creatures of the high Arctic, typified by the barren ground subspecies. Yet it is an extraordinary thought that it was once possible to see herds of caribou in the forests of New Hampshire and Vermont.

Similarly, American bison are now seen as icons of the Great Plains, but in early colonial times, they also trampled trails through the forests to favored salt licks in herds measured in many hundreds of animals. When Daniel Boone forged his famous trail through the Appalachians, he was, more often than not, following well-marked buffalo trails, and at Blue Licks, he found buffalo paths converging on the salt licks from every direction that "were cut deep into the earth like the streets of a great city."[14]

More than twenty-five years before Daniel Boone blazed the Wilderness Trail, when settlements on the coastal plain were already burgeoning, Thomas Walker was charged with scouting out routes that would take settlers across the Blue Ridge and Alleghenies and into the fertile lowlands of the Ohio Valley. The journal of his trip through the Cumberland Gap gives some idea of the numbers of game animals, including bison, which he encountered. "We killed in the Journey [4 months] 13 Buffaloes, 8 Elks, 53 Bears, 20 Deer, 4 Wild Geese, about 150 Turkeys, besides small game. We might have killed three times as much meat, if we had wanted it."[15]

In early colonial times, bison roamed as far east as Pennsylvania and New York, possibly even as far as New England. These herds were much smaller than those that darkened the plains, usually only a few hundred animals, but nonetheless impressive to the first people to see them. They certainly seem to have occurred in such numbers in West Virginia, Kentucky, and Ohio. In Scott County, Kentucky, for example, a historic marker near Stamping Ground suggests that it was named because buffalo had trampled down all the vegetation around a nearby spring.

However, the full extent of their historic range is still debated. A plethora of "buffalo" place names throughout North Carolina is used as evidence by some that large herds occurred here and possibly followed the valleys as far south as Georgia. I've even been told that Interstate 40, cutting west across the Appalachians from Asheville, follows old buffalo trails in places. But convincing evidence is hard to come by.[16] Indeed, the historic status of these eastern bison is often confusing and difficult to unravel.

There are two subspecies of bison in North America: the plains bison and the wood bison. The wood bison lives to the north of the plains subspecies, a distribution centered on the aspen parklands and conifer forests of Alberta. A few people have claimed that it was the wood bison that lived in the eastern forests, though it's now clear it was the plains subspecies. And it was probably a recent immigrant.

There are records of bison east of the Mississippi from the 1500s, although some people now think that big numbers didn't arrive in the eastern forests until the turn of the eighteenth century.[17] This was also the time that Indian populations were collapsing due to war, disease, and displacement, and the two events are in all probability linked. It seems that the arrival of the Europeans and the subsequent demise of Indian hunters allowed the plains bison to colonize the eastern forests, but within three hundred years, those same people had wiped it out. There were none left in the forest by the early years of the nineteenth century.

Smaller mammals were also widespread and abundant in the eastern forests—otters, martens, fishers, and beavers. Beavers were everywhere, from the boreal forests right down into the southern hardwood forests, and their dam-building had major effects on all these forests. Flooding killed the trees, creating open patches in the forest. Insects are more numerous along these forest edges, and these in turn supported high numbers of forest birds. There are references to beaver dams half a mile long, which might not be much of an exaggeration since there is a reliable record of one in Montana that was over two thousand feet long. Beaver ponds, large and small, were an integral and vital part of the forest and in no small measure helped increase the diversity and numbers of both plants and animals.

Unfortunately, beavers, along with many other forest mammals, made the mistake of wrapping themselves against the cold New World winters in thick, warm fur, which was soon seen as a valuable commodity by those looking for profits from the Americas. Hunting for commercial markets was one of the first ways that Europeans began to change the nature of the eastern forests, and one of the first people to recognize the commercial potential of these forests was Captain John Smith.

After surviving the early years of Jamestown, he spent a few years back in England publicizing the New World with unending optimism. Then, in 1614, the unconquerable captain was back in the Americas, exploring the northern coasts, where he found Indians willing to trade the pelts of beavers, martens, and otters. He picked up 1,300 skins "for trifles" and realized that there were good profits to be had from these forests. He wasn't the only one. A few years earlier, Henry Hudson, an Englishman heading up a Dutch expedition, sailed into New York Harbor. Here he found magnificent forests teeming in wildlife. He supposedly landed on an island where rabbits were so abundant he called it Coney Island. Then he landed on an island the local Indians called Manna-hata, where there were plentiful freshwater streams: "pleasant and proper for Man and Beast to drink, as well as agreeable to behold."[18] I wouldn't try that today.

He headed on up the river that now bears his name, as far as modern Albany, and all the way he found plentiful, fur-bearing game. This voyage would be the basis of the Dutch claim to the "New Netherlands," and the abundance of furs soon drew merchants and adventurers from Holland. They had already set up trading posts in the northeastern forests by the time Smith began his explorations of the area. Keen to promote England's rival claim to this part of the continent, Smith realized that the wealth of furs could be one incentive to establish English settlements here. When Verrazzano had sailed along this coast in the sixteenth century, he called the area Norumbega, but to encourage exploitation by the English, Smith, ever the publicist, renamed it New England. Yet, despite his attempts to promote the establishment of commercial fur-trading posts here, it would be a very different set of colonists that arrived in 1620.

The arrival of the Pilgrims brings into sharp focus two related factors that dramatically reshaped the eastern forests and after that the rest of the continent. One was the commercial market in New World commodities—a market that began long before the foundation of Plymouth with the cod shoals of the Grand Banks, though one which was integral to the Pilgrims' mission. The other was a philosophy of what a Christian civilization should look like.

Long before this time, problems of a religious nature had been brewing in England. In Elizabethan times, there were many that felt the English church had become too politicized and too Catholic in its doctrines. By setting out to purify the church, these people earned themselves the title "Puritans." But since the established church remained heavily intertwined with state affairs, and the state continued to appoint high-ranking church officials, the Puritans gradually formed their own sets of doctrines and practices. In the eyes of the establishment, this amounted to antistate, revolutionary thinking that led to the Puritans being increasingly persecuted as the seventeenth century dawned.

One group from Nottinghamshire had fled to the town of Leyden, in more tolerant Holland, but, as both England and Holland learned more of this New World across the Atlantic, these people saw an opportunity for a new beginning—new communities that could be founded upon a truly purified church. But it was painfully obvious by now that setting up new colonies was both expensive and dangerous. The only way the Puritans were going to get to the New World was if the venture was also a commercial enterprise. However, many of these Puritans were already trained in commerce and trade, so they understood the requirements of the markets. When the Mayflower eventually arrived in New England, only thirty-five of the one hundred "Pilgrims" were actually from the Leyden community. The rest were traders, farmers, and the like. But, with its core of Puritans, this colony should have a better chance of surviving than many earlier attempts.

Unlike many of those on the Jamestown venture, the Puritans were used to hardships and a simple life, and they had a God-given determination to succeed. Yet, right from the outset, they made what in hindsight look like basic mistakes. They refused to take John Smith with them. Perhaps not surprisingly, they thought his proud and boastful nature would not fit well with their intentions of establishing cities of godliness. Even so, he'd had many years of experience in surviving in the New World; he was the nearest thing England had to an expert. And when they finally arrived off Cape Cod, they had made the same mistake Smith had in the Chesapeake. They had brought no useful fishing gear.

And if Smith had been peddling both the Chesapeake and New England as an earthly Paradise, the Pilgrims didn't necessarily see it that way. They arrived late in the year when, as William Bradford, later governor of the colony, described it, everything bore "A weather-beaten face, and ye whole countrie full of woods & thickets, representing a wild & savage heiw."[19] For the Pilgrims, this wasn't Paradise, at least not yet. It was the savage wilderness beyond the

Garden of Eden. In some ways, this was the start of a much more realistic way of looking at the New World. Unbelievably abundant it might be, but it is also a hard place to live; a wilderness like this is no place for civilized people. Yet everywhere that explorers traveled up and down the coast, they found plenty of Indians, who were surviving very happily here.

One of the reasons why so many colonies failed amid the New World's abundance was that the settlers' mindset prevented them from living like Indians. They were happy enough to trade with them, or even steal from them, but they could not bring themselves to live like the Indians. Learning to build brushwood weirs to trap fish shoals was one thing, but adopting the real key to Indian success—mobility—was another. The whole intellectual foundation of European civilization was fixity—a worldview profoundly different from the Indians, who thought nothing of moving around to make the most of different food sources.

The Pilgrims, like the Jamestown settlers, quickly found out that the natural abundance here is seasonal. Even though Cape Cod was named for the enormous cod shoals found in the surrounding waters, the Pilgrims found none. They had arrived at the wrong time of the year—even if they had brought fishing gear. Many other colonists—before and after—were similarly fooled by the Paradise publicity campaign for the New World, since, though the reports didn't always lie about what was here, they rarely made the great seasonal differences clear. The Indians, on the other hand, possessed enough ecological knowledge to know how to exploit different food sources at different times of the year.

Along the coast of Maine, to the north of the Pilgrims' first colony at Plymouth, the Indians lived entirely off the natural abundance. Spring brought great flocks of waterfowl and shorebirds. In March, smelt would run up all the rivers in huge numbers, followed in April by alewives, then later by salmon and sturgeon. During the summer there were huge herds of seals on the coast and offshore islands and great banks of shellfish for the picking. Late summer saw the return of shorebirds and waterfowl and the ripening of berries and grapes. Winter was a hard time, but when it snowed, moose were fairly easy to track and kill with bow and arrow. And, if all else failed, the Indians seemed more than happy to go hungry, an attitude that the settlers found incomprehensible.

There was a lot variation across the vast forest region, especially away from the coast, but all Indians followed some kind of seasonal hunting and gathering cycle that meant they had to move around their territories, to be at the right place at the right time. However, around Plymouth and further south, the Indians also farmed. Most of them grew corn, beans, and squash—the three sisters—all three together in mounds of soil; and so their yearly round also included food from their fields, though they still depended to a great extent on hunting and fishing. William Bradford discovered this latter point very quickly. While still looking for a site to plant the colony, he blundered into an ingenious deer trap, which hoisted him off his feet in a most undignified manner.

Many accounts of these farming tribes suggest that they, like the hunter-gatherers to the north, didn't remain permanently in one place. And, although there's some evidence to the contrary, they also appeared not to fertilize their fields; they simply carved new ones out of the forest when soil fertility dropped. If true, perhaps this demolishes another of our cherished stories of colonization. The Indian Squanto was supposed to have helped solve the Pilgrims' early farming problems by suggesting they bury a fish in each mound of earth. But since the Indians' shifting agriculture didn't need fertilizer, this makes it unlikely Squanto was passing on an old Indian custom. He had been to Europe with previous expeditions to New England and may have learned this trick in a place where there was neither room nor inclination to keep moving to new fields.

However, not all researchers agree with this scenario. William Doolittle, at the University of Texas in Austin, has examined the firsthand accounts of pioneer settlers in the eastern woodlands with a fine-tooth comb, and says he can't find any really hard evidence that Indians practiced such shifting farming patterns. Instead, he thinks that fields were laboriously cleared of stumps and tree roots and cultivated on a permanent basis.[20] It was simply too time consuming and difficult to fell trees with stone axes, only to abandon the field after a couple of years. In this view, true shifting agriculture, or swidden, only developed after European metal axes made the job easier, and earlier patterns of farming had been disrupted by wars with the newcomers. But even if their fields were more or less permanent, the Indians still depended on hunting for a significant part of their food and that still entailed moving around their territory to make the most of seasonal abundances.

In fact, the situation may have varied from region to region. In some areas, the Indians didn't seem too bothered about removing the remnants of trees in their fields. Instead, they cleared off what they could by burning then girdled the really large trees to kill them. These were often left standing, according to some accounts. "Now, in the first clearing of their plantations, they only bark the large timber, cut down the saplings and underwood, and burn them in heaps; as the suckers shoot up, they chop them off close by the stump, of which they make fires to deaden the roots, till in time they decay."[21] Similar fields, dotted with the stumps of trees, are a common sight among Amazonian Indians today. As these fields become exhausted, they burn off new areas of forest or, more often, reburn old fields that have reverted to forest.

In a similar way, many historians speak of North American Indians abandoning both their fields and their villages on a regular cycle. Archaeologist Thomas Neumann described the Onondaga (part of the Iroquois Confederacy) as abandoning their fields after ten years and their villages after thirty years. In such cases, the abandoned sites are not wasted land. As the forest regrows, it produces tall thin trees, which, at about ten years old, provide poles for building houses and palisades around the new village,[22] part of their mixed economy of forest and field.

So a large part of the Indians' success was down to their willingness to move, which also lessened their ecological impact in any one area and therefore helped preserve the abundance that they depended on. However, a seminomadic lifestyle of hunting, fishing, and farming was not what the Pilgrims intended. For them, civilization meant the building of permanent towns and farms. The intellectual and religious underpinning of their world view was the biblical injunction to subdue the earth and till the soil. Indeed, they used this as part of their reasoning for how they could "legally" take over Indian lands. By their definition, land was only considered as owned if it was improved from its base natural condition by the sweat of the brow. Since the Indians could hardly be described as having improved this forest wilderness, any claims they might have to it were forfeit. Yet, the colonists were on slightly dodgy ground with this line of reasoning—on two counts.

First, Indians south of the boreal forest had considerable amounts of land under cultivation. John Smith records many areas of fields in his early explorations of the Chesapeake, and another writer, in 1620, considered that Indians in tidewater Virginia alone probably had between two and three thousand acres under cultivation at any one time.[23] Further north, Verrazzano saw large areas of fields right up into New England, especially among the Wampanoags of Narragansett Bay, who would later become neighbors of the Pilgrims. And virtually all the early European settlements only survived as long as they did because of Indian corn and beans.

Second, the Indians had, in fact, significantly altered and "improved" vast areas of the forest, but not in the obvious way of clearing trees to make farms. When Verrazzano cruised along the east coast, he made frequent reference to fires in the forest. Just north of the Outer Banks, he found an area where "the inhabitants being numerous, we saw everywhere a multitude of fires."[24] Many other early explorers frequently mentioned Indian-set fires, from New England all the way down to La Florida and inland across the mountains. These deliberate fires had major effects on both the appearance and ecology of the forests. They cleared away dense underbrush to create forests that were so open they reminded many Europeans of the great parks they had left behind. This also probably helped some of the trees grow to the enormous sizes that so impressed the first explorers. There is less competition from neighbors in a thinner forest, and certainly, in England, the discovery of a really large, old tree in woodland usually points to the fact that it was once heavily managed parkland or wood pasture rather than ancient woodland.

Indian fires also created large glades and meadows. In his explorations of Rhode Island, Verrazzano describes both these effects, though there's no evidence to suggest he connected these landscapes with Indian fires: "there are open plains twenty five of thirty leagues in extent, entirely free from trees or other hindrances. . . . On entering the woods we found that they might all be traversed by an army ever so numerous."[25] Likewise, around the Chesapeake, John Smith found "a man may gallop a horse among these woods any way, but where the creekes or Rivers shall hinder."[26] The same was true further south when an expedition explored along North Carolina's Cape Fear River in 1663: "We found a very large and good Tract of Land . . . thin of Timber, except here and there a very great Oak, and full of grass, commonly as high as a man's Middle, and in many Places to his Shoulders, where we saw many Deer and Turkies; one Deer having very large Horns and great Body, therefore we called it Stag Park."[27]

However, it didn't take long for Europeans to realize what the Indians were up to. Game animals like deer and elk were much easier to see in these open forests, and much easier to follow. William Wood quickly realized this in New England in the decade following the Pilgrims' arrival: "it being the custom of the Indians to burn the wood in November when the grass is withered and leaves dried; it consumes all the underwood and rubbish which otherwise would over-grow the country, making it unpassable, and spoil their much affected hunting."[28] Around the same time, another New England colonist observed that Indians "Burnt up all the underwoods in the Countrey, once or twive a yeare and therefore as Noble men in England possessed great Parkes . . . onely for their game."[29]

But burning does more than just increase the visibility of game. Grass springing up from the ashes in these open forests grew thicker and more lush than in unburned forest, and it grew even more luxuriantly in the meadows. As one observer noted in 1818 in Connecticut; "Where the lands were burned there grew bent grass . . . two, three and four feet high."[30] Not only did this attract game, but such improved grazing also increased the numbers of deer, elk, and the like. So the abundance of game animals that so astounded early explorers may have been down, at least in part, to Indian management of their land.

As Indians created open meadows, they also increased the amount of "edge habitat," just as beavers did with their ponds. In the same way, this increased both the diversity and abundance of other species, from bugs to birds. And fires helped create the illusion of Eden in other ways. Fruits and berries grew thick and ripe in the wake of fires, an abundance remarked on in many accounts. Even before the Jamestown colonists had entered the James River, George Percy was remarking on the local strawberries: "Going further we came into a little plat of ground full of fine and beautifull strawberries, foure times bigger and better than ours in England."[31] Later, the naturalist William Bartram, on his travels through the Carolinas, described his horse's hooves as being stained red by strawberry juice, while earlier in New England, William Wood had seen equally fine displays of an even greater variety of fruits of the forest: "There is likewise strawberries in abundance, very large ones, some being two inches about; one may gather half a bushel in a forenoon. In other seasons there be gooseberries, bilberries, raspberries, treackleberries, hurtleberries, currants, which being dried in the sun are little inferior to those our grocers sell in England."[32]

The other commodity of the forests frequently commented upon was the superabundance of nut-bearing trees: pecans, walnuts, oaks, and, most abundant of all, the American chestnut. In the fall, these forests rained nuts. There's some evidence that Indians spared valuable nut and fruit trees when clearing fields, or even planted them. They were certainly quick to plant European fruit trees around their villages, so they were hardly likely to have failed to notice the copious—and often equally delicious—bounty of their own native trees. Bartram, for example, noticed that Chickasaw plum trees were often much commoner in the forest close to Indian settlements than in the forest at large. In the forests of coastal North Carolina, Thomas Hariot found an unusual abundance of walnuts: "Walnuts are of two kinds, and there is an infinite number of both. In some of their great forests a third of the trees are walnut."[33]

It's even possible that, far from being a pristine wilderness, the eastern broadleaf forests were, in effect, one vast Indian orchard. It might seem inconceivable that Indians could have exerted such an influence over so great an area of the continent, but, if this seems far-fetched, some researchers are now arguing that a large part of the Amazon rainforest, that icon of pristine wilderness, is also a huge Indian garden—a form of agriculture with trees, so different from our own concept of farming with annual grasses that we simply didn't recognize it. And since it was a form of farming, it could support far greater numbers of Indians than conventional thinking would allow.[34] Perhaps the same was true of the deciduous forests of the East.

If Indian management of the land contributed significantly to the vision of Paradise that greeted the first Europeans, then it also contributed to the vision of this place as Hell on Earth. Such an abundance of animals like deer meant plenty of predators—wolves, cougars, lynx, and bobcat, as well as the omnivorous black bear. Some of these animals were hunted for commercial gain, but others were hunted out of fear and hatred. And one of these in particular stood out for seventeenth-century Europeans as the very embodiment of the devil on earth—the wolf.

Drawing on biblical symbolism, a holy war had already been waged against wolves right across Europe; after all, hadn't Christ sent his followers forth "as sheep in the midst of wolves"? These devils in fur were entirely exterminated in England by the early 1500s, while elsewhere across Europe, if not eliminated, they were forced to retreat into the most remote fastnesses. Symbolizing the struggle between civilization and wilderness, this long-running battle against wolves became the stuff of fairy tales and myth: cunning predators that would stop at nothing to devour their mortal enemy—*Homo sapiens*. But those myths must have transformed into reality for European settlers arriving in North America. The forests beyond their insubstantial settlements rang to the wild howls of creatures that "the Devil hath created to Plague Mankind."

So ingrained is a hatred of wolves that almost no one had a good word to say for them. Even early naturalists, who, in the flowery prose of their day, expressed their wonder for most aspects of the natural world, lambasted the wolf. Mark Catesby, in North Carolina, called them an "awful creature" that traveled "in droves by night and hunt deer like hounds, with dismal, yelling cries."[35] Those sentiments are echoed by writers from all periods of settlement and colonization, and from east to west across the continent. Yet those few who cared to look deeper than the antiwolf rhetoric found a creature very different to the one of myth.

John Lawson in his travels around the Carolinas in 1700 had plenty of chance to get to know a whole range of predators in the wild woods.

> When we were all asleep, in the Beginning of the Night, we were awaken'd with the dismall'st and most hideous Noise that ever pierc'd my Ears: This sudden Surprizal incapacitated us of guessing what this threatening Noise might proceed from; but our Indian Pilot (who knew these Parts very well) acquainted us, that it was customary to hear such Musick along that Swamp-side, there being endless Numbers of Panthers, Tygers, Wolves, and other Beasts of prey, which take this Swamp for their Abode in the Day, coming in whole Droves to hunt the Deer in the Night, making this frightful Ditty 'till Day appears, then all is still as in other Places.[36]

I like to think that Lawson would have listened to this nightly symphony with some degree of wonder, since he knew that the wolves were no real threat: "they are neither so large, nor fierce, as the European Wolf. They are not Man-slayers; neither is any Creature in Carolina, unless wounded." But Lawson's was a voice in the wilderness; no one wanted to change their ideas about wolves. Besides, they did kill deer and, later, European livestock, so the settlers saw every reason, both practical and philosophical, to wipe out wolves as fast as possible.

Ten years after they landed, the Puritans were offering generous bounties on wolves, and other settlements followed almost as soon as they were established. By 1648, a single wolf was worth forty shillings, the equivalent of a week's wages for a farm laborer. Yet even with such incentives, wolves remained far too common for comfort around the frontier settlements. So people responded by killing wolves in as many ways as they could devise. Poison bait was laid indiscriminately over wide areas and succeeded in killing all kinds of creatures, including the settlers' own dogs. Later, cumbersome metal traps were hauled into the forest and again killed indiscriminately. One Pennsylvania frontiersman, William Long, claimed to be able to attract wolves by howling and by 1790 was said to have killed more than two thousand. At the same time, the settlers began to clear any dense vegetation where a wolf pack might lie up. Slowly wolves became rarer where people were commonest. But there was to be no let up.

Experience taught the settlers that wolves quickly repopulated an area even if only a few stragglers were left. Every last wolf had to be eliminated, and drives were a particularly successful way to mop up the last individuals. Often hundreds of people turned out for such a drive, to surround a large area of woodland, then march toward the center carrying burning torches and making a terrifying din. As the wolves panicked and tried to break through the tightening cordon, they were shot. Not only did this clear the area of its last wolves, it also provided "pleasant amusement," as one participant put it. By 1800, wolves had gone from southern New England and many of the other more populous areas. They were still common enough further north and to the west, on the Great Plains and in the Rockies, though the frontier was inexorably heading their way.

The howls of wolves might have sent shivers down the spines of early settlers and caused them to huddle just a little closer to their fires, but the night was full of other terrifying noises too. According to William Wood, the bass section of this demonic chorus was provided by lions: "some . . . likewise being lost in woods, have heard such terrible roarings, as have made them much agast; which must eyther be Devills or Lyons."[37] William Wood was at least partially right. There was a large feline hunting deer in the forests, but it wasn't at all clear to the first settlers what it was. It didn't have a mane like male lions from Africa or India. Even so, the belief that the eastern forests were infested with lions persisted for some time, another confusion between the Old and New Worlds. The lack of any specimens with manes was explained by the simple fact that so far only females had been caught. But slowly it became clear that this was a new animal. It took English naturalist John Ray, considered the greatest taxonomist before Carl Linnaeus, to settle the matter, in 1693.

He described this animal as uniquely American and called it after a local Brazilian Indian name—*cuguacuarana*—mercifully shortened today to "cougar." As more became known of this elusive creature, it was obvious that William Wood's (and other) accounts were a little embellished. Cougars are not capable of producing "terrible roarings," or indeed roarings of any sort, as

William Byrd described in 1728, in his *History of the Dividing Line:* "his Voice is a little contemptible for a Monarch of the Forrest, being not a great deal lowder nor more awful than the mewing of a Household Cat."[38]

In actual fact, the truth lies somewhere between—cougars can scream loud enough to make the hairs on the back of your neck stand up if they want to. They are also incredibly successful animals. Ranging throughout most of North and South America, they have the widest distribution of any American mammal. Adapting to such widely different circumstances, the cougar has evolved into a number of separate subspecies. The one that so terrified Wood and others was later called the eastern cougar—*Felis concolor couguar.* But like wolves in the East, they didn't last long in the face of European settlement. In the early 1700s, Cotton Mather, who did much to set the moral tone of the New England colonies, saw their mission as clearing the woods of "those pernicious creatures, to make room for better growth." The settlers were diligent in these duties. In 1739, Virginia botanist John Clayton summarized the general retreat of larger forest creatures: "Panthers [cougars], Buffaloes and Elks and wild cats [bobcats] are only to be found among the mountains and desert parts of the countrey where there are as yet few inhabitants."[39]

Most wildlife biologists now accept that the eastern cougar finally became extinct in the first half of the twentieth century—though it flatly refuses to lie down. Indeed, the eastern cougar is causing as many hassles now as it ever did in early colonial times. The problem is that people keep seeing cougars in remote areas of forest. The official line up to the 1990s was that these were about as real as the "terrible roarings" heard by Wood's informants. Then, with better techniques for DNA analysis, more and more of those sightings were verified as flesh and blood cougars. The "establishment" view has now changed; these are western cougars (which are still plentiful enough) that have escaped from collections or pets outgrown their welcome. But a growing band of people support the fact that these sightings could represent remnant populations of eastern cougars. And this is not just an academic debate. Eastern cougars are listed on the Endangered Species Act, but western cougars aren't. If there really are relic populations of eastern cougars in some remote valleys of the Appalachians or Alleghenies, then they would receive immediate federal protection and funding.

Camped on a remote ridge in the Great Smoky Mountains a few years back, I fell asleep wondering whether a genuine eastern cougar might have slipped silently by in the night, giving my tent and snuffling horse a wide berth, never breaking cover even in the darkness. But next morning it was another of the forest's large mammals I had to contend with. The previous day, I'd followed the best advice in books by hanging my camera pack from a rope slung between two trees, since it had in it several packets of jerky intended to see me through the next day or so. What no one told me is that the bears hereabouts have also read those same books. All last night there was no sign of bears, which was a pity since we were here trying to film them. But as soon as I lowered my pack to the ground, one appeared from nowhere, grabbed the pack and made off into the woods. Figuring that he was more likely to be after my jerky than my camera, I trailed him for nearly three quarters of a mile, picking up various bits of camera equipment en route. I finally even found the pack itself, a little chewed and devoid of jerky, plastic wrapping and all.

Like wolves and cougars, black bears were also viewed with fear by many in colonial times, and not without reason. They could certainly kill a person if they were wounded, cornered, or protecting cubs, and they existed in great numbers—"that plague of beares," as they were described by early settlers. It's possible to get an idea of just how numerous they were from early hunting records. In 1750, Canada's Anticosti Island was uninhabited by people, but thick with bears, until a hunter called Thomas Wright arrived: "The Bears, who are the principal inhabitants of this island, are so numerous that in the space of six weeks we killed fifty three and might have destroyed twice that number had we saw fit."[40]

In New England, settlers described bears as congregating in groups of twenty to forty during the mating season and setting up a terrible din. In New York State, there is a report from a French explorer describing an even more incredible scene: "There comes out of a vast forest a multitude of bears, three hundred at least together, making a horrid noise, breaking small trees, throwing the rocks down by the waterside. The wildmen [Indians] told me that they never heard their fathers speak of so many together."[41] Almost certainly this last account is an exaggeration, since it happened at night, though even so it describes a spectacle that must have been truly extraordinary to behold. But, like the wolf and cougar, the bear symbolized the wild and untamed forest outside the Garden of Eden.

Although black bears provide good fur, good meat, and useful fat they were also hunted simply to tame the woods. Near Otsego in New York, one bear had the audacity to interrupt a Sunday church service. All the men immediately grabbed their guns and dashed out in pursuit, leaving the Reverend

Daniel Nash in mid-sermon. Once they had killed the bear, they returned to hear Rev. Nash finish a hastily improvised sermon, in which he told his congregation that it was a good Christian act to destroy dangerous animals on the Sabbath. Killers of bears, wolves, cougars, and other dangerous creatures were given hero status in the colonies, and some are still famous today. Daniel Boone—described by Farley Mowat as "that insatiable butcher"—reputedly killed two thousand black bears in his time, as he helped open up the great forest for settlement.

But whatever the settlers thought, this was no howling wilderness, untainted by humanity; humans were an integral part of this landscape, and a few of the early settlers understood the nature of Indian life, at least in part. Thomas Morton arrived in New England in 1624 and helped found a settlement called Mount Wollaston on the site of present day Quincy, Massachusetts. He wrote profusely on all aspects of life in the New World and posed a riddle to his English readers. Why, if this place was so extraordinarily abundant, did the Indians live like paupers?

The answer, Morton pointed out, was that they didn't live like paupers; they only seemed to do so to English eyes. In fact, their itinerant lifestyle gave them everything they needed or wanted. The Indians had an alternate worldview, but one no less valid than the Europeans—indeed, one admirably suited to life here. This was not the kind of thing the Pilgrims wanted to hear, and Morton came under increasing persecution for his views, from the very people who had themselves only recently come here to escape such intolerance. The Pilgrims, and in fact all the English colonists, intended to import their Old World view into this New World.

As the numbers of settlers increased, they began to change the balance of the local ecology, both intentionally and unintentionally, and the first major change was entirely unintentional, often preceding any real attempts at colonization. When Europeans came here, they brought not only their old world views but also Old World diseases, the vast majority of which, from smallpox to the common cold, were unknown here. And with no previous exposure, the Indians had absolutely no resistance to any of these diseases; they died in their droves.

The figures for Indian deaths during repeated epidemics are truly horrendous; historian David Stannard has called it the "American Holocaust." But it's extremely hard to put exact figures on these deaths, particularly in the early years. Diseases often traveled ahead of the first explorers, so there was no one to record the tragedy for posterity. In broad terms, by 1700, the Indian population was probably reduced to 60–90 percent of its size in 1600,[42] but the number of deaths between 1492 and 1600 is the subject of much heated speculation. It's hard to grasp the true impact from such cold calculations; it's much easier to relate to the horrors in microcosm—at the scale of individual humans.

Squanto, the Indian who was so helpful to the Pilgrims, had traveled to England in 1605. He was a member of the Patuxet tribe, and his real name was Tisquantum. After some lively adventures in England and Spain, he finally returned to New England in 1619. But when he stepped ashore, there were no Patuxet waiting to greet him. Every last member of his tribe had been wiped out in an epidemic two years earlier. A whole Indian nation gone in just a few months, and with them went their knowledge of the land and how to live here. Such tragedies would be repeated in every one of the hundreds of nations, right across North America.

So, when the Pilgrims arrived in New England, much of the land was deserted. To their eyes this was a sign that God intended them to have this land. Not only had the Indians failed to improve the land, and therefore forfeited any rights to ownership, but God was now clearing vast tracts of forest in preparation for cities of godliness to rise up out of the wilderness.

For the Indians, on the other hand, the loss of such a large proportion of their population plunged them into an ecological crisis. Large areas of their forest now remained unburned, and a dense tangle of underbrush grew up, making hunting a lot more difficult and further undermining their way of life. The rapid disappearance of so many Indians also had a big effect on many forest creatures, though the nature of these effects was far from simple.

So far, I've painted a picture of a forest managed by Indians to increase harvests of nuts and fruits and of game and to make game easier to see and hunt. But the picture might be more complex than that. Archaeologist Thomas Neumann has come up with a very intriguing thought, that abundant deer, raccoons, bears, and turkeys would all have been competitors with the Indians for the wild harvest from the trees, as well as for the maize they grew in their fields. He thinks that Indians, far from managing the land to increase the population of game, actively tried to reduce their numbers.

Neumann suggests that Indians sought out pregnant or nursing whitetails and hunted turkeys in the spring before females laid their eggs, both strategies that would have a bigger impact on populations than more carefully con-

sidered hunting. Even as early as 1622, John Smith was surprised at how indis-
criminate Indian killing appeared: "for at all times of the yeere the never spare
Male or Female, nor old nor young, egges nor birds, fat nor leane, in season
or out of season with them, all is one."[43] Neumann goes on to point out that,
though easier to hunt and no less appetizing, possums make up a much smaller
proportion of remains in archaeological deposits than raccoons. Possums, he
suggests, were not competitors for mast in the same way that raccoons were
and so weren't targeted. He sees a consistent pattern in all of this, and con-
cludes that, far from Indians deliberately trying to increase game abundance,
they were intentionally trying to keep many species of game below maximum
levels.[44] Yet, at the same time, management of the forests themselves, by burning or encouraging mast trees, would likely increase game abundance, so the
ecological role of Indians was far from simple.

If Indians were actively reducing game populations to remove competition
for wild and domestic crops, then game populations could be expected to rise
as Indian numbers fell, which may have been the case with the eastern buffalo.
It may also explain the comments, made above, concerning black bears, that
"The wildmen [Indians] told me that they never heard their fathers speak of
so many together." Indeed, some scientists now suggest that much of the extraordinary abundance that greeted the first settlers was down to the fact that
so many Indians had been wiped out by disease. The basis of such a view is not
new; indeed in 1622, John Smith was already arguing that Indian hunting was
so profligate that destroying them would promote wildlife abundance: "the
Deere, Turkies, and other Beastes and Fowles will exceedingly increase if we
beat the Savages out of the Countrey."[45] Others have suggested that the loss
of grazing smothered by underbrush in the aftermath of decimated Indian
populations decreased the population of deer and other large game. So, in
one scenario, the huge abundance of game at first contact was due to Indian
management of the land; in the other, to the lack of Indians. This contradic-
tion on the Indians' role in creating the vibrant ecology of the eastern forests is difficult to reconcile. For example, the view that historic abundance
depended on the destruction of Indian populations doesn't take into account
that the very first explorers to land on these shores, people like Verrazano,
described abundant populations both of Indians and of game.

To summarize these two viewpoints: on the one hand, Indians managed
the forests to increase the numbers of game animals. On the other, they would
no doubt have recognized that many of these species were direct competitors

for other forest resources and for crops in their fields and so acted to reduce competition. Yet deer, bears, raccoons, and the like were not just competitors; they too were valuable resources. If there is truth in both of these views (and there is good evidence for both), then the Indian role in the ecology of the forests seen by the first explorers and settlers must have been a very complex one. Which effects prevailed must have varied from place to place and from time to time creating an ever-changing pattern in the mosaic of the eastern forest. But whatever the case, that pattern was about to change dramatically.

Apart from disease, the settlers brought something else that would alter the forest ecology—livestock. As much as ploughing the earth, domestic animals were a symbol of settled civilization. In the early years, hogs did especially well, since they are really only half domestic. They can forage for themselves in the forest, and big boars can put up a spirited defense against marauding wolves or cougars. In fact, they did rather too well. In South Carolina, at the start of the eighteenth century, hogs were described as swarming "like Vermine upon the Earth,"[46] a pattern repeated throughout the eastern forests.

The pig family, Suidae, is not native to North America. In the Southwest, there are peccaries, piglike creatures that belong to the related family, Tayassidae, but no true pigs. So European pigs were as happy as, well, pigs in mud—which is what their rooting did to the forest: turned large areas into muddy wallows. They also destroyed the fields of settlers and Indians alike, forcing the Indians to fence their fields, something that they never did before. Such changes gradually drove the Indians into a more sedentary lifestyle, and that helped reinforce the rapidly changing ecology. Pigs became such a nuisance that they were trapped and re-released on offshore islands, where they were out of the way, but could be harvested when needed. Here they did even more ecological damage. They virtually wiped out the huge banks of clams and oysters around these islands, as well as eggs and nestlings of nesting birds—another source of Indian food gone.

Other kinds of livestock needed much more looking after. Cattle had to be fed during the harsh winter, and that meant growing hay. At first the settlers cut the coarse grass of natural salt marshes or harvested native meadows, but as the numbers of livestock increased so to must areas of hay meadow. Old or abandoned Indian fields were used, but the best meadows sprang up as beaver numbers declined. Untended dams eventually collapsed, draining the lakes and ponds, and the accumulated silt at the bottom of these beaver ponds provided rich earth for growing hay to feed domestic beasts.

Although scarce at first, numbers of domestic animals rose quickly. By 1634, William Wood was able to report: "Can they be very poor where for four thousand souls there are fifteen hundred head of cattle, besides four thousand goats and swine innumerable?"[47] Increasing numbers of domestic animals began to compete with the native grazers. And on top of that, forest creatures were also hunted for food as well as for their skins, in numbers that seem incredible.

The skins of white-tailed deer were the most favored in a trade that was centered on the southern colonies. White-tailed deer were perhaps the most important animals to Indians right throughout the eastern forests, and they were also hunted for food and skins by Europeans from the very start of colonization. But the deer skin trade was given a major impetus in the early eighteenth century, when disease ravaged the cattle herds of France. England banned the import of diseased leather and replaced it with the skins of deer from the "infinite herds" of Virginia. By the middle of the eighteenth century, half a million skins a year were being shipped from the colonies. Most of the hunting was done by Indians, particularly the Creek, Choctaw, Catawba, and Cherokee.

The Eastern Band of the Cherokee Nation still occupies some of its ancestral lands in the southern Appalachian Mountains of North Carolina, a place that is beginning to feel like a second home to me. Eddy Bushyhead, a traditional-minded Cherokee who is striving to keep his language and culture alive, lives in a small cabin high on an isolated hillside on the Qualla Boundary Reservation, and as we sat on his porch a while back, overlooking a fiery display of fall colors, he told me a very poignant tale.

When the first Cherokee came to the Appalachians, animals, plants, and people all spoke the same language, and all got along well. But gradually, as the Cherokee grew in numbers, they began to kill more and more game. Worse, they showed the animals no respect and killed indiscriminately. Eventually, the animals called a council and agreed that, from then on, if any Cherokee killed an animal without showing it proper respect, that animal would inflict the hunter with disease. In this way, for example, a hunter killing a deer without saying a prayer and making an offering to the deer's soul would be very quickly struck down by arthritis. But the plants remained friends with the Cherokee and agreed in their own council to produce a cure for each of these diseases.

This story hints that in the past the ancestors of the Cherokee may have faced hard times by depleting game populations; it provided a powerful reminder to each and every Cherokee hunter of his obligations, not only to his clan and tribe, but to the animals that he depended on. To Indians before Columbus, animals and plants were not just commodities; they were also part of the spiritual fabric of their lives.

Indian morality dictated that they should only take what they needed, a fact often remarked on (even if the morality was ignored) by early settlers. In the middle of the seventeenth century, Nicolas Denys noted that among the hunter-gatherers of northern New England "they killed animals only in proportion as they had need of them. They never made an accumulation of skins of Moose, Beaver, Otter, or others, but only so far as they needed them for their personal use."[48] This philosophy is anchored in practicality. People who need to move frequently simply cannot accumulate masses of personal possessions. But such prudence was also reinforced by their spiritual beliefs.

These observations, though, appear to be at odds with the idea that Indians saw game animals as competitors for their nut, fruit, and maize harvests. If, as it appears, there are elements of truth in both these viewpoints, then clearly the Indians' philosophical relationship, as well as their practical relationship, with their environment was an extremely complex one, a point that becomes apparent as the Indians were drawn into the deer skin trade.

In the southern forests, where the deer trade was at its largest, John Lawson, at the beginning of the eighteenth century, commented of the local Indians that "They have thousands of these foolish Ceremonies and Beliefs of which they are strict Observers."[49] This suggests that many Indians held to their traditional relationships even as the deer trade was beginning to explode. So why did they become so embroiled in a trade that would only further undermine an ecological relationship with the land that had served them so well for thousands of years?

First, most Indians believed that, so long as the right prayers and ceremonies were performed, the soul of a hunted animal would return to the spirit world to be reclothed in new flesh, then return to Earth to be hunted again. In this philosophy, the natural resources of the eastern forests didn't just look infinite, they really were infinite. But second, and perhaps more importantly, many Indian nations could no longer live in their traditional way

Epidemic disease had repeatedly decimated their populations, and the face of the landscape was being transformed by an ever-growing tide of Europeans. Trade goods from Europe in return for skins from their never-ending herds made their lives easier, so given the circumstances many Indians entered into this new deal with enthusiasm. Even so, some Indians saw that they were being sucked into a relationship that could only end in disaster. One such was Skiagunsta, a headman of one of the Cherokee towns: "What are we red people? The clothes we wear we cannot make ourselves, they are made to us. We use their ammunition with which we kill deer. We cannot make our guns, they are made to us. Every necessary thing in life we must have from the white people."[50]

But there was nothing that leaders like Skiagunsta could do, and the deer trade continued to grow. In some areas, the deer herds held up remarkably well, but in others numbers fell fast—so fast that Massachusetts had to declare a closed season on deer hunting as early as 1694; this in an area where, a few decades earlier, colonists could see a hundred deer in the space of a mile. Further south, the deer trade started even earlier. It was so intense that, by 1631, Virginia's colonial authorities had to outlaw the commerce, as too many colonists were forgetting to grow the crops they needed for survival. But colonial regulation failed to curb the enthusiasm for money making from the deerskin trade. Many of these people had come here for the express purpose of getting rich, and the abundance of the New World very quickly gave them rebellious thoughts toward any authority that tried to control their free market. In many ways, it was the abundance of nature here that led to revolution—or independence—depending on which side of the ocean you sat.

By 1661, Maryland had set up its first deer reserve to protect the dwindling herds, but by the end of the nineteenth century, the white-tailed deer was a rare species. And the herds of elk and buffalo had faired a lot worse. The last buffalo east of the Appalachians was shot at Buffalo Cross Roads, near Lewisburg, Pennsylvania, in 1801, thus giving the name of the place an instant poignancy. The elk survived a little longer, but eventually also succumbed. Like the buffalo and the cougar, the elk of these forests was a distinct form, the eastern elk, which, by the late 1800s, was also extinct.

The end of the nineteenth century was a low point for American wildlife. Ruthlessly exploited for profit, some species and subspecies had been wiped out entirely, and many others brought to the very brink of oblivion. Writing at the time, Henry Osbourne, president of the New York Zoological Society, summed up the gloomy prospects: "nowhere is Nature being destroyed as rapidly as in the United States . . . an earthly paradise is being turned into an earthly hades; and it is not savages nor primitives who are doing this, but men and women who boast of their civilisation."[51]

These ecological changes might have reached a climax in the late nineteenth century, but they started as soon as the Europeans arrived. Just how quickly is obvious from a speech made by a Narragansett leader called Miantonomo in the first half of the seventeenth century: "our fathers had plenty of deer and skins, our plains were full of deer, as also our woods, and of turkies, and our coves full of fish and fowl. But these English, having gotten our land, they with their scythes cut down the grass and with axes fell the trees; their cows and horses eat the grass, and their hogs spoil our clam banks, and we shall all be starved."[52] This is a startlingly accurate—and poignant—summary of the ecological changes following in the wake of European settlement, and, as Miantonomo points out, it wasn't just hunting and competition from livestock that threatened the Indians' wild larder. Their woodland home was also rapidly disappearing. Both fields for crops and hay meadows for livestock meant an assault on the forest itself, to clear space. One way the early colonists achieved this was by a profligate use of wood.

These people had come from a continent where the remaining forests needed careful management to provide enough wood and seem to have responded to the endless forests of the New World by using more wood than anyone in Europe would have thought possible. Visitors described hearth fires in the humblest of homes in New England as grander than anything that even the most affluent could afford back home. A typical New England house probably burned an acre of wood each year.[53] However, New England's bitter winters made these luxurious fires more of a necessity than those back home.

The colonists made everything, no mater how utilitarian, from the very best wood. Prime trees might be surrounded by many of lesser value, but these were simply destroyed just to get at the best trees. There are descriptions of kitchen tables made from single planks, two and a half feet wide, without a single knot or blemish. And of course timber could be exported back to a country desperate for it.

In the early seventeenth century, England imported much of its big timber, for buildings or masts, from the Baltic region, but war with Holland had made this very unpredictable. So England turned instead to the forests of New England, where the trees were bigger and more plentiful anyway. Further south, the colonies around the Chesapeake also began to export their forests—this time to the Caribbean Islands, already denuded of trees to make way for tobacco and sugar plantations.

The forests disappeared remarkably quickly from the most densely settled areas and the great white pines, in demand for ships' masts, were first to go. White pines, like longleaf pines, are resistant to forest fires and so depended to some extent on Indian burning to prevent their being smothered by hardwoods. But with the crash in Indian numbers, white pines could no longer compete, and so once they were gone, they were gone. At the end of the eighteenth century, Timothy Dwight, president of Yale College, lamented the passing of these mighty trees. "There is reason to fear that this noblest of all vegetable productions will be unknown in its proper size and splendor to the future inhabitants of New England."[54]

The forest was assailed for many reasons, both practical and spiritual—to beat back the wilderness; cleared for fields and meadows; felled to provide building material, fuel, and profit from export; and to clear away the last sanctuaries of wolves, bears, and cougars. On the 240-mile journey from Boston to New York, Timothy Dwight reckoned he passed through no more than twenty miles of forested land. New England was rapidly living up to its name, being transformed into a copy of Old England, perhaps in ways that the settlers would later regret.

As the forests retreated west, the colonists found themselves facing a wood crisis—too many people spending too long in one place. The Indians knew all about the problems of staying put for too long. One of the reasons they kept on the move was to make sure they always had plentiful supplies of wood near to hand. Indeed, when the first settlers arrived in New England, the Indians assumed that they must have moved here because they had exhausted their forests back home.

But such a view—of the inevitable sweep of ecological devastation—is too simplistic. In reality, some English settlements appear to have achieved a balance in New England's landscapes—different from that of the Indians, but potentially as sustainable. Their story provides a context in which to understand the processes that did eventually lead to the ecological devastation described by the likes of Henry Osbourne at the end of the nineteenth century. This different vision of the colonial past has emerged from the meticulous work of environmental historian Brian Donahue, who used detailed tax returns, along with other sources, to analyze the ecology of farming in and around Concord, Massachusetts, over a period of nearly two centuries.[55]

The farmers of Concord took the mixed husbandry of their Old World heritage and changed it to fit the New World. These farmers were no longer newcomers struggling to survive in an unfamiliar world, but people adapting successfully to a different ecology. Instead of wheat, they grew Indian corn along with some of the more hardy Old World grains and raised cattle for milk, cheese, and beef. These different aspects of their economy were all linked through one vital resource—manure.

To grow crops in permanent fields, especially those underlain by New England's acidic soils, meant fertilizing them with cow manure. But the quantity of manure available depended on the number of cows kept, which in turn depended on how much hay could be cropped from the meadows. So the sizes of pasture, arable land, and meadow were all inextricably linked. Woodlands also came into this equation, since wood was needed for building and fuel. Woodland had its own value, sometimes greater, sometimes less than that of pasture depending on the fine details of the balance of landscapes. Cut woodland was allowed to regrow, producing poles useful for building and fuel—a New World version of coppicing that changed the nature of some of the forest but nevertheless maintained a substantial proportion of land under woodland cover.

Ultimately, meadow land, and therefore dung, was in limited supply, which set an upper limit for how much land was worth clearing and plowing for crops. Such local limitations imposed a balance of different land types and dictated the pattern of farming around Concord. The pattern was more or less stable for nearly two centuries, during which time, many generations of farmers achieved a good subsistence living without degrading the land. It was, though, a different balance of landscapes than that under Indian stewardship.

As the population grew, there was inevitable pressure on these resources but no short-term incentive to disrupt the system—any change in the balance of landscapes would create a negative impact on one aspect of the mixed economy, which in turn would affect the whole. There was, however, room to improve the system a little. Instead of mowing natural meadows, the farmers could import English hay, a mixture of English grasses and clover that gave better yields and allowed more cows to be overwintered. This changed the landscapes a little further as these alien species became established, but the overall pattern remained and to judge from the tax returns seemed to be sustainable. Whether it was as sustainable in the long term as the Indian system clearly was, we'll never know, since in the end this local system became connected to the wider economy, which transformed it beyond recognition.

As the area around Concord filled up with self-sufficient yeoman farmers, they were faced with a limited number of options. Further intensification of the subsistence system would help a little, as would limiting the number of children. The next generation of yeoman farmers could also emigrate to recreate this system in virgin territory. The good folks of Concord seem to have tried all these in varying degrees, though this last option was the only one which offered a long-term solution. However, setting up new colonies needed money, which meant the yeoman farmers would have to become commercial farmers in order raise capital to fund their children's futures.

They switched to commercial dairy farming and grew corn to feed their enlarged herds. With money earned, they could buy wheat and wood from distant sources, and, no longer constrained by local limiting factors, there was every financial incentive to clear as much land as possible for cattle rearing. As Brian Donahue points out, Concord's sustainable system of husbandry was remade by agricultural capitalism, a system that, until then, had been protected from consumption by raw global capitalism through local ecological feedback and community obligations.

The new generation of commercial farmers looked back on their yeoman ancestry with disdain, a view that has masked their forebears' achievements in producing a sustainable system of farming in the New World, at least until now. Perhaps parallel systems sprang up elsewhere in the colonies, areas that haven't yet received such a rigorous analysis. For example, the Moravians that settled around Salem in the eighteenth century seem to have created a similar dynamic with the landscape, one which was instantly noticeable to travelers passing through: "The moment I touched the boundary of the Moravians, I noticed a marked and most favourable change in the appearance of buildings and farms, and even the cattle seemed larger, and in better condition."[56]

The Moravian and Concord farmers illustrate that changes to the New World landscapes were more complex than just a broad sweep of inevitable environmental disaster. But, in the end, these episodes were just temporary deflections from an inevitable trajectory. Even though the details of the processes vary from place to place, the arrival of the European market economy and commercial enterprise in whatever guise eventually spelled the demise of the eastern forests.

The area to the south of New England, around the Chesapeake colonies, illustrates that point. On the eve of the American Revolution, Ben Franklin was complaining that wood that had been "at any man's door" was now so scarce it was hard to obtain, though the forests here had disappeared for different reasons. The Virginia colonies were anxious from the start to provide profitable commodities for the commercial companies that had backed the settlements. Early on, Jamestown shipped sturgeon back to England, and later colonists supplied wood to the Caribbean plantations, but none of this was big money to the merchant venturers. However, in the early days of the colony, John Rolfe had begun experimenting with a plant that the local Indians used both practically and spiritually.

The Chesapeake Indians called it *uppewoc*, and they inhaled the smoke from its dried leaves or used the smoke to carry their prayers to the spirit world. A different variety grew in the Caribbean, where they called it *tobacco*. The smoke of this species was much more pleasant to the taste, so Rolfe began cultivating tobacco around Chesapeake. He produced several good experimental harvests, which were compared favorably with the product from the Spanish Indies by an increasing band of discerning smokers back in England.

Then, as now, there was big money in tobacco, so the Chesapeake colonists took to planting it in a major way—so much so that at times legislation had to be introduced to stop them spending all their time planting crops for profit. They seem to have quickly forgotten the starving time, and that they couldn't eat tobacco. Despite protestations from King James, who hated the habit of smoking with a passion that would impress any modern antismoking lobbyist, the tobacco economy of James's town really took off. But the tobacco plantations had a major impact on the local ecology.

First, they needed a lot of labor, which meant the population in the area rose, at first with indentured servants, then with African slaves. Second, tobacco is an extremely hungry crop; it completely exhausts the soil of nitrogen in just a few years. This meant that new plantations had to be hacked from the forest all the time, and the frontier of civilization moved quickly westward. As the centers of population moved west, so too did the colony's capitals, first Jamestown, then Williamsburg, and finally Richmond.

The land left behind looked like it had been ravaged by a biblical plague. As early as 1649, the south side of the York River revealed the barren aftermath of tobacco culture, and great tracts of Maryland would likewise come to resemble a wasteland. Forests took a long time to recolonize the exhausted ground, which instead grew rank and thick with shrubs and weeds. Soil eroded from the bare land began to choke the waters of the rivers and bay and reduce populations of fish and shellfish. No one wanted to waste land on grass or clover, so livestock was also scarce—all of which meant that large parts of Virginia and Maryland were not at all pleasant places to be at the height of the tobacco boom.

As the population grew and moved west, so the forests were felled for farmland and for timber for the ever-growing cities of America. The fate of the forests was now intimately tied to events, both national and international. In the aftermath of the Civil War, vast tracts of southern forest reverted to the federal government, which meant there was no one to pay local taxes on this land. An Alabama congressman, Goldsmith Hewitt, recognizing that these forest lands were not paying their way, pushed a bill through that allowed for their sale. They were snapped up by northern forestry companies, often for as little as $1.25 an acre, who were soon hard at work converting trees to cash.

Half a century later and another conflict put further pressure on these southern forests. As American troops arrived in Europe during World War I, the Southern Pine Association placed placards in the forests to encourage their rapid exploitation, which read:

> To Lumbermen: For the support of our soldiers in France the Government must have wooden ships. Without ships the war cannot be won. Without timber ships cannot be built. Our country looks to you.
>
> Every swing of the axe, every cut of a saw may score as heavily as a shot fired from the trenches. Help our boys in France. With them win the war. Make the world safe for Democracy.

The last forests to fall were in the most inaccessible places, but so great was the demand for timber that by the late nineteenth century, even these forests were worth exploiting. Railroads penetrated the heart of the Appalachians and Alleghenies to take loggers into the last stands of old growth forest.

At the Forest Service headquarters in Asheville, North Carolina, there is a small room lined with filing cabinets in which it is possible to lose yourself for hours at a time. The cabinets contain an archive of the logging industry in the southern Appalachians, which happened late enough for it to have been recorded in photographs. The first drawer that I open gives a glimpse of what William Bartram or John Lawson must have seen, as loggers pose in front of the forest giants they are about to fell. With men to give them scale, these photographs show just how big these trees really were. But pull out the bottom drawer and see what these forests looked like after the loggers had done their work. The scenes captured in these photographs look like the aftermath of a nuclear holocaust.

Trainloads of huge logs snake their way through a devastated landscape that stretches across whole mountainsides. By some accounts, just 2 percent of the eastern forest escaped the axe, or later the whipsaw and chainsaw, though it wasn't all felled at the same time. Secondary growth sprang up in the wake of the devastated old growth, replacing the giant trunks with insubstantial poles, but which nevertheless provided shelter for hard-pressed forest plants and animals. The growth of secondary forest on previously logged areas provided a refuge for these creatures, but the peak of logging in the eastern forests coincided with the greatest hunting pressure on many forest animals. The real wonder is that so few creatures followed the eastern elk and eastern cougar into extinction. Perhaps they would if unregulated logging continued, but the scenes of devastation across so much of the landscape prompted the government to act.

Passing the Forest Reserve Act in 1891 allowed the creation of protected forest reserves and paved the way for the formation of the Forest Service, part of the Department of Agriculture, with a remit to manage logging in parallel with wildlife conservation on its reserves—no easy task. Its first chief, Gifford Pinchot, was one of the first utilitarian conservationists, espousing a practical philosophy to guide the human relationship with nature. He was an early member of the Boone and Crocket Club, set up by Theodore Roosevelt to promote sustainable hunting of game, and Pinchot applied the same philosophies to forests and timber. "Conservation is the fore-sighted utilisation, preservation and/or renewal of forests, waters, lands and minerals, for the greatest good for the greatest numbers of people for the longest time."[57]

In many ways, he was simply restating in modern terms how the Indians related to their lands, but he stood in stark contrast to the "preservationists," like John Muir, who we'll meet later, across the continent in California. The Forest Service has come in for much criticism, particularly from the preservationist school, over the years as it tried to juggle its almost impossible remit, but one thing is for certain: forests once again clothe the Appalachians and Alleghenies as well as large tracts of the lowlands toward the coast, and many of these are national forests, the successors to the forest reserves. In these forests, many of the creatures that came so close to annihilation at the end of the nineteenth century have bounced back, and none more so than the white-tailed deer.

Even in the early part of the twentieth century, there were gloomy predictions for this deer in the East. But by the latter years of the twentieth century, there were somewhere between 15 and 25 million white-tailed deer in the United States. It's widely reported in the popular press these days that whitetails are overabundant: a plague of deer. But comparing the best guesses for historical numbers (24–33 million) with estimates for the current population shows that whitetails haven't yet rebounded to historical levels. However, the ecology of the eastern forests has changed considerably since those days. There isn't as much forest either, so in the remaining forests the deer might well be at higher population densities than the Pilgrims and the Jamestown settlers found. Today, hunters kill 2–3 million a year, and cars kill another half a million, but that hasn't affected their population growth.[58] In the East, with no wolves or cougars to kill them, there is mounting evidence that whitetails are damaging forests.

In Catoctin Mountain Park in Maryland, the beautiful purple-fringed orchid has all but been eliminated by hungry deer. They can also eliminate favored tree species, like eastern hemlock, while browsing and grazing opens up the forest floor, promoting the growth of grasses over shrubs. This makes the nests of ground and shrub-nesting birds easier to find by predators. There's also less food for birds in these kinds of forests. In heavily grazed forests, ovenbirds, for example, have to defend bigger territories than they do in denser forests, and many other birds appear to live in lower densities where deer numbers are greatest.[59]

But to reestablish the balance that existed in precolonial times is unthinkable, because it means reintroducing that devil in fur, the gray wolf, along with cougars. The wolf reintroduction program in the vast open spaces of the West has, as we will see later, caused enough problems with livestock owners. Besides, most people today, like the Pilgrims four centuries ago, like their wilderness to be safe. The magnificent elk, on the other hand, would be a boon to tourists and hunters alike.

In recent years, there have been attempts to reintroduce elk to the Appalachians and Alleghenies, using animals of a different form from the Rocky Mountains, where it is still common. Some of these herds appear to be successful, so in a few places, like the Smoky Mountains of Tennessee, it is once again possible to hear the whistling call of rutting elks echoing through the red and gold forests of a fall dawn. But these evocative sights and sounds only serve to emphasize the differences between my first views of the vast forests of the Blue Ridge and those of the first explorers. Gone are the big trees and the big predators. And gone too are the lifestyles of Indians from New England to Florida, from the Carolinas to the Mississippi that helped create the forests in the form that Giovanni da Verrazzano, John Smith, and William Bradford encountered.

People are inevitably part of the ecology of the land they live on, and different lifestyles create different balances. European and Indian worldviews and lifestyles were very different at first encounter—so different that long-term coexistence was impossible, and as European attitudes and technologies came to dominate, so the face of the land changed. But perhaps the most succinct summary of the differences is not from modern ecologists or biologists, but from an eighteenth-century Cherokee leader called Corn Tassel, whose insight deserves the last word: "The Creator has given each his lands. He has stocked yours with cows, ours with buffalo, yours with hogs ours with bears, yours with sheep ours with deer. He has indeed given you an advantage in this, that your cattle are tame and domesticated whilst ours are wild and demand not only a large space for a range but art to hunt and kill."

CHAPTER 8

Poll, Ben, and Martha

The eighteenth century, as the Age of Enlightenment blossomed, must have been a wonderful time to be a naturalist. There was still so much to find out as well as some astounding spectacles to see. Traveling to distant lands was becoming, if not exactly easy, then at least more feasible than in earlier times, and a passionate desire to catalogue the natural world and eulogize its spectacles drove the curious to the furthest parts of the globe, to leave us with a glorious legacy of writing and painting. In North America, this age of naturalists produced some extraordinary works, books of paintings and writings that portrayed not just the valuable commodities of the New World but a more complete natural history. Such works and the naturalists behind them will be our guides to the abundance of birds in the eastern forests.

But there were also more practical reasons behind the desire to understand the natural world. As European colonies spread across North America with increasing pace, so European governments wanted to know what natural resources lay in their paths and which parts of the continent were worth fighting over. So intrepid naturalists were encouraged to travel into remote areas of the continent on extended collecting journeys—a motley collection of souls from widely different backgrounds, with different personalities and skills, but united in their enthusiasm for the nature of the New World.

At the center of all this activity stands an extraordinary man, the epitome of a man of the Enlightenment—Thomas Jefferson. Passionately interested in science and natural history, he was also a diplomat and social philosopher. His biographer, James Parton, said he could "calculate an eclipse, survey an estate, tie an artery, plan an edifice, try a cause, break a horse, dance a minuet, and play the violin."[1] And in addition to all of this, he somehow found time to be the main author of the Declaration of Independence and become the United States' third president, between 1801 and 1809. After Independence, he encouraged the exploration of the new United States as well as clandestine visits to territories still owned by European powers.

I place him at the center of the growing understanding of New World natural history for two reasons. Chronologically, his life spans the middle of the period of great naturalists, from Mark Catesby to John James Audubon. But more importantly, he stands at the opposite philosophical pole to the first explorers and settlers. When colonists arrived at Jamestown or Plymouth, St. Mary's City or St. Augustine, they saw the New World in terms of the old; their mission was to build Europe in America. Jefferson, on the other hand, was fascinated by the uniqueness of the American fauna.

At the same time, there was an idea in Europe that New World animals were somehow inferior to their Old World counterparts. This seems surprising in the light of the glowing descriptions that had been emerging from the New World since the fifteenth century, but nevertheless, at the end of the eighteenth century, these were the theories backed by an influential French scientist, George LeClerc, Comte de Buffon. In 1786, de Buffon came up against a patriotic Thomas Jefferson, then U.S. minister to France. Jefferson, driven by pride in his newly born country, refuted de Buffon by the simple expedient of having a moose specimen shipped over from America, to compare with a European elk. A suitably chastened de Buffon promised Jefferson that he would revise his theory in the next volume he published, though he rather conveniently died before he could do so.

Jefferson's pride in the uniqueness (as well as the superiority) of New World nature also manifested itself in his importing and planting of New World trees in Paris gardens. Having absorbed the work of two generations of naturalists in America, Jefferson was excited by the New World's differences rather than its similarities and the period around Jefferson's life saw a flourishing of natural history exploration, painting, and writing that left evocative descriptions of the eastern forests, much of it encouraged by Jefferson himself.

Traveling through the forests east of the Mississippi, the naturalists of the eighteenth and nineteenth centuries saw magnificent woodlands inhabited by an abundance of animals unknown in Europe. But of all the natural wonders that they described in their journals, it was birds that most often left them speechless; some of the bird spectacles they witnessed would have been unsurpassed anywhere on the planet. Two figures in particular left us vivid descriptions, both in painting and in words, of the bird life in the eastern forests, and since they will form the focus of our birding trip to the eighteenth- and nineteenth-century forests, it is worth spending a little time to flesh out their stories. One was a Scot, the other a Frenchman.

Alexander Wilson was born in Paisley, near Glasgow, in 1766. His father was a smuggler, who had recently turned to weaving, to take advantage of the rapid growth of the industry as Paisley became one of Britain's first major manufacturing centers. In time, Alexander Wilson followed his father into weaving, though his heart lay elsewhere—in writing poetry. Unfortunately, he was no great poet, though some of his satirical works, attacking the barons of the weaving industry, earned him a little jail time. This, together with his restless nature, set him on a road that would eventually lead to America and to his being considered the father of American ornithology. But at first the road merely led him on a peddler's life around the southwest of Scotland, selling cloth and writing more mediocre poetry—the traveling, at least, good preparation for his long treks through the American wilderness in years to come. In 1794, the road led him to Belfast Dock and on board an American ship called the *Swift*. He would never return to Scotland.

His life in the New World started out in pretty much the same way as his life in Scotland finished. After a short period of work as a weaver in Philadelphia, he took to the road again on selling trips. As he traveled around he found that teachers were in short supply and despite having no qualifications soon found himself teaching, a job he much preferred to weaving. In his spare time he hunted the marshes along the Delaware River where he saw those great clouds of ducks and geese arriving from the north each fall. And so began his lifelong love affair with the birds of North America. But the difficulties in his private life continued, particularly over several failed love affairs, and he frequently found solace for his melancholic soul in nature. He spent long periods in silent contemplation in the woodlands around his home, slowly absorbing the riches of the birdlife. This growing passion for American nature became much more sharply focused in 1802 when he returned to Philadelphia and met William Bartram.

William Bartram was the son of naturalist John Bartram and an extremely accomplished botanist in his own right. His father had started taking him on collecting expeditions when William was just fourteen, and straightaway he was gathering plants and preparing the skins of birds. Curiously, John was never very enthusiastic about his son being a full-time naturalist, but although he tried to turn his son into a businessman, William's heart lay in the American wilderness. In 1773, he found sponsorship from a Dr. Fothergill to collect plants in Florida and began his career as a naturalist.

Between collecting trips he developed a botanic garden in Philadelphia, and it was there in 1802 that Alexander Wilson came for support. He received much encouragement from the kindly William Bartram, as well as other naturalists who frequented the gardens. Philadelphia was definitely the place to be for an eighteenth- or nineteenth-century naturalist. In 1803, Wilson met Merriwether Lewis, who was visiting Philadelphia in preparation for his expedition along the Missouri River. Being immersed in the heady atmosphere of Philadelphia must have started Wilson thinking, because in the same year he announced his intention, despite lacking any experience, of painting every species of North American bird and describing their behavior—such an immense undertaking, even for a practiced artist, that most people thought it was impossible, or at best impossibly expensive. It was only to be hoped that Wilson would prove to be a better painter than a poet.

His first efforts at painting were rather awkward, but after observing live specimens in captivity he began to produce more acceptable results that encouraged him to apply some serious effort to his daunting project. He devoted all his free time to traveling and painting, but had yet to face up to the problem that preparing the engravings of the paintings for printing would be prohibitively expensive. He had to become a peddler again, this time traveling the roads selling subscriptions to his monumental, multivolume *American Ornithology*. It was hard work, but when an enthusiastic President Jefferson signed up, other subscriptions followed. Over the years he continued his travels, gathering further subscriptions and describing the lives of the birds he found. In 1809, he found himself in Louisville, Kentucky, where he had heard that the local storekeeper had an interest in ornithology—another possible subscriber. His name was John James Audubon.

Audubon and Wilson were very different characters: the Scot prone to periods of melancholic reflection though with a wry sense of humor, Audubon quick to anger and quick to laugh—an altogether more flamboyant character who never quite fully mastered the English language. If Wilson is the father of American ornithology, it is Audubon's name that is more widely familiar today, both through his own monumental works on American birds and mammals as well as having his name attached to one of America's largest conservation societies (though Wilson does have prestigious and long-running ornithological bulletin named after him). Yet the life of the man attached to this famous name is often one of mystery, mystery promulgated by John James himself. He claimed he was born in Louisiana to a wealthy Spanish Creole lady, though in reality it seems he was born, in 1785, the son of a French sea captain called Jean Audubon and a servant girl called Jeanne Rabine. His mother died soon after giving birth, so Audubon was raised for a while by the captain's mistress on his Caribbean plantation.

The family had to flee the Caribbean during a slave uprising, when Audubon seems to have acquired his third mother, Captain Audubon's presumably very tolerant wife back in France. Both son and father conspired to cover up this early colorful history, so his true background may never be entirely certain. However, John James Audubon was definitely in Valley Forge, Pennsylvania, in 1803, having arrived to manage his father's estate at Mill Grove, and at the same time avoid being drafted into the French Army. Here he proved himself about as adept at business as Alexander Wilson and William Bartram and so spent a lot of his time hunting in the local forests instead.

Eventually he decided to move to Kentucky, to open a store with a friend called Ferdinand Rozier. Not surprisingly, Ferdinand was more often behind the counter, while John James was off exploring the banks of the Ohio River. Wilson was probably lucky to find Audubon at the store when he called by in the summer of 1809. The story then goes that Audubon was about to subscribe to Wilson's work when Ferdinand Rozier pointed out that Audubon's own paintings of birds, from his hunting trips in Pennsylvania and Ohio, were better than Wilson's. So instead, Audubon decided to produce his own work on American birds, in a different style to Wilson.

His technique was to use wires inside stuffed specimens to arrange the birds in more dynamic and lifelike poses than was usual in the staid scientific illustrations of the day. He, or one of his assistants, also added detailed backgrounds, and, perhaps his boldest decision, Audubon became obsessed with portraying all his specimens life size. The largest sheets available for printing at the time were "double elephant" folios, just about large enough to squeeze on a life-size flamingo or spoonbill, so long as it performed some slightly unnatural contortions.

Today, it is generally accepted that Audubon's paintings are better—more vibrant and dramatic—than Wilson's, though a couple of Audubon's paintings do look to me like he caught the moment of impact of the bird with an unseen windowpane. Wilson was constrained by budget and tried to cram as many different birds on to each page as possible, so his work was often described as cluttered in comparison to Audubon's immense paintings. But Wilson was working in a style that is now very familiar to anyone using a modern field guide, and as an inveterate collector and peruser of such works, my vote would go to Wilson—if forced to choose. Certainly no one in their right mind would ever consider using Audubon's elephants as a *field* guide. In reality though, the work of both men is extraordinary—a stunning and vital link to the forests of just a few centuries ago. And how different those forests were.

A few springs ago, Bill Duyck was giving me an impressive demonstration of "pishing." We were in the car park at Whitewater Falls in the southern Appalachians, to film the highest waterfall in the eastern United States, and Bill was busy making the hissing noises that almost always draw small birds (and in this case plenty of curious tourists) out of hiding to investigate. The first bird to break cover looked like it had coated its head in yellow pollen and dribbled streaks of red ochre from its eyes right down its sides to its tail—a chestnut-sided warbler. I remember thinking that Audubon would have been very excited about this. He only ever saw five chestnut-sided warblers in all his travels, and all of those he shot on one day.[2] We saw more than that around one car park in just one day, and I've seen dozens since. Clearly, things have changed since Audubon and Wilson walked through these forests.

Chestnut-sided warblers do well in scrub and secondary forest growth, and so benefited considerably as the eastern forests were cleared and grew back in the eighteenth and nineteenth centuries. Other birds, which were more dependent on open grassland and are today commoner in the West, also existed in large numbers in the East as the forest was cleared for farmland—birds like meadowlarks, bobolinks, and dickcissels. Audubon describes such numbers of bobolinks on farmland in New York and Connecticut that they "plunder every field, but are shot in immense numbers."[3] He reckoned that every year, professional hunters shot millions of them at roost sites. But were these birds just pests, responding to the new opportunities created as European-style farms opened up vast tracts of the forest? Conservation biologist Robert Askins thinks not.[4]

It's still sometimes said that before 1492 a squirrel, if it had the inclination, could travel from New England to Arkansas without ever touching the ground. But we've already seen that the eastern forest was not such a squirrel-friendly continuous canopy of trees. There were great sweeps of solid forest, but the squirrel's journey, though possible, would have been circuitous as it wound its way around the edges of frequent glades, sometimes of considerable extent, maintained by a combination of Indian fires and grazing.

Many early explorers attest to the size of some of these grasslands. In the 1600s, for example, the treeless Hempstead Plain on Long Island covered more than fifty thousand acres. A fragment still exists, and it looks for all the world like tallgrass prairie. The scale of this east coast prairie was probably due to the thin coastal soils, but there are plenty of records of smaller, though still substantial, grasslands throughout much of the eastern forest.

Riding near Hopkinsville, Kentucky, in 1812, one traveler reported: "one vast deep-green meadow, adorned with countless numbers of bright flowers."[5] It is clear from such descriptions that we need to see the historic eastern forest as a mosaic of woodland interspersed in places with substantial grasslands, which suggests that the grassland birds that so impressed Audubon were part of the precolonial ecology. In fact, their history probably goes back much further.

Even before Indian management, beavers would have created many open meadows as their ponds dried. In some areas as much as one fifth of the terrain is open marshy meadow created by beavers.[6] And earlier still, there is good evidence that, immediately after the ice age, North America's mammoths and other grazing megafauna would have opened up and maintained large grasslands in the midst of the developing eastern forest. There are remains of grassland megafauna together with such archetypal grassland birds as sharp-tailed grouse in subfossil deposits in Pennsylvania that attest to the existence of such a mosaic. In addition, many eastern "grassland" species are distinct subspecies from their western counterparts, also suggesting a long residency in the area.

But grassland birds in the East are in serious decline as open areas are turned into malls or houses, or are reclaimed by secondary forest growth. Robert Askins points out that much has been made of the decline of some of the woodland birds in the East, but much less attention is paid to grassland species, since they are regarded as more recent colonists, taking advantage of the changes wrought by colonial farming and forest clearances. The long view suggests a different story. It's now clear that part of the wonderful abundance and diversity of birds in the eastern forests depended on this mosaic of woods and grass, maintained by Indian management.

As European settlements spread, that balance changed. Indian burning ceased, and more and more of the forests were cleared. Yet, at the end of the previous chapter, I remarked how few animals from the eastern forest became extinct, despite extensive logging. This was because, although virtually all of the eastern forest was logged, it wasn't all cleared at the same time. At the peak of logging at the end of the nineteenth century, 50 percent of the land was still covered in trees from regrowth, providing vital refugia for forest wildlife.

Also, many of the species of the eastern forests range more widely across North America, in which case the species as a whole was likely to survive even if local extinctions occurred in the East. But the story is a little different for those creatures restricted or largely restricted to the eastern forest. Several abundant and spectacular forest birds did disappear entirely, despite refuges of secondary growth. Their stories are both poignant and informative.

In 1809, Alexander Wilson was engaged on one of his more difficult journeys from the mouth of the Ohio down to Nashville, through "some of the most horrid swamps I had ever seen." He did, however, have a companion—a beautiful and lively creature called Poll. She was a bird, shining green with a bright yellow head and orange cheeks—North America's only native parrot—a Carolina parakeet. She had been wounded when Wilson had shot some of her flock, but always keen for live specimens, Wilson took her along for the ride. She traveled wrapped in a silk handkerchief stuffed into Wilson's pocket, though as Wilson struggled through horrendous terrain she made frequent escapes. "The path through the wilderness between Natchez and Nashville is in some places bad beyond description. There are dangerous creeks to swim, miles of morass to struggle through, rendered almost as gloomy as night by a prodigious growth of timber, and an underwood of canes and other evergreens. In some of the worst of these places, where I had, as it were, to fight my way through, the Paroquet frequently escaped from my pocket, obliging me to dismount and pursue it through the worst of the morass before I could regain it."[7]

When it was time for feeding, Poll exacted revenge for her undignified treatment: "We generally had a quarrel; during which it frequently repaid me in kind for the wound I had inflicted, and for depriving it of liberty, by cutting and almost disabling several of my fingers with its sharp and powerful bill." Wilson's commentary is wonderfully personal and makes it easy to imagine the world he was traveling through. But these descriptions are made all the more poignant because Poll and her kind no longer exist. Carolina parakeets are extinct, even though when Wilson and Audubon trekked through the eastern forests their flocks were so numerous they were regarded as pests when they descended on crops.

Carolina parakeets were highly social, and when Wilson arrived at a settler's house and gave Poll a respite from her silken confinement by finding her a cage, it didn't take long for wild birds to hear her calls and flock to her side. In the wild, such flocks of parakeets were a tremendous sight. "They came screaming through the woods in the morning, about an hour after sunrise. . . . When they alighted on the ground, it appeared at a distance as if covered with a carpet of the richest green, orange and yellow; they afterwards settled, in one body, on a neighboring tree, which stood detached from any other, covering almost every twig of it, and the sun, shining strongly on their gay and glossy plumage, produced a very beautiful and splendid appearance."

As settlers moved into their habitat, Carolina parakeets reciprocated and moved into the settlers' habitat in spectacular numbers, as Audubon noted, with a similar metaphor to Wilson: "The stacks of grain put up in the field are resorted to by flocks of these birds, which frequently cover them so entirely, that they present to the eye the same effect as if a brilliantly covered carpet had been thrown over them."[8] Many other explorers and naturalists described similar scenes, from Florida and southern Texas north to southern Michigan and central New York, though these noisy and conspicuous birds weren't common throughout the whole of that range. The biggest flocks were found in mature bottomland forest, especially where great sycamores grew. They also brightened the magnificent swamp forests of bald cypress in the south. In the north of their range, they were tough enough to survive freezing winters, and the sight of such tropical-looking birds frolicking in snow covered trees stopped a few early settlers in their tracks.

Dutch settlers near Albany, New York, were so astounded by such a spectacle in the winter of 1780 that they thought the sight must portend "nothing less than the destruction of the world."[9] In a sense, they were right, but it was the parrots' world that was about to be destroyed. Just how such an abundant and adaptable creature managed to vanish from the face of the Earth is still something of a mystery, but we owe it to Poll and her kind to seek lessons from their passing. Their extinction should leave some legacy.

It's hard to guess at their numbers before the coming of the settlers. They certainly occurred in flocks of thousands, especially at saline springs or salt licks in the Midwest, where they came for the minerals. Here they were joined by immense flocks of passenger pigeons and herds of bison in what must have been one of America's most amazing wildlife spectacles. Some earlier estimates put their total population in the millions, and Noel Snyder, who has produced the most recent detailed account of the species, suggests that these kinds of numbers would not have been impossible, though they remain essentially guesswork.[10] The exact date of their extinction is equally just a matter of guesswork. The last captive specimen, Incas, died in Cincinnati Zoo in 1918, though it is generally accepted that the species clung on in a few wild places until the 1920s. However, there are quite a few tantalizing records after this, many of which sound very plausible.

Most frustrating is a record from Georgia's Okefenokee Swamp in the late 1930s. An Audubon lecturer called Dee Jay Nelson acquired an old movie camera from his boatman during a field trip to the swamp sometime in the 1950s, and with it he got eight rolls of exposed film. He didn't bother to look at the film for fifteen years, but when he did, he was amazed to find thirty seconds of footage of Carolina parakeets. Although the footage wasn't great, Nelson was convinced of the birds' identity. The film was shown at a 1970 American Ornithologists' Union meeting, where there was general agreement with Nelson's assessment. Since the film was in color, it had to have been shot after about 1936, when the first color films became available, but this priceless archive has subsequently disappeared, misplaced, or lost. If ever there was a time to check your attic . . .

There are other "late" records from the mid-1930s from along the Santee River in South Carolina, a vast untrodden swamp and ideal parakeet country. There is even a tantalizing record from the 1940s in North Carolina, not far from the Santee River swamp, that came to light in a remarkable letter in 1981 to Roger Tory Petersen. The letter was from Stanley Kolosky, who remembers traveling on a troop train through North Carolina in 1944. While the train was stopped in the middle of a swampy region, Kolosky was surprised by what he saw: "I looked out and was startled to see a green parrot with a yellow head and bright red disc around his eyes. It was perched in a tree not more than 20 feet away. I said, Damn, someone's parrot got away! My seatmate laughed and said; no, that's a Carolina Parokeet. . . . He said we were about 30 or 40 miles from his home. . . . He said these birds were common in this area of the swamp."[11] Lucky Mr. Kolosky. He might have been one of the last people to see a Carolina parakeet alive. So what happened to them?

Many early naturalists noted the abundance of Carolina parakeets in what we today would call "old growth" forest, particularly among the massive sycamores that grew along the river bottoms. So the first obvious suggestion for their demise must be habitat destruction, as primary forests were cleared for timber and farms. Yet in the early years, they seemed quite happy around human habitation. Noel Snyder interviewed several old residents of Florida who remembered Carolina parakeets roosting in barns and outhouses, and Audubon describes great flocks descending on fields and orchards.[12] Indeed, Audubon, Wilson, and many others describe the parakeets as being particularly fond of the seeds of cocklebur and sandspur, two weedy plants that sprang up in open ground to plague the first settlers. So habitat destruction alone seems unlikely to have caused their extinction.

But the birds were also shot. Wilson and Audubon took more than their fair share of parakeets in their collecting trips, and both describe a habit that made them particularly vulnerable to shooting. "Having shot down a number, some of which were only wounded, the whole flock swept repeatedly around their prostrate companions, and again settled on a low tree, within twenty yards of the spot where I stood. At each successive discharge, though showers of them fell, yet the affection of the survivors seemed rather to increase; for, after a few circuits around the place, they again alighted near me, looking down on their slaughtered companions with such manifest symptoms of sympathy and concern, as entirely disarmed me."[13]

Many birds show this strange tendency to flock around fallen companions, which at first sight seems self-destructive, but which, in natural circumstances, makes good evolutionary sense. It gives young birds a chance to memorize the predator responsible and avoid it in future. But it's not such a good strategy when faced with a more recent evolutionary innovation—an ardent naturalist armed with a gun. Yet even the most enthusiastic naturalist is unlikely to have made much impact on their numbers.

Farmers too have been accused of shooting these birds as agricultural pests, but again it's not really that straightforward. From early descriptions, like those of Audubon, it sounds like the appearance of a flock of parakeets would have filled a farmer's heart with dread:

They cling around the whole stack [of grain], pull out the straws, and destroy twice as much of the grain as would suffice to satisfy their hunger. They assail the pear and apple-trees, when the fruit is yet very small and far from being ripe, and this merely for the sake of the seeds. As on the stalks of the corn, they alight on the apple-trees of our orchards, or the pear-trees in the gardens, in great numbers, and, as if through mere mischief, pluck off the fruits, open them to the core, and, disappointed at the sight of the seeds, which are yet soft and of milky consistency, drop the apple or pear, and pluck another, passing from branch to branch, until the trees which were before so promising, are left completely stripped.[14]

Yet the birds also gorged themselves with equal vigor on the seeds of sandspur and cocklebur, two rampant and poisonous weeds of farmland, a fact that early farmers can hardly fail to have noticed. Carolina parakeets were as much allies as enemies of farmers, reflected in the fact that the parakeets never had any form of bounty placed on their heads. European settlers were quick to deal with any perceived threat to the expansion of farming, so the absence of parakeet bounties suggests that they weren't seen as major pests, and there are no historical records of systematic destruction. Yet despite this, it seems that the population began to fall very quickly after colonization began. Audubon was one of several people to comment on their early disappearance from certain areas. "Our parakeets are very rapidly diminishing in number, and in some districts, where twenty-five years ago they were plentiful, scarcely any are to be seen. . . . I should think that along the Mississippi there is not now half the number that existed fifteen years ago."[15] If it wasn't the settlers themselves that were causing this, perhaps it was something they brought with them.

Honeybees are not native to the New World, but spread rapidly from the first hives, taking over tree cavities to build their combs. Could they have driven the parakeets from their nest holes? Some researchers have suggested this, though from what is known of parakeet nest holes, they were probably too small to be of much interest to a swarming colony of bees looking for a new home. But even though competition with introduced bees can't be entirely ruled out, the settlers did bring something else to the New World, something that we've already seen wreak havoc here—disease.

It is possible that a bird disease arriving with infected poultry could have been fatal to the parakeets. Certainly, some aspects of their decline point to disease, such as the rapid early fall in numbers. Also, many of even the latest sightings included juveniles in their distinctive plumage, which suggests that whatever the problem was, it was affecting mortality rather than breeding success, again compatible with some form of disease. The fact that flocks were often drawn to human habitation would only have made disease transmission all the more likely. Yet there's no direct evidence for mass mortality of parakeets apart from occasional descriptions of birds afflicted with something resembling "apoplexy." So, in the end, the reasons for the demise of the Carolina parakeet must remain conjecture. However, the cause of the final demise of Poll is much better documented: "In this short space she had learned to know her name, to answer, and come when called on; to climb up my clothes, sit on my shoulder and eat from my mouth. I took her with me to sea, determined to persevere in her education; but destined to another fate, poor Poll, having one morning, about day break, wrought her way through the cage, while I was asleep, instantly flew overboard, and perished in the Gulf of Mexico."

But Poll wasn't Wilson's only traveling companion. His technique of drawing live birds meant he would often keep any that he had only slightly injured, and one in particular made quite an impression—literally—on Wilmington, North Carolina. "This bird was only wounded slightly in the wing, and, on being caught, uttered a loudly reiterated and most piteous note, exactly resembling the violent crying of a young child; which terrified my horse so, as nearly to have cost me my life. It was distressing to hear it. I carried it with me in the chair, under cover, to Wilmington. In passing through the streets, its affecting cries surprised every one within hearing, particularly the females, who hurried to the doors and windows with looks of alarm and anxiety."[16] Enjoying the joke, Wilson rode up to an inn and asked whether the landlord had accommodation for himself and his baby. When the landlord merely stared blankly at him, Wilson produced the noisy creature from his bag. It was an ivory-billed woodpecker, the largest and most spectacular species in North America and certainly the noisiest.

Wilson locked his prize in his room and left to get his horse taken care of. He returned to find that his woodpecker had used its substantial ivory bill to demolish parts of his room: "The bed was covered with large pieces of plaster; the lath was exposed for at least fifteen inches square, and a hole, large enough to admit the fist, opened to the weather-boards." Next time, Wilson took the precaution of tying his woodpecker's leg to a heavy mahogany table, before leaving to find his destructive companion some suitable food. Big mistake. Not for nothing are woodpeckers called woodpeckers. "As I reascended the stairs, I heard him hard at work again, and on entering, had the mortification to perceive that he had almost entirely ruined the mahogany table to which he was fastened."

Even in the wild ivory-billed woodpeckers are the most prodigious peckers of wood, as Wilson recalls from his travels: "Wherever he frequents, he leaves numerous monuments of his industry behind him. We there see enormous pine trees, with cart loads of bark lying around their roots, and chips of the trunk itself in such quantities, as to suggest the idea that half a dozen axemen had been at work for the whole morning . . . one can hardly conceive it possible for the whole to be the work of a woodpecker." I imagine it was a lot easier to conceive after he'd seen the state of his room.

An individual ivory-bill is spectacular, nearly two feet long, painted in bold strokes of black and white and topped off with a startling red crest. Audubon considered it was colored in the style of the great seventeenth-century Dutch master, Van Dyck. Whenever he saw one, he would say to himself, "there goes a Vandyke!" The sight and sounds of these magnificent creatures in towering swamp forests sent Wilson back to his poetic roots: "[It] seeks the most tow-ering trees of the forest, seemingly particularly attached to those prodigious cypress swamps, whose crowded giant sons stretch their bare and blasted, or moss-hung, arms midway to the skies. In these almost inaccessible recesses, amid ruinous piles of impending timber, his trumpet-like note, and loud strokes, resound through the solitary, savage wilds, of which he seems the sole lord and inhabitant."

And if all this wasn't enough to whet your appetite, ivory-bills seemed sometimes to gather in small groups. Audubon saw five feeding together, but another observer was lucky enough to find eleven, in the late 1800s, near the Gulf Coast of Florida—sights and sounds that must have been truly unfor-gettable.[17] It's certainly feasible that the ivory-bill was sometimes a social species since there are other social woodpeckers, where ecological circum-stances allow.

The acorn woodpecker of the Southwest and California cooperates to store large quantities of acorns in "granary trees." Working in family groups, these woodpeckers drill holes, each big enough to insert a single acorn. A well-stocked granary tree provides plenty of food for the whole group, which can then cooperate to defend their precious winter store more effectively. The granary trees become valuable resources, passed from generation to genera-tion, a pattern of inheritance that makes another good reason to live in ex-tended family groups. The largest granary ever seen, and doubtless the work of many generations, had fifty thousand holes drilled in it.[18] Ivory-bills didn't store acorns, but they did seek out big, recently dead trees infested with nu-merous, large, and juicy larvae of longhorn beetles. A group of woodpeckers working together might stand a better chance of discovering such an isolated resource, and the demolition capabilities of several woodpeckers working together would soon uncover their favorite food, no matter how deeply the beetle larvae had burrowed into the wood.

Throughout their southeastern range, ivory-bills were a relatively common sight. Audubon found plenty on his escapes from behind his store counter, traveling the Ohio River as far as its confluence with the Mississippi: "after which, following the windings of the latter, either downwards towards the sea, or upwards in the direction of the Missouri, we frequently observe it." Yet only a few decades after Audubon published his descriptions of this woodpecker, it was clear that it was in trouble. By 1895, archaeologist and naturalist Charles Conrad Abbott was predicting a gloomy future. "The probabilities are that it will soon be extinct, so far as the United States is concerned. It is too handsome not to tempt every collector, taxidermist and millinery establishment in the country, and he who protests will be laughed at for his trouble."[19]

Unlike the still mysterious disappearance of the Carolina parakeet, it seems to have been the ivory-bill's need for a particular kind of forest that proved its undoing. Ivory-bills favored open woodland, through which they could fly their lazy looping flight, flashing black and white. Indian fire management kept many of the forests open and clear of undergrowth, which suited the ivory-bill just fine. But this fire management largely ceased with the death of so many Indians from disease. Changes in the lifestyle of those remaining also meant that the forests rapidly became impassable as shrubs grew up. In addition, ivory-bills needed big trees. They liked to build their nest holes high off the ground and a twenty-two-inch bird makes a substantial hole. Only big, old trees were large enough at the heights favored by the woodpeckers to accommodate the birds' nest holes, but these mighty giants were usually the first to be targeted by loggers.

Finally, ivory-bills also seemed to need a lot of ground. Back in the 1940s, estimates were made of the density of birds in different locations. In the Singer Tract, in Louisiana, there was an average of about one bird per seventeen square miles. In the California Swamp in northern Florida the density was around one bird per ten square miles, and on the Wacissa River in the Florida panhandle, ivory-bills were crammed together at one bird per 6.25 square miles.[20] Clearly, birds that needed such a lot of space were not going to do well as the remaining forests became fragmented.

Prime ivory-bill habitat is bottomland forest along the region's river valleys. These forests grow on rich soil and so were the first to go as farmers cleared land for crops. They were more thoroughly cleared than other types of forest, so bottomland specialists were particularly hard hit. Bachman's warbler, for example, which lived in the extensive canebrakes along bottomlands, is in all likelihood extinct. And by the 1920s, many people thought the ivory-bill was also extinct. However, the species gained a reprieve in 1932 when a single male was shot in the Singer Tract, a vast, impenetrable swamp forest in Louisiana. It turned out that the locals had known about the woodpeckers here for some time, but the existence of a specimen now prompted some people, at least, to take action to ensure a future for the ivory-bill.[21]

In 1937, a young ornithologist called James Tanner, funded, appropriately enough, by the newly renamed National Audubon Society, began a study of these Van Dyck–painted birds while there were still some left to study. He also worked with Aldo Leopold and the Audubon Society to have this last known refuge of the ivory-bill turned into the Tensas Swamp National Park. But by 1939, while his study was still in full swing, loggers from the Chicago Mill and Lumber Company had moved in. Tanner and the Audubon Society pleaded with the lumber company to spare the woodpeckers, but to no avail. Then the Japanese bombed Pearl Harbor.

The Second World War created a surge in demand for timber and gave the loggers all the incentive they needed. The last official sightings of ivory-bills were in the mid 1940s, though the species also occurred on Cuba, where it lingered a little longer. But despite being declared officially extinct, unconfirmed sightings continued to tantalize those who believed the species might yet survive in some remote swampy forest, untrodden by loggers or birders.

The Cache River National Wildlife Refuge in the Big Woods of Arkansas doesn't, at first sight, seem to fit that bill. Only sixty miles from Little Rock, Interstate 40 thunders right past it. Yet, take your eyes off the busy road for a brief second, and you'll see bayous tantalizingly winding their way from civilization to wilderness. On February 11, 2004, Gene Sparling of Hot Springs, Arkansas, was paddling along one of those bayous when a large woodpecker flew toward him and landed in a tree. Its size and its bold black-and-white pattern convinced Gene that he was witnessing something special.

A week later he was given the third degree by Tom Gallagher, of the Cornell Laboratory of Ornithology, and Bobby Harrison, of Oakwood College in Huntsville, Alabama, who tracked him down as soon as they heard of his experiences in the swamp. They were so convinced by his descriptions that all three set off to the same bayou. On February 27, as they paddled through the swamp, a great woodpecker, flashing black and white and decked out in the style of a Van Dyck, flew across the bayou, just seventy feet in front of them. A simultaneous cry of "ivory-bill" echoed through the swamp. After they had finished their immediate field notes, the emotion of the moment hit both scientists. Bobby Harrison just sat and sobbed, "I saw an ivory-bill, I saw an ivory-bill." Tom Gallagher was too choked with emotion even to speak.

Later they returned to the swamp and managed to get some rather shaky video footage of the bird. As far as many were concerned, this was more than enough proof that the magnificent ivory-bill had, against all odds, somehow managed to see the dawning of the twenty-first century. Shaky it may be, but it is both amazing and emotional to watch a real, live, twenty-first-century ivory-bill in action, albeit for only four seconds. In 2005, the ivory-billed woodpecker had its extinction officially revoked—a second reprieve.

Although the Cache River sighting was trumpeted in the press as a miraculous return from the grave for the ivory-bill, evidence of its continued existence had been around for some time, indeed right back to the point when it was presumed lost after the Singer Tract was logged. Feathers, nest holes, and excavations were recorded from a number of locations along with unconfirmed sightings, though many ornithologists didn't see this evidence as entirely convincing.[22]

One problem is that a glimpse of an ivory-bill is hard to distinguish from a glimpse of the widespread pileated woodpecker. Indeed, David Sibley, author of one of the best field guides to North American birds, and others are convinced that the shaky footage from the Cache River is in reality just that—a common pileated woodpecker.[23] As the debate heated up, Cornell University sent out teams to gather more evidence, though the 2006–2007 field season found no sign at all of the elusive ivory-bill in Arkansas. Was David Sibley right, or had this phantom bird simply disappeared again?

Perhaps. But perhaps ivory-bills are nomadic, only staying in one area for a short time, which would certainly help explain how they had survived for so long after their "extinction." The lure of this charismatic bird is so strong that people continued to scrutinize suitable habitats, and in May 2005 ornithologist Geoff Hill, together with two research assistants, found an ivory-bill in mature swamp forests along the Choctawhatchee River in Florida's panhandle. In the following year, they clocked up fourteen sightings and heard the bird's distinctive calls and knocking sounds on dozens of occasions.[24] So, even if the Cache River bird was a phantom, the species does seem to have returned from the dead.

The story of the ivory-bill is clearly a long way from ending, and it could yet go either way, but it inevitably raises the question as to whether there might be some remote tract of forest where Carolina parakeets still clamber through the lofty branches in their colorful troops. They always seemed to be less shy of human company than ivory-bills, so one might think any survivors would have made themselves known. But Noel Snyder doesn't put their survival as completely beyond the bounds of possibility.[25] I think, however, that you would be hard pressed to find anyone who still lives in hope of finding survivors of the most spectacular bird of the eastern forests.

Imagine sitting with your back resting against the vast trunk of a tulip poplar, whose thick leafy branches arch sixty feet over your head. The sun is dipping, the forest darkening, but full of the sound of bird song. Beyond the gentle hush of leaves blown by the wind, there's a new sound, like a stronger wind stirring the forest—a storm front approaching? The storm grows louder and louder, building to a roaring gale, though the leaves above your head are hardly moving—image and sound eerily out of sync. The sky grows darker and the storm arrives.

Birds are everywhere, sweeping through the open forest to the limits of your vision, filling the great boughs above your head. The rush of air from beneath their wings swirls leaves on the forest floor, and their droppings rain down like an early snowstorm. More and more birds pile in until you think the air can hold no more. They pile on to the branches, a solid mass sometimes four or five birds deep, the whole stack fluttering to keep balance, adding to the general mayhem. A resounding crack and a bough, maybe two feet thick, crashes through the canopy, torn from the tree by the sheer weight of birds. It rips through the birds crowded on branches beneath it. Leaves and dead birds flutter to the forest floor. It's hard not to think of this spectacle as one giant organism, each individual just an insignificant part in this vast whole, but pick up one of the dead birds. Its colors glow with subtlety, rose pink on the breast grading imperceptibly into shades of gold, green, and crimson over the rest of its body. From intimate beauty to staggering spectacle—you are standing under a roost of passenger pigeons.

Passenger pigeons were the most numerous birds in North America, possibly in the whole world, and they could turn up almost anywhere throughout the eastern forests, literally out of the blue. They existed in such prodigious numbers that many naturalists felt that true descriptions of their flocks might not be believed. Audubon inserts into his account of the species just such a disclaimer. "The multitudes of Wild Pigeons in our woods are astonishing. Indeed, after having viewed them so often, and under so many circumstances, I now feel inclined to pause, and assure myself that what I am going to relate is fact."[26] And the facts that he relates are truly astonishing. In the fall of 1813, he saw one of the biggest flocks he had ever seen on his way to Louisville, Kentucky.

> The air was literally filled with pigeons; the light of the noon-day was obscure as by an eclipse, the dung fell in spots, not unlike melting flakes of snow; and the continued buzz of wings had a tendency to lull my senses to repose. . . . I cannot describe to you the extreme beauty of their aerial evolutions, when a Hawk chanced to press upon the rear of a flock. At once, like a torrent, and with a noise like thunder, they rushed into a compact mass, pressing upon each other towards the centre. In these almost solid masses, they darted forward in undulating and angular lines, descended and swept close over the earth with inconceivable velocity, mounted perpendicularly so as to resemble a vast column, and, when high, were seen wheeling and twisting within their continued lines, which then resembles the coils of a gigantic serpent.

Remarkably, even after the danger had passed, the birds continued to follow the serpentine route laid down by the initial panic, as if the birds had no mind but that of the group. Yet, each individual was a thing of singular beauty, which, multiplied a hundred million times, sent Audubon into further raptures. "During their evolutions, on such occasions, the dense mass which they form exhibits a beautiful appearance, as it changes its direction, now displaying a glistening sheet of azure, when the backs of the birds come simultaneously into view, and anon, suddenly presenting a mass of rich deep purple."

Because of their immense size, these flocks were forced into a life of perpetual travel, scouring the forested landscape for places with enough food to sustain their hundreds, perhaps thousands, of millions. The forests were full of trees that bore nuts and fruits, but some trees, like American beeches, don't produce their seeds in the same numbers every year. Instead the trees muster their resources, and then, every few years, all the trees in the neighborhood produce an enormous crop, designed to satiate any seed predators and still leave some seeds on the ground to turn into new beeches. Whether such a strategy worked with passenger pigeons is open to question, so great were their numbers. Areas with such "masting" trees were exactly what all those hundreds of millions of eyes were on the look out for—enough food to sustain the flock, even if only for a day or so—then off again to find the next area, which could be tens or hundreds of miles away. Such a nomadic lifestyle meant that the pigeons could turn up anywhere.

When they found an area of forest rich in nuts or fruits, the whole flock descended in a terrifying mass. But even now, the flock was not at rest. The thick mass of birds at the back were continually flying forward, pushing their way to the front, to grab what food they could before they too were overtaken by the next wave. Ohio ornithologist John Maynard Wheaton described such scene in 1882. "This movement soon became continuous and uniform, the birds from the rear flying to the front so rapidly that the whole presented the appearance of a rolling cylinder having a diameter of about 50 yards, its interior filled with flying leaves and grass. The noise was deafening and the sight confusing to the mind."[27]

Audubon describes a similar scene six decades earlier. "When alighted, they are seen industriously throwing up the withered leaves in quest of the fallen mast. The rear ranks are continually rising, passing over the main body, and alighting in front, in such rapid succession, that the whole flock seems still on the wing." And when the day's foraging was finished, the birds set off to roost. Alexander Wilson takes up the story. "I was suddenly struck with astonishment at a loud rushing roar, succeeded by instant darkness, which, on the first moment, I took for a tornado."[28]

Roost sites also drew a similar comparison from Audubon, even before the birds arrived. This one was on the banks of the Green River, in Kentucky. "I rode through it upwards of forty miles, and, crossing it in different parts, found its average breadth to be rather more than three miles. . . . The dung lay several inches deep, covering the whole extent of the roosting place. Many trees two feet in diameter, I observed, were broken off at no great distance from the ground; and the branches of many of the largest and tallest had given way, as if the forest had been swept by a tornado." And then the birds arrived: "The Pigeons, arriving by the thousands, alighted everywhere, one above another, until solid masses were formed on the branches all around. Here and there perches gave way under the weight with a crash, and, falling to the ground, destroyed hundreds of birds beneath, forcing down the dense groups with which every stick was loaded. It was a scene of uproar and confusion. I found it quite useless to speak, or even to shout to those persons who were nearest to me."

The pigeons lived their entire lives in these unimaginable numbers. This is what Chief Simon Pokagon, a remarkable elder of the Potawatomi tribe, observed in the late 1800s as the birds arrived at a "nesting," well worth repeating in full.

> I was startled by hearing a gurgling, rumbling sound, as though an army of horses laden with sleigh bells was advancing through the deep forest towards me. As I listened more intently I concluded that instead of the trampling of horses it was distant thunder; yet the morning was clear, calm and beautiful. Nearer and nearer came the strange comingling of sounds of sleigh bells, mixed with the rumbling of an approaching storm. While I gazed in astonishment, I beheld moving toward me in an unbroken front millions of pigeons, the first I had seen that season. They passed like a cloud through the branches of the high trees, through the underbrush and over the ground, apparently overturning every leaf. . . . They fluttered all about me, lighting on my head and shoulders; gently I caught two in my hands. . . . I now began to realize that they were mating, preparatory to nesting. . . . In the course of the day the great on-moving mass passed by me, but the trees were still filled with them sitting in pairs in convenient crotches of the limbs, now uttering to their mates those strange, bell-like wooing notes which I had mistaken for the ringing of bells in the distance. On the third day after, this chattering ceased and all were busy carrying sticks with which they were building nests in the same crotches of the limbs they had occupied in pairs the day before. On the morning of the fourth day their nests were finished and eggs laid.[29]

As with everything else to do with this bird, the size of the nesting colonies defies belief. Of those actually measured, one in Petoskey, Michigan, in 1878 was thirty to forty miles long and three to six miles wide. The largest recorded was in central Wisconsin, in 1872, and formed an L shape, with the long arm stretching for seventy-five miles and the short arm for fifty miles. The width varied between six and eight miles.[30] Such huge aggregations of nesting or roosting birds were an irresistible draw to local settlers and farmers, who took enormous quantities of birds. Audubon was not the only one present at the roost he described on the banks of the Green River. There were also: "a great number of persons, with horses and wagons, guns and ammunition. . . .

Two farmers from the vicinity of Russelsville, distant more than a hundred miles, had driven upwards of three hundred hogs to be fattened on the pigeons to be slaughtered. Here and there, the people employed in plucking and salting what had already been procured were seen sitting in the midst of large piles of these birds."

Alexander Wilson also witnessed the scale of destruction at roost sites. "When these roosts are first discovered, the inhabitants, from considerable distances, visit them in the night with guns, clubs, long poles, pots of sulphur and various other engines of destruction. In a few hours they fill many sacks and load their horses with them." The sulfur was burned under the roost trees to poison the birds. They were also trapped in the daytime in spring-loaded nets, drawn into range by a "stool pigeon," a captured bird, often with its eyes sewn shut and tethered to a perch or "stool." It was made to flap its wings to attract the attention of a passing flock, and it was quite usual for each trapper to catch upward of five hundred birds in each release of the net and maybe five thousand birds in a day's work. As Audubon recorded, there were usually far more birds killed than could be transported from the site, so hundreds of hogs were turned loose, to gorge on the piles of dead birds littering the ground.

Yet at first, it is doubtful whether even this level of carnage had much effect on their numbers. Today, eared doves in Argentina nest in flocks up to ten million strong and are poisoned or shot as agricultural pests. Yet, even though perhaps 10 percent of the colony is killed, their numbers continue unabated.[31] And Wilson estimated some of the flocks of passenger pigeons he saw to contain several *billion* birds. Audubon performed some similar calculations and came up with a figure of over 1 billion birds in a single flock that he watched near Louisville, Kentucky. A flock in Ontario thirty years later took several days to pass and was later estimated to contain nearly 4 billion individuals.[32] It is extremely difficult to get an accurate census of such enormous populations continuously on the move, but Wilson's and Audubon's figures were worked out from his firsthand experiences of these massive flocks. More recent conservative estimates suggest the total population to have been between 3 and 5 billion birds.[33]

That the forests could support such extraordinary numbers is testament to the sheer productivity of the mast-bearing trees. But was there enough to go round? There have been recent suggestions that the Indians of the eastern forest would not have stood back and watched nutritious nuts disappearing down millions of pecking beaks in the way that Chief Pokagon described.

We've already met the idea that perhaps the Indians saw deer, turkeys, squir-rels, raccoons, and bears as competitors for a valuable food resource. Some researchers now suggest that Indians and pigeons were in direct competition for mast and that mast use by the Indians acted to keep pigeon populations at lower levels before the coming of the Europeans.

In this view, the astounding spectacles that awed Audubon and Wilson only came about because Indian populations were decimated by disease, al-lowing the pigeons to achieve their full potential. It has even been suggested that the vast flocks may have rebounded to levels that were unsustainable in the long term. Yet, to me, passenger pigeon biology suggests that they were adapted to—and needed to—live in huge numbers. Their ultimate demise was down to their inability to live in mere hundred of thousands. If Indian competition really did keep their numbers lower, perhaps they weren't that much lower and the "rebound," if there was one, was only to a state that the pigeons and the forests had evolved to cope with. So were these enormous flocks of billions of birds stable in the long term or were the world's great-est bird spectacles merely temporary aberrations that would have declined again without human intervention? We'll never know, because humans did, undoubtedly, intervene.

There were ready markets for these birds in the big cities back east. In 1805, Audubon saw schooners laden with pigeons caught further up the Hudson River docking in New York City, where the birds fetched one cent each. "In the month of March 1830, they were so abundant in the markets of New York, that piles of them met the eye in every direction."[34] Even so, Audubon didn't believe there was any real threat to their numbers. But when railroads pen-etrated pigeon country, things changed. By the end of the Civil War, most of the country east of the Mississippi was within reach of a railroad, which meant easy transportation of pigeons to the markets of big cities. Telegraph lines followed the railroads, which meant that it didn't take long for news of a big nesting to reach a growing band of professional pigeon hunters. Even as early as 1851, nearly 2 million pigeons arrived in New York City from one nesting in upper New York State. Apart from food, thousands of live pigeons were shipped to the cities to serve as living targets on shooting ranges. A million birds could easily be lost at a single nesting, but is that enough to threaten such an abundant species? Like all the birds we've looked at so far, the story is much more complex.

Audubon thought that no direct assault on their numbers would ever cause the population to drop. "Persons unacquainted with these birds might naturally conclude that such dreadful havoc would soon put an end to the species. But I have satisfied myself, by long observation, that nothing but the gradual diminution of our forests can accomplish their decrease." Habitat loss, as suggested by Audubon, looks a likely candidate for the near extinction of ivory-bills, but is less likely to be the case, at least on its own, for the pigeons. They were gone long before the forests. Today, there are two broad schools of thought on the demise of the passenger pigeon. One is that the birds needed to be part of huge flocks, and once the numbers fell below a certain threshold, the pigeons were inevitably doomed.

This phenomenon is common in ecology, where it is termed the Allee effect, after the person who outlined the principles, ecologist Warder C. Allee. In broad terms, he showed that the reproductive output of each individual is related to the size of the population (through a variety of behavioral and physiological mechanisms). At low populations, each individual produces few offspring, through, for example, difficulty in finding mates. As the population rises, the number of offspring per individual also rises to some maximum value, before declining again at higher population levels. We've seen this effect in previous chapters where the growth of cod stocks is dependent on existing population size, even though each female can produce millions of eggs. The importance of this effect is becoming increasingly clear for conservation,[35] and in the case of passenger pigeons perhaps it was just a question of scale—birth rate falling below death rate at relatively high populations—and once this happened extinction was a mathematical certainty.

But why should this effect kick in at such high population levels? The answer lies in the specific biology of the passenger pigeon. To nest successfully, the birds had to find areas in the vastness of the forest where mast was abundant enough to support them through the whole nesting period. More eyes meant greater likelihood of finding such patches, so when numbers began to decline, it was possible that the pigeons simply couldn't find food patches fast or frequently enough to successfully raise their chicks.

The other explanation for the demise of the passenger pigeon is that hunting and, more importantly, nest disturbance was responsible. There are several records of nestings being abandoned due to disturbance, including the last one ever recorded, in Wisconsin, in 1887.[36] This, together with the slaughter of nestlings that had somehow managed to hatch, would have meant that the birds were no longer able to replace their numbers. And here, railroads and telegraphs really made a difference. Once the whole area east of the Mississippi was linked by rapid communication and transport, no nesting was safe from hunters. Even a nesting in 1881, in Oklahoma, which was over a hundred miles from a railroad, was discovered and raided by professional trappers.

Of course, both problems—hunting pressure and Allee effects—could have worked together to hasten their ultimate demise. On top of that, burgeoning populations of hogs would have competed with the pigeons—and with other wildlife—for mast. This food crisis would have been exacerbated by deforestation and may have helped finally push the pigeons over the edge. As the forest was cleared, the remaining fragments may not have been large enough to support such huge flocks. They may have needed the whole eastern forest ecosystem intact to find enough patches of masting trees. By the early years of the twentieth century, the passenger pigeon was gone. Between 1910 and 1912, the America Ornithologists Union organized searches throughout its range, even offering rewards of up to $2,000. But the rewards went unclaimed. The last passenger pigeon of all, a bird called Martha, after the wife of George Washington, died in captivity in Cincinnati Zoo in 1914.

Passenger pigeons and Carolina parakeets passed from existence with no real effort to save them. At the start of the twentieth century, species conservation was a newly born philosophy, with little hard science or public support to back it up. But another formerly abundant bird did receive considerable efforts to preserve it in its dying days. And its passing did begin to stir the public conscience.

In the early days of colonization, several sorts of grouse were abundant throughout the forests, but one was particularly favored for the table—the heath hen. So abundant was it, especially in scrubby open forests, that there are tales, like those relating to salmon, that servants demanded they were fed heath hen no more than a few times a week.

Heath hens were a subspecies of prairie chicken, which existed in even more prodigious numbers on the open grasslands to the west. Originally, the heath hen, a smaller, darker bird than its western cousins, ranged from Maine to Virginia, and was probably another creature that benefited from Indian management of the forest. But a combination of hunting and changes to the forest gradually led to lower and lower numbers until it finally disappeared everywhere—except the island of Martha's Vineyard.

Here the birds still continued their habits of old, the males gathering each spring in open meadows to display by erecting tufts of feathers on their head, inflating orange "balloons" on their necks and strutting around making strange booming noises at each other. Heath hens were one of many grouse species that lek. That is, the males all gather together on a display ground and defend small personal territories. The best territories are deemed to be in the center of the lek, so visiting females can quickly work out just who the best males are. The meadows on Green Farm, near West Tisbury on Martha's Vineyard, were one such "booming ground."

It was clear from its demise on the mainland that, even by the late nineteenth century, the heath hen was in big trouble. It was given full protection on Martha's Vineyard, which reduced hunting, even if it didn't exactly stop it completely. One Boston marketman reported to ornithologist William Brewster, in 1885, that he still got some twenty birds a season from "the Vineyard."[37]

In 1908, the Manuel F. Corellus State Forest was created in the center of the island as a heath hen reserve. Birds were also removed from the island in an attempt to reintroduce the species to the mainland, though all these attempts very quickly failed. In desperation, western prairie chickens were also released on Long Island and in Massachusetts, but these birds, too, quickly disappeared.[38] Yet on Martha's Vineyard, conservation measures seemed to be working. From around fifty birds the population in the reserve had risen to several thousand birds by 1915. But in reality, this is still a tiny population, and the heath hen illustrates the extreme dangers to a species when it is reduced to such small, localized populations.

The heath hen was wiped out by a series of unfortunate incidents. In 1916, a fire destroyed most of their habitat. This was followed by a severe winter, which further reduced the birds' numbers. To add insult to injury, that winter saw an influx of goshawks, for which heath hens were ideal sized prey. Following that, most of the remaining birds succumbed to disease brought to the island with domestic turkeys. The last record of any young being born was in 1924, when there were still around fifty adult birds.[39] By 1927, there were thirteen birds, only two of which were females, and by the spring of 1928, the entire world population of heath hens consisted of three males—not exactly good news for conservation.

Only two of those males returned to Green Farm in the autumn, and then, sometime after that, there was one. He was nicknamed Booming Ben, though he didn't have much to boom about. He did however return to the meadows of Green Farm each spring for several years, where his plight moved locals to suggest bringing him a female prairie chicken, not so much in the hopes that this would save the heath hen, but more out of genuine compassion for the last-ever heath hen, wandering alone around meadows that once resounded to exuberant, booming birds. It's not recorded whether he ever received this gift. Instead, in 1931, Ben was trapped and banded, for reasons I can't quite fathom. But he was also filmed and photographed. On March 11, 1932, James Green watched Ben scurry into some low vegetation on his farm, and that was the last anyone saw of the heath hen.

But the poignant images taken the year before began to create a wider public awareness of the plight of many other species at this time in North America. Earlier observers of nature frequently commented that the idea of protecting threatened species was met with derision, or at best incomprehension. But Ben's passing and the failure to protect ivory-bills in the Singer Tract just a few years later did at least help to get conservation measures taken more seriously. The real legacy of Poll, Ben, Martha, and others was a growing list of legislation designed to prevent similar crises in the future.

The politics of the growth of species conservation in the United States and Canada would be a weighty tome in its own right, but it culminated in the Endangered Species Act (1973) in the United States and the Species at Risk Act (2002) in Canada, both designed to give immediate protection to any species of plant or animal considered threatened with extinction. Both acts are valuable weapons in the armory of conservationists, though the ESA in particular has been something of a political football for most of its existence. Nonetheless, such acts have had notable successes, with several species being brought back from the brink, enough to be "de-registered." However, neither act fully takes on board the lessons of history.

They both represent "last ditch" thinking in species conservation. A species has to be severely threatened before the full weight of the law is mustered to help it. Though they shared a similar fate, passenger pigeons, heath hens, Carolina parakeets, and ivory-bills (though these latter currently have a reprieve—hopefully not temporary) disappeared for a variety of different, often still not fully understood, reasons. To wait until a species is already rare and declining is to invite the unfortunate coincidences that finally did for the heath hen. But worse, it doesn't give long to work out the different, usually complex reasons behind each species decline and then do something about it. At the moment, as far as individual species protection goes, they are the best we have got, but is it the best we can do? Many conservationists today advocate the "precautionary principle"—if in any doubt, don't do it—and history certainly suggests this is a wise course. But, despite these lessons, most people are very good at brushing evidence under the carpet and looking the other way, often until too late.

Will we be more successful with the ivory-billed woodpecker today than we were with those in the Singer Tract or with the heath hen? Hopefully, we have come a long way since the chief executive of the Chicago Mill and Lumber Company explained his reasons for refusing to stop logging in the Singer Tract: "We are just money grubbers. We are not concerned . . . with ethical considerations."[40]

But the ivory-bill will still test our resolve and the weight of the law to the full. We now know it is a shy bird that needs large areas of old growth forest, so to ensure its future means protecting vast areas of forest and allowing trees to mature to the size needed by these birds. The by-product will be the protection of the whole, rich bottomland ecosystem, but it will be hugely expensive. And that's another problem with such conservation triage: it is far more expensive to enact these last minute measures than it is to protect the future of species when they are less threatened.

Such were my thoughts as I stood in silent contemplation in front of the cage in Cincinnati Zoo that once held Martha, the last-ever passenger pigeon—one pigeon out of maybe 5 billion. I've read stories that toward the end of her life, her keepers had to rope off her cage to prevent visitors from throwing stones to make her move. The experience was made all the more poignant by the fact that we know *exactly* when the passenger pigeon became extinct. Martha was found dead, on the floor of the very cage I was looking at, at precisely 1:00 p.m. on the first of September 1914. In more ways than one, she died alone.

CHAPTER 9

Souls and Furs

During the seventeenth century, English colonies sprang up all along the eastern seaboard, from New England to the Carolinas, and then spread into the great eastern forests along the main rivers. The numbers of settlers increased rapidly, and their ways of seeing and exploiting this new world profoundly changed the nature of life here, for Indians as well as for the plants and animals of the coasts and forests. But to the north of the English settlements, a somewhat different relationship was being forged between the newcomers and the ancient lifeways of the New World. It too would have major impacts on the ecology of North America, though these would unfold in different ways from those happening in the south.

The main focus of French exploration was the St. Lawrence Seaway and River. Initially seen as a likely candidate for the elusive route through the continent to the Pacific, this great gash in the coastline penetrated deep into the interior and eventually connected to the Great Lakes, which quickly carried French explorers nearly halfway across the continent. As a water route to the Pacific, it proved a disappointment, but these difficult journeys were more than worth the effort. The French found their El Dorado here, not in gold and silver as the Spanish had in Central and South America, but in furs. The forests here abounded in fur-bearing game, but in particular with one creature that would shape the fortunes of New France—the beaver.

Beavers were abundant throughout large areas of North America, but thrived in the maze of lakes and waterways in New France. "Every River where the current was moderate and sufficiently deep, the banks at the water edge were occupied by their houses. To every small Lake, and all the Ponds they builded Dams, and enlarged and deepened them to the height of the Dams. Even to ground occasionally overflowed, by heavy rains, they also made dams, and made them permanent Ponds."[1] This report, from the latter half of the eighteenth century, shows that beavers are no ordinary creatures. They have been called "ecosystem engineers" and a "keystone species," a species at the hub of a complex web of relationships and on whom the integrity of the web depends.[2]

Their dams affect the flow, temperature, and chemistry of the streams and rivers they occupy. The flooded ponds behind the dams kill trees and open up the forest to sunlight. This in turn warms the large expanse of water, which in turn warms the streams below the dams as water percolates through. This makes life difficult for some creatures, like brook trout, which prefer cooler water. And since these fish can't live at all in the slow, silty conditions created in the ponds themselves, beavers are not good news for brook trout. But their activities benefit a far greater variety of plants and animals.

Nutrients settle out in the slow water of the ponds, instead of being swept downstream. This increases plant productivity in and around the ponds, which in turn supports increased numbers of animals such as waterfowl. A study in Maine showed that untrapped areas supported more Canada geese, hooded mergansers, and mallards than did areas where the beaver population had been reduced, and all nests of black ducks were within active beaver colonies.[3] Elsewhere, Canada geese and trumpeter swans even use the beaver's lodge as a nesting site, and it's not just waterfowl, but a whole host of forest birds that are more abundant around beaver ponds.

These ponds produce an abundance of protein-rich insects, which can support dense populations of breeding birds.[4] Dead and dying trees, killed by the rising water, also provide nesting sites for woodpeckers, and when these holes are abandoned by their original tenants, they provide homes for nuthatches, tits, flycatchers, tree swallows, owls, and wood ducks. And these are just the most obvious strands in the complex ecological web radiating from the industrious beaver. Some of the more obscure threads show just how far the ecological engineering of beavers extends.

Young white pine trees growing in the shade of aspens are rarely attacked by the white pine weevil. But aspen is a favorite food of beavers, and they frequently clear them from the edges of their ponds. Now exposed, the white pines are severely attacked and damaged by the weevils.[5] Beavers also eat cottonwoods, which regrow from the base. But once attacked, these trees produce higher levels of phenolic glycosides, poisonous chemicals meant to deter herbivorous mammals. However, a particular leaf beetle, *Chrysomela confluens*, seems not only immune to these chemicals, but reuses them in its own defense. These beetles grow faster and survive better on cottonwoods that have been attacked by beavers.[6]

Beavers continue to affect the local ecology long after they have abandoned a particular pond. If the dam doesn't break, the pond will gradually silt up and dry out, producing a fertile meadow. The rich growth of vegetation on these beaver meadows is cropped by white-tailed deer, moose, elk, and black bears, which are all more abundant in areas where beavers are common. In turn, this abundance of large prey animals encourages higher populations of predators. Elk are a favored prey of wolves, though beavers themselves are important backup items on their menu, and there's some evidence that wolf populations declined in areas where beavers were removed.

Slowly, a beaver meadow should return to forest, but even now the beaver is still exerting its influence. Firs are often slow to recolonize these meadows since it turns out that fir trees have a symbiotic relationship with a particular fungus, which cannot endure the low oxygen conditions that existed while the soil was at the bottom of the beaver pond. So why doesn't the fungus recolonize the soil once it has dried out? The answer depends on yet another link in this increasingly complex story—the red-backed vole. It seems that the fungus depends on the voles for dispersal, and red-backed voles are reluctant to venture out on to beaver meadows. But, despite their effects on firs, beavers, overall, increase the diversity of vegetation through their engineering. One study found that fully one quarter of the plant diversity of an area was due to wetlands created by beavers.[7]

I could fill many more pages with similar examples, but it should be clear by now that beavers really are ecosystem engineers par excellence, their effects felt at every ecological level, from whole landscapes to the intimate lives of tiny insects. But they are just as much engineers of history. They have reshaped the distribution and fortunes of Indian tribes, altered the balance of power among European nations and helped draw the political map of the continent. Not bad for a rodent!

Their historical engineering began with the fact that the French needed the Indians to catch beavers. Several early fur traders commented on the fact that beavers were far too smart to be caught by Europeans, and even if this was tongue-in-cheek, beaver trapping was far more efficient and profitable for Europeans when plugged into the Indian's extensive trade network. This need for Indian allies demanded a different approach to colonization. The French didn't sit in palisaded settlements but went out into the northern forests to live with the Indians, to learn their languages and their ways of life, and very often to take Indian wives. From these partnerships, the fur trade grew into a massive and successful global business, though not for the Indians on whom it depended. They ended up nearly exterminating the beavers, along with a number of other animals, and in so doing destroyed their own lives—and this from people who had such an intimate relationship with the land and its animals when the French arrived.

In the past, North America's Indians have carried the mantle of "noble savages," an idea that stemmed from the Romanticism of philosophers like Rousseau. Such ideas arose in the latter part of the eighteenth century as a revolt against the cold rationalism of the Enlightenment. In this view, Indians lived a life unsullied by civilization; they still dwelt in the Garden, in harmony with the natural world. Although Indians are often still seen like this in popular culture (witness the antipollution campaign in the 1970s that featured a crying Indian), it is fashionable in more academic circles to strip that "nobility" away. And seeing Indians as real humans instead of caricatures of a European ideal certainly paints a more complete picture of North America's past. But this should not obscure the fact that Indians did see their world in a very different way to Europeans.

When the French first explored along the Gulf of St. Lawrence and across the Great Lakes, they encountered a large number of different Indian nations, from the Miq'mac around the entrance to the Gulf, to the Huron, Ottawa, Ojibwa, and Menominee inland. Some of these nations lived too far north to farm so had to rely entirely on hunting, fishing, and gathering. These nations were linked with the farming nations to the south through a complex market economy in which they could trade furs and skins for products of the fields, often through an intermediate universal currency of wampum—shell beads made by the nations bordering Long Island Sound.

Yet even farming tribes also relied on hunting, and all these people had, like the Indian Nations we've already met in the south, a pact with the creatures they hunted. The details of how this pact arose and how it was maintained varied from nation to nation, but, in essence, all were based on a mutual obligation between nature and humanity. Both sides had a set of behaviors to which they had to adhere and if either side broke this contract, catastrophe would result.

Nature, as seen by the Ojibwa, for example, consisted of a whole series of societies, equivalent in all ways to those of the Ojibwa themselves. Each kind of animal or plant had its own home and family and a leader known as a master or keeper. Such "keepers of the game" were usually larger than their ordinary brethren and often white. It was these spirit creatures, or manitous, that were responsible for their particular family keeping to their side of the pact.

Just as with the Cherokee, the masters of the game could also inflict punishment, usually in the form of disease, if they discovered any transgressions from the Indians. On the Indian side, each and every hunter became responsible for their side of the pact when he reached puberty. The rites of passage into adulthood, and the responsibilities that these brought, were therefore of prime importance in allowing Indians to continue to survive by hunting. As anthropologist Alfred Hallowell describes in his 1955 book *Culture and Experience*, the hunter must only take what he needs for food, clothing, and warmth for his family, he must not be destructive or greedy, and he must never torture any animal. If he breaks this pact, the keepers of the game will withhold animals from him, and in the end, he will destroy himself since neither material nor spiritual sources of life will be available to him.[8] Yet, after the French arrived, that is exactly what many nations did. How did this happen?

The story starts in the 1530s with Jacques Cartier, the Breton sailor who made several voyages of exploration around the Gulf of St. Lawrence, looking for a passage to the Pacific, but also cataloguing the resources of the continent that lay beyond the great cod fishing grounds. He was not, at first, impressed. "If the soile were as good as the harboroughes are, it were a great commoditie: but it is not to be called The new Land, but rather stones and wild cragges and a place fit for wilde beastes, for in all the North Land I did not see a Cart-load of good earth. . . . I believe this was the Land that God allotted to Caine."[9] But he soon changed his mind as he explored further on a second trip. He was determined to reach as far inland as a village called Hochelaga, though the autumn was rapidly approaching as he traveled up the St. Lawrence. Along the way, they "beganne to see as goodly a countrey as possibly can with eye be seene, all replenished with very goodly trees, and Vines laden as full of grapes as could be all along the river." When he finally arrived in Hochelaga, he found "the fairest and best countrey that possibly can be seene, full of as goodly great Okes as are in any wood in France, under which the ground was all covered over with faire Akornes."[10]

Hochelaga was at the base of a large hill, from the top of which Cartier could gaze across the Laurentian Highlands, an endless expanse of forest in the glory of the fall, the dark green of the conifers splashed with the reds and yellows of oaks, maples, and other broadleaf trees. So splendid was the prospect that he named the hill "Royal Mount," *Mont Réal,* eventually to become Montreal. But when Cartier stood here, it was called Hochelaga—beaver meadows.

By now, Cartier had already begun to realize that the "wilde beastes," that at first he so disparagingly described, could well be useful commodities. Almost as soon as he approached the shores of the New World on his first voyage he was surrounded by canoes belonging to Miq'mac Indians eager for trade: "they . . . came on land, and brought some of their skinnes, and so began to deale with us, seeming to be very glad to have our iron ware and other things. . . . They gave us whatsoever they had, not keeping any thing, so that they were constrained to go back againe naked, and made signes that the next day they would come againe, and bring more skinnes with them."[11]

The fur trade was nothing new to these Indians; by the time Cartier arrived, they had been trading furs, as well as other commodities, among themselves for many centuries. But the overenthusiastic transactions described by Cartier could be seen as the birth of the French fur trade, even if it didn't become really big business until the beginning of the next century. As the English were finding out to the south, setting down permanent roots here was fraught with difficulties.

On his second voyage, Cartier overwintered at a village nearer the mouth of the St. Lawrence, a place called Stadacona. It was a tough time, and to make matters worse scurvy broke out. He would have lost more men than he did if the Indians hadn't given them a bark tea to cure them. Despite the hardships, Cartier tried to set up a permanent settlement here as a base for future colonization and exploration, though it soon failed, succumbing to the harsh New World winters after Cartier returned to France. In the intervening decades, the French tentatively tried to plant settlers elsewhere in North America, though, in 1600, they again tried to set up a colony on the shores of the St. Lawrence at Tadoussac, a place Cartier had visited and described more than half a century earlier. It too didn't survive long, though it was later reoccupied and is still a small village today.

Three years later, Samuel de Champlain began a series of wide-ranging travels through the whole region, south along the coast to Cape Cod, then inland along the St. Lawrence where he went well beyond Hochelaga and explored the eastern shores of Lakes Huron and Ontario. In 1608, he returned to the site of Stadacona, now completely deserted by the Indians, to set up a permanent base. This time it did survive, earning Champlain his epithet of the "Father of New France." Today, Stadacona is called Quebec, and it was founded just one year after Jamestown on the Chesapeake.

Now the way was open for the trade to expand. Champlain sent a companion, Etiene Brule, deep into the hinterland to live with the Huron Indians and to learn their trade routes; the first of an extraordinary breed of Frenchmen, the coureurs de bois—the runners of the woods—who lived more like Indians than Europeans. The coureurs expanded on the existing Indian trade network for beavers and began to build trading bases, to which Indians could bring their skins in exchange for European goods.

Hochelaga itself, like Stadacona, was now also abandoned by its Indian inhabitants and was settled by the French in 1643, eventually to become modern Montreal. By then Jean Nicollet had penetrated even further than Champlain into the heartland of the continent, crossing the Great Lakes as far as Lake Michigan then traveling down from Green Bay, on the western side of Lake Michigan, almost as far as the future site of Chicago. He laid claim to this whole area for France. With the help of their Indian allies, the French quickly gained extensive knowledge of the vast territories of New France. And what they found was remarkable.

Pierre-Esprit Radisson, one of the better known coureurs, called Lake Nippising the "Lake of Castors" (beavers), so abundant were they. And not just beavers: "We came to a place where weare abundance of otter, in so much that I believe all gathered to hinder our passage."[12] Otters were as abundant as this right down to the coast, and just as happily fished in salt as in freshwater. In the late sixteenth century, fishermen visiting the Newfoundland coast said, "Of otters we may take like store [with bears] everywhere, so you may kill them as oft as you list."[13]

These coastal otters were joined by an altogether more mysterious creature, described in Newfoundland by no less a figure than the English naturalist Joseph Banks as "bigger than a fox, tho not much, in make and shape nearer compared to an Italian Greyhound, legs long, tail long and tapering . . . [it] Came up from the Sea."[14] William Wood also saw this creature, describing it as an aquatic marten. It seemed destined to be another unsolved mystery until its bones were dug up from an Indian midden in Maine. It turned out to be a distinct species of mink, now called the sea mink, which grew to perhaps twice the size of the American mink. A later find of bones showed that this almost unknown species ranged as far south as Massachusetts.[15] These bones were in an Indian ceremonial site, suggesting that this impressive beast may have been eaten in rituals, but otherwise virtually nothing is known about it. It seems to have lived along the coast, catching a wide range of fish, and like the coastal otters had valuable fur. Living on the Atlantic coast, these were the most accessible furbearers so their numbers quickly dwindled. The coastal otter survived—just, but the sea mink became extinct at the end of the nineteenth century.

Intriguingly, this creature might be responsible for the curious name of a smaller relative, the fisher. Fishers were extremely abundant throughout the northern forests, hunting a wide variety of prey. But the one thing they don't do is catch fish. Farley Mowat thinks that the sea mink may have been the original "fisher," but since it declined very quickly its name was transferred to a similar-looking relative.

As explorers and traders pushed into the northern forests they left more descriptions, of abundant deer, moose, elk, lynx, fishers, mink, and martens. The trading network established by the coureurs allowed Champlain and his associates to buy twenty-two thousand skins in 1626 alone—for just $2 each.[16] The fur trade soon dominated the lives of people here, and few were interested in pursuing any of the original priorities for the exploration of New France, such as finding a sea route to Asia or, if this failed, at least giving France its own claim on the new continent. As one observer noted: "The officials in canada are looking not for The western sea but for The sea of beaver."[17]

Beavers were so valuable because their dense underfur makes a very good waterproof felt, perfect for making hats. This industry had existed for some time, fed by a slightly different species of beaver from Europe. But European beavers were growing ever more scarce. They had been extinct in England since the thirteenth century and gradually retreated across the rest of Europe until they could be found in abundance only in the most remote areas. Before the arrival of American beavers, the hatters of Europe depended on beavers from Russia, but now even that supply was drying up. So when Champlain for France, Smith for England, or Hudson for Holland saw the sheer abundance of furs in the New World, they knew they were on to a good thing. A large industry already existed back home, a ready market for North American furs.

Because it was the underfur that was turned into felt, the long guard hairs had first to be removed, usually with lethal chemical concoctions based on mercury. This heavy metal damages the central nervous system and is therefore responsible for the expression "mad as a hatter." But there was even more good news from the New World, at least as far as the sanity of hatters was concerned. The brittle guard hairs eventually fall out of older furs that have been repeatedly worn. The Indians were delighted to find that Europeans would pay good prices in trade goods for their old worn out cloaks—so-called coat beaver. As far as they were concerned, it was the traders, not the hatters, that were insane.

But harvesting the abundant furs wasn't going to be that easy. Many of the nations here were as eager for trade in European goods as the Miq'mac were with Cartier, but, unfortunately, this enthusiasm manifested itself in an escalation of existing rivalries between major groups of Indians.

Sometime after Cartier had left and before Champlain arrived, five Iroquoian tribes came together in a confederacy to provide mutual aid against their rivals and to better resist the erosion of their traditional lifestyles. Later a sixth nation, the Tuscarora, joined, after being driven from their own lands by spreading English settlements in the south, giving the confederacy its modern English name of the "Six Nations." The name adopted by the six nations themselves is *Haudenosaunee*—the People of the Long House. Although they are more familiarly known as the Iroquois, this (like so many commonly used names for the First Nations) is derived from a less than complimentary expression from a rival tribe, in this case a Huron word for "black snakes." And the Huron had good reason to think of the Haudenosaunee in that way.

The two groups had been rivals for some time. It's likely that Stadacona was deserted when Champlain founded Quebec on the site in 1608 because it had been wiped out by a Haudenosaunee attack. A year later, Champlain became embroiled in this battle when he helped the Huron defeat a Haudenosaunee raiding party with the help of superior European firepower. Lines of loyalty were rapidly being drawn. The French and the English had also been at war, on and off, for centuries, so First Nations and European nations were drawn into each other's rivalries. The whole thing began to escalate, culminating in the late seventeenth century with the French and Iroquois Wars. At stake was not only the possession of territory in the New World, but access to the lucrative fur trade. Not for nothing is this series of conflicts also known as the Beaver Wars.

The situation was made all the more complicated by that fact that some Indian groups played the French, English, and other Europeans off against each other as they sought the best value for their furs. Raids into other nations' territories for beavers frequently sparked off another conflict in the ongoing

Beaver Wars. When beavers on their own lands were becoming scarce, the powerful Haudenosaunee expanded into Huron territory, displacing them. Likewise, in the west of New France, the Dakota, moving into better fur territory, also displaced local tribes. The map of Indian America was being redrawn by the beaver and its fur-bearing kin.

Often, exploration and exploitation of new beaver territory was halted as these conflicts flared into all-out war, but these were only short stays of execution for the beavers. Such an unstable situation made it very hard to develop a sustainable market, though this is one case where such a market should have been possible, since beavers can multiply very quickly. Instead, never knowing which territory might belong to which tribe tomorrow, or who would be allied to whom, the motto of the beaver trade became "trap out and get out." But this political situation still doesn't explain the apparent shift in Indian philosophy and in their spiritual relationships with the creatures they were hunting.

The coureurs weren't alone in their rapid expansion through the St. Lawrence and Great Lakes country. They were accompanied by Jesuit priests, called "Black Robes" by the Indians. The Catholic Crown of France was interested in the profits from the fur trade to fill its coffers, but equally in the extension, settlement, and civilization of New France. And, just as for the Pilgrims to the south, civilization meant Christianity. The situation was succinctly summed up by the Comte de Frontenac, the governor of New France when he said: "There are but two businesses in New France, the conversion of souls and the conversion of beaver."

But these twin thrusts of French ambition were not always easy bedfellows. Civilization meant settlements, the fixed existence of towns and villages carved from the wilderness. The fur trade, on the other hand, needed preservation of the wilderness, even coming to terms with it, which is what the coureurs did so well. Yet despite this tension, these two objectives, working in parallel, would become an irresistible force, a combination symbolized by the frequent partnerships between individual coureurs and missionaries, who set off together to explore the wilderness. And we can be glad they did, since most coureurs were illiterate and would have left no record of the vast territories they explored if not for the writings of their Jesuit companions.

For forty years, accounts of the travels of missionaries and coureurs were published as the *Jesuit Relations,* a truly extraordinary body of work containing priceless insights into the land and people at the point of contact with

Europeans, albeit through the filter of Catholic doctrine. A Huron friend once told me that when traditional-minded Huron were trying to revive some of the old ceremonies that had long since been forgotten, their only sources of information were the *Jesuit Relations*. I'm not sure what the Jesuits would have thought of their records being used in this way, but as an insight into the world of seventeenth-century Canada, the *Relations* are unsurpassed.

They also document in detail the early years of the fur trade and the missionizing work of the fathers. They allow us to piece together how the Indians' lives changed as they became more deeply enmeshed in trade relations with the French. For the Jesuits, the first stage in the "conversion of souls" was to target a critical point of contact between the Indians' heathen spiritual world and the world of humans. The pact between Indians and animals was in constant flux, with transgressions on each side of varying degrees of seriousness. So it was vital to keep lines of communication open between the Keepers of the Game and other manitous and the hunters of the tribe.

This was the job of the shaman, an individual who, by various means, could communicate with the manitous, to find out who had transgressed and repair the damage. Maintaining the ecological balance that existed when Europeans arrived here was a hard spiritual job demanding constant vigilance and practice. The Jesuits, on the other hand, saw the manitous as devils, and since the shamans were the ones on speaking terms with these devils, they were targeted first. But the job of undermining the shamans was a lot easier than the Jesuits might have imagined.

The *Jesuit Relations* contain evidence that several tribes were already in a state of spiritual chaos when the Black Robes made first contact. They had probably been hit by epidemics of diseases carried by Europeans who had been landing all along the cod coast from as early as the late fifteenth century. Since disease was a symptom of some kind of transgression in the pact between people and animals, it was the shamans' job to sort it out. But these new diseases were beyond treatment by any traditional means. As elsewhere on the continent, people died in their droves, often wiping out whole villages and undermining faith, both in the shamans' abilities and in the traditional worldview. On the other hand, the Jesuits and coureurs often survived such epidemics, so it began to look like the God of the Black Robes was more powerful. But accepting this new God meant accepting a new, dualistic philosophy of the world, one which separated humanity from all other forms of life. In this philosophy, the rest of Creation had been laid out for the sole use of people.

Accepting this new worldview may have removed any need to worry about the old pact. But even this might not be the whole story. At the beginning of the eighteenth century, the Miq'mac were observed to pluck out the eyes of fish, birds, or mammals that they had killed, supposedly to blind the animal's spirit to the irreverence of overexploitation. They don't seem to have practiced this in earlier times, which suggests that the Miq'mac, at least, hadn't entirely abandoned their old worldview even this late in the trade. Such actions recall the descriptions of John Lawson in Carolina, of southern Indians performing rituals over deer killed for the deer trade. Yet all these Indian Nations, from the Carolinas to Canada, had become embroiled in the systematic destruction of the very resources on which they used to depend. Just as with the southern Indians, destruction of their societies by European diseases made it hard, even impossible, to maintain their old ways of living. They may have had little choice but to trade for European goods and embark on the road to dependence.

But the fur trade may also have just been a stimulus to escalate an ancient battle. Among some nations at least, there is intriguing evidence that the Indians might have been waging a spiritual war on the beaver. This idea, though controversial, was outlined in the late 1970s by Calvin Martin in his classic book on Indians and the fur trade, *Keepers of the Game*. The evidence comes from two highly knowledgeable and reliable explorers from around the turn of the nineteenth century. David Thompson lived and traveled with the Cree Nation for many years, and Alexander Henry, the Elder, was an adopted Ojibwa. According to Thompson, "This continent from the Atlantic to the Pacific Ocean, may be said to have been in the possession of two distinct races of Beings, Man and the Beaver."[18] By the time Canada was being explored by Europeans both Thompson and Henry's informants suggest that beavers were gaining the upper hand. Thompson summarizes the situation: "Thus all the lowlands were in possession of the Beaver, and all the hollows of the higher grounds . . . the dry land with the dominion of Man contracted, every where was hemmed in by water without the power of preventing it."

Just why the Cree thought beavers were taking over the world is not entirely clear. It's possible that as disease reduced Indian populations and removed traditional hunting pressures on the beavers, beaver numbers would have increased. Beavers are certainly prolific and capable of reaching high numbers very quickly, to judge by the recent surge in numbers to "nuisance" levels in certain parts of their range. Such an idea fits with those that we've already met in the forests to the south, that some of the abundance that greeted early colonists was in fact a recent phenomenon, created by massive declines in the Indian population.

But, whatever the reason, this increase would have been seen by the Cree as a breach of the pact. In conversation with two aged Cree from the Lake Winnipeg area, Thompson learned the following: "I have told you that we believed in years long passed away, the Great Spirit was angry with the Beaver, and ordered Weesaukejauk to drive them all from dry land into the water; and they became and continued very numerous; but the Great Spirit has been, and now is, very angry with them, and they are now all to be destroyed."

From his contacts, Alexander Henry learned that animals had entered into a conspiracy against humans: "At the head of the conspiracy was the bear; and the great increase which had taken place amongst the animals rendered their numbers formidable."[19] Henry went on to discover that *Kitchi Manitou* (the Great Spirit) had removed the power of speech from the beaver to stop them from becoming superior in understanding to humans. Calvin Martin puts these ideas together to suggest that some Indians might have seen the arrival of European technology as a way of gaining the upper hand again in this battle with the animals. If so, overhunting could easily have escalated, driven by a positive feedback loop: kill animals, trade their skins for better weapons that can kill more animals and provide more skins to trade for even more weapons in order to kill even more animals.

But whether the Indians were deliberately overkilling animals or not, the system wouldn't have worked without a demand for furs. And here another positive feedback loop kicked in. The production of high-quality beaver and felt hats sparked a growing demand in Europe. It has been calculated that in 1700, in England alone, the potential market for hats was nearly 5 million. Throughout the century, that demand grew as fashion shifted to beaver hats, not just in England, but all across Europe. It took the fur from one prime beaver skin to make one hat, and in 1700, around seventy thousand beaver hats and the same number of felt hats (beaver fur mixed with other furs such as rabbit) were exported from English ports. By the middle of the century, exports had risen to half a million beaver hats and 370,000 felt hats.[20] This demand was met by rising numbers of furs passing through the trading posts and by pushing ever further into unexploited fur country.

It is clear that, despite different objectives, the conversion of souls and the conversion of beaver were closely bound—the one drove the other. And that meant beavers and other fur bearers were soon hunted out once the trading posts arrived. Beavers had gone from Lake Simcoe, to the north of Lake Ontario, as early as 1635. Further south, in New England, declines in beaver numbers were also noted around the same time, and by the end of the century, the beaver trade here was already dead. This story was repeated in more and more remote locations as the trade spread out across the Northeast and down the Ohio and Mississippi Valleys. The comment below, made by an English fur trader, was echoed endlessly across the country within a few decades of the first trading posts being erected: "A few years ago beaver were plenty on the upper part of these forks [the confluence of the Red and Rat Rivers] but now they are nearly destroyed."[21]

Another comment, from the area around Lake Nipigon, shows how the trade responded to such extinctions: "I am, however, sorry to remark that this part of the country is now very much impoverished since; beaver is getting scarce, but I have nevertheless managed to keep up the average of returns by shifting from place to place every year and increasing the number of posts."[22]

As with the fish off the coast, increasing scarcity meant increasing value, which made it worthwhile to pursue beavers with increasing vigor even as numbers declined. A growing demand also pushed up prices, which began to rise from about 1730 onward, increases that were mirrored through the middle years of the century by a rising number of furs arriving at the trading posts.

The Indian trappers were caught up in this ultimately self-destructive economic system. It is sometimes said that as fur prices rose, Indians needed to bring in fewer furs. They had fixed requirements for European trade goods and adjusted their hunting of furs accordingly. However, records show that in reality they took advantage of price rises and a strong market to bring in more furs, enabling them to increase their purchase of luxury items. This in turn drew them ever deeper into dependency on the Europeans and their markets.[23]

As effective as the twin aims of converting souls and beavers were in tandem, the tensions between the need for settlement and the need to push ever deeper into the hinterland did result in some problems. The Jesuits and their missions were backed by the French Crown and the government, who were concerned that without permanent towns the task of converting the Indians to settled civility would be that much harder. In addition, lack of a densely populated colony would make it even harder to hang on to New France in the face of rivalry from the rapidly growing colonies of England.

The Crown granted licenses to traders, and as part of the conditions for being allowed to trade, the license holders had to agree to establish colonies in New France. Furthermore, to keep people in the new towns, the Crown forbade exploration west of Montreal. The free-living, half Indian, unlicensed coureurs were outlawed from trade, but life in the wilds of the northern forests doesn't exactly breed respect for staid authority. So great was the lure of beavers, that many coureurs continued to do what they always had. Two of the most famous were Pierre-Esprit Radisson and Médard Chouart Des Groseilliers. In 1654, Des Groseilliers had returned to Ottawa with fifty canoes, all filled with furs. Later, he and Radisson teamed up for another expedition to seek yet more new fur territory.

Despite the restrictions on travel, they headed west as far as Lake Superior and the headwaters of the Mississippi. It was worth it. They acquired an enormous quantity of furs, and set off back to Montreal in August 1660 with a hundred canoes. The *Jesuit Relations* for that year describe the scene: "40 [canoes] turned back and 60 made it through, loaded with 200,000 livres worth of pelts; they left 50,000 livres worth in Montreal and carried the remainder to Trois-Rivières."[24] They finally arrived in Quebec to salutes from the cannons on the battery to celebrate their contribution to the wealth of New France, and then the governor promptly had them arrested, thrown in jail, and their cargo confiscated for trapping without a license.

While trading with the Indians, they had heard of untouched fur territory between Lake Superior and the shores of a great northern sea. But now was obviously not a good time to discuss it with the governor. In fact, they subsequently failed to get backing to explore this area from anyone in France. French officials were now much more concerned with keeping all efforts at colonization firmly focused on the St. Lawrence. After several failed attempts, they turned to the English, who were very interested, both in a new source of furs and in slapping France in the face.

In 1668, Prince Rupert, cousin to King Charles II, along with several other partners, sponsored an expedition, led by Radisson and Groseilliers, to look for a northwest passage to the Pacific. At the same time they could check out those rumors of a great wealth of furs around the shores of the northern bay. Radisson was forced back to Plymouth by storms, but Groseilliers, commanding the *Nonsuch,* made it into a great inlet of the sea that had first been explored in 1610 by Henry Hudson. Hudson had spent some time sailing around the shores of this bay searching for a northwest passage leading out of it, but found none. His crew eventually mutinied, and Hudson was never heard from again. Groseilliers had no more luck in finding a passage from Hudson's bay westward to the Pacific, but he did find the wealth of furs that he had been told about by Indian trappers—so many furs that Prince Rupert and the other backers set up a company by Royal Charter in 1670—the "Governor and Company of Adventurers of England Trading into Hudson's Bay," later known as the Hudson's Bay Company. The company claimed a vast swathe of land, called Rupert's Land, that extended south and west from the bay, skirting the St. Lawrence and Great Lakes, but reaching nearly as far south as present day Minneapolis. It enclosed and overlapped with the territory of New France. Having redrawn the map of tribal territories, the beaver was about to start redrawing the political map of the New World.

The Hudson's Bay Company provided as good an insight into the ecology of seventeenth- and eighteenth-century Canada as the Jesuits, but for very different reasons. Prince Rupert and many of his fellow company members also belonged to the Royal Society in London, one of the oldest scientific bodies in the world. As the Company set up bases around the remote shores of Hudson Bay, its investors encouraged its employees to become part-time naturalists, collecting and describing the local fauna.

The Boreal Forest reaches up around the southern part of Hudson Bay, though open patches of barren ground become more frequent to the north. Around Churchill, on the western side of the bay, the forest is dwarfed by wind and cold and gradually gives way further north to open tundra and birch scrub. According to the Hudson's Bay Company's naturalists, this mixture of coniferous forest and open ground supported a wonderful abundance of both mammals and birds. One of the most careful observers, indeed a naturalist well ahead of his time, was Samuel Hearne. He spent time in the 1770s around Hudson Bay itself as well as in the forests inland and, unusually for his time, was as much an observer as a collector. He extended his behavioral observations by keeping a broad selection of the local wildlife as pets—from snow buntings and eagles to mink and foxes. He even had pet beavers, which became as tame as dogs.

He also made an epic journey north with Indian companions, as far as the Arctic coast. It's often quite hard in our modern world to appreciate the sheer guts it took to explore North America; the evocative descriptions that help us build up a picture of this world don't always convey the hardships endured by these remarkable people. But Sam Hearne, after many days of hard trekking through bleak terrain, often with no food, leaves us in no doubt as to what it took to see the sights back then: "My feet and legs had swelled considerably. The nails of my toes were bruised to such a degree that several of them fell off. The skin was entirely chafed off from the tops of both my feet, and between every toe. For a whole day I left the prints of my feet in blood almost at every step I took." What he found was worth it. Beaver, mink, and foxes all produced valuable furs, and their numbers were, at times, astounding. Sam Hearne reckoned that within half a mile of Churchill, it was possible to kill forty Arctic foxes in a night. In mid-October, he observed these little foxes moving south along the coast of Hudson Bay to congregate around Churchill, where they fed on the carcasses of whales washed up on the shore. The foxes were left in peace for a month or so, until their winter coats were in prime condition.[25]

Today, Churchill is better known as the polar bear capital of the world. In the autumn, bears gather here as they wait for the bay to ice over, allowing them to hunt their favorite prey, ringed seals, out on the open bay. A tourist industry has grown up around this annual congregation, giving people close encounters with curious bears from the safety of bear-proof tundra buggies, complete with toilet facilities. I'm sure Sam Hearne would have appreciated this luxurious way of exploring the land around the bay; his was a much harder existence and his encounters with bears much closer.

Further south on the bay, where the forests grow thicker and taller, Sam's men killed eleven black bears in one day on a journey between the trading posts of York Factory and Cumberland House. In the January of 1775, his men brought thirteen sled loads of elk meat into Cumberland House. But perhaps the best indication of the abundance of life here is from the official records of the Hudson's Bay Company. Between 1700 and 1720, an average of nineteen thousand beaver skins were brought into the trading post at Fort Albany each year. For a while the average dropped to just five thousand a year, then rose in the middle of the century to twenty-three thousand a year. Another post, York Factory, saw similar averages of skins, though in peak years nearly sixty thousand skins passed through their gates.[26] Lynx, too, were extremely abundant, to judge from records of skins shipped to Europe to keep the fashionable warm. Between 1853 and 1877, over *half a million* lynx skins were sold in London. Such an extraordinary abundance of predators shows just how rich the boreal forests were. But this is not the whole story.

There were wide fluctuations in numbers of skins from year to year. In some years as few as four thousand lynx skins made it to the London marketplace, then a few years later more than seventy-five thousand were sold.[27] Some of this has been put down to variations in demand from Europe, but some undoubtedly reflects the fact that animals weren't abundant everywhere and all the time. There were times on his voyages that Sam Hearne went hungry as well as lame, though it was another of Hudson Bay's part-time naturalists, Peter Fidler, who first spotted the reason behind this. There appeared to be periodic cycles of abundance and scarcity in some of the animals. "There are in some seasons plenty of rabbits [snowshoe hares], this year in particular—some years very few—and what is rather remarkable the rabbits are the most numerous when the cats appear. . . . The cats are only plentiful at certain periods of about every 8 or 10 years and seldom remain in these southern parts in any number for more than two or three years."[28]

Subsequently, ecologists have used the extensive records of the Hudson's Bay Company to investigate this curious phenomenon, and they found that it's not just lynx and snowshoe hare numbers that rise and fall over a ten-year period. So too do the populations of red fox, ruffed grouse, spruce grouse, muskrat, fisher, pine marten, northern goshawk, and great horned owl. Voles and lemmings also show population cycles, though at a different frequency of around four years. At the peak of these cycles, numbers can be extremely impressive: "Every little thicket has a Rabbit in it; they jump out at every 8 or 10 feet; they number not less than 100 to the acre on desirable ground . . . The Rabbits of the Mackenzie River Valley reached their flood height in the winter of 1903–04 . . . in 1907 there seemed not one Rabbit left alive in the country."[29] Rupert's Land was obviously a naturalist's paradise, but you would have to have timed your visit carefully to see it at its most impressive.

All these cycles are linked. Lynx, for example, reached their peak a year after the hares, though coyotes peaked in the same year as the hares and spruce grouse a year earlier. One of the founding fathers of ecology, Charles Elton, made a careful statistical analysis of fur trade records and plotted the exact timing of the cycles for different species, all of which he found to vary slightly. It was assumed that the cycles of predators and prey drove each other, the prey multiplying, allowing the predator to multiply, until increased predator numbers knocked back the prey, causing a subsequent drop in the predators themselves. But many aspects of these dramatic cycles remain unexplained, not least why some populations are cyclic and others aren't, or why some cycle over ten years and others over four. And why, for example, does building a fence around a population of red-backed voles cause their population to grow—even though the fence doesn't exclude predators? As Charles Elton wrote, now more than six decades ago, "the cycle of abundance and scarcity has a rhythm of its own."

But superimposed on these cycles was, inevitably, a familiar pattern of decline, reflecting that seen earlier by the French on the more accessible fur grounds around the St. Lawrence and Great Lakes. This created problems for many of North America's First Nations since by now many Indians were dependent on the fur trade for survival, particularly as intertribal and intercolonial conflicts continued to escalate. Indeed, by the mid-eighteenth century, tensions were building to breaking point. The spark, however, didn't come from the northern fur territories, but from the Ohio Valley, long since claimed by the French as part of New France and another valuable fur territory.

British colonies were now spilling over the Appalachians, laying rival claims to this rich land. The French responded by building forts to defend New France and to launch attacks to push out the British. So the British sent a young and promising Virginia officer, called George Washington, with a letter to demand French withdrawal, which, not surprisingly, failed. However, on his journey, Washington came across a point of land where the Allegheny and Monongahela rivers join to form the Ohio. Here, he thought, was the perfect place to build a British fort to counter the French. The Colonial leaders agreed and began work on Fort Prince George in early 1754, unknowingly laying the first foundations of the city of Pittsburgh. But before it became Pittsburgh, it would become Fort Dusquesne, as it was taken over and completed by the French.

When Washington heard of the surrender of Fort Prince George he led a preemptive strike against French troops in the area, the first battle in what would become the French and Indian War, the war that shaped the future of North America. Washington won that engagement, but was defeated in a counterattack, and so the war, officially declared as such in 1756, swung back and forth, with the French taking the upper hand in the early years. Indian allies were drawn into this conflict from the start, escalating old tribal rivalries. But they were also being played as pawns in an Imperial war for possession of their country. As much as some Indian leaders could see the inevitable results of this, they were powerless to do anything about it. They had been drawn into a dependence from which it was impossible to break free; the best they could hope for was to pick the winning side.

In 1758, the British began to gain the upper hand and consolidated their position by negotiating a peace treaty with Indian Nations of the Ohio Valley, effectively cutting off support for the French. The turning point came with Wolfe's famous scaling of the Heights of Abraham and the fall of Quebec. With the seat of French power in the New World gone, the whole house of cards began to tumble. In 1760, the last two French strongholds, Montreal and Detroit, were taken and all of New France fell to the British.

The new political map was confirmed in 1763, with the Treaty of Paris, which gave all of North America east of the Mississippi (except New Orleans) to the British. In a further bit of land bargaining, Britain gained Florida from Spain, who, in return gained control of Louisiana, a name that then referred to a vast tract of land west of the Mississippi. But, despite the peace in Europe, disruptions to Indian life went on. Many tribes remained hostile to the British, resulting in the Pontiac Rebellion in 1764. After this, peace reigned, but only briefly. Less than a decade later, there was another rebellion; this time the British in America declared war on their own Crown.

But what did the Treaty of Paris mean for the beavers and other furbearers? Since the declaration of Rupert's Land, the Hudson's Bay Company had been engaged in frequent conflicts with the French. The Treaty of Paris removed that threat, but brought in its wake a more serious one in the form of the North West Company, formed in 1779 as a cooperative of Montreal-based fur traders. Economic rivalry between these two fur-trading companies was so intense that it frequently broke out into conflicts as violent as any between England and France. So not much changed for the Indian trappers, and therefore for the beavers. The best policy was still to "trap out and get out." Relations between the two companies got so out of hand that in 1821, pressure from the British Government forced them to merge.

The records of the new company, still called the Hudson's Bay Company, show a continued decline in furs being traded. This was due in part to the disappearance of the furbearers, the aftermath of more than two centuries of overhunting, and in part due to a fall in the demand for furs. The end result of both effects was the same for the Indians. Nations decimated by disease, torn by conflicts often of European origin, and now largely dependent on Europeans and new Americans for many of the staples of life had only one thing left to sell—their land.

Beavers, on the other hand, have regained much of their former territory. The fall in demand for their fur allowed this prolific rodent to quickly regain lost ground and spread back across much of the United States from wilderness areas in the north. In places like Minnesota, they seem to be everywhere again. In the "Land of 10,000 Lakes" (actually nearer 12,000), there seems to be a beaver lodge in almost every one you come across. If you are prepared to give blood, Minnesota style to feed the local mosquitoes, and sit by a pond during a fall dusk, you'll almost certainly see these big rodents going about their business in the half light, repairing their lodge for the coming winter and dragging aspen branches to underwater larders.

But many of the locals don't view these sights with the same enthusiasm that I did. Just as the early explorers described, beavers will dam almost anything wet. Rivers or steams, drainage ditches or culverts, it doesn't matter to a beaver. Near Lake Itasca, one woman I talked to had her home flooded several times by these enthusiastic ecosystem engineers. Further south, they are returning to a much more populous country, where they can be even more of a problem.

In 1984, an Amtrak train derailment in Vermont was blamed on a series of beaver dams that had collapsed and washed out the track. In North Carolina, a survey revealed that three times as many people complained about beavers than saw their benefits in increases in waterfowl and other creatures that live around beaver ponds or in just the simple pleasures of watching them.[30] Yet there *are* people who appreciate the return of the beaver. A couple I once visited in North Carolina had beavers living in a most uninviting looking ditch behind their house. But they had created a feeding platform, lit with low-intensity lights, and trained a camera on the scene that linked back to their computer in the house. The camera took a frame every few minutes, so each morning they could check on the whole night's activity over breakfast. If we still had wild beavers in Britain, that's what I would have done.

Beavers are a keystone species; their demise during the peak of the fur trade helped transform the land. But unlike some of the critical species we've seen so far, beavers are clearly resilient. They quickly recolonize lost ground when given the chance and for this we should be grateful. It doesn't take them long to begin their ecological engineering, and all this restoration work doesn't cost conservation bodies a single cent.

CHAPTER 10

Gathering of Waters

On a late April or early May day in 1541, the conquistador Hernando de Soto found himself gazing across a mighty river—"bigger than the Danube," as one of the chroniclers of his expedition put it. Another chronicler described in more detail the scene that lay before the exhausted army of conquistadors, who had been trekking through the forests and swamps of the Southeast for nearly two years. "The river in this place was a mile and a half in breadth, so that a man standing still could scarcely be discerned from the opposite shore. It was of great depth, of wonderful rapidity, and very turbid, and was always filled with floating trees and timber carried down by the force of the current."[1]

De Soto was not impressed by this river. It was a major obstacle in his search through the Southeast for gold and treasure. He had been with Pizarro during the conquest of the Inca Empire in Peru and through kidnapping and looting had amassed a personal fortune. He had also learned some barbarous techniques for surviving in the wilderness and coaxing information from the natives—skills that he put to good use in North America. Yet two years' worth of maiming, torturing, and brutal executions had failed to reveal a second El Dorado, and now he was facing this enormous obstacle. It took him a month to build enough rafts to ferry his army across and continue his bloody search.

De Soto's expedition, or invasion as some have preferred to call it, is recorded in four accounts, three by people that traveled with him and one based on later interviews. These accounts don't always agree on distances traveled, place names, and the sequence of events, so reconstructing the conquistador's route has been fraught with difficulties, making it a fascinating story in its own right. However, many people now think that when de Soto witnessed the scene described above, he was standing on the Chickasaw Bluffs and looking across the Mississippi River, at a site that is now just north of the city of Memphis, Tennessee.

When I visited this same area more than four and a half centuries later, the river lay a long way from the edge of the bluffs. It was probably different in de Soto's day. The Mississippi was a contrary river, forever picking a new course over its broad floodplain. But, even though today the river has been tamed by dams and levees, at least for most of the time, the bottomland forest on the floodplain below the bluffs is still a magical place for a naturalist, full of standing pools of water, thick with crayfish burrows and darting dragonflies. It's several miles from the base of the bluffs to the river, and when you arrive, it's a little disappointing to find the bank lined with rocks and concrete, a river in a cage. Nevertheless, the Mississippi is still special; it runs through American history and culture like no other river. Linking the dark coniferous forests of the north to the humid swamp forests of the Deep South, it also carried explorers and settlers through the heart of the continent.

De Soto's chronicler was right about this river. It is bigger than the Danube—around 2,300 miles long, compared to the Danube, Europe's longest river, at only 1,780 miles in length. But on these figures the Mississippi is only the fourteenth longest river on the planet and not even the longest river in the United States, being beaten to first place by the Missouri, which runs into the Mississippi at St. Louis. But the way we have named these rivers downplays the scale of this river system. Usually a river is defined and named from its most distant source, and in the case of the Mississippi, that should really be the source of the Missouri on the eastern slopes of the Rockies. By this reckoning, de Soto was actually standing on the banks of the fourth longest river in the world.

This massive river system drains a huge area of land, somewhere between 1.2 and 1.8 million square miles (the Danube's watershed is only around half a million), or about 40 percent of the entire continental United States as well as parts of two Canadian provinces. A drop of rain falling into a stream that tumbles through the rich forests of the western Appalachians and one landing in a stream cascading down the steeper slopes of the Rockies could eventually meet in the maze of channels that form the Mississippi's delta in Louisiana. Without doubt, the Mississippi is the vast aorta at the heart of this continent. So it is somewhat surprising that after de Soto's visit no other Europeans followed up on his discovery for well over a century, a fact remarked on in typical lyrical style by perhaps the most evocative chronicler of the great river, Mark Twain:

After De Soto glimpsed the river, a fraction short of a quarter of a century elapsed, and then Shakespeare was born; lived a trifle more than half a century, then died; and when he had been in his grave considerably more than half a century, the SECOND white man saw the Mississippi. In our day we don't allow a hundred and thirty years to elapse between glimpses of a marvel. If somebody should discover a creek in the county next to the one that the North Pole is in, Europe and America would start fifteen costly expeditions thither: one to explore the creek, and the other fourteen to hunt for each other.[2]

The next Europeans to see this river were Frenchmen. In 1673, Father Marquette, a Jesuit priest, and explorer Louis Jolliet headed up a small expedition to chart the course of a huge river that they had heard about from Indians visiting French fur traders in New France. No one yet knew the scale of the interior of North America, and all the European nations still hoped for some convenient passage between the Atlantic and Pacific. If the great river flowed westward, maybe this was it. So the Comte de Frontenac, at the time vice-regent to Louis XIV, saw Jolliet and Marquette's expedition as the first step in establishing a French empire stretching from the Atlantic to the Pacific.

But their journey began on another enormous freshwater system that, by Jolliet and Marquette's time, was already reasonably well known — the Great Lakes. By this period, the French were well, if thinly, established across vast tracts of what is now southern Canada and the northern United States. In the century since Cartier had first pushed up the St. Lawrence and gazed over the endless forests around Mont Réal, French priests and coureurs had traveled the maze of lakes and rivers with Indian guides and outlined the main features of the Great Lakes.

Like the Mississippi River, the Great Lakes are another of North America's world beaters. Splashed across the northeastern United States and southeastern Canada like a giant Rorschach ink blot, these lakes contain about one fifth of the surface freshwater of the entire planet, one of the largest freshwater systems on Earth. Put another way, if the Great Lakes were tipped out across the continental United States, they would cover the whole area with nearly ten feet of water. Landlocked Michigan has a longer coastline than any coastal state except Alaska. Together, the Great Lakes and the Mississippi river system form the focus of this chapter, exploring the extraordinary abundance and diversity of freshwater life that greeted the first explorers and sustained the local Indians.

Around the southern Great Lakes, the climate was mild enough for the Indians to be farmers, though they also hunted the forests and fished the waters of the lakes. But further north, many nations had come to rely almost completely on an aquatic harvest—of wild rice from infinite marshes or fish from apparently endless shoals.[3] As Jesuit missionaries and fur traders paddled their way along the rivers and coastlines, they began to learn from the Indians just how abundant fish were. Antoine Cadillac was commander of the outpost at Michilimackinac, a fort and trading post overlooking the Straits of Mackinac, which connect Lakes Huron and Michigan. In 1695, he recorded: "The great abundance of fish and the convenience of the place for fishing have caused the Indians to make a fixed settlement in those parts. It is a daily manna which never fails."[4] He saw nets filled with "as many as a hundred whitefish and further observed that a hundred different kinds of fish abound at this part of the lake." And it wasn't just numbers. As on the Atlantic coast, the fish here were often extremely large as well. A Jesuit father called Gabriel Sagard left us a good summary from 1623: "For indeed in this Fresh-water Sea there are sturgeon, Assihendos [whitefish], trout and pike of such monstrous size that nowhere else are they to be found bigger, and it is the same with many other species of fish that are unknown to us here [in France]."[5]

As Cadillac suggested, there is a rich diversity of fish here, and Sagard has outlined some of the key species. To his list, we might add American eels, Atlantic salmon, blue pike, and lake herring. All were extremely abundant, and all were harvested by the Indians, though each needed its own techniques.

Whitefish are primitive members of the salmon family. The smaller species are often called ciscoes, and one in particular, also known as the lake herring, existed in almost unbelievable numbers. However, for commercial fishermen descending on the Great Lakes in the nineteenth century, the most important whitefish was the biggest—the lake whitefish, which in those days often reached twenty pounds. The immense shoals were described by one such fisherman as being like "bright clouds moving rapidly through the water." The Indians often caught them when they moved into rivers to spawn, fishing them out of even the most powerful rapids with a hoop net, in spectacular fashion, as Father Dablon noted in the *Jesuit Relation* of 1669: "Dexterity and strength are needed for this sort of fishing: one must stand upright in a bark canoe, and there, amongst the whirlpools, with muscles tense, thrust deep into the water a rod, at the end of which is fastened a net made in the form of a pocket, into which the fish are made to enter . . . and when they have been made to enter the net, raise them with a sudden strong pull into the canoe."[6]

Techniques for harvesting eels were even more elaborate, and kept the Baron Lahontan amused on a 1688 tour of the upper St. Lawrence:

> The Inhabitants that are setled between Quebec and fifteen Leagues higher, diverted me very agreeably with the fishing of eels. At low water they stretch out hurdles to the lowest Water-Mark; and that space of ground being then dry by the retreat of the Water, is covered over, and shut up by the Hurdles. Between the Hurdles they place at certain distances Instruments called Ruches, from the resemblance they bear to a Bee-hive; besides Baskets and little Nets belag'd upon a Pole, which they call Bouteux, and Bouts de Quievres. Then they let all stand in this fashion for three months in the Spring, and two in the Autumn. Now as often as the Tide comes in, the Eels, looking out for shallow places, and making towards the Shoar, croud in among the Hurdles, which hinder 'em afterwards to retire with the Ebb-water; upon that they are forced to bury themselves in the abovementioned Ingines, which are sometimes so overcram'd that they break. When 'tis low water, the Inhabitants take out these Eels, which are certainly the biggest, and longest in the World.[7]

Each of the Great Lakes has its own individual character and therefore its own unique suite of species. Lake Ontario, the easternmost lake, connects the whole system to the St. Lawrence and so had a distinct flavor of the east coast. It had its own landlocked population of harbor seals and an enormous population of Atlantic salmon. These fish ascended the rivers flowing into the lake to spawn, just like their coastal kin, but their offspring never left the lake. Forgoing a rich marine diet, these fish may not have reached such great sizes as the coastal ones, but even so there are descriptions of fish weighing nearly fifty pounds.

The sheer numbers of salmon can best be gauged by accounts of their spawning runs into Lake Ontario's rivers. The superintendent of fisheries for Upper Canada witnessed some amazing spectacles: "I have seen them from 1812 to 1815, swarming the rivers so thickly, that they were thrown out with a shovel, and even with the hand."[8] A report from Wilmot's Creek in Ontario, where the inhabitants often hauled out a thousand salmon a night, conjures up an even more bizarre sight: "They were so plentiful . . . that men slew them with clubs and pitchforks—women seined them with their flannel petticoats."[9] These are not techniques you see used much among salmon fishermen today.

The largest and most impressive fish of the Great Lakes is the lake sturgeon. One of eight or nine (depending on which taxonomy is followed)[10] sturgeon species in North America, these monsters can reach eight feet in length, though nowhere near as long as the mighty Pacific white sturgeon, at twenty feet. Like all the fish mentioned so far, sturgeon existed in great abundance in the early days of exploration but were important to the local Indians as more than just food.

They feature in the Menominee creation story, and as shoals gathered near the shore each spring, prior to running up river to spawn, they were welcomed back with ceremonial dances and songs. The Menominee knew the spawning sites, where these huge fish crowded into the shallows, thrashing the water in their breeding frenzy. Many observers have commented on lake sturgeon rolling at the surface or even leaping into the air at such times. I've seen spawning aggregations of smaller specimens, but I can only imagine what these historic spawning runs must have been like.

Lake sturgeon weren't at first valued as a commercial harvest by Europeans. On the contrary, they were seen as nuisance fish. Since they are specialists at feeding from the lake bottom, they were accused of hoovering up the eggs of more valuable species. As one Lake Erie fisherman, back in 1894, put it: "A sturgeon is like a hog in a hen roost. They go around and suck up all the spawn there is."[11] Some of that spawn would have belonged to lake trout, a far more valuable fish than sturgeon in the early days. Unlike whitefish and lake herring, lake trout shun big shoals; they are solitary predators. They belong to a small, but elite, group of salmonids sometimes called char to distinguish them from other trout and salmon.

Char prefer to live in cold, oxygen-rich water, the most extreme being the arctic char, which has been recorded feeding in seawater below the freezing point of freshwater. True to their kind, lake trout in the Great Lakes favor colder, deeper water, and in the coldest and deepest of the lakes, Lake Superior, there is even a unique form, called the siscowet, which lives at depths of over a thousand feet. Their solitary habits made lake trout much harder to harvest in big numbers, except in the fall when they moved into shallower water or up into rivers to spawn. Jesuit missionaries living with Great Lakes

Indians in the seventeenth century often described enormous lake trout of fifty to sixty pounds.

So these were the Great Lakes that Jolliet and Marquette knew back in the seventeenth century as they prepared for their epic voyage to find and explore the Mississippi. They left Michilimackinac in the May of 1673 and paddled their canoes south along the abundant shores of Lake Michigan and into Green Bay. Here they spent time in the Menominee Nation and learned more of the natural resources on offer from the Great Lakes. They also relied on the Indians to guide them through vast marshes as they ascended the Fox River from Green Bay: "The way is so cut up by marshes and little lakes that it is easy to go astray, especially as the river is so covered in wild oats that one can hardly discover the channel."[12]

Today, the wild oats described by the two French explorers are more widely known as wild rice, though in some respects Marquette and Jolliet's description is more accurate. Wild rice is more closely related to cereal grasses than it is to true rice. Since it grows in dense stands and reaches heights of thirteen feet, it's not surprising that Marquette and Jolliet needed some expert local help to navigate through the rice marshes. Later explorers estimated some of these "fields" to be five miles long and two miles wide, while at the top of the Fox River "as far as the eye can reach, there is a stretch of wild-rice swamp."[13] This is the heart of wild rice country, and both Menominee and Ojibwa Indians depended heavily on this natural harvest. The tribal name *Menominee* derives from an Indian word, *manomin,* for wild rice, and the Menominee were frequently referred to as the "wild rice people."

As the grain ripened in autumn, entire communities headed for the marshes. It was a man's job to pole his canoe into his family's section of the marsh, taking two women to do the actual harvesting. Each used two long poles to bend the rice stalks over the canoe and knock off the grains. It didn't take long to fill a canoe in these dense stands, and the precious cargo was then returned to the lake shore for processing. The grains had to be dried, either under the sun or over a low fire, then pounded and winnowed before they could be stored. If a family wanted to leave grain in an area they knew they would return to, they buried it in a dugout canoe, on a south facing hillside. The slope meant that rainwater would quickly run off, and the sun kept the hillside dry. Stored like this, the grain could last for two years.

Together, fish and wild grain supported large populations of Indians around the Great Lakes, and many Europeans commented on both the bounty and beauty of this place. French fur trader Pierre-Esprit Radisson had overwintered in Green Bay twenty years before Marquette and Jolliet paddled through and reported: "I can assure you I likes noe country as I have that wherein we wintered: for whatever a man could desire was to be had in great plenty; viz staggs, fishes in abundance and all sort of meat."[14] Father Marquette would echo Radisson's thoughts as he and Jolliet entered the Fox River: "We left this bay to enter the river that discharges into it; it is very beautiful at its mouth, and flows gently. It is full of bustards, ducks, teal and other birds, attracted thither by the wild oats, of which they are very fond."

But Marquette and Jolliet couldn't stay in this paradise. They had an unknown river to find and chart, and a mission to extend French presence in the New World. Traveling up the Fox River, they entered Lake Winnebago, pioneering a water route that would later be used by many other explorers heading into the unknown center of the continent.

A century after Jolliet and Marquette passed through here, an English explorer called Jonathon Carver traveled this way. A lot had changed in that century. New France now belonged to the English, and though the Crown wanted the settlers to consolidate their position in the East, the colonials were naturally keen to explore their new possessions. Carver passed through Lake Winnebago, flying a Union Jack from the stern of his canoe and displaying a calumet—a peace pipe—at the front. He traveled later in the year than Marquette and Jolliet, and so witnessed the fall migration of waterfowl. "The Lake itself abounds with fish, and in the fall of the year, with geese, ducks and teal. The latter, which resort to it in great numbers, are remarkably good and extremely fat and they are much better flavoured than those that are found near the sea, as they acquire their excessive fatness by feeding on the wild rice which grows so plentifully in these parts."[15]

Having exchanged the customary presents with the Winnebago Indians, Carver's expedition headed to the point where the Fox flows into the lake, to continue their journey upriver, as Jolliet and Marquette had done one hundred years before. In October, the upper Fox River was spectacular: "This river is the greatest resort for wild fowl of every kind that I met with in the whole course of my travels; frequently the sun would be obscured by them for some minutes together. Deer and bears are very numerous in these parts and a great many beavers and other furs are taken on the streams that empty themselves into this river."[16] Jolliet and Marquette traveled this route in summer and so missed the waterfowl spectacles. They were eventually guided to the head of the Fox River where they had to carry their canoes the short distance across a portage into the drainage of the Wisconsin River. From here, the Indians told them, they could float downstream and find the huge river that the Ojibwa called Mesipi—a "Gathering of Waters."

Traveling down the Wisconsin River, they passed through yet more vast marshes and lakes filled with life. But the character of the land bordering the river was changing. The forest frequently gave way to open meadows, or "prairies" as they are called in French. Indeed, the name "Wisconsin" reputedly comes from a local Indian word meaning "grassy place." "On the banks one sees fertile land, diversified with woods, prairies and hills. . . . We saw there . . . many deer, and a large number of cattle."[17] These cattle, boeuf in the original French, were actually bison, though they are still better known by a corruption of the French word for cattle—"buffalo." The French explorers were gaining a foretaste of the vast grasslands that lay to the west of the Mississippi.

Father Marquette had learned what he could of the journey ahead from the Indians around the Great Lakes. Even before the arrival of the French fur traders, there was an extensive Indian trade network, linked by the maze of lakes and waterways, so the Menominee had been able to describe in some detail what the explorers would find. In fact, they had tried to dissuade them for making the journey, explaining that "the great river was very dangerous, when one does not know the difficult places; that it was full of horrible monsters, which devoured men and canoes together; that there was a demon, who was heard from a great distance, who barred the way, and swallowed up all who ventured to approach him."[18] But Marquette was undeterred and entered the Mississippi on June 17 "with a joy that I cannot express."

It didn't take them long to find the Menominees' monsters. "From time to time we came upon monstrous fish, one of which struck our canoe with such violence that I thought it was a great tree, about to break the canoe to pieces." This giant river was, appropriately enough, filled with giant fish. Father Marquette had probably just had a close encounter with a catfish. Mark Twain picks up the story: "I have seen a Mississippi catfish that was more than 6 feet long and weighed 25 pounds; and if Marquette's fish was the fellow to that one, he had a fair right to think the river's roaring demon was come."[19]

Huge catfish were often reported from the Mississippi in the nineteenth century, and these weren't just fishermen's tales. The chairman of the Missouri Fish Commission, a Dr. J. G. W. Steedman, bought a pair of blue catfish from a fish market in 1879 that weighed 150 and 144 pounds. They had been caught in the Mississippi near St. Louis. The river still yields impressive catfish, and specimens over the one-hundred-pound mark have been turning up ever more frequently in the last few years, though still not the size of Steedman's pair. But catfish aren't the only monsters in the river.

There's a wonderful old black-and-white photo that I first saw published in David Etnier and Wayne Starnes's book, *The Fishes of Tennessee*.[20] It shows an exhausted-looking man sitting behind a makeshift trestle table on which is lying a truly monstrous alligator gar. This unbelievable beast was pulled out of Moon Lake, Mississippi, sometime around 1910—and probably not without considerable effort. Based on the photo, these two fish biologists estimate it to have been ten feet long, making the alligator gar the biggest fish in North America after the white sturgeon. Alligator gars are by far the largest of the seven gar species, all of them prehistoric-looking fish confined to North and Central America.

The alligator gar is found mainly in the southeastern United States, extending up the Mississippi Valley and into the lower reaches of the Missouri and Ohio Rivers. In the early nineteenth century, botanist, ichthyologist, and prolific writer Constantine Rafinesque recorded in his book *Ichthyologia Ohiensis:* "This is a formidable fish living in the Mississippi, principally in the lower parts, also in Lake Pontchartrain, the Mobile, Red River, &c. It has been seen sometimes in the lower parts of the Ohio. It reaches the length of eight to twelve feet, and preys upon all other fishes, even Gars and Alligators. Mr. John D. Clifford told me that he saw one of them fight with an alligator five feet long and succeed in devouring him, after cutting him in two in its powerful jaws."[21]

Because of its size and ferocious appearance the alligator gar has often been accused of attacking people as well. It's hard to pick truth from fiction and bravado in most of these accounts, and just as hard to find any real evidence of unprovoked attacks. However, big gar certainly have big, sharp teeth and can undoubtedly cause nasty injuries if they are carelessly handled by fishermen, so perhaps these were the "devouring demons" of which Jolliet and Marquette were warned. The intrepid travelers, though, didn't describe anything like an alligator gar. But they did catch other Mississippi giants. "When we cast our nets into the water we caught sturgeon, and a very extraordinary kind of fish. It resembles the trout, with this difference, that its mouth is larger. Near its nose, which is smaller, as are also the eyes, is a large bone shaped like a woman's busk, three fingers wide and a cubit long, at the end of which is a disk as wide as one's hand. This frequently caused it to fall backward when it leaps out of the water."[22] At this point in their journey, Jolliet and Marquette could have been catching any one of three species of sturgeon. Lake sturgeons extend into the Mississippi river system, where they are joined by two other species of this ancient family, the shovelnose and the pallid sturgeon. The "trout-like" fish, though, was nothing of the sort. It belongs to another ancient family of which but two species still survive—the paddlefishes. American paddlefishes occur widely in the Mississippi system, but their only living relative is found in China, a strange disjunct distribution that reflects their ancient heritage. American paddlefishes can reach seven feet in length, perhaps more in precolonial times and in those days also swam in the Great Lakes.

Marquette and Jolliet continued down the Mississippi, which they found to be heading stubbornly southward, until they reached the confluence with the Arkansas River. Here they were made welcome in a village of Acansa Indians, from whom the river and, later, the state were named. The Acansa told them that the river continued to flow south for several more days before emptying into the ocean. This convinced the explorers that the Mississippi was not the great route westward they had hoped for. And, worse news, the Indians told them that there were already Europeans around the river mouth. Father Marquette realized these must be Spanish, so to avoid running into a potentially hostile force, they decided to head back up the river to New France. They returned to the Great Lakes by a different route, following the Illinois River to a portage near present day Chicago, the same route chosen by the next Frenchman to paddle down the Mississippi Valley, a decade later.

Rene-Robert Cavelier, Sieur de la Salle, trained as a Jesuit, but left the order and went to Canada in 1667. He became a fur trader and explorer, traveling extensively throughout the Great Lakes. He lived with several groups of Indians, learned their languages and customs and left us with yet more descriptions of the abundance of fish, fowl, and fur around the waterways of the north. And he was nothing if not ambitious. Bored with the fur trade, he received approval from Louis XIV to explore the Great Lakes and travel further down the Mississippi than Marquette and Jolliet had reached. By claiming the whole area for France, he could press a claim on the northern Spanish territories, but not for him exploration from Indian birchbark or dugout canoes.

He set about building a large ship, the *Griffon*, on Lake Erie, just above Niagara Falls. To the watching Indians the billowing sails seemed to drive the vessel across the water by magic, with no effort from paddle or pole—a symbol of the power of the god of the Black Robes and of the people who served him. But for the moment, this new power was tempered by the natural forces of the New World. The *Griffon* was lost in a vicious storm that swept across the Great Lakes. Nor would it have been much good for the Mississippi expedition. La Salle had already explored the Illinois River in the wake of Jolliet and Marquette and knew exactly what to expect: "It runs through vast marshes, winding so much that, although the current is rather strong, they sometimes found after paddling a whole day that they had not advanced two leagues in a straight line; as far as the eye could see they saw only marshes covered with reeds and alders, and for more than forty leagues of their course, they would have found no place to encamp but for some mounds of frozen ground upon which they rested and lighted their fire."[23]

In the winter of 1681, La Salle set off in earnest, to follow the great river all the way to its mouth. As he descended the Illinois and then the Mississippi, he described similar scenes to those witnessed by Jolliet and Marquette; large herds of deer and buffalo, great flocks of waterfowl, and abundant beavers and otters. In the middle of March, 1682, the expedition left the Acansa village that Marquette and Jolliet had visited and passed the point where the earlier explorers had turned back. They were entering a very different landscape, where new animals began to make their appearance. "The first day we began to see and kill alligators, which are numerous, and from fifteen to twenty feet long."[24] As they moved south, the journals make further references to large numbers of very big alligators, which must have made exploring the flooded forests particularly exciting. On April 18, as they camped on a tiny island, a few of the intrepid Frenchmen climbed the trees and saw what they thought was open water in the distance. "La Salle went with two men to see if it was the sea. On his return, La Salle said he had found brackish water. There were a great many land crabs burrowing in the ground."[25]

It isn't clear from this what kinds of crabs La Salle saw, but, presuming that he made his observations during daylight, they were most likely fiddlers, made conspicuous by the antics of the males as they wave a brightly colored, enlarged claw in ritual combat with nearby rivals. Several species of these little crabs live around the Gulf coast, and probably existed in truly enormous numbers before their coastal habitats were invaded by sun-seeking humans. In more remote locations, I've seen a few places where fiddler crabs carpet the mud in a continuous layer, which parts with a strange rattling rustle as you walk through them. But if he had explored at night, or at dawn, he might well have seen equally large numbers of blue or red land crabs.

These are much bigger than fiddler crabs, reaching eight inches across. They rarely move far from their burrows in the tangled, mosquito-infested undergrowth of the back swamps, except during high spring tides in summer, when they march en masse to the sea to release their eggs. Both kinds of land crabs still reach impressive densities in some places around the Caribbean, and their spawning migrations are a real spectacle.

Coastal developments in the more populous United States have reduced their numbers here considerably, although I have seen fair numbers marching across U.S. 1A, the road that runs along the barrier islands offshore from Fort Pierce, Florida. But Sherry Reed, who lives in Fort Pierce and works on these crabs at the Smithsonian lab there, has seen so many crabs on some nights that the road had to be closed. She even has a few that have taken up residence in her lawn. As successful as these suburban crabs are, the Gulf and Florida coasts would have had even larger populations when La Salle was exploring the area. Fueled by the high productivity of swamps and estuarine mudflats, land crabs have the potential to reach truly astronomical numbers.

La Salle was getting close to his goal now. The river began to break into confusing channels as it picked its way across the rich delta wetlands. As the explorers tried to find a route through the maze, they came across large numbers of herons: "We camped opposite an island on the left. On this island we killed a great many white crow, red heron, and others that had duck feet, long beaks and short necks, and on their backs, down like silk. They perch in trees."[26] Again, it is not entirely clear which species these are. Red herons could be roseate spoonbills, beautiful in their pink and red breeding plumage at this time of the year, or perhaps the reddish egret which is always engaging to watch as it races back and forth at the waters edge in manic pursuit of those small crabs. White crows might be snowy egrets, pure white herons that, while not looking a lot like crows are, at least, about the right size and make harsh calls.

The last species is a mystery. In part the description could be that of an anhinga, which does have webbed feet, a long bill and downlike plumage on its back. But it also has a very long neck. It's a curious bird, which hunts underwater where it uses its long neck to great effect for spear fishing. It can fold its neck back on itself in a tight S curve, and then lunge its long, sharp bill forward to stab fish. It's then a wonderful site watching a successful anhinga try to slide the impaled fish off its bill and down its throat without dropping it in the water. On land, they often rest with the neck folded, which could make the bird look short-necked, but if La Salle was describing a specimen he had shot, and looked closely enough to spot its "duck feet," he can hardly have failed to notice its long neck.

La Salle gave us our first glimpse of the rich wetlands of the delta, but it is frustratingly incomplete. There must have been huge populations of herons and egrets, brown pelicans and spoonbills, all feeding in their own individual ways in the teeming waters. It's still possible to get a sense of La Salle's delta in some places. The Cypress Island Preserve near Lafayette is home to thousands of nesting herons and spoonbills, and some of the barrier islands just off the coast are covered in nesting brown pelicans. But the backdrop to the pelicans and their reptilian chicks these days is one of large tankers and oil platforms. Three hundred years ago, there was just a handful of Frenchmen, struggling to erect a large wooden cross bearing the arms of Louis XIV. In a short ceremony on one of these islands, La Salle claimed the entire area for France and named it for his king—Louisiana.

Mission accomplished, he set off back upriver. Arriving in what is now northern Louisiana and northern Mississippi he camped near towns of the Taensa, Coroa, and Natchez Indians, as he had on the way down. And he quickly realized that these people were very different to the hunters and fishers of the Great Lakes with whom he had spent a great deal of time.

They lived in well-made houses in large towns. Their societies were divided into nobles and commoners, and some of the nobles lived in elaborate ceremonial complexes centered on large earthen mounds. These societies were the direct cultural descendants of a civilization that thrived along the Mississippi long before even de Soto arrived. Mound building here dates back five thousand years—one thousand years before the first Giza pyramid was constructed in Egypt. Indeed, the large bird effigy mound at Poverty Point, built around three thousand years ago, has a similar base area to the Great Pyramid at Giza.[27]

But mound building reached its greatest development with the emergence of the "Mississippian culture" around AD 900 in cities like Cahokia, near the confluence of the Missouri, Illinois, and Mississippi rivers. At its peak between AD 1000 and 1200, Cahokia had as big a population, or perhaps bigger, than Paris or London of the same period.

Cahokia was one of the first true "Mississippian" centers to emerge and grew to be the most impressive, but this sophisticated, mound-building civilization spread widely along the Mississippi and its tributaries and throughout the Southeast. The rapid expansion of population that accompanied the rise of the Mississippian culture was supported by crops grown in the fertile soils of the rivers' floodplains. Each mound city, with its priests and nobles, must have been served by great numbers of farms that would have transformed the surrounding countryside.

But the cities were also built on the natural abundance of the rivers. Fish and shellfish were plentiful, and, just as importantly, timber for building these cities grew thickly on the bottomlands. The stretch of floodplain south of the Illinois River is called the American Bottom, an especially rich, eighty-mile swathe of forest fertilized by silt from three great rivers—the Illinois, Missouri, and Mississippi. Here, deer, bears, and game birds were particularly abundant. It is no coincidence that Cahokia and the Mississippian civilization flowered in this area. This was America's Nile.

But after flourishing for three hundred years, Cahokia began to decline a full three centuries before de Soto trekked through the area. The Natchez, Taensa, and others visited by La Salle might have been descendants of the tribes that made up the Mississippian culture, but La Salle saw nothing to rival Cahokia. What had happened?

There are plenty of theories, and the truth is probably a combination of several of these. There is some evidence that the really big centers, like Cahokia, needed so much wood for building that the bottomlands were denuded. They had to go further and further for a supply of wood, until it eventually became both impractical and uneconomical. That this can become a critical problem has already been illustrated—by European settlers on the east coast as their numbers swelled in the eighteenth century, causing the likes of Ben Franklin to complain about how hard it was to get timber from what used to be an endless forest.

Likewise, game would also have been severely depleted by the growing numbers of people. A large population with elaborate divisions of labor, of nobles and artisans, depends on the production of a surplus of food by the farmers, fishers and hunters, so the disappearance of natural resources would have created real problems for these people.

Another more recent suggestion is that the Cahokians grew to be so numerous that they outstripped their local water supply, which was just a small creek. You can see downtown St. Louis, on the other side of the Mississippi, from the top of the largest mound at Cahokia, but it's a long walk to Ol' Man River from here, especially carrying enough water for the multitudes. So it's possible that the citizens of Cahokia diverted a larger creek into theirs to improve the water supply closer to the town. If so, then it's likely that, especially with so much land cleared of forest, floods would have become a major problem, carrying away much of their maize crop in some years.[28]

Ahead of de Soto, the arrival of European diseases wouldn't have helped any remnants of the Mississippian culture. It was hard enough for the more modest townships of the eastern forests to maintain their traditional lifestyles after being decimated by disease. It would have been impossible to maintain a complex civilization. There's also a suggestion that for some of those remnant Mississippian tribes close to the patches of prairies, the arrival of Spanish horses made a nomadic life in pursuit of buffalo a more attractive option.

So, due to a combination of some or all of these factors, the great Mississippian centers had vanished before the Europeans arrived. La Salle saw only a pale reflection of these societies when he visited the Natchez Indians in Mississippi on his return from the delta. Even so the Grand Village was an impressive sight, as he was escorted to the top of a large flat topped mound, crowned with a ceremonial building, and ushered into the presence of the Great Sun, the hereditary chief. Natchez society was highly evolved and divided into different classes, with the Great Sun at its head—not perhaps as grand as La Salle's own Sun King in his palace at Versailles but still a glimpse into the past glories of the Mississippian civilization.

If the Mississippians had overexploited their local resources, nature had certainly bounced back by the time Marquette, Jolliet, La Salle, and others explored the area in the seventeenth and eighteenth centuries. Game abounded and the riverine forests, often impenetrable, also grew magnificent trees. On returning to Canada, La Salle summarized his findings on the Mississippi:

> The banks are almost uninhabitable, on account of the spring floods. The woods are chiefly poplar, the country one of canes and briars and of trees torn up by the roots; but a league or two from the river is the most beautiful country in the world, prairies, open woods of mulberry trees, vines and fruits that we are not acquainted with.
> ... there is a large number of buffaloes or bears, large wolves, stags, sibolas [buffalo], hinds, and roe deer in abundance.[29]

There was also another abundant resource that many tribes along the Mississippi and its tributaries made use of—freshwater mussels. They existed in such huge numbers, that they formed extensive banks, or shoals. The town of Muscle Shoals in Alabama, though misspelled, was named after the great banks of mussels along the stretch of the Tennessee River on which it now stands. Further north, it was possible to walk across the upper Ohio River on the backs of mussels; back then, in the early 1800s, the average depth was only one foot, thanks to thickly growing beds of mussels.[30] Tribes living along the major rivers made good use of this resource, judging by the enormous numbers of shells found in waste heaps.

These "middens" form large mounds sometimes containing millions of shells accumulated over the centuries. Many were around three hundred yards long, perhaps thirty to forty yards wide, and often reached heights of over ten yards; and some stretched for nearly half a mile. There are hundreds of such middens scattered up and down the river, and the vast number of shells in these ancient mounds has suggested to some that the local Indians were overexploiting the mussel beds. Certainly, evidence for shellfish consumption disappears around 1000 BC, which, though it's is hardly an unequivocal proof, may have been due to the increasing scarcity of mussels. However, mussel use began again around AD 900, during a cultural transformation stimulated by the arrival of maize from Central America. At this time, Indians found a new use for mussels as they began making shell-tempered pottery.

The start of maize agriculture probably effected mussels in other ways as well. This period is marked in the archaeological record by a decline in elm pollen. Elm was a major constituent of the bottomland forests, which were also the best places to farm, so the elm decline is seen as marking widespread forest clearances as maize agriculture spread.[31] Increased silt running into the rivers from cleared land would probably have had an impact on the most sensitive species of mussels.

A careful analysis of the different layers of shells in the middens can yield valuable clues to the historic environments in the area and this does seem to show that one group of mussels (*Epioblasma spp.*) declined in relative abundance as Archaic cultures gave way to the later Woodland and Mississippian cultures. These species are all sensitive to too much sediment in the water, and although it is far too early to be sure, one possibility is that increasing silt in the water was caused by deforestation along the river banks. It might be that these mussels record the growing exploitation of resources as Mississippian cultures arose along the major rivers.[32]

Either through direct exploitation or through environmental changes, the Indians along the Mississippi and its tributaries may at times have had a large impact on the great mussel beds. Yet even so, there were still vast numbers when the first biologists arrived to document them. And, just as incredible as their numbers, there was also an extraordinary variety of species. Constantine Rafinesque alerted the world to this biological treasure chest in an 1820 paper, which described eighty species living in the Ohio alone. Across North America, there are more than three hundred species, the vast majority of them occurring in the Mississippi drainage. This is about a third of all species worldwide, making the United States the mussel capital of the world. The river systems of the Southeast contain the greatest diversity, but this extraordinary natural spectacle is largely unsung and uncelebrated, except by a handful of mussel enthusiasts.

One such is Paul Johnson, of the research wing of the Tennessee Aquarium, based in an out-of-the-way lab on the borders of Tennessee and Georgia. Here, he has row upon row of gravel trays, flushed with clean, clear water from a spring bubbling up a few hundred yards away. And in these trays are representatives of some of the rarest animals on earth. He pulled out one specimen and handed it to me, explaining that it was the only specimen of that particular mussel that he knew of. In such a poignant moment, several thoughts hit me at once. First—don't drop it. Second—this should rank alongside seeing the last Carolina parakeet or passenger pigeon. But it doesn't, Paul lamented. It's hard to get people as worked up about mussels as about wolves or eagles, bison or black-footed ferrets. And that's a pity—on several counts.

First, mussels have great names; the world is a far better place for being inhabited by the turgid blossom, the finerayed pigtoe, and the snuffbox. Second, mussels exhibit some great biology. Freshwater mussels have a risky breeding strategy. Their larvae must live as parasites on the gills of fish; the problem is how can a sedentary mussel attach its larvae to a fast moving fish? The answer is to persuade the fish to come to the mussel.

Some species of mussels have fleshy outgrowths of the mantle that can be extruded beyond the edge of the shell. These protuberances bear an uncanny resemblance to different kinds of aquatic insects, an impression made all the more convincing when the mussel waggles its lure in a fish-tempting fashion.

The mussel's larvae, called "glochidia," are contained in packets within the lure, which explodes in the face of any fish that tries to grab the "insect."

A few mussels have gone even further. They package their larvae into a pair of structures called conglutinates, which are attached to long lines. As a mussel lets out its line, the packages drift downstream, for perhaps a yard or so. The conglutinates at the end of this line look very much like a pair of silvery minnows, and when they catch the current, they twist and turn around each other, looking so much like spawning fish that they would fool any fisherman. Any fish fooled by this display, however, will get a face full of glochidia for its trouble.

Some mussels only parasitize one or two kinds of fish, while others are less fussy. And these latter mussels, with more catholic tastes, have plenty of choice. The Southeast's fish fauna is just as varied as its mussels. There are some three hundred species of fish in the Tennessee and Cumberland rivers, making these the richest rivers outside the tropics.

One of the most diverse groups of fish, and one targeted by many species of mussels, is the darters. Many of these are stunningly beautiful fish, more than a match for any tropical species. They are all relatively small fish, prompting biologist Stephen Forbes, in 1880, to describe them as not so much dwarfed as concentrated fishes—a description that has never been bettered.[33] With the help of modern genetic techniques, new species are being discovered all the time, including five in the last few years by scientists from the Illinois Natural History Survey.

Overall, the aquatic fauna of the Southeast is one of the richest in the world, only bettered by a few hotspots in Southeast Asia.[34] Half the world's species of crayfish live in these rivers and streams, and around 10 percent of the world's salamander species are hidden under rocks and logs nearby. Taking all these aquatic creatures into account, the Tennessee River system contains more species than any other river in the United States.[35] But, as Paul Johnson is quick to point out, much of this diversity is now severely threatened. As far as he and other freshwater biologists are concerned, the Southeast is witnessing one of the greatest extinctions on the planet, but because it concerns obscure creatures, it is virtually unknown.

Muscle Shoals has lost nearly half of the seventy mussel species that occurred there historically, a story repeated in rivers throughout the United States. Ten percent of the mussel species of the Mississippi Basin have become extinct since 1900. We have seen the last of the Tennessee riffleshell, the Scioto pigtoe and Sampson's pearlymussel, to name but a few. Half of all the crayfish species are threatened with a similar fate, but the greatest extinction crisis is amongst tiny freshwater snails.

Obscure even by mussel and crayfish standards, very little is known about these creatures. They are hard to identify, and new species are still being found, while at the same time others are disappearing. It's even hard to know which species are really extinct. For some time, the tiny tulotoma snail of the Coosa and Alabama river systems was presumed extinct until new populations were found in 1990.[36] But there are twenty-six other species from this same river system that don't appear to have been so lucky.

Yet all of these creatures matter. Mussel shoals provided both food and shelter for many other creatures. Some fish, like the freshwater drum, feed almost exclusively on mussels and muskrat lodges often have piles of empty, though perfect, mussel shells around them. It's clear that mussels are an important part of their diet, even if it is less clear how muskrats manage to open the shells without damaging them. Crayfish too are on the menu for many more familiar animals, from raccoons to screech owls.

One reason for this biodiversity crisis is that rivers form one long, interconnected system, winding through a lot of territory. It's very hard to conserve just one bit, since it is an integral part of a much bigger whole. This problem is exemplified by one of the biggest problems facing mussels, crayfish, darters, and the like in the twentieth century—the widespread building of dams.

The greatest variety of mussels are found in clear stretches of water flowing over sand and gravel, the natural state of even some of the biggest rivers of the Southeast. But behind a dam, water flow slows and fine silt settles out. A few kinds of mussels prefer this habitat and have benefited from dam building, but a far bigger number of species disappear. Muscle Shoals' mussel shoals were drowned behind the Wilson, Wheeler, and Pickwick Landing dams. The once-shallow rapids now lie beneath ten feet of water, which is why half the mussel species have disappeared. And this might yet prove to be an underestimate.

Mussels can live for a long time, perhaps up to one hundred years. If conditions change, and, for example, their host fish vanish, they won't be able to reproduce, but they might survive through several generations of freshwater biologists, giving a false impression of their status. Yet these are doomed populations, the fateful day when they are added to the role call of extinctions merely postponed by their longevity.

Just occasionally, one of these obscure aquatic creatures catches the attention of the media and surfaces into public awareness. One such was the snail darter, back in the late 1970s. David Etnier discovered this little darter (nowhere near the prettiest of its kind, it has to be said) in the lower Little Tennessee River in 1973, the same year in which the Endangered Species Act (ESA) was signed into effect. And this obscure little fish almost killed the ESA at birth.

The snail darter may have been more abundant and widespread in the past, but in 1973, it looked to be confined to a short stretch of river, the very stretch, in fact, that would soon be drowned behind the Tellico Dam, due to be completed in 1979. The snail darter was listed under the ESA in 1975, which, in theory, made it illegal to finish the project, even though the dam was almost ready to be closed. Not surprisingly, those behind the dam, the Tennessee Valley Authority (TVA), were not impressed and took the case to court. This obscure little fish found itself at the center of a series of cases that ended up at the Supreme Court, which eventually decided in favor of the darter and the ESA. At that point, it really did look like the ESA was the landmark environmental legislation that it was trumpeted to be when Nixon signed it.

But the TVA wasn't finished yet. Senator Howard Baker from Tennessee and a supporter of the TVA's project was drawn into the battle and the debate on the Senate floor really got going. As it did, it became increasingly clear that many in the Senate saw the ESA as merely designed to protect iconic creatures. Senator Jake Garn of Utah commented that "I would be in favor of undertaking tremendous costs to preserve the bald eagle, and other major species, but that kind of effort is out of proportion to the value of the woundfin minnow, or the snail darter, or the lousewort or the waterbug or many others we are attempting to protect.[37] Senator John Chafee from Rhode Island concurred when he said "We who voted for the Endangered Species Act with the honest intentions of protecting such glories of nature as the wolf, the eagle, and other treasures have found that extremists with wholly different motives are using this noble act for meanly obstructive ends."[38]

Ecology depends as much on the obscure and boring as it does on the large and charismatic species—in fact usually far more—but the TVA's campaign held the snail darter up to ridicule. How could a drab little fish hold up the completion of a project that had already cost over $100 million? The snail darter had certainly been thrust into the spotlight; as David Etnier recalled, "snail darter types" had become synonymous with "ultra-liberal environmental activists." That such an insignificant creature could threaten large scale economic development began to worry some people. Perhaps the ESA was too good a piece of legislation.

If, as many assumed, common sense eventually prevailed and the dam was completed, then the ESA would have been rendered toothless in its first real test. Better a weakened Act survive than a strong one die. In 1978, the Act was amended to allow a committee to meet to discuss possible exemptions to the Act in cases like the Tellico Dam. The so-called God Committee would, in some cases, have the power to extinguish certain species. But the God Committee granted the snail darter life. They came out against an exemption for the Tellico Dam, though only in part because of the snail darter. They also argued that the economic projections of the TVA were flawed and the dam was not worth completing.

Baker was undeterred and continued his campaign: "Mr President, the awful beast is back. The Tennessee snail darter, the bane of my existence, the nemesis of my golden years, the bold perverter of the Endangered Species Act is back." The darter also became the bane of the Carter administration, which was split on the issue. Other, apparently more important, issues such as the Panama Canal Treaty were pressing on Jimmy Carter. He needed Senate support on such problems, so, on September 25, 1979, he expediently signed an exemption for the Tellico Dam.

But nature had the last laugh. The obscure little snail darter refused to lie down and die. David Etnier found another population in South Chickamauga Creek in 1980 and others in the mainstream of the Tennessee River in 1981 and 1982. Also, specimens from the original threatened population were transplanted to other streams, and some of these seem to have been successful. In 1984, the snail darter was down-listed from endangered to threatened—a successful conclusion to this fishy tale.

So, was all the fuss and heated debate, legislation and lobbying, pointless? Not at all. It served as a clear illustration of the problems of conserving the less charismatic species that occupy our planet—some of which may well be of greater ecological importance than more endearing creatures. And in this sense, the snail darter's story—and the ESA—was a dismal failure.

Before the era of dam building, there were other problems for freshwater creatures. One that faced mussels in particular came from Germany, in the form of John F. Boepple. In 1891, he arrived in Muscatine, Iowa, and set up the first pearl button factory, making buttons from the shells of freshwater mussels. It was so successful that the industry quickly expanded. By 1916, the industry was worth $12.5 million and employed twenty thousand people. The harvest was unregulated, and the numbers dredged from the river astonishing; in some places, nearly two thousand pounds a day were being hauled up. Yet, such was the abundance of mussels that some biologists don't think their numbers were seriously affected by this harvest. The pearl button industry ran its course and eventually collapsed in the face of the plastics revolution. The last factory, again in Muscatine, closed in 1967. But well before pearl buttons became fashionable, mussels had already had to face another crisis.

In 1857, some lucky soul found a pearl in a freshwater mussel in Notch Brook, a small stream flowing past Paterson, New Jersey. It was sold at Tiffany's for $2,500, enough to spark a pearl rush. People descended on Notch Brook in their droves and in two years removed every single mussel. In doing so, they made around $115,000, and as news spread that such treasures were hidden in the mussel beds, no river was safe. At the height of the pearl craze in about 1890, rivers from Vermont to Florida and west to the Rockies were being plundered in an unbelievably wasteful practice.[39]

Like the pearl button industry, pearl harvesting has now declined, but the pearl industry isn't through with North America's mussels just yet. Since the 1950s, rivers from Wisconsin to Alabama have supplied most of the shells needed by the cultured pearl industry. Fragments of these shells are inserted into marine oysters to stimulate the growth of high-quality pearls. Unfortunately for the mussels in the rivers of the Southeast, their particular shells have just the right hardness to produce the best nuclei for such pearls. So great is this new threat, that some states—Ohio, for example—have banned commercial collecting. Yet so lucrative is the business, that such regulations are often ignored; in one recent case, poachers were caught with two tons of living mussels stolen from just one bed.

But the most recent and perhaps the greatest threat to mussels, indeed to the whole Mississippi basin, doesn't come from people, but from another mussel, an invader from the Caspian region on the borders of Europe and Asia—the zebra mussel. Zebra mussels do extremely well in the Mississippi, in places carpeting the bottom, outgrowing and overgrowing native mussels. In some surveys, ten thousand young zebra mussels were found attached to each native mussel. The natives are both starved and smothered by the invaders.

Zebra mussels followed pretty much the same route into the Mississippi as La Salle. Their port of entry into the United States was Detroit on Lake Michigan, in 1986, carried in ballast water of commercial ships. From there, they spread rapidly throughout the Great Lakes and used Chicago's canal system to get into the Illinois River. By 1991, they were in the upper Mississippi River from where thousands of miles of rivers lay open to them. By 1993, scientists were recording unbelievable densities of fifty thousand mussels per square yard. There has been a recent respite in the form of an unexplained mass die-off in the summer of 2001, though in a few places, like Lake Pepin near Winona, Minnesota, big populations somehow survived and will no doubt serve as a base from which a new assault on the river can be launched.[40]

Their effect on the Great Lakes has already been devastating. Like all mussels, the zebras feed by filtering the water for phytoplankton. But they exist is such unimaginable numbers that they have almost cleared the water of these microscopic pastures, at least in the shallower areas of the lakes, and other creatures, which used to graze them, have simply starved. One of these is a little crustacean called *Diporeia*.

Diporeia are amphipods, small shrimplike creatures that crawl through the bottom mud, feeding on diatoms that sink down from the surface. They used to exist in countless numbers, making up 70 percent of the biomass of the lake bottom, and were therefore a key food for whitefish and young lake trout among others. Now deprived of the rain of algae from above, *Diporeia* numbers have collapsed, and in consequence the fish that depended on them are also suffering.

Paradoxically, the situation has been made worse by environmental improvements. Following the passage of the Clean Water Act, the last few decades have seen a reduction in the runoff of agricultural fertilizers into the lake. This is further reducing the productivity of the algae in surface waters of the lakes.[41]

The combined effect of mussels and pollution controls has effectively shifted the site of productivity in the lakes from the midwater to the bottom, which has fundamentally altered their ecology.[42] This is the exact opposite of the situation that we've created in the Chesapeake, where destruction of the vast oyster beds has shifted productivity from the benthic zone to the midwater. We've created a similar shift in the basic ecology of the northwest Atlantic, so oceanic, coastal, and freshwater systems have all been affected at very fundamental levels. These examples show that human influence hasn't just made a few species rarer, it has created deep-seated changes in ecology which will be much more difficult to reverse.

Nor have the changes finished. Zebra mussels are still spreading, and now they've been joined by another even more insidious invader—the quagga mussel, from the Dneiper River in the Ukraine. It too arrived with commercial shipping in Lake Michigan probably in the late 1980s and now blankets much of the lake bottom. It can tolerate colder water and more varied substrates than the zebra mussel, so can invade the deeper parts of the lake. This gives it the potential to reach even higher populations than the zebra mussel, which is a cause of great concern for Great Lakes ecologists, many of whom think that quaggas will have a much greater impact on the lakes than even the zebra mussel. And these are just two of 139 foreigners that have made some kind of impact on the Great Lakes.[43] But not all these invaders are accidental introductions. Some are part of a deliberate policy to manage fisheries in the lakes.

The abundant fish resources of the Great Lakes were hardly likely to escape the attention of commercial fishermen. Fisheries here started out as family affairs, but quickly spiraled out of control. In the words of historian Margaret Bogue, "between 1850 and 1893, commercial fishing on the Great Lakes evolved into a wasteful, exploitative, profit-oriented and market-driven industry"[44]—none of which was good news for the fish.

Throughout this period and into the twentieth century, four main species were targeted: lake whitefish, lake trout, lake sturgeon, and lake herring. Whitefish were most highly prized, and soon their numbers began to drop. So fishermen turned their attention to the next species in line. The scenario was not difficult to predict, as Samuel Wilmot, superintendent of fish culture for Canada did in 1894: "Formerly Lake Erie was called 'Whitefish Lake' by the fishermen and Fish Dealers Everywhere: This was on account of the vast quantities of whitefish that were at one time taken in that Lake;—the Whitefish are now largely fished out, and Erie is called by the Fishdealers the 'Herring Lake'—with the same overfishing of Herring, and with no close season for protection, it will soon lose its character as a 'Herring Lake' and become a Blue Pickerel Lake."[45] It did. Lake Herring stocks collapsed in 1925. Blue pike, not a true pike but a close relative of the walleye (possibly even just a distinct form of this species) were, as Wilmot predicted, next in line. Between 1950 and 1957, blue pike catches fluctuated between 2 and 26 million pounds a year. In 1959, the fishery collapsed. No one has seen a blue pike for certain in the last few decades, despite intensive searches. It is now presumed extinct.

Following the collapse of the lake herrings, which were important food for other lake fish as well as for people, rainbow smelt were introduced into Lake Erie, in 1935. Filling the niche left vacant by the herring, their populations exploded. By 1959, 7 million pounds were landed by fishermen, and they had become a new staple for the lakes' predatory fish.[46] Alewives have also found their way into the Great Lakes, either accidentally or deliberately, and now also swim in vast shoals.

But, despite a new source of food, the Great Lakes predators continued to decline. The demand for fish during World War I had a devastating effect, backed by a campaign from the U.S. Food Administration, with the slogan: "Save the products of the Land. Eat more fish—they feed themselves." Many species were struggling to recover from this when, in the 1930s, the sea lamprey struck. There were possibly some sea lampreys, at least in Lake Ontario, as far back as the 1830s, but a century later the population exploded. It's not entirely clear why, but the usual explanation is that enlargement and improvement to the Welland Ship Canal gave much easier access from the sea for these parasitic fishes. But, however they got here, they had a huge effect on the lakes' fishes, particularly species like the lake trout. From the 1920s through to the 1950s, lake trout fisheries collapsed in each of the Great Lakes, due to the combined assaults of fishermen and sea lampreys.

Meanwhile, rainbow smelt and alewives were doing rather too well in the absence of predators. The alewives, in particular, were proving a real problem. Great numbers died off after spawning in the autumn, and, as stinking heaps of carcasses piled up on lake shores, local people began to complain. The Great Lakes needed their predators back. After much expensive research a chemical is now available that kills lampreys but not other fish and that produced a good measure of control over the sea lamprey problem. So it's just a question of putting the lake trout back in the lake, isn't it?

Lake trout restoration began in Lake Superior in the 1950s, in the 1960s in Lake Michigan, in the 1970s in Huron and Ontario, and in the 1980s in Lake Erie, but only in Lake Superior is there any real evidence of a self-sustaining population developing from these introductions.[47] That could be in part because lake trout now have some competition from other salmonids that don't belong here.

Some sporadic introductions were carried out as early as the late 1800s, but beginning in the mid-1960s, both Americans and Canadians began introducing nonnative salmon in earnest to the Great Lakes—brown trout from Europe and rainbow trout, chinook salmon, coho salmon, kokanee, and others

from the Pacific rivers of North America. There were two official motives behind this: to control the immense populations of alewives and smelt and to
develop new sports fisheries.

The new salmon did extremely well, and the sport fishery boomed, so
much so that maintenance of this lucrative fishery became far more important
than controlling nuisance populations of alewives. In 1993, stocking levels of
chinook salmon and lake trout were reduced, to prevent a crash in the population of alewives—which is exactly what they were supposed to do. The mo-
tive behind these management changes was largely to preserve the chinook
fishery.[48] The lack of any real will to try and return the Great Lakes to their
original natives is clearly illustrated by the sheer numbers of Pacific salmon
released over the years—some 745 million fish between 1966 and 1998; that's
an average of sixty-one thousand fish released *every day* for thirty-three years.[49]
And neither Canadian nor American fisheries agencies bothered to carry out
any studies on the potential effects of such a major ecological experiment.

The ecological implications may be very serious. With such extreme stocking levels, the numbers of salmonids in the Great Lakes may be higher now
than when La Salle, Jolliet, and Marquette described these rich waters. But
most of these introduced fish are generalist predators, eating any fish small
enough to fit into their mouths, so they not only eat the introduced smelts
and alewives, but also native species like sculpins and yellow perch. Further,
some of these Pacific salmon have developed breeding populations. So the
struggling lake trout faces competition both for food and for spawning sites.

On Lake Ontario, there are major efforts to reintroduce the native Atlantic
salmon, but into a lake already heavily stocked with Pacific salmonids. One,
the steelhead trout, is a close ecological equivalent to the Atlantic salmon, and
research suggests that steelheads compete with Atlantic salmon, particularly
on the spawning grounds. Some fisheries scientists and ecologists are now
calling for a halt in nonnative fish stocking, but the sport fishery is so lucrative, it's hard to see such a thing happening.[50]

The restoration of the Great Lakes to their state when the missionaries
and coureurs of France first saw them is, of course, an impossible dream. The
lakes are now surrounded by huge urban areas, they are no longer fished solely
by subsistence communities of Indians, and, most critical of all, a number of
species simply don't exist any more. At least four kinds of ciscoes—blackfin,
deepwater, longjaw, and shortnose—have joined the blue pike in extinction,
and the combined effect of overfishing, pollution and alien invaders has com-

pletely, perhaps irrevocably, altered the whole ecosystem. Each might be surmountable on its own, but together the picture is much bleaker.

For example, after passage of the Clean Water Act of 1972, the water quality began to improve, allowing lake whitefish and lake trout populations to build up again. In places this resurgence was dramatic. In eastern Lake Ontario whitefish regained their historic abundance by the early 1990s, but began to decline again, as zebra mussels spread throughout the lake. Lake whitefish have been forced to shift their feeding from highly nutritious *Diporeia,* which formerly made up to three-quarters of their diet, to zebra mussels, to judge from the stomach contents of fish examined in a 1999 survey. Often, the guts of these fish contain a lot of mussel shell, which has no nutritional value whatsoever.

So what does the next decade hold for the Great Lakes? In truth, it's impossible to predict. Despite legislation, new invaders arrive all the time. In the last few years tube-nosed and round gobies have arrived from the Caspian region and are multiplying at phenomenal rates. Changes continue to happen so fast across the Great Lakes that managers barely have time to react to one before another begins.

The history of the Mississippi has followed a slightly different course. Although La Salle mapped out the river down to its mouth in 1682, it was some considerable time before the source of this mighty river was known. And long before the source was finally discovered, La Salle's Louisiana would change hands a few times. After the French and Indian War, the defeated French ceded Louisiana to Spain—rather that than let the victorious English have it. But after the English became Americans, and looked to follow their manifest destiny westward, the Spanish grew nervous. They still claimed large tracts of North America in the West, so they secretly gave Louisiana back to the French, hoping they would act as a buffer between the expanding United States and New Spain.

Meanwhile, England and France were again at war—one of the great constants of European history. Once more in danger of losing its American possession to the hated English and in financial crisis over the costs of the war, the Emperor Napoleon found a willing buyer for Louisiana in the United States. So, on April 30, 1803, the United States doubled its size, all for a mere $15 million—one of the best real estate bargains of all time. One reason that Thomas Jefferson jumped at the French offer was that he realized the value of the Mississippi and its major tributaries as a transportation network. But he needed to know exactly where these rivers would transport his countrymen. In 1804, he dispatched Lewis and Clark to follow the Missouri back to its source and to document the resources of the new land. A year later, Zebulon Pike was dispatched to find the source of the Mississippi.

Pike's expedition moved north late in the season and into what today is called the Headwaters Region, a glorious part of North America, especially in the fall. There are extensive tracts of red and white pines interspersed with dazzling glades of maples, an eye-aching contrast to the dark conifer forests at this time of the year. And everywhere there are beaver ponds. Sit quietly by one at dusk and soon there are tell-tale ripples distorting the perfect reflections of the pines and maples. Within a short time the whole family is out, checking their pool thoroughly before getting on with their night's work.

As we've already seen, beavers are now doing very well in Minnesota—too well according to many locals. Their industrious damming of drainage ditches is not at all appreciated, but it's nothing to what Zebulon Pike found: "10th Oct. Thursday : Came to large islands and strong water early in the morning . . . passed a cluster of islands, more than 20 in the course of four miles; these I called Beaver islands, from the immense sign of those animals, for they have dams on every island and roads from them every two or three rods."[51]

The Mississippi headwaters twist and turn as if deliberately trying to throw an exhausted explorer off the trail. Eventually, Pike reached a point where the Mississippi emerged from a large lake (today's Leech Lake) and convinced himself that this was the source of the river. He was wrong, and it would be nearly three more decades before anyone of European descent knew where North America's greatest river began its life. The local Chippewa Indians could have told them, but no one bothered to ask until Henry Schoolcraft came along in 1832. When he asked this question of a Chippewa by the name of Ozawindib, the Indian simply produced a map and pointed to a lake called *Omashkoozo-zaaga'igan*—Elk Lake.

After some negotiation, Ozawindib agreed to take Schoolcraft there, and in repayment, Schoolcraft officially renamed the lake "Itasca." It might sound Chippewa, but it's as European as you can get, derived from Latin, from *veritas caput*—the "true head. In reality, French coureurs had already visited this lake in the past, but they would have had to look hard to spot the Mississippi. It began as a barely discernible overflow through dense marshes, hardly a noble birth for so mighty a river. So, in the 1930s, the source was moved and improved. The surrounding swamp was drained, a new, more obvious channel was dug and a small stone dam erected at the edge of the lake, so the Mississippi could begin by tumbling over a miniature waterfall. Millions of bare feet must have waded across this manicured stream in the belief that it is the source nature intended. But the minor readjustments to the river at Itasca are nothing in comparison to the way it has been reshaped over the rest of its journey to the sea.

The Mississippi and its tributaries were the original interstates. For generations, they were used by Indians, who had developed an elaborate trade network that spanned the continent by the time de Soto arrived. La Salle described Indians on the Mississippi with shell ornaments that came from the east coast. A soft stone, called catlinite, quarried in Minnesota and used for making the bowls of calumets, was exported extensively along the waterways. Scarlet macaws from Mexico turn up in large numbers in excavations of old Pueblo sites in Arizona and New Mexico. Northern Indians traded excess furs for the products of the agricultural south that they couldn't grow themselves, and by La Salle's time, Indians on the Mississippi were already growing European fruit trees, brought in from either the Atlantic colonies or, more likely, the Spanish settlements in northern Mexico. But the new Americans saw the Mississippi system as transporting much more than just birchbark and dugout canoes.

The problem was that the Mississippi was a willful river, frequently changing course, often full of dangerous snags and sand bars, interspersed with shallow areas of impassable rapids and all made worse during periodic drops in water level. As Mark Twain pointed out, the river that he traveled as a steamboat captain was not the same one that La Salle descended. "At Hard Times, La., the river is two miles west of the region it used to occupy. As a result, the original SITE of that settlement is not now in Louisiana at all, but on the other side of the river, in the State of Mississippi. NEARLY THE WHOLE OF THAT ONE THOUSAND THREE HUNDRED MILES OF OLD MISSISSIPPI RIVER WHICH LA SALLE FLOATED DOWN IN HIS CANOES, TWO HUNDRED YEARS AGO, IS GOOD SOLID DRY GROUND NOW. The river lies to the right of it, in places, and to the left of it in other places."[52] Such an unpredictable nature is of no help to the advance of civilization. In 1824, Congress approved funds for the removal of snags and so began the taming of the continent's greatest river. Shortly afterward, the Army Corps of Engineers began building wing dams along stretches of the river where rock was easily available.

These are structures that extend from each bank toward the center of the river. By restricting the river's flow to the center, they increase the current here, which scours the bottom of silt and keeps a navigation channel open. This also stops the river from meandering, firmly fixing it in place. But the increasing scale of riverboats soon outstripped this first stage of improvement.

In 1907, Congress appropriated more funds for the six-foot channel project, to create a minimum depth of six feet along the whole navigable stretch of river. This meant thousands more wing dams, shore protection, additional dredging, and the construction of two new locks. But even before the six-foot channel was completed, it was abandoned in favor of a nine-foot project. This immense engineering project was again the responsibility of the Army Corps of Engineers and required the construction of dozens of dams and locks that would eventually transform the nature of the river completely.

No ecological considerations were given to any of these projects, yet ecological changes inevitably followed in the wake of all these phases in the taming of the river, though not all of them detrimental, at least initially. Silt settling out behind wing dams created good conditions for some river invertebrates, while others, like crayfish, found the rocky foundations of the dams much to their liking. This in turn boosted populations of fish such as smallmouth bass and walleye and turned the wing dams into world class fishing piers. But construction of the closing dams for the nine-foot project flooded large areas of bottomland forest. The trees here thrive on a seasonal inundation that brings fertile silt from the river, but permanent flooding is too much of a good thing and kills many species. On the other hand, the new pools behind the dams created large areas of habitat for waterfowl. Not only that, but aquatic plants sprang up in profusion.

In summer, the pools' edges were colored red with smartweed, a marsh plant that produces vast quantities of seeds that are relished by waterfowl. In Weaver Bottoms, Minnesota, tall Phragmites reeds covered vast areas, recalling descriptions from La Salle and Marquette. This sea of reeds was a magnet for waterfowl. But both Phragmites and smartweed, like the bottomland trees, need to have their feet dry occasionally. Since the purpose of the dams was to maintain a constant water level, this explosion of marsh vegetation didn't last. By the mid-1960s, Weaver Bottoms had become an open expanse of water, no longer attractive to ducks or duck hunters.[53] Likewise, the swathes of smartweed have long since disappeared. And the dams have also brought changes to the forested islands and bottomlands that weren't flooded. The lock and dam system, with its carefully regulated water levels, means that these forests are no longer flooded at all, which had caused a shift in species composition; mile after mile is now dominated by silver maple.

In the lower Mississippi, the problem isn't so much maintaining channel depth, but of stopping the river meandering around its floodplain. It's no good building an expensive riverside facility only to find the river has other ideas about where it wants to be. And the floodplain is very wide in the Deep South, which means that many river towns and cities are at risk from floods. The answer has been to contain the river behind thousands of miles of levees. But the Mississippi is a powerful force, not so easily tamed. Floods are still frequent and occasionally disastrous.

Between May and September of 1993, states from North Dakota to Illinois were inundated by the waters of the Mississippi, the Missouri, and their tributaries as thousands of levees failed. Fifty people died, ten commercial airports were flooded, and all railroad traffic in the Midwest was halted. The cost ran to $15 *billion*.[54] In August 2005, Hurricane Katrina swept ashore over New Orleans and left a scene of horrendous devastation. But most of the damage was done by the river, not the hurricane. In its natural state, the delta region was a place where land and water merged, just as La Salle described. Flood surges were absorbed in a myriad channels and in broad tracts of bottomland forest. But as cities like New Orleans grew, natural vegetation was cleared and the river was contained and constrained behind barriers. Katrina destroyed those barriers and released the river, flooding four fifths of New Orleans to depths of nearly thirty feet.

But if the river was a serious threat to populations along the river, so too growing numbers of people were a threat to the river. Lying alongside this major transport route, many of the Mississippi's towns grew quickly into cities, then into large conurbations. As the population grew, so too, inevitably, did effluent from these cities. The Mississippi doubled as the continent's largest sewer. The problem of treating sewage from so many people seemed so insurmountable that even as late as the 1970s, a number of politicians thought that the United States couldn't afford to build treatment plants for all these cities and, at the same time, pursue the cold war. Since the cold war was clearly more important, there were serious suggestions to condemn the Mississippi to becoming—in the words of river biologist Calvin Fremling—"Uncle Sam's colon." During this time, the river below the Twin Cities, one of the biggest contributors of sewage, was devoid of all fish as well as most invertebrates. Luckily sense, and sewage treatment, prevailed and gradually water quality began to improve. As it did, fish and invertebrates began to return.

To get a sense of the potential productivity of the river, take a walk along its banks somewhere like Winona, Minnesota, or La Crosse, Wisconsin. If you pick the right summer's evening you may end up wading knee deep through mayflies. In summer, billions of larvae of *Hexagenia* mayflies emerge from the soft mud on the bottom, where they have lived for several years, and rise to the surface. Here they molt into winged forms that smother the surrounding bushes and trees. Mayflies are unique among insects in that this first winged form (a subimago to entomologists or a dun to fly fishermen) must molt again to reach true adulthood. Now the swarm can take to the air, males using their enlarged eyes to seek out females which they grab in midflight with elongated front legs. It's a living blizzard and almost claustrophobic to walk through a really dense swarm.

Unfortunately, the mayflies are drawn from their dance by the bright lights of cities and pile up in thick, confused masses, sometimes feet thick on roads and sidewalks. Although roads by the river sometimes have to be closed, these mind-boggling swarms are in reality a good thing. Mayflies are sensitive indicators of water quality, and the return of these summer swarms to the upper Mississippi is a testament to the improvements in water quality.

In a similar fashion, *Hexagenia* swarms have returned to Lake Erie—with a vengeance. The swarms were so big they caused power outages by shorting out transformers in Detroit in 1995 and Toledo in 1996.[55] They had disappeared from Lake Erie in 1953, at the same time that the blue pike vanished, and were virtually absent from the lake for four decades. Their dramatic reappearance began in the early 1990s and may well be part of the reason behind resurgences of sturgeon, lake whitefish, lake herring, and silver chub that began around the same time.[56] In the summer of 1999, a vast cloud of mayflies was picked up over eastern Lake Erie by the Doppler weather radar of a local television station, which revealed the swarm to be ten to fifteen miles long and two to three miles wide.

The return of the mayflies is an event that should be celebrated by all along the banks of the Mississippi or the shores of the Great Lakes, but the natural history of both these vast freshwater systems has been so altered that La Salle or Marquette would hardly recognize it. Overfishing, pollution, and dam building have taken a great toll, but at least these are under our control—to some extent. And the reappearance of the *Hexagenia* swarms on both river and lakes shows that we can make a difference. But the most worrying problem facing these two great aquatic systems is the deliberate and accidental introduction of alien species. Some of these creatures are now well beyond our control, causing cascades of ecological changes. We were lucky with sea lampreys—a technological fix has lessened, if not removed, the problem. But what of zebra and quagga mussels, round and tube-nosed gobies? And what has just jumped ship, as yet unseen and unknown, from some exotic port?

Freshwater species are disappearing from North America as fast as species from tropical rainforests—123 species gone since 1900. Freshwater snails, fish, amphibians, and mussels are dying out five times faster than land species.[57] But this is a largely unseen crisis. Wading through swarms of mayflies shows that there is a lot we can do, but solving this particular environmental crisis will be an uphill slog until people put the same value on a pink pearly mucket or a tulotoma snail as they do on a black-footed ferret or a bald eagle.

CHAPTER 11

A *Sea of* Islands

I've been making wildlife films for twenty-five years and sometimes that means living in stifling rain forests; feeding the local fauna on blood, sweat, and tears; or camping on tropical seabird islands, infested with cockroaches that insist on sharing your sleeping bag. And sometimes, luckily, it doesn't. One of the latter was a month, back in the mid-1980s, spent filming the creatures that live in Sargasso weed, a floating seaweed that spends its entire life drifting on the currents of the Atlantic, making a great circular journey around the center of the ocean on the Atlantic gyre. One of the best places to intercept its migration is off the coast of Belize, and to do so meant living on the tiny island of South Water Cay, around fifteen miles off shore from Dangriga. And I mean tiny. You can walk around the whole island in just a couple of minutes. It's nothing more than a low sandy spit, barely rising from the azure water, covered in coconut palms that shelter a couple of small huts belonging to a fisherman and his mother—a picture postcard idyllic tropical Paradise. Sometimes this job is just Hell, but someone has to do it!

The daily chore was to take our little boat off shore, jump into the water and gather handfuls of Sargasso weed to pick off the crabs, prawns, toadfish, and other denizens of this floating jungle. And all the time, beneath us, was the Belize Barrier Reef. In one of his less widely known books, *The Structure and Distribution of Coral Reefs,* Charles Darwin described it as "the most remarkable reef in the West Indies." But Mr. Darwin was underselling it. This is the second largest barrier reef on the planet, after Australia's Great Barrier Reef, and it's wonderfully diverse. Three hundred species of fish dart among the branching stagshorn coral or shelter in rocky crevices, out of a total of 2,500 for the whole of the Caribbean. Definitely a most remarkable reef, though in the past the whole marine world of the Caribbean was just as remarkable, with populations of fish, reptiles, birds, and mammals that defy belief, and it's these creatures that form the focus in this, the first of two chapters on the region.

The Belize Barrier Reef, like all the reefs around the Caribbean and indeed around the world, is now in serious trouble. Most of the big fish have gone, and the coral itself is dying. They are afflicted by a litany of diseases—white pox, white band disease, black band disease, and coral wasting disease, most of which have only appeared in the last few decades.[1] One third of all the coral around Florida has died since 1996, and right across the Caribbean, reefs have suffered 40 percent damage since 1998. Now climate change is only going to make matters worse. But these recent disasters are just the end of a long line of problems for the Caribbean Sea. Successive waves of Indians, island-hopping along the Caribbean's island arcs, soon began to reduce the populations of some species. But the pace of change accelerated dramatically after 1492, when Cristobal Colon ran into the Bahamas.

On the evening of October 11, 1492, Colon, better known now as Columbus, leaning on the rail of the *Santa Maria*, thought he saw a light on the horizon. A few hours later the keen eyes of Rodrigo de Triana, lookout on the *Pinta*, spotted the low outlines of an island. A small flotilla of three ships, the *Niña*, *Pinta* and *Santa Maria*, had left Spain thirty-three days before and were now poised to change the history of the world. But not just yet—it was getting too dark. The next morning, a landing party went ashore and set foot on a new world. Columbus called this island San Salvador, the starting point for Europe's American adventures. But exactly which of the many Bahamian islands he was on is still much debated. Watlings and Cat islands are among the favorites, and the modern inhabitants of Watlings Island were so convinced of their claim that they changed the island's name to San Salvador. They can't have been too pleased when the National Geographic Society suggested another island altogether—Samana Cay.

Of course, Columbus was not the first European to stand on these shores, wherever they were. Many Vikings had preceded him to the New World, and Columbus himself would not stand on the mainland until his third trip, six years later. But this encounter was different. The Vikings' knowledge was lost along with their colonies, victims of the deteriorating climate at the start of the second millennium. But now Europe, and Spain in particular, was ready for exploration, expansion, and colonization. The Spanish had just managed to evict the last of the Moors from southern Spain, after more than eight centuries of trying, and energy spent fighting the Moors would soon be poured into exploring the two vast continents that lay a few days sailing from the beach where Columbus stood with his men.

On San Salvador, Columbus also met Taino Indians, sometimes also called Lucayo, who were part of a large network of Arawak-speaking people that he would meet on the much bigger islands he was being told about further west. He left the Bahamas, looking for an island that some of the Taino had called *Cuba*. Luckily that name has stuck, so we know exactly where he was. But Columbus didn't. Cuba was so large, and full of tales of grand kings, that he thought he must have reached the mainland of China.

Leaving Cuba, Columbus sailed to the south and east where he found a large island that he called La Isla Española, the Spanish Isle, later known as Hispaniola, and later still as Haiti and the Dominican Republic. He was very impressed: "This island and all the others are very fertile to a limitless degree, and this island is extremely so. . . . Its lands are high, and there are in it very many sierras and very lofty mountains, beyond comparison with the island of Teneriffe . . . all are accessible and filled with trees of a thousand kinds and tall, and they seem to touch the sky."[2] He gave similar glowing descriptions of almost all his landfalls around the Caribbean. One valley on La Isla Española so impressed him, he called it Valle del Paraíso—the Valley of Paradise.

Three further trips from Spain, with more ships and more people, began to outline the main features of the Caribbean; the tangled mangrove shores of the Central American coast, forming the western boundary of the sea and the Yucatan Peninsula pointing toward the large, east-west island chain of the Greater Antilles: Cuba, Hispaniola, and Puerto Rico, together with Jamaica lying to the south of Cuba. To the north of this axis lies the Gulf of Mexico, cradled in a great circular sweep of coast north of Yucatan, all the way round to Florida.

On his second voyage, Columbus landed on the Lesser Antilles, a chain of much smaller islands sweeping south from the Virgin Islands to the coast of South America and marking the eastern boundary of the Caribbean. This last arc of islands was divided by later explorers into the windward and leeward islands. The winds here generally blow from southerly directions toward the north, so the southern part of the chain became the Windwards, and the northern, the Leewards. Included, ecologically, in this complex network of marine and island habitats is the southern tip of the Florida peninsula, pointing from mainland United States to within a hairsbreadth of Cuba, and the smear of Bahamian islands and shallow reefs, running above the Greater Antilles. In all there are seven thousand islands and cays in the Caribbean, a sea of islands as much as of water.

The Antilles were named for Antilia, a mysterious island paradise. At one time or another, virtually everywhere along the eastern seaboard of North America was sold to the folks back home as Paradise, but South Florida and the Caribbean islands are still marketed like this today. And there's some truth in this view. Ecologists have identified the Caribbean as a biodiversity hotspot, a place where evolution just seems to be showing off.

It's one of twenty-five such hotspots, listed in 2000 by Conservation International, based on work by ecologist Norman Myers. In 2005, another nine regions joined this elite group. These are areas that are both biologically rich and threatened—places where scarce conservation dollars might be most effectively spent. To qualify, an area has to have at least 1,500 species of plants found nowhere else and have lost around 70 percent of its original habitat. The Caribbean more than qualifies on the first criterion, with 6,500 of its endemic plants confined to single islands. Sadly, it also more than qualifies on the grounds of habitat loss.

Diverse plants foster diverse communities of animals. The Caribbean has six hundred species of birds, of which about one quarter are found nowhere else. Nearly half of the ninety mammal species are endemics as are an extraordinary 94 percent of its reptiles. More than a third of freshwater fishes, fifty-six of 160 species, are also uniquely Caribbean. That's a head full of figures, but the take-home message is simple: the Caribbean is a very special place.

Some of this exuberant life is big and showy and reminiscent of a Caribbean carnival, but to my mind the real Caribbean gems are at the opposite end of the scale, world beaters because of their *small* size. The world's smallest hummingbird, the bee hummingbird, is found in Cuba and the world's smallest lizard, a tiny gecko, is found in the Dominican Republic. The world's smallest snake, a thread snake called *Leptotyphlops bilineata,* is found only on Barbados, St. Lucia, and Martinique, but very rarely. The biggest ever found was a gigantic four and a half inches long and could have crawled through a pencil if the lead was removed. And there's a tree frog on Cuba that grows to just less than half an inch. For me, it's these perfectly formed miniatures that represent the real wonder of nature.

I doubt Columbus spotted any of these tiny creatures, but the staggering variety of the Caribbean was certainly obvious to him, even on his first voyage. "There are birds of many kinds and fruits in great diversity.[3] In addition, there are trees of a thousand kinds . . . and they all give off marvellous fragrance."[4]

The world beneath the keel of the *Santa Maria* was just as rich. "Here the fishes are so unlike ours that it is amazing; there are some like dorados, of the brightest colors in the world . . . colored in a thousand ways."[5] He saw more evidence of this diversity during his second voyage, when he also began to really appreciate the marine abundance. On an island near Santo Domingo, on Hispaniola, he saw creatures he called "sea wolves" and ordered his crew to kill eight of them for supplies. What his crew were later to feast on were West Indian monk seals.

There were three species of monk seals around the globe, unusual in being found in warmer latitudes than most other kinds of seals. As Columbus was picking his way through the Caribbean, Hawaiian monk seals were hauling up in large numbers on this Pacific archipelago, while the Mediterranean monk seal would surely have already been familiar to Columbus who sailed the Mediterranean from an early age. This species also ventured beyond the Straits of Gibraltar and into the Atlantic along the North African coast. And on the opposite side of the Atlantic, the West Indian monk seal swam in enormous numbers around the Caribbean. It ranged over an area bounded on the east and north by the Lesser Antilles, the Bahamas, and Florida. Its bones have even been found in middens on the coast of Texas, though it's likely they got there through trade; there's no compelling evidence that West Indian monk seals occurred naturally this far north in the Gulf of Mexico.

The fact that bones are found in middens shows that they were being hunted long before Columbus's men dined on sea wolves. And there are also eyewitness accounts. In 1549, a young boy named Hernando D'Escalante Fontenada, only thirteen at the time, had the misfortune to be shipwrecked on South Florida's perilous shore. He was taken captive by the local Indians, the Calusa, and ended up living with them until he was rescued at the age of thirty. In that time, he traveled extensively throughout their territory. In his memoirs, he records that these Florida Indians caught sea wolves but that only the "principal persons" ate them. Whether such native hunting had an effect on numbers is hard to judge at the remove of half a millennium, though when Europeans began to explore the Caribbean further, they found plenty of places where monk seals still existed in great abundance—and it was just as well.

In 1524, Hernan Cortes, remembered today for his conquest of the Aztec, sent an expedition across the Caribbean to put down yet another Indian insurrection, which unfortunately didn't go exactly as planned: "A ship loaded with supplies of meat, bread, wine, oil, vinegar, and other provisions was lost with everything, and left only three men on an islet in the ocean that is five leagues from the land, for whom I later sent a ship. And they were found alive having maintained themselves on many seals that are on the islet, and on a fruit that they said was like a fig."[6]

A later description, from the early 1700s, describes a similar abundance on the Bahamas: "The Bahama Islands are filled with seals; sometimes Fishers will catch 100 in a night."[7] One hundred seals a night is more than most sailors could eat. But by now, seal hunting wasn't merely for subsistence or dire necessity. They were being taken for oil as much as for meat, a commercial value that forged a link between the seals on their isolated Caribbean islets and the vast, insatiable markets of Europe. Demand and supply.

Similar nightly catches would have been happening at most of the monk seal colonies throughout the Caribbean. It's been estimated that, in Columbus's day, the population of monk seals was somewhere between 230,000 and 680,000 individuals.[8] The wide margins of these "guesstimates" are because there are no hard and fast censuses for the time. The scientists that put these figures together had to draw on trade reports, ships' manifests, and a critical reading of historical accounts like those above as well as ecological knowledge. This work is being carried out at HMAP (History of Marine Animal Populations), an association of around one hundred scientists from a number of countries who are trying to piece together what the oceans should really look like. As imprecise as the HMAP figures might be, they do at least tell us that there were a lot of monk seals in the Caribbean in 1492. An equally imprecise, though undoubtedly real, measure of their abundance and productivity is that it seems to have taken quite some time for commercial hunting to have had a noticeable impact on their numbers.

But that effect was certainly noticeable by 1878, when another visitor to the Bahamas recorded: "Some few seals are to be found in that vicinity, and hunting has reduced their numbers throughout the Caribbean."[9]

Even so, there were so many small, isolated cays scattered around this sea of islands that a few colonies hung on. As late as 1886, forty-nine were collected in just three days from a chain of small cays, and it was from examining these specimens that most of our knowledge of the biology of this species comes. Despite all the hunting, no one bothered to record much about the natural history of this species, and by 1952, it was too late to find out more. That was when the last-ever West Indian monk seal was seen on the remote Seranilla Bank, between Jamaica and Nicaragua.

There have been reports of West Indian monk seals since then, though none have been confirmed. They were rumored to be living of the Yucatan Peninsula in the 1970s, but a thorough survey in 1973, which covered around four thousand miles of coast, failed to see any at all. Another survey, in 1980, produced the same result. Yet, isolated sightings of seals continued to surface around the Caribbean and some of these were eventually confirmed by experts. There really were seals still swimming in the Caribbean, but not monk seals.

In 1993, and again in 1996, scientists found hooded seals off the coast of Puerto Rico, a long way from their icy Arctic home. Over the last decade, the number of hooded seals sighted in Caribbean waters has steadily risen. All these animals were emaciated and, not surprisingly, suffering from heat exhaustion. No one has any idea what these seals are doing so far south of their normal range, in waters so unsuitable for their survival, but it's probably not good news. It also suggests that many of the isolated "monk seal" sightings in recent years may well have been wandering hooded seals. With that in mind, the International Union for the Conservation of Nature (IUCN) pronounced the West Indian monk seal extinct in 1996. And, incidentally, the other two monk seals are not far behind.

Monk seals weren't the only big marine mammals that impressed Columbus. He also came across a creature that we still call by its Taino Indian name — *manatee.* Columbus found an abundance of manatees in a bay on the southern coast of Cuba, a place that gained notoriety for a rather different reason nearly five hundred years later — Bahia de Cochinas — the Bay of Pigs.[10] Just to set the record straight, it's not a bay of pigs at all. Although *cochinas* can mean pigs, it also refers to the orangeside triggerfish, suggesting that Columbus's manatees were swimming amongst great shoals of fish in the Bay of Orangeside Triggerfishes.

West Indian manatees belong to a group of animals called sirenians, or sea cows, an appropriate enough name since they munch their way through great quantities of aquatic vegetation to support their huge frames. Everything these massive animals do is in slow motion, surely one of the most laid-back creatures on the planet. And you can't help being lulled into a similar soporific trancelike state when you are in the presence of these gentle animals. In the Crystal River and Homosassa Springs area of Florida, manatees are now big business, drawing thousands of tourists each winter for close encounters with nature. Florida is about as far north as these tropical creatures can live year round, though they do venture as far north as Virginia in the summer months.

Manatees living around Florida are sometimes described as a separate subspecies, but if they are, they haven't really adapted to the winters in Florida. Humans migrate to Florida in the winter to enjoy the balmy, subtropical climate, but the open waters around the northern half of the peninsula can sometimes get too chilly for the sensitive manatees. They need to seek the sanctuary of freshwater springs, where water bubbling up from the limestone foundations of Florida remains at a constant, comfortable temperature in the low seventies. They also make good use of our modern world, gathering in the warm water outflows of power stations during the winter. In fact, in some areas, they've come to rely on these places. When one power station went off-line during a cold snap in 1977, a lot of manatees died. The biggest herd, though, still relies on nature's more reliable warm water outflows in the Crystal River area. And seeing manatees here during the winter is a magical experience.

At dawn, mist rises from the warm water and creates a dramatic light show, picking out the shafts of sunlight playing over patterns of ferns and palms. Out over the crystal clear pool, a deep sigh and a puff of breath, almost lost in the mist, is usually the first glimpse of a manatee. But, it's only when you enter their world that you can really appreciate their extraordinary appeal. It's often said that manatees, or their close relatives, dugongs, are the reality behind the myth of mermaids. These same books then go on to point out the irony that such an ugly creature could ever be mistaken for a beautiful mermaid, and presumably only by sailors who have been away from their wives and girlfriends for far too long. The order of mammals to which they belong, the Sirenia, also gets its name from a similar myth, that they were the original sirens, luring sailors to their doom with their beauty.

When Columbus saw his first "sirens," off La Española, he reckoned: "They are not as beautiful as they are painted."[11] That's a little harsh on the manatee. I'm prepared to admit that they're not pretty (in the conventional sense), but, permitting myself a little anthropomorphism, they are hugely endearing and charming. Nose to nose with that melancholy, bristly face, ceaselessly hoovering up mountains of greenery with rubber lips, it's impossible not to become a manatee fan. But such intimate moments inevitably stir my imagination. If this experience is so amazing now, what was it like in the past? For one thing, there would have been a lot more manatees.

William Dampier, an English traveler, naturalist, and sometime buccaneer, saw plenty in his journeys around the Caribbean toward the end of the seventeenth century. "I have seen of the Manatee in the Bay of Campeachy, on the Coasts of Bocca del Drago and Bocco del Toro, in the River of Darien, and among the South Keys or little islands of Cuba. I have heard of their being found on the North of Jamaica a few, and in the Rivers of Surinam in great Multitudes."[12]

As with the monk seal, it's hard to know exactly how abundant manatees were in the past. For one thing, as William Dampier has pointed out, they didn't occur everywhere in the same abundance. They can only survive where there are big enough beds of aquatic vegetation to sustain their constant munching. But in these favored locations there's every chance that they really did exist "in great Multitudes." There's good evidence for spectacular herds of the closely related dugong in Australia. In 1883, one herd in Moreton Bay in Queensland was estimated to be three hundred yards wide and fully three miles long. There's no reason to think West Indian manatee herds couldn't have reached the same size, though they were hunted by Indians, which may have kept their populations below maximum. In fact, Indians throughout the manatee's range had come up with a whole variety of ingenious ways of catching them.

Sometimes they were just hauled ashore and butchered, but other Indians used more inventive methods. Off the coast of Nicaragua, William Dampier watched Miskito Indians hunting manatee with an ingenious harpoon system

> The Mosquitoes, two in a canoe, have a staff about eight feet long, almost as big as a man's arm at the great end, where there is a hole to place the harpoon in. At the other end is a piece of light wood, with a hole in it through which the small end of the staff comes; and on this piece of bobwood there is a line of twelve fathoms wound about, the end of the line made fast to it. The other end is made fast to the harpoon, and the man keeps about a fathom of it loose in his hand.
>
> When he strikes, the harpoon presently comes out of the staff, and as the manatee swims away the line runs off from the bob; and although at first both staff and bob may be carried under water, yet as the line runs off it will rise again. When the creature's strength is spent they haul it up to the canoe's side, knock it on the head and tow it ashore.[13]

Indians in Guiana used a moku-moku flower as bait. This flower, hung above the water, seemed to be an irresistible temptation to the ever-hungry manatee, and when one reached up to grab it, the waiting Indians unleashed a hail of arrows. But most remarkable of all were the Indians of Cuba, who were said to use remoras to catch manatees.[14] These fish are often seen attached to sharks, hitching a ride. They hang on with a specially modified dorsal fin, which has been turned into a disk capable of sealing itself to the shark's skin and creating a negative pressure. The power of this suction has been measured and is surprisingly strong, particularly on shark skin. But no one has yet tested whether the Arawaks of Cuba really could hang on to manatees using tethered remoras.

Caribbean Indians hunted the manatee for meat, as well as for its surprisingly tough hide. Europeans also found plenty of uses for its hide, as William Dampier recounts: "The skin of the manatee is of great use to privateers, for they cut them out into straps, which they make fast on the sides of their canoes, through which they put their oars in rowing, instead of pegs. The skin of the bull, or of the back of the cow, they cut into horsewhips, twisted when green and then hung to dry." Manatee tail, soaked in brine, also became something of an unlikely delicacy, and soon manatees became big business. In 1660, a Jesuit priest, Father Antonio Viera, recorded that twenty Dutch ships a year were sailing from northern Brazil, loaded with manatee meat. These could have been either West Indian manatees or a very similar species, the Amazonian manatee, which ranges to the south of the West Indian species and inland along South America's great rivers.

Inevitably, commercial exploitation resulted in a decline in numbers. Though West Indian (and Amazonian) manatees haven't yet followed monk seals into extinction, in some ways they might as well have. There are still enough to give tourists pleasure in Florida's warm springs, but not enough to be a functioning part of the Caribbean ecosystem. They are ecologically extinct in most of their range. And they used to exist in such large numbers that they were an important part of the whole, a key factor in maintaining and shaping the vast beds of sea grass that grew in the clear shallow waters.

Sea grasses are a strange and wondrous group of plants: flowering plants that live in shallow seas and that really do flower—underwater. Their pollen is carried on currents of water rather than the wind. Although generally lumped together, there are several sorts of sea grasses. The commonest is turtle grass. Not far behind is manatee grass, with long cylindrical leaves, rather than the flat blades of turtle grass. Shoal grass is another widespread species, and all formed vast undersea pastures, grazed by vast herds of manatees, though manatees would have been greatly outnumbered by another grazer of these marine grasslands: green turtles.

Based on estimates of hunting and the number of large rookeries, there may have been up to 39 million green turtles in the pre-Columbian Caribbean, an impressive number that translates as a fifteen- to twenty-fold greater biomass than the spectacular herds of large ungulates on East Africa's plains. Another estimate, based on the carrying capacity of the vast beds of sea grass, suggests that an astounding 660 million green turtles could have swum in the Caribbean.[15]

Once adult, green turtles are fairly immune to predators. In ecological parlance, their populations are regulated from the bottom-up rather than top-down—limited more by food than predation—and it's quite feasible for such species to approach the carrying capacity of their environment. Certainly, reports of explorers and pirates support the idea of such an extraordinary abundance. Off southern Cuba, sailors on Columbus's second voyage found: "the sea was thick with them [turtles], and they were of the very largest, so numerous that it seemed that the ships would run aground on them and were as if bathing in them."[16]

Some populations undertake long migrations, from feeding grounds to breeding beaches, where they laboriously haul their way up the sandy shore to lay their eggs. Turtles feeding off the coast of Brazil somehow manage to find a tiny speck of land, nearly a thousand miles away and smack in the middle of the Atlantic, called Ascension Island, which is where I first saw breeding green turtles. Back in the 1980s, Ascension was not an easy place to get to, even for humans. A Royal Mail Ship sails every few months, conveniently from Bristol, in the southwest of England, where I live. Alternatively, the Royal Air Force flies there, to a major military base on the island. There's also a big U.S. Air Force base there, so with such strategic importance, it was hard to get permission to disembark there. However, apart from the military, the British Broadcasting Corporation also has a base there, transmitting its World Service alternately to South America and Africa. Since, at the time, I was working for the BBC, it was possible to get permission, as well as a Land Rover—and a chance to explore this extraordinary volcanic island.

The day job was filming the various species of tropical seabirds that nest here, but after a hearty evening meal in the mess, and a few cold lagers, there was nothing more pleasurable than an after dark stroll along a beach of black volcanic sand. With nothing to interrupt their progress, mighty Atlantic rollers crash into these beaches in roiling foam and erupt in white sheets of spray over lava outcrops. But it doesn't take long to spot a dark shape emerging from the thundering breakers, seemingly oblivious to the pounding. Another green turtle has managed to find this volcanic dot in the endless Atlantic.

Sitting next to that turtle for the next few hours was a wonderful experience. She didn't seem at all bothered by the red lights of our head torches as she slowly and methodically began her task of scooping out a nest hole with her hind flippers. Frequent collapses of her excavations caused her no consternation; she just carried on regardless, her flippers working alternately to shovel up a load of sand and then throw it as far as possible, usually over the enthralled observers. Eventually satisfied with the depth and moisture content of her hole, she began to lay her eggs—an erratic stream of ping-pong balls that tumbled into a rough pile in the bottom of the nest. All that remained was to backfill the hole, then she could drag herself back to the supporting waters of the Atlantic. By the time she began to heave her bulk down the beach, her eyes were streaming with tears. This is one of the reasons why many people find watching these great beasts, toiling under the unfamiliar weight of gravity, such an emotional experience—an empathy, across the evolutionary gulf from mammal to reptile, for a creature struggling to fulfill her maternal duties. In fact, she is merely secreting excess salt, an elegant adaptation to life in seawater. Nevertheless, the effort she has just made was very real and worthy of admiration.

The green turtle was of crucial importance in the exploration and conquest of the Americas. They existed in extraordinary numbers, and since they are far from sprightly when they're hauled up on a beach, they were extremely easy to collect. They also tasted good and could be stored alive for several weeks by the simple expedient of turning them on their backs, in which position they are entirely helpless. So, vessels in the Caribbean always stocked up on turtles before setting sail for Europe. And it wasn't difficult to find breeding beaches in those days.

In 1513, the Spaniard, Ponce de Leon, set out to explore the as yet unknown lands to the north of Spain's Caribbean bases. He was acting on information from Indians who had described a large island to the north of Cuba, perhaps another source of gold, silver, or slaves. On his voyage, he came across a small, isolated chain of islands that soon became known as the Dry Tortugas, a name that tells you everything you needed to know. There was no water here, but plenty of turtles. "They reached the chain of islets which they named Tortugas because in a short time of the night they took, in one of these islands, a hundred and seventy turtles and might have taken more if they wished, and also they took fourteen seals."[17]

More than twenty years previously, on his first voyage, Columbus had already named another island, off the northwest tip of La Española, *Isla de la Tortuga*, presumably after the numbers of turtles there. Soon, many other "Tortugas" began to appear on the maps, a reflection of the abundance of sea turtles right across the Caribbean. The Cayman Islands were also, at one time, called Tortugas after a huge turtle rookery that Columbus found on his fourth and last voyage. This same colony was also later described by John Hawkins, another English privateer, and was probably the largest of all green turtle rookeries. So many turtles crowded around this island that sailors could use the noise of their splashing to navigate. "it is affirmed, that vessels, which have lost their latitude in hazy weather, have steered entirely by the noise which these creatures make in swimming, to attain the Cayman isles.[18]" We can only imagine what Columbus or Hawkins would have seen if they had sat out all night on that beach, since, apart from their impressive numbers, green turtles grew bigger back then. Today they reach around 450 pounds, but may have grown to twice that size in the past.[19] Certainly their size impressed Peter Martyr, writing in the mid-sixteenth century: "They tell marvellous thynges of the monsters of the sea aboute this Island, and especially of the tortoyies. For they saye that they are bigger then great round targettes."[20]

As the Caribbean was explored and settled, the exploitation of green turtles followed a now all too familiar pattern. No longer used just as provisions for homeward journeys, they became valuable commercially, for their meat and skin as well as for the green fat that gives them their name. By 1688, forty sloops from Jamaica were working full time to ferry turtles back from the giant rookery on the Cayman Islands. This probably amounted to about thirteen thousand turtles a year, a plentiful supply of food that was critically important in building Britain's most important Caribbean base at the time. By the late seventeenth century, numbers in the Cayman rookery were so low that the fleet had to move on to Cuba and then to the Miskito Cays off Nicaragua. This pattern of exploitation and decline was almost universal, though with a few notable exceptions.

Green turtles also climbed the beaches of Bermuda in large numbers and were, at first, exploited there just as enthusiastically as elsewhere. But seeing what was happening, and recognizing the long-term value of the turtles, the Bermuda Assembly passed one of the New World's first environmental laws, *An Act Agaynst the Killinge of Ouer Young Tortoyses,* in 1620. This prohibited the taking of turtles less than eighteen inches in breadth, on pain of a hefty fine of tobacco, which is a tougher law than it might sound today. In the seventeenth century, tobacco was virtually a form of currency. In 1711, Jamaica also passed a law that prohibited the destruction of turtle eggs, but neither law had much effect on the subsequent history of turtles in the Caribbean.

Elsewhere, the slaughter continued. Even taking a more conservative historical estimate, the population is now probably only around 3–7 percent of its original size. Green turtles are still with us, but in such reduced numbers that they are, like manatees, ecologically extinct. Such vast numbers of big grazers had a major effect on the great undersea pastures of sea grasses, and in that sense, they were key species.[21] Drifting over sea grass beds today, all looks well, a carpet of long leaves slowly blowing back and forth in the current. But dive down and take a closer look. The fronds are covered in algae and slime, and piles of decaying leaves have smothered some patches. This buildup of detritus also contributes to turtle grass wasting disease, which is killing off large areas of these undersea grasslands. All around the Caribbean, sea grass beds are dying off because they are not being grazed by turtles and manatees. If Columbus had snorkeled over these areas, he would have seen a low, tightly cropped turf with few or no decaying leaves, a very different habitat to the one that exists today. Clearly, the Caribbean needs its turtles back.

There have been many efforts to restore turtles around the Caribbean. One of the earliest was led by Archie Carr, as eloquent a spokesman for sea turtles as there ever was. In 1959, with the help of the U.S. Navy, he began collecting eggs from Tortuguero, a nesting beach in Costa Rica. These eggs were then hatched, and the young turtles flown by the Navy's Grumman aircraft, that were able to land on the Tortugeuro River, to beaches around the Caribbean, where, it was hoped, they would return when mature to found new breeding colonies. Operation Green Turtle was stopped in 1968, in part because the war in Vietnam was seen as a more critical use of the Navy's resources. But there were also questions as to how effective this plan was. By then, 130,000 turtle hatchlings had been shipped and there were worrying signs that the Tortuguero population was declining. In addition, few released turtles were ever seen again. But even if Operation Green Turtle did not achieve its aims of establishing new colonies, it did raise public awareness on the plight of Caribbean turtles, and the reasons behind its failure taught turtle conservationists some valuable lessons.

When young turtles hatch, they make a frenzied dash to the sea, under cover of darkness to avoid the watchful eyes of predators. Once in the water, they swim like overwound clockwork toys until they are out of the dangerous shore zone. This "swim frenzy" period is preprogrammed into the little turtle's physiology and lasts slightly more than a day. Then the tiny hatchlings continue their migration at a more leisurely pace, to ocean nursery grounds where they can feed and grow.[22] Once mature, most will return to breed on the beach where they hatched. So, that mad dash to the sea still must have still given them enough time to memorize cues that will guide them back to a single beach across a vast expanse of ocean, many years down the line. Exactly how they do this isn't yet fully understood, but probably involves a combination of scent and magnetic cues.[23]

One reason for the lack of success of Operation Green Turtle was that the hatchlings were held beyond their swim frenzy period and may not have had the drive to get clear of the shore when they were finally released in their new home. It's also possible that the window for imprinting on a future breeding beach is quite short and limited to the first few days of the young turtle's life, in which case, the relocated hatchlings wouldn't have been able to find their new home again, even if they did make it out to the mid-ocean nursery grounds. This understanding has benefited later turtle conservation programs for other species, as we'll see shortly.

Meanwhile, more conventional conservation measures at Tortuguero, such as nest protection and control of beach development, have encouraged a satisfying increase in the number of nesting females. Tortuguero is now the largest green turtle rookery in the Caribbean, and one of the largest in the world, a feat for which Costa Rica can be rightly proud. There is, however, no room for complacency. Increasing numbers of turtles are being found with fibropapillomas, a form of tumor probably caused by a virus. In addition, in this very real Paradise, beach development is a constant threat. Even development along the top of the beach can prove lethal.

Baby turtles are guided on their run to the sea by the lighter horizon over the ocean. The lights of homes and bars above the beach cause them to run in the wrong direction, and when dawn breaks, they are easy targets for a long list of predators, who find turtles just as tasty as those early sailors. Nevertheless, Tortuguero shows that, given the right measures, turtles can bounce back. In fact, there seems to be more good news in recent years for the green turtle. The numbers nesting on Ascension Island, where I saw my first-ever green turtle, have risen threefold since 1970 according to one turtle specialist, Annette Broderick, from the University of Exeter in the United Kingdom. She thinks this is now around the same population that nested here before the British Navy arrived two hundred years ago. She also feels that green turtle populations are now so healthy that they should be removed from the IUCN's endangered list, even though the IUCN itself reconfirmed the green turtle's endangered status in 2006. So, what should the overall aim of turtle conservation policies be?

The IUCN's guideline is to aim for population levels that existed three generations ago. For green turtles, this translates to 100–130 years ago. But by then the population was already only a fraction of its pre-Columbian abundance. This is another example, this time built into the guidelines of a major international conservation body, of the problem of shifting baselines, a problem that we've already met in our exploration of the once-abundant northwest Atlantic. We humans are very limited in our perceptions. Our clearest insight on the changing natural world comes from comparing the world of our earliest memories to that we experience now. This powerful gut feeling, very real and objective in a subjective way, is such a strong perception that it makes other comparisons so much less vivid — which is why it's so important to realize how different the world was not just three generations ago, but ten or a hundred. Realizing what's gone is vitally important. It stops us from accepting a depauperate world as pristine, untrammeled nature. Those that see the world's population of green turtles as healthy and no longer endangered estimate the global population as "in excess of 2.6 million."[24] And while that probably does mean that there's little danger of losing the green turtle as a species in the immediate future, a global population of 2.6 million falls a long way short of a possible 660 million in the Caribbean basin alone.

However, understanding these lessons from history and recreating that history are two very different things. The world has changed so much since Columbus that it may not be possible to see turtles or manatees in such numbers again, no matter how hard we try. Perhaps a more realistic aim should be to bring these species back from ecological extinction and return them to service in maintaining the sea grass beds, which are so critically important for a whole host of other creatures. In its own way, though, that's just as hard as recreating the pre-Columbian world. It demands a detailed ecological knowledge of each species' role in its ecosystem and how it relates to other species. Yet this is the only real way forward for conservation. As John Donne so succinctly put it, "No man is an island"—nor is any other species, even in this sea of islands. Single-species conservation has had some showcase successes—we'll meet plenty in this book—but in the end, environmental policies have to embrace whole ecosystems if they have any hope of long-term success.

The numbers of green turtles in the Caribbean were extremely impressive, but they weren't the only species of sea turtles swimming in these waters. Hawksbills, loggerheads, Kemp's ridleys, olive ridleys, and leatherback turtles were also here in large numbers, and these species all play a very different role in their habitats. They are carnivores, eating sponges, jellyfish, shellfish, crustaceans, and a variety of other marine creatures. Carnivores, higher up the food chain, are usually less numerous than herbivores, and that proved to be the case with turtles too. The pre-Columbian population of Hawksbills, for example, was estimated to be around 5 million animals. However, hawksbills have the bad luck to be protected by highly valuable shells, from which commercial tortoiseshell is made. Weight for weight, tortoiseshell was more valuable than ivory, so it's not surprising that the hawksbill is also ecologically extinct across much of its range. Hawksbills eat mainly sponges that grow in abundance on the reefs, and their ecological demise has allowed sponges to proliferate and overgrow the corals, adding to the other problems faced by West Indian reefs.

Rarer still are Kemp's ridley turtles. Yet these were one of the most spectacular of all the Caribbean turtles. Although they didn't exist in the same abundance as green turtles, they made their numbers felt. They nest during the hours of daylight and invade their breeding beaches in vast aggregations, called *arribadas,* or arrivals. Even as late as the middle of the twentieth century, some of these arribadas were truly amazing sights, and we know this because one was filmed back in 1947, at a beach called Rancho Nuevo in Mexico, about one hundred miles south of the Texas border. It's thought that there were forty thousand turtles hauled up on Rancho Nuevo on the day that a Mexican architect, called Andrés Herrera, decided to record the event for posterity.[25] When the film was rediscovered in 1963 and shown to Archie Carr, he was enthralled at the sight of turtles so tightly packed that they were clambering over each other to find bare sand and digging up each others nests as they tried to lay their own eggs. He pronounced the film more important and more epic than anything he'd ever seen from Hollywood. "It made Andrés Herrera in my mind suddenly a cinematographer far greater than Fellini, Alfred Hitchcock, or Walt Disney could ever aspire to be."

Despite a few records of nesting from elsewhere, this stretch of Mexican beach is where virtually all Kemp's ridleys nest. So a dramatic fall in numbers in the later decades of the twentieth century was extremely worrying. At low points, only around 750 turtles were seen at one time, though the situation probably wasn't as bad as these raw figures alone suggest; numbers of nesting females have always varied tremendously from year to year. But even during better years, only around two thousand nesting females were seen at a time. Some scientists have recently questioned the estimates of numbers based on Herrera's film, but even allowing for an overoptimistic interpretation of the film, there must still be close to an order of magnitude drop in nesting females and plenty of reason to worry.

The evidence of Herrera's film suggests that the problems facing Kemp's ridleys are more recent than those facing green or hawksbill turtles. And that turned out to be the case when it was discovered that Kemp's ridleys were particularly at risk from being caught and drowned in the nets of shrimping boats. Numbers of shrimping boats have increased dramatically in the Gulf of Mexico in recent years and seem to be a major factor in the decline of Kemp's ridleys. In response to this, a Turtle Excluder Device (TED) was invented and it is now mandatory for U.S. shrimpers to fit these devices to their nets. The United States is also trying to force other countries fishing in the Gulf of Mexico to follow this example by threatening bans on imports from any that don't comply. However, this has yet to have a major impact, since, in the face of economic and political expediency, deadlines are extended and exemptions granted. Further, TEDs don't always work, and quite a few Kemp's ridleys are still drowned in shrimpers' nets.

Nevertheless, Kemp's ridley turtles have responded to these measures by arriving at Rancho Nuevo in ever-increasing numbers. In 2005, ten thousand nests were counted. And, with a little help from conservationists, they are also reclaiming some of their old nesting grounds. Between 1978 and 1988, a joint Mexican-U.S. project was set up to reestablish a rookery at Padre Island National Seashore near Corpus Christi, Texas, where there were historical records for breeding Kemp's ridleys. Using the lessons learned in Operation Green Turtle, eggs were collected on Rancho Nuevo beach and incubated in Padre Island sand. The young hatchlings were released to run down the beach at Padre Island and allowed a brief swim in the Gulf of Mexico, before being recaptured. Hopefully now imprinted on Padre Island, the youngsters were then "headstarted" by being fed in captivity, so avoiding their first dangerous year in open waters full of predators. After a year, the young turtles were tagged and released into the Gulf. Although the value of headstarting has been questioned,[26] the other improvements over Operation Green Turtle seem to be paying off. In 1996, the first two tagged Kemp's ridleys returned to Padre Island, and numbers have increased ever since. The year 2004 saw twenty-five nests on the beach and forty-two nests in total in Texas.[27] Five nests were found on the same day—not yet an arribada, but a step in the right direction. The good news continued in 2005, when twenty-eight nests were recorded on Padre Island, and another twenty-six recorded on other U.S. Gulf Coast beaches. In 2007, 115 nests were dug, the largest number since recording began in the 1980s.

The largest of the sea turtles, the leatherback, is a really impressive beast. It can reach six feet in length and weigh in at 1,200 pounds, a true leviathan that, with its leathery, ridged shell, would not look out of place swimming in a sea full of plesiosaurs and ichthyosaurs. It was called the trunk by British settlers in the Caribbean, who found that trunk oil was a valuable commodity. Again, hunting caused an alarming decline in this species, and again, recent protection seems to be having a positive effect, though the increase in numbers is painfully slow. On the British Virgin Islands only three leatherbacks nested in 1990. At this point, British government officers began patrolling the beaches, to gain a more accurate picture of the nesting population. This also seems to have helped the turtles, by putting off the few trunkers that were still hunting leatherbacks. In 2001, they found a total of sixty-three nests.

The Caribbean is vitally important for sea turtles on a global scale. Apart from Tortuguero being one of the largest green turtle rookeries in the world, one of the biggest remaining concentrations of leatherbacks lives around Suriname and French Guiana. The seas off Yucatan support globally important populations of hawksbills, and Rancho Nuevo remains the largest nesting colony of Kemp's ridleys. There are reasons for hope with all these turtles, though absolutely no room for overconfidence. The seas are still the most abused habitats on our planet, and it's not hard to imagine that unforeseen consequences of our depredations on the oceans might still reverse all the good work. When Archie Carr wrote *The Windward Road* in 1955, now a natural history classic about his search for green turtles across the Caribbean, turtles were in deep trouble. He spearheaded both a scientific and public awareness campaign to highlight the problem. And the importance of understanding the full scale of the problem—of just how different the modern Caribbean is—was clear to him when he said, "What they all overlook is the fact that they came to know Chelonia long after it had been cut down to a mere trace of its primitive abundance."[28] The news is certainly much better now for sea turtles, but Archie Carr's sentiments are as valid now as when written half a century ago. Sea turtle populations in the Caribbean are still only ghosts of those that existed when Columbus sailed these waters.

As Columbus explored the Caribbean, he also found lots of people. Not every island was inhabited, but most were. On his first voyage, he met Arawak Indians who had probably moved up the Lesser Antilles chain from South America, eventually to occupy the big islands of the Greater Antilles. Almost invariably, Columbus described these people as charming and friendly, though that didn't stop him from suggesting their use as slaves to help the Spanish better exploit the Arawak homelands. Sometime after colonization by the Arawak, a second wave of people used the Lesser Antilles as stepping stones into the Caribbean. These were later known as Caribs or Canibas. The former name became immortalized in the name of the region, the latter as cannibal, since these people were reported to eat human flesh.

Just how many Arawaks and Caribs lived around the Caribbean? That's a hot topic among anthropologists and archaeologists, and estimates vary widely. We will probably never know for certain, though the earliest accounts, including Columbus's own, suggest there were a lot. The most telling reports are those of Bartolomé de las Casas, who became something of a champion for the Indian cause early in the sixteenth century, in the face of Spanish exploitation and atrocities.

His first encounter with Indians was in 1493, as a nine-year-old boy in Seville. He was watching Columbus's triumphant parade through the city and got his first glimpse of the exotic Caribbean—Taino Indians and startlingly colored parrots that Columbus had brought back. He was hooked. Nine years later, he went to the Caribbean with his father, and eight years after that became a priest on La Isla Española. He wrote several books based on his experiences and observations in the Indies, including *A Brief History of the Destruction of the Indies,* only published after his death, a powerful attack on the way the Spanish had treated the Indians. Even today, Las Casas remains a figurehead for native rights throughout Latin America and was said to have inspired the revolutionary Simon Bolivar among others. But his importance in our context is that he was there, on the ground, right at the start of Spanish colonization of the Caribbean. And what he saw when he got there was a land teeming with people. "There are other great and infinite Iles round about [Hispaniola], and in the Confines on all sides: which we have seen the most peopled, and the most fullest of their owne native people, as any other Countrie in the World may be." In a later section of his *Destruction of the Indies,* he tries to put some figures to these observations. "And I doe verily believe, and think not to mistake therein, that there are dead more than fifteene Millions of soules."[29]

Fifteen million dead, from disease and enslavement. Las Casas had a point to make, so we shouldn't rely too heavily on his actual figures; most modern scholars wouldn't accept such high populations. Some put the Caribbean population at only one hundred thousand, in keeping with the generally low estimates for the Americas. But now, with each passing year, numbers seem to be creeping up. Some suggest that three hundred thousand people were living on Hispaniola when Columbus arrived.[30] Others suggest that 1–2 million people lived here with 6–8 million people across the whole of the Caribbean.[31] There are also firsthand descriptions, including those of Columbus himself, that back up the premise that there were plenty of people here.

Columbus also mentions several times that he never saw any large animals that could be hunted, so how did all these people survive? Even on his first voyage, Columbus described large fields around the towns and sometimes whole valley floors that were cultivated. But, particularly on the smaller islands, the marine harvest was vitally important. Indians hunted manatees, seals, and turtles, possibly in enough numbers to reduce their populations. But there were other marine resources that existed in vast quantities and that were extremely easy to collect.

Walk along any beach in the Caribbean and you'll soon find shells or fragments of the West Indian top shell. This large black-and-white patterned shell belongs to a marine snail that must have existed in enormous numbers, to judge from the quantities found heaped in Taino middens on some islands. It usually lives in shallow water of three feet or less, which must have made it very easy to collect and therefore an important part of the Taino diet. It's still eaten today, when it's generally just called "whelk." In fact the taste for whelk wiped out these snails in Bermuda. This was bad news for the West Indian top shell, but equally bad news for the purple-clawed hermit crab that uses an empty top shell as home. However, a reintroduction program has successfully reestablished the top shell in Bermuda and at the same time alleviated the hermit crab housing crisis.

Whelks may have existed in prodigious numbers, but they were only the second most important shellfish in the region, beaten into runner-up position by the queen conch. Conch are huge shellfish, up to a foot long. They are very much scarcer today than when the Taino harvested them, but it's still possible to watch them lumbering through sea grass beds with their peculiar, even slightly comical, gait. They don't glide along on a fleshy foot like most other snails. Instead they have a short spine attached to the foot, which they use as a lever to pole themselves along. Watch a conch for long enough and it will suddenly lurch forward with an un-snail-like hop, before stopping to contemplate the world again.

The size of their historical population defies belief, but some sense of their abundance is still easy to find in southern Florida. Here, the Calusa Indians built huge mounds from conch shells to create islands in their swampy home. In the center of their territory, one island in every five is artificial. The largest of these, at Chokoloskee, is 150 acres in extent, is twenty feet high, and contains millions of shells. Many of these mounds still exist, and if you are prepared to brave the mosquitoes to finds areas where the mound has been excavated, the sheer numbers of shells used to build it are readily apparent. But the real testament to the abundance of the Caribbean's waters is not these impressive mounds, but the entire Calusa culture.

In 1896, Frank Cushing, an archaeologist from the Smithsonian Institution, got quite a surprise. He was excavating a Calusa site at Key Marco in Collier County when he began to turn up some stunningly beautiful artifacts. "After the first day's work . . . I was no longer left in doubt as to the unique outcome of our excavations. . . . To me, the remains that were most significant . . . were the carved and painted wooden masks and animal figureheads."[32] Studying these elaborate artifacts, Cushing began to realize that the Calusa lived in a highly sophisticated society that had enough resources to support artisans and priests as well as labor to build the great shell mounds. His problem was that, up to this point, archaeology taught that only farming societies, like those at Cahokia on the Mississippi, could muster enough resources to feed a complex society. Here in South Florida, the Calusa clearly didn't need to farm. The shallow waters around the coast provided more than enough food with enough ease to free up members of their society to specialize in other jobs, such as carving and painting ceremonial figures. A similar tradition of elaborate and evocative art is found along the western coasts of Washington, British Columbia, and Alaska, where it was supported by a superabundance of Pacific salmon running up the rivers.

The Calusa relied mainly on estuarine areas, where freshwater flowing from the swamps mingled with the sea. Such areas are particularly fruitful; they can produce four to ten times as much organic matter as a field of corn. So, there was hardly any point in farming. Based on this marine abundance, the Calusa built their massive shell mounds, whose construction was every bit as sophisticated as the rest of Calusa society. The base was formed from conch shells hammered into the ground point first. Then layers of conch shells were built up on this foundation, and the finished mound faced with oyster shells laid on the outside like tiles.

These mounds seem to have had a variety of uses. Some were topped with elaborate ceremonial complexes, but one at least was also an ingenious fish trap. Sandfly Island, which covers about seventy-five acres, is built in the shape of a donut with a channel cut into the center. Water entered the hole in the donut at high tide, and then, as the tide ebbed, the Calusa strung nets across the channel to trap fish. For the Calusa, there was food everywhere, a fact that was immediately obvious to Hernando Fontenada. During his captivity, he recorded a varied and plentiful diet. "The common food is fish, turtle and snails (all of which are alike fish) and tunny and whale. . . . There is another fish which we here call langosta [lobster] and one like unto a chapin [trunk fish]."[33]

Conch is still a popular item on menus particularly across Florida and the Bahamas, but overharvesting of this easy-to-collect snail has severely reduced populations. To judge from the Calusa mounds, conch must have carpeted the floor of Florida Bay in their millions in the past, but the commercial fishery in Florida had to be closed in 1975 as numbers declined to low levels. Ten years later, all recreational fishing was also banned. But the stocks have showed only minimal signs of recovery, so Florida state scientists decided to lend a hand, with a restocking program of captive bred conch. As with sea turtles, it's not just a question of dumping juveniles into the sea and hoping for the best. Extensive research resulted in a successful formula that sounds more like it has come from some ancient fairy tale than a modern biology lab.

The free-floating larval stage can be persuaded to metamorphose into tiny sedentary snails by exposing them to an extract of red seaweed. The resulting young conchs did best when released in the fall on a full moon and after they had been previously exposed to caged predators and "taught" how to bury themselves in defense. And, in response to all this effort, numbers of conch do seem to be rising in the spawning aggregations that the scientists have been monitoring, though an estimate in 2003 for the Florida Keys spawning aggregations was still only thirty-five thousand animals—not enough to build a very large mound. And there's a real cost to these conservation efforts. The Florida scientists have worked out that every ten-centimeter conch that survives to reach fifteen centimeters will have cost $9. Such a value on each conch, I suppose, would have made every Calusa a millionaire many times over.

The Calusa's elaborate culture wasn't the only one that was supported by the marine wealth of the Caribbean. It also helped build a much bigger and more widely known one—the Mayan civilization. Famed for its wonderful temples, now reclaimed by Yucatan's rainforests, the Maya were just as dependent on the sea as the land. Columbus met huge Mayan canoes on his last voyage, later described by Las Casas in another of his works, *Historias de las Indias.* "There arrived a canoe full of Indians, as long as a galley and eight feet wide. It was loaded with merchandise from the west, almost certainly from the land of Yucatan."[34] These canoes were very impressive indeed and could hold twenty-five merchants, together with their wives and children, sheltering under a palm roof in the center. After Columbus's encounter, there were frequent reports of canoes, carved from massive mahogany logs, easily holding fifty people.[35] At the height of the Mayan civilization, such canoes regularly traveled eighteen miles off the coast of Belize to trade for fish and shellfish, presumably from fishermen not too dissimilar to the one that looked after us so well on South Water Cay.

The flowering of great civilizations, like that of the Maya, meant increasing exploitation of the Caribbean, but there's evidence that Indian populations had already had some noticeable effects before this.[36] The archaeological record, from remains found in middens, shows that the biggest Nassau groupers and similar predatory fish had become scarcer, while smaller fish, like parrotfish and surgeonfish had consequently become more abundant. Likewise, the biggest of the conchs disappeared, and the land crab population also seems to have fallen. In parallel, numbers of West Indian top shells rose, though the size of individuals found in middens decreases as time passes, showing that the population was under pressure from exploitation.

So Columbus's paradise might already have been somewhat tarnished in 1492. But the Indians could just turn to other abundant resources, like tuna and jack. The Caribbean is a very diverse place, and it seems that there was always something else just as tasty swimming in those warm seas. But that very diversity might well be the reason why, suddenly, in the last few decades, reefs and sea grass beds alike are in big trouble. Diversity can mask ecosystem wide effects until it is too late.

Diversity is nature's redundancy. If some species of herbivores or carnivores are reduced to ecological extinction, then similar members of the food chain can take over their job. This delays any effects on the ecosystem as a whole, but if exploitation continues with the next in line, then it's only a postponement of the inevitable—when the last link is broken and the chain finally snaps. The problems facing the Caribbean's reefs are a case in point. In the intact ecosystem a variety of grazers, from urchins to parrotfish, kept down algal growth and allowed the corals to flourish. But one after another, the grazers were reduced, until only one was left—a sea urchin called *Diadema antillarum*.

To judge from historical records, *Diadema* was always extremely abundant.[37] It's not clear whether the removal of other algal grazers allowed its population to rise, though either way, they seem to have managed to keep algae under control. But recently, they've been struck down by disease, and their population has collapsed. Now unchecked, algae are rapidly overgrowing the reef and destroying corals, such as stagshorn and elkhorn, two of the major reef builders here. There was a massive die-off of corals in the 1980s, with losses ranging from 80–98 percent of the population.[38] In the last few years, nearly half the remaining reefs are showing some form of damage, a situation so severe that stagshorn and elkhorn have now been formally suggested as candidates for listing under the Endangered Species Act.

In Discovery Bay, Jamaica, *Diadema* urchins have made a comeback and by the start of 2000 had cleared large areas of algae. Perhaps their earlier population crash was part of a natural cycle of abundance and decline, as has also been suggested for the destructive crown-of-thorns starfish in the Pacific. But Diadema's population crash would not have had such a huge impact on reef ecosystems if the other grazers hadn't already become ecologically extinct. The recovery in Discovery Bay shows that some of these ecosystem scale effects can be reversed, but as welcome as this news is, reefs are facing ever-increasing problems.

In recent years, corals have been suffering from outbreaks of devastating diseases. Eighty-five percent of elkhorns around Florida have died since 1996, mostly due to "white pox" disease.[39] Research has now confirmed that this is caused by a bacterium called *Serratia marescens,* which is more usually found in human feces and has probably infected the corals from sewage flowing into the sea. "Black band" disease, first seen in corals off Belize and Bermuda in the mid-1970s, also seems to be caused by bacteria from human feces, and new diseases are cropping up with an alarming frequency. In 1997, "rapid wasting" disease was seen off Bonaire and has since spread with worrying speed.

Many marine biologists now predict that 70 percent of reefs worldwide will die in our lifetimes. For anyone who has hung weightless over a colorful reef teeming with a confusing diversity of fish and invertebrates, that's an unthinkable tragedy. But marine ecologist Jeremy Jackson has pointed out that anyone who has had that pleasure has only ever witnessed an impoverished version of a reef. Wholesale changes to reef ecosystems started long before scuba gear was available, so divers are faced with an extreme form of the shifting baseline syndrome. The realization that the Caribbean was, despite centuries of heavy exploitation by Indians, such a remarkable place five hundred years ago places the current plight of its marine world in an even more stark perspective.

The lessons from a five-hundred-year perspective on the Caribbean point to the same conclusions as for all the ecosystems we've looked at so far. Attempting to control the demise of reefs and sea grass beds by protecting individual species or groups of species is never going to work. The problems need to be tackled at a more fundamental level. Jeremy Jackson and his colleagues laid the problem bare when they said that we need to stop arguing about which problem, overexploitation, pollution, disease, or climate change, is the most important and tackle all of them.[40] So far our efforts have been piecemeal, and our targets too conservative. Now that we have a clearer picture of what the Caribbean should look like we can see the true scale of the problem. We can set targets for conservation measures that make ecological sense, but whether politicians and legislators in all the Caribbean countries can see that sense is a whole different problem.

CHAPTER 12

Islands in the Sea

The moment that Columbus left his boot prints on San Salvador's coral sand beach a new era began. The New World would never be the same again, but neither would the Old. Contact was a two-way process. From his log entries, Columbus seemed convinced he had made it to Asia, so he never called this the "New" World. But, just before he died, he did call it the "Other" World, since he'd been so forcefully struck by its differences.

> I saw neither sheep nor goats nor any other beast, but I have been here but a short time, half a day; yet if there were any I couldn't have failed to see them.
> All the trees were as different from ours as day from night, and so the fruits, the herbage, the rocks and all things[1]

As Europeans explored the Americas, they found more and more differences. It was one of the reasons why early settlements had such trouble surviving. For settlers trying to cling to their precarious toeholds in the New World, these differences were a matter of life and death, but for those back in Europe, they proved even more serious. They had the capacity to wreck the foundations of Western civilization.

Contact is a two-way process, and the "discovery of America" is far more accurately described as the "Columbian Exchange."[2] That exchange began in the Caribbean, and the effects of Old World animals, plants, and ideas arriving on Caribbean islands in the wake of Columbus are the main focus of this chapter. But I will begin with ideas that flowed the other way, from America to Europe.

Western civilization was underpinned by Christian philosophy, backed by the authority of the Bible. Aristotle had long since provided a scientific and philosophical framework that many church authorities found entirely compatible with their own and, almost as importantly, with the Bible. Everything, from the Creation to Noah's Ark, was nicely worked out and embedded into the culture. Then Columbus saw that light flickering on the far western horizon. For anyone who thought about it, the New World shook those comfortable beliefs right down to their very roots. And a Jesuit priest called José de Acosta certainly thought about it.

Why were there no records of jaguars or raccoons, alpacas or guanacos listed among the inhabitants of the Ark? And, if these creatures, all abundant at the time of first contact, had so successfully survived the flood on their own, what on Earth was the point of building an Ark in the first place? "That which I speak of these Pacos and Guanacos may be said of a thousand different kinds of birdes and beasts of the forrest, which have never beene knowne, neither in shape nor name; and whereof there is no mention made, neither among the Latins nor Greeks, nor any other nations of the world."[3]

José de Acosta was a priest and theologian, born in Spain in 1540, in the same year that Ignatius of Loyola founded the Society of Jesus. By the age of thirteen, Acosta was a novice in that Society, and on his way to becoming one of the most widely respected of all Jesuits. In 1569, he traveled to Lima in Peru and from there proceeded to acquaint himself thoroughly and personally with the land, the people, and the natural history of the Americas. He published several key works including his best known, *Historia Natural y Moral de las Indias*. The New World fired his formidable intellect and imagination and, even though a priest, forced him to speculate well beyond the bounds of orthodoxy. "I say for example, if the sheepe of Peru, and those which they call Pacos and Guanacos, are not found in any other regions of the world who hath carried them thither? If they have not passed from some other Region, how were they formed and brought forth there? It may be that God hath made a new creation of beasts!"[4]

A *second* creation! But a single creation is fundamental to Christianity. And who were those people that greeted Columbus so warmly? Orthodoxy dealt with this problem by suggesting that Indians were descended from the lost tribe of Israel, so fitting them neatly into the established framework and answering a few long-standing questions into the bargain. But Acosta was not so sure.

The problem of the Americas continued to plague science and philosophy for several more centuries. Even as late as 1857, zoologist Philip Sclater's philosophy was still forcing him to consider a second creation.[5] Although the idea that species could change through time was already being discussed, and would be thrust into public consciousness just two years later, with the publication of *The Origin of Species*, Sclater still believed in the immutability of species. And that led him to think that the unique plants and animals of the New World must have arisen exactly where they live today, in a separate creation.

Actually, Acosta already had the germs of the right answer three centuries earlier as he was busy thinking yet more unthinkable thoughts. As an alternative to a second creation, he wondered whether animals might wander away from where the Creator put them and then postulated land bridges that allowed animals and people to colonize the Other World. His observant mind had soon registered that many of the big mammals were absent from the Caribbean islands, implying that they couldn't cross water. The abundant and diverse birds, on the other hand, could easily have flown. If water was such a barrier to big mammals, he reasoned that their presence on the mainland might mean they got there via a land bridge from the Old World. In this, Acosta was far ahead of his time, perhaps the first person to think like a modern biogeographer.

It was this kind of thinking that lead the way from the myth-laden Middle Ages to the Renaissance and eventually to the ultimate heresy of evolution, from the pens of Charles Darwin and Alfred Russel Wallace, both of whom also explored the Caribbean and Central America. But the ultimate irony is that, even as the New World's differences were challenging Western orthodoxy, Westerners were busy transforming this Other World into a much more familiar one.

When Columbus arrived in October 1492, he brought seeds of European crops. And on Christmas morning he was glad he did. The *Santa Maria* was wrecked off the coast of Hispaniola, forcing Columbus to set up a small makeshift colony, which he called La Navidad. When the two remaining ships returned to Spain, Columbus left seeds with the colonists so they could grow familiar crops in this unfamiliar land. La Navidad disappeared and presumably so did any crops. But in November of 1493, Columbus was back, with more ships, more men, and more seeds. These seventeen ships and 1,200 men were a very serious attempt at setting up permanent colonies here, and the settlers would soon find that many of the plants and seeds they were carrying would spring out of the Caribbean earth with an extraordinary vigor. José de Acosta reckoned that "oranges, being fallen to the ground, and rotten, their seeds did spring, and of those which the water carried away into diverse parts, these woods grew so thicke."[6]

However, not everything prospered in Paradise. Wheat, a semidesert grass and the staple of the European diet, failed, which ensured that the Spanish suffered their own "starving time" in the early days. But in the long run, these were minor glitches. In 1493, Columbus also brought sugar canes from the Canaries, and they certainly prospered, sowing the seeds, so to speak, of the Caribbean's future economy. In 1516, bananas were brought from the Canaries and in just a couple of decades were widespread, according to another chronicler of the early Caribbean, Gonzalo de Oviedo. In 1535, Oviedo published his *Historia Natural y General de las Indias,* sometimes seen as the start of a European natural history tradition that led to the great learned societies of the next century. Even by the time Oviedo was putting pen to paper, bananas had gone bananas and "multiplied so greatly that it is marvellous to see the great abundance of them on the islands and in Tierra Firme [the mainland], where the Christians have settled."[7]

Not much more than a century after Columbus, many of the Caribbean islands looked a lot more like southern Europe or North Africa—and a good thing too, according to the likes of Bernabe Cobo, another priestly naturalist. Cobo was one of the most thorough students of Latin American nature in the seventeenth century, but he stuck to his Eurocentric views: "All regions of the globe have contributed their fruits and abundance to adorn and enrich this quarter part of the world, which we Spaniards found so poor and destitute of the plants and animals most necessary to nourish and give service to mankind."[8]

Bananas, sugar, and tobacco, along with various exotic fruits, came to clothe many of the islands as well as vast tracts of the Central American mainland. Sugar, tobacco, and fruit businesses grew as vigorously as the plants that supported them and by the nineteenth and twentieth centuries had given rise to massive corporations, like the United Fruit Company, so powerful that they had a major impact on the politics and economics (and hence the environment) of many areas in Latin America and the Caribbean. The United Fruit Company was the archetypal example of those corporations that gave rise to the expression "banana republic." To create these banana republics, land had to be cleared of its original vegetation.

Each time Columbus landed on a new island, he fell into raptures about the beauty of the native vegetation. On his first voyage, he eulogized the Bahamas, Cuba, and Hispaniola. As he explored the Bahamas, each island seemed more like Paradise than the last.

Though all the others we had seen were beautiful, green and fertile, this [probably Crooked Island] was even more so. It has large and very green trees, and great lagoons, around which these trees stand in marvellous groves. . . . The singing of small birds is so sweet that no one could ever wish to leave this place.[9]

You can even smell the flowers as you approach this coast; it is the most fragrant thing on Earth.[10]

Of course, he and his crew had been sailing across an unknown ocean for more than a month, so any patch of dry land would seem like Paradise. Nevertheless, ignoring the hyperbole, his descriptions still conjure up extraordinarily rich and beautiful places.

On his second voyage, he came across the Lesser Antilles, landing first on Dominica: "all that part of the island which met our view, appeared mountainous, very beautiful, and green even up to the water, which was delightful to see." Then he landed on Marigalante: "This island was filled with an astonishingly thick growth of wood; the variety of unknown trees . . . was surprising, and indeed every spot was covered with verdure."[11]

On almost every island that he stepped foot on, Columbus stood, awestruck, in tall, verdant forests, which, despite extensive areas of Indian agriculture, still clothed most of the islands. There were great mahoganies (a Taino word) and cascarillas, whose bark provides one of the flavorings for Campari. There were brazilletos, which supplied dye wood and were much sought after by the best cabinetmakers. The Spanish soon began a lucrative trade in these trees. In areas of drier and poorer soil, there were great tracts of pine forests, containing trees of a size to interest Columbus the sailor: "so large and wonderful that I cannot exaggerate their height and straightness, like spindles, both thick ones and slender ones. I knew that ships could be made from these . . . and masts for the largest vessels of Spain."

And these forests were full of life, though, as Acosta has already noted, there weren't any large terrestrial mammals on these islands. The problem is partly one of geography, as he surmised, and partly one of ecology. On the smallest islands, there just aren't enough resources to support a viable population of big mammals. Instead their place is taken by reptiles—snakes, lizards, and tortoises.

The reason for this is that reptiles are cold-blooded, which is actually a very poor description of their physiology. They are better called "ectotherms," which differ from the likes of you, me, and the family dog (all endotherms) in not generating heat internally to maintain their body temperature. Instead, they use the sun's heat to raise their body temperature when they need to. At times they are as warm-blooded as any mammal, but they don't have to burn food to provide that heat. In other words, reptiles can get by with much less food than mammals. And on islands, they often reach impressive sizes. In the past, there were three-foot-long tortoises and six-foot-long rock iguanas in the West Indies, though these disappeared a long time ago.[12] Nevertheless, there were still some pretty impressive rock iguanas around when Columbus arrived. And, thanks to their ectothermic nature, they also existed in some pretty impressive numbers.[13]

There are eight species of rock iguanas scattered around the Greater Antilles, and another kind of iguana (*Iguana delicatissima*) living in a similar way on the Lesser Antilles. In some places, the scenes that greeted the Spaniards must have been reminiscent of the famous images of the Galapagos, with herds of loafing iguanas covering exposed rocky areas. In others, their population may already have been reduced, since the Indians often ate all kinds of reptiles. "There are great numbers of small snakes, and some lizards, but not many; for the Indians consider them as great a luxury as we do pheasants."[14]

Although reptiles prospered on the Caribbean islands, there were also plenty of smaller mammals as well. Rice rats occurred on all the islands of the Lesser Antilles, seemingly of different endemic species or subspecies on each island. Evidence from Indian middens suggests that populations fluctuated, possibly doing well as Indian agriculture turned forests into more open terrain and declining when those same Indians turned to hunting them.[15]

Columbus found many creatures about the size of rabbits, and similar enough to the familiar rabbits back home for the Spanish to call them coneys. "No four-footed animal has ever been seen in this [Hispaniola] or any other islands, except some dogs of various colors [native dogs] . . . and also some little animals, in color and fur like a rabbit, and the size of a young rabbit, with long tails and feet like those of rat; these animals climb up the trees, and many who have tasted them, say they are very good to eat."[16] The Indians called these animals *utia*, and today they are still known as hutias. They are rodents though only distantly related to rats and mice. What Columbus couldn't have known was that he was only seeing the tip of a hutia iceberg; there were, at one time, twenty different species throughout the Caribbean, many of which reached high densities. One even grew to the size of a bear, at a time when the lower sea levels of the ice age made the islands much bigger. Half are now extinct, from climate change at the end of the last ice age and from later hunting.

Some species are only known from subfossil bones found in Indian middens, though whether Indian hunting caused their final demise is hard to say. Indians also carried live hutias in their canoes, as a fresh supply of meat on long trading trips, much as European sailors stored live turtles. They also seem to have introduced agoutis from the mainland on to some islands as well as carrying with them guinea pigs,[17] a rodent that is still a common domestic animal in many Andean kitchens. Hutia may also have been semidomesticated by Caribbean Indians. Certainly, they would be good candidates for domestication, since they have very high rates of reproduction, at least in captivity, and, as Columbus pointed out, they're very tasty. Indeed, they used to be kept in barns in colonial Cuba and reared for the pot, and even today wild hutia are still hunted on Jamaica.

These tough little rodents get all the water they need from the vegetation they eat, which means they can even live on small cays with no standing freshwater. One such was the Bahamas hutia, which used to be found in great abundance on many of the low sandy Bahamian cays and islands. Yet, despite its abundance and isolation, it was thought extinct by the 1930s—and so it was believed until 1966, when Dr. Garrett Clough decided to spend a night on the eastern island of the Plana Cays.

As darkness fell, hundreds of extinct hutias emerged from their burrows all around him. This wasn't just a case of a few wary individuals somehow surviving unseen. The place was swarming with hutias. There are perhaps ten thousand crammed onto just 1,100 acres, defying ecological sense by reaching nearly the same biomass as rock iguanas. Some of these were later transplanted to remote islands in the Exuma Cays, where they have proceeded to eat themselves out of house and home by destroying most of the vegetation. This is also strange since hutias certainly occurred on these islands prehistorically[18]—and probably much later—another unforeseen pitfall of restoration ecology.

Although, historically, both hutias and rock iguanas were heavily hunted by humans, we weren't their main problem, at least not directly. Both occurred in such abundance because there were no mammalian predators on most of the Caribbean islands (apart from Indian dogs). After Columbus, all that changed. These islands were definitely Paradise for the cats, rats, dogs, and mongooses that came with the colonists and planters and subsequently ate their way through an unwary island fauna. It was feared that mongooses had dined on every last Jamaican rock iguana until one was caught by a pig hunter's dog in the Hellshire Hills in 1990—another species back from the dead, but only just. At most there are only fifty to two hundred left, making this rock iguana one of the rarest lizards in the world.

And it doesn't take long for introduced predators to wreak havoc on animals that have evolved no defenses against predators. On Pine Cay, a population of five thousand Bahamas rock iguanas was almost completely wiped out by cats, rats, and dogs in just three years. Then a natural sand spit formed between Pine Cay and the adjacent Little Water Cay, and the killers crossed over. In 2000, a last ditch campaign was mounted to transfer the remaining rock iguanas to uninfested islands. In addition, since both rock iguanas and hutias breed well in captivity, several programs are now under way to restock depleted islands with captive bred stock. And for once nature seems to be helping. These captive bred animals appear to survive extremely well in the wild, even with no prior conditioning.

Rock iguanas also face a genetic threat: hybridization with introduced green iguanas. It's possible that green iguanas were introduced from South America by Indian colonists, along with agoutis and guinea pigs, as a source of food, but these big lizards are also popular as pets and have traveled even more widely in recent years. With such problems, it's not surprising that every one of the remaining species of rock iguanas can be counted among the most endangered lizards on the planet.

Although introduced predators have caused severe problems for some of the native fauna, it's the introduced herbivores that have changed the Caribbean beyond recognition. Cattle, horses, and omnivorous pigs arrived with the first conquistadors, multiplied at astounding rates and quickly formed free-ranging herds. Just six years after Columbus's first voyage, a renegade on Hispaniola found he could survive quite easily in the "wilderness" by catching feral cattle and could simply help himself to horses from the roadside. Soon, the herds of cattle on Hispaniola were bigger than those in Spain. Gonzalo de Oviedo saw many herds of five hundred head and some up to eight thousand.[19] Well before the end of the sixteenth century, two hundred thousand cattle hides were exported annually from Hispaniola.[20] By the end of the century, feral cattle had been deliberately released onto a great many islands as emergency rations in case of shipwreck. Marooned sailors smoked the meat over a grate called a boucan—the first of the buccaneers.

Wild horses roamed over open grass and scrublands on Hispaniola in such numbers that these natural savannas were soon destroyed by overgrazing. But pigs, as always, did best of all. In 1514, Diego Velázquez de Cuéllar, who had sailed with Columbus on his second voyage and then settled on Hispaniola, wrote the king to say that the few dozen pigs he had brought with him had now grown to thirty thousand. Yet, as quickly as European animals multiplied, the Indians were disappearing.

Most books tell us that the Taino eventually became extinct, though quite a few people around the Caribbean still vociferously claim descent from Arawak roots. As elsewhere in the New World, the biggest killer was disease, though around the Caribbean, slavery added to their woes. The Spanish had ambivalent attitudes to the Indians. Some saw them as outside the framework of biblical history; they were not humans and therefore had no rights. Others campaigned for their human rights and eventually succeeded in getting the pope to declare that Indians too were descended from Adam.

This ambivalence was already evident by the time of Columbus's second voyage, when the *encomienda* system was set up. In essence, this granted trusteeship of parcels of land to Spanish overlords, *encomonderos*, though not outright ownership. The Spanish Crown recognized that the Indians still owned their land, but they were now subject to taxation by their new guardians, who could also call on them for labor, to increase the wealth of the colonies. This was, in theory, a more enlightened approach than other nations, who simply seized the land they wanted either by force or fraudulent treaties and in justification declared that God had sent disease to clear the land of Indians for them. In reality though, the encomonderos produced the same results. Most of them ruthlessly exploited the Indians as slaves to work the land or mine silver and gold to line Spanish pockets, reasoning that savages had no real use for wealth as such. In parallel to the encomiendas, there were also plantations, which were owned by the Spanish, and which also ran on Indian slave labor, until disease forced the owners to look to Africa for replacements.

The lack of Indians as much as the presence of cattle and pigs changed the Caribbean landscapes. Savannas that escaped overgrazing were invaded by scrub that Indians would normally have cleared. Pigs damaged the remaining forests, and their ability to regenerate was reduced by the demise of seed dispersers. Rock iguanas ate large quantities of fruit and were probably key agents in transporting seeds around the forests. Such wholesale changes to the landscape inevitably stressed the web of ecological relationships that existed before 1492 and produced the ecological equivalent of diseases—plagues.

Twice (that we know of) ants created havoc in the Caribbean. The first plague was on Hispaniola from 1518 to 1519, the second on the Lesser Antilles, lasting from 1760 to 1770. Edward Wilson of Harvard University, one of the world's leading ant experts, thinks he has worked out the culprits and causes of these two plagues.[21] The first plague was probably of the tropical fire ant, *Solenopsis geminata*. This is one of those fascinating ants that guards herds of plant-sucking bugs and "milks" them for their sweet honeydew secretions. Their population exploded when they could expand their herds with imported plant bugs on the ever-spreading crops, a parallel in microcosm to the plague of real cows overrunning the islands.

But, under ant protection, the herds of plant bugs multiplied far faster than mere mammals ever could, and as they did, pomegranate, orange, and cassia crops were destroyed "as though a fire had fallen from the sky and scorched them."[22] The ants themselves were so numerous that the planters and farmers had to resort to standing the legs of their beds in pots of water—a wise precaution. Fire ants are well named; I can personally attest from several encounters that they have an extremely painful bite. In the Lesser Antillean plague, the ant itself was probably also an immigrant, possibly the big-head ant, *Pheidole megacephala*, from Africa. On Barbados, every sugar cane plant along the twelve-mile stretch from St. Georges to St. Johns was destroyed. But these were very temporary setbacks for Caribbean farmers. In the long run, the richly diverse forests continued to give way to monocultures of bananas and sugar canes.

When Columbus saw these forests, he was continually struck by the numbers and varieties of birds. On the Bahamas, he noted that the "small birds of so many species are so different from our own that it is a wonder."[23] Later, he found the same was true of the larger islands: "There are, both in this [Hispaniola] and other islands, an infinite number of birds like those in our own country, and many others such as we had never seen."[24] He frequently remarked on beautiful bird songs that filled these forests, but the forests also rang to the raucous screams of multitudes of parrots. On the Bahamas, Columbus reckoned that there were so many parrots that their flocks darkened the sun.

Later, Bartolome de Las Casas observed the same on Hispaniola. "There are in this island . . . vast numbers of green parrots."[25] That's a sight I would dearly love to have seen. A single parrot locked in a cage is the saddest sight imaginable once you've sat under a fruiting rainforest tree full of chuckling birds, deftly plucking fruits, continually chattering to each other, and occasionally taking a break from feeding to swing by their beaks from a branch just for the hell of it. Flocks the size of those seen by the Spanish must have been utterly entrancing.

Las Casas's green parrots were Amazons of which several different species occur in the Caribbean, some confined to single islands. In all there were at least twenty-eight different kinds of parrots in the Caribbean when Columbus arrived,[26] though the exact number is still debated. That's because today around half that number have vanished. The most spectacular were undoubtedly several species of macaws, none of which survive on any Caribbean islands today. Luckily, other kinds of macaws have survived in South and Central America, and, in the wild, these birds truly merit the word "awesome."

On one occasion, while making a long, slow journey up the Iriri River in Brazil's Amazon in a sputtering canoe (another Taino word, by the way), a pair of hyacinth macaws flew out of the forest on the far distant bank. These birds are huge and a most extraordinary intense blue in color. The pair flew low over the broad river, engaged in a deafening conversation, and passed right over our canoe. Two such animated birds seemed the epitome of joy, so instantly infectious that it sent a wave of similar emotion through me.

Those macaws that had made it from the Central and South American mainland to the Caribbean islands had evolved into a number of different species, some of which were found on only one small island. Exactly how many kinds there were is still uncertain because our knowledge of these birds is somewhat hazy. The Jamaican red macaw is only known from a painting by the nineteenth-century naturalist Philip Henry Gosse, based on a specimen shot by a Mr. Odell around 1765. That specimen, along with the rest of the species has since vanished, and because there are no museum specimens either, we are left to speculate as to whether this was a unique Jamaican species or a variety of the Cuban macaw. This decision is made all the more difficult since the Cuban macaw is also extinct. When zoologist Walter Rothschild visited Cuba in 1875 to collect specimens, he was told he was about ten years too late. The last Cuban macaw was apparently shot about 1864, and the species rendered extinct "for food purposes."[27] There are, though, about fifteen specimens of this species in collections around the world, so at least we know what we are missing.

We just have to guess what the St. Croix macaw looked like. It's known only from one leg bone on this tiny island in the U.S. Virgins group, and that was found in a kitchen midden. But, despite such clear evidence of hunting by Indians, both for food and for making ceremonial items, early reports suggest that many species still existed in large numbers at first contact. In a rare book published in Strasbourg in 1534, a German traveler called Huttich described what can only be macaws on the island of Guadeloupe: "The island has psytacos [parrots] larger than our pheasants . . . they are red in color and are present in such numbers as grasshopper are with us."[28]

The local Indians also kept Guadeloupe macaws to fatten them for the pot: "although the forests are full of psytachen, they feed some of them so that they are better to eat. . . . When our people entered their houses they found utensils in which human flesh was cooking together with psytachen, geese and ducks."[29] As to the last remark, these were obviously Carib—or Canibas—Indians. No specimens of Guadeloupe macaws exist, and we have no idea what they looked like. Like several of their relatives, they are mere ghosts of species. And there are more such ghosts (possibly) on Dominica, Martinique, and Hispaniola, though a recent rereading of the contemporary accounts suggests that the Hispaniolan macaw might have been a figment of an overenthusiastic interpretation of those accounts.[30] Such difficulties illustrate how hard it is to reconstruct the extraordinary parrot fauna of Columbus's Paradise. But at least some of those parrots have survived.

Huge flocks of Amazon parrots greeted Columbus when he stepped ashore on Puerto Rico, a species that today is known as the Puerto Rican parrot. Some scientists think that there may have been around a million of them on the island in 1492,[31] though others suggest a mere hundred thousand or so. Either way, they impressed Columbus. It took time for their population to fall, since the Spanish didn't have much impact on Puerto Rico for some time; their population remained in the hundreds right until the middle of the seventeenth century, though after that it rose exponentially. In parallel with this rapid late growth of settlements, the forests were cleared and the Puerto Rican parrot forced to retreat in the face of an advancing tide of sugar cane. In 1836, a German naturalist called Moritz reported much reduced numbers and by 1968, just a few dozen were left, confined to a small area in the Luquillo Mountains, where remnant rainforests formed islands in a vast sea of cane.

Once a species has been reduced to such low levels, it takes only one unfortunate accident to push it into oblivion. It happened with the heath hen on faraway Martha's Vineyard, and it nearly happened to the Puerto Rican parrot. In 1989, after an intensive effort to build up the numbers of parrots, Hurricane Hugo swept ashore and wiped out half the birds. The parrots struggled back to thirty-nine birds by the middle of the 1990s, though there were still only a precarious six breeding pairs. As part of the recovery program, parrots are being bred in captivity and released, with enough success that a second release zone is now being set up in the hope of starting a second population. Artificial nest cavities have also been designed that exclude nest competitors and predators, to give the chicks a better chance survival. Parrots, being smart birds, have really taken to these artificial nests, and by 2002, all wild nesting birds were using artificial cavities.

A smaller parrot, the Puerto Rican parakeet, has not been so lucky. It too retreated with its forest home, but it was also shot. West Indian ornithologist, James Bond, who loaned his name to his friend Ian Fleming for his secret agent, thought that Puerto Rican parakeets were finally pushed into extinction by pigeon hunters from the United States who visited the island during the nineteenth century, after it had fallen under American ownership. The story of the extinction or near extinction of birds has been repeated on many of the Caribbean islands, and not just with parrots.

Islands of all sizes around the Caribbean provided safe nesting sites for vast colonies of seabirds. Twenty-one species occur around the Caribbean, some still in spectacular colonies, but overall the population is probably only 10 percent or less of its historical size.[32] But even Columbus saw only a shadow of the true exuberance of nature at these colonies. Seabirds were so densely packed and so easy to harvest that when the first Indians arrived, starting around seven thousand years ago, they were easy meat. There is good archaeological evidence that seabird numbers fell dramatically after this time. In North America, the great wave of extinctions that happened at the end of the ice age has also been blamed on the arrival of humans, though the evidence here is still debated. The climate was also changing rapidly at this time and with it the pattern of habitats. Some now think that, on the mainland, climate change may have been more to blame than the Indians' ancestors. But on the Caribbean's islands, it's easier to separate these two factors.

By the time Indians began to settle the Antilles from South or Central America, rapid climate change had largely finished. In detailed excavations on Antigua, in the Lesser Antilles, scientists found a number of species from around seven thousand years ago that were never recorded by European explorers. Other species disappeared from Antigua, though survived elsewhere. The pattern is complex, but it looks as though Indians were responsible for a number of extinctions when they arrived on the islands.[33] And it seems that they also had a major impact on seabird colonies.[34] So it's left to our imagination to picture what these colonies would have looked like before humanity. They must have been quite breathtaking, since, even today, there are some spectacular seabird colonies dotted around the Caribbean, though they are now largely confined to remote cays and tiny islands.

It was quite late in the day when our small fishing boat arrived off one such remote chain of cays, the Dry Tortugas, a national park seventy miles west of Key West in Florida. As we headed for the moorings on Garden Cay I could hear a tantalizing cacophony coming from nearby Bush Cay, made by noddy and sooty terns. It was getting too dark to explore, but every now and then the cacophony rose several decibels and so did my anticipation of filming the birds next morning. The rise in volume accompanied a mass takeoff of birds, and I could just make out swirls of dark shapes over the colony in the fading light. They kept up their chattering all night, a perfect lullaby. During the nesting season, Bush Cay is the sole preserve of the birds; not even wildlife filmmakers are allowed to set foot on the island, though the park authorities were quite happy to let us film from the shallow water surrounding the cay.

So, next morning, we loaded all the camera gear into a small boat and set off through the shallows, towing the boat behind us as we circumnavigated Bush Cay to find the best angle in the early morning light. The sea was sumptuously warm, and thousands of brown noddies and sooty terns were going about their noisy business, ferrying fish from the sea to the gaping mouths of chicks. Resting and nonbreeding birds were perched in artistic arrangements on gray driftwood along the beach and paid not the slightest attention to two humans towing a small boat, who were—quite literally—wallowing in the experience.

Noddies get their name from their confiding behavior; noddy is an old term for "stupid," and sailors reckoned, with good reason, that anything that didn't stay well clear of people certainly couldn't be very smart. But that same behavior meant we could get some fantastic close-ups of these beautiful birds, without ever stepping foot on the island. We spent two days filming these tropical terns, and on the last night, as I was rocked to sleep by a gentle swell, the vivid memories of the past few days made it easy to conjure up the excitement felt by another visitor to Bush Cay, more than a century and a half before me.

John James Audubon could hardly contain himself as he approached the Tortugas on board the *Lady of the Green Mantle*. Her captain had been filling his head for days with tales of the abundance of both sooty and noddy terns on the cays. "He assured me that both species were on their respective breeding-grounds by millions. . . .'Before we cast anchor' he added 'you will see them rise in swarms like those of bees.'"[35] The captain obviously knew what he was talking about: "As the chain grated the ear, I saw a cloud-like mass arise over the 'Bird Key.'. . . On landing I felt for a moment as if the birds would raise me from the ground, so thick were they all around, and so quick the motion of their wings. Their cries were indeed deafening."[36]

In those days, sailors always made sure they stocked up on fresh eggs or meat whenever they passed a seabird colony, and the crew of the *Lady* was no exception: "Some of the sailors, who had more than once been there before, had provided themselves with sticks, with which they knocked down the birds as they flew thick around and over them. In less than half an hour, more than a hundred Terns lay dead in a heap, and a number of baskets were filled to the brim with eggs."[37] The Tortuga colonies were also exploited commercially by Cubans, since they were only a short hop across the water as Audubon soon found. "At Bird Key we found a party of Spanish eggers from Havana. They had already laid in a cargo of about 8 tons of eggs of this Tern (Sooty) and the Noddy."

Eggers probably reduced the numbers of these terns and in some places wiped out colonies entirely,[38] though both species occur widely throughout the tropics and are not endangered globally. Sooty terns in particular are very numerous, with a world population still around 60–80 million birds. Some colonies today reach a million birds, so Audubon's captain may not have been exaggerating as they approached the Tortugas.

Yet even the largest colonies can be threatened if feral cats make it to their island sanctuaries. I saw for myself the scale of damage that cats can inflict on a big sooty tern colony on Ascension Island, in the middle of the Atlantic Ocean. On my first visit, the terns had just arrived at their colony on the ragged black lava fields around Mars Bay. The ground was carpeted in terns, shuffling about on their short legs as they found places to lay their eggs. They don't bother with a nest, but make a shallow scrape, each one carefully spaced just beyond pecking distance of their nearest neighbors. Since these black-and-white birds are quite conspicuous, it is easy to see the vast size of their colony. But Ascension has long been a port of call for the British Navy, and it didn't take long for cats to become established and build up a large population.

My second visit to Ascension was about six weeks later, in time to film the birds feeding chicks. But I could barely believe the sight that greeted me when I stepped out of the Land Rover at the end of a bumpy journey over lava fields. Instead of tightly packed, bickering birds there were just carcasses strewn everywhere. The cats had started at the outside edge of the colony and worked their way in, eating only small parts of each of their victims. They hadn't reached the center of the colony yet, which was still a din of birds feeding spotty, fluffy chicks, but they were surrounded by a grizzly ring of carnage some two hundred yards wide.

In fact, there was a precarious balance between sooty terns and cats on Ascension. Outside the breeding season, sooty terns live over the deep ocean and, once the colony leaves, the cats starve. So they can't ever build up a big enough population to wipe out the tern colony entirely. Each year, birds at the center of the colony are able to fledge their chicks and take them to safety over the open ocean. But this stalemate between cats and birds depends on the fact that all the other seabird colonies, of boobies, tropic birds, and frigate birds, have long since vanished from the main island, so no food remains when the terns are at sea. This is hardly an ideal state of affairs, so, in the last few years, a huge effort has been made to eradicate the cats. The last one was removed in 2004 and now other seabirds, from their refuges on offshore islands, are rejoining the sooty terns on the main island.

All seabird colonies are just as vulnerable to introduced predators, and such carnage must have been repeated right across the Caribbean. Introduced rhesus monkeys wiped out all the seabirds breeding on Desecheo Island, off Puerto Rico. Mongooses were introduced onto many islands to control snakes but found seabirds easier to hunt. They were also supposed to control rat numbers, but here they failed miserably. Rats are still the biggest problem for most seabird colonies. Almost invariably rats find their way on to any island that their human benefactors land on, and once there, they can reach plague proportions. There are records of one such plague on Bermuda, which devastated people's livelihood as well as the local seabirds.

Before Europeans found it, the islands of the Bermuda group hosted vast seabird colonies, but the whereabouts of these tiny specks in the Atlantic were known by the early sixteenth century. Their discovery is usually attributed to the Spanish explorer Juan de Bermudez, and for the rest of that century, both Spanish and Portuguese vessels used Bermuda as a refueling stop, though no settlements were ever established. The sailors said the islands were haunted by screaming devils. Then, in 1609, George Somers was wrecked on this Isle of Devils. He was on his way to newly established Jamestown as governor when storms drove the *Sea Venture* onto Bermuda's reefs. With him was William Strachey, who published an account of the ordeal, *A True Repertory of the Wracke*. His writings are thought to have inspired Shakespeare's *The Tempest*, which contains reference to the "still vexed Bermoothes." But more importantly, at least in our context, he left us some early observations on Bermuda. This was no Isle of Devils; it was teeming with life.

The shores around the group of islands abounded in fish and lobsters. The sailors made nets and hauled five thousand fish at a time: "Wee have taken also from under the broken Rockes, Crevises sometimes greater than any of the best of our English Lobsters; and likewise abundance of Crabbes, Oysters, and Wilkes . . . no Iland in the world may have greater store or better fish."[39] And the islands themselves swarmed with birds. "Fowle there is in great store . . . we found divers Ayres, Goshawkes, and Tassells, Oxen-birds, Cormorants, Balde-Cootes, Moore-Hennes, Owles and Battes in great store."

But there were also strange nocturnal bird: "A kind of webbe-footed Fowle there is . . . and in the darkest nights of November and December (for in the night they onely feed) they would come forth . . . hovering in the ayre, and over the sea, made a strange hollow and harsh growling." For their nightly hooting, the sailors called these birds sea owls, and they existed in prodigious numbers. Here was the reason why the Spanish thought these islands to be inhabited by screaming spirits and why they never settled here. But for the shipwrecked English sailors, these devils and spirits helped keep them alive. "There are thousands of these birds, and . . . at anytime wee could . . . bring home as many as would serve the whole Company." And they weren't difficult to catch. William Strachey tells us that if the sailors made loud whooping and hooting noises, the birds would fly to them and land on their arms and shoulders. In this way, the men could feel how heavy the birds were and select only the plumpest for the pot.

These birds were petrels, tiny relatives of the great albatrosses that ride the winds over the southern oceans and the north Pacific. In particular, they were Bermuda petrels, sometimes called cahows in imitation of their ghostly calls.

Outside their breeding season they range over the open ocean, but every last one of them returns to breed on the tiny group of islands that make up the Bermuda archipelago. There were probably a million birds here before Juan de Bermudez, nesting in burrows and crevices all over these islands, which were too far from the mainland of America to have any mammalian predators.[40] Elsewhere in the world, some petrels still exist in such vast numbers. Wilson's petrels, for example, beautiful little birds about the size of starlings, with bright yellow webbed feet, may well be the most numerous birds on the planet. But cahows haven't been that lucky. After Somers, Strachey and their crew made it to Jamestown in a boat they built from the wreck of the *Sea Venture* and local timber, Bermuda was claimed by the British and settled in 1612. The birds and their eggs were collected for food, but a far bigger problem was the arrival of domestic livestock.

In reality, this problem predates settlement. Gonzalo de Oviedo had tried to release hogs on Bermuda, as emergency rations, soon after its discovery but was unable to land because of weather. This was, however, only a short stay of execution for the cahows. Later sailors obviously succeeded where Oviedo failed, and by the time of Strachey's unscheduled stopover, hogs were already everywhere. They provided food for the shipwrecked sailors, which of course was the original intention of releasing them here: "our people would goe a hunting with our Ship Dogge, and sometimes bring home thirtie, sometimes fiftie Boares, Sowes, and Pigs in a week."[41]

The hogs fed on whatever they could find to eat, including cahows and their chicks, whose burrows were easily sniffed out and ripped open by the hog's formidable snout. When George Somers and his crew wanted to vary their diet with fowl, they had to cross over to the smaller islets; the hogs had already destroyed all the cahows on the main island. Still, to judge from Strachey's writings, these must have been impressive colonies. Then the inevitable happened. Black rats jumped ship to vex the Bermoothes still further. Doubtless, rats were among the survivors of the wreck of the *Sea Venture* and just a few years later had multiplied to reach plague proportions. In 1614, the ever-itinerant John Smith reported from Bermuda that "The Rat Tragedy was now terrible: some fishes had been taken with Rats in their bellies, catched as they swam from Ile to Ile."[42]

Now, none of the islands would be safe. In 1616, Richard Northwood was dispatched from London to carry out a survey of Bermuda and found, in masterful understatement, "a wonderful annoyance by silly rats." He considered this to be a plague sent by God, though it was definitely brought by man. They destroyed crops as fast as they destroyed seabirds, and the people of Bermuda began to starve. In desperation, the inhabitants decided to try an early form of biological control. "We used all diligence for the destroying of them, nourishing many Cats, wile and tame, for that purpose."[43]

The cats, of course, were just as fond of petrels as they were of rats, and the petrels were a lot easier to catch during their nesting season on the islands. Under the combined onslaught from cats, rats, hogs, and people, the cahow vanished from its only known breeding colonies, possibly as early as 1620 or 1621. And so the cahow was presumed extinct for three hundred years, our only source of knowledge the descriptions by people like William Strachey and Richard Northwood and fossil bones, the sheer quantities of which corroborate those early eyewitness reports of teeming abundance. Then, in 1906, a living specimen was collected on the tiny islet of Castle Island. It caused quite a stir in ornithological circles, as spectacular as finding a living dodo. Another specimen turned up in 1935, but still nobody knew where they were breeding. There are, after all, 138 islands making up the Bermuda archipelago, all of which might need searching at night and in the right season to find the elusive cahows. But after more cahows began turning up, an expedition was mounted to start a thorough search of the most likely islets.

On the expedition was a fifteen-year-old schoolboy called David Wingate, and what he saw out there changed the course of his life. They were lucky enough to find a few breeding cahows, but so few that they were teetering on the brink of extinction. At that moment, David Wingate decided to dedicate his working life to rescuing Bermuda's dodo. He ended up as head of the Bermuda government's cahow recovery program until his retirement in 2000, and his hard work has slowly paid off. By 2002, those precious few pairs had crept up to sixty-five and reared a record thirty-five chicks. They now nest on four tiny islands, but their combined nesting colonies still cover less than one hectare in total. It's vital to encourage the birds to spread to new islets so, beginning in 1962, Nonsuch Island has been slowly cleared of predators. It is now the Nonsuch Living Museum and returned to its precolonial state—well, almost. All it lacks now are clouds of cahows filling the night air with their devilish cries. There are, though, plans afoot to lend nature a helping hand and move chicks there.

Petrel chicks grow rapidly, as they're stuffed with crustaceans, fish, or squid by their parents. Soon they are bigger than the adults, at which point their parents abandon them. Once left on their own, the chicks just sit tight in their burrows until hunger forces them to leave and take their first flight over the ocean. So there's very little risk in moving them during this period and, hopefully, such transplanted chicks will return to the place where they fledged to breed. This trick worked well with Gould's petrel off the coast of New South Wales in Australia, so there's every hope that cahows will become the star exhibit in the Nonsuch Living Museum.

Two other petrels lived in great numbers in the Caribbean proper; the black-capped petrel and the Jamaica petrel. Both bred on quite large islands, in crevices or burrows high up in the mountains in the center of the islands, a most unexpected place to find seabirds. The Jamaica petrel was first described in 1789, when it was considered plentiful in the mountains of that island. The black-capped petrel or diablotin was more widespread through the Greater Antilles and as far as the Lesser Antilles, where it existed in enough numbers to be a major source of food in the sixteenth and seventeenth centuries. "Its flesh is so delicate that no hunter ever returns from the mountains who does not ardently desire to have a dozen of these "devils" hanging from his neck."[44] In the eighteenth century, petrels became a staple of the slave diet during the season that they flocked to the mountains: "It may be said that these birds are a manna that sends every year for negroes and for the lowly inhabitants, who do not live on anything else during the season."

The birds were also victims of the distorted taxonomy of the Catholic Church, who frequently redefined the natural world to suit its needs: "Those who read these memoirs will doubtless be surprised that we should eat birds in Lent, but the missionaries who are in these islands . . . after serious deliberation and consultation of a medical man have declared that lizards and diablotins are vegetable food and that consequently they may be eaten at all times."[45]

This very convenient, if not very conventional, biology means that Jamaican petrels are now feared extinct, though there are occasional reports of strange noises at night in the John Crow Mountains of Jamaica. Black-capped petrels have been exterminated from many of their island colonies, though a few still nest in Haiti, where poverty prevents the widespread sale of firearms.

Despite a long history of hunting by Indians, there were still many spectacular seabirds colonies dotted around the Caribbean in the sixteenth and seventeenth century. English privateer John Hawkins saw vast colonies on the Cayman Islands, called Tortugas in his day for their equally impressive numbers of sea turtles. "The fifth of July we had sight of certaine Islands, called the Tortugas . . . and found such a number of birds that in halfe an houre he laded her [their boat] with them; and if they had been ten boats, they might have done the like."[46] We will never know exactly what species Hawkins saw, though he would have certainly come across big colonies of magnificent frigatebirds, otherwise known as man o' war birds or alcatraces (alcatraz in the singular). They often nest on mangrove islands, where the males can be seen blowing out their large red throat pouches in a colorful display to passing females. There are still quite a few places around the Caribbean where the dark, sinister shapes of frigatebirds can be seen hawking over mangrove cays. Bird Cay, off Belize, is one such: a tangle of red mangroves, whose arching roots make it almost impossible to move between the trees, especially with a heavy tripod and camera. The ragged silhouettes of frigatebirds, visible through the heavy foliage above our heads, paint a very primeval image. They somehow bring to mind flocks of pterodactyls from a lost world. Even today, they are a memorable sight, but back in 1801, Alexander von Humboldt saw huge colonies.

Humboldt was an extraordinary man, remembered today for the ocean current off South America named after him. But his extensive explorations in South and Central America also left a legacy of dozens of species bearing his name, from penguins to orchids, as well as twenty volumes of observations and theories on all aspects of natural history. In his book *The Island of Cuba,* he described the wanton destruction of young frigatebirds.

> While we were engaged in botanising our sailors sought for sea crabs, and irritated with ill success, they soothed their anger by climbing the mangroves and committing terrible havoc among the young alcatraces, which were snugly ensconced in pairs in the nest. . . . The young birds defended themselves valiantly with their bills . . . while the old ones flew above our heads uttering hoarse and mournful cries.; but the streams of blood continued to trickle down the trees, for the sailors were armed with clubs and cutlasses. . . . The ground was covered with wounded birds, struggling with death, so that this retired spot, which before our arrival was the abode of peace, seemed now to exclaim, Man has entered here.[47]

Yet other colonies were destroyed by mining for guano. Each year, as birds such as boobies returned to nest, they added a new layer of nitrogen and phosphorus-rich droppings to the islands. Over centuries, this guano accumulated into thick valuable deposits, which make great fertilizer or gunpowder, depending on your particular vocation. The biggest and best deposits were off the coast of Peru, created by birds feeding in the rich upwellings created by Humboldt's current. But several islands in the Caribbean had big enough and old enough seabird colonies to have built up thick layers of guano, well worth mining as agriculture in North America spread westward and spilled onto the Great Plains. Just how important guano was before the days of chemical fertilizers was illustrated in 1856, when the United States passed the Guano Islands Act. This allowed any U.S. citizen to claim as U.S. territory an uninhabited guano island anywhere in the world, and it empowered the president to use the U.S. military to defend those claims. In all, more than fifty islands were claimed, and some are still disputed. Navassa Island, off the coast of Haiti, was claimed in 1857 by an American sea captain called Peter Duncan. Today, it's still U.S. territory, a status hotly disputed by Haiti.

The guano on such islands was mined by black slaves in utterly horrendous conditions of killing heat and choking, toxic dust. On Navassa, conditions were so bad that in 1889 the slaves revolted and killed several of their overseers. After that, guano mining continued, but at much lower levels, until, with the advent of modern fertilizers, the island was finally left to the boobies again. A few pairs of boobies have taken up the invitation and are nesting again, now under the watchful eyes of the Fish and Wildlife Service who look after Navassa.

In other places, boobies still live in spectacular colonies. At Booby Pond Nature Reserve on Little Cayman, twenty-thousand red-footed boobies give more than enough justification for its name. Birds returning to nests at sunset create a truly memorable sight, as do the magnificent frigatebirds on Bird Cay and the brown noddies and sooty terns of the Tortugas. But the Caribbean islands would have hosted many more and much bigger spectacles before there were human eyes to appreciate them. All that's left of these is the dry archaeological record of their passing and the knowledge that nature can create such vibrancy when left to her own devices.

CHAPTER 13

La *Florida*

Although I have spent more than twenty years of my life working in television, a medium that is now, to say the least, ubiquitous, it was a strange and rare thing in my youth. We didn't get our first TV set until I was eight, a great wardrobe-sized box, or so it appeared to my wondrous eyes, with a tiny glass screen sunk into its front face—a window onto a new and entirely unsuspected world. Nor was television the infinite choice of incessant, bland mediocrity that so much of it is today. A single decision was all that was necessary. A choice of just two channels, both of which only broadcast in the evenings, meant channel hopping wasn't a major problem for early program makers. Besides, the remote control was years away from being invented, so even if you had wanted to channel hop between these two channels, you would have got more exercise in one evening than most TV couch potatoes today get in a lifetime.

So for me, television was something of a treat, watched sparingly between the equally important pursuits of catching butterflies or digging up worms in the garden. But my own private window on the world began to show me that there was more to life on Earth than butterflies and worms, more than our garden, more even than the moorland that rose into cleaner air from the smoking industrial tangle of England's northeast, where I grew up.

Peter Scott, with *Look* and later *Faraway Look,* showed me creatures and places that only whetted my appetite for more. Then, later in the 1960s, an American television show appeared on the screen. It followed the adventures of a young boy called Sonny and a dolphin called Flipper. The show was set in and around somewhere called the Everglades, and Sonny's father, Ranger Ricks, patrolled this vast swamp on something that looked like a cross between a boat and a plane, something I soon learned was called an airboat. That was the life for me, roaring across an exotic swamp full of equally exotic creatures.

Even before I'd made the acquaintance of Flipper and the Ricks family, I knew, with that simple certainty of childhood, that I would spend my life working with wild creatures, even if I hadn't yet figured out exactly how. But here was a taste of what must be possible. The Everglades became first on my still-growing list of must-see places. And though I never did get a ranger's job working in the Everglades National Park, things didn't work out too badly. I have sped across the Glades, piloting my own airboat, on many occasions since then, tracking down Florida's unique wildlife for various film projects.

Yet, despite the weekly problems facing the Ricks household, I never really understood back then just how much trouble the Everglades was in. I had no idea at the time that the Everglades might not even exist if I didn't get a move on and find a way to go see it soon. And I certainly didn't know that less than a century before Ranger Ricks was crossing these swamps in comfort (well, comfort is not exactly the right word for airboat travel), this whole area was a vast blank on the map, unknown and unloved. How could somewhere so big, so impenetrable and so uninviting move from obscurity to oblivion in so short a time?

The Everglades takes the story of our relationship to North America's natural world a stage further. So far, much of the impact of Europeans on America's abundance has been through commercial exploitation of a range of individual species. But here in southern Florida it was the land itself that came under attack. Much as the wolf symbolized an untamed and dangerous nature, so the great swamps of Florida were seen as an affront to civilization, of no possible use to humanity except that, in their destruction, civilization could be held up as an inevitable conquering force.

Many years after Flipper and Sonny had had their last adventure (somehow a recent feature film revival just didn't have the same original magic), I finally got to visit the Glades. I was staying in Homestead, a small town south of Miami that became a familiar home for several long periods while I was filming in the swamps. But on this first occasion, all I knew was what the map told me — that it was conveniently close to one entrance of the national park. As I drove toward my destination, nothing could have looked less like Ranger Ricks's wild world. Flat, featureless fields of mud and crops separated by slime-filled ditches stretched away on either side of the road. Occasional groups of migrant farm workers, bent double in their backbreaking labor, were often the only signs of life. Then, finally, rising from the dusty earth was a wall of green, a thick, subtropical forest and a blessed relief from the monotony of fields.

A cool, dark tunnel swallowed the road and brought me to the gateway to another world. In the dimmed light, the National Park Service's familiar brown sign announced the boundary to a more ancient Florida.

The tunnel disgorged me into dazzling sunshine and heat once again and revealed a transformation that was remarkable for its apparent absence. Flat brown land still stretched away to a heat-rippled horizon, though no longer covered with exotic crops. Now it was sawgrass and marl prairie that stretched to the distant horizon. There are none of the jagged peaks that tower over visitors to Rocky Mountain National Park, no steaming geyser basins that draw the multitudes to Yellowstone. Instead there is just a sheet of water and sawgrass that extends to infinity, reflecting a perfect sky and sometimes dotted with dwarf swamp cypresses that would grace any Japanese garden. And it is truly wonderful.

The first stop for most visitors using this entrance is Anhinga Trail, but it's worth admiring the car park before heading down the trail. It's situated on a small island topped off by some magnificent royal palms, a particularly large and spectacular species. The Glades are dotted with such small islands that rise imperceptibly from the flat sawgrass plains. They're called "hammocks," and those few feet of elevation make all the difference. It's almost impossible to spot the rise in the land itself, but you will certainly spot the change in vegetation, from prairie to rainforest. You are now parked on Royal Palm Hammock and a century ago this same hammock became a favored spot for one of Florida's pioneering naturalists—when it was a lot harder to get here.

Charles Torrey Simpson moved to Florida in 1902, when he was already fifty-six, and spent the remaining thirty years of his long and productive life studying plants and animals here. A contemporary of perhaps now better known figures like John Muir, he certainly did for the Everglades what Muir did for Yosemite. His knowledge was deep and wide ranging and his writing evocative.

Royal Palm Hammock was part of an area called Paradise Key, and for good reason according to Simpson: "My eyes have never rested on any spot on Earth as beautiful as Paradise Key." On Royal Palm Hammock, he described one group of the eponymous palms that rose one hundred feet above his head: "a picture of unsurpassed beauty set in a wonderful frame. The whole effect is glorious beyond the power of description."[1]

Royal Palms were much more widespread in the past. William Bartram described them along the St. Johns River in northern Florida in his *Travels*, published in 1791 but perhaps these northern ones were eliminated in one of Florida's rare freezes. Prolonged freezing temperatures have blighted this subtropical paradise on six occasions (that we know of) during the nineteenth century,[2] any one of which may have eliminated the sensitive royal palm from the northern peninsula or, perhaps more likely, they were simply felled by settlers. Either way, one of the easiest places to admire these wonderful trees today is the car park at Anhinga Trail.

Anhinga Trail itself is a wooden walkway raised on stilts above the swamp—by far the least painful way to explore. It takes you along Taylor Slough, one of the rivers that run through the Glades, though in this landscape it's a somewhat debatable point as to where the swamp ends and the river begins.

Early on a winter's morning, huge numbers of black and turkey vultures roost here, rising into the air in spiraling masses as the sun coaxes thermals from the warming ground. Anhingas hang themselves out to dry on bushes and snags, alligators cruise stealthily through the dark water, herons sit patiently on low branches, and everywhere there are dragonflies and butterflies. But to really appreciate these swamps means getting wet and dirty. A swamp is all about the interplay between land and water, and that's where you have to be to get to grips with it—at the interface between wet and dry.

Down here, in subtropical Florida, there are just two seasons—summer is warm and wet, and winter is dry. Each transforms the Glades, and each brings its own particular joys and miseries. In the dry season, the water level drops, exposing the rough limestone foundations of the swamp. The remaining water and most of the fish are concentrated in ponds, alligator holes, and sloughs, all of which become magnets for herons and egrets. Mrazek Pond, about an hour's drive south of Royal Palm Hammock, is always a great place to spend a warm winter's day in Florida, watching the way the various waterbirds divide up the dry season's opportunities.

Spoonbills sweep their spatulate bills from side to side as they walk slowly forward, trapping minute animals. Wood storks wade through the water with their heavier bills agape, ready to snap shut on anything that triggers their lightning-fast reflexes. Snowy egrets patrol the shallows, often pausing to stir up the mud with their bright yellow feet. Green herons sit immobile in pondside vegetation, with boundless patience, waiting for a shoal of small fish to pass within reach. It's ecology in action and quite easy to lose a whole day here without even trying.

The summer wet season brings spectacular downpours that replenish the marshes and turn the Glades into a land of sky and water. Towering purple thunderheads are reflected in shallow still water, and when a last glimpse of sun lights the foreground prairie, it paints the perfect picture of the Everglades—Pa-Hay-Okee, "grassy waters," in the admirably succinct language of the Seminole Indians. This is the time to experience the swamp—working off the beaten track with researchers who know it well, wading through knee-high water and getting cut to ribbons either by the sharply serrated leaves of the well-named sawgrass or by stumbling into unseen cracks in the jagged limestone. Stand still, and the torture continues as uncountable hoards of mosquitoes follow the trail of carbon dioxide on your breath to find their target. Swamp angels they were called, with a pioneer's sense of humor. And one early entomologist, with even more patience than a green heron, caught 356,696 in one night to prove how miserable this swamp could be. Charles Torrey Simpson summed up the joys of exploring the Everglades: "The wilds of Lower Florida can furnish as much laceration and as many annoyances to the square mile as any I've seen."[3]

So it's not, perhaps, as instantly pleasurable as walking through cool groves of pines in the Sierra Nevada or through the dappled shade of a Smoky Mountain fall. But every painful step is rewarded with something new—a giant apple snail laying eggs, or perhaps a glimpse of an amphiuma, a strange eel-like amphibian. Then there is the thrill of the alligator's roar or the nighttime wails of limpkins, like lost souls abroad in the dark swamp. All of these experiences are still possible in today's Glades, but Charles T. Simpson's own agonizing explorations, just a century ago, have left us with the exhilaration of a more pristine Glades: "Bear, deer, otter, raccoons, various wildcats and the opossum were abundant, while every swamp and stream was full of alligators. Vast numbers of roseate spoonbills, snowy herons, American egrets and the great white heron . . . winged their way over the pineland as they visited the swamps for food. And food was everywhere abundant, for the waters were swarming with small fish and the lowlands contained unnumbered millions of pond snails."

Simpson explored the Glades at the beginning of the twentieth century, when much of this enormous ecosystem was still largely unknown. At this time, explorers could turn up at one of the luxury hotels recently built on the higher, drier ridge of land along the east coast and walk about a quarter mile to the west to find a swamp that stretched unbroken for seventy miles across the peninsula and 130 miles from left to right.

In 1920, John Kunkel Small, head curator at New York Botanical Garden, set off with Stanley Hanson, a bird inspector with the U.S. Biological Survey, to explore Big Cypress Swamp, not far from today's Naples. Their description sounds more like an expedition to some remote tract of the third world. And, in essence, it was, as their trusty Ford bogged down on sandy trails or bumped over trackless prairie. As Small described it: "Only a score or so of surveyors, hunters and prospectors, out of the hundred million inhabitants of the United States, have any definite knowledge of its physical geography. Miami and Fort Myers are about 120 miles distant from each other, in a direct line, but the intervening area could have been conveniently . . . traveled only in an aeroplane."[4]

The reason that the Everglades remained unknown for so long was partly one of scale. South Florida was one vast swamp, and a unique one at that, well deserving of its own chapter in our story. I think Gifford Pinchot would have agreed: "It is a region so different that it hardly seems to belong to the United States. It is full of the most vivid and most interesting life on land, in the air, and in the water. It is a land of strangeness, separate and apart from the common things we all know so well."[5]

In 1947, Majory Stoneman Douglas wrote *the* classic on the plight of the Everglades, poetically rendering the Seminole's name as *The River of Grass*. She opens her book by pointing out that there are no other Everglades in the world, a sentiment echoed, more in desperation than in wonder, by a U.S. soldier struggling through unfamiliar terrain to find and expel the last remnants of the Seminole Nation. "No country that I have ever heard of bears any resemblance to it. It seems like a vast sea filled, with grass and green trees."[6] Actually, Douglas's analogy is more apt; it really is one huge grassy river, a product of the flat limestone landscape of Florida. The Everglades begin (or rather began) life in a chain of linked lakes in central Florida, imaginatively called Chain of Lakes. In turn, they fed into the winding Kissimmee River, which flows south. In winter, this river once attracted countless thousands of waterfowl to its overflowed banks, and all year round great flocks of herons and egrets fed themselves on swarms of bass and bluegills in its waters.

The Kissimmee itself flows into a huge shallow lake — Okeechobee — once also crammed with catfish and bass. But no river leaves Okeechobee — though two almost do. The Caloosahatchee rises three miles to the west and flows to the Gulf of Mexico, while the St. Lucie begins twenty miles to the east and flows to the Atlantic. They'll play a key role in the Glades' later story, but first we must return to the swamp system as it might have been described by an ecologist a century and a half ago—if such a thing had existed.

With no outlet, water simply slops over Okeechobee's southern lip, like an overfilled tub, and creates a vast shallow sheet of water flowing almost imperceptibly to the south and west. The sheet eventually forms two broad rivers, Shark Slough flowing southwest towards Ten Thousand Islands and Taylor Slough, which we've already explored, flowing south into Florida Bay. In the wet season, though, water flows across the whole landscape as a seventy-mile-wide river of grass. However, if you were being botanically picky, you should really call it a "river of sedge," since sawgrass, which covers most of the deeper areas, actually belongs to the sedge family.

Dotting this flat landscape are thousands of hammocks, all elongated in the direction of water flow and covered in a watered down version of West Indian rainforest. Diluted they might be, but in their pristine state, these islands of tropical rainforest were still pretty impressive. Charles Torrey Simpson spent many years exploring these hammocks, searching for the beautifully patterned West Indian tree snails that had become his passion since his move to Florida. But he also found and collected a huge range of spectacular orchids, which existed in almost unbelievable quantities just a hundred years ago.

On a trip to Snake Hammock, near Flamingo on the southern tip of the Florida peninsula, he was joined by botanist John Small—and I wish I'd been able to go along with them too. Small found that "this hammock is the most marvelous natural orchid garden in the United States. All but one or two of our native epiphytic orchids grow there . . . in greater profusion and to greater size than I have ever seen them elsewhere."[7] He photographed one specimen of a cigar orchid (*Cyrtopodium punctatum*) on which he counted 31 four-foot flower spikes carrying hundreds of blossoms. These magnificent floral displays were sometimes likened to swarms of bees and gave rise to an alternative name, the bee swarm orchid. When Small and Simpson collected orchids in south Florida, bee swarm orchids were everywhere, and their depredations would have been unnoticeable, but overcollecting has now reduced cigar orchids and many of their relatives to extreme scarcity.

Traveling south through the Glades and approaching the coast, the first tiny mangroves appear, struggling to survive on the wet prairies but slowly growing in stature as the water turns saltier until they rise into a tangled intertidal forest, accessible only along water channels and infested with an unimaginable number of particularly fierce mosquitoes. All these habitats are thick with life, but none more so than the mangrove fringed estuaries. As one early visitor noted of fish, crabs, and lobsters: "You can at one glance, through this crystal water, see over fifty varieties. The colors would put to blush the palette of an impressionist."[8]

The swamp itself was largely reviled and feared. Only a century ago, the general consensus was that people wouldn't move from Hell to south Florida, an attitude that can hardly be reconciled with today's flood of people inundating the Sunshine State. But, back then, most people simply avoided the Glades and speculated wildly about what might be hidden there. As far back as 1565, John Sparke thought that there were unicorns in the center of Florida, though he never bothered to go and find out. Others felt sure that three-headed serpents lurked there. Much more recently, Okeechobee itself was the subject of much rumor and speculation. Some thought that such a vast inland lake didn't exist at all, others that it was surrounded by 150-foot cliffs and infested with monkeys. Florida was also rumored to be the site of a fountain of youth, something that attracted the attention of an ambitious conquistador called Juan Ponce de Leon back in 1513.

Ponce de Leon was governor of Puerto Rico until 1511 when he was removed from office for brutality toward the remaining Indians. During this time, he had extracted tales from the local Taino Indians of a large wealthy island to the north called Bimini, containing this magical fountain. Before the Spanish, the Tainos traded widely around the Caribbean and had developed a good working knowledge of its geography so there was no reason not to trust their information.

Ponce de Leon was probably in his fifties at the time, so may have been tempted by such stories of eternal youth, but he was also a practical, hardheaded fellow and probably far more interested in the possibility of gold, silver, and slaves than in a way of regaining his lost years. But, whatever drove him, he set off in the early spring of 1513 and around Easter sighted what was, as far as he was concerned, another large Caribbean island. For the Spanish, Easter was the "Flowery Festival" or the "Feast of Flowers"—Pascua Florida, and so this new island was christened to commemorate the date of its discovery. Actually, he may simply have meant "Florida" to refer to the lush vegetation he saw there, which, to me at least, seems more appropriate.

He landed at several places around this "island," but like most who followed him over the next three and half centuries, Ponce de Leon didn't explore inland. He had a good excuse; he was greeted by very aggressive—and very large—Indians. "The Natives of the land . . . very austere and very savage and belligerent and fierce and untamed people and not accustomed . . . to lay down their liberty so easily."[9] No slaves here then. These were the Calusa people that we've already encountered briefly in our exploration of the Caribbean and that broke the rules of conventional anthropological thought. They developed complex societies that lived on large artificial islands in the swamp and that had plenty of time to make exquisite carvings—all without the support of farming. Enough food existed in the swamps and estuaries for all their needs.

When archaeologist Frank Cushing excavated one of their mounds at Key Marco in 1896, he found a great variety of beautifully carved and painted animals superbly preserved by lying in anoxic waters. Lacking the technology to preserve these wooden figures after excavation, the paint quickly faded and the figures dried and crumbled, though luckily Cushing had made accurate watercolors of his finds. These were later used by the University of Florida in Gainesville to make replicas of many of the carvings.

I've filmed some of these replicas, and they are truly beautiful. It's easy to understand Cushing's passion, and I quite concur with his view that one of the most stunning is a deer's head. "In form . . . it portrayed with startling fidelity and delicacy, the head of a young deer or doe. . . . [The ears] were also relatively large . . . fluted, and their tips were curved as in nature . . . they were painted inside with a creamy pink-white pigment . . . and the black hair tufts at the back were neatly represented by short black strokes of paint . . . it was evident the primitive artist who fashioned this masterpiece loved, with both ardor and reverence, the animal he was portraying." White-tailed deer were abundant throughout Florida, particularly on tracts of higher ground in and around the river of grass. Panfilo Narvaez, a conquistador who explored central Florida shortly after Ponce de Leon discovered it, described forests filled with game of all sorts. But south Florida has its own special form of white-tailed deer—the key deer.

As their name suggests they live along the Florida Keys and probably got there during the ice age, when sea levels were lower and Florida, consequently, a lot larger. The Keys would have all been connected to each other and to the mainland as a continuation of the ridge of higher land that runs down the eastern coast. Rising sea levels marooned the deer here, but they continued to thrive. During their isolation on these small islands, they adapted by evolving a smaller size and are now the smallest of twenty-eight different subspecies of whitetail. Their existence was certainly a surprise to Hernando Fontenada, the young captive of the Calusa. "But what was a great wonder . . . was the existence of deer on the Islands of Cuchiyaga (The Lower Keys)."[10]

They were hunted by Indians, but even such small, isolated populations weren't hunted to extinction. After their discovery by Europeans, there were still plenty to be hunted by sailors from passing ships. A survey in 2000 revealed around seven to eight hundred remaining, a low enough population to be of concern, though, confined to this chain of small islands, these deer could never have reached enormous populations. But in and around the Key Deer National Wildlife Refuge on Big Pine Key, these little deer don't exactly feel rare. A short walk down one of the garden-lined back streets will soon reveal a key deer munching its way through someone's carefully tended plants.

In his excavations on Key Marco, Cushing also unearthed a carving of an even rarer creature. The carving looks more like something from the Egypt of the pharaohs, a kneeling catlike figure. And although this was not Bast, the Egyptian cat-headed god, it does seem to have been an object of reverence. Cushing said it was "carved from a hard knot, or gnarled block of fine, dark brown wood. It had either been saturated with some kind of varnish, or more probably had been frequently anointed with the fat of slain animals or victims. To this, doubtless, its remarkable preservation was due." The Key Marco cat is a Florida panther, another subspecies of puma, the Americas' most widespread cat. The Florida panther is the southeastern counterpart of the eastern cougar that roamed the forests of the east coast, but unlike that subspecies, Florida panthers still definitely exist—if only just.

Once they were just as abundant as eastern cougars, ranging widely through the forests of all the southeastern states, but the last few, probably no more than fifty or sixty of them, are now confined to the southern half of the Florida peninsula. If not for the remoteness of the southern swamps, they would almost certainly have been eradicated by the advance of civilization, just as their eastern cousins seem to have been.

The Calusa have also bequeathed us exquisite carvings of pelicans, wolves, alligators, and sea turtles, all creatures that must have been important to them both practically and spiritually. Most of what we know about these extraordinary people comes from such archaeological speculation, though there are a few firsthand accounts. Perhaps the most informative is that of Fontenada, who spent many years as a captive of the Calusa and traveled widely with them throughout their large territory. There were also occasional official meetings between Calusa leaders and those of the Spanish, usually to negotiate the release of captives like Fontenada.

Pedro Menendez de Avila was Florida's first governor, charged by the crown with establishing contacts with the Indians. He managed to engineer a meeting with the Calusa, after which he described their large decorated houses and plentiful food supply, confirming the existence of a surprisingly sophisticated civilization in a land that looked anything but appealing to European eyes. He also managed to secure the release of Fontenada, after nearly twenty years of captivity.

But, most of the time, the Calusa simply repulsed any attempted intrusion. Even other nations bordering their territory were wary of encouraging contact with Europeans for fear of reprisals from their powerful and xenophobic neighbors. This was another reason why the interior wasn't explored for so long and why it remained the fancied abode of unicorns, three-headed serpents and swarms of monkeys. In fact, very little was known about Florida's unique swamplands for three centuries after Fontenada was rescued. But that didn't stop Florida itself becoming a pawn in European politics.

In the space of six decades, it passed from Spain to England, then back to Spain and finally to the ever-expanding United States. Each country in turn tried to encourage its own citizens to settle in order to consolidate their political claims. Though these efforts were largely concentrated in north Florida, European and American wars didn't bypass the Calusa altogether.

In 1702, England was at war with France and Spain again, this time over who would succeed to the Spanish throne. Inevitably the war spilled over into the New World, where it is known as Queen Anne's War. Here, it pitted Spain in the south and France in the north, together with their Indian allies, against the British colonies with their Indian allies. In north Florida, as the combined forces of the British and Creek nations overcame the Spanish and their Appalachee allies, defeated Indians began to drift down the Florida peninsula. This created an effect like falling dominoes, which eventually ran into Calusa territory in the far south.

European disease had by now also weakened the once-invincible Calusa, and their leaders began to realize that drastic action was needed. No longer able to protect their swamp heartland, many headed south to Cuba. The nation as a whole faded from official history around the middle of the eighteenth century, though small bands, under other names, may have survived in south Florida's swamps until the first half of the nineteenth century. Records of Calusa children being born in Cuba raises the possibility of Calusa blood surviving there, though this is thought unlikely by most researchers. In any case, the Calusa, long known as the "Fierce Ones," vanished from Florida's swamps.

But the swamps didn't stay empty of Indians for long. Bands of the Creek Nation had moved into Spanish north and central Florida to escape constant conflicts, where they became known as Seminoles. There's some debate over the origin of the name, but it is popularly assumed to derive from the Spanish *cimarrones*, a term originally used for runaway African slaves (or maroons). So in this sense it meant "outlaws," or, if you were on the other side of the fence, it meant "those who would not be subdued."

William Bartram visited the Seminole in north Florida in the early 1770s and found them living a good life on rich lands, but their alliance with the British would earn them nothing but enmity from a nascent United States. On top of that, General Andrew Jackson, hero of the Creek Wars, felt that Florida was vital to U.S. security and that it was manifestly destined to become part of the United States. He led raids into Florida against bands of Indians that were attacking settlements in Georgia, possibly at the behest of the Spanish—raids that eventually became the First Seminole War. At the end of this, the United States effectively controlled Florida, so in 1821, Spain sold Florida to the United States for $5 million, in return for which the United States agreed to give up their claim to Texas—at least for the moment.

The new owners of Florida did not want to share it with the Seminole, and initially they tried to persuade them to move south, into the unoccupied swamps. But even the Indians were reluctant to enter this land of water. A Seminole leader called Neamathla tried to plead their case: "We hope you will not send us south to a country where neither the hickory nut, the acorn, nor the persimmon grows." The Seminole were farmers, and the way the Calusa had lived was as foreign to them as it was to the new Americans. But soon they would have no choice. When Jackson became president, he signed into effect the Indian Removal Act, designed to banish all the major tribes of the southeast to Indian Territory, across the Mississippi. Any that refused to leave voluntarily were rounded up by the army and marched west along routes that collectively became known as the Trail of Tears.

For the Seminole, the only escape was south, into that unknown blank on the map called the Everglades. Two distinct but related groups, the Micco-sukee and the Seminole, began to create a new lifestyle for themselves here, based on farming the drier hammocks and hunting the swamps and estuaries for those same creatures that sustained the Calusa. They also created a major headache for the United States.

Although no one as yet had any conceivable use for the swamps, Jackson's vision was for an Indian-free Florida. His life had been saved by a Cherokee called Junaluska at the Battle of Horseshoe Bend, during the Creek Wars, so he ought to have had some sympathy for the situation that the southeastern Indians found themselves in. And indeed some think that Jackson himself may have thought he was doing the Indians a favor with the Indian Removal Act. It allowed them to move beyond the frontier, to a place where they could remain undisturbed to continue their traditional lifestyles in peace. In reality though, the Trail of Tears led to a very different landscape from the one in which southeastern cultures evolved and most Indians already knew that the Great River wasn't going to stop the inexorable spread of the United States.

Bribes and coercion persuaded some to abandon the swamp, until a charismatic warrior called Osceola persuaded the remainder to stay and fight. And fight they did. This Second Seminole War became America's first Vietnam. The fight drew soldiers deep into the sawgrass and the swamp cypress forests, and it is from this period that most of the earliest descriptions of the wild Everglades come. Most make the place sound like Hell on Earth, as indeed it was for the hard-pressed soldiers, fighting an unseen enemy that ambushed the conspicuous, slow-moving columns and then melted back into the swamp. Not even the vibrant natural world seemed to restore the soldiers' spirits: "At night as we lay down the uproar around us was fearful. Birds of all kinds were making the night hideous with discordant sounds."[11]

No doubt they were hearing the harsh cries of night herons and the eerie wailing of limpkins. The Seminole, on the other hand, grew to know the swamps intimately. This uncharted and unexplored wilderness was the best protection they could have imagined. They were never defeated by the U.S. Army, and they never surrendered. Their descendents live there today.

The Seminole may have remained unconquered, but Pah-Hay-Okee wouldn't be so fortunate. The army's incursions into the southern swamps were the first steps in turning the grassy waters to a more productive use. As news of this vast landscape began to reach the wider world, resourceful Americans began to see possibilities for making money here.

One resource turned out to be those noisy birds. The whole area teemed with herons, ducks, egrets, spoonbills, and pelicans. On the Kissimmee River, a mass takeoff of these flocks could easily be mistaken for thunder. Further south, Audubon wreaked havoc amongst these flocks as he collected specimens for his magnum opus.

> The flocks of birds that covered the shelly beaches, and those hovering over our head, so astonished us that we could for a while scarcely believe our eyes. Our first fire among a crowd of Great Godwits laid prostrate sixty-five of these birds.[12]
>
> On the 31st of May, 1832, I saw an immense number of these birds on an extensive mud-bar bordering one of the Keys of Florida, about six miles south of Cape Sable . . . Four or five guns were fired at once, and the slaughter was such, that I was quite satisfied with the number obtained, both for specimens and for food.[13]

He also saw flocks of thousands of wood storks, which he called ibises. "After the sun had disappeared, the broad front of a great flock of Ibises was observed advancing towards us. They soon alighted in great numbers on the large branches of the dead trees; but whenever one of the branches gave way under their weight all at once rose in the air, flew about several times, and alighted again. One of my companions, having a good opportunity, fired, and brought two down with a single bullet." Sandy Island, near Cape Sable, was covered in a great variety of birds, including white ibises. "As we entered that well-known place, we saw nests on every bush, cactus, or tree. Whether the number was one thousand or ten I cannot say, but this I well know: I counted forty-seven on a single plum-tree." Such grand bird spectacles continued to amaze those with the endurance to visit these swamps, long after Audubon. And for some, life didn't get much better. "Here I felt I had reached the high-water mark of spectacular sights in the bird world." Another visiting ornithologist could only echo those sentiments. "It was a truly wonderful sight, and I have never seen so many thousands of birds together at any single point."

Despite pages more of such evocative descriptions, it's still difficult to put any firm numbers on the population of waterbirds in south Florida's swamps. One estimate suggests that there could have been 2.5 million back in 1870.[14] But James Kushlan, who has spent much of his career studying waterbirds and was one of the authors of that estimate, has also pointed out that attempted estimates of the historic abundance of Florida's wading birds vary widely and dramatically.[15] And often, observers gave up trying to produce firm figures, simply holding up their hands and declaring it impossible to count birds in such difficult and inaccessible places. So a true picture may never be known.

Kushlan also suggests that figures for waterbird populations could well have been "massaged" for political ends as the great bird spectacles of south Florida's swamps and marshes became an early focus in the battle between a rapidly growing conservation movement and commercial interests. The ability to find or create a market for almost any and every natural spectacle on the continent has been—and still is—one of the most remarkable talents of those who came here, from Columbus onward, and waterbirds were no exception.

Male egrets are decked out in filigree plumes in the breeding season to impress potential mates. And for some reason, female humans thought they might serve them for the same purpose. Even in Audubon's day, flowing plumes adorned the hats of the fashion conscious. "The long plumes of this bird [the Great White Egret] being in request for ornamental purposes, they are shot in great numbers while sitting on their eggs or soon after the appearance of the young. I know a person who, on offering a double-barreled gun to a gentleman near Charleston, for one hundred White Herons fresh killed, received that number and more the next day."[16]

The craze grew beyond herons and beyond the delicate, flowing aigrettes into a mad scramble for whole birds, skinned and mounted in strange postures on hats that looked more like exhibits from natural history museums with every passing year. At least, that's what Frank Chapman must have thought and he was well placed to judge.

An ornithologist from the American Museum of Natural History in New York, he found he could now do his bird-watching on the streets of Manhattan. On two walks through a fashionable district, he counted forty species of birds perched in coquettish poses on the heads of passersby. The numbers taken were immense. In 1886, the American Ornithologists' Union estimated that 5 million birds had become milliners' trappings. At the height of the trade, in 1897, *Harper's Bazaar*—or perhaps it should be "bizarre"—reckoned: "That there should be an owl or ostrich left with a single feather apiece hardly seems possible."

But herons and egrets were the main targets. At the start of the twentieth century, plumes were worth $32 an ounce—about *twice* the price of gold. Not surprisingly, Florida and the Gulf coast saw a plume rush, and the great rookeries were decimated. The slaughter was bloody and cruel, but as news of the carnage leaked out of the swamps, the millinery trade tried to present a more wholesome image. They claimed that most of the feathers were simply collected from the rookery floor after the birds had finished with them and molted. But the truth out in the swamps was very different.

Molted plumes were worth only a fifth of the price of "harvested" ones. Instead, plumes were torn from dead or injured birds and their chicks left to starve in the scorching heat. When Frank Chapman went to Florida to visit one of the heron's few protectors, a man called Guy Bradley—and maybe to see some live birds for a change—he was shown a rookery on Cuthbert Lake that had been entirely destroyed. In the immediate aftermath of the carnage, Bradley told him: "You could've walked right around the Rookery on those bird's bodies—between four and five hundred of them."[17]

But not all women were seduced by this fashion craze. In 1896, Harriet Hemenway, a pillar of Boston Society, read about the bloody slaughter of egrets in faraway Florida and immediately called on her cousin, Miss Minna Hall. The two women were appalled at the true cost of those stylish bonnets and decided to act. They perused the Boston Society Register to compile a list of the city's most fashionable ladies and then ran a series of afternoon teas. Society teas in Boston might not sound like a lot of help to egrets nesting in sweaty, mosquito-infested swamps over a thousand miles, and a whole world, away, but the legacy of those teas survives to this day.

These two women began to persuade influential figures to boycott the plume trade, though they soon realized that this was never going to be enough. The millinery trade in the United States at the turn of the twentieth century was enormous. It employed one in every one thousand Americans. A new plan, and the enlistment of the opposite sex, was necessary.

Hemenway and Hall convened a meeting of both men and women to form a society to tackle the plume trade head on. They called it the Massachusetts Audubon Society, which is slightly ironic, given the number of these birds that the great man himself had blasted out of the sky during his career. To be fair though, that was the nature of science back then. As an old Victorian natural history saying has it—what's hit's history, what's missed's mystery. But, under the banner of this famous figure, the new society began to have some effect, though Hemenway and Hall weren't the first women to be moved by the senseless slaughter of Florida's birds.

Harriet Beecher Stowe is probably more famous for her antislavery novels, *Uncle Tom's Cabin* and *Dred,* than as a conservation campaigner. But two decades after she stirred America's conscience to the injustices of slavery, she used her literary skills on behalf of beleaguered herons and egrets. Traveling around Florida, she had been appalled by the quantities of birds shot, and not just for the plume trade. On the steamboats that chugged along rivers like the St. Johns, she watched in horror as passengers blasted away at anything that fluttered within range, simply out of boredom. In 1877, she published *Protect the Birds*, though it didn't have quite the same effect as *Uncle Tom's Cabin*. But two decades later, the Massachusetts Audubon Society seemed to capture a new mood, at a time when massive environmental degradation right across the settled United States could no longer be ignored.

As the idea caught on, other states formed their own Audubon Societies. This was a seminal moment, a groundswell of people opposed to a free-for-all exploitation of nature and the first dawnings of the application of moral principles to the continent's natural resources. Many at the time credited this new, more nurturing, view of nature to the growing involvement of women. "Do women who wear birds ever stop to think what an injury to the . . . moral influence of our sex they are inflicting." Whereas Gifford Pinchot, with the development of forest reserves, focused on the practical aspects of conservation, Audubon's growing army of women focused on the moral aspects. But the sheer scale of the plume trade meant that moral indignation would need to be backed by the law if the herons were going to be saved.

The feather trade was centered on New York, but the supply came from a thousand miles away, across many state boundaries. Several states in the Deep South had enacted laws to protect their dwindling heron and egret populations, but plenty of feathers were still reaching the markets in the north. So in 1900, Congress enacted the Lacey Act, designed to enhance existing state laws by outlawing the movement of protected species across state boundaries.

But, despite this nick-of-time intervention, Florida's birds were still disappearing fast. Brown pelicans, which thronged Florida Bay when the Calusa immortalized them in wooden and stone carvings, were now down to their last breeding colony, on Pelican Island. But, luckily, the White House was now occupied by the imposing frame of Theodore Roosevelt, who shared with the Audubon Society the growing worries about the state of nature in the country under his stewardship. His desire to stem the hemorrhaging of natural resources was firmly rooted in the practical school of conservation. He saw the wholesome and manly pursuit of hunting as integral to the American character, though he also recognized the spiritual value of wild places and natural spectacle. So when Frank Chapman went to him in 1903 and told him about the plight of Florida's pelicans, he listened. In fact, he did more than that; he declared Pelican Island to be the first federal bird reserve—the first in what would later become the National Wildlife Refuge system.

The Lacey Act and federal reserves certainly helped, but feathers and birds were still finding their way onto hats in all too large numbers. In response, the Audubon Societies began paying for wardens to protect the colonies, a dangerous business against armed plume hunters. Three wardens, including Guy Bradley, who Frank Chapman had met, were killed by hunters. But the presence of wardens, many as tough as the plume hunters they faced, did work. Just how effective they were can be judged by the fact that when the Audubon Society had to withdraw their warden from the Alligator Bay rookery because they didn't have the money to pay his salary, it was almost immediately obliterated.

At the same time, the millinery trade was busy campaigning to have the Lacey Act repealed, on the grounds that it would create economic hardship and upheaval if such a huge business was strangled to death. But, despite these efforts, conservationists won deciding victories in 1911 in the key state of New York, with the passage of the Audubon Plumage Bill, which finally banned the sale of all plumes of native birds, and again in 1913 with the Migratory Bird Treaty Act.

The milliners lost their appeals yet, despite all the predictions of economic doom and gloom, no one lost their jobs. The women of America simply adorned their hats with silks and ribbons instead. In hindsight, it's a bizarre fact of life that, taking beaver felt into consideration as well, fashion-led crazes for headgear has had such an extraordinary effect on the wildlife of North America over the centuries.

In fact, not all waterbirds were so badly hit by the plume trade. White ibis and wood storks don't produce fine plumes, and those of the tricolored and little blue herons were small and dark and therefore less sought after. These species survived the years of the plume trade relatively unscathed and still existed in impressive numbers in the early decades of the twentieth century, as John Small discovered when he ventured into Florida's swamps in 1920. He was overwhelmed by their numbers, just as Audubon was. "We went down to the slough afoot just as the thousands of birds in the rookery were awakening. The birds mostly represented several species of ibis, and were present by the hundreds and thousands on the large cypress trees. In fact, they were so crowded on some of the giant cypresses that they were continually falling off for want of sufficient room to stand."[18] But, safe from the hatters of New York, snowy egrets (which almost became extinct) and great egrets—the two most targeted species—also began to recover. Yet, even as the various Audubon Societies, now collaborating under a National Committee in Washington, celebrated better protection for the herons themselves, a new question arose as to whether the increasing numbers of birds would have a home for much longer.

The other thing that soldiers fighting the Seminole War had seen was land—that endless flat horizon of the Glades. Most of it was underwater, but a few ambitious people were daring to suggest that it could be drained, and the muck from which the river of grass grew turned into first class soil in a first class climate. These dreams of a new agricultural empire were kicked off by the Swampland Act of 1850, which opened the way for some of the biggest land scams in American history.

The idea was that any land defined as swamp could be turned over from the federal government to the state, and the state could then sell the land to private enterprises who agreed to turn worthless swamp into productive farmland. It was something of a scam from the start since in state surveys, the definition of "swamp" was very loosely interpreted so the state could get its hands on as much public land as possible.

In Florida, an Internal Improvement Board was set up to dispose of land to people who would drain it. In reality, though, it became a huge land give-away to people with the right connections. One regular beneficiary was Henry Flagler, a railroad tycoon, who was handed thousands of acres of Florida that he rarely bothered to drain. But he did build an ambitious railroad down Florida's east coast, which started ferrying hopeful farmers down the peninsula. The place that was once described as Hell on Earth was now being sold as a subtropical paradise, but in these early days, many prospective farmers who bought land from the real estate companies that had benefited from the land grab found their land was better measured in gallons than acres.

Even so, as settlements along the drier eastern ridge of the peninsula grew, so did calls to get serious about draining the swamps. In fact, progress, albeit slow, was already being made in central Florida, where the river of grass is born. The Kissimmee River area had been drained by turning the river into a straight canal, flushing water straight into Okeechobee.

But a new impetus to tackle the southern swamps came when a dashing and flamboyant governor took up office in Florida. If anyone could conquer these swamps, it would be someone with the imperial name of Napoleon Bonaparte Broward. He reckoned that his Empire of the Everglades could be created for the cost of a dollar an acre and all the industrious Floridians had to do was to "knock a hole in a wall of coral and let a body of water obey a natural law and seek the level of the sea."[19] As he frequently reminded them, "water runs downhill." In Florida, however, it turned out that Mark Twain's more cynical observation was more accurate—that "water runs uphill—to money."

To achieve his dream, Broward built massive dredges to cut canals into the limestone foundation of the Glades and carry the water to the sea. These were gargantuan, noisy, steam-powered machines that looked like they might have emerged from the pages of *War of the Worlds*. A preserved one now lies silently on the roadside along the Tamiami Trail and gives some idea of the scale of Broward's thinking. But draining the swamps never proved as easy as Broward had promised. It was going to take a lot more than a few canals cut through the eastern ridge. Even so, some land was emerging from the water, and it did grow lush crops, so more and more people began supporting the idea of reclaiming the Glades.

Yet, even in the 1920s, there were still vast tracts of swamp remaining, full of life, as John Small saw as he explored the hinterland in his trusty Ford: "we sped westwards through pinelands and across the Halpatiokee Swamp, where countless turtles and snakes basked in the sun about the water."[20] On the drier ground, he found an abundance of one of my favorite birds: "Perhaps the most interesting creature on these prairies was the burrowing owl. This bird honeycombed the prairie in many places with its burrows. . . . The owls were so tame that we could almost pick them up." I've filmed burrowing owls in Florida, and I can tell you that they are nothing like as abundant these days. They are, though, the most charismatic little owls you can ever meet, aggressive beyond their diminutive size toward anything that ventures too close to their burrow.

But when Charles Torrey Simpson joined John Small on one of his later trips, the fate of the swamps was becoming ever more obvious. "There is something very distressing in the gradual destruction of the wilds. . . . Soon this vast, lonely, beautiful waste will be reclaimed and tamed; soon it will be furrowed by canals and highways and spanned by steel rails. A busy, toiling people will occupy the place that sheltered a wealth of wildlife."

In 1916, Simpson saw one of his favorite places, Paradise Key, gain some measure of protection as Royal Palm State Park, but this was no more than a token gesture, a tiny fragment of the whole interconnected Everglades system. And as new inroads were made into the swamps, that whole system began to break down. Dikes built across the bottom of Lake Okeechobee prevented water from spilling over into the river of grass, and canals joined Okeechobee to the St. Lucie, so excess water could be drained to the sea, bypassing the whole of the Glades. Mile upon mile of land south of Okeechobee was converted from sawgrass to sugar and oranges. Growing sugar here was seen as vital to U.S. security, to wean sweet-toothed Americans off their dependence on Latin American sugar. So it had huge backing and grew to be a massive industry with plenty of friends in high places.

In 1928, the Tamiami Trail opened, connecting Tampa to Miami—hence the name. To do so, it cuts east to west right across the center of the Glades, creating another barrier to whatever water found its way into the river of grass. The Trail crosses several sluice gates that allow water under the road, but they were rarely opened, since watering the sawgrass was not as important as watering the sugar further upstream. The Everglades was in deep trouble, though at this stage few knew about it. Agriculture was big business and converting swamps to productive land was all part of the impetus of the Progressive Era. Then, in 1947, Marjory Stoneman Douglas wrote *The River of Grass.*

It had the same kind of impact that Rachel Carson's *Silent Spring* would have fifteen years later. More and more people began to realize that a unique part of America—of the world, in fact—was rapidly disappearing under the assault of agriculture. Even before Douglas's now-classic work, a few people, who were already aware of the Glades' dire situation, had been working hard to try and gain protection for at least part of the Glades and a month after publication of *The River of Grass,* the Everglades National Park was dedicated.

It was centered on the tiny Royal Palm State Park but still only preserved 20 percent of the original wetlands, since most people didn't want anything to limit the massive flow of people into the Sunshine State. There was even a chunk of agricultural land left in the middle of the park—the so-called hole in the donut. The park boundaries were the final compromise of much hard bargaining, but in reality, it was nowhere near enough to guarantee a future for the Glades. The whole complex system was now badly fragmented, and what was the point of creating the Everglades National Park in the south if all the water was being siphoned off by thirsty sugarcane fields in the north? These were the problems that Marjory Stoneman Douglas alerted the world to.

In the year that saw the creation of the Everglades National Park, as if in protest at such inadequate measures, nature retaliated. After a decade of drought, she dumped one hundred inches of rain on Florida and flooded almost all of the reclaimed land, washing away crops. But her plan backfired. Agribusiness simply saw this as a reason to intensify efforts to control the flow of water and bend it to human needs. A year later, the Army Corps of Engineers started the Central and Southern Florida (C&SF) project, a plan to manage the unruly flow of the river of grass. Ten years later, the C&SF project had cut off the northern Everglades to create the Everglades Agricultural Area.

Despite agreements to supply the lower Glades with vital water, a period of drought at the beginning of the 1970s showed where the priorities lay. At the end of this decade, south Florida's water managers finally agreed to pump water from the Everglades Agricultural Area to slake the southern Glades, but this brought new and unforeseen problems. The water was laced with significant amounts of phosphorus from agricultural fertilizers. The sawgrass marshes had evolved under low nutrient conditions so this enriched water encouraged the growth of cattails, which are now spreading rapidly and invading the river of grass. In one area, in just four years in the early 1990s, the area of cattails increased by 350 percent, and wading birds find it much more difficult to find food in these dense growths.[21]

The problem may have been made worse by the disappearance of so many of the characteristic tree islands of the central Everglades. Drainage canals and the construction of levees and dams to create water conservation areas have so altered the natural flow patterns that in some areas nearly 90 percent of these hammocks have disappeared.[22] Phosphorus levels on the tree islands are up to one hundred times higher than in the surrounding marshes and marl prairies, in part because the greater evaporation of water from the layers of shrub and tree leaves draws in water from the rest of the marsh and concentrates phosphorus in the hammock soils. So the tree islands may play a role in keeping phosphorus levels in the marsh low and therefore in maintaining the dominance of sawgrass. There is no more telling illustration of the fact that the Everglades is one enormous, delicately interlinked system. It may have seemed to be a vast, impenetrable wilderness to the first explorers, but those complex linkages make it very fragile.

As changes to this intricate system cascaded, the extraordinary Marjory Stoneman Douglas remained active and fighting for the Glades. She formed the pressure group Friends of the Everglades in 1970, at the age of eighty. Through the 1960s and 1970s, the environmental movement was gaining ground, and once enough people became aware of the issues and there were therefore votes to be had, politicians also became interested. In the same year that Douglas founded the Friends, Richard Nixon founded the Environmental Protection Agency—a reflection of the rising tide of environmental awareness. But the Glades were still being reclaimed, starved of water or flooded with agricultural waste water.

The battles were becoming increasingly acrimonious as agricultural interests clashed with environmentalists. A huge amount of time and huge sums of money were spent on hammering out deals that eventually resulted in a new act to set minimum standards on pollutants in water released to the Glades and to time the release of that water better, when the swamp needed it rather than when the sugar fields didn't.

This looked like being a step forward, a landmark piece of legislation that was to be called the Marjory Stoneman Douglas Act, to honor her role in fighting for so long and so hard for the Glades. But when the 103-year-old Douglas read the final deal, she thought that "Big Sugar" had used its political clout to make the Act a far better deal for agriculture than for the Glades. She flatly refused to have her name associated with it, so the Act became law as the Everglades Forever Act instead.

It can certainly be argued that the Act has had some effect. By 2003, phosphorus levels had fallen from two hundred parts per billion to thirty. Forty thousand acres of the Everglades Agricultural Area had to be taken out of cultivation and turned into water filtration and purification marshes to achieve this. But phosphorus levels need to be below ten parts per billion to return the Glades to its former state, so the sawgrass marshes are still being choked by cattails, just more slowly. The deadline to achieve this critical level was 2006, a deadline that was extended when 2006 came and went, prompting many environmentalists to rename it the Everglades Whenever Act.

The problems facing the whole ecosystem are both widespread and fundamental, a fact that became all too apparent in 2004, when a hurricane churned up the waters of Lake Okeechobee. This huge lake has been a dumping ground for agricultural waste for a long time, and the sediments on the bottom are now heavily polluted by phosphorus. In the aftermath of the hurricane, water managers panicked at the thought of all this pollution rising into the water column and turning the lake into a dead zone. They flushed the water out through the canals into the St. Lucie's estuary, where it stimulated a deadly red tide. And it's not the first time something like this has happened. Earlier, in 2002, a cloud of black water drained into Florida Bay and wiped out *half* the coral there.

It's going to take a lot of money to solve these problems—over eight billion dollars according to the latest plan to save the Everglades.[23] The Comprehensive Everglades Restoration Plan (CERP) was the result of yet more hard bargaining and more time and money spent on arguing cases. As with the Everglades Forever Act, it is a compromise between competing interests. Even though it has been billed as the greatest restoration project in America, many biologists think that yet again it benefits agriculture more than the natural Glades. However, the more pragmatic among the biological community think that something is better than nothing. Otherwise, there was the very real danger that both sides would have sat arguing until there was nothing left of the Glades.

So the compromise was put into action in 2000. The difficulties faced by such a bold and ambitious plan, delicately balancing the needs of so many different parties, cannot be overstated and vested interests threatened to wreck the delicate balance from the start. Plans to release more water into the Everglades National Park, to improve conditions for the colonies of wading birds were opposed by both Miccosukee Indians and some biologists on the grounds that to do so would mean raising water levels in the central Everglades which would further threaten the tree islands.

By 2005, this enormously expensive plan was overbudget and making slow progress; its long-term future must be a cause for concern. In 2000, a federal budget surplus lent optimism to CERP. Since then, the U.S. economy has slowed, and wars in Iraq and Afghanistan have drained federal resources. Yet there is more at stake here than just the Everglades.

The plan to finally save the Glades forever was trumpeted from Washington and Tallahassee as the greatest piece of restoration ecology that the country—perhaps the world—has ever seen. Around 50 percent of the Glades has been irrevocably lost, so there's no hope of recreating the whole original ecosystem, the best that can be hoped for is that the worst environmental problems are mitigated by "getting the water right." Yet this would still be an incredible achievement. If Florida can get it right, it would point a way forward for so many other critical areas around the planet. And the world is watching.

CHAPTER 14

. . . To *Shining* Sea

In 1893, Katherine Lee Bates, a schoolteacher on a vacation traveling around the United States, struggled up Pikes Peak in the Rocky Mountains. Relieved to have made it at all and elated at the view, she composed a poem inspired by the country that stretched away beneath her feet. The immense panorama visible from the "purple mountain majesties" on which she sat helped her conjure up the phrase "from sea to shining sea" in a poem which later, set to music, became a popular rival to the official national anthem, "The Star Spangled Banner."

But when Katherine Bates wrote "America the Beautiful" she almost certainly had no idea how apt her phrase was. In 1827, Auguste Duhaut-Cilly, a French merchant on a trading trip to California, at this stage still part of Mexico, found the western sea to be quite literally shining—with iridescent blue and gold. "While we went along by this shore, we found the sea almost everywhere covered with asphaltum, now in the form of round flat slabs of some thickness, now in that of large sheets of oil and tar, spread over the water and displaying yellow or blue reflections."[1] He was later told by locals that these oily slicks came from pits of molten tar that bubbled up in the hills inland. The most famous today are known as the Rancho La Brea tar pits, and there's nowhere, from sea to shining sea, that you could find a place of such stark contrasts. Wilshire Boulevard and Los Angeles' Miracle Mile have grown up around these ancient eructations. Beyond the boundary fence, the ultramodern hustle and bustle is relentless, but inside, La Brea bubbles and oozes as it has done for thousands of years.

Since their discovery, scientists have hauled out the remains of all kinds of extinct creatures, beautifully preserved by being sealed in tar. Many are now on display in a splendid museum at the site and give a glimpse of a much earlier America, from long before Columbus, from long before even the first Indians, from a time when mammoths and saber-toothed cats wandered through Tinseltown and Rodeo Drive. And that's the wonderful thing about California. It's a land of such extreme contrasts: you can literally smell the past at La Brea, and you can definitely smell the present if you roll down your window while stationary on one of Los Angeles' twelve-lane car parks that sometimes doubles as a freeway. We'll meet other such contrasts as California forms our base camp for an exploration along the Pacific coast over the next four chapters.

Look at any map of North America and one thing is obvious: it's a very, very long way from sea to shining sea, at least for the French and English settling and exploring along the east coast. By good fortune, though, New Spain tapered away to almost nothing at the Isthmus of Panama, just before South America balloons out again to continental proportions. So as early as 1513, a Spaniard by the name of Vasco Nuñez de Balboa had crossed this narrow neck of land and stood knee-deep in the Pacific to claim this "South Sea" for Spain. Not that it was a Sunday afternoon walk in the park. Balboa had to fight his way through thick rainforest and several hostile tribes and then struggle over a mountain range to make his discovery.

He was driven on through all this hardship by the same thing that motivated much early Spanish exploration, the rumor of gold along the Pacific shores. But as he stood rusting his armor in the Pacific's salty water (if some early depictions of this event are to be believed), he could not have known that the real riches along this coast were not an inert, yellow metal but vibrant, living ones.

Nor could he have known that the shores on which he stood ran for six thousand miles to the north, from tropical shores to the frozen Arctic. For most of that length, the coast and offshore islands are washed by highly productive waters that once supported some of the greatest wildlife spectacles on the planet. But the Spanish wouldn't have all these resources to themselves; as they were venturing north from New Spain, so Russian explorers had crossed the Bering Straits and were pushing south from Alaska. However, since the first recorded glimpses of this abundant natural world were through Spanish eyes, our journey begins in New Spain.

Just eight years after Balboa had waded into the Pacific, the Aztec Empire fell to Hernan Cortes and his tiny army of conquistadors. Spain had now acquired a major mainland colony to add to her Caribbean empire, as well as plenty of treasure and slave labor. Her New World possessions were proving very lucrative and drew ever more people eager to make a quick fortune. And there was no shortage of incentive to explore farther and farther afield. First, there were perpetual rumors of cities of gold and silver, always tantalizingly over the next horizon, and second, there was still the notion that a northwest passage cut across this continent somewhere to the north. If no one had found the Atlantic entrance yet, then maybe the Pacific exit would be easier to find. In fact, confidence was so high that this outlet had already been given a name—the Straits of Anian.

In 1532, Cortes sent ships to explore north along Mexico's Pacific coast—and they were never heard of again. A year later, Fortún Jimenez, a Basque pilot, guided another expedition north, to see what happened to the first. He ran into land off Mexico's coast, which he—quite reasonably—assumed to be an island, but which later proved to be the tip of the seven-hundred-mile-long peninsula of Baja California. Unfortunately, he was killed by Baja's Indians, along with most of the rest of his crew. Just two survivors made it back to report their exploits to Cortes and to tell him that, though they hadn't found the lost ships or any gold, they had found huge beds of pearl-making oysters.

The existence of pearl oysters along the Pacific coast wasn't news; Balboa's expedition had seen them and realized their potential. But the beds that the Jimenez expedition found were enormous. The land itself might not have been very encouraging, unless you liked cacti, but the existence of such immense beds of pearl oysters was more than enough incentive to mount new expeditions.

In 1539, Francisco de Ulloa went much further than Jimenez. He sailed right up into the head of the Gulf of California, proving that Baja was not an island but a fingerlike peninsula. Surprisingly, not everyone seemed to take much notice. Although Baja appeared on some maps as a peninsula soon after Ulloa's discovery, it continued to appear on many maps as an island, and the reason seems to have been its name.

It will come as no surprise to many of its current inhabitants that California was Paradise, or at least a close neighbor to it. The Island of California was originally a mythical land across the Atlantic: "Know, that on the right hand of the Indies there is an island called California very close to the side of the Terrestrial Paradise; and it is peopled by black women, without any man among them, for they live in the manner of Amazons."[2] This, the first mention of California in writing, is from a popular romance novel called *Las Sergas de Esplandián*, written in 1510. It's not entirely clear who first thought to apply that name to the "island" that Jimenez found; some say it was Jimenez himself, some that it was Francisco de Bolanos, another explorer who sailed about halfway up the peninsula in 1541. Either way, the name stuck and so did the idea that California must therefore be an island, despite all the evidence to the contrary. And while the land itself might not have initially lived up to the abundance of Paradise, the oceans most certainly did. First, there were all those pearl oysters.

Pearl oysters belong to a different family (Pteriidae) from the edible oysters (Ostreidae) that made up the great reefs of the east coast and Chesapeake Bay. However, names can be deceptive, and pearl oysters are actually just as edible, which is why the Indians of Baja and the Central American coast collected them. They simply threw the oysters onto a fire to roast them, with the result that any pearls they might bother to keep were blackened and not worth much to European eyes. Two species were common along these coasts, *Pinctada mazatlanica* and *Pteria sterna*, and both formed reefs to rival those of the Chesapeake's ostreid oysters.

After hearing the reports from the survivors of the Jimenez expedition, Cortes himself mounted an expedition to the southern tip of Baja, to fill his pockets with pearls on top of Aztec gold and silver. The year was 1535, and the expedition was a disaster. The colony was abandoned in 1536, and there's no evidence that Cortes brought anything back apart from a few black pearls obtained from the Indians, though he did leave his name for the sea enclosed by the gulf, the Sea of Cortez.[3]

Sixty years later, Sebastian Vizcaino, who would later make his name exploring upper or Alta California, applied for permission to set up a pearl operation in Baja California and in 1596 set off to make his fortune. He found a bay of mercifully calm water with reasonably friendly Indians at the southern end of Baja, both of which reasons prompted him to call his landfall the Bay of Peace—later contracted to La Paz. Just like Cortes, he failed, though La Paz would eventually become a major center for pearl production. And its rise to that position began in the early years of the next century, by which time Caribbean pearl oysters had largely disappeared and the focus of the pearl industry shifted to the Gulf of California.[4]

The search for new pearl beds encouraged the further exploration of the Gulf of California, and in 1613, the Cordona Company in Spain sent out six vessels to establish pearl-harvesting operations. First though, they had to stop in the Caribbean to pick up black slaves, since a royal decree in 1585 had forbidden the use of Indians to dive for pearl oysters. The Spanish Crown, under some pressure from the Jesuits, and in particular from that resolute campaigner for Indian rights, Bartolomé de las Casas, was growing increasingly worried about the brutal treatment of North America's natives at the hands of their empire builders, a concern that didn't seem to extend to Africa's natives.[5] In fact, Las Casas himself suggested a switch to African labor, a position that he did, however, later recant.

The Cordona Company's vessels finally began exploration of the Pacific coast and the Gulf in 1615, when the expedition reported: "Over a distance of one hundred leagues all that one sees are heaps of pearl oysters."[6] These heaps were the remains of Indian feasts, and the Spaniards used them to locate likely positions of oyster reefs offshore.

Over the next few centuries, the fishery expanded. In 1846, Edwin Bryant arrived in California, having led a wagon train of 250 wagons and 1,500 people from Independence, Missouri, to a new life in California. He stayed and explored, and published the results of his observations in a book with a title that what it lacked in imagination, it made up for in clarity. In *What I Saw in California*, he described the pearl-fishing industry that had grown up around La Paz since Vizcaino's failure. "Pearl-fishing is the chief employment of the inhabitants of the bay, and the pearls are said to be of superior quality. I was shown a necklace, valued at two thousand dollars, taken in this water."[7]

The Spanish royal decree had clearly been forgotten in the 250 years since it was pronounced, since Bryant found that Baja's Indians were the mainstay of this extremely hazardous industry: "They are all found by diving. The Yake [Yaqui] Indians are the best divers, going down in eight-fathom water. . . . Why it is a submarine diving apparatus has not been employed in this fishery, with all its advantages over Indian diving, I cannot say. Yankee enterprise has not yet reached this new world." But soon after Bryant's visit, Yankee enterprise, and newfangled diving equipment, did arrive in Baja, which greatly increased the efficiency, though not the safety, of pearl collection. After 1880, the use of air pumps and diving apparatus had completely replaced free diving, allowing pearl divers to reach deeper beds. La Paz became the pearl capital of the world. But this technological revolution produced a glut of pearls that drove down the price; in response the pearl industry simply increased its output to try to maintain profit margins with the inevitable result that pearl oysters began to disappear. In fact, alarming declines had already been noticed as early as the end of the seventeenth century, but in 1938, the remaining oysters suddenly all but vanished. The fishery had collapsed, but not before two and half *billion* pearls had been exported from the Gulf of California.[8]

When the first Spanish explorers ventured into the Gulf, it wasn't just the reefs of pearl oysters that amazed them. Fish, seabirds, turtles, fur seals, sea lions, and whales were all just as spectacularly abundant. Francisco de Ulloa, picking his way around the peninsula in 1539, found extremely large fish that were very easy to catch: "they found a fishing which was very wonderful, for they suffered themselves to be taken by hand; and they were so great that every one had much ado to find room to lay fish in."[9]

A few years later, another explorer witnessed the abundance of the Gulf. "In this port [Cabo San Lucas Bay] they take very much sardine that, running from the big fish it gets so close from land, that lads can take a great quantity in just two palms deep." What they were probably seeing were schools of ocean predators running baitfish up against the beach to trap them. And the fact that it seemed to be a common fishing technique here suggests that those ocean predators were very abundant. Indeed, Ray Cannon, an ex–silent movie star turned journalist writing in the early twentieth century, reckoned to have counted four billfish (swordfish, marlin, or sailfish) in every one hundred square feet across a patch of ocean twenty miles in diameter offshore from the town of Guaymas.

Other descriptions give an impression of the size of these shoals: "shoals of fish frequent the shores in such abundance, that the surface is often agitated for hundreds of yards by a school playing almost within an arm's reach of the sands."[10] Ray Cannon described even more incredible scenes in an area of the Sea of Cortez he called the "midriff." Here a group of islands and a bulge on the coastline together constrict the gulf. Tides running through this narrowed area produce whirlpools and currents that churn up nutrients from the sea floor to feed shoals of fish that defy imagination; "The words 'schools' or 'shoals' fall far short of describing the mass movements of fish populations in and around these islands. They must be visualized as hosts, armies or clouds when seen churning the surface from horizon to horizon in all directions."[11]

After Vizcaino's failed attempt at pearl fishing he returned to Baja in 1602, this time trying to find, among other things, the Straits of Anian. He explored much further north than on his last voyage, and he too found vast shoals of fish. He also described how the Indians supplemented the staples of their fields with a varied diet of seafood. "Their food is commonly fish and maize, for there are great quantities of fish of many kinds. They fish with enclosures of sticks, catching in this way many mussels and shell fish." When the time came for his own men to catch their supper, they couldn't believe how easy it was. "Orders were given to make ready the net for catching fish, but it was not necessary, for God granted that there should be cast upon the beach as many sardines as all could eat, with many left over."[12]

Sudden drops in ocean temperature are known to kill huge numbers of sardines and anchovies, which is probably what Vizcaino's men had found. However, there is also a fish in these waters that deliberately throws itself onto the beach. Like capelin on the opposite corner of the continent in Newfoundland, grunion struggle out of the water to bury their eggs on the beach, out of reach of ocean predators. Unlike capelin though, grunion spawn only at night. But take a torch onto a beach in the right season and you'll be amazed.

Grunion occur all the way from San Francisco to the southern half of Baja California, though today they are most abundant south of Point Conception, where California's coast takes a sharp turn to the east about eighty miles from Santa Barbara. But perhaps the best place to have a grunion experience is on Cabrillo Beach, near San Pedro, right next to the Port of Los Angeles. It might not seem the most romantic place to spend a moonlit night on California's coast, but the Cabrillo Marine Aquarium is right at the top of the beach and their experts run grunion nights during the spawning season.

With such expertise on hand, this seemed to be the best place to head when I wanted to film the grunion's strange spawning behavior. These little fish spawn between March and August, for two to six nights after a full or new moon, just after high tide, and we had timed our visit for the second night, on the assumption that we could first watch the whole event with the folks from the Aquarium to work out the best way of filming the fish.

At the appointed hour, the grunion duly made their appearance, and within half an hour, the beach was a mass of squirming silvery fish. Each female twists and writhes until the back half of her body sinks into the wet sand, and as she lays her eggs, a male curls himself around her protruding head, releasing sperm to fertilize her eggs. We cautiously illuminated this frantic scene with filming lights to check their response, but not a single fish broke off from its vital task of creating a new grunion generation. However, the forty or so people who'd turned up to watch the evening's events certainly appreciated the additional light, which revealed grunions surfing up onto the beach as far as the lights pierced. This was the last evening of the Aquarium's public program, so the next night we would only have to share the beach with the grunions.

We arrived at the beach just after dark, set up the cameras, but left the lights turned off in case they discouraged the fish from starting their spawning runs. We found ourselves a cozy hollow in a low dune and settled down in the pitch dark to wait for the tide to drop—around midnight. As we sat there quietly, we began to hear all kinds of strange noises coming from the grassy park at the top of the beach. Eventually, the cameraman's curiosity got the better of him and he crawled to the top of the dune to scan the park with our low-light imaging equipment.

After a few seconds, he slid back down to my position to report that the grunion weren't the only creatures engaged in reproductive activity tonight—the park seemed to be attracting ever-increasing numbers of the good citizens of San Pedro. By now, both of us were dreading the moment that the fish came ashore, and we turned on the filming lights. After all, some of Los Angeles' citizens have been known to shoot each other for minor traffic offenses, so I wasn't at all sure that they'd see the funny side of finding their ever-growing orgy suddenly floodlit.

I've never been so glad of nature's unpredictability. Not a single fish bothered to throw itself onto the beach that night, and when the spawning period finally came and went fishlessly, we could quietly—very quietly—dismantle the equipment and sneak back to where we had left the car. Thank you, grunion.

When the Spanish first explored California's shores, they probably wouldn't have been so lucky. Grunion, like many other fish, were incalculably more abundant. They were an easy source of food during the summer months, and, much as Indians must have done in the past, California's present inhabitants still scoop grunion off the beaches today. Spawning nights draw thousands of people to beaches up and down the coast, some to be amazed and some to eat the grunion.

There is hardly any commercial exploitation of grunion, but at the start of the twentieth century, there was a big enough recreational fishery to cause a drop in the numbers of spawning fish. After a closed season was enforced, the population seemed to recover. However, today there are no catch or size limits for grunion and just a brief period in April and May when the fishing is closed. The official line from the California Department of Fish and Game is that grunion stocks are now stable, though casual observations by volunteer "Grunion Greeters" (well, it is California) suggest that spawning tails off in the open season, perhaps due to disturbance.

But there have been much clearer changes among some of the other fishes of the Gulf of California and the Pacific coast. Really big Gulf and goliath grou-

pers were extremely common in the Sea of Cortez in the early days of exploration, and they remained so right until the 1960s, when a market developed in
North America, which very quickly consumed all the big fish. As we've seen
elsewhere, it's the big fish that go first, a warning sign of the early stages of
overexploitation, which usually goes unheeded and which is, therefore, in too
many cases a prelude to the total collapse of that particular species.

Mexico's attempt to regulate the grouper fishery is yet another illustration
that fisheries policies often take too simplistic a view of ecology. For statistical analysis, all grouper catches were lumped together, even though sixteen
different species of groupers occur around Baja, some of which are much
larger than others. The total weight of groupers landed has risen over the last
few years, which has been taken by policy makers as an indication of healthy
stocks. In reality, catches are now made up from greater numbers of smaller
individuals, which probably means that the largest species that so impressed
early travelers are now severely threatened.

Those exploring the Gulf and Pacific coast in the early days were much less
impressed by the extraordinary abundance of sharks. Bull sharks and ham-
merheads were the bane of pearl divers so ship owners were obliged by law
to carry equipment to kill as many of these "marine monsters" as possible.
These sharks were also huge, some being "as large as middling sized California
whales."[13]

Sharks also plagued those who were trying to fish in the Gulf's swarming
waters or out in the Pacific. "No sooner was a line thrown into the water than
hundreds of fish would dart towards the bait. . . . We had been fishing only a
short time when many sharks appeared about us and did much damage to our
gear . . . sharks were exceedingly abundant and troublesome, and the utmost
care had to be exercised to prevent their carrying away our gear."[14]

We've already seen that Atlantic sharks have been reduced to a tiny fraction
of their historic abundance, but that story has been repeated in every ocean
basin and sea. However, the Gulf's remote location meant that it survived as
a biological hotspot longer than many places. Commercial fishing didn't really begin until the start of the twentieth century, when a market developed
in China for the swim bladders of a fish called the totoaba (or sometimes to-
tuavu),[15] which were used in making a special soup called *seen kow*. Dried swim
bladders were worth $5 a pound at the time, a fortune for the Mexican fish-
ermen. Totoaba belong to the same family as the more modest-sized croak-
ers but grow to the size of marlin, perhaps one of the giant fish encountered

so frequently by the Spanish. Certainly, at the start of the twentieth century, they were numerous enough to be easily spearfished.

The lucrative market in these monster swim bladders was followed by a growing demand for their plentiful, firm, white flesh and spurred the development of three fishing ports in the upper Gulf. Unfortunately, the upper three hundred miles of the Gulf is the only place on the planet where totoaba live, so it didn't take long for numbers to drop steeply. In theory, totoaba fishing has been illegal in Mexico since 1975, but large numbers are still poached. Funding from the Mexican government for research on totoaba has recently dried up, so scientists can't even tell you how many of these fish still swim in the upper Gulf. And their swim bladders are now worth $100 apiece in China, enough to make poaching in the poorly patrolled waters well worth the risk. One estimate suggests that the illegal fishery is worth around $2.5 million a year, providing plenty of totoaba meat to market places, even in the United States, where its import was banned in 1977.[16] Here it's often sold under the name of "white sea bass," actually a closely related species that is almost impossible to distinguish from totoaba on the market table.

Following the establishment of the totoaba fishery, shrimping boats began to move into the Gulf in the 1940s and, as well as shrimps, accidentally caught lots of young totoaba, which didn't help the plight of this giant fish. In 1940, John Steinbeck took a cruise in the Sea of Cortez with his friend, marine biologist Ed Ricketts, who was the inspiration for Doc in *Cannery Row*. He published the account of this trip as *The Log of the Sea of Cortez* in which he describes the destruction caused by shrimp trawls, not just to young totoaba but to all marine life:

> they were doing a very systematic job, not only of taking every shrimp from the bottom, but every other living thing as well. . . . Any animals which escaped must have been very fast indeed, for not even the sharks got away. . . . The big scraper closed like a sack as it came up, and finally deposited many tons of animals on the deck—tons of shrimps, but also tons of fish of many varieties; sierras, pompano of several species; of the sharks, smooth-hounds and hammerheads; eagle rays and butterfly rays; small tuna. Catfish; puerco; tons of them. And there were bottom-samples with anemones and grass-like gorgonians. . . . Fish were thrown overboard, and only the shrimps kept. The sea was littered with dead fish and the gulls swarmed about eating them.[17]

After the 1970s, the scale of commercial fishing and its effects on Gulf eco-systems escalated well beyond that seen by Steinbeck. Yet despite this, the Gulf of California still attracts dive enthusiasts from all over the world to en-joy its spectacular marine sights. Sinking below the waves in one of Baja's dive hotspots, it's easy to believe that all's right with the world. But such sights and experiences shouldn't blind us to the fact that they are but shadows of the spectacles that existed just a century ago. It's yet another case of shifting baselines, where we have no real "gut" way to compare our own observations with those of previous generations.

A study carried out in 2005 tried to quantify this effect among the fishermen of the upper Gulf of California. Scientists interviewed three generations of fishermen and asked them to describe their own experiences of the changing state of the Gulf's fish populations. The study showed clearly that the base-lines the fishermen were using to gauge the extent of the decline in fish stocks had shifted rapidly between each generation, to the extent that there was out-right disbelief from the youngest generation at the stories of past abundance from the oldest.[18] As interesting as this is as a sociological study, it also goes to the heart of modern problems of conservation. If it's hard even for fishermen or field naturalists to grasp the true scale of the problems, what chance have politicians in air-conditioned offices thousands of miles away?

Just as with the Caribbean, the waters of the Gulf also swarmed with turtles: green, loggerhead, ridley, and hawksbill. And again like the Caribbean, it had its own Tortuga islands, named for this abundance. As on Florida's Dry Tor-tugas, sailors around Baja reported catching a hundred turtles a night with ease on nesting beaches. Close to Cabo San Lucas, one explorer in the late eighteenth century reported that the sea "was almost covered with turtles and other tropical fish."[19] Because Baja was more remote and less densely settled than the Caribbean, big numbers of turtles lasted longer. A research trip in 1889 caught 167 turtles in a single haul of their seine net.

And just as on the other side of Central America, there is a species of ridley turtle that hauls up on spawning beaches in prodigious numbers. The olive ridley is a close relative of the Kemp's ridley that we met in the Gulf of Mexico. It's sometimes called the Pacific ridley, which isn't such a helpful name since this species also occurs in the Indian and Atlantic oceans and the Caribbean. However, its Atlantic populations are in serious decline and there it is a rare and endangered species.

Not so in the Pacific and Indian oceans, where many researchers consider it to be the commonest of all turtles, indeed the most abundant sea turtle on the planet. Nevertheless, we need to remember that its numbers today are nothing compared to a century or two ago. And although they still spawn on many beaches along the Pacific coasts of Mexico and Costa Rica, it is only in a very few areas that their numbers are great enough to form the spectacular arribadas or mass spawnings. The beaches around Nancite and Ostional in Costa Rica and at Escobilla in Mexico all have spectacular arribadas, though numbers at Nancite have fallen rather worryingly in recent years, from two hundred thousand in the early 1980s to just thirty thousand in the 1990s, for reasons not yet fully understood.[20]

Some of the problems facing olive ridleys earlier in history are much less mysterious. In the 1970s, both Mexico and Ecuador began trading turtle leather particularly with Italy. The trade seems to have been stimulated in part by an increasing scarcity of crocodile leather,[21] and the number of ridleys taken quickly rose into the hundreds of thousands per year.[22] In the face of falling numbers, Mexico gave all its sea turtles total protection in 1990, though a substantial black market still exists for turtle products of all kinds, from leather and meat to the translucent tortoiseshell of the hawksbill.

But in Costa Rica, olive ridleys are still being exploited, though this time for their own good—at least in theory. At Ostional, an innovative conservation measure was introduced in the early 1980s—the commercial harvesting of turtle eggs. The rationale was to encourage a legal trade in olive ridley eggs that undercuts prices paid for poached eggs. And of course an economic value attached to the arribadas at Ostional would give the local people a good reason to make sure the turtles kept coming.

The biology behind the economy is just as interesting. So many turtles nest on the arribada beaches that older nests are often dug up and eggs scattered around. These beaches are patrolled by all kinds of creatures with a taste for turtle eggs, from vultures to coatis, so any exposed eggs are soon devoured. Furthermore, surviving nests are so closely packed that lack of oxygen for the developing embryos might become a problem, as might bacterial infections started by damaged and decomposing eggs. This may explain why only 15 percent of the eggs at Ostional hatch, compared to 90 percent from solitary nests on other beaches.[23]

What evidence there is suggests this reasoning is sound. A recent study at Nancite, where the population of nesters is falling, suggests that low oxygen levels and high carbon dioxide levels as well as the higher temperatures experienced by eggs developing at higher densities really does depress hatching success.[24] Perhaps the sheer numbers of turtles nesting here is contributing to their current decline. Ostional's experiment in economic conservation does seem to be sustainable on current evidence, though it is not without its problems, mostly resulting from a lack of a sufficiently strong organization behind the project.[25] Strict control of the harvest is critical to its success and to avoid a free-for-all that would be disastrous for the turtles. Yet it would be a great boost to other such schemes to see the people of Ostional reaping long-term benefits from the extraordinary natural spectacle on their doorsteps. Studies from many parts of the world show that conservation schemes can often be more successful if the local people both benefit directly and are in control of operations.[26] On top of the commercial harvest, Costa Rica's arribada beaches are also a magnet for ecotourists, another valuable source of income in a country which is leading the world in sustainable ecotoursim.

Another natural spectacle is also proving a money-spinner for Baja, drawing an ever-increasing number of people to the shallow lagoons around the peninsula, such as Magdalena Bay. They come here for close encounters with gray whales, which migrate to these lagoons in winter to give birth to their calves. Tourists are taken out in small Zodiacs, which allow them to get eye to eye with the whales in a way that isn't possible in most other whale-watching areas. For thousands of tourists each year, it's the experience of a lifetime, but most of them simply wouldn't believe what whale watching tours here might have been like a century or two ago.

On his second voyage along the California coast in 1602, Vizcaino's crew saw so many whales they feared no one would believe them. "In ancient maps this place is called 'Ensenada o Seno de Ballenas' and this is because along the coast until Mendocino Cape [whales] are so abundant that counting will be impossible and you will not believe it unless seen by you."[27] And later in the voyage: "there are, as I have said infinite numbers of great whales and great abundance of great sardines, that are, as is said, the common food of whales, and may be, for this reason there are here such a great abundance."

Visiting Monterey Bay in 1786, French naval officer Jean François de Galaup, Comte de La Pérouse, found his vessel surrounded by great schools of whales: "One cannot put into words the number of whales that surrounded us nor their familiarity; they blew constantly, within half a pistol shot of our frigates, and filled the air with a great stench."[28] There are similar descriptions from elsewhere of whales so confiding and so numerous that ships and crews were sprayed with water as they spouted and engulfed in great clouds of bad breath.

In 1836, Richard Henry Dana described all the bays along this coast as filled with coastal gray whales in the right season, including the bay that would eventually become Los Angeles Harbor.[29] And these were big whales. The captain of one of the ships on the Ulloa expedition recorded three large pods (of which species we can't be certain), each above five hundred whales that followed his ship for an hour "which were so huge, as it was wonderful."

Commercial whalers found these huge whales by the end of the eighteenth century, and they too were amazed by the size. In 1790, James Colnett was commissioned by the British Crown to look into the sperm whale fishery in the eastern Pacific. But even his experienced crew was often unable to identify whales in the Gulf because they were so much bigger than expected. "I am ready to confess that I was deceived respecting the species of whale which I saw . . . the humpback whale was so much larger than generally believed . . . that the most experienced fishermen I had on board believed them to be black whale [sperm whale]."[30]

Even as they destroyed these great whales, the whalers left us with descriptions of astounding abundance, and one person in particular has also left us with intriguing descriptions of behavior and biology. His name was Charles Scammon, and he was an extraordinary character. He was a whaler who became a naturalist. The spectacles he saw inspired him to become one of the foremost authorities of the period on marine mammals. As he is at pains to point out in the preface to his classic book, *The Marine Mammals of the Northwestern Coast of North America,* published in 1874, he had originally become a whaler by necessity.

> Being on the coast of California in 1852, when the "gold fever" raged, the force of circumstances compelled me to take command of a brig, bound on a sealing, sea-elephant and whaling voyage, or abandon sea-life, at least temporarily.
>
> The objects of our pursuit were found in great numbers, and the opportunities for studying their habits were so good, that I became greatly interested in collecting facts bearing upon the natural history of these animals.[31]

Scammon certainly took those opportunities and left us graphic accounts, both of the abundance of sea mammals off the Pacific coast and their slaughter. He found whales "huddled together so thickly that it was difficult for a boat to cross the waters without coming into contact with them." Just as in the Atlantic, some Indians hunted gray whales, but, as Scammon points out, they didn't take many. Even the slaughter of a single one was a time of great celebration and of accolades heaped on those who managed to kill it. The "civilized" whalers, as Scammon calls his fellows to distinguish them from savages, were driven by a different market.

Yet even as the whalers raked in their profits, it was clear to someone as intelligent as Scammon what the future held. The whalers had developed a whole range of different techniques to hunt these coastal whales, in their Arctic feeding grounds, on their migrations, and in their subtropical calving grounds: "As it approaches the waters of the torrid zone, it presents an opportunity to the civilised whalemen—at sea, along the shore and in the lagoons—to practise their different modes of strategy, thus hastening the time of its entire annihilation."[32] Scammon's prediction was deadly accurate for the Atlantic gray whale, and very nearly correct for western Pacific gray whales, now down to only a hundred or so, but luckily he was wrong about the eastern Pacific stock. Nevertheless, at the end of the nineteenth century, gray whales, along with humpbacks, bowheads, right whales, and a host of smaller species all became vanishingly rare. Some are showing no real signs of recovery, probably because, as we saw in the Atlantic and Caribbean, the ocean ecosystem has been radically changed. But gray whales in the eastern Pacific have done better than most.

Reduced to a few thousand at the start of the twentieth century, by the end of the century, their population had bounced back to somewhere between nineteen and twenty-three thousand. Scientists from the National Ocean and Atmospheric Administration (NOAA) now regularly count the number of calves that migrate north each spring with their mothers, which is a good way of monitoring the health of the population. A worrying drop in the number of calves between 1999 and 2001 seems to have been a temporary blip, and in 2006, the NOAA scientists counted 1,018 young of the year, up from a low of three hundred in 2000 and 2001.[33]

So satisfactory is their recovery that the gray whale became the first marine mammal to be taken off the Endangered Species List with some saying that they have now regained their historic abundance. Some whales are now turning up malnourished which has also been used as evidence that the gray whales population has rebounded to the carrying capacity of their environment. But, as impressive as it is to see gray whales passing off Monterey Bay or lolling in the shallow lagoons of Baja, I know of nowhere that matches the historical accounts above. And science would seem to back up the evidence from history.

Using an analysis of the genetic variation of gray whales, similar to that described for Atlantic whales, scientists have concluded that the historic gray whale population was up to five times larger than the current population.[34] This puts the modern conservation achievement in context and also causes a few worries. The fact that some gray whales now appear malnourished points to deeper changes in their ecosystem that we have yet to address.

Most of the people that flock to Magdalena Bay to commune with gray whales have probably never heard of one of the rarest of all cetaceans—and the smallest. The *vaquita*, or little cow, is a tiny porpoise that never grows much longer than four feet. It lives right at the head of the Gulf of California, where the Colorado River, or what's left of it, empties into the Sea of Cortez. And this is the *only* place it lives. It is thought by many scientists to be the most endangered cetacean in the world, especially since its closest rival for this position, the baiji of China's Yangtze River, is now presumed extinct.[35]

They behave a little like miniature gray whales; they are often seen in water so shallow around the delta of the Colorado that their backs protrude above the surface, though this could also be mistaken identity with bottlenose dolphins. Indeed, just about every aspect of the vaquita's life is as difficult to untangle as this. We've only known that we've been sharing the planet with this extraordinary little porpoise since 1958, when three skulls washed up on one of Baja's beaches were identified as a new species, distinct from the similar but much larger harbor porpoise. Even so, it wasn't until the 1980s that serious efforts to study the biology of vaquitas began, and we still know very little about this tiny cetacean. What we do know came from examining just a few tens of specimens and suggests that like harbor porpoises, they feed on the fish and squid that abounded in the Sea of Cortez. Remarkably, it seems to have been unknown in its remote haunts, even by people living along the shores of the Gulf.[36]

It may have been more widespread in the past, but since science didn't differentiate it as a separate species until the middle of the twentieth century, it's almost impossible to interpret early reports. Scammon described porpoises as being much more widespread throughout the Gulf, and later descriptions concur, calling them common in places. Since harbor porpoises don't occur in the Gulf today, it's possible that these reports refer to the diminutive vaquita.

Fishermen interviewed in 1976 said they remembered the vaquita as being "very abundant," but since they also had difficulty in distinguishing this species from bottlenosed dolphins, which are common in this area, their testimony can't be taken as reliable.

On the other hand, genetic analysis suggests that the vaquita may always have been rare. Its closest relative is Burmeister's porpoise, which lives around the southern tip of South America, and vaquitas seem to be a relic population, derived from a few individuals of this species that crossed the equator and became isolated in the upper Gulf perhaps ten thousand years ago. It may never have been abundant, but its population has now been severely reduced. There are probably just 150 left in a small area of four thousand square kilometers of ocean at the top of the Gulf—and the population is still falling.[37]

It's possible that changes in the Colorado River are part of the problem. The delta of the Colorado River at the head of the Gulf of California was at one time one of the most remarkable places on the continent. Aldo Leopold paddled his canoe through the intricate maze of channels of a "river reluctant to lose his freedom in the sea" in the 1920s and left evocative descriptions: "Fleets of cormorants drove their black prows in quest of skittering mullets; avocets, willets and yellowlegs dozed one-legged on the bars; mallards, widgeons and teal sprang skyward in alarm. . . . When a troop of egrets settled on a far green willow, they looked like a premature snowstorm."[38]

That once-mighty river has now been reduced to a trickle by dams and irrigation schemes in the U.S. Southwest, and the delta ecosystems have collapsed. Using shell remains in the sediments, it seems that shellfish populations, which supported much of the abundance of the delta, are now reduced to just a few percent of their abundance when Leopold paddled over them.

However, the biggest threat to the vaquita is fishing, not for the little porpoise itself, but for other species. They are often caught in nets set for sharks and totoaba or in nets towed behind shrimping boats. One estimate in 2000 suggests that between thirty-nine and eighty-four individuals were killed like this. Totoaba fishing has been illegal since 1975 (apart from some "experimental" fisheries), so it's a severe indictment of law enforcement in the area that between 1985 and 1994, seventy-six vaquitas are known to have died in illegal totoaba nets.

Time may be running out for the vaquita. Very little action has been taken to protect this little porpoise since its discovery and a paper published in 2007 suggested that we have at most two years to act before the population is reduced to such a low level that a single unfortunate event could wipe them out. By the time you read this, the vaquita might well be in this precarious position.

The vaquita illustrates a common problem for conservation in poorer regions. Certainly, the existing laws need to be enforced, for the sake of both the vaquita and the totoaba. But many local people depend on fishing for their livelihood. The fishermen of the upper Gulf are not supported by subsidies and don't have the options of, say, Canada's generous payouts to fishermen who can't fish. The only way that creatures like the vaquita can be saved is by working directly with local fishermen to change fishing practices or to find other ways of making a living. And that's just what CEDO is doing.

CEDO, the Spanish acronym for the Intercultural Center for the Study of Deserts and Oceans, is based at Puerto Peñasco on the northeastern shore of the Sea of Cortez, where the Sonoran Desert sweeps down to the coast. It is a nonprofit organization, working to protect the desert and marine habitats of the Gulf and promote sustainable ecotourism to the area. This is grassroots conservation, right at the cutting edge and of a kind that often makes a real difference, yet which is so often starved of cash. On their limited resources, CEDO have already managed to promote a series of self-managing fisheries around the gulf.

In the early 1990s, a market grew in Asia for the meat and opercula of black murex snails. These beautiful marine snails gather in large spawning aggregations of perhaps five thousand or more on the bed of the Sea of Cortez. But with a rapid increase in collection for this new market, numbers began to fall. This was especially worrying as new research on the murex suggested it was a pivotal species in Gulf ecology. CEDO arranged meetings in several fishing communities to present the latest information on the murex and its role in the ecosystems on which they all depended for their livelihood, and they found a great willingness among local fishermen to establish mechanisms of their own to control the fishery. These included voluntary closed seasons and even a voluntary reserve or "no-take" area.[39] They policed the fishery themselves, and the results have been very encouraging, not least because they suggest that the exploitation of a common resource doesn't always have to end in tragedy.

When Garret Hardin published his seminal paper on the "Tragedy of the Commons" in 1968, he assumed that the drive to maximize short-term profits from a shared resource would always overrule common sense and long-term sustainability. Work like that of CEDO, as well as Costa Rica's experiments in harvesting the eggs of marine turtles, suggests it doesn't always have to be the case. The hope now is that a similar arrangement can be found for those fishermen whose nets are drowning the vaquitas before it's too late.

The early accounts of the sparkling Sea of Cortez conjure up images of teeming waters, fished by amazing numbers of seabirds. But the Gulf of California wasn't particularly special. Such spectacles were reported right along America's west coast. In 1542, Juan Rodriguez Cabrillo, he for whom my grunion beach was named, set out northward along the Pacific coast. He had been with Cortes in 1521, in his conquest of the Aztec and two years later had gone with Pedro de Alvarado to conquer what is now Guatemala. By the 1530s, he was one of Guatemala's wealthiest citizens—but a conquistador can never be too rich. Exploration brought with it the chance of more wealth, and Cabrillo put together a small fleet to push further along the coast than anyone had before.

On September 28, he took shelter from a storm in a large bay, which he named San Miguel. Sixty years later, Vizcaino visited this same bay and renamed it after his flagship—the *San Diego*. So Cabrillo was the first recorded visitor to Alta California, later to become the state of California, and his visit here is commemorated in the Cabrillo National Monument on Point Loma, with panoramic views over Cabrillo's safe haven and the city that grew up there.

He headed north from San Diego, though historians still debate how far he actually got. He recorded the latitude in his log, but it's known he was using inaccurate tables to do the calculations, so he probably wasn't where he said he was. It's possible he got to Monterey Bay or Drake's Bay before he was driven back by storms to San Miguel Island, off today's Santa Barbara. Here he broke his arm (or his leg according to a second account of the voyage). Either way, he eventually died from an injury that today would be little more than an inconvenience—a reminder of just how dangerous these trips were. His pilot took the ships north again and may have reached the California-Oregon border. The Pacific coastline was gradually being filled in on Spanish maps.

The notes from this voyage were used two decades later, to set up the longest and most dangerous trade route in the world. In 1565, the Spanish had begun trading with Manila in the Philippines. Gold and silver from the mines in Mexico and Peru were loaded up at Acapulco ready for the hazardous voyage across the Pacific to Manila, where they were traded for Chinese silks and perfumes, porcelain, gems, and spices—all worth a fortune in Europe. But, to protect Spain's own trade with the Far East, the Manila run was limited by law to one voyage a year. So the Manila galleons were loaded to the gunnels with as much treasure as they could cram on board, before sailing back to the New World.

To reach New Spain, they sailed on a northerly route to catch the prevailing winds, which usually meant making landfall somewhere around Cape Mendocino in Northern California. The galleons could then use the southerly flowing California Current to carry them back toward Acapulco. A safe harbor along the coast of Alta California would be extremely useful for repairs or shelter after the long and perilous Pacific crossing and the search for such a harbor stimulated further exploration, at first by the homeward bound galleons themselves. But, when one sank while exploring a possible harbor, the Spanish realized that this could be a very expensive way of charting the coast.

The search for such a safe haven was yet another reason that Sebastian Vizcaino was sent north in 1602, and he did succeed in finding a suitable bay, which he called Monterey after the viceroy of New Spain. He described the bay as being surrounded by forests of tall trees, suitable for repairing storm-battered galleons. But that wasn't the only natural resource they found. Along the coast they saw islands teeming with fur seals and sea lions. In 1539, Ulloa, in circumnavigating the Gulf of California had already "found so many seals that were I to say there were a hundred thousand I think I would not be exaggerating. For this reason we name it 'Puerto de los Lobos' [seals and sea lions were often referred to as sea wolves—hence the name]."[40] Later explorers saw similar sights: "Through the night strange noises, like dogs tending livestock were heard from the shore. At sunrise we saw a small white island. . . . We found a great number of sea lions, so many that we almost could not reach the shore without passing over them."[41]

Within reach of these early Spanish explorations, there were both sea lions and the related fur seals. These are not true seals, such as the harp and monk seals we've already met. They are instantly distinguishable, at least when close enough, because they still have the remains of their external ears, now just two little fleshy flaps, on the sides of their heads. For this reason, with the unerring logic of biologists, they are sometimes called eared seals to distinguish them from true seals. Sea lions and fur seals also differ from true seals in that they can turn their hind flippers forward and underneath their bodies, allowing them to move with more agility on land than true seals, which are reduced to crawling like overweight caterpillars. They also move differently when in their true element, underwater. True seals cruise by gently paddling their hind flippers while eared seals fly through the water using their enlarged front flippers like wings.

The differences between fur seals and sea lions are much less obvious. Sea lion males are usually much bulkier and more heavily built and have more squat faces than fur seals. But, most importantly for those looking for wealth in these waters, fur seals have a double layer of fur, with a thick, dense under-fur. This made their pelts more valuable though, since both kinds yielded oil, both were hunted commercially. Incidentally, there isn't really a convenient common name that encompasses all sea lions, fur seals, true seals, and walruses, so they are generally referred to as pinnipeds, meaning "winged feet."

Two species of sea lions, Steller and California sea lions, are both widespread along the coast, and the California sea lion also has a distinct subspecies that inhabits the Galapagos and another one in Japan, though the latter is probably extinct. There are also five species of fur seals along the Pacific coast of the Americas. Two, the Galapagos fur seal and the Juan Fernandez fur seal are restricted to their island archipelagos—the Galapagos off the coast of Ecuador and the San Felix and Juan Fernandez Islands off Chile. The South American fur seal is much more widespread and occurs along both the Pacific and Atlantic coasts of South America.

None of these three species, strictly speaking, reach into our area of exploration, though it's worth noting that there are plenty of descriptions of islands and coasts covered in amazing numbers of these creatures. For four years, the Juan Fernandez Islands were also the home of a marooned sailor called Alexander Selkirk and the islands were later made famous by Daniel Defoe who based his character Robinson Crusoe on the exploits of Selkirk. When Defoe was penning his famous novel, 4 million fur seals called Crusoe's island home.

The Guadalupe fur seal lived on Guadalupe Island, 150 miles off the Baja coast as well as along the coast of Baja itself and as far north as the Channel Islands off Santa Barbara. According to some estimates, there were two hundred thousand on Guadalupe Island alone. The northern fur seal has a much wider distribution, from San Miguel in the Channel Islands, right up the west coast of the United States and Canada, across the Aleutian Chain and down the western Pacific coast. Across this range there were perhaps 4.5 million of them. Some of the seals observed by Spanish explorers were probably this species, not least since there were two hundred thousand of them on the tiny cluster of rocks off the coast near San Francisco known as the Farallon Islands. But they were first officially described in the north of their range by a German naturalist called Georg Steller traveling with a Russian expedition led by a Dane.

After their early expeditions, and with little sign of much gold or silver, Spanish interest in exploring the Pacific coast waned, at a time when the Russians were becoming very interested in finding out what lay to the east of Siberia and where Asia stopped and America started. Steller had traveled to Russia to work at the St. Petersburg Academy of Sciences, but in 1738, left to travel east. In 1740, he finally arrived in Okhotsk on Siberia's far eastern coast where he met with a Danish sailor called Vitus Bering. Bering had joined the Russian Navy some thirty years earlier, and though he was getting a little long in the tooth, he'd been sent by Peter the Great to explore the Kamchatka Peninsula and find a route eastward to America. To cut a long story short, Steller ended up being appointed naturalist on the venture, though to judge from his journals of the expedition, Steller didn't get on with Bering or with the crew— and the feeling seemed to be mutual. Bering was getting old and didn't always command with authority. Yet the officers generally ignored anything Steller suggested, even though he was often proved right.

The two ships that made up the expedition were soon separated in a storm, so Bering and Steller, on board the *St. Peter*, sailed eastward alone. Seeing certain kinds of seaweeds washing past the *St. Peter*'s bows, the naturalist knew they must be close to land, somewhere to the north, but Bering refused to change course to investigate. In consequence, they sailed parallel to the Aleutians, the chain of islands that forms a convenient series of stepping stones from the Old World to the New, without ever seeing them. Finally, a mountainous island slowly revealed itself over the horizon. They presumed they had come far enough for this to be part of America, but Bering didn't seem too bothered about finding out.

Bering had no intentions of exploring much. He was perpetually worried about the weather in this part of the world and was keen to turn tail and head back to Kamchatka as soon as possible. Initially, he even refused a frustrated Steller permission to land and collect specimens. Eventually, he relented and allowed Steller to go ashore with a landing party sent to collect freshwater, but he was only to stay on land as long as it took to fill the ship's barrels. In reply, Steller complained that they seemed to "have only come to take American water back to Asia."[42]

He didn't have time to find much, but a Cossack he had taken on as his assistant and hunter did provide him with proof that they had made it to America: "Luck, through my hunter, placed in my hands only a single specimen, which I remember having seen painted in vivid colors and written about in the newest description of Carolina plants and birds published in French and English not long ago in London and whose author's name eludes me. This bird alone sufficiently convinced me that we were really in America."[43]

Steller was recalling Mark Catesby's *Natural History of Florida and the Bahamas,* and the bird he thought his Cossack had brought him was the blue jay. In reality, blue jays don't occur here; instead, the bird he was holding is now called Steller's jay in his honor, and it was just as good a proof that they had crossed the invisible line that divides Asia from America. He was standing on what would later be called Kayak Island, separated from the mainland of Alaska by nothing more than a narrow channel of water. But his time was up. Although many of the *St. Peter*'s officers wanted to continue on, Bering had made up his mind to return to Kamchatka. In his journal, the irritated naturalist fumed: "Ten years the preparation for this great undertaking lasted, and ten hours were devoted the work itself."

They headed west again, making occasional stops for provisions, when Steller's advice was again consistently ignored. The crew took water from a foul but easy supply near the beach, even though Steller had found a fresh spring further inland. The crew also refused to follow Steller's example of eating antiscorbutic plants, so, not surprisingly, disease spread through the crew, and even Bering fell ill. And they finally ran into the foul weather that Bering had feared. "Every moment we expected the shattering of our ship. . . . No one could remain at his station, but we were drifting under God's terrible power wherever the enraged heavens wanted to take us. Half our men lay sick and weak, and the other half was healthy out of necessity, but thoroughly crazed and maddened by the terrifying movements of the sea and ship."[44]

Clearly, things were not going well. After enduring several such storms, they finally sighted land. The optimistic among the crew, which seemed to be most of them apart from Steller, convinced themselves that it was Kamchatka's coast that lay before them, so they beached the badly damaged and barely seaworthy ship in the shallows and went ashore.

Wherever they were, this was as far as the *St. Peter* was going to take them. But Steller's naturalist's eye soon told him that this was definitely not Kamchatka: "since I saw . . . on the beach many manatees, which I had never seen before—nor could I know what kind of animals it was since half of it was constantly under water—and since my Cossack . . . answered that this animal existed nowhere on Kamchatka . . . I came to doubt that this could possibly be Kamchatka."[45]

Again he was right—well, almost. They certainly weren't on Kamchatka, but, though the creatures he described were sirenians, no manatee could survive in these cold northern waters. They were sea cows and much bigger than any manatee the Spanish had seen in the Caribbean. Steller estimated their length at nearly thirty feet. And they existed in large numbers around this island. "These animals are found at all times of the year everywhere around this island in vast numbers such that the entire coast of Kamchatka could continually supply itself plentifully from them with both fat and meat."

This was a rather prescient comment from Steller. Twenty-seven years after Steller first saw this creature, it was extinct, something of a record, though an unenviable one. All that we have now are the pages of Steller's journal to conjure up in our minds what it was like to encounter the creatures that eventually came to be called Steller's sea cow.

The crew repaired one of their small boats so they could hunt sea cows, and Steller records a heartrending description of how these animals help an injured companion: "they have indeed an extraordinary love for one another, which extends so far that when one of them was cut into, all the others were intent on rescuing it and keeping it from being pulled ashore by closing a circle around it. Others tried to overturn the yawl. Some placed themselves on the rope or tried to draw the harpoon out of its body. . . . We also observed that a male two days in a row came to its dead female on the shore and inquired about its condition."[46]

Unfortunately for the sea cow, both its meat and its copious insulating layer of fat were tasty and could be stored for some time before becoming rancid. "The boiled fat itself excels in sweetness and taste the best beef fat, in fluidity and color like fresh olive oil, in taste like sweet almond oil, and of exceptionally good smell and nourishment."

These herds seemed to be confined to the small group of uninhabited islands on which the *St. Peter*'s crew found themselves marooned, today called the Commander Islands, about 150 miles off the coast of Kamchatka. They may already have been hunted to extinction elsewhere by native hunters. So it didn't take long for well-armed Russian hunters, following in the wake of the *St. Peter*, to wipe out these last remnants.

The crew were stranded on this tiny island in November and so had to face a bitter winter. Bering finally died of his ailments in this remote spot, a place afterward called Bering Island, an insignificant speck at the southern edge of the cold sea that also bears his name. Those that survived had to live on the local fauna, which included the spectacled cormorant, a bird described by Steller as being sufficient to feed three starving men. That's because they were large birds, clearly evolving in the direction of the great auk. They were almost flightless and might have eventually become the north Pacific's answer to the great auk if they hadn't been so easy to catch. Steller was the only naturalist to see this bird alive; it was extinct by the middle of the nineteenth century, about a hundred years after Steller ate his first one. The Russian exploration of the eastern Pacific wasn't getting off to a great start—at least as far as the local fauna was concerned.

In fact, Steller and the crew of the *St. Peter* weren't doing a lot better. At first, life on Bering Island was extremely hard, but Steller built shelters for the sick and set about turning his naturalist's knowledge into a survival skill. They began by hunting ptarmigans, of which there was a plentiful supply, though often a hard day's hunting was wasted when the local Arctic foxes helped themselves to the spoils.

Arctic foxes were incredibly numerous on Bering Island. On one single day, the crew killed sixty of them, but that didn't stop the rest from becoming a real problem as they grew ever bolder in their exploits.

The foxes which now turned up among us in countless numbers, became accustomed to the sight of men and, contrary to habit and nature, ever tamer, more wicked, and so malicious that they dragged apart all the baggage, ate the leather sacks, scattered the provisions, stole and dragged away from one his boots, from another his socks and trousers, gloves, coats.

It also seemed that, the more we slew and the oftener we tortured them most cruelly before the eyes of the others, letting them run off half skinned, without eyes, without tails, and with feet half roasted, the more malicious the others became. . . . At the same time, they made us laugh in our greatest misery by their crafty and comical monkey tricks.[47]

Buoyed by this bizarre mixture of cruelty and empathy, many of the crew survived the winter and with spring came the possibility of a welcome change to the menu. Northern fur seals began to haul up on their breeding beaches. The first few were

> followed later by innumerable herds, which within a few days filled up the whole beach to such an extent that we could not pass by them without danger to life and limb—nay, in some places since they covered all the ground, they forced us to scale the mountains and to continue our way up there.
> During the whole of May and half of June, we lived on the meat of young and female fur seals.

These were the first detailed description of this species but once word got out about these resources, the inevitable hunting for fur and oil began. Gavril Pribilof was a captain sailing for the Russian-American Company, a Russian fur-trading enterprise, and in 1786 was exploring the north Pacific when he ran into the island that now bears his name. He can hardly have been able to believe his eyes. Pribilof Island was covered in northern fur seals—2.5 million of them. He'd just found the largest concentration of marine mammals anywhere on the planet. More than half of the entire world population of this fur seal was hauled up on Pribilof's beaches.

By 1914, that population was down to two hundred thousand. The scale of the slaughter had been immense and often very wasteful. In 1803, one company destroyed seven years' worth of pelts when they found that they had spoiled. They had been holding them back to prevent a glut on the market knocking down prices. How many fur seals were pointlessly sacrificed to these blind market forces?

Similar scenes were repeated along thousands of miles of coast, right down to South America. It's been estimated that 3.5 million Juan Fernandez fur seals were taken between 1793 and 1807, after which they was considered commercially extinct. A tiny group of animals was discovered on Isla Robinson Crusoe in 1968, since when their population has crept back to a mere twelve thousand. By 1883, the Guadalupe fur seal was also considered commercially extinct, and after 1894 it was presumed totally extinct, since no more could be found. Then, in 1926, two fishermen rediscovered a few animals on Guadalupe. They managed to catch several alive and sold them to San Diego Zoo. But one of the fishermen got into an argument with the director of the zoo and in a fit of pique returned to Guadalupe and slaughtered every fur seal he could find. Again it was presumed extinct, this time at the hand of a single irrational human being, an ignominious end for any creature.

But the Guadalupe fur seal must count itself the luckiest species on the planet. It has returned from the dead twice. In 1949, a lone male was seen on San Nicholas Island in the Channel Island group, and inspired by this, a thorough search was made on Guadalupe. Finally, a small colony was located, hidden in a sea cave, safe from sealers and irate fishermen. And more importantly, the colony had pups. Under protection from the Mexican government, numbers have recovered to around seven thousand at the last count.

The most spectacular of the pinnepeds along the Pacific coast must undoubtedly be elephant seals, which bred in large numbers on many of the islands off California. Here they hauled out from December to March, when, in defending their territories, the massive bulls would launch themselves at each other, blubber quivering, like giant sumo wrestlers. Each male defends a harem of females, who have in turn to defend their not insubstantial pups from being accidentally crushed by their twenty-foot-long, three-ton fathers. Then, breeding over, they head off to sea to feed and recuperate from the arduous days ashore. The males forage as far north as the Aleutians, the females usually further south but they all must haul out again sometime between March and August, this time on different beaches, to molt.

These huge creatures were regarded with some enthusiasm by the oil men of the nineteenth century. All that quivering blubber yielded plenty of oil, in quality second only to sperm whale oil, and, unlike sperm whales, elephant seals thoughtfully exposed themselves to shore-based seal hunters twice a year, when each large bull might yield two hundred gallons of oil. The scale of hunting, as well as the sheer abundance of pinnepeds, is apparent from Scammon's accounts. On Isla de Cedros, off Baja, he found that the

> surrounding shores teemed with sealers, sea elephant and sea otter hunters.
> A few years ago great numbers of Sea Lions were taken along the coast of upper and lower California, and thousands of barrels of oil obtained. The number of seals slain exclusively for their oil would appear fabulous,

when we realize the fact that it requires on average, throughout the season, the blubber of three or four Sea Lions to produce a barrel of oil.[48]

All the pinneped populations were reduced to mere remnants by the onslaught of seal hunters, but some now suggest that the Indian populations of California and Oregon may have had a substantial impact on populations before this. Archaeological evidence implies that, more than two thousand years ago, many breeding colonies of northern fur seals existed on the mainland coast of western North America as well as on offshore islands. The fact that these colonies didn't seem to exist in the heyday of sealing has been put down either to prior overhunting by Indians or to climate change, or perhaps a combination of both.

However, a detailed analysis of middens on the Channel Islands, off the California coast south of Santa Barbara, suggests that, in this area at least, marine mammals were a relatively small part of the diet in comparison to fish over long periods of history.[49] So perhaps changes in marine mammal numbers were more likely to be caused by climate changes. This coast is severely affected by climatic swings caused by El Niño Southern Oscillation (ENSO) events. Temperature changes in the ocean cause massive die-offs or movements of bait fish, which in turn impacts on predators. In the 1983–84 ENSO, 60 percent of fur seal and sea lion pups died.

In contrast, others now consider that coastal Indians had a major influence on the numbers and distribution of some marine mammals. They see the abundance described first by the Spanish and later by the Yankee whalers as due to the widespread decimation of Indian populations by disease and a subsequent "bounce back" by the animals they hunted. These scientists suggest that deadly European diseases could have swept out of the first Spanish colonies in Mexico, long before the first explorers themselves ventured into California. These epidemics reduced Indian populations to a fraction of their former size, so that, in the time it took for the first expeditions to arrive, animal populations had chance to rebound to unexploited levels.

We've met versions of this argument before, with the abundance of deer in the eastern forests and even the mind-boggling flocks of passenger pigeons. Certainly on the Pacific coast, some of the Indians encountered by Spanish and Russian explorers had the technology to hunt fur seals and sea lions, in the form of sophisticated harpoons and impressive sea-going canoes from which to use them. They could have followed fur seals and sea lions out to some of their offshore colonies if the coastal rookeries had been wiped out, but such canoes were also used for hunting seals at sea, as a member of Sebastian Vizcaino's expedition observed: "With this artifice[canoes and harpoons] the Indians capture very large fish and many seals."[50]

The Chumash, living around the Santa Barbara area, had particularly remarkable oceangoing canoes, made from planks sewn together with milkweed fiber and caulked with the tar-pitch mixture that conveniently oozes out of the ground in California. Further north, the Aleuts, living along the Aleutian Chain, used one-man canoes, called *baidarkas* by the Russians, which had an opening sealed with skin to prevent shipping water in rough seas.

But to judge from evidence in middens and elsewhere, hunting patterns weren't the same all along the coast, so the effects of native depredations on marine animals were probably complex and difficult to fit into generalizations. We'll look in more detail at these theories of Indian overhunting when we follow the first Spanish explorers into California's hinterland in the next chapter, but one thing is already abundantly clear. The newcomers to these shores had a much bigger influence: they virtually eliminated pinneped populations entirely.

The population decline was so severe that by 1834 the Russians, within their sphere of influence, had implemented a few protective measures. Later, in 1867, the United States bought Alaska from Russia and two years later set aside the Pribilof Islands as a reserve for fur seals, though not as a sanctuary to allow numbers to recover unmolested. It was an attempt to control the harvest; the U.S. Treasury now issued sealing licenses to favored operations. But it didn't help much, since around the same time pelagic sealing had started. Out at sea, away from any hope of regulation, this was immensely destructive. Many pregnant females were taken, and many more fur seals were killed than actually recovered. Most populations were reduced to commercial extinction by the start of the twentieth century and some close to total annihilation.

In 1911, the North Pacific Fur Seal Convention was set up between Canada, Japan, Russia, and the United States to control hunting on land and to ban pelagic sealing—though most pelagic sealing had already stopped two years earlier since so few could be found. Now only males on land were to be taken. In these species, where a few dominant males guard all the females, most males don't ever get a chance to mate, a surplus that doesn't contribute to population growth and that should therefore represent a sustainable harvest. Under treaty protection and control, numbers did indeed begin to grow until the convention was abandoned as Japan entered World War II.

Another convention was signed in 1957, after which numbers began to build again, until the Fur Seal Commission decided that numbers were growing too large on the Pribilofs. By then, the Pribilofs were home to maybe 870,000 animals, a long way short of the sights that greeted Gavril Pribilof. With no regard for this historic abundance or the role which that abundance played in the ecology of the northern Pacific, the Commission decided to reduce the population and "stimulate productivity" by killing females. This bizarre experiment ended in 1968 with, not surprisingly, a declining population once again.

Globally, the population of northern fur seals did recover to around the 2 million mark in the first half of the twentieth century, but fell again to 1 million for reasons not fully understood—though killing females on the Pribilofs could hardly have helped. But on these islands, the worrying decline continued, even after cessation of the cull. The number of pups born there dropped from 450,000 in the mid-1950s to 253,000 in 1992. Further protection came when the Fur Seal Act was passed in the United States in 1966, which banned all hunting for fur seals apart from subsistence hunts by Indians, Aleuts, and Inuit. In 2002, the world population was estimated to be 1.2 million and rising slowly, but the bottom line is that it's not rebounding at anything like the rate expected under total protection.

The population of Steller sea lions in the Bering Sea has been falling since the 1970s. One explanation—and one that might also apply to fur seals and whales—is that the Bering ecosystem has been fundamentally altered by human exploitation and is now no longer capable of supporting the historic populations of marine mammals.[51] The series of events that led to this may have been something like this. The virtual elimination of whales and eared seals and the later depletion of Pacific herring and Pacific ocean perch led to more food being available for groundfish like walleye pollock, which rapidly increased in abundance—so much so that it is now the largest fishery in the United States. Historically, sea lions took smaller species like capelin and Pacific herring, which are now kept at low numbers by the predatory pollock, forcing the sea lions to switch to pollock, a much less preferred species. Periods of high pollock abundance do seem to coincide with the worst times for the sea lions, added to which the size of sea lions has also decreased, particularly at the peak of the decline in the 1980s. So it looks like Steller sea lions don't do well on their second choice menu.

The reason seems to be that herring contain much higher levels of fat than pollock and pollock take more energy to digest. Both of these factors mean that sea lions get less sustenance from pollock.[52] The pollock also seem to have occupied the niche left vacant by the great whales, which might explain why so many species of whales seem to be struggling to make a comeback.

Elsewhere, some populations of Steller sea lions seem stable while others are suffering similar worrying declines to those in the north. The colony at Ano Nuevo, in California, for example, has declined by 85 percent since 1987, whereas those in southeast Alaska are increasing.

This inconsistent pattern can also be seen in different populations of northern fur seals. All two hundred thousand of them on the Farallons were killed between 1807 and 1840, since they were living rather too conveniently close to San Francisco. It took a long time for northern fur seals to reclaim this breeding site; it wasn't until in 1992 that a birth was recorded, the first pup on the Farallons in a century and half. Intriguingly, several colonies have now also established themselves on the mainland, lending weight to the argument that their earlier absence was due to Indian overhunting and/or climate change.

But one species in particular shows just how fast pinnepeds can respond in favorable conditions. Elephant seals were almost totally wiped out, since they yielded so much high-quality oil. They were commercially extinct by 1860 and thought to be completely lost by 1884, when no more could be found. But in 1889, Charles Townsend, a collector for the Smithsonian Institution, found eight animals, again on Guadalupe, which seems to have been the ark that saved several Pacific species. Seven of these precious few creatures were killed for scientific specimens, the thinking at the time being that it was better to have some decent specimens of an extinct species rather than let the last few corpses rot in the deep. As Townsend himself observed, these specimens could have been "the last of an exceedingly rare species."

But, just as with the Guadalupe fur seal, a few more must have survived, perhaps a few tens of individuals somewhere off the coast of Mexico. And these few began to increase at a phenomenal rate, some 6.3 percent per year on average. In 1922, 250 elephant seals were counted, and by 1955 that had grown to thirteen thousand. Their population explosion continued, reaching thirty thousand in 1977 and perhaps 150,000 by the turn of the new millennium.[53] They recolonized their old breeding sites in droves and continued to swim north, expanding into sites where there is no archaeological evidence for previous occupation. At Ano Nuevo Point, not far from San Francisco, elephant seals have established a breeding beach, now the largest mainland colony in the world.

Such a rapid population explosion does suggest that some species, at least, would have been capable of bouncing back to much larger numbers in the time between the decimation of Indian populations and the arrival of Spanish chroniclers. It also means that, today, many elephant seal beaches are so packed with these huge creatures as to be reminiscent of the scenes that would have greeted Vizcaino.

Meanwhile, back in 1742, George Steller was still trying to survive the rigors of Bering Island. One of the creatures that kept them alive, and the first mammals they caught after being shipwrecked, were sea otters. The crew of the *St. Peter* would have been familiar with these creatures, since they occurred along the coast of Kamchatka, although much more rarely than here. Sea otters are one of the cutest animals you'll ever see, especially the babies, with their surprised black eyes peering out of a face full of unruly fur. Back in the nineteenth century, an American sailor obviously agreed, when he wrote that "nothing can be more beautiful than one of these animals when seen swimming."[54]

It's not hard to spot sea otters anchored in the beds of giant kelp in Monterey Bay and in Elkhorn Slough, which flows into Monterey Bay, they bob like furry corks around the boats in the marina. This is a wonderful place to sit as the evening light picks out the sprays of water sent everywhere by sea otters trying to smash clams as they hammer them on a stone carefully balanced on their furry chests. Instead of rocks, some of the females may have tiny babies cradled on their chests, rocked to sleep by the gently rolling swell. Steller also admired these creatures, though for him sea otters were also a matter of life and death.

Even so, he had time to record valuable scientific observations of a sea otter population on a remote, uninhabited island, before they learned to fear these strange creatures walking on two legs. Steller frequently came across vast rafts of them lounging some way up the beach. He also saw them giving birth on land, something they never did in Kamchatka or the Kurile Islands where they were heavily hunted. Later explorers also described enormous assemblies of sea otters blackening the shore with their numbers, perhaps areas where, like Bering Island, disturbance by Indian or Aleut hunters was less. Steller's sea otters were certainly confiding—at least in the early days: "In the beginning we needed little diligence, cunning, and agility since the whole shore was full of them and they lay in the greatest security. But after that, they were so wise to us that we saw them go ashore warily and with the greatest care."[55]

They were hunted on Kamchatka, not for food as the crew of the *St. Peter* were doing, but for their fur, possibly the finest on any mammal. It's twice as dense as fur seal fur, or, to put it another way, an average human head has a total of about six hundred thousand hairs, whereas a sea otter has three hundred thousand hairs per *square inch*, making it both luxuriant and warm. Even as Steller was catching them for the pot, their pelts were worth $80–$120 each on the Chinese market. Stranded on their remote island, the sea otter's meat was far more important to the crew than the value of their furs, though they knew well enough what the furs would be worth back in Kamchatka, and the lower ranks soon found an economic use for sea otter pelts, even in this remote spot. The crew wiled away the long winter by gambling, using pelts as currency, and ended up killing large numbers just to obtain their stake in the next game. But many of the valuable furs were left to rot, since no one bothered to preserve them.

When spring finally came, Steller and the crew turned their minds to getting off the island. They built a somewhat leaky and unseaworthy craft by cannibalizing the remnants of the *St. Peter* and completing it with whatever local material they could lay their hands on. They set off on their precarious voyage repairing leaks as they went until they finally reached Kamchatka. They arrived with stories of superabundant sea otters and the proof of their tales stored in the hold. Steller knew they owed a lot to this cute little creature—they had, after all, eaten their way through seven hundred while on Bering Island: "this animal deserves the greatest respect from us all, because for more than six months it served us almost solely as our food and at the same time as medicine for the sick." But they didn't get much respect. Word was out, and a year later Russian fur hunters, or *promyshleniki*, were on Bering Island, catching as many sea otters as they could. The ensuing fur rush would help shape the political future of the west coast.

The Russians didn't usually hunt the otters themselves. They employed, or rather coerced, Aleuts to chase them down in their swift baidarkas. The Aleuts had been hunting and trading sea otters for millennia, so knew exactly how to catch them, but this new Russian trade was brutal, to otters and Aleuts alike. If the Aleuts weren't inclined to help, the Russians destroyed their villages or kidnapped their wives, and there was little the Aleuts could do against Russians armed with guns and cannons. A successful revolt on Umnak Island in 1761 gave the local Aleuts a few years of freedom, but the Russians were soon back, this time in force, and the reprisals were terrible. Sea otter numbers fell rapidly, forcing the Russians to turn to the less valuable fur of fur seals or to push south in search of virgin sea otter populations.

They found plenty of sea otters along the coast of California, and though their fur was not quite so luxuriant as those in the colder north, they were certainly worth exploiting. It soon became apparent that the Russians needed a base in California, both to exploit the local fur-bearing creatures and as a farm to grow supplies for the more northerly colonies, where colder weather and less fertile soil made self-sufficiency impossible. After several exploratory trips, the Russians decided on a location about seventy-five miles north of San Francisco and set about establishing Fort Ross, named after *Rossiya*, the name for Russia in the days of the tsars. They even brought Aleuts, with their baid-arkas, to hunt Californian sea otters.

Fort Ross lasted from 1812 to 1841 and has been rebuilt recently as Fort Ross State Park, an intriguing glimpse into California's Russian past. But back then, California was still Spanish territory, and the Spanish were not at all happy with their new neighbors, despite the fact that one of the first Russians to visit the Spanish in San Francisco had diplomatically married a Spanish woman. In reality though, Alta California was nothing more than an outpost of New Spain, and the Spanish weren't able to effectively patrol their coasts to chase every Russian fur pirate. One they did catch, however, confessed to taking 955 sea otters from the tiny San Nicolas Island, in the Channel Islands, which shows the numbers available.

But the Russians wouldn't be a Spanish problem for much longer. In 1821, the inhabitants of New Spain won their independence, after a struggle that lasted more than a decade, and California changed from being an outpost of New Spain to being an outpost of Mexico. The new rulers had a much more relaxed attitude to the trade in sea otter pelts, which therefore flourished in the first years of the new country. When Charles Scammon observed the sea otter trade shortly after Mexican independence, he gives some idea of its value: "The number of Sea Otter skins taken annually is not definitely known, but from the most authentic information we can obtain, the aggregate for the past three years has been five thousand, one thousand of which came from the Kurile Islands; and valuing each skin at fifty dollars, amounts to the sum of two hundred and fifty thousand dollars."[56]

Soon, the California sea otters were heading the same way as their northern cousins in the Bering Straits: "The hunting of them on the coast of California is no longer profitable for more than two or three hunters, and we believe of late some seasons have passed without any one legitimately engaging in the enterprise."[57] Though Scammon mentions one area in California where he had heard of recent successful hunts and where the sea otter population might have been increasing, their numbers had dwindled to almost nothing along most of the west coast. But even someone as observant and knowledgeable as Scammon still found it hard to believe that such an infinite resource could ever run out. Just as we've heard argued for several other species in earlier pages, Scammon preferred to believe the sea otters had simply moved elsewhere: "may it not be that these sagacious animals have fled from those places on the coast of the Californias where they were so constantly pursued, to some more isolated haunt, and now remain unmolested?"

In truth, the $50 price tag on their luxuriant pelt meant there was nowhere to hide. In 1910, no one could find any to hunt. A year later, and not a moment too soon, they received protection under the 1911 Fur Seal Convention. Somehow, a tiny population had managed to survive, but it stayed perilously small for four decades, showing no signs of real increase until after World War II. Then they began a rapid and welcome growth in population—well, welcome by everyone except one group of people—commercial abalone and urchin fishermen.

This conflict derives from the fact that sea otters are another keystone species, pivotal in the balance of the coastal ecosystem. Sea otters relish red abalones and urchins, and an abundant population of sea otters keeps numbers of abalones and urchins in check. Remove the sea otters and the population of urchins and abalones explodes. Urchins are grazers and in increased numbers scour the rocks of all algae, creating urchin barrens and destroying even the largest sea weeds. And along the California coast there are some of the largest seaweeds in the world.

Giant kelp, feather boa kelp, and bull kelp form towering underwater forests that sway to the rhythm of the Pacific swell. The fronds of giant kelp can reach 175 feet in length and to reach such impressive sizes grow at two feet a day. The fronds reach the surface and form great slicks that worried early explorers. "From the extreme end of Loma begins a long sheet of seaweed, stretching for more than a league to the south-southwest. It is so thick on the surface of the water that, if one undertook to pass it with a light breeze, he might find himself stopped by this obstacle which, however, offers no other danger, for there is everywhere a depth of fifteen to twenty fathoms."[58]

But despite their prodigious rates of growth, these kelp forests soon disappear under the onslaught of hungry urchins. Along the Aleutians, there have been several episodes of urchin barrens. Archaeologists excavating Aleut middens have found periods in prehistory when the remains of large sea urchins became abundant. The size and number of these animals, along with only sparse remains of sea otters, suggests that the offshore habitat must have switched to an "urchin-barrens" state, probably because sea otters had been overhunted.[59] Certainly, Aleuts had the technology and capacity to all but eliminate sea otters, since they did so in later times under extreme coercion from the Russians.

This second period of urchin barrens, as sea otters almost disappeared during the fur trade of the eighteenth and nineteenth centuries, may also help explain the surprisingly rapid demise of sea cows. These vegetarians depended on easy access to huge quantities of plant matter, so starvation in the aftermath of the sea otter collapse may well have added to hunting pressure and helped push them into extinction. Another episode of barrens is much more recent, as sea otters around the Aleutians declined by 80 percent between 1990 and 2000.[60]

This last decline has been attributed to killer whales switching their diet to sea otters, as has the decline in Steller sea lions. Historical documents contain many accounts of killer whales attacking larger whales, and they still take a toll of gray whale calves as they migrate north from Baja. So as the great whales disappeared, killer whales may have been forced to switch diet. Using their energy requirements and the calorific value of sea lions and sea otters, it's possible to work out that killer whales could easily produce the observed effects on the populations of both sea otters and sea lions. Just forty killer whales could account for the drop in Steller sea lion numbers, and a pod of five are all that's needed to reduce sea otter numbers,[61] an illustration of the unpredictable cascade of events following the removal of even just one strand in the complex web of life.

In the south of their range, the role of sea otters is even more complicated. The kelp forests here are more diverse, and there are other predators of sea urchins, fish like sheephead as well as spiny lobsters, so the loss of sea otters doesn't always result in the immediate appearance of urchin barrens. However, these other predators have now also been overfished, so large tracts of kelp forest have subsequently disappeared, creating barrens in which urchins and red abalones are unnaturally abundant. And that's the situation that commercial urchin and abalone fishermen walked—or swam—into. With the return of sea otters, the population of abalones and urchins falls as the original balance is reestablished, but it looks to the fishermen as if sea otters are merely serious competitors for their livelihoods.

Under the combined pressure of otters and people, red abalone numbers dropped. However, there are several other species of abalones in these waters, and divers switched to each of these in turn and, just as for the reds, the populations of black, green, and pink abalones also collapsed. So, in the 1970s, commercial divers went after a less accessible, deeper water species, the white abalone. At this time, white abalones lived in large beds that reached densities of ten thousand individuals per hectare. In 1972, seventy-two tons of white abalones were landed, but after that the catch dwindled. Now divers are lucky to find one or two individuals per hectare. In May 2001, the white abalone had the dubious honor of becoming the first marine invertebrate to be listed on the Endangered Species Act, but some scientists even see this as pointless. They say there aren't enough white abalones left to establish a captive breeding and reintroduction program and that extinction is all but inevitable.

The problem for the remaining wild white abalones is that they are scattered too thinly. To breed, they simply release sperm and eggs into the water and fertilization occurs as they mix. This only works if the abalones are close enough together—no problem when they covered the bottom in dense carpets. But even an athletic abalone can only manage a few feet a minute and with the population now so sparse, it's unlikely that any white abalone will ever encounter another of its species.

Abalones provide another good example of why it is difficult for a free market to produce sustainable harvests. As they became rarer, prices rose, and though the commercial fishery was closed in 1997, today abalones can change hands for $200–$300 each—more than enough incentive to hunt down the last individuals. Compare this situation to the locally managed fisheries in the Sea of Cortez and the turtle egg harvests in Costa Rica. The difference lies in local people, who have few or no alternative livelihoods, putting a long-term value on their resources. And that also seems to have been the basis of the economy of many of the original inhabitants of these western shores.

By now, it should be clear that the Indian's relationship with their land and the animals and plants that lived on it was far from simple. But the Chumash, who lived in Central California, may have achieved a particularly sophisticated level of understanding and ecological management. Archaeological evidence suggests that the Chumash attained one of the highest population levels known for hunter-gatherers. So a team of anthropologists and ecologists have taken a look at how they affected their local ecology in one neatly defined area, San Miguel Island in the Channel Islands.

Looking at middens around the island, the team found that the ancestors of the Chumash had been hunting sea otters here for around nine thousand years. In one continuous time sequence that they carefully unearthed, sea otter remains were present from three thousand years ago right up to AD 1800, when the last Chumash were removed from the island. So the Chumash clearly hadn't exterminated sea otters even from the limited population on the island, though of course, immigration from other colonies could have supplemented the local population.

However, the archaeological evidence also shows that there are more red abalones in those middens from more recent times, suggesting that the sea otter population, though not wiped out, was gradually lowered. The Chumash, too, saw value in the sea otters fur, for their own use and for trade inland. One possibility suggested by the researchers is that, rather than seeing this as yet another example of human overexploitation inevitably eliminating a resource—another "tragedy of the commons"—perhaps it should be seen as a form of management. The Indians may have reduced the numbers of sea otters around their village sites, where it was convenient to collect abalones, but allowed the population to flourish elsewhere.[62]

This is exactly the approach now being suggested for the management of the red abalone fishery—to create sea otter sanctuaries in some places, but to prevent them from reestablishing themselves in other areas, to create enhanced populations of red abalones for the commercial fishery.

From the historical point of view, this research again shows that Indians didn't live lightly on the land. They were key elements in shaping the New World's ecology in ways that we are only just beginning to realize, and in ways that were both complex and varied. But perhaps the best places in the whole of North America to appreciate this are not the coasts and islands. Inland, the rolling hills and grasslands, the high mountains and deserts, supported a greater diversity of cultures than anywhere on the continent. Here, California truly was Paradise.

CHAPTER 15

Blessings Fit for the Use of Man

In a novel from the sixteenth century, California was an island paradise. This was the first-ever mention of the name; here Queen Calafia ruled over a land rich in gold and populated solely by women—certainly a vision of paradise in some eyes. But the idea of California as an island has some truth in it, at least ecologically, as the title of Elna Bakker's classic work on the natural history of California, *An Island Called California*,[1] suggests. Biologically, California is the richest area in North America; fully one quarter of the continent's biodiversity can be found here. And, just like many real islands, much of this wealth is found nowhere else; one third of California's flora, for example, is endemic. In fact, it has more unique plants and animals than any other state.[2] And like an island, California also *feels* like a place separated from the rest of the United States, especially if you drive there along one of the busy interstates. Instead of a small green sign marking the state line, there are large border posts, more intimidating than crossing between many sovereign countries in Europe. They are not there to inspect passports, but to check for fruit and other produce that might introduce alien pests to the extensive farms and fields, orchards and vineyards that now clothe a large part of the state. But they are a little too late.

Almost as soon as European explorers arrived here, so too did European plants and animals, and they found this "island" paradise much to their liking. Early explorers described riding through thousands of acres of European wild mustard plants, higher than their heads even when mounted on horseback. And the mission fig, initially planted around the first Spanish missions along the coast, soon found its way into riverine forests. Other species followed, some intentionally introduced and some accidentally. Over the centuries, alien plants transformed landscapes throughout California, and alien animals now threaten both valuable commercial crops and the unique diversity of native species.

One reason for California's extraordinary wealth of species was its varied landscapes. The fertile coasts teemed with fish and marine mammals, and above the shoreline, running from Morro Bay to the Oregon border, coastal prairies were a carpet of wildflowers. The Coastal Range, clothed in forests of giant conifers—redwoods and Douglas firs—separates these grasslands from those of the vast Central Valley, which used to be California's own private version of the Great Plains. The Central Valley runs north to south for four hundred miles, following the rivers that drain into San Francisco Bay, north along the Sacramento and its tributaries and south along the San Joaquin. All these rivers were lined with tall riverine forests, often containing enormous valley oaks, and, further from the rivers, the valley became an open prairie of long-lived bunch grasses interspersed with great marshes of tule reeds. Several of the rivers flowing into the Central Valley had no permanent outlets and simply ended in vast shallow lakes on the valley floor. The largest was Tulare Lake, at seven hundred square miles in extent, the biggest lake west of the Great Lakes.

Traveling east across the valley floor, the land is gently folded into the foothills of the Sierra Nevada, beautiful, rolling country of open parkland dotted with oak trees that produce vast crops of acorns in the fall. Then the traveler rises into the ice-carved granite of the Sierra Nevada itself, which flanks the Central Valley on its eastern border. The slopes are again clothed in giant trees; this time sequoias, the largest living things on our planet—if you discount giant fungal mycelia or superclones of aspen. Ice age glaciers have cut spectacular valleys into the Sierra's hard granite, valleys that later carried crystal clear rivers over impressive waterfalls. Rain to feed these rivers and falls is wrung from moisture-laden winds blowing in from the coast, as they're forced up over the peaks and cooled. But most of this rain falls on the western slopes. To the east, in the rain shadow of the high mountains, the land is desert. Travel further east still, over the lower ranges of the Panamints and the Inyo Mountains, and the desert becomes extreme. In summer, hot winds whipping across the floor of Death Valley scorch exposed skin, yet in its own way this landscape is just as beautiful as the high Sierras, abstract patterns of eroded and folded rocks, painted in the colors of drought and heat.

To the north and south, the mountains close ranks and obliterate the Central Valley—the transverse ranges of the Tehachapi to the south and, to the north, the Cascades, which then continue the spectacular mountain scenery right along the west coast, up through Washington State. Along the whole of the Pacific coast, there are historical descriptions of giant Douglas firs cloth-ing mountain slopes, and of teeming estuaries and marshes along the rivers that flow from these mountains to the ocean. But most spectacular of all was the land that would one day be called California—still a land of superlatives today. The highest mountain in the Lower Forty-eight, Mount Whitney, is un-der two hundred miles from the lowest point in the western hemisphere, the evocatively named Badwater, at the bottom of Death Valley. Both the largest and the tallest trees in the world, sequoias and redwoods, respectively, grow in Californian soil, and the smallest and largest birds on the continent, the cal-liope hummingbird and the Californian condor, fly through its skies.

Not surprisingly, such a large range of productive habitats in such close proximity has allowed a great variety of Indian cultures to flourish. In fact, California's cultural diversity is just as impressive as its natural diversity; one hundred mutually unintelligible languages were spoken here, one quarter of all the languages in North America. There were, perhaps, five to six hundred different tribes, or at least independent political units, within the modern state's boundaries. But the Indians hadn't just adapted to an existing natural diversity; they had played a major part in creating it. Through varied hunting and harvesting practices, and by irrigation and burning, sowing and trans-planting useful species, they shaped the landscapes that so impressed early visitors. And this carefully husbanded wealth of natural resources meant that Indians could live here in large numbers. The average population density has been estimated at one person per two square miles,[3] among the highest any-where in the world for indigenous people and certainly the highest density north of Mexico at the time of European contact.

Modern California retains its record. It is still the most populous state in the Union, and that dense population has transformed the landscape over the last two centuries. Even so, it's still possible to be enthralled by nature here. Early in the year, when rain soaks into the dry earth of California's desert valleys, annual flowers spring briefly into life—California poppy, owl's clo-ver, and goldfield, the latter a most apt name. In a good year, the hills look as if someone has carelessly splashed them with yellow paint. But in the past, these displays were larger and more widespread and conspicuous. Even when viewed from the deck of a heaving galleon several miles offshore, the brilliant hues of the coastal hills and prairies were clearly visible. The yellow of Califor-nia poppies, erupting across the spring landscape, inspired the Spanish to call this coast the "Land of Fire." And when the first explorers traveled into California's interior, the botanical extravaganza continued. One explorer found "an infinity of rosebushes in full bloom,"[4] while the first expedition to view the site of the future city of San Francisco found the Presidio to be "very green and flower-covered, with an abundance of violets."[5] Across the bay, the site of the first campus of the University of California, at Berkeley, was covered in blue lupines and gold poppies, the origin, so it is said, of the university's own striking colors.

With so many flowers, insects also thrived in such numbers that they were included in the Indians' varied diet. Some drove large swarms of grasshoppers into pits, where they could easily be collected. Others fired the grasslands, which, though usually seen as increasing the quality of grazing for big game, also yielded a good harvest of small game. In the 1870s, one observer watched Yokuts gathering a rich source of protein like this, though it's one that wouldn't tempt many western palates. "In the mountains they used to fire the forests, and thereby catch great quantities of grasshoppers and caterpillars already roasted, which they devoured with relish."[6]

I've never really understood the mentality that balks at eating insects and yet savors crustaceans. As a fellow of the Royal Entomological Society of London, I've been served roast locusts at the annual Verrall Supper, and I've munched on caterpillars in South Africa and beetle larvae in Australia, all of which are just as palatable as prawns or shrimps. The vast numbers of insects in California's grasslands and forests were (and some still are) an easy—and sustainable—source of high-quality protein of which the Indians made good use. Those caterpillars that survived the fires went on to turn into equally protein-rich pupae and then into butterflies or moths, which at times existed in great clouds. In 1806, Gabriel Moraga led a Spanish expedition through the Sierra foothills and camped in one place where there were "myriads of butterflies of the most gorgeous and variegated colors, perched about on the surrounding trees."

The butterflies were so numerous that they named the place after them— Mariposa. But, according to the expedition's diarist, a Franciscan priest called Pedro Muñoz, not everyone enjoyed the spectacle: "This place is called Mariposas because the great multitudes of these, especially at night and in the morning, could not be more troublesome, their eagerness to hide from the rays of the sun reaching such proportions that they pursued us everywhere, so much that one got into the ear of one of the Expedition Leaders, causing him great discomfort and not a little effort to extract it."[7] The name stuck, and

Mariposa today is a lovely small town, on the banks of the Mariposa Creek, not far from the tourist magnet of Yosemite. But for which butterfly was Mariposa named?

California tortoiseshells are well known for their population explosions followed by spectacular migrations, often in large numbers to new territories. But California tortoiseshells are colored dull orange and brown, subtly exquisite to an entomologist, but unlikely to be described as "gorgeous and variegated" by a disinterested explorer. On the other hand, tortoiseshells were much more abundant in the past, which may have impressed them on the minds of Moraga and his men. They were so numerous that Mono Indians used to collect their pupae as food. Even today, some elders of the tribe can remember big swarms of tortoiseshells occurring every year, whereas now they are only, at best, seen in these areas every decade or so and often not at all for several decades.[8] So perhaps I do the members of Gabriel Moraga's expedition a disservice in suggesting they didn't appreciate the understated beauty of the California tortoiseshell.

Father Muñoz's description sounds as if they had camped in the midst of a butterfly roosting site, and one butterfly famously assembles in such roosts to pass the winter. The monarch is also "gorgeously variegated" in orange and black, to advertise the fact that it is packed full of foul-tasting and toxic chemicals, obtained from the plants it fed on as a caterpillar. Monarchs migrate from as far north as Canada to spend the winter in more benign climates. Their main overwintering sites are in the Sierra Madre Mountains in Mexico, where tens of millions assemble in just a few isolated groves, in numbers so great that they weigh down the branches of the pines. On some mornings, if the sun warms the butterflies and rouses them from their overnight torpor, they cascade from the branches as a living waterfall of orange and black. They end up carpeting the forest floor, until the day has warmed up enough for them to take to the wing. Now they fill the sunlit glades with a shimmering wall of fluttering wings as if the air itself had become pure color. And more remarkable than such impressive sights, the sound of ten million butterfly wings is quite extraordinary.

The western populations of monarchs head to California's coast, rather than Mexico, where they winter in more modest numbers scattered across many more sites. There are around two hundred such winter roosts known at present, and though none have the millions of Mexico's Sierra Madre, they are still spectacular places to visit. The largest is located near Pismo Beach, with well over one hundred thousand butterflies in some years, though numbers vary dramatically from year to year. But I doubt that Moraga saw monarchs at Mariposa. He was there at the end of September, a little too early for wintering monarchs and a long way from the known sites along California's coast, where the cool winter air allows them to conserve their reserves of energy. So I'm still not entirely sure which of California's many butterflies Moraga witnessed. After all, even many of today's rarities would have been abundant enough in the past to impress footsore Spanish explorers.

But it was a long time before Spanish eyes gazed in wonder on California's interior. Until the second half of the eighteenth century, it was a neglected outpost of New Spain, and all we have to go on are glimpses from the coast and occasional forays a short distant inland. In 1542, Cabrillo gave us the first foretaste when he sailed into San Diego Bay. He found the waters teeming with small sturgeon, ready to make their spawning runs up river, a hint of the productivity that later explorers would discover. But as he explored along the coast, he was not tempted to explore further inland. Mountainous waves buffeted the tiny ships, and fog shrouded them for much of the time, forcing Cabrillo to stay a safe distance from dangerous cliffs and rocks.

Next, it was the turn of the English to explore the Pacific coast. In 1579, we get a few more substantial glimpses of California's riches when one of England's great heroes, Francis Drake, appeared off the coast. He was a man of many talents—privateer, explorer, navigator, slave trader, politician, civil engineer, and bane of the Spanish. He's famous in English school history books for deciding to finish a game of bowls on Plymouth Hoe before popping off to defeat the invading Spanish Armada in the English Channel in 1585 and thus saving England from a terrible fate. What many fail to realize is that the Armada was there in the first place in no small part because of Drake's exploits in the Caribbean and Pacific.

In 1577, Elizabeth I sent him to plague the Spanish settlements on the Pacific coast of America. He'd already done such a good job in the Caribbean, and made himself rich into the bargain, that he was the perfect man for the job. He sailed, with renewed enthusiasm for his life's work, from Plymouth, down the east coast of South America and through the Magellan Straits that separate Tierra del Fuego from the rest of South America. On this voyage, he sailed further south than anyone before him. Indeed, his record wouldn't be broken until 1773, by that other great English navigator, Captain James Cook.

There were rich pickings for a privateer in the Pacific. He sacked Valparaiso, on the coast of Chile, but this was just small beer. The top prize in this ocean was the Manila galleon, and in 1579 he hit the jackpot. He ran into the *Cacafuego*, which was carrying enough gold, silver, and other valuables to put England's economy back into the black. No wonder Elizabeth called him "my pirate." Drake then headed for the California coast to carry out much needed repairs on his heavily laden ship and to keep his navigator's eye open for the still-elusive Straits of Anian. At first, he wasn't at all impressed. He was probably off the coast of Oregon when he ran into "thick stinking fogs, which nothing which the Wind could remove." A fairly typical summer's day along that coast. So he sailed on south, even though "neither for 14 Days could they see the Sun for the Fogginess of the Air."[9]

Eventually, he found what he was looking for, a protected bay where he could beach the *Golden Hind*. More than that, it was fringed with white cliffs that reminded him of the White Cliffs of Dover and home. So he claimed this chunk of Spanish territory for England and called it Nova Albion. But the white cliffs were where the resemblance ended. On landing they found "How unhandsome and deformed appeared the face of the earth itself . . . showing trees without leaves and the ground without greenness in those moneths of June and July."

They were the first to observe, if not understand, that California is one of a small handful of places around the world with a "Mediterranean" ecology. The others are the Western Cape of South Africa, the area to the south of Perth in western Australia together with Eyre's Peninsula in South Australia, parts of the Chilean coast, and of course the shores of the Mediterranean itself. They all have hot, dry summers followed by warm, wet winters, and although the actual plants that grow in each of these places are different, they all bear an uncanny resemblance to each other—like different actors performing the same play in different theaters. And thanks to the similar climate in each of these zones, it's possible to spend the evening in any one of them reminiscing over a great day's botanizing while sampling some of the finest wines on the planet. Paradise indeed!

Drake also began to appreciate California when he ventured a little further inland. "The inland we found to be farre different from the shoare, a goodly country, and fruitful soyle, stored with many blessings fit for the use of man." This was a very prophetic vision of the future for California's natural history. The fruitful soil and benign climate would indeed grow just about anything.

But before the farms and agribusinesses, Drake found "The whole Countrey to bee a warren of a strange kinde of Conies."[10] Conies (or coneys) were rabbits, but it is doubtful whether these were anything a biologist would call a rabbit. From later descriptions, they were probably pocket gophers, which still honeycombed the ground with their burrows in such prodigious numbers that they plagued the early days of commercial agriculture. Several kinds of ground squirrels also existed in phenomenal numbers and added their earthmoving efforts to those of the gophers. And there were real rabbits here too. Many explorers described large numbers of hares (jack rabbits) and rabbits (cottontails), though only one of these, the pygmy rabbit, actually digs its own burrows in the way that European rabbits do. Doubtless, pygmy rabbits would have also been digging extensive warrens when Drake landed on these shores, though today they are endangered and very scarce throughout most of their range.

Drake also found plenty of larger animals in his brief exploration of California: "infinite were the company of very large fat deer, which there we saw by the thousands as we supposed in a herd."[11] He was watching elk. In all, there are six subspecies of this large deer across North America, two of which, the eastern and Merriam elk, are now extinct. The great herds ranging over California's grasslands were tule elk, the smallest variety, named after the great tule marshes that lay scattered across the grasslands and that were dominated by tall sedges called tule reeds. But in reality tule elk favored the open grassy plains; the impenetrable tule marshes were simply their last refuges from European American hunters in the nineteenth century.[12]

Elsewhere in California and through Oregon, Washington, and British Columbia, there were large numbers of Roosevelt elk in the Pacific forests and Rocky Mountain Elk further inland. These large deer were joined by equally impressive numbers of smaller varieties: black-tailed deer along the coast and inland the mule deer. These last two deer are closely related, perhaps just distinct subspecies of the same species,[13] although other authorities suggest that mule deer are in fact just that—hybrids between black-tailed and white-tailed deer.[14] All of these deer were extremely abundant, but according to some, tule elk provided a spectacle to rival that of the game herds on East Africa's Serengeti plains. And that certainly sounds feasible from the descriptions of explorers who followed Drake.

One nineteenth-century traveler saw tule elk "as far as the eye could reach," while another "saw bands of elk, deer and antelope in such numbers that they actually darkened the plains for miles and looked in the distance like great herds of cattle."[15] The valley grasslands may have supported up to half a million elk and uncountable numbers of smaller mammals and birds, as Sebastian Vizcaino reported just twenty years after Drake: "up country were found geese, ducks, quails; rabbits and hares were also here in great numbers."[16]

Later explorers often made particular comment on immense flocks of California quail. William Dawson, an ornithologist who wrote the classic *Birds of California* in the 1920s, described flocks of one to five thousand as commonplace, and another observer in San Mateo County "saw quail by the thousands everywhere; every canyon, gulch and ravine contained quail . . . and the whole country seemed to be alive with them."[17] All the early reports describe similar abundance, both along the coast and as far inland as these mariners dared to venture. But Spain didn't bother much with detailed exploration of this outpost of empire; it didn't look like being a source of gold in the same way as Mexico and Peru.

But then the Russians began taking a serious interest in Alta California, and the Spanish suddenly felt the need to establish a firmer presence there. So, in 1769, nearly two centuries after Cabrillo first landed in Alta California, Gaspar de Portola led an expedition on foot along the coastal ranges and prairies to find an overland route to Monterey Bay, which had already been charted by mariners exploring this coast.

The expedition was a massive undertaking. As Portola left Baja California, three supply ships sailed north, two to rendezvous with the overland expedition in San Diego and the third to resupply them in Monterey Bay. Unfortunately, this last ship disappeared at sea and was never seen again, but from Portola's point of view it didn't matter too much, since on this first trip he failed to find Monterey Bay anyway. But the overland expedition did at least meet up successfully with the two supply ships in San Diego Bay. When he arrived in San Diego, Portola discovered that the crew of these two vessels had had a much harder time getting there than he did. Many of the sailors had died from lack of food and water, and most of the survivors were suffering badly from scurvy.

In contrast, the overland expedition usually had a plentiful and varied diet. Along the coast, Portola's men met large numbers of Indians living well on surf and turf. As well as all those rabbits, quails, and other creatures of Southern California's desert scrub, they had seagoing canoes to harvest the abundant marine resources: "These canoes landed on the beach . . . and brought an abundance of bonito and bass . . . in such quantity that we might have loaded the pack animals with fish if we had the facilities to salt and prepare it."[18]

After leaving San Diego, and heading north for Monterey, they passed through open country and began to see large herds of deer and pronghorn. Many early explorers called these latter creatures "antelopes," or sometimes "goats," because these were the only familiar animals that they resembled. But in reality they are neither—they are the only surviving members of an ancient family, the Antilocapridae. The first scientific description was made by Lewis and Clark as they crossed the Great Plains, but other early travelers tell us that they were widespread and abundant across California's grasslands as well, and often very easy to approach.

George Yount, who moved to California in the 1830s, is renowned as the first person to plant a vine in the Napa Valley, and although the place is now swamped with them, when George first arrived it was covered with spectacular herds of game. "The deer, antelope and noble elk . . . were numerous beyond all parallel. In herds of many hundred they might be met, so tame they would hardly move to open the way for the traveler to pass."[19] This unexpected tameness has been interpreted by some scientists as further evidence for the idea that such spectacles only existed because Indian hunting pressure had been drastically reduced, since these animals quickly lose their fear of humans in the absence of hunting. This "historic overkill" hypothesis is given further support from the excavation of ancient midden sites. Tule elk vanish from this record quite early, while in the mountains, the remains of bighorn sheep are replaced by those of yellow-bellied marmots as time progresses. Large elk and sheep would have been the preferred prey for local Indians so their disappearance from midden sites may have been caused by overhunting, though there are other possibilities. For example, elk are so big that they may have been butchered where they were killed and only the edible parts taken back to the village. However, one researcher goes so far as to suggest that California's Indians may at times have reduced game to levels that today we would consider endangered.[20]

But, as with the marine animals in the previous chapter, the situation is complicated. For example, the archaeological evidence shows a resurgence of black-tailed deer in at least one region. Possibly a decline in more desirable species might spark an increase in intertribal warfare, which in turn might create no-go areas between tribal territories, where it is too dangerous to hunt. These would then serve as game reserves, allowing game numbers to build again. This certainly seems to have been the case on the Great Plains, as we will see in a later chapter. The Indian relationship with the land was clearly a continuously shifting and dynamic one, driven partly by their own effects on the natural world and partly by long-term climate change over the ten millennia or so since the ice age ended. Yet, whatever the details of that relationship, the natural world continued to support large populations of Indians right up to the eve of European contact.

Part of the problem in understanding the extent of any historic overkill, or any subsequent bounce-back after decimation of the human population, is that it is difficult to know exactly how quickly epidemics spread. The idea is that disease spread through the Indian population well ahead of actual contact, which, of course, meant there were no European observers to record the effects. When such observers finally did arrive, game animals had already multiplied to spectacular populations and grown tame in the process.

Yet, when the first explorers landed in Alta California, they found large Indian populations in many places, still managing the land in a traditional manner. Cabrillo called San Pedro Bay *Bahia de los Fumos*—the Bay of Smokes—since there were so many Indian fires burning. Even as late as the mid-eighteenth century, when Portola began his epic trek along the coast, he found many places that were thickly populated. One of the Franciscan fathers, Father Serra, who traveled with him, noted that "We have seen Indians in immense numbers, and all those on this coast of the Pacific contrive to make a good subsistence on various seeds, and by fishing."[21]

There were places where the expedition also came across large populations of game, both mammals and birds, yet there were other places where he and his men went hungry—all of which points to a complex pattern of Indian interactions with the rest of California's ecology. And, as elsewhere, ethnographic evidence doesn't always agree with archaeological evidence.

Kat Anderson, in her detailed examination of the ecological relationships of California's Indians, *Tending the Wild,* says that, in her experience, most Indians across California followed two basic rules—leave some of what is gathered for other animals and do not waste what is harvested.[22] A Maidu elder told her that she always left some acorns on the oaks, some berries on the bushes, and some tubers in the ground for "the birds and squirrels and other animals." Ritual and ceremony also guided native Californians in their use of resources. Just as for Indians across the whole continent, they didn't see nature as something "out there," distinct from humanity. On the contrary, humans were an inseparable part of it, their actions dictated by pacts with the other inhabitants of a shared world.

In practice, of course, life was never that perfect. It seems likely that Indians did reduce the population of some game animals and certainly caused the extinction of a few. The demise of a spectacular, flightless, goose-sized diving duck (*Chendytes lawi*) along the California coast around 2,800 years ago seems to have been due to overhunting for its temptingly large drumsticks, though it should be noted that *Chendytes* did survive hunting for eight thousand years even though Indians had watercraft and were able to reach many of its offshore island homes throughout this period.[23] Many of the morality stories, passed down through tribal history across the whole continent, suggest past overexploitation followed by an attempt to reestablish some kind of balance. After all, they wouldn't have had numerous religious sanctions against destroying nature if they didn't have the capacity to do so. All of these aspects of indigenous life contributed to the very dynamic relationship between Indians and the landscapes they lived in—a relationship that at times may have reduced abundance and diversity, but at other times enhanced it.

One action that would have increased game was burning, which created and maintained the coastal prairies and improved the quality of forage for elk. We've heard the same arguments applied to white-tailed deer in the eastern forests. Such forms of landscape management help promote some species (those that were most useful to the Indians) at the expense of others. And Indians today are very clear that their forebears knew exactly what they were doing, as Kat Anderson was told in 1989 by a Chukchansi/Choynumni: "My husband's family . . . burned to keep things clear. They also burned for the animals—the deer, bear, rabbits and squirrels. The new growth the following spring gave them better and higher-quality foods such as buck brush."[24]

As Portola's expedition began their search for the land route to Monterey, they came across more evidence of California's carefully tended resources. Near the Santa Ynez River, not far from modern Santa Barbara, they saw some very large bears and evidence of many more, to judge from the numbers of tracks. Nearer San Luis Obispo, they entered a canyon: "In this canyon we saw a troop of bears; they had the land plowed up and full of holes which they make in searching for the roots they live on."[25] Impressed by such numbers, they called this place Cañada de los Osos—Canyon of the Bears—and the town that later grew up near this canyon is still called Los Osos. Modern visitors to this pleasant little dormitory town on Morro Bay are still welcomed by a bear, though this one is a large statue. There are no living California grizzlies around Los Osos today—nor anywhere else for that matter. This distinct variety of grizzly bear is now extinct, though ironically, they still appear on California's state flag. They did however remain plentiful for some time after Portola passed this way.

When George Yount came to California in the early nineteenth century, it was quite possible to see fifty or sixty in a day, and many explorers reported seeing them moving in large herds. California's grizzlies were obviously more social than those elsewhere, and perhaps they had to be; grizzlies reached their highest population densities in this area. To someone who has spent many days traveling around the best grizzly country today—Yellowstone, for example—to see one or two bears, the thought of whole herds of bears is an extraordinary concept. And on top that, there were other predators to thrill or terrify. Around San Francisco Bay, visitors were warned about "the bears, wolves or tiger-cats which are very plentiful on these woods."[26]

Even jaguars reached up into the modern state of California before livestock farmers declared all out war on anything with fangs. There are plenty of reliable eyewitness reports of jaguars here up to the mid-nineteenth century and descriptions of Indians stealing prey that jaguars had hidden.[27]

The Indian relationship with such predators was somewhat more complicated than that of the Europeans, typified by the Indian attitude to the large herds of formidable grizzlies that wandered through their territories. Many tribes, like the Wiyot and Cahuilla, for example, were reluctant to hunt grizzlies, or antagonize them in any way[28]—a sensible approach to even a solitary grizzly, in my opinion. If a Cahuilla met a grizzly, the trick was to talk soothingly to him, saying, "I am only looking for my food, you are human and understand me, take my word and go away."[29] And the bears, for their part, seemed to have had the same attitude as the Cahuilla. There are several reports of explorers camping in good bear country who woke to find bear tracks around their camp, but no attempt by the bear to attack.

Other tribes hunted them. Back in the 1950s, Tracy Storer and Lloyd Tevis wrote the definitive work on California grizzlies in which they documented a mass of evidence of Indian hunting, as well as the reasons why Indians would undertake such a dangerous task armed with just spears or arrows.[30] One reason, they suggest, is that the omnivorous grizzly was competing with the Indians for vital resources. This idea has recently seen a revival, based on evidence that some Indians in the eastern forests deliberately overhunted white-tailed deer, turkeys, raccoons, and anything else that might eat the hickories, wal-nuts, and acorns before the Indians could get their hands on them.

Many early reports from California describe bears trooping into valleys to graze on clover "like herds of swine." Maidu Indians also ate such herbs, and one early observer was astonished to see Indians "spread out over the plains and gathering & eating different kinds of herbs like the beasts." The Maidu were one of those tribes that regularly killed grizzlies, since they also com-peted for an even more vital resource—acorns: "Indians and bear . . . thrash down acorns, which is almost as effectively done by one as by the other."[31]

Since California grizzlies were one of the largest subspecies, killing one needed careful forethought and planning. One technique was to dig a pit beneath a tempting oak tree and cover it with a light layer of brush. A bear trapped in such a pit could then be dispatched with arrows or spears. Even so, hunting grizzlies also demanded courage as well as cunning and several tribes, like the Pomo and Kato, gave the title of "Chief Grizzly Bear Hunter" to their war chiefs.

Yet, when not being hunted, California grizzlies seemed remarkably peace-ful. In 1900, Joaquin Miller, sometimes called the "poet of the Sierras," pub-lished a book called *True Bear Stories* in which he recalled his travels in the mid-nineteenth century: "In the early 50's, I, myself saw the grizzlies feeding together in numbers under the trees, far up the Sacramento Valley, as tran-quilly as a flock of sheep. A serene, dignified and very decent old beast was the full-grown grizzly as Fremont and others found him here at home."[32] But by then, war was being waged on California's bears, a war that started shortly after Portola's expedition. Just three years after this pioneering expedition, when the first Spanish missions were struggling to gain a foothold in Alta Cal-ifornia, settlers around Los Osos sent nine thousand pounds of grizzly meat to the northern missions, to fend off starvation. But it was as grisly entertain-ment that many of California's bears met their demise.

Many of the missions staged fights between bears and bulls and catching the unwilling participants allowed young men to show their bravado. This entailed riding up to a group of bears, singling out a likely combatant and lassoing it. At this point, the trick to staying alive long enough to watch the upcoming fight was to get several other ropes onto the bear as quickly as pos-sible, preferably one on each paw, so it could be stretched out by the horses. Thoroughly trussed up, the bear could then be transported to an arena set up in the mission grounds. Here, one end of a rope was tied to one of the bear's back legs and the other to the bull's front leg, to make sure the two combatants were only able to retreat a few yards from each other. A spectator at one of these fights in 1846 described the scene: "The bull roared, pawed the earth, flung his head in the air, and at every moment his opponent seemed inclined to escape, but the lasso checked his course, and brought both of them with a sudden jerk to the ground."

If, as in this case, a bear was reluctant to fight, it was goaded with a "nail fixed in the end of a stick." Eventually, the bull would charge the bear, and the bear, more often than not, would deliver an agonizing bite to the bull's nose. Now all Hell broke loose: "The noise was terrific and the dust rose in clouds, whilst the onlookers shouted as they saw that the fight was deadly and witnessed the flow of blood." The outcome was by no means certain. If the bull could gore the bear early in the contest, it stood a good chance of finishing off its wounded opponent, but if the fight went on for some time, the bear's sheer power would likely win out. With teeth and claws, the bear could rip the bull until it bled to death or the bear's strong paws might twist the bull's head and break its neck. One witness described the end of a fight in which a badly gored bear, dragging its entrails around the arena, still managed to bite off a bull's ears, tongue, and most of its lower jaw; presumably such a close fight rated highly on the entertainment scale.

Over time, the missions spread and became large farms. Now, all large predators were targeted with increasing efficiency, not just for bullfights, but to protect the ever-expanding herds of livestock. The last known California grizzly was shot by a rancher in the southern Sierra Nevada in 1922, and though there was a report of one being seen in the Sequoia National Park in 1924, it is now officially extinct.

Back in 1769, Gaspar de Portola was still trying to find Monterey Bay, with little success. His expedition, though, was amassing some very impressive natural history observations. It was October, and as they tracked the Coastal Range north they found themselves in a forest of giant trees. "We directed our course to the north-northwest, without withdrawing far from the coast, from which we were separated by some high hills very thickly covered with trees that some said were savins. They were the largest, highest, and straightest trees that we had seen up to that time; some of them were four or five yards in diameter. The wood is of a dull, dark, reddish color."[33] Because of this distinctive color, the Spanish called this tree *palo colorado*—"red wood," which is how they are still known today. This rather dry description came from the expedition's engineer, but it was the first description of the world's tallest trees.

Father Serra was so impressed that he decided he would like a redwood coffin when the time came for him to reap the rewards of his pious life. And as part of that pious life, Father Serra returned to this area with Portola a year later to found the first mission and military base in Alta California—the Mission and Presidio of San Carlos de Borromeo de Monterey. Although the mission was soon moved to Carmel, a small stone chapel, completed in 1794, remained to service the military presidio. It still survives today, as the oldest continuously functioning church in the state ... or the smallest cathedral in the continental United States ... or California's first cathedral, depending on which of these carefully crafted superlatives you prefer.

Yet, despite these attempts at hype, the little church is undoubtedly a very significant historical monument. So it's ironic that the main threat to its continued existence comes from the trees that so impressed its founder. A group of redwoods planted near the church is now undermining it, as their roots burrow through the foundations. The guardians of California's rich human and natural heritage are faced with the unenviable task of deciding whether to preserve the church or the trees.

In the fall of 1769, the Portola expedition made perhaps their most important discovery: "Thursday, 2 November.—Several of the soldiers requested permission to go hunting, since many deer had been seen. . . . They said that to the north of the bay they had seen an immense arm of the sea or estuary, which extended inland as far as they could see, to the southeast; that they had seen some beautiful plains studded with trees; and that from the columns of smoke they had noticed all over the level country, there was no doubt that the land must be well populated with natives."[34]

They might not have been able to find Monterey Bay, but they had done even better. They had found the huge expanse of San Francisco Bay, which had been missed by all previous explorations along the coast, though not without good reason. Fogs frequently hid the shore from ships and the entrance to the bay, today spanned by the Golden Gate Bridge, is very narrow. There are also islands inside the bay, like Angel Island and Alcatraz, that make the coastline seem continuous when seen from some distance out to sea. So it's not too surprising that the existence of this vast natural harbor remained unknown, despite many previous expeditions along the coast.

Portola's men arrived here in the fall, when countless skeins of geese were dropping out of the sky on to the extensive marshes and lakes. The expedition passed through one area that they called *Llano de los Ansares*—Goose Plain—because of the sheer numbers of geese. A few weeks earlier, as they had marched passed Monterey Bay without realizing it, they had seen other migrants arriving in large numbers. At the north end of Espinosa Lake, " [We] pitched our camp between some low hills near a pond where we saw a great number of cranes—the first we had seen on this journey. . . . This place was given the name of Laguna de las Grullas (Crane Lake)."[35] These were sandhill cranes. But as the fall progressed, the marshes and lakes were overwhelmed with more migrants from the north. The expedition camped along Major's Creek: "During these days we killed many geese; it was impossible to estimate the number of flocks of these birds, which were seen at every step; so no lack of food was felt in the camp."

A later Spanish explorer, Juan Bautista de Anza, pioneering an overland route from New Spain to Alta California, came across San Jacinto Lake. He arrived in spring before the birds had left, when it was "As full of white geese as of water . . . it looked like a large white grove." A century later, George Yount described similar scenes on the marshes around San Francisco Bay. "The wild geese, and every species of waterfowl darkened the surface of every bay . . . in flocks of millions. When disturbed, they arose to fly, the sound of their wings was like that of distant thunder."

Just as on the east coast, many of the white geese were snow geese, though in this case a different subspecies, the lesser snow goose. Unlike the greater snow geese that gather on the marshes of the east coast, a substantial proportion of lesser snow geese are not white at all, but blue-gray in color, the so-called blue phase. So when a flock of lesser snow geese erupts into flight, it has a hypnotic, salt-and-pepper appearance as blue birds mingle with white in ever-changing patterns.

Another white goose, Ross's goose, also visits California. George Yount would undoubtedly have seen large numbers of these birds, even though to him, and the Spanish before him, they were all just white geese. But Ross's goose, the smallest of the white geese, was known as a distinct species by the time William Dawson wrote the *Birds of California* in the 1920s, in which he recalled the spectacle of Ross's geese in California's past: "It is scarcely possible to exaggerate the number which frequented this region before the advent of the white man. It must have run into the millions, and may easily have reached the tens of millions. Practically the entire population of the North, breeding and bred on the Arctic shores of British America, in Banks Land and , presumably, upon the still undiscovered Hyperborean land mass, poured across the defiles of the Sierras in late September and early October, and covered the central California landscape as with a quivering white blanket."[36]

In Dawson's day, the Ross's goose may have been recognized as a distinct species, but no one still had any idea where the hordes that descended on California came from. It turned out that their nesting grounds were, as Dawson speculated, somewhere in that undiscovered Hyperborean land mass, though it wasn't until 1940 that the exact locations were known, when Angus Gavin of the Hudson's Bay Company found them nesting around the Perry River in Canada's central Arctic.[37] Today, some Ross's geese are changing their old habits and pioneering new wintering areas in Arkansas, Louisiana, New Mexico, and Texas, but, historically, the entire population wintered on the marshes and grasslands of California's Central Valley. Here, they and the snow geese were joined by equally impressive numbers of greater white-fronted geese and Canada geese.

Just as with the large game mammals, some researchers have recently suggested that such impressive numbers of birds were the result of a relaxation of Indian hunting pressure. Like the game herds, the waterfowl flocks were often very easy to approach, so easy, in fact, that they offered no real sport to sportsmen like William Thomes, who "found no pleasure in shooting such tame game."[38]

Geese, in particular, are very smart birds and soon adapt to hunting pressure—or the lack of it. I recently spent a week of wonderfully crisp autumn weather filming lesser snow geese at Sand Lake in South Dakota, a stopover for birds heading further south along the Mississippi. But at this time of year the birds are hard to approach as they are hunted with some enthusiasm. The motel in Aberdeen, the nearest town to the refuge, was geared up to register gun dogs as well as people, and we felt somewhat out of place with just a pile of camera cases. Walking across the parking lot after dark set off a fearful howling from the long ranks of trailers, as we inadvertently woke their slumbering inhabitants. As dawn broke the following morning, the fence lines outside the refuge looked like scenes from the trenches of the First World War, lined with hunters trying to read the minds of geese that were leaving the lake to forage on farm fields.

Spring used to be very different. There was no hunting and the birds knew this, the refuge manager, Bill Schutze, explained to me as we used every ounce of field skill we possessed to get within shooting range (film, that is) of the wary flocks. In spring you could pretty well just drive up to the flocks, he said. I'd had similar experiences on Delaware Bay in the past. When hunting pressure was less you could use a van as a mobile blind and get within twenty yards of the leading edge of the flock. But, as we've already seen, snow goose numbers have exploded in the last few decades, and as part of an attempt to control what are seen as runaway numbers, spring hunting was introduced on Sand Lake. Almost overnight, the birds became just as nervy in spring as in the fall. There's just no fooling those geese, and as we tried to film the ever-alert flocks around Sand Lake, I was quickly convinced they would have given William Thomes a very good run for his money.

So, the tameness of flocks back in the nineteen century could easily have been a reflection of a lack of hunting, since by then, Indian populations had fallen dramatically. But were the flocks just as tame when the first Spanish arrived? There is less evidence from this period, though some accounts mention herds of deer or pronghorn that were very hard to approach and were therefore presumably intensively hunted. Yet, as with the flocks of geese and cranes, the Spanish frequently described large numbers of these animals, suggesting that, even though they were still being hunted enough to select for wary behavior, there were still plenty around. Again, there is little doubt that Indians had a great impact on their environment, but their role in the local ecology must have been a complicated one.

Portola's men found this out the hard way. Even in the Paradise of California, food wasn't always so abundant that it was there just for the taking. At Carmel Bay, the going got much tougher: "At this place, however, the men were much worse off than the animals, for the land had plenty of pasture for the latter but lacked everything necessary for the former. The sea, which did not yield even a single mussel, was no less barren, although it abounded in gulls and pelicans—the only fishermen on this shore—to which our people gave no truce, for they ate as many as they killed."

They finally found a landmark that they recognized from the mariners' descriptions, the conspicuous white cliffs of Drake's Bay, and they realized they had somehow walked right past Monterey Bay. There was nothing for it but to head south again, where they ran into more trouble over food. "All these towns, which on our outward journey had plenty of fish and furnished us with much of it, were now without any, and we saw that they were in great need."

At another point, the Spanish decided to emulate the Indians and harvest the hugely abundant acorn crop. Unfortunately, they didn't know about the high levels of tannins in acorns, put there by the oak to protect its seeds — to prevent exactly what the Spanish were intending to do with them. In this instance, the oaks won: "Our men, being without meat or seeds, tried the acorns, but most of them suffered great injury to their health, indigestion and fever." The Indians knew how to prepare acorns, by flushing them with copious quantities of water to leach out the tannins, after which they could be turned into nutritious flour.

But despite these problems, most of the expedition made it back to San Diego. They may not have achieved their objective of opening a route to Monterey Bay, but they had given the rest of the world a really good look at the resources that had lain hidden in California's hinterland. Portola and the Franciscan fathers retraced their journey a year later, and this time recognized Monterey Bay. It was time for phase two of the Spanish plan for Alta California — the establishment of a chain of missions to serve as centers to civilize the inhabitants of California and show the Russians and the English that California was firmly in Spanish hands.

Shortly after the pioneering efforts of Portola, Juan Bautista de Anza set off from New Spain to establish a more direct overland route to Alta California and to open the way for building the chain of missions. His route eventually became known as the Camino Real — the Royal Road — linking a chain of twenty-one missions, mostly along California's coast. And, as the Mission Era began, life changed very quickly for California's Indians and the land they tended.

The purpose of the missions was primarily to Christianize Alta California's heathen hordes, though they also served as military bases to protect Spanish interests. The idea was to encourage Indians to settle around the missions, convert to the new religion, become honest farmers and help support the Spanish presence in the region. After ten years, the missions could then be turned over to the Indians, now diligent farmers and good Christian citizens of New Spain. However, in reality, there was no way that, after building up a lucrative farm, the padres would ever contemplate giving it all away. A mission could make anything from $10,000 to $50,000 a year in agricultural produce, and in hindsight, it's clear that the missions were really just a dressed up version of the encomienda system that had served the Spanish so well in the early days of empire, and which in turn was just a dressed up version of the slave plantation system by which other European powers exploited the New World. In other words, in California—the continent's greatest flowering of human diversity—hundreds of distinct, locally adapted cultures were to be reduced to uniformity and conformity. There was bound to be trouble.

European domestic animals were introduced and, just as in the Caribbean, went wild. As usual, hogs did really well and mopped up a large proportion of the acorn crop each year. But it wasn't long before great herds of wild horses and cattle were also a common sight. By 1832, mission records show that there were nearly half a million cattle, 320,000 sheep and goats and sixty thousand horses and mules grazing California's grasslands. They competed with elk and deer and began to have a serious impact on the prairies.

At the same time, annual grasses from Europe replaced the native perennial bunch grasses. Since the missions were concentrated along the coast, it was the coastal prairies that suffered the most. Not only were they overgrazed, but as Indians were drawn into mission life, the coastal prairies were no longer burned, which allowed scrub to invade the grasslands. The millions of water-fowl that came to California's marshes and prairies were forced to turn to the missions' crops as wetlands were drained for farmland. The mission fathers responded by poisoning hundreds of thousands of them with strychnine spread across the fields.

The end result was that, in the vicinity of the Spanish, traditional Indian life became increasingly difficult and many Indians were forced to move into the squalid settlements around the missions where they became dependent on the beneficence of the mission fathers. Any that tried to escape were caught and brutally punished.

Crowded together in such close proximity with Europeans, disease became a major problem, and several devastating epidemics ravaged the Indian population. Mission records show that between 1779 and 1833, twenty-nine thousand births were recorded among mission Indians, and sixty-two thousand deaths—hardly a sustainable way of life. At the height of the mission system, there were seventy-two thousand mission Indians, but by 1830, only eighteen thousand still survived—though presumably since those fifty-four thousand lost souls had been converted to the one true faith, they had all gone on to a better life. From the Jesuits in New France to the Franciscans in New Spain, the attitude was "better a dead Christian than a living heathen."

Unsurprisingly, under such conditions, revolts and rebellions were frequent, especially as it became clear to the Indians that they were essentially just slave labor. As early as 1775, Kumeyaay Indians destroyed Mission San Diego, and in 1781 Quechan and Mojave Indians along the Colorado River destroyed two missions and effectively closed Anza's overland route to Alta California.

In 1821, it seemed as though this hard fight against enslavement by the church might have been worthwhile. Resentment of Spanish rule in New Spain had been growing since 1810, when the hero of Mexican Independence, Miguel Hidalgo, himself a parish priest, marched on Mexico City. He failed in his attempt to overthrow the government and was executed for his trouble, but resistance sputtered on for a decade, fueled by his loyal followers. It didn't look like succeeding until a strange turn of events, beginning in 1821.

King Ferdinand VII was deposed in a coup d'etat in Spain and forced to sign a new, more liberal constitution. Suddenly, the leading lights of New Spain saw their own position threatened by this liberal charter, and thinking it safer to be free from the mother country, formed an unlikely alliance with the rebels. A tenuous compromise was agreed among this unprecedented union, which was enough to guarantee Mexican independence, but which would soon come back to haunt the new country. The First Mexican Empire lasted just a few years before it was replaced by the Republic of Mexico.

This should have been good news for the suffering Indians on the fringes of the new republic. Its leader, Guadalupe Victoria outlawed slavery and gave Indians citizenship in this new republic, with rights to vote and hold public office. He also began a process of secularizing the missions, since many Mexican citizens resented the church's monopoly on this lucrative venture. But yet again, the reality was different. Vested interests kept the mission slave system more or less intact for some time and when the system finally began to collapse, it was only because Mexican citizens, by being granted grazing leases, were muscling in on the same act.

In 1846, Mexico ran head first into Manifest Destiny in Texas and came off worse. By 1847, the U.S. Army was in Mexico City and in 1848, in the treaty of Guadalupe Hidalgo, the United States was expanded by the addition of Texas, New Mexico, and Alta California. But the fate of the Indians and of California's diversity was about to take another turn for the worse. Alta California had long been neglected by New Spain. It may have possessed an extraordinary natural wealth, but the Spanish didn't exploit this in the same way that France or England did in their New World possessions. From the Spanish point of view, it didn't have the fabulous wealth in gold and silver that they had looted from the empires of the Aztecs and Incas.

Then came one those quirks of fate that makes history almost as interesting as biology. At the same time that the treaty of Guadalupe Hidalgo was being signed, a man called James Marshall picked up a nugget of soft yellow metal from the bed of the American River in the foothills of the Sierra Nevada Mountains. In turned out that Alta California really did live up to the mythical land of Queen Calafia—there really was a fortune in gold here. But a local Nisenan chief warned Marshall that the gold belonged to a demon who devoured all who searched for it. How right he was.

CHAPTER 16

Rivers of Fish

The year 1849 gave a name to those who began one of the worst episodes of environmental destruction in North America's history—"forty-niners." The discovery of gold the year before on the American River sparked a massive invasion of California, and mining on such a scale that the state still bears the scars today. But initially, the first prospectors were drawn to the rivers, which had already done the job of scouring out gold from the hillsides. When they arrived, they found these rivers teeming with life, with so many fish that it was almost impossible to believe. A forty-niner on the Bear or Yuba rivers could easily pitchfork an unlimited quantity of fifty-pound salmon on to the bank. In 1848, the year that gold was discovered, a sport's fishermen took thirty-five "splendid" fish out of the American River in one afternoon. On the Sacramento River, another visitor hauled out 3,500 pounds of river perch in a single day.

There were also prodigious numbers of eellike lampreys and a kind of smelt called eulachon that choked west coast rivers in the same way as river herrings did on the east. Indians made use of all these fish. Eulachon are also called candlefish, since they were so full of fat that they could be threaded with a wick and lit as a candle. They could also be rotted down and boiled to extract their oil, which kept for long periods without spoiling, making it valuable both as food and as a trade item. A few good candlefish runs remain in some northern rivers, still harvested by several of Canada's First Nations.

And there were spectacular numbers of other creatures in the West's streams and rivers. Shasta crayfish were so numerous in Coyote Creek in California that they gave rise to an extensive fishery in the middle of the nineteenth century, supplying the San Francisco fish markets. By the turn of the century, there were none left, though the species still survives in low numbers in the Pit River, in Shasta County, where it is listed as endangered.

Some of the Pacific rivers were particularly prolific, as one intrepid band of explorers discovered in 1805. Exhausted and hungry, they had been led over the daunting barrier of the Rockies and into the drainage of the Columbia River by Capts. Meriwether Lewis and William Clark on a trail that would eventually lead them to the Pacific coast at what is today the border between Oregon and Washington. Since no one had managed to find the Straits of Anian, Lewis and Clark had been sent by President Thomas Jefferson to find an alternate way to connect the ever-expanding United States with the Pacific Ocean and the lucrative trade to Asia. But this was no easy route—there would be none until the invention of the airplane. Lewis and Clark didn't know how far they would have to travel or over what kind of terrain, but when an Indian gave Lewis a piece of salmon, he knew enough fish biology to realize that they must have crossed the continental divide and that the river they were following must flow to the Pacific.

That river already had a name, the Columbia, so named by Captain Robert Gray who had explored its mouth seven years earlier. As the expedition descended, they soon began passing through large numbers of native fisheries. Everywhere they looked, there were split salmon drying on scaffolds. William Clark observed: "The multitude of this fish is almost inconceivable." And he wasn't exaggerating. The Columbia used to support one of the biggest salmon runs of all time, possibly 10–16 million salmon and steelhead trout though the Klamath and Sacramento rivers weren't far behind, and the rivers flowing into the Puget Sound further north may have been even more spectacular.[1] So abundant were salmon, that Lewis and Clark's men soon tired of eating them and instead used them to trade for Indian dogs to vary their diet. But for other inhabitants along these rivers, such a superabundance of protein was not to be sniffed at.

Large numbers of bears feasted on the salmon as they ran up stream, and so did wolves. In places where they still occur, wolves continue to catch salmon during spawning runs, though with such small prey, they no longer need to hunt as a pack. Each wolf slowly works its own way upstream, so it can grab any unsuspecting salmon from behind. Often, wolves eat only the salmon's head, though their fussiness might have more biological sense behind it than that of Lewis and Clark's men. It may be a way of avoiding infection by parasites that spend part of their life cycle in fish.[2]

Such huge numbers of salmon swimming upstream to die also have a major effect on the forests along the river banks. As they decompose, the fish release nutrients that allow trees close to the river to grow more than twice as quickly as those further away.[3] Salmon nutrients can even end up deep in the forest since, as the old saying goes, bears shit in the woods — and so do wolves, eagles, and a host of other predators and scavengers of salmon. Nutrients from dead adult salmon also stimulate productivity in the streams, which in turn will feed the young salmon as they hatch — a legacy from parents to a next generation that they will never see.

Lewis and Clark would have seen similar sights had they had picked any of the rivers of British Columbia, Washington, Oregon, or Northern California to follow to the Pacific. Since Alaska's rivers also fill with salmon in the appropriate seasons, Pacific salmon made their way in multitudes back to the streams, lakes, and rivers where they hatched along more than five thousand miles of coast — a far wider geographical range than Atlantic salmon on the eastern shores. And that doesn't include salmon runs on the Asian side of the Pacific.

These western salmon runs also involve more species: five kinds of salmon and the closely related rainbow trout. All of these fish belong to a single genus, *Oncorhynchus,* as distinct from *Salmo,* the Atlantic salmon and trout, though like their Atlantic cousins, the Pacific *Oncorhynchus* are all stunningly beautiful fish. When feeding at sea, they are sleek and silver, shot through with subtle colors, and when they enter freshwater, they transform to deep red or shades of red, blue, and green depending on species. It was Georg Steller, naturalist on the first Russian expedition to America, who first described the various kinds of Pacific salmon and gave them all Russian names, now immortalized in their scientific names. But why so many more species here than in the Atlantic?

One look at the classic volcanic cone of Mount Rainier, visible from Seattle on those joyful days when the rain lifts, or even just the general appearance of the west coast's spectacular mountain scenery, tells you that this place is geologically active. And devastating earthquakes, from San Francisco to Anchorage, only serve to confirm this fact. The west coast is evolving, and at a fast pace, at least to the geologist's mind. And with it, so too are Pacific salmon. Georg Steller didn't know it, but in naming these different kinds of fish, he was documenting evolution in action. Each of the various *Oncorhynchus* species, though confusingly similar to the nonenthusiast, occupies a slightly different niche.

Chinook are the least abundant though largest of the Pacific salmon, named after the Chinook Indians whose domain Lewis and Clark passed through on their way down to the Pacific. Chinook salmon make their way into larger rivers, like the Columbia, to spawn. Sockeye salmon (not named for their eyes, but from a corruption of an Indian name for the fish) travel long distances upriver to spawn in lakes, or in the rivers feeding into them, while pink and chum salmon are content to spawn in or just upstream from the estuaries of those same rivers. Coho salmon spawn in small tributaries off the main river channel and have the very photogenic ability to leap the log jams that frequently block these streams. But this is only the start of the fun in unraveling the lives of *Oncorhynchus*.

There is great variety in these basic habits. For example, most chinook spawn in the autumn, but there are many distinct populations, some of which spawn in every month of the year. The length of time spent in the river and feeding in the sea also varies between different populations, except for pink salmon, which are always two years old when they return to spawn. Yet even with this apparently simple species, there are still two distinct populations, "odd year" fish and "even year" fish, which never meet or interbreed. Such differences in timing divide up all these species into subpopulations, another spur to evolution in this already confusing group. And added to this complexity is the most confusing of all, the rainbow trout, given its own distinct genus by Russian taxonomists but included with the other Pacific salmon by Western scientists.

Most of its many varieties and subspecies are confined to freshwater, though a few, like the steelhead and the redband steelhead, run to the sea to feed and return to rivers to spawn like the other Pacific salmon. One reason for the confusion surrounding this complex group is that some are called trout and others salmon, when they are all closely related. But the real reason is that they exhibit an astounding natural diversity. There are dozens of distinct populations, each genetically adapted to local conditions, not so much a gene pool as a whole series of gene puddles.

However, the first people to describe these astounding fish runs weren't so much impressed by their genetic variability as by their numbers. Three decades after Lewis and Clark, a second major expedition, the U.S. Exploring Expedition, made its way through Oregon. Its leader, Charles Wilkes, saw Indians fishing at The Dalles, on the Columbia, where "It is not uncommon for them to take twenty to twenty five salmon in an hour."[4] Wilkes later saw Indians using large baskets to catch salmon. "This basket, during the fishing season, is raised three times in the day, and at each haul, not infrequently contains three hundred fine fish."

Clearly, there were lots of Indians taking substantial numbers of fish. As we've seen in earlier chapters, this has led to suggestions that such exploitation must have reduced their prey and that the rivers packed with fish that greeted Lewis and Clark and Charles Wilkes were the direct result of dramatic reductions of Indian populations. Certainly, in 1833, when malaria swept through the Central Valley and decimated tribes there, salmon numbers seemed to rise, though, as with previous cases, a wider perspective shows the situation to be far more complex.

In the case of salmon, it's possible to trace their abundance with reasonable certainty across great swathes of time, by measuring the relative abundance of a particular isotope of nitrogen in lake sediment cores. One form of nitrogen, N^{15}, is derived mainly from marine algae and gets into lake sediments when returning salmon die after spawning. Analyses of sediments from different depths, and therefore different periods of history, show that salmon populations didn't just drop, but followed complex cycles of abundance. These cycles seem to be tied as much to long-term climate changes and shorter climatic cycles (such as the Pacific Decadal Oscillation and the El Niño Southern Oscillation) as to Indian fishing pressure. For example, on Kodiak Island, changes in salmon abundance correlate both to climatic and cultural changes.

Abundance has also changed on longer timescales. In the northeast Pacific prior to AD 800, warmer ocean water created lower marine productivity and therefore fewer salmon. Conversely, cooling conditions after AD 1200 meant lots of salmon. And, as the salmon population rose, archaeological evidence shows that Indians around spawning rivers developed technology to catch the fish and, as they did so, became increasingly dependent on the fish harvest.

So, rather than causing changes in abundance, in this particular case, the Indians seem to have been responding to natural variations in salmon numbers. However, once the technology existed to fish efficiently, Indians could have overfished the rivers—they are, after all, only human and almost certainly made mistakes during their long history of occupation of North America. But the important point is that Indians have been salmon fishing for a very long time; at some sites, fishing nets have been discovered that are three thousand years old, and the first archaeological evidence for salmon eating is nine thousand years old.[5] In all that time Indians haven't eliminated the fish, and that's not just because salmon were so superabundant and widespread. Some of those individual gene puddles were quite small, yet all that complex genetic variability survived to puzzle the ichthyologists of the last century.

One reason is that Indians have cultural mechanisms in place that limit the harvest. Many of the tribes that fish for salmon still hold a First Salmon Ceremony to welcome the fish back to the river, a long tradition that was more than just an excuse for a party and a barbecue. In some tribes, there was a ban on salmon fishing for days or even weeks after the ceremony, to allow at least some salmon time to spawn, and Umatilla Indians went as far as refraining from catching any fish until the majority had spawned. This was more of a sacrifice than it appears, since physiological changes in the salmon as they come into breeding condition cause the muscles to waste and turn to a mushy consistency.

Klamath people left their fishing weirs in place for only ten days, and the ethnographic literature documents similar examples all around the Pacific coast. Many of these researchers see no evidence to suggest that Pacific salmon were ever seriously overfished by Indians.[6] That such cultural mechanisms have an important part to play in resource management is clear from the fact that the most elaborate rituals have evolved where salmon are the most important part of the diet. Elsewhere, such as in Central and Southern California, where the acorn harvest was of greater significance than salmon, the most complex rituals grew up around the oak trees.

In addition, Indians often assigned private rights to those resources that were most critical. The development of such private rights for fishing was most developed along the Klamath where salmon were a critical resource.[7] This is one way around a free-for-all and another tragedy of the commons, since people that own a resource have a far greater incentive to protect that resource in the long term. The details of how Indians saw such property rights differed from the European view, but nevertheless many ecologists today are suggesting that the most effective way to conserve our heavily depleted marine fisheries is to assign them to private ownership.

In other areas, fish, acorns, and game were seen as common property, but even here a tragedy of the commons wasn't inevitable. As across the whole of the continent, Indians needed the blessing of the hunted in order to make a kill. Numerous pacts existed between humans and the rest of the natural world, upon which depended the success of hunting. These pacts were mediated by shamans or priests, who could dictate hunting quotas, and there were few who would dare transgress such treaties with a powerful and unpredictable spirit world.

So, through a combination of rights and rites, salmon stocks seem to have survived at least nine thousand years of exploitation. But less than ten years after Lewis and Clark, the Pacific Fur Company was already reporting on the commercial potential of the salmon runs; Pacific salmon were about to encounter a new kind of economy. One reason for this unseemly haste was that salmon stocks in the Atlantic rivers were rapidly disappearing. But the discovery of the Pacific salmon rivers only reinforced the idea that North America was infinitely abundant. An attitude prevalent throughout much of North America's exploration—and one that still, worryingly, pervades too much thinking today—is that as soon as any one particular resource was used up, another would be found to take its place. For many, the discovery of the West's salmon rivers proved that very point.

But at first, the resource was too far from civilization and too locally abundant to have any real commercial value. Ezra Meeker, one of the first to head west by oxcart along the Oregon Trail, was one of many pioneers who could think of no better use than to dump fish on the fields as fertilizer. "I have seen the salmon so numerous on the shoal water of the channel as to literally touch each other. . . . At certain seasons I have sent my team, accompanied by two men with pitchforks, to load up from the riffle for fertilising the hop fields."[8]

Not much else could be done with these remote rivers, at least until the invention of canning, a technique that was perfected in 1809, when a Frenchman discovered a way to preserve food for Napoleon's army in glass jars. It wasn't long before tin cans replaced the fragile jars, and by the 1830s, Scotland was canning salmon. By the 1840s, Maine was also canning its salmon, which helped hasten the demise of Atlantic salmon and refocus attention on Pacific salmon runs. In 1883, 43 million pounds of chinook were shipped from the Columbia alone. As chinook numbers fell, sockeye and coho were targeted. Around the same time, there were twenty-one canneries operating on the Sacramento River in California.

As elsewhere, Indian nations were drawn into commercial fishing. Klamath Indians in California joined this wider market economy in 1876, the Quileute in Washington in the late 1800s. At the same time they abandoned their First Salmon Ceremonies. There were two treasures in the Pacific rivers—gold and fish—and this new market treated them both in the same way, even though fish and gold are fundamentally different. While there's not much to be gained from leaving any gold behind, there is a real value in leaving some fish in the river; gold won't make more gold, but fish can certainly make more fish.

This difference was implicit in earlier Indian ecologies and made manifest through ritual and ceremony. But there is no market mechanism that rewards individuals for leaving fish. Remember the "Lord's oysters" in the Chesapeake? Why leave any, if someone else will later benefit by collecting them? Better grab them all now. Economists call this version of the tragedy of the commons the "Fisherman's Problem," and it wasn't difficult to predict the results of such a problem, as this report on California's salmon fisheries did in 1936: "California's salmon fishery, the oldest and once the most important fishery in the state, continues to decline and it is inevitable that our two species of salmon, the king [chinook] and silver [coho], will become extinct in California unless more protection is given them . . . too large a portion of the run is caught before the salmon can get in the river."[9]

But was it really that inevitable? Archaeological evidence suggests that Indians had harvested large quantities of fish, possibly even as much as the commercial operations on rivers like the Columbia in the late nineteenth and early twentieth centuries.[10] Perhaps it was the timing of the harvest since Indians let at least some fish spawn before taking them. But, as the commercial harvest got under way, there were also other changes on the rivers, from mining pollution to logjams and dams, that interacted in complex ways with the fishery and caused salmon numbers to plummet.

One response was to control the fishery, though this was largely ineffective, in part because the rapidly evolving salmon hadn't paid much attention to the equally rapid evolution of the political landscape in North America. They were now happily swimming across international boundaries in their ocean wanderings. Canadian fishermen were catching salmon at sea that were bound for rivers in Washington and Oregon, and U.S. fishermen were hauling out salmon that had been born in Canadian rivers. It took fifteen years of earnest negotiations (while salmon were still being caught in large numbers) until 1985, when Canada and the United States signed the Pacific Salmon Treaty. Yet for most of the 1990s, the two countries failed entirely to agree on how many of the remaining salmon each should be allowed—and the stocks continued to dwindle. Finally, some measure of agreement was achieved in 1999, and funds allocated to restore and enhance stocks. But this wasn't the end of the problems, since by now a lot of damage had already been done—some with the best intentions in mind.

Even as early as the nineteenth century, it was clear that Pacific salmon needed help. But the future of the fish and the industry they supported was seen to lie, not in conservation of wild stocks, but in hatcheries. Technology to the rescue. A farsighted and well-intentioned man called Livingston Stone began experimenting with artificial culture of salmon on the McCloud River in California in 1872, because he'd seen how much damage was being done, particularly by gold mining operations that turned once-clear rivers to mud and suffocated salmon eggs. The visionary Mr. Stone wanted the McCloud as a preserve, both for the salmon and for the Wintu Indians who depended on them. But he was too far ahead of his time; his preserve is now beneath three hundred feet of water, part of Lake Shasta, contained behind the second highest concrete dam in the United States.

But the idea of hatcheries caught on; they were seen as critical in saving Pacific salmon because they were so much better than nature. Around 95 percent of hatchery eggs produce fry, compared to only about 5 percent in the wild—surely a no-brainer when it comes to the best way of conserving salmon? One of the largest, the Central Hatchery, built on the Columbia in 1909, could handle 60 million eggs each year, and the progeny released wherever they were needed. But no one at the time knew anything about all those distinct gene puddles.

Biology doesn't make it easy for legislators (or biologists for that matter). A key piece of environmental legislation in the United States is the Endangered Species Act (ESA), designed to protect those individual species under the greatest threat. But the only constant in biology is change and the neat definition of a species in the minds of either a biologist or a legislator doesn't necessarily exist in nature. Reality is a lot more complicated.

So, for rapidly evolving species like Pacific salmon, legal and scientific brains combined to come up with a new category—the Evolutionary Significant Unit (ESU), defining in essence those individual gene puddles.[11] And while no species of Pacific salmon is listed as endangered, several ESUs are now covered by the act, thanks in part to random stocking of hatchery fish. Just as for Atlantic salmon, it's now clear that mixing the genes of wild and hatchery-bred salmon can harm wild salmon stocks, though it is also argued that rivers full of hatchery fish can take the fishing pressure off wild salmon.

A heated debate on the value of supplementing natural populations with hatchery fish is still going on, but trying to improve on nature is fraught with problems, as is demonstrated by two alternative approaches to salmon conservation. In the United States, the Lower Columbia River Fisheries Development Program has become increasingly focused on hatcheries. So far, about $3 billion has been spent on salmon recovery in the Columbia, a further $50 million slated for new hatcheries and $1 billion for adapting dams to allow passage of adult fish upstream and juveniles down.[12] In all, 80 percent of the Columbia's salmon production is from hatchery stock, but, despite all this effort, fish runs in the Columbia are only 5 percent of their historic size.

On the Fraser River in British Columbia, managers took regard of all those gene puddles. Individual stocks were managed separately and natural production nurtured through habitat management. Over the same period as the recovery program on the Columbia, the Canadians spent $23 million and by 1990 were recording runs of 22 million sockeye. Clearly technology is not an answer. Indeed, in a recent report prepared for the Wild Salmon Center, biologist Bill McMillan of the Wild Fish Conservancy described the efforts on the Columbia as possibly being "the greatest, and certainly the most expensive, failure in the history of fish and wildlife restoration that has ever occurred."[13] Certainly, if one of the aims of hatchery releases is to reestablish self-sustaining populations, then their track record isn't great. From scores of such projects, only three populations are maintaining themselves after stocking ceased.

U.S. managers placed their faith in hatcheries and stocking programs in part because such techniques were seen as compatible with other demands on the West's river systems, such as damming for hydroelectric power and irrigation. It appears from these examples that relying on just one approach to recovering salmon is too blunt an instrument for the subtleties of *Oncorhynchus;* dams and salmon just don't mix.

Early in their history, both Oregon and Washington passed laws to prevent their valuable salmon rivers from being blocked by dams, but this legislation was largely ignored as the west coast developed. There are now dozens of dams on the Columbia and its major tributary, the Snake, which make the way upriver all but impassable, particularly for species like sockeye that travel a long way upstream. Redfish Lake, Idaho, named after the glowing red of sockeye in breeding dress, was at the end of the longest of all sockeye runs, but in 1992 just one fish made it past the eight concrete dams that now obstruct the run.

Poignantly dubbed Lonesome Larry, the fate that awaited him after his nine-hundred mile journey was to be dispatched for his valuable sperm, to fertilize eggs in a breeding program that had been started a few years earlier. There were other Lonesome Larrys in 1994, 1996, and 1998, and no sockeye at all in 1995 and 1997. The few fish that made it contributed to a more enlightened hatchery program that at least now recognizes the distinctiveness of this particular population of sockeye. In 2001, ninety adult, captive-bred, Redfish sockeye were released into the lake. In 2006, an estimated 79 Redfish Lake sockeye entered the Columbia, and the estimates for 2007 were three hundred fish, a step in the right direction, though this particular gene puddle remains perilously close to drying up.

Dams are more than just physical barriers to upstream or downstream migrations. Water in the impounded lake warms up and when released can kill salmon downstream or trigger disease epidemics. Such an event happened on the Klamath in 2002, when seventy thousand chinook and an unknown number of coho salmon died. Apart from power, the dams provide water for irrigation, and when large amounts are siphoned off, river flow falls. Such a conflict between farmers and fish might seem to be intractable, yet there is hope. Many of the dams are up for relicensing, and since a number of salmon stocks are now listed on the ESA, this would have to involve expensive modifications to include fish ladders, which, even if completed, might still be inadequate for salmon recovery. Instead there are discussions about removing some of the dams that would otherwise become uneconomic.

Together dams, hatcheries, fishing, and habitat destruction are usually seen as the most important factors in the decline of Pacific salmon. These have been called the "4 H's"—hydroelectric, hatcheries, harvest, and habitat—and all four interact in complex ways.[14] But there are yet other factors emerging that also need to be considered by those attempting to find the best way forward for salmon recovery.

Like most waterways in North America, the West's rivers are now occupied by a host of alien species. One example will suffice to show the complexity and subtlety of ecological interactions and the scale of the problems facing those charged with protecting Pacific salmon. On their downstream migration, juvenile salmon are eaten by a native species, the pike minnow. In the Columbia, these little predators are responsible for devouring more than 16 million young salmon each year, yet in other rivers they hardly eat any. The difference depends on whether there are nonnative fish, like walleye, small-mouthed bass, or channel catfish present. In pristine rivers, pike minnows feed largely on crayfish, insects, and small, bottom-living fish called sculpins. Young salmon only make up about 2 percent of their diet. But walleye, catfish, and bass compete with the pike minnow for its favored prey, forcing it to switch diet to young salmon.[15]

With so many factors involved, it's obvious that salmon recovery will be a difficult task. And all these ecological factors have to be weighed against economic and social factors by the politicians who will make the final decisions. But there are some useful lessons emerging.

Understanding the history behind these problems is vital, but it's not enough just to reverse those factors; ecology is rarely that simple. For example, removing fishing on some rivers led to an increase in salmon, but on others it didn't. That's because many different factors are acting in concert, in complex and often unpredictable ways. It's often been tempting (for simplicity's sake or for ease) to focus on just one aspect of the problem, in the hopes that a solution will at least improve the situation. But that rarely works; witness the failure of hatcheries as a long-term solution. As for fisheries elsewhere, it is vital that politicians understand the uncertainty inherent in such complex systems in the advice given to them by scientists. Science is too often seen as providing precise and accurate answers, yet in the case of Pacific salmon, the complexity of the problem means that scientists are as deeply divided over an answer as in any religious debate—in the words of one salmon recovery group.[16] With such uncertainty, the "precautionary principle," erring on the side of caution, must surely underpin any strategy.

While these discussions go on, salmon numbers continue to fluctuate. Good river and ocean conditions in the 1990s improved many salmon runs, but in 2001 a severe drought saw numbers fall again. That decline has continued in a number of endangered ESA-listed stocks, including Snake River steelhead, spring chinook, and fall chinook and Upper Columbia River chinook and steelhead.

But, elsewhere, winter run chinook in the Sacramento, which fell to just two hundred fish in the 1990s, now have runs of up to seven thousand in good years, and a fair number of other stocks around the northern Pacific have shown similar signs of recovery. The pattern is complex, not surprisingly for a group of species that shows such genetic diversity and microadaptation, but it should still be remembered that throughout the Pacific West, from British Columbia to California, many runs are at best only 10 percent of their historic size, often much less and a great many no longer survive at all.[17] In the light of historic descriptions of the west coast's rivers of fish, it's a sobering thought to realize that salmon have vanished from 40 percent of their range and half of the remaining populations are at risk.[18]

CHAPTER 17

Wilderness Cathedral

The mountains of the Sierra Nevada are sublime: granite domes and spires buttressed by giant trees and flanked by glorious flower meadows, all illuminated by an ever-changing palate of light. Yet these same landscapes witnessed one of the worst episodes of environmental vandalism in the history of North America—the California gold rush. The mad scramble for gold turned a vision of Paradise into one of Hell. Yet out of this Hell was born a new and more enlightened philosophy. In the blasted landscapes after the gold rush grew the seeds of the modern environmental movement. The story of the Sierra Nevada is, in microcosm, the story of the birth of environmentalism and of our various modern relationships with the natural world.

Some of the first Spanish expeditions in to the Southwest had seen a thin white line rising above the desert horizon, a distant range of snow-capped mountains they called the "snowy range"—the Sierra Nevada. But it was as the "Range of Light" that the landscapes of the Sierras would make their greatest impression: "it seemed to me that the Sierra should be called, not the Nevada or Snowy Range, but the Range of Light. And after ten years of wandering and wondering in the heart of it, rejoicing in its glorious floods of light, the white beams of the morning streaming through the passes, the noonday radiance on the crystal rocks, the flush of the alpenglow, and the irised spray of countless waterfalls, it seems above all others the Range of Light."[1]

John Muir steeped himself in the Sierras and wrote more passionately and evocatively than anyone on his Range of Light. His writing and his zeal played a critical role in preserving the beauty of the Sierras as well as helping to erect one of the pillars of modern environmentalism. This much is probably familiar to anyone interested in nature writing. It's less well known that, despite his years in the mountains, during which he gained an understanding of the deep history of the Sierra that was well ahead of his time, Muir still never fully

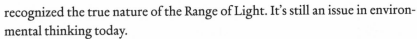

recognized the true nature of the Range of Light. It's still an issue in environmental thinking today.

The Sierra Nevada flanks the eastern boundary of the Central Valley. All its wonders are contained in just four hundred miles of crests and valleys—nothing compared to the Rockies, the backbone of the continent that stretch over three thousand miles. Yet it is the Sierra Nevada that contains the highest peak in the Lower Forty-eight—Mount Whitney—as well as the glories of Yosemite Valley, Mono Lake, and Tuolumne Meadows. A rich diversity of life inhabits these peaks and valleys, in part because the two flanks of the mountains are so different.

The western slopes rise gently out of the Central Valley to the rocky crests, while the eastern slopes drop more precipitously into the Great Basin. Indeed, the drive up to Lake Tahoe from Reno, Nevada, is such a rapid ascent that the different ecozones, from sagebrush desert through dark pine and fir to colorful montane meadows, flash by in a blur. The famous heart of the Range of Light is Yosemite Valley, which, for Muir, was a cathedral of nature, capturing all the transcendent beauty of the Sierras. Those that lived here before Muir, people of the Miwok Nation, saw it in a similar light

> The Great Spirit gathered a band of his favourite children and led them on a long wearisome journey until they reached the Valley now known as Yosemite. Here the Great Spirit made them rest and make their home. Here they found food in abundance for all. The streams were swarming with fish. The meadows were thick in clover. The trees and bushes gave them acorns, pine-nuts, fruits and berries, while in the forests were herds of deer and other animals which gave them meat and skins for food and clothing. Here they multiplied and grew prosperous and built their villages.[2]

This Miwok paradise has changed somewhat these days, in ways which epitomize California as a land of extremes. It's still possible to marvel at fleeting rainbows drifting on curtains of spray from Bridalveil Falls, or at Half Dome, glowing red in the half light, yet the bottom of the valley is choked in tourists, catered for by mountains of pizzas and burgers. Here is the paradox at the heart of the Sierra Nevada and at the heart of nature conservation. It was the birth of mass tourism that helped save this place and many others throughout the range. But standing at the bottom of Yosemite Valley made me think about why we conserve nature—for its own sake, for ours, or for both—and how, therefore, we go about balancing the different interests in this vital task. These questions came into sharp focus in the Sierras at the start of the twentieth century, and they still haven't been fully resolved today.

The eastern slopes of the Sierras were harder places for Indians to live. Moisture-laden winds blow in from the Pacific, but, as they are forced to rise over the mountains, most of that moisture condenses and falls as rain, to water the western slopes of the Sierras. The eastern slopes lie in the rain shadow of the mountains, dry enough to have created searing deserts like Death Valley. Even so, enough meltwater flowed from the snowy peaks down the eastern slopes of the southern section of the Sierras, to feed an impressive river—the Owens River. Watered by this river, the Owens Valley was rich and fertile. It lies parallel to Death Valley and just sixty miles to the west, but it couldn't have been more of a contrast; descriptions from the end of the nineteenth century are enough to make a naturalist's mouth water: "Here are cress, blue violets, potentilla, and, in the damp of the willow fence-rows, false asphodels . . . native to the mesa meadows is a pale iris, gardens of it acres wide, that in the spring season of full bloom make an airy fluttering of azure wings . . . full fields have the misty blue of mirage waters rolled across the desert sand."[3] The Owens Valley Paiute gathered many of these wild plants and indeed were partly responsible for such astounding displays. They dug channels to irrigate fields of blue dicks and other wild plants, but the Owens River meant they could also farm their land in more conventional ways.

The river had no outlet to the sea; instead the Sierra meltwaters pooled into a huge lake at the end of their journey down the valley. With no outlet, Owens Lake became more and more alkaline. The streams and rivers feeding it brought dissolved salts, which gradually increased in concentration as water evaporated from the vast lake surface. Such alkaline lakes have their own fascinating ecology, but it's no good expecting to learn about it at Owens Lake; it dried up many years ago. It is possible, though, to get a glimpse of what it must have been like.

To the north of the Owens Valley lies Mono Lake, another alkaline lake that has fared a little better. And it's just as well: Mono is a truly extraordinary place. Columns of tufa rising from the water give it an otherworldly feel, and the black line around the edge of the lake is not a strand line—it's alive. It's a solid mass of brine flies. The larvae of brine flies live in the lake in uncountable numbers where they graze the bacteria-covered rocks. Strangely, the adults also feed on these same underwater bacteria, which means you can pass a fascinating afternoon watching a succession of flies alight on a rock then deliberately walk underwater. Each traps a silvery bubble of air around its body as it submerges: its own scuba gear. The air makes the flies buoyant, so they have to cling tightly to the rocks as they scrape off the bacterial film. Then, when satiated, they can just let go and pop back to the surface to fly off to join a few million of their fellows basking on the shore.

Walking through these basking flies, they rose around my legs like a living mist, before settling back quickly behind me. And sometimes I saw a similar black wave surging along the far shoreline for no apparent reason. The first one I saw took me by surprise. I had no idea what was causing it, though through binoculars I thought I could make out a shape, obscured by a haze of flies. Then, as the wave rolled toward me, the shape revealed itself to be a California gull, running as fast as it could, head bent forward and beak snapping wildly to the left and right. It was trawling the air for flies. Since then, I've seen Laysan teal feeding in the same manner on salt lagoons in Hawaii, and, believe me, a duck running flat out through a swarm of flies is an even more amusing sight. But both birds were engaged in a very serious pursuit, taking advantage of an apparently limitless supply of food thanks to the simple but spectacular ecology of alkaline lakes.

No fish can survive in these waters, so, with no predators, brine flies, along with brine shrimps, multiply to astounding numbers, fueled by simple photosynthesizing bacteria. The flies then feed the gulls, which come here in enormous numbers to breed. In some years, sixty-five thousand California gulls nest here, making Mono Lake the second largest rookery for this species after the Great Salt Lake. But even with such numbers of gulls, there's plenty left for other birds. In midsummer, Wilson's phalaropes begin to arrive. A few nest around Mono Lake, but most are migrants, the first to arrive being females.

Phalaropes have switched the standard roles of the sexes, and the females arriving at Mono have left their mates on the marshes and bogs of the western United States and Canada. There, the males have the sole responsibility for rearing the chicks while the females feast on Mono's brine flies and shrimps. Eventually, the males and young arrive at this refueling and molting stop, and the number builds to between eighty thousand and 125,000 birds, before they all head off together to South America.

As spectacular as this is, eared grebes arrive here in even bigger numbers—up to 1.6 million of them. Here they double in weight on the infinite swarms before moving on to wintering grounds in the southwest United States and

Mexico. It's impossible not be impressed by Mono's bird spectacles (not to mention its insects and crustaceans), so it's all the more remarkable to realize that they were once even more impressive.

Although it's still possible to see tens of thousands of waterfowl here, a survey carried out as recently as 1948 recorded 1 million of them using the lake. Katherine Clover, a resident along Rush Creek before 1940, stated that "the sky would go black with huge flocks of ducks. There were so many!"[4] The ducks formed a solid black line, ten feet wide along the lake's shore, and when they moved, it looked like the shore was moving. I suppose you get an impression of what that must have looked like from the brine flies—but imagine it with ducks. And then try imagining that in the past there were even more flies.

In the middle of the nineteenth century, William Brewer, chief botanist of the California Geological Survey traveled extensively around the state and eventually published his extensive notes as *Up and Down California in 1860–1864*. At Mono, he was overwhelmed by the numbers of flies: "No fish or reptile lives in it [Mono Lake], yet it swarms with millions of worms, which develop into flies. These rest on the surface and cover everything on the immediate shore. The number and quantity of these worms and flies is absolutely incredible. They drift in heaps along the shore—hundreds of bushels could be collected. They only grow at certain seasons of the year."[5] Such a rich harvest didn't go unnoticed or unused by the local Indians—as Brewer goes on to describe. "The Indians come from far and near to collect them. The worms are dried in the sun, the shell rubbed off, when a yellowish kernel remains, like a small yellow grain of rice. This is oily, very nutritious and not unpleasant to the taste."

John Muir also found Indians harvesting the flies as well as other abundant insects: "In the season they [the Indians] in like manner depend chiefly on the fat larv of a fly that breeds in the salt water of the lake, or on the big fat corrugated caterpillars of a species of silkworm that feeds on the leaves of yellow pine."[6] As I've already pointed out, insects are extremely nutritious. Later observers, biased by the eating habits of their own cultures, thought that the sight of Indians reduced to eating insects was a sign of how hard life was for them when, in reality, they were making good use of a highly sustainable resource. As Muir observed, for the Indians, fly collection was a serious business: "Strange to say they seem to like the lake larv best of all. Long windrows are washed upon the shore, which they gather and dry like grain for winter use. It is said that wars, on account of encroachments on each other's worm-grounds, are of common occurrence among the various tribes and families. Each claims a certain marked portion of the shore."[7]

It's not far from the moonscape of Mono to Tuolumne Meadows, the largest of the subalpine meadows that nestle around the domes and crests of the Sierras. Like all the remaining high-country meadows, it is an utterly entrancing place. I once lost a whole day there, photographing wildflowers; every time I managed to raise my eyes from yet another stunning plant, there was another equally stunning view of the Cathedral Range, and I don't remember seeing another soul the whole time I was there. Not surprisingly, Muir was equally entranced: "Of all Nature's flowery carpeted mountain halls none can be finer than this glacier meadow. Bees and butterflies seem as abundant as ever. The birds are still here, showing no sign of leaving for winter quarters though the frost must bring them to mind. For my part I should like to stay here all winter or all my life or even all eternity."

I can only say I agree. But, like many other areas, these magnificent meadows are not entirely natural. Indian management has helped maintain them, by clearing invading conifers to keep open what amounted to fields where they could harvest wild plants. Such management was widespread through many habitats in the mountains, from the high-altitude meadows to the rolling oak-covered foothills. In fact, there were probably few areas that weren't in some way shaped by their Indian inhabitants.[8]

Lower down, the resource was acorns, one of the most important plant foods for the local Indians. The oaks grow in a beautiful open savannah, which was maintained by burning. And in response to good management, the oaks produced a plentiful crop of acorns in late summer. So abundant are acorns in these oak forests that many animals—chipmunks, chickarees, acorn woodpeckers, scrub jays, wood rats, and band-tailed pigeons to name a few—also depend on them. And, if Indians were responsible for maintaining the structure of the habitats, then many of these animals lent a hand by dispersing and planting oaks.

Back in 1923, ornithologist William Dawson watched western scrub jays burying acorns in caches for later use, but didn't fully understand their importance when he said; "Doubtless this miserly trick has served nature's purpose now and then in producing new trees."[9] A decade later, Joseph Grinnell, a professor of zoology at Berkeley, watched industrious western scrub jays ferrying acorns of black oaks uphill all day long and realized that such birds were actually crucial in spreading oaks. But the role of birds in maintaining these oak savannas had long been understood by Indians. C. Hart Merriam was told by the Miwok that Steller's jays plant acorns so that oaks come up everywhere. And the Indians also knew that, before they could eat the fruits of all these oaks, the acorns needed processing.

Acorns are filled with tannins, which must be leached out in specially dug pits that are continuously flushed with water. After that, they can be ground into flour. The technology to process acorns seems to have developed around 1,400 to one thousand years ago and encouraged settlement of the western slopes, where perhaps ninety to one hundred thousand people may have been living when the Spanish arrived. A long way from the Spanish missions along the Camino Real, these Indians escaped being drawn into the sphere of Spanish influence for longer than those of the Coast and Central Valley. But their isolation couldn't last forever.

The nature of the mountains helped sustain large populations of Indians. Big variations in altitude means lots of different habitats—and lots of different resources—in close proximity, and the Indians of the Sierra Nevada were adept at using this variety. But the first Europeans to come here didn't see this rich tapestry. Instead they saw a great stone barrier barring their way to the Pacific. They crossed the mountains as quickly as they could and headed on to the coast. But gradually a few people lingered.

In the early nineteenth century, fur trappers began exploring the Sierras, looking for new beaver supplies. When one of the more famous of these "mountain men," Jeddediah Smith, came here in 1826 he encountered a much darker side of the Range of Light. Engulfed by a spring storm, his description shows why the mountains were so feared by those trying to reach a new life on California's coast:

> It was one of the most disagreeable days I have ever passed. We were uncertain how far the Mountain extended to the East. The wind was continually changing direction and the snow drifting and flying in every direction. . . . Our poor animals felt a full share of the storm and 2 horses and one mule froze to death before our eyes. . . . Night came and shut out the bleak desolation from our view but it did not still the howling wind that yet bellowed through the mountains bearing before them clouds of snow and beating against us cold and furious. It seemed that we were marked out for destruction and that the sun of another day might never rise to greet us.[10]

Another description, somewhat more to the point than Smith's, sums up a common sentiment of those early visitors to the Sierra Nevada, and it certainly doesn't sound like he was enjoying himself: "Shit, Hell and Granny with a cock and bollocks Damnation and Hellfire Camphire Fox Fier and all else that is low, mean and shitting."[11] It's hard to imagine a more stark contrast with Muir's descriptions of the Range of Light—and Muir's eloquence for that matter. Yet at the same time, many of those people who experienced the dark side of the mountains were still in awe at the scenery. As one put it: "The scenery around us last night would put at defiance the artist's pencil."

Zenas Leonard was one of the first trappers in the region and one of the first to see Yosemite Valley and to describe its amazing scenery and gigantic trees. "In the last two days of traveling we have found some trees of the Red-wood species, incredibly large—some of which would measure from 16–18 fathoms round the trunk at the height of a man's head from the ground."Despite huge trees and grand scenery few came to stay though, a decade or so after the first fur trappers, some did begin to settle around the foothills. John Sutter, one such immigrant, arrived in 1839. By then, the fur trappers had found what they were looking for, an abundance of beavers and other fur bearers and in his first years in California, Sutter saw trappers for the Hudson's Bay Company take an annual toll of three thousand beavers from the Sacramento and San Joaquin rivers.

At this time, California was still part of Mexico, so, in 1840, Sutter became a Mexican citizen in order to set up a farm and fort with the help of local Maidu and Miwok Indians. In doing so, he became one of the first of European descent to farm the Central Valley. Sutter's fort would eventually become Sacramento, California's state capital, so Sutter could be seen as the symbolic start of the transformation of the Central Valley to an agricultural plain. But his lumber mill, on the American River near present day Merced, was the very real start of the biggest environmental disaster to hit the Sierra Nevada.

The giant sequoias, along with various species of pines, were valuable resources, and it was to exploit these that Sutter built his mill in the Sierra foothills. He engaged James Marshall to construct the mill, and while Marshall was excavating the tail race for the mill in 1848, he picked up a nugget of gold. Sutter and Marshall tried to keep the find quiet, but, even without the help of e-mail or Internet, the speed with which this "secret" spread was remarkable. Within the year, it reached Australia and China, and sparked the California Gold Rush.

A decade before this, when Sutter arrived, there were only around a thousand Europeans living here, among tens of thousands of Indians. News of the discovery of gold would dramatically reverse that ratio in just a few years. Between 1849 and 1854, three hundred thousand people came to California in the hope of making their fortunes. In 1857, J. Ross Browne, hired to report on the fate of Indians in the face of this stampede, summed up his findings: "The wild Indians inhabiting the Coast Range, the valleys of the Sacramento and San Joaquin, and the western slopes of the Sierra Nevada, became troublesome at a very early period after the discovery of the gold mines. It was found convenient to take possession of their country without recompense, rob them of their wives and children, kill them in every cowardly and barbarous manner that could be devised, and when that was impractical, drive them as far as possible out of the way."[12]

In 1859, more gold, as well as silver, was found in the Virginia Mountains of Nevada. Again, the Indians were moved out of the way to accommodate the gold diggers; this time the Northern Paiute were relocated to a reservation at Pyramid Lake, where they still live today. Here, the tribe runs an elegant and beautifully designed museum dedicated to the long history of the Paiute along the eastern fringes of the Sierra Nevada.

At first, individual "forty-niners"—at least the lucky ones—could simply pick up surface deposits of gold. But soon, bigger companies got involved in more ambitious schemes. To expose gold eroded from hillsides and now lying hidden on river beds, entire rivers were diverted. And when that source ran out, the big mining companies simply increased the rate of erosion—by blasting apart the hillsides with water.

Hydraulic mining was engineering on an audacious scale. First, high-altitude lakes were created by damming rivers. Then, thousands of miles of wooden sluices and flumes, which consumed many of the local pines, brought this water to the mining site lower down. The large difference in altitude meant that the water was delivered to specially constructed nozzles under enormous pressure. Such was the force of water gushing from these nozzles, it was said that a strong man couldn't swing a crow bar through it. The water velocity was around 150 feet per second, enough to kill a man two hundred feet away from the nozzle and more than enough to blast apart the sides of the hills.

The rivers ran thick with mud, so thick that one eyewitness said they could scarcely run at all. But mud was only one problem. To recover the smallest particles of gold, the miners used liberal quantities of mercury, a deadly heavy metal that soon wiped out life from long stretches of the rivers. Nor is all this just of historical interest. Much of that mercury is still around today and so are the effects of all that mud washed down from the hillsides. Some of the hills are still barren moonscapes, and several estimates suggest that the rivers won't be finally clear of mud and silt until the year 3000.

Not all miners got rich; it was a hard and risky life. Far more people got rich from the miners. A vast influx of hopeful forty-niners created new markets, and supplying this market became more lucrative that mining itself. In some areas, close to the centers of mining, 90 percent of the saleable timber was removed, for flumes, pit props, or buildings. Large areas were clear-felled, though logging had even wider impacts on the drier, eastern slopes. Here, the rivers rarely ran deep enough to transport logs to the mills, so splash dams were built. These dams raised the water level behind them to create temporary lakes in which cut logs were floated. When enough timber had been accumulated, the dam was breached and the surge of water carried the logs downstream. It also carried away most of the riverbanks, scoured the river bed, and killed all the fish. The mills themselves produced vast amounts of sawdust, which frequently blocked the rivers in rotting, fetid piles.

Apart from building material and fuel, the miners also needed feeding. When Marshall picked up his gold nugget from the American River, wildlife was generally still abundant through California. Now it was seen as a larder for hungry miners, and as this market grew, its effects spread well beyond the immediate vicinity of the mines. Before the gold rush, San Francisco was a small town. Afterward, it transformed rapidly into a busy metropolis. And just twenty miles offshore—on the Farallon Islands—was the largest seabird colony in the continental United States. When Cabrillo first visited these islands, they were covered in uncountable numbers of common murres, which were subsequently used by generations of sailors for supplies. Even so the colonies were still thriving in 1849, when a Dr. Robinson founded the Pacific (sometimes called the Farallon) Egg Company. The sheer scale of the flood of people into California meant that Robinson's company went from strength to strength as miners and other immigrants ate their way through millions of murre eggs. To ensure fresh eggs for their customers, the Pacific Egg Company's collectors used the same trick as those living off great auk eggs off the northeast coast three centuries earlier. First smash all the eggs you can find, then wait for the birds to relay and collect these new eggs.

Such were the profits from these eggs that rival collectors began to poach on those parts of the Farallons claimed by the Pacific Egg Company. In 1863, this rivalry erupted into violence in the so-called Egg War—though since the only actual shoot-out lasted a mere twenty minutes, it must be one of the shortest wars in American history. The practice of destroying as well as collecting eggs had a devastating effect on the murre colonies. Egg collecting was finally stopped in 1881, when the federal government took over the islands to run a lighthouse.[13] But by then, the murre colony was a fraction of its former size.

Even though egging ceased more than a century ago, recovery hasn't been straightforward. Oil spills and drowning in commercial fish nets have all added to natural fluctuations caused by El Niño events, so the population has swung wildly over the last few decades. At the moment, around sixty thousand murres are nesting on Southeast Farallon Island,[14] still an impressive sight until one remembers the historic size of this colony.

There were also other large seabird colonies right in San Francisco's backyard. *Alcatraz* is Spanish for pelican, and before the city's rapid growth, the tiny island bearing this name in San Francisco Bay was covered in them. In 1827, the French traveler, Auguste Duhaut-Cilly described just how abundant they were: "A rifle shot we fired across these feathered legions made them rise in a dense cloud with a noise like that of a hurricane."[15]

In addition to pelicans, the meadows and marshes around San Francisco Bay were teeming with waterfowl, which soon found their way into the growing city's markets, along with other abundant game birds like quail. Elk and big horn sheep, also numerous at first, were hunted relentlessly, and not always just to feed California's growing population—as William Brewer observed: "Elk were here in great numbers . . . They were mercilessly killed by hunters, killed not for their flesh, but for the fun of the killing. All are now exterminated, but we find their horns by the hundred."[16]

This is a story we've seen repeated right across the continent. So abundant were North America's natural resources that, whenever Europeans first encountered them, they were described as infinite. So, no matter how much they were exploited, they could never diminish. The following comment, by an awestruck German visitor to the redwood forests of Mendocino County, is but one of dozens, probably hundreds, expressing the same sentiment: "As far as the eye could reach, a seemingly interminable forest lay at our feet. . . . It was sufficient to convince me that California will for centuries have virgin forests, perhaps to the end of Time!"[17] It took just decades to make a nonsense of such statements. Raymond Dasmann, in *The Destruction of California*, describes the period between 1850 and 1910 as one of massive faunal change. And that's probably an understatement. Writing at the end of this period, Joseph Grinnell, the first director of the Museum of Vertebrate Zoology at Berkeley said, "Throughout California we had been forcibly impressed with the rapid depletion everywhere evident among the game birds and mammals."[18]

To feed California's rapidly expanding populations, farms began to spread over the Central Valley, and even the smallest mammals began to feel the effects. When Francis Drake landed on California's shores, he was amazed by the number of animals he called "conies," which were probably pocket gophers. Ground squirrels existed in equal abundance, but none of these little digging and seed-eating machines were much appreciated by farmers, who began a major control campaign by spreading bait poisoned with thallium. The quantities used were incredible. In 1929, fifteen California counties laid down an average of forty thousand pounds of thallium-treated grain each.[19] Few at the time questioned the necessity of controlling these rodent hordes, though it soon became clear that this large-scale and enthusiastic use of thallium was adding to California's problems.

In 1931, an already long-running and well-respected ornithological journal, *The Condor*, carried a report by Jean Linsdale on the collateral damage in this war against rodents.[20] He interviewed dozens of farmers about their perceptions on changes in wildlife populations around their farms. On collating the results, he realized that thallium was killing indiscriminately and threatening some of California's predators, like coyotes, that happily scavenge dead squirrels. One of his informants reported: "In this locality coyotes were formerly very numerous. During the last eight months, I have not seen a live coyote and I am out on the range almost every day."

Other animals were targeted deliberately. In the fig and apricot orchards, drinking fountains were provided for birds such as orioles and grosbeaks, in which the water was laced with arsenic. Such changes turned California's unique Central Valley prairies into the familiar endless miles of profitable farmlands that you drive through today. Rodents are still poisoned, though now, in theory, with much tighter controls. Even so, some of those once-abundant rodents are now severely threatened.

The San Joaquin antelope squirrel once ranged over nearly 3.5 million acres of arid grassland of which just a few tens of thousands of acres still exist in the southern San Joaquin Valley and Elkhorn Plains. Most are in tiny blocks less than thirty acres—too small to support the squirrels for long. The impressive giant kangaroo rat is in a worse predicament, confined to a few even smaller, precariously isolated populations.[21]

So farming and mining are beginning to look like a double-barrel shotgun aimed unerringly at California's unique and abundant natural resources. But the story is not that simple. The effects of hydraulic mining in the Sierra Nevada didn't take long to filter down to the lowlands. Rivers were turned to mud, and dams broke, sending devastating floods to wash away orchards, farms, and, sometimes, whole towns. So it was the farmers of the valley that became one of California's first organized environmental groups.

In 1878, they formed the Anti-Debris Association of the Sacramento Valley, to campaign against the hydraulic mining companies. Not that their concern was to preserve the pristine beauty of the Sierra Nevada—they were simply trying to protect their own livelihoods. Nevertheless, their campaigns resulted in the "Sawyer Decision," a significant milestone in environmental legislation. In 1884, Judge Lorenzo Sawyer heard the case of *Woodruff vs. North Bloomfield Mining Company* and ruled that the mining company had to prevent their debris from washing into rivers and affecting the livelihood of others living downstream. This ruling didn't ban hydraulic mining, but since it was impossible to prevent mud and rocks washed from the hillsides from entering rivers, it effectively closed it down.

But, in the late nineteenth century, mining was only one of a legion of environmental problems plaguing California. The marshes of the Central Valley were being drained and its vast grasslands converted into fields and orchards. In the mountains, forests were being clear-felled at an alarming rate, and rivers polluted by rotting piles of sawdust. North America's population was growing rapidly at this time, as the tired and poor of many nations flocked to this land of opportunity and dreams. Cities grew exponentially, using up the continent's natural resources faster than ever before, which made a growing number of people realize that the abundance of this Paradise Land was definitely not infinite.

And, as urban centers grew and spread, people were beginning to yearn for wild places. As early as 1852, smack in the middle of the gold rush, Assemblyman Henry Crabb tried to protect California's giant redwoods and sequoias by making them the common property of all California's citizens, such that they could not be subjected to trade or traffic. Unfortunately, his idea was just a little too far ahead of its time. But, as the frontier disappeared, the notion of preserving some of the "wilderness" that had helped define the nation was an idea whose time was definitely approaching.

However, in a world driven by economics, the birth of this idea had to wait until commercial interests found a way to exploit it. Eventually, people realized that money could be made from tourists, shipped in by rail and road to get a breath of fresh Sierra Nevada air before returning to crowded, smoky cities. And the place they began to flock to was a valley that had escaped the worst of the gold rush. Luckily, the Merced River had no significant deposits of gold, so the valley that it ran through still survived in all its splendor—Yosemite.

When newspaper editor Horace Greeley came all the way from New York to see this spectacular valley he claimed that no single wonder on Earth could match Yosemite, just the kind of publicity that the railroad companies wanted to hear. Greeley's glowing reports echoed the kind of "Paradise publicity" that had drawn the first settlers to the New World, and, eagerly embellished by railroad companies and tourist operators, such reports sparked a tourist industry that has never looked back. Yosemite Valley was ceded to the state of California, so it could protect and manage it to exploit its tourist potential.

The first tourist structures in Yosemite were built in 1856, while the valleys around were still being torn apart by the lust for gold. But this new way of exploiting the natural world brought its own problems. In order to provide tourists with a better spectacle, one thoughtful operator blocked off all the side cataracts of Nevada Falls, to make the main falls more impressive. And well into the twentieth century, such areas were managed by shooting predators to protect the more popular creatures like deer.

But the seeds of another kind of conservation were also beginning to germinate in the Sierra's towering forests—actually an old idea, well recognized by the Miwok who hunted the valley and meadows—that nature provides for all people's needs, both practical and spiritual. Recently, Edward Wilson, of Harvard University, has coined the term "biophilia" for our deep-seated need for contact with nature and examined its origins and evolutionary value. If not for biophilia, I doubt I could have made a living producing wildlife documentaries for the past twenty-five years. There is an endless appetite among people of all countries to experience natural spectacle, even if only a flickering facsimile on the end of a cathode ray tube. Our appreciation of the spiritual value of wild nature is not new, but it was popularized by the nature writers of the nineteenth century, such as Henry David Thoreau and Ralph Waldo Emerson. None, though, went as far as John Muir.

Muir was an immigrant from Scotland, initially to Wisconsin and then, in 1868, to California, where the Sierra Nevada changed his life. His father was a "fire and brimstone" Scottish minister and, inspired by the mountains, John became something of a sermonizer himself—a John the Baptist figure preaching lessons from nature in his wilderness cathedral of granite and sequoias. His was one of the loudest voices calling for the preservation of wilderness for its own sake as well as ours. He was one of the first of the preservationists. At the same time, as we've already seen, another school of conservation was evolving out of the environmental disaster that was late nineteenth- and early twentieth-century North America. This was the "wise-use" brigade, championed by people like the forester Gifford Pinchot. And at first, both strands of conservation worked well together.

Muir also became something of an expert in glaciology, which helped him come to the conclusion that his magnificent cathedral had been carved and shaped by glaciers during the ice age. His work was ridiculed by some scientists of the day, like J. D. Whitney, state geologist and Harvard professor, who thought that the valley's origins lay in tectonic earth movements, and although neither theory was exactly right, Muir's hypothesis comes closest to the modern idea.[22] Muir also disagreed with Gifford Pinchot; Muir was convinced that some areas needed to be set aside, free from exploitation of any kind by people, except those seeking spiritual refreshment—true wilderness, just as nature intended. He never really understood that many of the landscapes he admired were as much a product of all those who lived here before as they were of the glaciers of the ice age. And the removal of those people was already causing changes.

Many meadows and oak forests were no longer burnt—and a good thing too according to some of the new managers of these landscapes. For one thing, fires threatened buildings and other tourist facilities. On the other hand, ranchers and foresters frequently used fire as a tool, as the Indians had before, so fire soon became a hot topic of debate. In the end, a policy of fire suppression won out, particularly on public use lands, and it didn't take long for these landscapes to begin to change—Smokey the Bear has a lot to answer for.

The open parkland, rich in game, that covered the floor of Yosemite began to grow rank. Miwok Indians that returned to the valley considered that it had been ruined by its new guardians. When the grand daughter of

Chief Tenaya of the Southern Sierra Miwok came back to the valley after a seventy-eight-year absence, she merely shook her head in disappointment and said, "Too dirty—too much bushy."[23]

It wasn't that people didn't see the hand of humanity in these landscapes. In the 1880s, an artist called Constance Gordon-Cummings visited Yosemite and warned, "Indeed, there is a corner of danger, lest in the praiseworthy determination to preserve the valley from the ruthless 'improvers,' and leave it wholly to nature, it may become an unmanageable wilderness."[24] A decade later, Galen Clark, who knew the Sierra Miwok well, also tried to convince the managers of Yosemite to reinstate burning. But a seductive, if incomplete, view of North America was emerging from the pens of Muir, Emerson, Thoreau, and the like. Muir's wilderness was free of significant human impact; the Indians that had lived there before the coming of the Europeans had lived there lightly, as noble savages in a Garden of Eden.

These were idealized Indians not real ones. Indeed, the abject figures of real Indians at the turn of the twentieth century often disappointed Muir. And so did the current management of Yosemite Valley by the state of California.

At state level, there were just too many vested interests in making money in the valley for Muir's comfort. He wanted Yosemite to be handed back to the federal government, where a more dispassionate view from a distance of three thousand miles might manage the place more appropriately. He got enthusiastic backing and support from Robert Underwood Johnson, the editor of *Century Magazine,* after Muir had taken him camping in Tuolumne Meadows. As they sat among the magnificent displays of flowers, they decided to campaign together for a national park, bigger than the current reserve, based on the precedent set in Yellowstone, the nation's first national park, declared in 1872. Muir was a canny Scot and used this trick several times—letting the landscapes of the Sierra Nevada speak more eloquently than he ever could. He also took Theodore Roosevelt camping there, a time that Roosevelt later recalled as one of the best in his life. In this way, Muir created many influential devotees of the Sierra Nevada.

One of the problems that Muir and Underwood saw in Yosemite and elsewhere on the range was domestic livestock. This problem dated back to the first Spanish settlements, when cattle, hogs, and horses found California much to their liking. By the mid-nineteenth century, there were 3 million cattle in California, though they were subsequently cut to only half a million by droughts. Sheep, however, are much tougher. They survived the droughts, and by 1875 there were 5.5 million of them. After his first fleeting visit to the Sierra Nevada on his arrival in California, Muir went back there as a shepherd—any excuse to return to the place that had captured his imagination. But he soon realized the destructive power of the creatures he came to call "hoofed locusts."

Sheep were now so numerous that they were eroding the grasslands around the headwaters of the Sierra streams. Apart from turning high-altitude meadows to desert, snow also melted quicker from this eroded land, meaning that, by summer, in the growing tourist attraction of Yosemite Valley, the Nevada Falls, Bridalveil Falls, and Yosemite Falls didn't have much water.

While Muir and Underwood were raising awareness of Yosemite's problems, other like-minded people were fighting to preserve the Sierra Nevada's giant trees. George Stewart, editor of the *Visalia Delta,* headed up an organization to campaign for protection for the Giant Forest. Mining and the building of cities like San Francisco had used up great tracts of forest, while the railroads that brought tourists to the mountains were also a conduit for Sierran timber to markets as far away as Salt Lake City. And even though the recreational value of the mountains was now being recognized, that interest took a few bizarre turns.

In the Calaveras Grove, one of the largest trees was felled and its stump turned into an elevated dance floor. Another three-hundred-foot specimen was killed by the removal of all its bark, so that it could be reconstructed in the East (and then in London) to show people just how amazing these trees were. Others were being felled for timber, though this was extraordinarily wasteful since, as Muir pointed out, when the biggest trees are felled "the sequoia breaks like glass." He reckoned up to half the wood was unusable in sawmills.

But on public lands there was one small ray of hope for Stewart and his fellow campaigners. Land could be claimed by individuals in 160-acre plots to farm, which included the right to cut timber. But, given the expense of processing timber, it was difficult to make a viable lumber business on a plot of this size, so few claimed any land in the forest. That slowed down private incursions, at least until 1885.

In this year a group of fifty stalwart socialists arrived and turned the allotment system to their advantage, by establishing a miniature communist state in the heart of California. The Kaweah Cooperation Colony came into being when all fifty individuals pooled their land grants in and around the Giant

Forest. It was to be managed along solid socialist principles, and the colony issued its own promissory notes instead of cash, for work done in the common good. And, if anyone was in any doubt as to the ideology behind their enterprise, they named the largest sequoia in the forest "Karl Marx."

Stewart fought this new threat to the forests and in 1890, his efforts were rewarded with the passage of a bill through Congress to protect key areas of sequoia forest, the embryo of today's Sequoia National Park, though, for some strange reason, the Giant Forest was excluded. Perhaps Stewart had come to have some sympathy for the struggling Kaweah Colony.

Meanwhile, Muir and Johnson had also managed to get a bill through Congress to protect the areas around Yosemite Valley. It passed five days after Stewart's bill, and for reasons still not fully understood, the Yosemite Bill also vastly increased the size of the Sequoia protected area, and this time the Giant Forest was included. By now, the Kaweah Colony was in decline, and when it finally ceased to exist, Karl Marx had its name changed to General Sherman.

General Sherman still stands there today, renowned as the world's most massive living organism. Actually, botanical pedants today point to a grove of aspens in Utah, the Pando Grove, as the true bearer of this honor, since what looks like a grove of trees is actually a single organism, connected by a single set of roots. But, as I stood at the base of General Sherman a few years back, craning my neck to see the top and wishing I'd brought an even wider angle lens, I was prepared to skip this technicality. These sequoias *feel* like they're the biggest things you'll ever see, and that's good enough for me.

The seeds of Yosemite and Sequoia National Parks might have been sown, but there were still problems, not least the fact that the acts that created them contained no provisions to actually protect them. There were no penalties for transgressions and misuse and no one to enforce the rules even if they had some power to do so. The Sierra Club was set up, in part, to lobby for some real clout in protecting the parks. But the only solution in the short term was the same as for Yellowstone — send in the army.

Yosemite's first ranger force was the Fourth Cavalry, under the command of Capt. Abram Epperson Wood. He set up his headquarters at Wawana, where, incidentally, there is still a campground today, called Camp A. E. Wood after this first protector of Yosemite. It didn't take Wood long to come to the same conclusion as Muir — those hoofed locusts were one of the biggest threats to Yosemite. "The last days of May the sheep commenced their annual migrations to the mountain grazing grounds, and by the 10th of June there were fully 60,000 of them close to the southern and at least 30,000 near the western boundaries of the Park."[25]

At first, he tried to frighten the sheepherders with threats of arrest, but they soon realized that, legally, there was nothing Wood could do. Wood, however, won a brief victory by evicting trespassers from the opposite side of the park from where they were arrested. This meant the sheepherders might be away from their flocks for up to ten days, by which time the flock would have scattered and some fallen prey to predators—a real financial incentive to avoid detention by the Fourth Cavalry. But even that didn't last long; the shepherds just got sneakier. Sheep continued to overgraze the Sierras and would soon drive apart the two main strands of conservation, even as they were evolving.

At the same time as California's first national parks were being created, so too were forest reserves, later to become national forests. These were not wilderness areas, free from humanity, but areas where resources could be used wisely. Gifford Pinchot became head of what would become the National Forest Service, and initially Pinchot and Muir were allies in the campaign to protect the Sierra Nevada from reckless exploitation. But Pinchot thought that sheep grazing was one of the wise uses of the mountains and allowed grazing on the forest reserves. Muir vigorously disagreed, and two of the founding fathers of conservation fell out irreconcilably. The balance between these two points of view is just as contentious today.

Muir's vision of the Sierra Nevada as a wilderness free of human interference, where people can touch the soul of nature, is a seductive one, but it would have been a nonsense to the Indians of the Sierra. By now, it should be clear that vast swathes of North America were not wilderness at all, even when the first Europeans saw it. As one Indian orator so succinctly put it—the Wild West wasn't wild until the white man came.

Many of the landscapes that so entranced Muir and like-minded thinkers were human landscapes. Yet, the idea of wilderness touched a need in early twentieth-century Americans, who wanted places to escape the expanding cities. So, in 1956, Howard Zahniser, executive director of the Wilderness Society drafted a bill to protect at least some of the nation's remaining wild areas in a way in which Muir would have approved. Unfortunately, he died before his bill became the Wilderness Act of 1964, which was designed to protect lands "untrammelled by man" and to keep them in that state. No roads or structures would be built in these areas, no permanent dwellings and no mechanical transport, no commercial activities of any sort.

Initially, 9.1 million acres were covered by the act, but more wilderness areas are being declared all the time. Surely this a good thing—huge chunks of wild America preserved for all to enjoy: "an area where the earth and its community of life are untrammelled by man, where man himself is a visitor who does not remain." As I stated in the opening chapter, of course it is, but we need to understand what it is that we are preserving. Many of these areas were not untrammeled by man, at least not until European diseases and outright war decimated Indian populations. It's not the America that existed before Columbus, nor for thousands of years before that. Yet, under the Wilderness Act, I can go into a wilderness area with my stills camera for private enjoyment, but I can't take in a movie camera to shoot for a commercial nature documentary. OK, so that's a bit of a personal gripe, but, nonetheless, it's symptomatic of what can happen without a full appreciation of the true nature of North America.

Similarly, Muir's vision was somewhat blinkered. The role of Indians in the landscapes of California was known to those who bothered to look, even in his day. But the two camps of preservation and utilization, epitomized by Muir and Pinchot, were already set on different tracks, a philosophical divide that grew to be a chasm over Hetch Hetchy.

Hetch Hetchy was another beautiful valley, watered by the Tuolumne River and named, in the Miwok language, for the grass that carpeted its floor. Muir described it as a second Yosemite: "I have always called it the 'Tuolumne Yosemite,' for it is a wonderfully exact counterpart of the Merced Valley, not only in its sublime rocks and waterfalls but in the gardens, groves and meadows of its flowery, park-like floor. . . . The walls of both are gray granite, rise abruptly from the floor, are sculpted in the same style and in both every rock is a glacier monument."[26]

But, just over three decades after Muir first saw Hetch Hetchy, San Francisco was hit by a massive earthquake. After 1906, the city had to be rebuilt from the ground up, and better than before to show nature who was in control here. To improve the water supply of the reborn city, they applied to the Department of the Interior for water rights in the Hetch Hetchy valley and specifically to dam the Tuolumne River. John Muir and the Sierra Club led a seven-year battle to prevent the flooding of the valley, and it's clear from his comments that he—like the Sierra Miwok before him—regarded these as sacred landscapes: "Dam Hetch Hetchy! As well dam for water-tanks the people's cathedrals and churches, for no holier temple has ever been consecrated by the heart of man."

But Muir's arguments for the sanctity of nature were outweighed by the practical need for water for a rapidly growing city. In 1913, the Raker Act permitted the building of the Hetch Hetchy Dam, which was completed in 1923, at which time Muir's second Yosemite was drowned under the waters of the new reservoir. Almost as worrying as the flooding itself, Hetch Hetchy was part of the newly created network of national parks in the Sierra Nevada, and the flooding of the valley caused many to question the worth of the fledgling system.

The battle for Hetch Hetchy's water certainly further divided the two conservation camps, but it also split the Sierra Club itself, in part prompting Muir and his preservationists to form the Society for the Preservation of National Parks. But this wasn't the first battle in California's water wars. That battle, perhaps even more famous than Hetch Hetchy thanks to feature films like *Chinatown* (1974) and books like Mark Reisner's *Cadillac Desert,* concerned the growing thirst of a city in the middle of a desert—Los Angeles.[27]

A desert is defined by its lack of water, so Los Angeles was a strange place to begin building what is now the most populous county in the whole of the United States. But there is a definite mentality in the desert Southwest that to accept the limitations of desert life is somehow to admit defeat for *Homo technicalis.* Deserts are for conquering, for proving our superiority over nature. The ultimate monument to this attitude was erected at Fountain Hills, near Phoenix, Arizona, where the world's largest fountain sprays great columns of water into desert air that sometimes reaches 110 degrees. A substantial portion of the water never reaches the lake again, evaporating in the desert heat long before it falls to earth. Yet this ostentatious display of technology over nature wasn't the first time that water had been brought to these deserts.

Around Phoenix, the Tohono O'Odam built fiendishly clever irrigation systems, while on the eastern flanks of the Sierra Nevada, Owens Valley Paiute irrigated their fields with water from the Owens River. But all these desert people used what water they could find locally. Later settlers in the Owens Valley expanded on this tradition, turning the Owens Valley into a miniature version of the agricultural Central Valley. But a rapidly expanding Los Angeles had its eye on the water in the Owens River.

Amid accusations of deceit and trickery, the city began to acquire water rights in the valley and by 1913 had completed the first aqueduct to carry water 226 miles across the desert to LA. It was an extraordinary engineering achievement, but that didn't impress the farmers of the Owens Valley as their agricultural Eden began to dry up. In the 1920 drought, Los Angeles began pumping groundwater from the Owens Valley, and the farmers retaliated by blowing up the pumps. But to no avail. So much water was diverted from the river that Owens Lake began to dry up, creating vast alkali flats, which still produce choking dust storms when the wind blows—the largest source of polluting dust in America.

LA continued to grow and to demand more water from the Sierras. In the 1930s, the city bought water rights at Mono Lake and began to siphon off the streams that fed it. And, just as at Owens Lake, the water level began to fall. This created big problems for the vast colony of California gulls that nested there. Causeways formed and connected their inaccessible nesting islands to the mainland, allowing predators like coyotes to cross over and feast on eggs and chicks. Gull numbers plummeted, but waterfowl numbers were also beginning to drop. Water evaporating from the lake surface was no longer replaced by freshwater flowing in from the streams and the salt concentration in the lake began to rise. Before the diversions, the salt content of the lake was around one and a half times that of sea water—a comfortable zone for the inhabitants of alkaline lakes. But by the 1960s, it had risen to twice that—three times as salty as seawater and too salty even for brine shrimps to thrive and far too salty for waterfowl.

A survey carried out in November of 1948 counted around 1 million waterfowl using the lake, but by the early 1960s there was just half that. In the 1970s and 1980s, only a few thousand came to the lake. The lake reached its lowest level in this period, just half of its prediversion volume and well on the way to following Owens Lake into oblivion. This prompted several lobby groups to press for legislation to control exploitation of Mono's water.

A 1994 law set a minimum volume of freshwater that must reach the lake from its feeder streams and at the same time called for its volume to be stabilized at a level twenty feet above the low point that it reached in the previous decade. Since then, the lake level has risen slowly. There is still a problem with land bridges to some of the islands, but the latest counts show that up to sixty-five thousand gulls are now managing to nest there, on more remote islands. Waterfowl numbers, though, still fall short of those spectacles described by early observers. Today, tens of thousands are using the lake again—spectacular, but a long way from the flocks that turned the sky black in the 1940s. Despite this, Mono Lake has, at least, escaped the fate of Owens Lake. But there's now even a new air of optimism in the Owens Valley, bled dry nearly a hundred years ago to water a city 250 miles away.

In December 2006, a crowd of spectators gathered to watch Los Angeles mayor Antonio Villaraigosa open a new sluice gate on one of the Owens River diversion dams and send a trickle of water down the Owens River Valley for the first time in a century, the start of one of the most ambitious restoration projects in the West. The restoration of the Owens Valley has been planned for a long time, but, much like the even more ambitious Everglades restoration project, the Department of Water and Power fell behind many of its target dates. It took a law suit and fines of $5,000 a day to finally start water flowing in the Owens River again, and it's still going to be a long haul before willows replace brittle bush and the waterfowl and shore birds return in the numbers that the first explorers saw here. But it's a start.

In 1913, William Mullholland, engineer with the LA Department of Power and Water, whose vision the LA aqueduct was, addressed a forty thousand strong crowd assembled in the San Fernando Valley, at the bottom end of the aqueduct. As the first gush of water splashed out, he said, "There it is! Take it!" In December 2006, only around five hundred people witnessed the rewatering of the Owens River, but in true Tinseltown style, David Nahai, president of LA's Water and Power Board of Commissioners had prepared an equally succinct statement: "There it is . . . it's yours!" Mayor Villaraigosa added an equally uplifting statement: "We are here today because we need to change course. We need to move with these waters."

California's history has swung between extremes of environmental degradation and protection, worthy of any melodramatic Hollywood script. Indeed, quite a few such scripts have been based on this history. This, the most populous state in the Union, has seen some of the worst environmental tragedies imaginable. For a while, in other states, bumper stickers saying Don't Californicate Our State were amusingly popular. Yet, because of this history, it has had to pioneer a whole range of groundbreaking environmental protection measures. And it still is.

There are now serious discussions concerning the possibility of breaching the dam holding back the waters of Hetch Hetchy and restoring the valley to its former glory. *Paradise Regained* is the title of the report outlining this ambitious project, though it will be extremely expensive to restore the paradise of Muir and the Miwok. However, even Governor Schwarzenegger's office has said the plan is at least feasible. And, in facing the new environmental problems of the twenty-first century, California's Republican governor has also surprised and pleased many by parting from the "head in the sand" philosophy of his party, to tackle the problems of climate change through state legislature.

Yes, that's California!

CHAPTER 18

The Great Stillness

On July 22, 1793, a British explorer called Alexander Mackenzie stood on the shores of a long narrow inlet of the Pacific Ocean, not far from the present site of the small town of Bella Coola, in northern British Columbia. Cooling your heels in the Pacific wasn't exactly new at the end of the eighteenth century; British, Russian, and Spanish explorers had been doing so since the sixteenth century, and Mackenzie never even made it to the end of his inlet to the open Pacific. Yet this moment was special. To commemorate the event, Mackenzie painted a memorial in grease and vermilion on a nearby stone— "from Canada by land." His graffiti is faded but still legible, marking him as the first person to cross North America by land, north of Mexico. His journey more or less laid to rest the idea of an easy Northwest Passage linking the Atlantic and Pacific, but his trip set in motion the exploration, mapping, and settlement of one of the last big blanks on the North American map, the great American prairies.

Mackenzie's exploits were later published as *Voyages from Montreal* and were avidly read by one of the nineteenth century's keenest students of North American geography—Thomas Jefferson. No doubt he was fascinated by the detailed descriptions of the land and its peoples, but the last few pages worried Jefferson. Here, Mackenzie advocated a British Empire in North America, extending from sea to shining sea, linked by a series of forts and trading posts that would give the empire builders the command of the whole of the North American fur trade. Fur-bearing animals had driven the exploration of the continent and shaped the course of New World empires, so Jefferson was wise to sit up and take notice.

Jefferson was already convinced that his own fledgling nation would only survive if it was free to expand westward. No one was using expressions like Manifest Destiny just yet, but the idea was already well established in the minds of the makers of the United States. And, just a year later, world events played right into Jefferson's expansionist plans. Napoleon, emperor of France, already stretched by a large slave revolt in France's Caribbean possessions, was facing an expensive war in Europe. When the U.S. government approached France about continued access to the port of New Orleans, in the French territory of Louisiana, France's foreign minister, Talleyrand, surprised Jefferson's negotiators by offering to sell to the United States the whole of Louisiana for just three cents an acre. As a parting shot, Talleyrand commented, "I suppose you will make the most of it." That was exactly what Jefferson intended to do.

Louisiana was a vast area, much larger than today's state of the same name. It was a great funnel of land, centered on modern Louisiana and extending in a broad wedge west of the Mississippi, up to Canada and across to the Rockies. In one action, the United States more than doubled in size, giving the young country all the breathing space it needed, at least for the moment. But even before Louisiana was officially part of the United States, Jefferson had been encouraging explorers to scope out the western regions of the continent. These clandestine missions weren't particularly successful and convinced Jefferson that small private ventures were not the way forward. He'd watched Britain mapping their world-spanning empire with elaborate military expeditions, like those of James Cook, and he realized that exploring the United States' new western frontier was so important to his own country that it, too, should be a military matter.

Of course, he still wanted to know about the natural history, geology, and peoples of Louisiana, but a military expedition could also assess the economic potential of the new possession and address its role in national security. Even before France surprised him by offering the territory for sale, Jefferson had been discussing such an expedition, but now he could come clean about it. He had chosen his private secretary and trusted friend Meriwether Lewis to lead this expedition, but the real stroke of genius, one that ensured the expedition would go down in history, was to appoint a coleader.

Lewis picked an experienced field soldier and son of a revolutionary war hero, a man called William Clark, and thus the names of Lewis and Clark became inseparably linked—bywords for exploration and discovery. When the expedition—the Corps of Discovery as it later came to be called—returned to civilization, they brought with them hundreds of specimens of unknown plants and animals and copious descriptions of the vast open plains that lay beyond the Mississippi.

Back in the late 1980s, I was working on a television series for PBS and the BBC called *Land of the Eagle,* about the discovery of North America's natural history. Our main consultant was Robert Peck, of the Philadelphia Academy of Natural Sciences—a man whose knowledge ranges widely through history and natural history, as befits someone working in the city that was such a focus of early natural history expertise.

On my first visit to the Academy, I learned that I had something in common with Jefferson: neither of us had ever seen the Great Plains. So Bob took me down to a basement room and unfolded a book of carefully pressed plant specimens from the West. These, he explained with a degree of understatement normally associated with we British, were some of the specimens that Lewis and Clark had brought back. That's the kind of thing to send a tingle down your spine. I looked at those specimens much as Jefferson must have done, intrigued by flowers and grasses that I'd never seen before, trying to imagine the vast landscapes that they had been growing in. Jefferson died without ever standing on America's prairies, but I knew then that I wasn't going to let the same fate befall me. I was off to find the last remaining fragments of America's grasslands, to try and get a sense of the scenes that must have greeted the first travelers beyond the Mississippi.

As soon as English settlers on the east coast pushed westward into Kentucky and the Ohio Valley, they began to get a foretaste of the land to the West. Grassy clearings, often called "barrens," opened up in the forest, though these weren't as bad as such a name might suggest. Back in England at the time, common grazing lands on the periphery of village fields were also sometimes called barrens, and Kentucky's barrens positively delighted those who stumbled on them, people who were enthralled by the "pleasing and rapturous appearance of the Plains of Kentucky. A new sky and a strange new earth seemed to be presented to our view."[1]

Thousands of deer, elk, and bison congregated at salt licks in these vast meadows, adding to the vision of Paradise. But the novelty would soon wear off. These tiny fragments of grassland could hardly prepare European sensibilities for what lay beyond the Mississippi. When people first experienced the Great Plains, they simply could not comprehend the scale and nature of these landscapes, which is not really surprising. They didn't know it at the time, but they were standing on the edge of the largest grasslands on the planet. The central sweep of the Great Plains themselves occupied more than 15 percent of the continent and merged with other prairies in and beyond the Rockies.

Clearing and settling the eastern forests was largely a recapitulation of European history, but there was nothing in western Europe to compare with the Great Plains. Standing at the center of an immense circular horizon, unbroken by the comforting shapes of trees, unsettled, not to say terrified, the first explorers. "I was perfectly alone and could see nothing in any direction but sky and grass. . . . I have often experienced this silence and solitude, but it struck me more forcibly in these boundless meadows."[2]

Perhaps the most telling phrase describing the European view of the Plains comes from fiction, from O. E. Rølvaag's *Giants in the Earth*, about Norwegian settlers in the Dakota Territory, where a character calls them "The great stillness where there was nothing to hide behind." The only Europeans to feel at home here were immigrants from the Russian steppes. For everyone else, there really was nothing to hide behind.

There *is* a great stillness about the Plains, but that's only a superficial impression. Take your cue from this and stop. Sit in the grass and the stillness resolves to endless activity. The sound of the wind in the grass, the call of a bobolink, the rustle of an unseen vole, the piercing cry of a red-tail hawk lost in a vast sky and, as a setting sun rim-lights the feathery heads of the grasses, the wild yips of coyotes. Nor were these plains just never-ending miles of unchanging grassland. They certainly are now (since both wheat and corn are grasses), but when the first west-bound explorers emerged from the forest, they found that the prairies were not so much a sea of grass as an ocean of flowers: "From May to October, they are covered with tall grasses and flower-producing weeds. In June and July, these prairies seem like an ocean of flowers, of various hues, and waving to the breezes which sweep over them."[3]

In the past, the prairies were a complex and ever-changing mosaic of different types of grassland, a fractal landscape with variations at every scale imaginable. To take just one example, vesper sparrows are happiest in recently burnt patches of grass, but as it grows taller, they are replaced by Henslow's sparrows. Clay-colored sparrows move in when a few shrubs take hold, before the whole system is reset as another fire sweeps through. These patterns in space and time are repeated for many other plains creatures. Viewed on longer timescales, the plains are a constant bustle of activity as different species come and go, searching for just he right microhabitat.

At these scales, it's clear that the Great Plains mosaic is incomprehensibly complicated. It's the reason why the plains supported such a diversity of life in an apparently monotonous landscape but, luckily, to appreciate the story of the plains, we need only to understand a much larger scale and a much simpler mosaic: three bands of grasslands running more or less north-south through the center of the United States and southern Canada.

In the east, the tallgrass prairie is, unsurprisingly, made up of tall grasses, rejoicing in such names as big bluestem, Indian grass, and switch grass, which sometimes reach twelve feet in height, too tall to see across, even for a man seated on a horse. On one early expedition, a young boy wandered off into this grassy jungle, and that was the last anyone saw of him for several days.

In the west, the shortgrass prairie consists of grasses like buffalo grass, hairy grama, and blue grama that grow to just a few inches in height. Some ecologists distinguish the shortest of the shortgrass prairies as a separate habitat, called shortgrass steppe, but either way, between the short and tall grasses, there's a third zone, an intermediate type of grassland known as mixed grass prairie. Yet, even at this broadest of scales it's hard to find that "great stillness." The prairie is still a dynamic place. The boundaries between all these types of grassland, as well as that between the tallgrass and the eastern forest, are always on the move.

The main reason for this is water. Shortgrass prairie grows where rainfall is less, while tallgrass grows lush in wetter areas. And the main factor determining where rain falls over the prairies is that great wall of stone and rock lying to the west—the Rockies. Most of the rain from moisture-laden air blowing in from the west falls on the western slopes of the Rockies, creating a rain shadow in the lee of the eastern slopes. Traveling east across the plains, this rain shadow effect gradually diminishes, allowing first mixed grass, then tallgrass prairie to flourish. So, in reality, nature doesn't fit exactly into our "black box" definitions; it's better to visualize the Great Plains as a continuum ranging from short, dry grasslands in the West to tall, lush ones in the East. Eventually, with increasing rainfall, trees can replace the grasses and the eastern forests begin.

Superimposed on this broad picture is the meandering, snakelike form of the jet stream, whose writhings high in the atmosphere bring cycles of wet and dry. During wet periods, the boundaries of all these ecosystems march westward, only to be driven back as drier years return. The boundary between trees and grass was also influenced by fire, both natural and Indian made. Tallgrass prairies often extended much further east than dictated by climate alone, as Indian burning kept trees at bay in favor of lush grazing.

The existence of the prairies was known long before the days of Lewis and Clark. Early French explorers learned of these vast grasslands when they questioned Indians about the great rivers that flowed into the Mississippi from the west. And paddling along the Mississippi itself, they frequently caught glimpses of small patches of prairies, complete with impressive herds of buffalo. Soon after this, fur trappers were exploring the upper reaches of those western rivers in search of virgin fur territory. Likewise, explorers from New Spain had been trekking across the southwestern grasslands since the sixteenth century and, even before they'd seen them in the wild, they'd come across bison in Moctezuma's private zoo in Mexico.

But these people had little impact on the plains themselves and left few descriptions of what they saw. When the United States was born on the east coast, the plains were still largely blank on the map of North America and little known, especially to English Americans. But Thomas Jefferson saw completing that empty map as a vital goal for his young country. For him, future exploration should be concerned with "filling up the canvas we begin." Lewis's little trip, as Jefferson called it, was nothing of the sort. It was the start of the next phase of growth of the empire of the United States.

Lewis's instructions were carefully worked out and very detailed. They ran to many pages, among which he was to "Acquire what knowledge you can of . . . the soil and the face of the country, its growth and vegetable productions . . . the animals of the country generally and especially those not known in the US . . . the dates at which particular plants put forth or lose their flower or leaf, times of appearance of particular birds, reptiles, or insects."[4] All this was to satisfy Jefferson's scientific curiosity as well as prepare the way for settlement. In addition, they were to establish friendly relations with the Indians and ascertain the possibilities for trade, particularly for furs. Jefferson also hoped they might discover a living giant sloth. The bones of this creature were well known to Jefferson, and his rational mind couldn't conceive of any reason why nature would be so wasteful and inefficient as to let a perfectly good species vanish. In his *Notes on the State of Virginia,* he concluded of Nature: "That no instance can be produced, of her having permitted any one race of animals to become extinct; of her having formed any link in her great work so weak as to be broken."

The Enlightenment produced rational minds, of which Jefferson's was one of the finest, yet in one way these minds were the same as those that went before. Nature was so indomitable and abundant that nothing humans could do would affect it. That was the attitude that arrived on the shores of the Chesapeake, and that was the attitude that was about to move west across the Great Plains.

With detailed instructions in hand, the expedition assembled at Camp River Dubois, where the Missouri empties into the Mississippi just north of St. Louis. When I visited this spot a few years ago, I found it hard to be impressed by the confluence of these two mighty rivers, at least from the wooded bank opposite the Missouri's mouth. But I dare say if I'd been sitting in the middle of the Mississippi in a flimsy canoe watching the roiling Missouri—the "big muddy"—disgorge giant tree trunks, I might have changed my mind.

Nearby, it's possible to get a more vivid insight into the past. Lewis and Clark's base camp has been reconstructed next to a comprehensive museum dedicated to the expedition and which gives a good flavor of the beginning of this epic voyage. But it can't convey the extraordinary difficulties they would face when they set off up the Missouri in the spring of 1804.

The expedition used a large keelboat and two pirogues (smaller flat-bottomed, canoe-like boats) to transport the men and the extensive equipment they needed to fulfill Jefferson's brief. Recently, for a film on the history of the Mississippi's and Missouri's wildlife, we reconstructed part of this journey along the Missouri, with a keelboat and a single pirogue during which I gained a new admiration for the achievements of the Corps of Discovery.

We headed off confidently into the Missouri near Onawa, with Iowa to our right and Nebraska to our left until a stiff plains wind caught the sails of the keelboat and sent us skimming sideways onto the nearest sandbank, before anyone could drop the sails. Our crew of actors, dressed in heavy serge, labored to pole the boat off the sandbank with a little help from the pirogue, which had thoughtfully been fitted with a motor. Back in open water again, the wind almost immediately caught the high cabin of the keelboat and spun us round and then onto another sandbank. More hard poling. Back out on the river, the crew tried using oars, as Lewis and Clark's men frequently had to do, to make headway against the current. No chance. After about thirty seconds of filming, we found ourselves back on the first sandbank, now with Nebraska to our right and Iowa to our left. This time we were stuck fast, so the actors, now browning nicely in the Nebraska (or was it Iowa) sunshine leapt over board, using ropes to pull the boat upstream through the shallow water, another technique needed by Lewis and Clark's men to move upstream. Their Herculean efforts moved us an impressive fifty yards upstream before the water became too deep, so they all hopped on board while the wind carried us—inescapably—back down to an increasingly familiar sandbar.

This time, we tried using the motorized pirogue to tow us upstream, so we could at least get some shots of the keelboat heading downriver under sail. Nice idea. Our captain told his crew to wait until the boat was pointing downwind before dropping the sails. Hopefully, they would billow out and carry us dramatically downstream. They billowed—and spun the boat sideways. Was that Nebraska or Iowa? Well, at least we knew where the sandbar, was and found it with unerring accuracy. We spent most of the day like this until our exhausted and disheveled crew towed us along the bank to find a safe place to tie up the boat for the night. It might be small consolation to them, but in the end, the sequence looked great. No amount of makeup could match the genuinely burnt and exhausted figures that we filmed hauling the boat up river. And it's exactly what the Corps of Discovery would have looked like at the end of most days of their twenty-eight-*month* expedition. Ours would have taken much longer. We tied up the keelboat about one hundred yards from where we began. I took some comfort from the fact that several accounts from keelboats, and even from steamboats, on the Missouri describe still being able to see their point of departure at the end of their first day.

But the efforts of Lewis and Clark's men would eventually prove more than worth it. The first part of their journey, though, was through known territory. There were even a few homesteads and settlements along the river, but eventually they began to move into the higher plains along the upper Missouri. Even here, they continued to meet with fur traders from the North West Company and the ubiquitous Hudson's Bay Company, whose initials, HBC, painted onto crates of their furs were said to stand for "Here Before Christ." But Lewis and Clark also began to find those animals that were "not known in the US" and that would therefore delight their president. "Discovered a Village of Small animals that burrow in the grown. Those animals are Called by the French Petite Chien."[5]

Clark preferred to call these "little dogs" barking squirrels or burrowing squirrels, both of which are actually better names than "prairie dog" since they are, like true squirrels, rodents. There are five species of prairie dogs across North America, but the Corps of Discovery had encountered the black-tailed prairie dog—by far the most abundant, even then. But just how many were there when Lewis and Clark wrote their descriptions? Ernest Thompson

Seton estimated that there were 5 billion of them,[6] and some of the colonies were certainly large enough to make that seem a reasonable estimate. In 1902, C. Hart Merriam described one prairie dog town in Texas that stretched 250 miles in one direction and one hundred miles in the other and may have contained 400 million individuals. Later researchers have worked out that prairie dogs must have ranged over somewhere between 40 and 100 million hectares of short and mixed grass prairies (we'll see shortly that prairie dogs hate long grass), though most now favor the lower end of this range.

If these estimates are correct, then the prairie dog's range has contracted by 99 percent since then, such an alarming reduction that the Fish and Wildlife Service proposed listing them under the Endangered Species Act (ESA). But in 2004, the black-tailed prairie dog was removed from the candidate list for ESA protection, since new research suggested that plague, which has been known to all but eliminate large colonies, was not necessarily always so devastating and that earlier estimates of their modern range were too conservative.[7]

Even so, these newer and more accurate estimates of present range are still only 2 percent of the prairie dog's range two hundred years ago, and two of the other, less widespread species of prairie dogs, the Utah prairie dog and the Mexican prairie dog, are already listed as endangered. However, as we've seen in other cases, absolute extinction is preceded by ecological extinction, which, in the long run, is a far more important criterion on which to base conservation action. So the discussion must turn again to the historical abundance of prairie dogs and from there to the exact role of these creatures in the ecology of North America's grasslands.

First, not everyone agrees with estimates of billions or their huge historic range over the grasslands,[8] and an accurate picture of the past is important since, apart from giving a baseline to judge how effective conservation measures are, it helps decide whether the black-tailed prairie dog is a keystone species—a species that has large and disproportionate effects on its ecosystem. Since nature doesn't fit things into neat black boxes the way that we do, it might seem that an argument over a definition is pointless, but the real importance is not what we call the prairie dog. It's over whether schemes to restore native grassland should include prairie dogs as a key element and even whether such schemes would be ineffective without prairie dogs. And that's contentious, because ranchers and farmers see prairie dogs as competitors for grazing.

Some wildlife scientists suggest that the large numbers of prairie dogs undoubtedly witnessed by biologists at the start of the twentieth century were an artifact of changes already under way. Prairie dogs prefer to colonize open ground where it is easy to see predators, and at this time, rapidly increasing numbers of cattle were grazing the grasslands flat, creating ideal conditions for prairie dogs and a boom in numbers. Others argue that, before cattle, bison would have performed the same job and that when the bison were all but eliminated, the grass grew, and consequently prairie dog numbers dropped. The rapid rise in numbers in the late nineteenth century was therefore just a rebound to former abundance, so biologists like C. Hart Merriam and Ernest Thompson Seton who made their observations during, or just after, this period were seeing something approaching the "natural" state of prairie dogs.[9] If so, then the next question is, how important are all these prairie dogs to the other creatures of the plains?

Paul Johnsgard is a biologist, naturalist, and award-winning writer, who, during his long career at the University of Nebraska in Lincoln, has written many evocative works on Great Plains natural history. In *Great Wildlife of the Great Plains*,[10] he lists fifty-six birds, eighteen mammals, ten reptiles, and seven amphibians using prairie dog burrows in Oklahoma, while a 1980 survey along an 828-mile transect across New Mexico to the Utah/Wyoming state line counted over one hundred mammals, birds, reptiles, and amphibians associated with prairie dog colonies. In all, 208 species have been recorded on or near prairie dog colonies, but for most of these, we don't have enough information to know just how critical prairie dogs are in their lives. This impressive number of associates doesn't include unstudied creatures like fleas, ticks, or lice—or a host of other invertebrates that may live with prairie dogs.

Many of these species can also survive without prairie dogs so perhaps the best that can be said at the moment is that, although the impact of prairie dogs on grasslands may have been misinterpreted or overstated in the past, these little rodents do seem to have a disproportionately large effect on grassland ecology and so should qualify as a keystone species.[11] If dog towns are vital parts of the grassland whole,[12] and their inhabitants part of a complex series of interrelationships with grassland animals and plants, what form do these relationships take?

Prairie dogs are obsessed with being able to see the horizon, but since they're tasty, bite-sized morsels for foxes, coyotes, and eagles, to name but a few, you can forgive their paranoia. Around the edges of their colonies, they clip tall plants, without eating them, to open up their view of the surrounding plains. They also keep the grass cropped into a well-manicured lawn, and as this grass regrows, it sprouts nutritious shoots that draw in bison. Some studies have shown that bison spend around 40 percent of their time in the suburbs of dog towns even though these represent only about 12 percent of their habitat. And this may be just part of a bigger reciprocal arrangement.

It's possible that bison grazed the area short enough for the dog town to become established in the first place. Now, as bison graze around the town, they fertilize the grass with copious quantities of nitrogen-rich urine, to the benefit of bison and prairie dogs alike. Indeed, as one ecologist has somewhat bluntly pointed out, America's grasslands are piss-driven ecosystems—one of the least romantic depictions of the Great Plains that I've come across.

Since prairie dogs and bison selectively eat grass, their grazing promotes the growth of nongrassy, nonwoody plants—called "forbs," for ease of discussion by ecologists. Forbs also grow better in the bare mud of the prairie dog's excavations, where they are free from competition with grass. And forbs are the preferred food of pronghorns. So prairie dog towns exert a kind of ecological gravity, drawing in life from the surrounding plains. And for some creatures, this gravity is so strong they can't escape. Of all the species associated with prairie dogs there are nine, which we know of at the moment, that depend on prairie dogs for survival and reproduction, though none more so than the black-footed ferret.[13]

With its bandit-like black mask, the black-footed ferret is probably a prairie dog's worst nightmare. They live in the prairie dog's burrow system and hardly ever appear above ground in daylight, perhaps just for a few minutes every few days.[14] They hunt mainly at night when they surprise sleeping prairie dogs in their beds, and since these unfortunate animals make up 90 percent of their diet, they are entirely dependent on prairie dog colonies. And it takes a large colony (probably one bigger than four thousand hectares) to support a viable population of ferrets. Since there are hardly any colonies of this size in North America, it will come as no surprise to discover that black-footed ferrets are critically endangered.

They're so secretive that Lewis and Clark never saw one. Neither did countless other explorers and pioneers; their existence wasn't widely known until Audubon and Bachman published a painting and description in *The Quadrupeds of North America*. However, local Indians caught them to use their skins for ceremonial purposes, and black-footed ferrets also occasionally turned up in the inventories of fur traders. But this time, neither Indians nor fur traders can be blamed for ferret's demise. The culprits were ranchers, who saw the prairie dog as a competitor, stealing the grass from the mouths of cattle and sheep. They waged war on these prolific rodents, an eradication campaign with bullets and poison that proved very successful.

But the campaign had a far bigger effect on the ferrets. By the 1960s, only one small colony remained in South Dakota. And when, for entirely mysterious reasons, this colony disappeared in the 1970s, this bandit ferret was presumed extinct. Its rediscovery, near Meeteetse, in Wyoming, was down to a ranch dog called Shep who brought one in as an offering for its master in 1981. This colony consisted of perhaps 130 animals, which was soon reduced to a mere eighteen by the double blow of sylvatic plague (lethal to prairie dogs) and canine distemper (lethal to ferrets) that struck the colony. In desperation, these last remaining animals were taken into captivity to found a breeding program, which, after a few early problems, eventually proved successful enough to begin rereleasing ferrets into the most suitable dog towns. But these reintroductions have met with poor success.[15] Ferrets are declining or have already disappeared from most reintroduction sites, often after plague strikes the prairie dogs, but perhaps also because most towns today are just not big enough.

At one site, in the Buffalo Gap National Grasslands in South Dakota, ferrets have increased slowly since their reintroduction in 1996. This colony has been mercifully free of plague during that time, but in 2004, the disease was identified on a nearby grassland, so the future of even this colony must be a cause for concern. In 2006, the minimum number of ferrets in the Shirley Basin in Wyoming, the largest remaining dog conurbation, was estimated to be 196, with around seven hundred living in the wild in other colonies and three hundred or so still living in captivity. But even if any of these colonies ever become self-sustaining, all these animals are derived from those original eighteen individuals taken into captivity, a genetic bottleneck that might render the whole population vulnerable to disease or fertility problems.

Protecting the grassland ecosystem is all about scale, that same scale that so overwhelmed the first to explore the prairies. The constantly shifting grassland mosaic is too big to be contained in anything but the very largest reserves. Unfortunately, there is, as yet, no Endangered Ecosystem Act, though many would love to see one. We have to work, via the ESA, with individual species. However, listing a keystone species, like the black-tailed prairie dog, would go a long way to restoring the whole ecosystem. So, many grassland ecologists were disappointed when the Fish and Wildlife Service (FWS) removed prairie dogs from the waiting list for ESA protection in 2004. However, the FWS didn't have much choice. The ESA is bound by very precisely defined conditions, which is both its greatest strength and its greatest weakness. Much woollier acts have not always been so effective, but there is no room in the ESA for a broader interpretation in cases like that of the prairie dog.

Removing prairie dogs from the candidate list saw an increase in poisonings, including at three of the largest remaining towns. Most conservationists now agree that farmers and ranchers must become part of the answer and not part of the problem, though at the moment, more than half of farmers and ranchers questioned wanted to see prairie dogs entirely eliminated from their land. And they do undoubtedly eat grass that could have been eaten by cows, but nature is never that simple. Regrowth after prairie dog grazing is often more nutritious, at least in younger colonies, and the rodents also keep down shrubs and brush that would make the pasture less attractive to cows. So, competition between prairie dogs and cattle may be less than it appears at first sight.

Poisoning is also expensive, and the costs of eliminating prairie dogs might well outweigh the advantages. It is also possible to give prairie dogs a positive financial value. In recent years, recreational shooting has become increasingly popular. Only a few of these people shoot prairie dogs for food, the rest for live target practice, as a way of spending time outdoors or just for fun. Such shooting now accounts for around 2 million prairie dogs a year. I'm personally deeply saddened that any human being could blow away a prairie dog just for the hell of it, but it's one of those ironies of conservation that if more landowners realize that prairie dogs have a commercial value, they might be more willing to tolerate colonies on their land. Whatever the case, Lewis's little barking squirrel is set to remain center stage in the battle to restore North America's grasslands.

When Lewis and Clark first saw them, they knew that these prairie dogs would delight their president, so they decided to dig one out and send it to him. After all, how hard could it be? "We attempted to dig to the beds of one of those animals, after digging 6 feet, found by running a pole down that we were not half way to his Lodge."[16] As part of our film, we decided we would reconstruct the efforts of the Corps of Discovery on the very site where they attempted to catch a prairie dog exactly two hundred years before. The site is recognizable since Clark described a rock formation, that he called "the steeple," overlooking the colony. Today, this is known as Old Baldy, a distinctive hill not far from the tiny town of Lynch, Nebraska. And, sure enough, there is still a prairie dog colony here, at the end of a bumpy ride over ranch trails, on the side of a hill with the broad expanse of the Missouri lying in the valley below, about half a mile away. Its inhabitants watched in what looked like startled amazement (though that's how prairie dogs usually look) as this new Corps of Discovery made its way, shovels in hand, to the center of the colony. We had no intention of trying to dig one out, since I don't think the present incumbent of the White House would appreciate prairie dogs in the same way as Jefferson did. All we needed was a few shots of our Corps digging near a burrow entrance and, yet again, we soon discovered how hard the original trip must have been. The ground was rock hard, and after an hour of digging and filming, we had barely scratched the surface. After digging down six feet in the heat of a Nebraska summer, Lewis and Clark's men must have been exhausted. But they still hadn't captured their prize for Jefferson.

If they couldn't outdig a barking squirrel, they would have to outthink it. They decided to flush one out of its burrow. But the only source of water wound its way through the valley below them, so the Corps formed a living chain, handing buckets along the line, from the Missouri to the mouth of the unfortunate prairie dog's burrow. Eventually the creature, presumably half-drowned, emerged into daylight and was promptly caught and caged. I doubt whether it appreciated the historical honor, but it would eventually become the first prairie dog to visit the east coast and meet a U.S. president.

As they struggled on up the Missouri, Lewis and Clark came across more and more strange animals. Now more than a thousand miles from Camp Dubois, they rounded the big bend of the Missouri in September and caught sight of a strange creature that they thought at first was goat. A week later, Clark managed to kill one of these strange animals and gain a closer look. "Verry actively made, has only a pair of hoofs to each foot, his brains on the back of his head, his Norstrals large, his eyes like a Sheep he is more like the Antilope or Gazella of Africa than any other Species of Goat." The fact that they couldn't decide whether it was a goat or an antelope was perfectly understandable. Neither could later scientists, when they gave this animal its own family—the Antilocapridae or goat antelopes. It was neither a goat nor a sheep—but a pronghorn, and the only living member of a family that flourished in the Pleistocene period. They might not have found any giant sloths for Jefferson, but if they knew then what biologists know now, this was the next best thing.

Pronghorns lived in impressive numbers on the plains, but they were never easy to approach. In the Pleistocene, the pronghorn's ancestors had to cope with America's very own cheetah and evolved an ability to run at high speed. "Verry actively made," as Captain Clark so rightly observed. In fact, as they got to know these animals, the pronghorn's speed really impressed the explorers. "I beheld the rapidity of their flight along the ridge before me it appeared reather the rappid flight of birds than the motion of quadrupeds. I think I can safely venture the asscertion that the speed of this animal is equal if not superior to that of the finest blooded courser."

The further west they traveled, the more they were also impressed by the increasing size of the bison herds. At first, they were overawed by the herds near the Mississippi, as the first French explorers had been. But as they headed west, the herds just got bigger and bigger and were joined by impressive numbers of other game animals: "this scenery already rich pleasing and beatiful was still farther hightened by immence herds of Buffaloe, deer Elk and Antelopes which we saw in every direction feeding on the hills and plains. I do not think I exagerate when I estimate the number of Buffaloe which could be compre[hend]ed at one view to amount to 3000." Finally, the sea of grass became a sea of bison: "from an eminance I had a view of the plains for a great distance. from this eminance I had a view of a greater number of buffalow than I had ever seen before at one time. I must have seen near 20,000 of those animals feeding on this plain."

Later explorers gave even more impressive descriptions of the sheer scale of these herds. In 1869, a pioneer settler in Kansas came across one such vast herd: "The herd was not less than twenty miles in width—we never saw the other side—at least sixty miles in length, maybe much longer; two counties of buffaloes! There might have been 100,000, or 1,000,000, or 100,000,000. I don't know. In the cowboy days in western Kansas we saw 7000 cattle in one round-up. After gazing at them a few moments our thoughts turned to that buffalo herd. For comparison, imagine a large pail of water; take from it or add to it a drop, and there you have it. Seven thousand head of cattle was not a drop in the bucket as compared with that herd of buffalo."[17]

Traveling along the Arkansas River in 1871, Colonel Richard Dodge, who later became better known for escorting a scientific expedition into the Black Hills to confirm George Custer's reports of gold, came across another such herd that passed by for almost a whole day. A few decades later, based on this description, Ernest Thompson Seton tried to calculate the number in that particular herd and then extrapolate from this to estimate the entire population of the Great Plains.

Seton undoubtedly had a head for figures—he once counted all the feathers on a grackle to satisfy his curiosity—and he was almost as obsessed with working out how many bison had once roamed the plains. He estimated that Dodge's herd contained 4 million animals and that, taking into account the distribution of other herds, the total population must therefore have been around 60 million. There have been even higher estimates; figures of 75 million are common in many books and pamphlets and sometimes even 100 million. However, several scientists have now converged on a more conservative figure of 30 million using several different methods of estimation, so this seems a more likely figure.

It might be only half of Seton's estimate, but it's hardly disappointing. Stop reading for a moment, sit back and try to imagine 30 million animals. It's still an astounding number—and quite impossible for the human mind (at least mine, anyway) to grasp. It's even hard to conjure up images of the size of individual herds. On today's Serengeti in Tanzania, around 1.5 million animals, mainly wildebeest, make a great circular annual migration. It's an incredible image, made familiar by countless wildlife programs through the decades, but bison are so much bigger and more imposing as individuals and some of their herds probably even larger.

You can get at least a glimpse of what Lewis and Clark or Richard Dodge must have seen when modern, managed herds of bison are rounded up for routine checking and culling. The herd in Custer State Park, in South Dakota's Black Hills, was used to create the impressive bison scenes for *Dances with Wolves*, so seemed like a good place to go when I wanted to recreate the huge herds seen by Lewis and Clark. The day of the actual roundup and corralling is now a major public event, a day when the park and the surrounding towns are choked with cars and curious sightseers, an incongruous sight in the normally deserted Dakotas. But before the big day itself, the herd has to be moved to a location close to the corrals, and to a position where tens of thousands of spectators are not going to have too close an encounter with a few thousand bison.

These preliminary movements of the herd, in the absence of thousands of people, seemed more appropriate images to conjure up Lewis and Clark's encounters so the herd managers helpfully stationed the cameraman and myself on the side of hill, close to where—they hoped—the herd would gallop past. It was a stunning high plains October day. The river in the valley below us was lined with cottonwoods glowing intense yellow in crystal clear air. To our right, the valley opened out into shortgrass prairie, rolling toward the horizon in carefully coordinated shades of brown. And there we sat, drinking in the intoxicating sense of space on the plains and lulled by a symphony of grasshopper chirps, until a burst of static from the radio reminded us why we were here.

The blue sky over the opposite side of the valley had already turned a hazy yellow, and as we watched, more and more dust rose, looking like smoke from a fire lit by prairie lightning. But it turned out to be prairie thunder, as the first of the herd crested the hill, in a gentle, effortless trot. Soon animals were pouring down the opposite slope, most of the herd just ghostly gray shapes in the swirling clouds of dust. But the thunder of hooves told us these were no ghosts—a thunder that can be both heard and felt gave an immediate sense of their power. The word "awesome" is overused today; its true meaning should be reserved for spectacles like this. And yet this was nothing compared to the herds witnessed by the first explorers. We were filming about 1,500 animals, and the spectacle lasted a matter of minutes. Imagine riding next to Colonel Dodge through such a spectacle that lasted all day.

It's easy to understand the awestruck prose of those who saw these herds, spectacles that, because they were so astounding, were also easy to exaggerate. That makes estimating the true scale of the bison herds a difficult task, made no easier by the fact that bison numbers have fluctuated widely in the past, thanks to their particular ecological history. At the end of the last ice age, as the grasslands began to take on their present form and distribution, they were populated by an extraordinary menagerie of creatures. I've already mentioned the American cheetah, but there were also lions, dire wolves, saber-toothed cats, and short-faced bears hunting a spectacular assemblage of grazers. This was the time of mastodons and mammoths, of giant sloths and giant armadillos. This impressive megafauna disappeared rapidly at the end of the ice age, though just what caused such a widespread extinction is still hotly debated.

The theories have been summarized in shorthand as "kill, chill, and ill." Either they were killed by humans newly migrating to the New World, by climate change, by some kind of pandemic, or by a combination of some or all of these. Since these creatures all predate the historical framework of this book, I won't discuss these events further, except to suggest that interested readers should pick up a copy of Tim Flannery's highly readable and thought-provoking book *The Eternal Frontier* for a much longer view of North America's natural history.

From our perspective, the important point is that the disappearance of the megafauna left a lot of space on the evolving grasslands—and nature abhors a vacuum. It might be hard to see the magnificent bison in this light, but it is, in essence, a weed species—able to expand its population quickly and make the most of any opportunities that arise. And the demise of the Pleistocene megafauna was a huge opportunity that propelled the bison to domination on North America's grasslands. Since the plains took on their modern form, they've been characterized by alternating periods of drought and higher rainfall, and the bison's weed ecology means they can respond to these changes by rapidly building their population when times are good. The archaeological record suggests that there were times when bison were extremely abundant and times when, long before Europeans could be blamed, bison were virtually absent from the plains.

As for many of the other natural spectacles that we've seen, some see the extraordinary numbers of bison witnessed by Lewis and Clark, Colonel Dodge, and the like as a direct result of the decimation of the Plains Indian nations, who had previously kept bison numbers much lower through hunting pressure. Yet others, using calculations of the number of animals needed for subsistence, backed up by first hand accounts, don't consider that Indians can have had much impact on bison numbers at all.[18]

Lewis and Clark themselves were well aware that humans had played their part in shaping the sights they were witnessing as they pushed ever westward. Spectacular herds of game were not abundant everywhere on the plains, and the Corps would find little game in the valley of the Columbia when they later crossed the Rockies. William Clark spotted one reason for this patchiness: "I have observed that in the country between the nations which are at war with each other the greatest numbers of wild animals are to be found." In other words, the no-go areas between tribes at war were, in essence, nature reserves—too dangerous to hunt, lest the hunter become the hunted.[19] In more secure areas, game populations could well have been depleted by hunting. Other explorers saw similar patterns elsewhere, so, while long-term fluctuations of the total population of bison are likely to be the result of cycles of wet and dry periods, the way that population was spread across the prairies may well be down to who was fighting who at the time. Given the complexity of these interactions, it would seem sensible to see the Indian-bison relationship as a constantly shifting and dynamic one. However, it's also possible that the awesome spectacle of grasslands blackened by endless herds may have actually have been created the Indians in the first place.[20]

In 1979, University of Alaska researcher Dale Guthrie heard about an ancient bison that had been uncovered in Alaska's permafrost. It was a remarkable creature, stained blue by vivianite crystals and therefore quickly nicknamed Blue Babe, after the story of Paul Bunyan and his legendary blue ox called Babe. Blue Babe lived around thirty-six thousand years ago, part of the Pleistocene megafauna, and was different from modern bison in many respects. He had massive horns, which were much larger than those of bison today and which swept out sideways, hence the species name of "long-horned bison" for Blue Babe and his kin. So much of Blue Babe was preserved that not only was Guthrie able to make a stew of some of Blue Babe's meat, but he could deduce a lot about how he had lived. And, critically, these studies suggested that long-horned bison lived in much smaller herds than modern bison. Since long-horned bison seemed to be the direct ancestors of modern bison, Guthrie wondered what caused the shift to living in vast herds. The usual ecological reason for opting for life in large herds, with all its disadvantages of having to compete with the crowds, is predation. And Guthrie points out that the only novel predator to arrive on the scene at about the right time walked on two legs and carried a sharpened stone spear. So, in one way or another, it seems that those great bison herds are artifacts of humanity.[21]

At times, the numbers of birds could be just as impressive as those of big game, as Lewis recorded in July of 1805: "we daily see great numbers of gees with their young which are perfectly feathered except the wings which are deficient in both young and old. My dog caught several today, as he frequently dose. the young ones are very fine, but the old gees are poor and unfit for uce." These were resident Canada geese, which had the unusual habit of nesting high in the cottonwood trees that lined the Missouri. When Lewis and Clark wrote their descriptions, the geese had begun their molt, a time when they lose their flight feathers along with the power of flight. But the explorers also witnessed the passage of large flocks of migrants, like lesser snow geese: "The white brant associate in very large flocks, they do not appear to be mated or pared off as if they intended to raise their young in this quarter, I therefore doubt whether they reside here during the summer for that purpose." They were right about these snow goose flocks. When the explorers recorded these notes in April of 1805, the geese were on their way back to Arctic breeding grounds.

But all of these spectacles pale into insignificance when the prairie skies were darkened by flocks of Eskimo curlews. We've already met this species as it dropped in on the coast of Labrador to feed on late summer berries before heading out over the Atlantic and on to wintering grounds in South America. In spring, the flocks returned to the Arctic by a different route, which took them along the Central American isthmus, over the Gulf of Mexico and then northward across the Great Plains.

On arriving in North America, these great flocks first descended on the coastal prairies of Texas and Louisiana, usually around early to mid-March. By late March, they had made their way north to Oklahoma, and by early April, to interpret contemporary accounts, they were flocking into Kansas, western Missouri, western Iowa, and Nebraska.[22] "The birds would arrive about the time the later willows began to bloom, being present in force for a week or 10 days only, for by the time all of the wild plum blossoms had fallen the birds were gone." The flocks seemed to follow areas of tallgrass and mixed grass prairie and descended in unbelievable numbers on recently burnt areas. The flocks were so dense that one observer concluded that he "could scarcely throw a brick or other missile into it without striking a bird."

Each flock might measure half a mile in length and more than one hundred yards in width and, when settled, covered forty or fifty acres. They also liked fields newly planted with spring corn, which served as a good substitute for burnt tallgrass. This should have been a welcome sight for those pioneer farmers, since the curlews were devouring large numbers of grasshoppers, which would otherwise reach plague proportions and devastate the crop. But their role as pest controllers didn't gain them much protection. In the late nineteenth century, wagons piled to the sideboards with the bodies of curlews trundled into expanding cities like Omaha.

Between 1870 and 1890, the numbers of curlews following the tallgrass corridor northward in spring dropped precipitously. The last large flock in Nebraska passed through in 1900, and after that small groups of a few tens of individuals were all that anyone saw. Through the 1940s and 1950s, there were only sporadic reports of lone birds or groups of two or three individuals. However, many of these were unconfirmed. Eskimo curlews are very similar to whimbrels and to an Asian species, the little curlew, so a good view is essential for certain identification. One was shot in Barbados in 1964, which was definitely a good enough view, but between 1945 and 1986, individuals and small groups were reported in only twenty-five of the forty-one years.[23] There have been no confirmed reports since the 1980s, but enough unsubstantiated sightings to give some people hope that the species is not yet extinct.

The Eskimo curlew is yet another species reduced from extraordinary abundance to the edge of extinction, and the reason seems to lie with events along its spring migration route, rather than its southward journey over Labrador.[24] Although they were hunted in the fall in Labrador, there weren't that many people there. More people hunted them in New England, but the curlew flocks didn't make landfall in New England every year. However, their passage over the Great Plains in spring took longer and exposed them to many more hunters. As the human population of the plains began to grow, there was a ready market for these birds in expanding cities. The once-infinite flocks of passenger pigeons were now in decline, and Eskimo curlews provided the perfect alternative—huge flocks of birds that were easy to kill in large numbers. And, although the flocks were enormous, the biology of Eskimo curlews meant that killing the birds on migration had an inordinate effect on their population.

The curlews were on their way to nesting grounds in the remote north of the continent, where they were exposed to the vagaries of the Arctic weather. Like most Arctic birds, they weren't able to nest successfully every year, so evolution compensated by making the birds long-lived, to give them better odds of having at least some successful years. This meant that Eskimo curlews could only raise enough young to maintain their population by living long lives, a strategy that proved disastrous when those lives were cut short by the guns of market hunters.

Changes in farming practices, such as a switch from spring-sown to autumn-sown crops, also made it harder for the flocks to refuel on their northward journey. Occasional sightings give some hope that the species still clings on, able to raise a few young on some unknown stretch of remote Arctic wilderness. But since it is these very areas that will bear the brunt of climate change, the future looks bleak for the little bird that may have guided Columbus to the New World.

Lewis and Clark never saw these vast flocks—they were in the wrong place at the right time. Even so, Lewis's little trip was extremely successful, even if not in its entirety. They did find a way over the Rockies, and like Mackenzie before them, stood on the shores of the Pacific. In a gesture to Mackenzie's earlier trip across Canada, Clark carved his own inscription into the bark of a tree — "William Clark, by Land, Nov 18 1805." They also found a wealth of furs along the upper Missouri, where Lewis declared he'd never seen so many beavers. But their transcontinental route was not the easy passage to the Pacific that Jefferson had hoped for. It was a long and hard trek, though the trip was hailed as a great success.

And even before Lewis and Clark returned, Jefferson was already thinking about filling in more of the blanks on the map of the United States. He was planning another expedition, this time along the Red River, on which he intended to correct a major oversight of the Lewis and Clark trip. On this expedition he was going to send a trained naturalist. Given Jefferson's thirst for knowledge, it seems extraordinary that he didn't send a trained naturalist with Lewis and Clark, though the Corps of Discovery was still more than worthy of its name.

The man eventually chosen for this task on the Red River Expedition was Peter Custis, possibly the least known of America's early naturalists, in part because the expedition was turned back by the Spanish after only a few hundred miles. Even though Custis managed to document many new species of plants and animals, the Red River Expedition never gained the widespread fame of the Corps of Discovery. Custis and his descriptions disappeared into obscurity, despite providing some enlightening comments on the history of the southern plains.

There was also no artist on Lewis and Clark's expedition. There are sketches in their notebooks, but nothing to convey the real spectacles of their journey apart from their text. A much more vivid insight into life on the Plains turned up in, of all places, the town of Neuwied in Germany just after the end of WWII. It was here that the director of the Museum of Koblenz uncovered a stash of four hundred paintings by the Swiss artist Karl Bodmer. They were in Germany because Bodmer, himself Swiss, had traveled with a German prince, Maximilian von Wied, on an expedition over the Great Plains in 1833.

Maximilian was an accomplished anthropologist, naturalist, and writer and, for his part, provided detailed descriptions of life on the plains to which Bodmer's painting served as illustrations. The paintings were really just "notes" to guide the production of aquatints to illustrate Maximilian's book of the journey, but the originals are quite breathtaking. Many now hang in the Joslyn Art Gallery in Omaha, Nebraska, and if you thought you'd never find a reason to visit Omaha, then here is one. The Art of the American West collection transports you through a history of the West on a wave of color and movement so vivid you can almost taste the dust. Here, Bodmer's works are hung with those of George Catlin, whose travels on the plains began around the same time.

Catlin's first trip, in 1830, was with William Clark, who was now superintendent of Indian Affairs for the Louisiana Territory, and on this and subsequent trips, Catlin produced some of the most stunning and vibrant portrayals of Indian life. Like the works of Bodmer, they are made all the more poignant by being painted just as life on the plains, for both Indians and wildlife, was undergoing a catastrophic change—as the West became the Wild West.

In fact, the changes that underlay the rapid transformation of the plains in the middle of the nineteenth century had begun several centuries before. One key factor is captured in two of my favorite Catlin paintings, *Catching a Wild Horse* and *Comanche Feats of Horsemanship*. Catlin, a good horseman himself, described the Comanche as the best horsemen he had ever seen—yet the horse was a recent addition to their culture.

Those archetypal images of an Indian surveying the wide-open plains, mounted on the back of a sprightly painted pony are the result of an ecological amalgam of cultures that began when the Spanish arrived in the Caribbean. The horses they brought with them prospered in the New World and soon established large feral herds, first in the Caribbean then in Mexico, California, and the southern plains. It shouldn't be too much of a surprise that horses did so well in the New World, since they evolved here in the first place, ranging widely over the grasslands at the end of the last ice age along with other members of the Pleistocene megafauna. Now back on their old turf, they spread rapidly. Before the middle of the nineteenth century there were at least 2 million mustangs between the South Texas and Arkansas rivers, and the Indian nations of the southern plains had another quarter million.[25]

Horses transformed the lives and the ecology of these Indians. They made bison much easier to hunt and enabled the Indians to select the best animals, which, for quality of hide and meat, were young cows. It was a seductive way of life and drew in many tribes who had previously lived on the periphery of the plains and depended more on farming, a change in ecology that precipitated a cultural shift. In the mixed economy of farming and hunting, women played an important role. Men hunted and women farmed, a division of labor that extended to the spiritual side of life as well as the practical. Hunting bison was a male pursuit, and as tribes adopted this lifestyle, women suffered a drop in status. It takes three days to process one hide, and as more and more became available, men began to take multiple wives, to cope with the workload, further eroding the woman's role. The women of several tribes tried to resist the shift to a nomadic life on the plains, but failed because their tribes were also being pushed onto the plains by problems originating in the East.

The multiple pressures of European colonization, wars, and trade alliances were forcing many tribes to move from their traditional territories. One important set of changes occurred when the Sioux moved out of their original home in the eastern forests and pushed other tribes, like the Cheyenne and Arapaho, further south on to the plains. At the same time, other tribes were emerging on to the grasslands from the mountains to the west.

Of course, the boundaries of Indian nations had always been fluid, responding to patterns of intertribal warfare, treaties, changes in ecology, and, particularly on the plains, the cycles of bison abundance. One Shoshone band, for example, emerged from the Rockies, probably during one of the bison's more populous phases, only to retreat to the mountain valleys again when the bison grew scarce. These people ventured back on to the plains when horses made bison hunting an attractive proposition once again. They were called "Komantcia" by neighboring Ute Indians, later changed to Comanche, the people who would swiftly become the finest horsemen on the plains, at least according to George Catlin. And they certainly became the biggest horse traders.

But this shift to a horse culture caused more changes in Comanche ecology. In the mountains, where resources could sometimes be limited, the Shoshone were reported to practice population control by infanticide. Horses provided a kind of ecological release, and the Comanche responded with a campaign to increase their population, a strategy to grow their market economy. It would allow them to maximize their use of the bison herds as well as defend their hunting territories against the ever-increasing number of tribes arriving on the plains. The Comanche fought long wars against the Cheyenne and Arapaho, who were trying to move in on the best horse country. But these conflicts were never really conclusive; the southern plains were very rich, as reported by Peter Custis on his brief trip along the Red River, and just too tempting for any tribe to ignore.

Did these major changes in Indian ecology have an effect on the bison herds, even before European hunters arrived on the scene in numbers? Calculating kills needed for subsistence (which are born out by historical observations) suggests that despite increased kills from horseback and the targeting of cows, the numbers taken were well within sustainable levels. Even allowing for trade with tribes surrounding the plains, the bison's "weed" ecology meant they could reproduce rapidly enough to maintain their population. And, as we've already seen, the zones between warring tribes, where it was too dangerous to hunt, provided refugia where game animals could multiply to prodigious numbers.

Yet there's also evidence, from as early as Lewis and Clark's expedition, that game was not always abundant everywhere, probably due to overhunting, which shows that Indian populations can have effects on game populations, at least at local levels. Also, the effect of other predators, like wolves, is not clear, and this new ecology of mounted Indians never had a chance to stabilize, so we'll never know whether, ultimately, it would have proved sustainable. Other forces were building that would destroy this way of life shortly after it had been born.

By middle of nineteenth century, there were increasing numbers of reports of starvation among many of the plains tribes, some of whom were reduced to eating their horses. So what had happened to the bison? In the mid-nineteenth century, the Indian population of the plains was boosted by the arrival of some eighty thousand Cherokee, Choctaw, Seminole, Creek, and Chickasaw Indians, who'd been marched west on the Trail of Tears. These were nations who had been evicted from their homelands east of the Mississippi after the passage of the Indian Removal Act in 1830. These tragic events shattered the lives of individuals and nations, but the Trail of Tears also dumped thousands of hungry mouths on to the southern plains, just at a time when the grasslands were entering another dry cycle. In the past, the fringes of the bison's range served as drought refugia, but now they were occupied by increasing numbers of people, both dispossessed Indians and colonists, which effectively stymied that particular adaptation. At the same time, the plains themselves were filling with horses, which have an 80 percent overlap in their diet with bison. So, all in all, things were not looking great for the future of bison-kind.

The increasingly hard times did at least have one positive effect for Plains Indians. They were forced into negotiating peace settlements with each other, but even this was more bad news for bison. With no war-zone refugia, bison could be safely hunted anywhere, and a new element in plains ecology was establishing itself along the rivers, one to which, with the cessation of war, all the Indian tribes would have access—traders of fur and hides.

In the early years of the nineteenth century, the fur trade had been depressed by the glut of skins reaching the markets but was revived by a new fashion for broad-brimmed stovepipe hats fashioned from beaver. By 1830, William Clark, as superintendent of Indian Affairs for the Louisiana territory, was writing of a "very perceptible decrease of the furred animals" that had been so abundant when he and Meriwether Lewis had explored the upper Missouri just a few decades earlier.[26] But in the process, men were making fortunes. The British fur companies had dominated the northern fur trade for more than a century, but the Americans had now also got in on this lucrative act. Perhaps the most famous was John Jacob Astor, who set up the American Fur Company in 1808. Although the heyday of the fur trade wasn't going to last much longer—and Astor wisely moved out of the business a few decades later—the American Fur Company stimulated exploration and exploitation of the plains and the Rockies. And the ensuing competition between the Americans and the British didn't do much for bison.

After the Hudson's Bay Company and the North West Company merged, they needed to encourage Indians to bring the pelts of ever-decreasing beavers to the British rather than the Americans and did so by also offering to buy the relatively worthless bison hides as well. A small market began to grow for these Indian-processed hides as they became fashionable as carriage robes. So Astor responded by shipping bison hides down the Missouri to St. Louis. But bison hides were much heavier than beaver, and at first relatively few could be shipped. Then, Astor launched a steamship, the *Yellowstone*, on the Missouri. On its maiden voyage, it carried George Catlin to paint the Indians whose lives would shortly be transformed by such technology and by 1840, one hundred thousand bison hides were being shipped back east each year.[27]

At first, many of these hides came from the Métis, a tribe whose origins lay in the intermarriage of French coureurs and local Indians. They were key to the northern fur trade and quickly shifted into bison hunting when a market developed. These Métis hunts were huge affairs. According to a very precise Alexander Ross, who witnessed a hunt in 1840 on the Red River, on the borders of South Dakota and Minnesota, 1,210 high-wheeled Red River carts carried 1,630 people to a hunting camp of which four hundred were hunters, responsible for chasing down bison on horseback. That hunt produced 1,375 tongues. Much of the rest of the meat went to waste, since it couldn't be transported, but the Red River carts hauled out the hides for the steadily growing market.

As happened with beaver, the sheer number of hides satiated the market and prices dropped. But by now, the Métis had become good capitalists and materialists, dependent on the luxury goods they acquired in trade. So they intensified the hunt, shipping more hides at lower prices so they could still afford their new lifestyles. By 1876, bison were commercially (and therefore presumably ecologically) extinct in the north and east of their Canadian range. The same events were repeated, with a few variations, among other tribes as the hunts spread south. George Catlin described his experiences with the Sioux in South Dakota:

> When I first arrived at this place [Fort Pierre] . . . which was in the month of May, in 1832 . . . [I was told] that only a few days before I arrived (when an immense herd of buffaloes had showed themselves on the opposite side of the river, almost blackening the plains for a great distance), a party of five or six hundred Sioux Indians on horseback . . . came into the Fort with fourteen hundred fresh buffalo tongues, which were thrown down in a mass, and for which they required but a few gallons of whiskey, which was soon demolished.[28]

The southern herds survived longer, partly because their hides weren't so thick and therefore not as much in demand. But that changed when an effective way was found to tan bison hide. The early trade relied on Indian-prepared hides, treated with the animals' own brains, since bison leather, treated like cattle leather, was not a very satisfactory product. But once techniques had been developed specifically for bison, it proved to be a really tough leather. The British Army marched into war in the Crimea on bison leather soles while bison leather machine belts were soon driving the engines of industry. But this process demanded raw or "green" hides, which are even heavier than treated hides. Luckily for the traders, if not for the bison, railroads had now penetrated the plains and provided the means to ship any number of green hides back east.

The insatiable markets of the East and of Europe meant that the herds disappeared rapidly, no doubt aided by further periods of drought during the second half of nineteenth century. Bison are quite capable of coping with the natural boom and bust cycle of the plains, but now a whole suite of new factors—increased subsistence hunting, competition, and diseases from livestock and worst of all, the market economy—prevented recovery.

There were protests and attempts to pass laws to preserve the herds, all of which failed. Official government policy at the time was not to have one. Bills introduced into Congress in the 1870s were just allowed to die, including one personally vetoed by President Grant. The underpinning philosophy of America during its Gilded Age was to let the markets take their course—a free market fundamentalism that is still the major driving force of the modern world.

There were also a number of people who would be glad to see the last of the bison. Historian Frances Parkman clearly had no liking for the beast: "the world may be searched in vain to find anything of a more ugly and ferocious aspect. At the first sight of him every feeling of sympathy vanishes; no man who has not experienced it, can understand with what keen relish one inflicts his death wound, with what profound contentment he beholds his fall."[29] Grant's interior secretary, Columbus Delano, was another who professed he would rejoice when the last bison was killed. As far as he was concerned, "The civilization of the Indian is impossible while the buffalo remains upon the plains."[30]

It's often stated that there was a deliberate campaign to eradicate Indians by eradicating the basis of their economy. Though one or two military commanders, like General Philip Sheridan, made this suggestion, it's not clear whether the Great Slaughter, as it has come to be called, was actually a widespread conspiracy of genocide. The market economy was all that was needed to reduce plains tribes to abject dependency—and the bison to virtual extinction. As in so many cases, it wasn't hard to predict. Catlin saw as much on his journeys on the *Yellowstone* along the Missouri. "This profligate waste of the lives of these noble and useful animals, when, from all that I could learn, not a skin or a pound of the meat (except the tongues), was brought in, fully supports me in the seemingly extravagant predictions that I have made as to their extinction, which I am certain is near at hand."[31]

Catlin's gloomy prediction very nearly came to pass. By the late 1800s, only a few hundred bison were left. Several small herds still survived in the newly formed Yellowstone National Park, according to the superintendent's report for 1880,[32] where they received at least partial protection—in theory. They could still be hunted as long as not for commercial gain, but they, along with the increasingly rare elk, bighorn sheep, and pronghorns, were also the targets of poachers. Between 1874 and 1875, Superintendent Philetus Norris claimed four thousand elk had been poached from the park, along with numerous bighorn sheep, pronghorn, moose, and bison.

This carnage in a so-called protected area ignited the ire of George Bird Grinnell, editor of the influential *Forest and Stream* magazine, and through him sparked a debate about what exactly national parks are for. In the long term, it helped shape the modern philosophy of national parks, but, in the short term, it didn't help the bison much. By 1902, there were only twenty-two left, in a broad and beautiful valley along the Pelican Creek, by now too precious to be allowed the freedom of this vast valley. They were rounded up into fenced enclosures to become the nucleus of a captive breeding herd.

Elsewhere a few small herds somehow survived on private land. One herd in Montana had its origins in a loose handful of orphaned calves that had imprinted on an Indian bison hunter called Samuel Walking Coyote. These animals bred happily in their semicaptive state, and the herd grew. Walking Coyote eventually sold his animals to two local ranchers, Charles Allard and Michael Pablo, who continued to expand the herd. Similar small private herds were also built up in Texas, Kansas, Nebraska, and South Dakota, mostly by individuals who thought the continent would be a poorer place if it lost this icon of the Great Plains. These were animals that had been bred in semidomestication for several generations and not truly wild bison like the remnant herd in Yellowstone. But beggars can't be choosers, and to build the Yellowstone herd meant buying in some of these animals to augment numbers.

Meanwhile, concerned scientists and sportsmen had formed the National Bison Society, to—among other things—persuade the government to take the bison crisis seriously. In 1908, President Roosevelt signed the bill enabling the National Bison Range to be established in Montana. Thirty-seven descendents of the Allard-Pablo herd were bought to stock the range, with money raised by the National Bison Society from donations right across the country, though, intriguingly not from Kansas, North and South Dakota, and Texas, the four states that could be considered the heartland of the bison's historic range.

The National Bison Range was far from perfect. It was essentially unwanted land and not, strictly speaking, true Great Plains prairie. It is one of the contiguous grassland types called palouse prairie, which is centered on southeastern Washington and Idaho, north of the Snake River, with tendrils extending in Montana, at least according to some definitions. Historically, palouse prairie didn't support bison, but that hasn't bothered the National Bison Range's herd, which thrived and therefore brought into focus another problem with the National Bison Range—its size. At eighteen thousand acres, it didn't take long for the bison to create a herd that was too big.

It's a problem facing all the remnant herds, which have to be managed to prevent their overgrazing the range, a symptom of the biggest problem facing the Great Plains. The largest grasslands on the planet have been reduced to tiny remnants, too small to accommodate the bison's traditional migration patterns or the vast towns of prairie dogs. These fragments of the sea of grass are now surrounded by a sea of agriculture or grazing land sown with alien grasses. And a great stillness has descended on the Plains.

CHAPTER 19

Devils in Paradise

There's nothing more magical than sunset over the tallgrass prairie. I saw my first at Tallgrass Prairie Preserve in Oklahoma, and as always when there are so many new plants, insects, and birds to meet, time loses its meaning. Standing among shoulder-high big bluestem, the autumnal yellows of goldenrod and sunflowers are emphasized by the glowing orange ball on the horizon. And then the evening performance of the song dogs begins. As coyote answers coyote, their exhilarating calls seem to bounce around the prairie horizon, wild yips and yodels that kept me sitting among the big bluestem until the sky had turned from deep blue to black. But, as I tried to find the car in the now almost complete darkness, it struck me that the sounds that kept me riveted until far too late should really have been the howls of wolves. The little song dog has done well across the United States because its larger cousin and serious competitor, the gray wolf, has all but disappeared.

The story of the gray wolf's demise is a long one, and it reveals much about our attitudes, both historical and modern, to the world around us. In the previous chapters, it has become clear that the reasons behind most of the devastating impacts on North America over the last five hundred years can be laid at the door of commercial exploitation, of what has now become the modern paradigm of a free market economy. But the story of the wolf highlights an entirely different philosophy, a mindset that sees the wolf as a symbol of wild nature, something to be loathed and feared—and something that must be vanquished as civilization prevails over wilderness. This is not a story of blind market forces but of blind hatred, and I've left this aspect of our relationship with nature until the final steps of our exploration because understanding this mindset is crucial to creating a new future for humanity in nature.

The story of the vanquishing of the wolf and the conversion of the prairies to farms symbolizes both the bending of the natural world to our will and humanity's separation from nature, or at least the *idea* that we are apart from nature, somehow special and immune to the vagaries of the natural world. Nothing could be further from the truth, but until that reality sinks in, we will make only faltering progress toward a viable future. And it's in our attitudes to the ultimate symbol of untamed nature that we can gauge our progress toward this vital understanding.

The story of the gray wolf began long before the Pilgrim Fathers stepped ashore and started their campaign to drive back the devils that inhabited this "waste and howling wilderness." By then, the wolf had already been exterminated across much of Europe. Now this campaign would spread with ruthless efficiency across the New World, though Canada's and Alaska's wolves fared far better in their remote forests and tundra than those in the rest of the United States or in Mexico. All predators and competitors for ranching and farming were targeted, but wolves were different; they touched a raw nerve in civilized humans. Their slaughter was carried out with a zeal that bordered on paranoia. And no death was too harsh or cruel. John James Audubon, for whom one of America's largest conservation organizations is named, described watching three wolves, captured by a sheep farmer, being hamstrung then torn apart by dogs. Audubon was astounded by the farmer's ingenuity in capturing the animals, but not by the mode of their death. This was appropriate treatment for wolves—the least that these devils in fur deserved.

A few years ago, I made a film, called *Animal Devil*, for National Geographic and NDR, a German TV network. It concerned the reasons why our culture (though not always others) saw certain animals as evil, and in the course of interviewing historians, psychologists, and zoologists, it became clear that the wolf's big problem was that it was never judged simply as a wolf. Instead, it had the worst attributes of humanity heaped on its head, the embodiment of all that was evil in human society. So, not surprisingly, it engendered a deep-seated fear and loathing that has never abated over the centuries.

Edward Wilson, of Harvard University, has pointed out a particular limitation of our perceptions that doesn't help when it comes to a rational view of wolves: "Ecological and evolutionary time, spanning centuries and millennia, can be conceived in an intellectual mode but has no immediate emotional impact."[1] Most people respond to the world primarily at an emotional level, and that leads to some serious misconceptions about nature. Wolves should be seen as wolves, as products of natural selection and not judged by human standards. Nothing in nature is evil. Good and evil, fairness and unfairness have no meaning at all in a world shaped by natural selection. But that's a hard, even frightening, concept for many people, so we continue to judge wolves by our own moral criteria, which is as pointless as accusing a virus of maliciously giving us a cold. It's also a view that meant wolves would never survive the coming of colonists to the plains. Of course, wolves, along with other predators, were a threat to the livelihood of farmers and ranchers, so there were rational reasons to hunt down these animals but the campaign against wolves was waged with irrational vigor.

The wolves of the central grasslands lasted longer than those on the east coast since the plains escaped early settlement. One hunter along the Arkansas River in 1859 saw a herd of eight thousand bison being trailed by forty "big gray wolves," and earlier still, in 1841, a large band of bison along the same river was accompanied by two hundred wolves.[2] Further north, Lewis and Clark saw so many wolves in some places that they declined to give estimates of their numbers, in case it cast doubt on the accuracy of their reports.[3]

Such numbers survived because the vast open spaces of the prairies did not entice colonists, who viewed the grasslands as a place to cross as quickly as possible. But by the time the United States came into being at the end of the eighteenth century, colonization of the West was seen as vital to the development of the nation as a true democracy, and Thomas Jefferson had a clear vision of exactly how that should happen.

In Jefferson's mind, the creation of a true democracy lay hand in hand with the creation of a West of yeoman farmers—bad news for the wolves, since farmers and predators have never mixed. Jefferson reasoned that if each farmer was given just enough land to feed his family and grow a small surplus for sale, they would be immune to the tyranny of the power hungry and become the foundation of a fully democratic nation. He once confided in James Madison: "I think our governments will remain virtuous for many centuries as long as they are chiefly agricultural; and this will be as long as there shall be vacant lands in any part of America. When they get piled upon one another in large cities, as in Europe, they will become corrupt as in Europe."[4]

The scaffolding on which this agrarian future would be built was the Jeffersonian grid, both a practical means of dividing up the western lands and a symbolic overlay of the rational mind on the vagaries of wild nature. Straight lines, east to west and north to south, were drawn across the map, dividing it into areas of six miles by six miles. Each block was then subdivided further into sections, and finally each section turned into four quarter sections, each of 160 acres—the exact amount of land, it was calculated, that would be needed by each farmer to build this Jeffersonian democracy. The legacy of this idea is still visible today. Look out of an airplane window flying across the Midwest and there's little left to see of the way nature designed the plains. Instead, there is a relentless grid of north/south and east/west roads, the manifestation of Jefferson's tidy and rational mind.

But there were substantial practical problems to overcome before this agrarian democracy could be born—not least the prairie itself. Tallgrass prairie, the nearest to the centers of civilization in the east and therefore the first to be settled, grew out of rich, deep soil, to which it clung tenaciously. Every square yard of grass was supported by twenty-five miles of roots and rootlets, packed so tightly that no plough could break through it. It would take new technology to break the prairie sod, but that was something that the United States, born out of the Age of Enlightenment, put great faith in.

The leaping yellow deer logo of John Deere is a familiar and frequent sight while driving anywhere in the Midwest, advertising modern, high-tech, and often immense machines for today's farmers. The first John Deere though, in 1837, was a more modest instrument, a new self-scouring plow, invented by the man himself, that made plowing more efficient as farmers began to tackle the tallgrass prairie. At the same time, carpenters in Chicago invented balloon frame houses, lightweight structures cleverly braced with small timbers, another technological fix to make life possible in a place where there wasn't enough big timber to build houses in the traditional style.

But even the John Deere plow often snapped in the prairie sod, and it wasn't until 1868 that John Lane, Jr.—a name you don't see while driving around the Midwest—invented a "soft center" steel plough that could cope with all those roots. Apparently, cracks as loud as pistol shots echoed across the prairies as the plough finally broke the sod and snapped the grass roots. But the farmers' efforts were worth it: the rich soils beneath the tallgrass yielded good crops. Establishing Jefferson's democracy further west would prove somewhat more difficult.

After Lewis and Clark, several other expeditions headed west along the Missouri and then along its tributaries, to explore more of the high plains and the short grass prairie. Major Stephen Long's expedition was accompanied by trained naturalists and artists, the first truly successful scientific exploration into the Louisiana Territory since the earlier Red River Expedition, with naturalist Peter Custis, had been turned back by Spanish soldiers in the disputed border zone in the Southwest. On the Long Expedition, Edwin James, Titian

Peale and Thomas Say, who was the great grandson of pioneering naturalist John Bartram, kept copious notes of their journey as they left the Missouri and followed the Platte through short grass country. They didn't seem to relish this country as much as Lewis and Clark, though at least the abundance of wildlife—of hares, eagles, badgers, ravens, and owls—"in some measure relieved the uniformity of cheerless scenery."[5]

Some of the wildlife proved less inspirational. Often clouds of insects filled the air, including some spectacular sounding (at least to an entomologist) horseflies. Titian Peale blamed these flies for the fact that their horses occasionally bolted off across the prairie. "June 29. Kenna returned at sunrise without the horse or having seen anything of her. On the prairies there is a species of green headed fly which torments horses and cattle so much that crossing the prairies in the day is next to impossible. This, I believe, was the cause of our horse running away. It is said that these flies will sometimes kill a horse, therefore in crossing prairies travelers mostly turn night into day and day into night."[6]

As they moved into higher and drier country, cacti became more frequent and so did comparisons to the deserts of Arabia, which, though a bit extreme, showed how they viewed the land they were crossing. When Long completed the maps of the territory that he'd surveyed, he labeled these short grass prairies as the "Great American Desert." As far as they were concerned, the land was totally unsuited to agriculture, though Edwin James conceded that "wells may be made to supply the deficiency of running water," which, in the end, would turn out to be a very prescient comment.

What was needed was a new way of approaching agriculture, a way suggested by John Wesley Powell. Powell is most famous for the brave (or perhaps foolhardy) act of shooting the then-unknown rapids on the Colorado River in wooden boats. He might have been better known as the creator of an agrarian West had his suggestions been taken seriously. Powell realized that the West was arid—not an Arabian-style desert but still too dry for a conventional approach to agriculture. In order to pursue the Jeffersonian ideal, he suggested that farmers should only have eighty acres, since that was all they could be expected to irrigate on their own, without having to resort to cooperatives to run bigger irrigation schemes, thus creating the conditions that might allow the development of big, powerful companies.

Most of the land he saw as suitable only as grazing and, since no one could realistically be expected to survive on 160 acres of short grass grazing, here he suggested that settlers were given four full sections, or 2,560 acres. And, most heretical of all, he made the outrageous suggestion that the Jeffersonian grid be ignored. Instead he suggested that the allotment of land should follow nature's contours, taking advantage of local geology, topography, and hydrology.[7] He also suggested that settlement in the arid West should be at a much lower density, following the model that was being established by one of the first groups of farmers to move west — the Mormons.

If anyone should have been able to break the rigid mold of thinking and adapt to the West, rather than imposing on it enlightenment ideals, it should have been the Mormons. They began by preaching a very different philosophy from most colonists. The Book of Mormon taught that Indians were descended from a lost tribe of Israel, the Lamanites, and had received a visit from Christ after his crucifixion. And the founder of the movement, Joseph Smith, preached that the Latter Day Saints were "not to kill any animals or birds, or anything created by Almighty God that had life, for the sake of destroying it." And more than anyone, they should have understood that the symbolic wolf was not the same as those that followed the bison herds on the plains, since they too had been labeled as wolves. Smith had founded a town in Illinois that he called Nauvoo, but, as time passed, people in the surrounding towns grew more intolerant of the Mormons and their strange ideas. These feelings culminated, in 1844, in what has sometimes been called the "Mormon War in Illinois." A large number of people gathered in the neighboring town of Warsaw, supposedly for a great wolf hunt, though everyone knew that the wolves they were hunting were in fact Mormons. The Mormons were driven from Illinois and began their trek to the West.

On the trail, they were harassed by real wolves and soon forgot the words of Joseph Smith. The exiled wolves began killing the wolves of the plains, and by their second winter in Utah, they had organized two teams of wolf hunters to stop "so much annoyance from wolves howling at night and depredations committed by foxes, catamounts [pumas], ravens and other animals." The two teams competed against each other to see who could kill the most predators, and the side with the smaller total would have to host a dinner and dance for the winners. The tally of just two months of hunting illustrates the number of wolves that loped through Utah's mountain valleys in the middle of the nineteenth century. The first team brought back eighty-four, the second 247. But, unwilling to stump up for the dinner and dance, the first team negotiated a four-day extension and came back with another 783 wolves. So, in the end, the attitude to wolves doesn't seem to have changed much in the time between the Pilgrim Fathers and the Latter Day Saints.

The Mormons moved west to reestablish the purity of Christianity as they saw it, and it wasn't long before the old biblical symbolism, of Christ as the Shepherd leading his flock, cast the wolf in the role of the Devil. But they also found another Bible story playing itself out in harsh reality, another threat to settled civilization even more immediate than wolves. When they arrived at the future site of Salt Lake City in 1847, they found the local Indians harvesting huge numbers of crickets and grasshoppers by driving them into fires. Dried and roasted, the crickets would provide winter food.[8]

Crickets and grasshoppers existed (and still do at times) in extraordinary numbers across the grasslands, a curse for farmers but an abundant source of food for those without the strange prejudices of Western civilization. One later group of Mormons, caught by winter as they crossed the plains, preferred to eat their leather shoes rather than resorting to insects. But if the Mormons refused to eat the crickets, the crickets certainly didn't turn their noses up (or rather their antennae) at the Mormon's crops. Just a year after they arrived, the Latter Day Saints faced a plague of truly biblical proportions.

The culprit is now known as the Mormon cricket, though it is actually a flightless katydid that in some years can appear in extraordinary numbers. One of those years was 1848, after the Mormon colony had struggled through their first tough winter in Utah. In late May, they watched as their crops were ravaged by marching hoards of Mormon crickets. One pioneer described "thousands of tons" of insects overrunning his crops, others stood helpless as they recorded armies reckoned in millions destroying their livelihood. All they could do was pray and on June 9, the Lord saw fit to answer their prayers. "The sea gulls have come in large flocks from the lake [Great Salt Lake] and sweep the crickets as they go; it seems the hand of the Lord is in our favor."[9] These were California gulls from the huge nesting colony on Great Salt Lake. They apparently ate the katydids then regurgitated them so they could eat more, until the plague was wiped out. The event became known as the "Miracle of the Gulls," commemorated in 1913 by the erection of Seagull Monument on Temple Square in Salt Lake City. Or so the story goes.

Mormon crickets still return to plague the mountain valleys in certain years, though usually without the intervention of divinely inspired gulls. In 1985, the katydid army was once again on the march in their millions, and though a few gulls watched with interest, they made no attempt to eat the insects.[10] Stick your nose close to a Mormon cricket and you'll smell a pungent aroma. That's because they're protected by a chemical defense that gives them an unpleasant taste, which explains why the gulls in 1985 left them alone. In fact, researchers in that year found no evidence of any vertebrate bothering with this foul-smelling food.

It could also explain why the gulls in 1848 regurgitated their first mouthfuls when they arrived on the Mormon fields. But why the difference in behavior between nineteenth- and twentieth-century gulls? It's been said that the gulls have simply lost their taste for Mormon crickets, though some biologists now think that Mormon cricket flavor is so disgusting that gulls never had the taste in the first place. A few California gulls have been recorded sampling an occasional mouthful, but not with enough enthusiasm to stop a plague in its tracks. Instead, the Mormon crickets of the great plague had probably reached the end of their life cycle. They had laid their eggs and simply died.

Plagues still happen, even today. One in 2001 caused $25 million damage to a million and half acres in Central Utah. But even these apocalyptic plagues don't always behave as our expectations dictate; they don't necessarily devour every last plant in their path. In 2005, researchers looking more closely at a one-kilometer-long army of Mormon crickets marching across Utah were surprised to find many plants left intact. The crickets were after protein and salt, devouring the protein-rich parts of plants such as seed pods, along with mammal feces and even urine-soaked soil.[11] And the most convenient package of protein and salt is another Mormon cricket. Any that fall behind the pace are soon devoured, so it seems that the marching millions are in fact marching to avoid being eaten by the katydids following up behind.

But mere millions of Mormon Crickets are insignificant when compared to the greatest insect spectacle of the plains—perhaps the greatest insect spectacle in the world. On June 15, 1875, Albert Child was standing on the porch of an office on the edge of the small frontier town of Cedar Creek in Cass County, Nebraska. He gazed out over the endless prairie and watched the horizon darken as clouds built up. At long last rain might fall and bring life to parched frontier farms—but instead these clouds brought death and destruction. As the cloud approached it was clearly moving under its own power, and Albert couldn't see any end to it in either direction.

And then suddenly it was on him, a trillion beating wings and biting jaws. Another swarm of Rocky Mountain locusts had descended from the mountains to plague hard-pressed frontier farmers on the plains. But Albert was no farmer. He was a scientist so he set about trying to measure the scale of the swarm—and what he found was truly astounding.

Using the telegraph, he sent messages up and down the line and found the swarm front to be unbroken for 110 miles. With his telescope he estimated the swarm to be over half a mile deep, and he watched it pass for "five full days." He worked out that the locusts were traveling at around fifteen miles an hour and came up with the astonishing fact that the swarm was 1,800 miles long. This swarm covered 198,000 square miles, or, if it was transposed on to the east coast, it would have covered all the states of Connecticut, Delaware, Pennsylvania, Maryland, Maine, Massachusetts, New Jersey, New York, New Hampshire, Rhode Island, and Vermont. And you thought Hitchcock's *The Birds* was frightening.

Albert Child had recorded the largest ever swarm—the biggest aggregation of animals ever seen on planet Earth. In contrast, the largest swarm of desert locusts in Africa covered no more than a few hundred square miles.

Albert Child was also a meteorologist, and so measured weather and wind conditions at the same time. This allowed later scientists to work out that it was a particular combination of drought and the strength and position of a conveyor belt of air called the "Great Plains low level jet" that gave rise to history's largest ever swarm. For these coincidences, University of Wyoming entomologist Jeffrey Lockwood has dubbed it the "Perfect Swarm."[12]

But although Albert's swarm was the largest, countless other vast swarms descended on struggling farmers through the mid- and late 1800s. Maybe some were even bigger, but went unrecorded by scientists. Indeed, Lockwood suggests that the Rocky Mountain locust shaped the nature of the American frontier. They were seen as an unstoppable plague, a natural force so powerful that it had the power to halt the westward expansion of civilization. They left nothing but desolation in their wake, eating everything "down to window blinds and the green paint." There are even horrific descriptions of sleeping soldiers being covered from head to foot in seconds by three-inch-long insects desperate for anything to eat. Occasionally swarms came to grief in places like the Great Salt Lake from where there are descriptions of vast mounds of putrefying insects lining the shoreline, creating unbearable smells for many miles downwind.

The scale of these outbreaks is astounding enough, but what makes this story truly amazing is the fact that by the start of the twentieth century, the Rocky Mountain locust had apparently disappeared—extinct. How could the world's most numerous species go from Albert's swarm, numbered in trillions, to oblivion in just a few decades? How did civilization conquer this overwhelming force of wild nature?

It took a long time to realize that the Rocky Mountain locust had indeed vanished, and even then no one could work out how or why it had happened. It was just too unbelievable. Many theories were put forward. Were they somehow linked to the great bison herds that roamed the plains, and that only just survived the locust's fate around the same time? Perhaps the disturbed ground left as the great herds passed was vital for successful egg laying. Or were they victims of climate change? Were they poisoned by the introduction of new crop plants? All these theories had some merit.

But no one at the time could have worked out the true answer, because no one at the turn of the century knew about a bizarre feature of the locust's life cycle. That part of the story took place in the 1920s, six thousand miles due east of Nebraska, around the Black Sea. A Russian scientist called Boris Uvarov, working on the migratory locusts that plagued local farmers, came to realize that two distinct species he had in his collection were in fact only one. One was a harmless grasshopper, the other the devastating locust of biblical plagues, but Uvarov worked out that when the density of the harmless grasshoppers became great enough it threw a genetic switch, causing the next generation to mature into long-winged, swarming locusts. And that clever piece of entomology got American scientists wondering.

Maybe the Rocky Mountain locust wasn't extinct after all. Maybe it still existed as a solitary grasshopper somewhere in the mountains. There were several possible candidates, each championed by different entomologists, but no one could be definitive. What was needed was genetic proof, but there are pitifully few Rocky Mountain locusts in insect collections, and these are all old and dried.

For some time there had been rumors that some of the glaciers high in the Rockies contained trapped and frozen insects, though no one paid them much attention until a few years ago when Jeffrey Lockwood wondered whether they could be the remains of swarms of Rocky Mountain locusts that had foundered on the great sheets of mountain ice. But now, at the start of the twenty-first century, solving the mystery of the locusts had become a race against time. Global warming is causing these glaciers to melt at alarming rates, dumping their precious, preserved cargo into muddy pools of meltwater where it rots away.

The journey to these glaciers is hard and dangerous, and the first few expeditions yielded nothing of great value. Finally, the team of scientists made the difficult ascent to Knife Point Glacier and hit the mother lode. Preserved in the fast melting ice were hundreds of bodies, which did indeed turn out to be Rocky Mountain locusts. They were well enough preserved for genetic analysis to prove that the Rocky Mountain locust was not hiding in the mountains in disguise. It really was extinct and after nearly a century the hunt for the cause was on again.

New analysis of all the old theories gradually ruled out each one until nothing was left. Nothing seemed big enough to account for the demise of something so abundant. It wasn't until Lockwood was driving with a colleague on one of those endless journeys across the plains, talking about anything and everything to stay awake, that he hit on an idea. The conversation had turned to the plight of another insect—the monarch butterfly. Once hugely abundant all over North America, its numbers have fallen dramatically in recent times, but there's no mystery here. Every year, monarchs from most of the continent migrate to a few groves of trees in the Mexican mountains, where they settle in spectacular swarms of tens of millions of butterflies. Despite protection, some of these groves are being logged illegally. In 2004, a mere 100 million butterflies were recorded, which sounds impressive until you realize that this is just 10 percent of the truly astounding numbers wintering here in the 1990s. After 2004, numbers have risen again, but illegal logging is also accelerating, so just a handful of desperately poor Mexicans could yet wipe out most of the monarch population of the entire North American continent.

What if the Rocky Mountain locust had a similar vulnerable period in its life cycle, perhaps when it existed in its solitary grasshopper phase? Wading through mountains of reports from the nineteenth century suggested to Lockwood that in all likelihood the solitary phase was confined to a few high mountain valleys, bordering rivers. It was from here that they would erupt every few years in uncountable numbers, but between swarms they existed over a very small range.

In the late 1800s, gold was discovered in the Rockies, and though the prospectors didn't head for the locusts' sanctuary, this vast influx of people needed feeding. Farmers followed the rush to exploit new found wealth by selling supplies—and *they* set up in the grassy river valleys. Plowing and trampling by cattle destroyed eggs, and careful calculations by the scientists showed that even such a relatively small number of farmers could have effectively removed the greatest threat to frontier farming (and the world's greatest insect spectacle). That an insect of such astounding abundance could be wiped out by so few people should sound the very loudest of alarm bells for the monarch.

Free of the scourge of locust plagues, farming would continue to change the nature of the plains. In the wake of the Mormons, more and more people traveled west, borne on the crest of a wave of blind optimism. The lack of trees should have warned them that this land was very different from the places they had left behind back east, but they were told not to worry—the climate was improving. Besides, it was thought that the action of iron wheels on iron railroads and electrical activity in the telegraph wires would stimulate clouds to drop rain on their labors. And later the saying that "rain follows the plow" became a very familiar refrain—the latest round in the centuries-old game of paradise publicity to encourage settlement and exploitation.

Yet, at first, rain really did seem to follow the plow. What the farmers didn't know was that, in the middle of the nineteenth century, they just happened to be moving west during one of the plain's wet phases. To encourage the development of Jefferson's agrarian democracy in the West, the middle of the nineteenth century saw increased calls to give free access to the 160-acre plots to would-be yeoman farmers. A Homestead Act enshrining in law the concept of free western land was the vision of many, but such an act was embroiled in dispute, particularly with the southern states, who saw it as part of the campaign against legal slavery in the new territories, and by big land companies, who had their own designs on all that free federal land out west.

The act may never have seen the light of day had it not been embraced by Horace Greeley, most famous for his advice to "Go West Young Man!" (even though these were originally the words of John Soule of Indiana). Greeley was the editor of the *New York Tribune* and an emancipation campaigner, which earned him the respect of Abe Lincoln. Lincoln's newly formed Republican Party championed the rights of poor working men in the east and embraced the idea of a Homestead Act, though not because of any hidden socialist ideals, but because it wanted a freer market, without unfair competition from the slavery economy in the South.

A year after Lincoln became president, the Homestead Act became law. But it was no victory for the little man. Large tracts of public land had already been sold to speculators and, as in Florida's swamps, railroad companies had received huge land parcels. Once they had run their railroads through this land, it could be sold at top dollar, since it was now connected to the rest of the world and to the market economy. A pamphlet, published ten years after the Homestead Act became law, trumpeted the fact that the Act had prevented a large-scale landgrab in the West, but was, in the words of western historians Robert Hine and John Faragher, a barefaced lie.[13]

The yeoman farmers that followed Greeley's advice started off at a disadvantage, since much of the best land had already gone. Later in the century, when a dry phase returned, many were driven back east in abject poverty. At the start of the twentieth century, the rains returned, and at the same time, a single event in Europe sparked a massive renewed migration back to the plains.

In the summer of 1914, Archduke Franz Ferdinand of Austria was assassinated in Sarajevo, triggering a cascade of events that led to World War I. That in turn led to a massive market for American wheat; the Great War drove the Great Plow Up, as the frenetic turning of the sod on vast acres of prairies was called. At the end of the war, western farmers were an integral part of the economy and encouraged through increasing mechanization and subsidies to expand production.

Then the jet stream shifted, the rains failed (again), and the winds came. Short grasses are only short above ground, and denuded of those countless miles of grass roots, the prairie soil simply blew away.[14] During the worst storms, in 1935, the visibility across most of the nation's midsection was virtually zero. The Dust Bowl years brought terrible hardships to the farmers, and as the dust storms blew into Washington, D.C., soil conservation measures were hastily enacted. Large areas of croplands were reseeded to grazing land, though usually with exotic species of grasses instead of the native bunch grasses.

Many of the stories we've seen in the previous pages show that history teaches powerful lessons in ecology, but none more so than the Dust Bowl. Yet, by 1968, Nixon's secretary of agriculture, Earl Butz, was urging farmers to plow from fence row to fence row, and industrialize their techniques to expand production. Unfortunately, the plains climate continues its ancient oscillation regardless of the aspirations of politicians. By 1982, croplands were losing an average of eight tons of top soil from every acre, every year—as bad as the more famous Dust Bowl of the 1930s.

And all these western farms depend on water pumped up from the ground on a scale so vast that—despite Powell's prescience in the previous century—the development of large corporations, and the inevitable concentration of power, was inevitable. The drive to industrialized farming has also meant fewer but larger farms, dependent on the oil industry for chemicals and fuels. It's been said that modern agriculture is merely a machine for turning oil into food and, in the process, further concentrates power in the hands of monolithic corporations. So much for the agrarian democracy. Market forces and subsidies have shaped a West as different from Jefferson's vision as is possible—he must be turning in his grave.

But farmers were only one force to change the nature of North America's grasslands. The other gave rise to the most enduring image of the open range—the cowboy. Cows have always done well in the New World. Large, semiwild herds were roaming the interior of the Caribbean Islands shortly after Columbus arrived, and it wasn't long before even larger herds were grazing the grasslands of California and the Southwest. In their semiwild state, they evolved into creatures that, like the bison, migrated over the plains in search of grazing and defended themselves against the plains predators. This impressive beast came to be known as the Texas longhorn and was said, by those who should know, to be fifty times as dangerous as a bison.

Cattle herding began in the Spanish colonies where it was influenced by the ideas of nomadic African pastoralists, brought to the New World in the holds of slave ships. Cattle ranches spread rapidly throughout New Spain, but the Great Plains proved perfect for this lifestyle: endless acres of grass from which the native grazers were being rapidly eliminated. It was here that the Spanish *vaquero* became anglicized to "buckaroo" and gave us the familiar cowboy, with his chaps and lariat, two of the many cowboy terms that are also derived from Spanish.

Cattle ranching became the new boom industry around the middle of the nineteenth century as thousands of inexperienced entrepreneurs drove vast herds onto the public lands of the West. A depression in the United States in the 1870s forced ranchers to sell their beef to the United Kingdom, which proved a very fruitful market—so successful that many British businessmen saw good business opportunities out west. Before long, these entrepreneurs controlled huge herds on America's plains. Granville Stuart, one such cattle baron, described how quickly the plains of Montana were transformed by this new industrial scale ranching. "In 1880, the country was practically uninhabited. . . . Thousands of buffalo darkened the rolling plains. There were deer, elk, wolves and coyotes on every hill and in every ravine and thicket. . . . In the fall of 1883 there was not a buffalo remaining on the range, and the antelope, deer, and elk were indeed scarce. In 1880 no one had heard of a cowboy in 'this niche of the woods'. . . but in the fall of 1883, there were 600,000 head of cattle on the range. The cowboy had become an institution."[15]

But, in the words of environmental historian Donald Worster, the first quarter century of ranching, between 1865 and 1890, was an unmitigated disaster.[16] Driven by the profits to be made from ranching, so many cattle were herded on to the plains that the grass gave out. Large areas were denuded, contributing (perhaps even a major contributor) to the dust storms that swept over the plains in later years. The half-starved herds, taken north in search of better grazing, were in no condition to face a freezing northern plains winter, and the cattle boom became a bust. Granville Stuart lost $20 million in the particularly vicious winter of 1885–86, and elsewhere there are descriptions of cattle carcasses filling ditches for miles on end. It took some time to recover, but as it did, short-horned cattle replaced the longhorns, which were themselves hunted to such an extent that, like the bison they replaced, they too needed a conservation program to ensure their future. In 1927, Congress passed legislation enabling a national herd to be established, though at the time only three bulls and twenty cows could be found.

The shorthorns brought more changes to the plains. Bred in wetter climates, they were much less suited to life on the dry plains and spent as much time as they could along streams and rivers, where they trampled the bankside vegetation into oblivion. Increased sediment in the rivers endangered native fish species, many of which are still rare today. Of 150 species native to the West, 122 are either extinct, endangered, or candidates for listing under the Endangered Species Act (ESA). The shorthorns also polluted the rivers with their waste. It's been estimated that cows grazing around the streams of the Greater Yellowstone Ecosystem produce as much sewage as a city of 1.6 million people, much of which ends up, untreated, in the water. These cows are also fattened on corn, to produce a more marbled, better flavored but ultimately unhealthier meat. Seventy percent of the corn grown in the Midwest goes to feed cows, a self-stimulating, mixed farming/ranching economy that has now spread over most of the plains.

The wolves that Granville Stuart described when he gazed over Montana's plains in 1880 could no more be tolerated by cattlemen (or sheepherders) than by farmers. They too waged all out war on wolves and other predators until the start of the twentieth century, when predator control was seen as so important to the national economy that the federal government took on the war using professional hunters working for the newly formed Bureau of Biological Survey. This war also benefited sports hunters, since herds of deer and elk, protected from the depredations of vicious predators, grew larger. Predators were also eliminated from national parks, on the grounds that people came to see nice animals like deer, not vicious predators.

The campaign against wolves would prove a great success. Eventually, they were completely eliminated from the lower forty-eight states, with the exception of a small population in Minnesota and another in upper Michigan. But the last few wolves on the plains proved very difficult to track down and kill. Wise to all the hunter's tricks, wary and suspicious, these wolves were often loners—necessarily so, after the rest of their packs had been killed. Many became celebrities, and their rise to fame helped engender a new attitude to the wolf and to the West.

At the time, these "last wolves" were usually described as larger, more cunning, and more vicious than their more mortal brethren. A South Dakota newspaper described one such wolf as "The cruelest, the most sagacious and most successful animal outlaw . . . the master criminal of the animal world." Another paper claimed that this wolf was the offspring of a mating between a wolf and a mountain lion with "the craftiness of both and the cruelty of hell." Such an animal deserved a name, and he was given one—the Custer Wolf.

He was reputedly responsible for killing five hundred horses, cows, and calves worth $25,000 and seemed unstoppable. A $500 bounty on his head (more than many human criminals) drew many eager hunters, though all failed. So when, in 1920, professional hunter Harry Percival Williams, was ordered by the Bureau of Biological Survey to go to South Dakota and not to come back until he had killed the Custer Wolf he knew he "was in for it."

Williams went to enormous lengths to fool the Custer Wolf. He boiled his traps for half a day then buried them in cow manure for several days to mask any human scent. Once prepared they were stored in cowhide bags, and when he was setting them he was careful to first throw down a cowhide before dismounting, so he didn't leave any scent on the ground. He also sprinkled the area with female wolf scent.

The Custer Wolf ignored all these traps, though near one he had begun to dig out a former den. Perhaps, Williams thought, stimulated by the female scent, he had hoped he might soon find another mate. Nothing Williams tried seemed to work, though he often caught glimpses of the wolf trailing him along a parallel ridge, stopping when he stopped. If Williams reached for his tobacco pouch, the wolf watched with interest, but if he reached for his rifle, the Custer Wolf simply vanished.

The wolf was sometimes warned of Williams's presence by a pair of coyotes, so to even up the sides a little, Williams shot the coyotes. Since he didn't want to let old Custer know that his early warning system was no longer operating, he tossed the bodies of the coyotes into a deep ravine, only to return the next day to find their bodies dragged back to the top and left in plain view for Williams to find.

Later, Williams found the Custer Wolf feeding at a carcass so he set his elaborately prepared traps around it. But more often than not, the wolf just pulled the carcass across the traps to spring them. It seemed to Williams that the wolf was playing games with him—and that gave him an idea. He dragged a carcass several hundred yards from where the wolf had been feeding on it, and sure enough old Custer dragged it back to where it was originally. So Williams dragged it back again, and this time set traps along the route. The next morning he found that the wolf had been so keen on playing his part of the game, he had carelessly stepped on one of the traps. In his panic he had dragged the trap off, leaving an easy to follow trail.

Old Custer had run for three miles encumbered by the heavy steel trap and when Williams caught up, the wolf was exhausted and dripping blood from a mouth full of cracked and broken teeth as he had tried to bite off the trap. Williams shot him and ended the seven-month game.

There's a photograph of the Custer Wolf, propped up in rigor, head bowed as if in submission, taken when this supernatural devil was shown to the local townsfolk. They were disappointed. He was just an ordinary-sized, ordinary-looking wolf, though perhaps with an extraordinary tenacity for life. Williams didn't say much at the time, but in an interview forty years later, he said: "I remember all the trouble and grief he'd caused. But I tell you I'd built up such a respect for the old devil that, if he hadn't had a trap on one foot, I just might not have killed him. I really think I might have let him go."[17]

There are many similar stories, of Old Lefty and Three Toes, Phantom and Snowdrift, and perhaps the most famous, Lobo of Currumpaw.

Lobo lived in New Mexico at the end of the nineteenth century, alpha male of a pack of around five animals, including the alpha female, Lobo's mate, Blanca. Like the Custer Wolf, Lobo avoided all traps and seemed to know which bits of a carcass had been poisoned. Eventually, Ernest Thompson Seton decided he would travel to New Mexico to hunt down Lobo and his pack. In time, he succeeded in trapping Blanca, who was roped head and feet and then killed by an effective, if overly brutal method: "We each threw a lasso over the neck of the doomed wolf, and strained our horses in opposite directions until the blood burst from her mouth, her eyes glazed, her limbs stiffened and then fell limp."[18]

As she died, Seton described hearing Lobo's howls for days afterward, with, he fancied, an unmistakable note of sorrow in it. Seton then set 130 steel jaw leghold traps in groups of four and dragged Blanca's body through the traps. Within a few days Lobo was caught, with a trap on all four legs. Seton took him back to a ranch and tied him up in a pasture where he lay quietly gazing at the prairie until, sometime during the night, he died.

Seton later made this story famous, first in *Scribner's Magazine,* then as part of his *Wild Animals I Have Known,* published in 1899. All the "last wolf" stories follow a similar, tragic pattern, somewhat overromanticized though based on actual cases. Seton, for example, described Lobo as dying of a broken heart, sentiments that earned him accusations of being a "nature faker" from William Hornaday, John Burroughs, and even Theodore Roosevelt. Seton responded by spending the next five years researching and writing the two-volume *Life Histories of Northern Animals,* which later was expanded to four volumes as *The Lives of Game Animals* and which earned him the last laugh by winning the John Burroughs Memorial Society's Bronze Medal. Nevertheless, Seton's writing illustrates a common theme in these "last wolf" stories. The animals are seen in a heroic, if tragic, light while humans are portrayed with brutal accuracy.

So, even as the last wolves were being hunted down, their stories sparked an unprecedented attitude to the gray devil (at least among those of European stock)—one that would have been incomprehensible to the Pilgrim Fathers and still is to a whole section of America today. But it was the work of one man in the middle of the twentieth century that did more to spur on this change than perhaps any other.

Aldo Leopold captured this widespread transformation in the moment of his own epiphany. He had been out with a party of men when they came across a she-wolf swimming across a river. On the far side she was greeted by an enthusiastic family of six cubs. Leopold and the others reacted instinctively—they blazed away at the family until the female lay bleeding on the bank and just one cub remained, mortally wounded, dragging itself on to the rocks. "We reached the old wolf in time to watch a fierce green fire dying in her eyes.

I realised then, and have known ever since, that there was something new to me in those eyes—something known only to her and to the mountain."[19]

As these last wolves died and the frontier disappeared, the wolf began to be seen as a nostalgic symbol of lost wilderness, at least among the growing urban masses. Yet wolves survived in good numbers in Canada and Alaska. Surely that symbol could easily be reestablished in the lower forty-eight?

The scheme to reintroduce a creature carrying the weight of so much symbolism—by now both positive and negative—is perhaps the most appropriate place to end our journey through North America's past abundance and the attitudes and forces that have reshaped it so dramatically. Biologically, reintroducing wolves couldn't be simpler. They breed quickly, spread rapidly, and are highly adaptable. They were one of the most successful and widespread mammals on the planet before humans began taming the wilderness. But the reintroduction program fired up many of the arguments and attitudes that we've seen throughout the preceding chapters and through five hundred years of European history in North America. Like all of those stories, it gives cause for optimism and pessimism in equal measure. For some, their attitude to the wolf has hardly changed since the days of the first colonists, while others see the wolf, through misty eyes, as the living embodiment of nature, wild and free, untrammeled by man and symbolic of pristine wilderness. And just a few see the wolf as a wolf and an integral part of the ecosystems that emerged out of the last ice age.

Aldo Leopold had been a game manager and an advocate of making more game available for hunters by eliminating the competition. But watching that dying wolf mother made him realize how impossible it was to manage ecosystems entirely to our own self-interested designs. "I was young then, and full of trigger-itch; I thought that because fewer wolves meant more deer, that no wolves would mean a hunters paradise. But after seeing that green fire die, I sensed that neither the wolf nor the mountain would agree with such a view."[20]

The Disney World–style national parks, free of nasty predators, would simply self-destruct or be prohibitively expensive to maintain. Yet returning the devils to Paradise has been (and still is) fraught with immense difficulties and not just with obvious "ranchers vs. environmentalists" problems. Feelings about wolves run deep, and even the government's own environmental departments couldn't agree over this contentious issue. In both the U.S. Fish and

Wildlife Service and the U.S. National Park Service, people lost their jobs for supporting wolf reintroduction.

Even so, the wolf was one of the first creatures listed when the ESA became law in 1974. But does the ESA have enough teeth for the job? The ESA was undoubtedly a piece of landmark environmental legislation when it was signed, but we've seen that political expediency (to put it politely) can blunt the act's teeth. So, the success or failure of wolf reintroduction was always going to be a stern test of the act's power.

In the past, not surprisingly for such a symbolic animal, a great many of the "facts" about the wolf were nothing of the sort. As always, the real wolf was hidden beneath its mythological guise. But a few people were interested in finding this real wolf. As far back as the 1940s, a pioneering wolf researcher, Adolph Murie, spent a lot of time getting to know the wolf packs around Mount McKinley in Alaska. He described their affectionate and cooperative behavior and their ecological relationships with their prey. But in the 1940s no one was much interested in "real" wolves, and besides, they were no longer a problem in the Lower Forty-eight. However, by the time David Mech published the results of his studies in 1970, public opinion was shifting. His book, *The Wolf,* was a well written but detailed scientific study of wolves, yet it sold widely, to an audience now eager to get to know wolves properly.

The rapid rise in popularity (and number) of wildlife films also helped. Some were sentimentalized and romanticized to a degree that would no doubt have John Burroughs and Teddy Roosevelt spinning in their graves, but many were detailed and intimate portraits of real wolves doing real things, including a beautiful film with Mech himself among the white arctic wolves of Ellesmere Island. All of this created a growing appetite to see wolves returned to the West.

Several areas were outlined as reintroduction zones—the northern Rockies, the western Great Lakes area, and a third area in New Mexico—to support the reintroduction of a different subspecies, the Mexican wolf. In the Rockies, Yellowstone National Park, largely in Wyoming, and the Selway-Bitterroot Wilderness Area, in Idaho, were selected. In addition, the Bob Marshall Wilderness/ Glacier National Park area in northern Montana, where wolves had already crossed the border from Canada under their own steam, was also listed.

Canadian wolves were already turning up in Idaho as well, but were usually shot as soon as they were discovered. As momentum gathered, the prowolf faction was split over whether just to encourage those wolves that were colonizing naturally or to catch suitable packs and shift them to release areas. While this was being argued out, the antiwolf faction was marshalling its own arguments and statutes. Ranchers gloomily predicted the decimation of their herds and the destruction of their way of life, and Idaho passed its own laws prohibiting state employees from assisting with the reintroduction process in any way. In the absence of local managers for the Idaho project, the Nez Perce tribe stepped forward to offer their help in bringing back wolves to the Bitterroots—the first time the U.S. Fish and Wildlife Service had formed a partnership with an Indian nation.

Finally, it was decided to jump-start reintroduction by relocating packs from Canada, but, trying to win round the ranchers, it was also decided to blunt the ESA's teeth from the start. If wolves had colonized naturally they would, in theory, have the full protection of the ESA. In the West, the antiwolf lobby is represented in powerful places, and it may have proved a test too far for the ESA. But translocated wolves could be classified as "experimental" and "nonessential," so giving more scope to eliminate those wolves that ran head-long into trouble.

Even so, ranchers and state officials fought long and hard in the courts to stop the wolves returning. But in January of 1995, wolves were back in Yellowstone. Caught in Alberta, they were moved to acclimation pens, where they could absorb their new surroundings before finally being released into the wild a few months later. Their arrival was greeted with both cheers and groans. The release in Idaho, around the same time, attracted much less publicity, though the Nez Perce organized a ceremony to welcome the wolves home. Tribal elder Horace Axtell, leader of the traditional Seven Drum Religion, offered this hope for the future. "We ask the Creator that wolves may be allowed to run free again, that they be able to live, to be a part of us, to be part of our land, to be a part of the creation for which they were intended."[21]

As expected, the wolves prospered, but the massive impact on ranching hasn't materialized. In order to mitigate livestock losses, the Defenders of Wildlife set up the Bailey Wildlife Foundation Wolf Compensation Trust, to repay ranchers for inevitable losses to wolves and thus blunt the main anti-wolf arguments. In 2006, the fund paid out only $148,000 in total, much less than even they expected.[22]

At this point, I can see some of the ranchers that I've spoken with glaring at me through steam rising off a fresh cup of coffee, paused in mid-sip. The fund only pays out on livestock losses that are confirmed as wolf kills, and a great many losses can't be proved one way or the other, though wolves were the likely culprits. This is certainly true; recent work suggests that wolves may be responsible for up to six times the number of "confirmed" kills. But payments of six times this compensation figure would still just be drops in the ocean of the world's largest economy.

Even for ranchers, losses to wolves (which they are at least partially compensated for) are tiny compared to losses for other reasons. The U.S. Department of Agriculture's own National Agricultural Statistics Service show that losses to wolves in recent years amount to fractions of a percent of the herds and pale into insignificance against losses due to bad weather and disease. And, in recognition of the difficulties inherent in fair payments under the compensation scheme, Defenders of Wildlife now make partial payments in cases where the killer can't be positively identified.

But this doesn't stop the antiwolf campaigners. At the time of writing, the Idaho Anti-Wolf Coalition is trying to gather enough signatures to bring about a vote on whether to eliminate all wolves from the state (again). In Wyoming, some politicians would like to reinstate an open season on wolves and want to see wolves eradicated from all parts of the state apart from a few tiny areas where they might attract tourist dollars.

The wolf reintroduction project may yet become a victim of its own success. As of 2007, there were four thousand wolves in the western Great Lakes recovery area, well above the ESA's stated recovery target of 1,350 wolves. Likewise, the Rockies target of three hundred has easily been surpassed; 1,300 wolves now run wild in the various recovery areas here and have even begun moving between areas. Odd wolves are also turning up in other states from these source populations. In March 2007, the western Great Lakes population was strong enough to be delisted, and the Rockies population followed a year later, in March 2008.

This should have been a cause of great celebration among prowolf people, but instead many wore looks of concern. Once no longer under ESA protection, the responsibility for managing the wolf population passes from federal to state control—and many senior politicians at state level are rubbing their hands in glee at the prospect. C. L. "Butch" Otter, governor of Idaho wants to reduce the Idaho population from 650 animals to one hundred, the minimum recovery figure for this population under the ESA—just enough for the state to remain in control of the wolves' fate. He has also stated that he wants to be the first person to legally shoot a wolf when the Rockies population is delisted. To be strictly accurate, the ESA does already allow wolves to be killed if they are caught harassing livestock, but I think Governor Otter's statement was meant to make his sentiments abundantly clear—which it does.

As part of their notice of delisting, the Fish and Wildlife Service stated that they were happy that each individual state in the range of the northern Rocky Mountain wolf population had committed to maintaining at least fifteen breeding pairs and therefore an overall population of between nine hundred and 1,250 animals. However, conservationists point out that no such commitments are enshrined in state law. And we also need to remember how small a fraction this is of the numbers that roamed here when Lewis and Clark passed through. Most telling of all, in the few months following delisting, a hundred wolves were shot in Wyoming, Montana, and Idaho. Worried by this, conservation groups challenged the ruling in the courts—and won. In July 2008, northern Rocky Mountain wolves regained protection under the ESA and were returned to federal management.

Hunting organizations and pressure groups are also worried about the success of wolf reintroduction. The arguments leveled against wolves by one such group, the Abundant Wildlife Society of North America, based in South Dakota, are very informative on how far our relationship with nature has (or hasn't) come in five hundred years. Apart from inflicting cruel deaths on livestock, wolves also reduce the quantity of game that could otherwise have provided targets for hunters. And, in doing so, they claim, wolves will not restore the "balance of nature."

In actual fact, wolves have been shown to significantly increase diversity by reducing overabundant species like elk. In Yellowstone, in the absence of predators, elk were spending a lot of time along river banks where they were trashing the streamside vegetation. Once wolves returned, the elk found themselves too easy a target here and were forced to disperse more widely. The elk may no longer be as abundant as the Abundant Wildlife Society would like, but the wolves have certainly improved conditions in the park.

It is also argued that wolf reintroduction is—plain and simply—a complete waste of money. First, wolves will reduce the populations of the other animals that the tourists want to see, and second, wolves themselves are so hard to see that most people will hardly ever encounter them. In reality, the Yellowstone wolves are far more visible than anyone thought, but the point is still made. What's the good in having wolves if not for our benefit? It's an argument that cuts to the heart of how we define our place in the natural world.

After staring into the eyes of a dying wolf, Aldo Leopold had an answer to that. "The practice of conservation must spring from a conviction of what is ethically right and aesthetically right, as well as what is economically expedient. A thing is right only when it tends to preserve the integrity, stability and beauty of the community and the community includes the soil, waters, fauna and flora, as well as people."[23]

We are still a long way from such an all inclusive view being commonplace, though a worldview that encompassed some of Leopold's philosophy was prevalent across the continent before the coming of the Europeans. But two such disparate ways of seeing the world were mutually exclusive. I'm not restating the case for the "noble savage" here. Such a stereotype is dehumanizing and as much an insult to real people (many of whom are personal friends) as any other stereotype. But let's not throw the baby out with the bath water. Keen to present a new view of Indians, revisionist historians sometimes present an image that then leans too far the other way.

When Horace Axtell welcomed the wolves home to Idaho, he did so with a wisdom that has been slow to dawn in Western minds. Our mentality has been to preserve and isolate sections of nature, in national parks or wilderness areas, separate from the human world. While that has preserved some wonderful and vital areas it has also fostered the dichotomy between people and the rest of nature. The bottom line is that we are just one part of nature. Whatever we might believe cocooned in our technology, we cannot exist in isolation—an enlightened and humbling perception that lies at the heart of both Indian philosophy and ecological rationale.

CHAPTER 20

A *New World*?

In the previous chapters, I've painted a picture of five hundred years of people and nature in North America in enough detail to illustrate the bewildering complexity of individual cases. The detail was important because it's vital to realize that our interactions with the rest of nature are both complex and varied. However, there is also a simple overarching thrust to the story, from abundance to scarcity. The plethora of historical reports that I've drawn on illustrates that nature was far more abundant in the past than most people realize, so this trajectory is a lot worse than it appears from the perspective of a single lifetime. In this final chapter, I will look for some underlying threads common to all these different examples across space and time to see what lessons they may hold for our future.

The bottom line is that people, like all other animals, are concerned first with their immediate survival and then with garnering as many resources as they can to make their future as secure as possible. But different cultures have different worldviews, and these varied philosophies affect the details of each particular relationship with the natural world. This is well illustrated in the New World: the "discovery" of America was in reality a clash of two very different cultures.

When the first explorers landed on the shores of the New World, nature was extraordinarily and wonderfully abundant, for reasons that were many and varied, but one common factor was often the Indians themselves. They managed the land in ways that weren't always recognized by Europeans, but which often increased natural abundance, at least of some species. In other cases, Indians seem to have reduced (or occasionally eliminated) resources by overexploiting them, though there is evidence from morality tales right across the continent that suggests many nations learned from these past mistakes and encoded the lessons into tribal stories to pass on to future generations.

On the other hand, it seems that some of the most extraordinary spectacles witnessed by explorers and settlers could have been the result of the demise of Indian populations. Released from hunting, animals as varied as fur seals, passenger pigeons, and bison bounced back to enormous populations. The evidence is stronger in some cases than others, so not everyone agrees with these ideas, and I've dealt with individual examples across the continent in the appropriate chapters. But the point I want to make here is that, even if populations were reduced, they were able to bounce back. Whatever stresses the ecosystems may have been under, they were still functioning well enough to recover, often in just a few years. But after Western philosophy swept across the continent this did not always remain so. Some ecosystems, particularly marine ones, have shown no signs of recovery, even under complete protection, while in others recovery has been perilously slow. The European ethos has had a much harder impact on the land, and five hundred years of history shows us why.

Central to the way Europeans saw North America was the emerging idea of capitalism. It began in the New World with private ventures, like those of Raleigh at Roanoke and continued with joint stock companies granted monopolies by the monarch, starting with the Jamestown venture. It evolved into a free market, spurred on in the New World by a growing resentment of control of American resources by a country on the other side of the ocean. Free market fundamentalism is now at the heart of modern capitalism, though ruthless competition still produces big corporations with a concentration of power and the ability to control markets in ways that don't fit entirely with free market ethics.

Skirting around that particular problem, economists like to point out that a truly free market economy should deliver the best deal both to people and their environment, although many examples in the previous pages show that this just isn't so. These economists argue that increasing scarcity should be reflected in increasing prices, which then forces a rise in efficiency in the way that resource is used and, as consumers look for lower priced alternatives, should also reduce its exploitation. In reality, the rise in price often means that it is still worth exploiting that resource especially since technological advances often increase the efficiency of exploitation of scarce resources and maintain, or even increase, profit margins. This is frequently made worse by subsidies, which further disconnect the market from the realities of ecology.

The paradigms of modern free market capitalism are enshrined in the so-called Washington Consensus, one element of which is an obsession with export-led development. The first stages of colonization and exploitation of North America show how destructive this can be. Almost as soon as the New World was discovered, it was connected to an enormous market in Europe and only a little later to another in Asia. These markets sucked up American resources at extraordinary rates.

An extended trading market was nothing new to Europe; trade around the Mediterranean and throughout Europe as far as the British Isles is as old as the Bronze Age and longer trade routes had opened to Asia before Columbus stepped ashore in the Caribbean. But these routes were difficult, overland treks, which meant volume was limited, and goods usually passed through intermediaries, which eroded profits. Indeed it was these difficulties that spurred exploration west across the Atlantic, to find an easier and more controllable sea route to Asia. The New World just happened to get in the way. But once the natural riches of this new land were known, the vast export trade from the Americas could be seen as the first real step on the road to globalization.

Some economists argue that such globalization is not only inevitable but again a good thing, both for people and their environments. It gives poor nations access to the world market, which should increase their prosperity and, as social conditions improve, so should those of the local environment. They point to figures that show declining poverty in the Third World, though in reality, most of these changes are accounted for in just two places—India and China. And in both places, environmental problems are still severe. China, indeed, has now reached the top of the league as the world's worst polluter—though to be fair, this is an absolute, rather than a per capita, figure.

Any good that globalization may do is undone by the very fact that it is global. The consumers are far removed from the effects of their consumption. None of the hat wearers of Europe saw the damage their headgear was doing to beavers, Indians, and environments in North America. None of the operators of factory machinery running on bison leather belts saw the transformation of the Great Plains. The situation is even worse today. It would be impossible to guess what impacts on what parts of the world a single aisle in a supermarket represents.

Another problem that has emerged in every chapter isn't, strictly speaking, the fault of the free market, but of the political system that supports it. Winston Churchill, who had an incisive way with words, summed up the problem in the best way I've heard when he said that democracy was the worst form of government except all the others that have been tried. The problem with democracy from an environmental point of view is that it works—of necessity—on short timescales. Ecology, on the other hand, doesn't. But it's very hard for politicians to make long-term decisions, especially when, in the short term (the term on which their reelection depends) these might result in people temporarily being worse off.

One way to mitigate this might be to hand resources over to private ownership. Owners of resources should, in theory, have a vested interest in maintaining the value of those resources into the future. This has been suggested, for example, with the intractable problem of fisheries. Trying to manage them as a common resource has certainly proved disastrous, one of the examples frequently used to illustrate the "tragedy of the commons." This idea suggests that any unowned resource will inevitably be overexploited, since it pays no one to exploit the resource sustainably, only to see a neighbor benefit from this by taking a larger share. But the world is not that simple. I've already pointed out that the "commons" from which the idea takes its name, the communal grazing areas of medieval England, were, in fact, very well managed. There's nothing inevitable about the tragedy.

But the difference between the medieval commons and modern ocean fisheries is again the difference between local versus global. For medieval peasants, the common land was their backyard; they could see the effects of transgressions and punish offenders. They also depended on the continued existence of the commons as much as if they owned the land themselves, since they didn't have the option of moving somewhere else. An ocean fishery could not be more different. It's a long way from home, and any degradation of the ecosystem is hidden beneath the waves. The ocean is also a big place, so even if resources dry up in one place, there's always another patch of ocean just over the horizon. Such attitudes, along with a lack of political bravery to make difficult, long-tem decisions, have reduced the oceans of the world to an abject state, particularly when compared to the teeming abundance of their pristine condition.

In some ways, it was this extraordinary profusion of nature in North America, on both land and sea, that caused its own destruction. Europeans were overwhelmed by the wealth of the natural world and concluded that it was so vast as to be indestructible. We've seen many examples of this attitude, from hunters to scientists and from the fifteenth to the twenty-first century. Yet, in every case, this optimism proved unfounded. Billions of passenger pigeons, hundreds of millions of green turtles, or tens of millions of bison—all were reduced to actual or ecological extinction. How could we be so consistently wrong?

This points to a fundamental misunderstanding of the natural world, and in particular of how ecosystems work. Modern ecology sees communities of plants and animals as being organized into a hierarchy of different layers, each nested inside the next level up. Elements in each layer can interact with each other and, to a lesser extent, with layers above and below. For example, leaves, of many different species, ages, and conditions, constitute one level, nested like a Russian doll in the next level up—trees. Trees themselves, of many species, are then nested in the next level—the forest. Such a model explains how ecosystems can remain stable in the face of constant perturbations. Each level acts as a filter, damping out short-term fluctuations, insulating the next level up, with the result that the highest level remains stable. Leaves get eaten, torn by the wind, die, and are replaced by new ones. All these short-term effects are damped out at the level of an individual tree, which don't show changes on such a short time scales. In a similar way, trees grow and die but the forest remains.

The problem comes when effects grow so great that they break through the filters of the different levels and impact on the highest level. When this happens the change can be sudden, dramatic, and completely unexpected. Sound familiar?

At this point, the ecosystem has reached a tipping point and can flip into an entirely new state, with a new hierarchy that can promote a stubborn stability in the face of attempts to restore the old one. It's almost impossible to predict these changes, since the web of interactions within and between levels is so complex that the whole system doesn't behave in a predictable, easy to understand, linear way. I think our canter through five hundred years of experiments with such systems shows just how unpredictable they are.

Spectacular collapses of ecosystems are still happening ,and they are still catching scientists by surprise. In fact, the global economy is making such problems both more frequent and more surprising as it has woven the whole planet into one vast web. Witness the potential collapse of ecosystems in the Great Lakes and the Mississippi caused by mussels and fish introduced from Asia in the ballast of cargo ships. And who could have imagined that a growing concern for environmental problems could have triggered an *increase* in deforestation of the Amazon? But that's what has happened as farmers in North America switched from growing soya to growing corn for biofuels, triggering a price rise in soya and creating an economic incentive to plant it in Brazil, in fields newly cleared from rainforest.

In 2002, Donald Rumsfeld said the following, for which he received no small amount of ridicule: "there are known knowns; there are things we know we know. We also know there are known unknowns; that is to say we know there are some things we do not know. But there are also unknown unknowns—the ones we don't know we don't know. And if one looks throughout the history of our country and other free countries, it is the latter category that tend to be the difficult ones."[1]

Actually, he was dead right, and the details of many of the interactions in hierarchical ecosystems are firmly in the "unknown unknowns" category. It is for this reason that I have repeatedly mentioned in previous chapters that all decisions regarding the exploitation of natural resources need to follow the precautionary principle. We don't know enough to make bold decisions about how much an ecosystem can take of our depredations. William Laurance, a biologist with the Smithsonian Tropical Research Institute, has succinctly summed up these dilemmas as "the perils of trying to make linear decisions in a non-linear world."[2]

This is also a good time for the snail darter to rear its obscure little head again, as just one example of how far we still have to go toward even the broadest understanding among decision makers of the complexity of our world. This little fish, restricted to just a few places in the Southeast, was threatened by dam building but was protected by the Endangered Species Act. So the dam builders and the fish ended up in the Supreme Court to argue their relative merits. Senator John Chafee became embroiled in the debate, and I repeat his quote from chapter 10 that shows how little our politicians comprehend the world that they hold in their hands: "We who voted for the Endangered Species Act with the honest intentions of protecting such glories of nature as the wolf, the eagle, and other treasures have found that extremists with wholly different motives are using this noble act for meanly obstructive ends."[3]

We can't pick and choose which animals and plants we want in our world and which we don't. To do so is like letting a child play with a box of matches. Most of the time we have no idea what role those obscure creatures are playing in their ecosystems, by the very fact of their obscurity. But it's much easier to get grants and public money to study the big and the beautiful favored by Senator Chafee. Such a case also illustrates the limitations—philosophical and practical—of "single species" conservation. Unfortunately, management of resources at the level of whole ecosystems is both difficult and expensive. So how do we proceed in the future?

One answer emerges from the underlying similarity of economics and ecology. The species that populate ecosystems in those complex hierarchies have evolved to do so by the wholly blind process of natural selection. This works on short-term self-interest, as those individuals that, by dint of random mutations, find themselves at an advantage are able to leave more copies of their genes in the next generation. The free market too is a system based on short-term self-interest, and the power of both systems is apparent in the previous chapters—as the extraordinary abundance and diversity of life and of the speed and completeness of its conversion into human wealth.

Both are also too complex to be easily controlled from above. The disastrous results of our attempts to manage ecosystems are evident in every chapter of this book, while the spectacular collapse of the Soviet Union illustrates the impossibility of controlling an economy effectively from the top down. This similarity should be food for thought for everyone. No capitalist would dream of suggesting that we know enough to control an economy so the same thinking should be extended to equally complex ecosystems.

The power of capitalism to devastate the natural world emerges very clearly from the previous chapters, but it's also apparent from the above that there is no real viable alternative as a means of running our world. So the only conclusion is as inevitable as it is unexpected—that we must turn to capitalism to rebuild nature.

This is not a new idea. In 1920, an economist called Arthur Pigou suggested a tax that reflected the external costs of manufacture—that is costs such as pollution or environmental destruction that don't normally appear in balance sheets. A free market is great at setting prices, but very poor at recognizing costs. Yet, as Pigou suggested, if the full environmental costs could be somehow built in to the equations, then the power of the free market could be turned to the advantage of the environment.

Since then, others have looked in more detail at the changes needed in our ideas of capitalism in order to harness its power to protect the natural world. These ideas are both fascinating and practical, and outlined by Paul

Hawken in *The Ecology of Commerce*[4] and Jonathon Porritt's more recent and well-thought-out *Capitalism as if the World Matters*.[5]

One change, which would only make the market freer, is the removal of subsidies, which cost taxpayers dearly, both in terms of money and in terms of the damage they do. Ecologist Norman Myers has worked out that the world's taxpayers already hand over between $950 billion and $1,400 billion in subsidies,[6] and for about 20 percent of this, we could run a truly effective global conservation program, which would enhance natural resources rather than destroy them.[7] Another way of improving capitalism's dismal environmental record is to foster the growth of local markets. When people can see the effects of their actions, they are far more likely to do something about it.

A criticism of loading true costs into the equation is that those costs would inevitably be passed on to consumers. Actually, each and every one of us is already paying the price, but in ways that are hidden. A true value on the resources we consume would most certainly open our eyes and would allow us a choice based on knowledge of the effects of our consumption. I believe there would be a big difference between people acting out of blind self-interest and those acting out of enlightened self-interest. The same critics also worry that such costs would also slow the economy. Good.

Terms like "sustainable growth" are tossed around with abandon across the media, but if anyone ever paused to think for a second, they would realize that such an expression is an oxymoron. Planet Earth is finite. The only way we can sustain a year on year growth of say 2 percent is if our planet was also growing at around 2 percent per year. A quick look at the latest geological texts suggests this isn't the case. Yet, when ecology inconveniently gets in the way it is swept under the carpet.

At the 1992 Earth Summit, the then President Bush said, regarding climate change, that the American Way of life was not up for negotiation. Take a look at the five-hundred-year assault on nature in your own country and project that trajectory into the future. The American (and European and the newly industrializing nations') way of life will have to change. The trick is to do so in a controllable way, by tweaking how capitalism works, as suggested by Paul Hawken, Jonathon Porritt, and a growing band of other people. These people are not suggesting that society stagnates. But growth, as a continuous increase in materialism, needs to be separated from its constant associate, development. And development should be about a lot more that just steadily increasing wealth—see, for example, *Development as Freedom* by Nobel laureate Amartya Sen.[8]

Many people already realize that simply becoming richer in money or possessions is no answer to life's questions. In one survey, 80 percent of Americans believed they consumed far more than necessary,[9] and many other studies have shown that increasing materialism does not bring increased happiness, which, after all, is what almost everyone is trying to achieve. I think we could all learn from Bhutan, which has switched its markers of national success from "gross domestic product" to "gross domestic happiness."

Nature makes a lot of people very happy in many different ways, from the deep-seated contentment of a desert sunset to the intimate experiences of hunting and fishing. Yet, in the history of our society, we have grown steadily apart from nature. In contrast to all the First Nations of America, Judeo-Christian religions teach that humans are separate from nature, a detachment that grew through the industrial revolution as life became ever more focused on cities. This attitude is, in no small part, responsible for the scale of the effects I have outlined in this book. Yet I see hope in all of this.

The more we have cocooned ourselves in cities, the more we miss nature. This was the theme of the last chapter, where I took the wolf as an appropriate symbol of these changing attitudes. While some still see the wolf as the devil incarnate, anathema to civilization, many now see the wolf as embodying all that we have lost. The green fire in its eyes suggests a vitality of nature that we have forgotten ever existed. There is a growing awareness of what we are losing, both practically and spiritually, though it will still take a massive effort to turn things around.

It was writer and poet Steve Turner who came up with the phrase: "History repeats itself. It has to; nobody listens." This book is a clear illustration of that. What we call today "environmental awareness" is nothing new. We've seen people throughout the history of North America comment on the foolishness of the profligate use of resources and suggest proceeding with caution. Yet in every age their words went unheeded as unbridled exploitation bled dry one ecosystem after the other. Have we now reached a tipping point in our own society? Is the groundswell great enough for our own culture to flip from one state to another—from squandering our extraordinary heritage to enlightened stewardship?

We have diminished nature far more than most people know. If we really did have a time machine, I'm convinced that every person alive today would be overawed by the true vitality of nature. They would also be shocked at the sheer scale of our impact on the planet. The true realization of what we have done would, I'm sure, spur enormous efforts to repair the damage, for the legacy of humanity to be more than just an impoverished planet.

I offer this book as that time machine.

Notes

CHAPTER 1: A DIFFERENT WORLD

1   T. Flannery and P. Schouten, *A Gap in Nature: Discovering the World's Extinct Animals* (New York: Atlantic Monthly Press, 2004).

2   D. Pauly, "Anecdotes and the Shifting Baseline Syndrome of Fisheries," *Trends in Ecology and Evolution* 10(1995):430.

3   D. Worster, "Transformations of the Earth: Toward an Agroecological Perspective in History," *Journal of American History* 76, no. 4 (1990): 1087–1106.

4   Ibid.

5   W. M. Denevan, "The Pristine Myth: The Landscape of the Americas in 1492," in "The Americas before and after 1492: Current Geographical Research," special issue, *Annals of the Association of American Geographers* 82, no. 3 (1992): 369–85.

6   J. Porritt, *Capitalism as if the World Matters* (Sterling, Va.: Earthscan, 2005).

7   D. Worster, *The Wealth of Nature* (New York: Oxford University Press, 1993).

8   Ibid.

CHAPTER 2: THE DISCOVERY OF PARADISE

1   J. Cartier, quoted in J. Bakeless, *America as Seen by Its First Explorers—the Eyes of Discovery* (New York: Dover, 1961).

2   From "The Saga of the Greenlanders," quoted in W. P. Cumming, R. A. Skelton, and D. B. Quinn, *The Discovery of North America* (London: Elek, 1971), p. 47.

3   H. Ingstad and A. Ingstad, *The Viking Discovery of America* (Facts on File, 2001).

4   Ibid.

5   F. Mowat, *Sea of Slaughter* (Boston: Atlantic Monthly Press, 1984).

6   N. Denys, quoted in ibid.

7   R. Behnke, *Trout and Salmon of North America* (New York: Free Press, 2002).

8   G. Cartwright, quoted in Mowat, *Sea of Slaughter*.

9   G. Cartwright and C. W. Townsend, *Captain Cartwright and His Labrador Journal* (Boston: Dana Estes and Co., 1911).

10 Mowat, *Sea of Slaughter*.

11 Quoted in ibid.

12 P. McGinnity et al., "Fitness Reduction and Potential Extinction of Wild Populations of Atlantic Salmon, *Salmo salar*, as a Result of Interactions with Escaped Farm Salmon," *Proceedings of the Royal Society (London) B* 270(2003):2443–50.

13 Ibid.

14 Atlantic Salmon Federation, "Atlantic Salmon Aquaculture: A Primer" (2000); available at http:www.asf.calbackgrounder/asfaquacbackgrounder.pdf.

15 R. L. Naylor, S. L. Williams, and D. R. Strong, "Aquaculture—a Gateway for Exotic Species," *Science* 294(2001):1655–66.

16 E. B. Taylor, "A Review of Local Adaptation in Salmonidae, with Particular Reference to Pacific and Atlantic Salmon," *Aquaculture* 98(1991):185–207.

17 C. Nielsen, G. Holdensgahrd, H. C. Petersen, B. Th. Björnsson, and S. S. Madsen, "Genetic Differences in Physiology, Growth Hormone Levels and Migratory Behaviour of Atlantic Salmon Smolts," *Journal of Fish Biology* 59(2001):28–44.

18 E. E. Nielsen, M. M. Hansen, and V. Loeschcke, "Genetic Variation in Time and Space: Microsatellite Analysis of Extinct and Extant Populations of Atlantic Salmon," *Evolution* 53(1999):261–68.

19 I. A. Fleming, K. Hindar, I. B. Mjølnerød, "Lifetime Success and Interactions of Farm Salmon Invading a Native Population," *Proceedings of the Royal Society (London) B* (2000):1507–23.

20 McGinnity et al., "Fitness Reduction and Potential Extinction of Wild Populations of Atlantic Salmon, *Salmo salar,* as a Result of Interactions with Escaped Farm Salmon."

21 D. Garant, I. A. Fleming, S. Einum, and L. Bernatchez, "Alternative Male Life-History Tactics as Potential Vehicles for Speeding Introgression of Farm Salmon Traits into Wild Populations," *Ecology Letters* 6(2003):541–49.

CHAPTER 3: ABUNDANT OCEAN

1   "The Saga of Erik the Red," quoted in W. P. Cumming, R. H. Skelton, and D. B. Quinn, *The Discovery of North America* (London: Elek, 1971), p. 50.

2   G. A. Rose and R. L. O'Driscoll, "Capelin Are Good for Cod: Can the Northern Stock Rebuild without Them?" *ICES Journal of Marine Science* 59(2002):1018–26.

3   D. Pauly, "Much Rowing for Fish," *Nature* 432(2004):813–14.

4   E. Evans, "Bristol and Newfoundland, 1490–1570," (paper presented at Cabot and His World Symposium Proceedings, St. John's, 1997).

5   J. Day letter to Lord Grand Admiral, Winter 1497–98, reprinted (in translation) in L. A. Vigneras, "The Cape Breton Landfall: 1494 or 1497; A Note on a Letter from John Day," *Canadian Historial Review* 38 (1957): 219–28.

6   R. de Soncino letter, reprinted in P. Cheyney, *Readings in English History Drawn from Original Sources* (Boston: Ginn & Co., 1908), p. 312.

7   P. Martyr, quoted in C. Roberts, *The Unnatural History of the Sea: The Past and Future of Humanity and Fishing* (London: Gaia, 2007), p. 34.

8   F. Mowat, *Sea of Slaughter* (Shelborne: Chapters Publishing, 1996).

9   Ibid., p. 165.

10 J. Mason, *A Brief Discourse of the New-Found-Land* (1620), reprinted in G. T. Cell, *Newfoundland Discovered: English Attempts at Colonisation, 1610–1630* (London: Hakluyt Society, 1982), pp. 8–9.

11 J. Cartier, *First Relation of Jaques Carthier of S. Malo, 1534* (1534), in *Early English and French Voyages, Chiefly from Hakluyt, 1534–1608,* ed, S. H. Burrage, p. 5 (New York: Charles Scribner's Sons, 1906); facsimile available at www.americanjourneys .org/aj-026/.

12 Ibid.

13 G. Cartwright and C. W. Townsend, *Captain Cartwright and His Labrador Journal* (Boston: Dana Estes & Co., 1911), p. 17.

14 T. Pitcher, "The Problem of Extinctions," *University of British Columbia: Fisheries Centre Research Reports* 12, no. 1 (2004): 21–28.

15 M. Vasconcellos et al., "Historical Reference Points for Models of Past Ecosystems in Newfoundland," *University of British Columbia, Fisheries Centre Reports* 10, no. 1 (2002): 7–13.

16 Thomas Butts, reported by Richard Hakluyt (1578).

17 Richard Whitbourne, circa 1600, quoted in Mowat, *Sea of Slaughter,* p. 28.

18 A. Thomas, quoted in T. Birkhead, "How Collectors Killed," *New Scientist,* May 28, 1994; available at www.newscientist.com/article/mg14219273.900.

19 Quoted in Mowat, *Sea of Slaughter.*

20 G. Cartwright and C. W. Townsend, *Captain Cartwright and His Labrador Journal,* pp. 318–19.

21 R. Kunzig, "Twilight of the Cod," *Discover Magazine,* April 1995.

22 F. Mowat, *Sea of Slaughter,* p. 167.

23 Ibid., p. 168.

24 Ibid.

25 Thomas Huxley, quoted in R. Ellis, *The Empty Ocean* (Washington, D.C.: Island Press, 2003).

26 T. Huxley (1883), quoted in M. Tsamenyi, "The International Legal Regime of Fisheries Management" (UNEF Workshop on Fisheries Subsidies and Sustainable Fisheries, Geneva, April 24–27, 2004).

27 R. A. Myers, "Testing Ecological Models: The Influence of Catch Rates on Settlement of Fishermen in Newfoundland from 1710 to 1833," *Research in Marine History* 21(2001):13–29.

28 C. Roberts, *The Unnatural History of the Sea: The Past and Future of Humanity and Fishing* (Washington, D.C.: Island Press, 2007).

29 J. A. Hutchings and R. A. Myers, "The Biological Collapse of Atlantic Cod Off Newfoundland and Labrador: An Exploration of Historical Changes in Exploitation, Harvesting Technology, and Management," in *The North Atlantic Fisheries: Successes,*

Failures, and Challenges, ed. R. Arnason and L. Felt (Charlottetown, Canada: Institute of Island Studies, 1995).

30 J. A. Hutchings, "The Cod That Got Away," *Nature* 428:899–900.

31 R. A. Myers et al., "Why Do Fish Stocks Collapse?" *Ecological Applications* 7(1997): 91–106.

32 C. Walters and J.-J. Maguire, "Lessons for Stock Assessment from the Northern Cod Collapse," *Reviews in Fish Biology and Fisheries* 6(1996)125–37.

33 Ibid.

34 Ibid.

35 M. Kurlansky, *Cod: A Biography of the Fish That Changed the World* (London: Vintage, 1999).

36 Ibid., p. 88.

CHAPTER 4: SEA OF WHALES

1 S. Levy, "What's Wrong with the Right Whale?" *New Scientist* 2211 (November 6, 1999): 38.

2 R. Mather, *Journal of Richard Mather* (1635), Collections of the Dorchester Antiquarian and Historical Society No. 3 (Boston: David Clapp, 1850).

3 J. Cartier, *Shorte and Brief Narration (Cartier's Second Voyage)* (1535–36), in *Early English and French Voyages, Chiefly from Hakluyt, 1534–1608,* ed. S. H Burrage, pp. 35–88 (New York: Charles Scribner's Sons, 1906), p. 45; facsimile available at www.americanjourneys.org/aj-027/.

4 C. Roberts, *The Unnatural History of the Sea: The Past and Future of Humanity and Fishing* (London: Gaia Thinking, 2007).

5 J. Roman and S. R. Palumbi, "Whales before Whaling in the North Atlantic," *Science* 301(2003):508–10.

6 A. Legardeur, le Sieur de Courtemanche, quoted in F. Mowat, *Sea of Slaughter* (Shelborne: Chapters Publishing, 1984), p. 210.

7 Ibid., p. 214.

8 A. Aguilar, "A Review of Old Basque Whaling and Its Effect on the Right Whales of the North Atlantic," special issue, *Report of the International Whaling Commission* 10(1986):191–99.

9 J. Rosier, *A True Relation of the Most Prosperous Voyage Made This Present Yeere 1605 by Captain George Waymouth* (1605), in *Early English and French Voyages,* pp. 355–94, quote on p. 392; facsimile available at www.americanjourneys.org/aj-041/.

10 P. J. Bryant, "Dating Remains of Gray Whales from the Eastern North Atlantic," *Journal of Mammalogy* 76(1995):857–61.

11 P. Dudley, "An Essay upon the Natural History of Whales," *Philosophical Transactions of the Royal Society of London* 33(1725):256–69.

12　T. Bartholin, quoted in O. Lundquist, *The North Atlantic Gray Whale: An Historical Outline Based on Icelandic, Danish-Icelandic, English and Swedish Sources Dating from ca 1000 AD to 1792* (St. Andrews, Scotland: University of St. Andrews Press, 2000).

13　P. J. Clapham and J. S. Link, "Whales, Whaling and Ecosystems in the North Atlantic Ocean," in *Whales, Whaling and Ocean Ecosystems,* ed. J. A. Estes, R. L. Brownell, D. P. DeMaster, D. F. Doak, and T. M. Williams (Berkeley: University of California Press, 2006).

14　T. Bartholin, *A Record of the Fishes of Iceland* (1675), quoted in O. Lundquist, *The North Atlantic Gray Whale.*

15　Quoted in R. Ellis, *The Empty Ocean* (Washington, D.C.: Island Press, 2004).

16　W. J. Bolster, "Opportunities in Marine Environmental Science," *Environmental Science* 11(2006):567.

17　T. Rastogi et al., "Genetic Analysis of 16th-Century Whale Bones Prompts a Revision of the Impact of Basque Whaling on Right and Bowhead Whales in the Western North Atlantic," *Canadian Journal of Zoology* 82(2004):1647–54.

18　W. Coats, quoted in W. G. Ross, "Distribution, Migration and Depletion of Bowhead Whales in Hudson Bay, 1860–1915," *Arctic and Alpine Research* 6(1974): 85–98.

19　Record from the log of the English whaler *Cumbrian,* Baffin Island (1823), quoted in Mowat, *Sea of Slaughter,* p. 242.

20　P. François-Xavier de Charlevoix, quoted in Mowat, *Sea of Slaughter.*

21　Department of Fisheries and Oceans Canada Web site, http://www.dfo-mpo.gc .ca/species-especes/species/species_belugaStLawrence_e.asp.

22　Mowat, *Sea of Slaughter.*

23　Quoted in ibid.

24　Quoted in ibid., p. 327.

25　Quoted in ibid.

27　Quoted in ibid.

27　B. Davies, *Red Ice: My Fight to Save the Seals* (London: Methuen, 1989).

28　G. B. Stenson et al., "Is There Evidence of Increased Pup Production in Northwest Atlantic Harp Seals, *Pagophilus groenlandicus?*" *ICES Journal of Marine Science* 59(2002):81–92.

29　"Canada's Seal Pups in Double Trouble," *New Scientist,* no. 2598 (March 28, 2007), p. 4.

30　D. W. Johnston et al., "An Evaluation of Management Objectives for Canada's Commercial Harp Seal Hunt, 1996–1998," *Conservation Biology* 14(2000):729–37.

31　R. T. Paine, "Food Webs: Linkage, Interaction Strength and Community Infrastructure," *Journal of Animal Ecology* 49(1980):667–85.

32 D. Pauly et al., "Fishing Down Marine Food Webs," *Science,* n.s., 279, no. 5352 (February 6, 1998):860–63.

33 H. Daly, *Beyond Growth* (Boston: Beacon Press, 1996).

34 J. Jackson, "When Ecological Pyramids Were Upside Down," in *Whales, Whaling and Ocean Ecosystems.*

35 B. Worm, H. K. Lotze, and R. A. Myers, "Ecosystem Effects of Fishing and Whaling in the North Pacific and Atlantic Ocean," in ibid.

36 Jackson, "When Ecological Pyramids Were Upside Down."

37 K. Kaschner, *Modelling and Mapping Resource Overlap between Marine Mammals and Fisheries on a Global Scale* (Ph.D. diss., Department of Zoology, University of British Columbia, Vancouver, 2004).

38 R. A. Myers and B. Worm, "Extinction, Survival or Recovery of Large Predatory Fishes," *Philosophical Transactions of the Royal Society B* 360(2005):13–20.

39 P. B. Best, A. Brandão, and D. S. Butterworth, "Demographic Parameters of Southern Right Whales Off South Africa," special issue, *Journal of Cetacean Research and Management* 2(2001):161–69.

40 H. D. Thoreau, *The Writings of Henry David Thoreau,* vol. 4, *Cape Cod, 1855–1865* (Boston: Houghton Mifflin, 1906), p. 188.

CHAPTER 5: LIVING IN PARADISE

1 B. Harrington, *The Flight of the Red Knot* (New York: W. W. Norton and Co., 1996).

2 Quoted in B. Lawrence, *The Early American Wilderness* (New York: Paragon House, 1991), p. 29.

3 Quoted in ibid., p. 34.

4 W. P. Cumming, R. A. Skelton, and D. B. Quinn, *The Whole and True Discovery of Terra Florida, by Captaine Ribauld* (London, 1563), reprinted in *The Discovery of North America.* (London: Elek, 1981).

5 Letter from a soldier on the Laudonnière Expedition, in ibid.

6 T. Hariot, *A Brief and True Report of the New Found Land of Virginia* (1588), p. 29; facsimile available at http://digitalcommons.unl.edu/etas/20.

7 J. Lawson, *A New Voyage to Carolina; Containing the Exact Description and Natural History of That Country* (1709); available at http://docsouth.unc.edu/nc/lawson/menu .html.

8 Ibid., p. 30.

9 G. Percy, *Observations by Master George Percy, 1607,* in *Narratives of Early Virginia, 1606–1625,* ed. L. G. Tyler, pp. 3–23 (New York: Charles Scribner's Sons, 1907); facsimile available at www.americanjourneys.org/aj-073/.

10 Ibid.

11 J. R. Wennersten, *The Chesapeake: An Environmental Biography* (Baltimore: Maryland Historical Society, 2001).

12 R. I. E. Newell, "Ecological Changes in Chesapeake Bay: Are They the Result of Overharvesting the American Oyster, *Crassostrea virginica?*" in *Understanding the Estuary: Advances in Chesapeake Bay Research*, ed. M. P. Lynch and E. C. Krome, pp. 536–46, Chesapeake Research Consortium Publication 129.

13 *Observations by Master George Percy, 1607.*

14 Wennersten, *The Chesapeake: An Environmental Biography.*

15 Quoted in ibid.

16 Quoted in ibid.

17 G. Hardin, "The Tragedy of the Commons," *Science* 162, no. 3859 (December 13, 1968): 1243–48.

18 O. Rackham, *Woodlands*, New Naturalist Series (London: Collins, 2006).

19 J. W. Ewart and S. E. Ford, "History and Impact of MSX and Dermo Diseases on Oyster Stocks in the Northeast Region" (Northeast Regional Aquaculture Center Fact Sheet No. 200, 1993).

20 T. Horton, *Turning the Tide: Saving the Chesapeake Bay*, rev ed. (Washington, D.C.: Island Press, 2003).

21 "Hungry Rays Thwart Effort to Restore Oysters in Piankatank," *Bay Journal*, July/August 2006.

22 J. Smith, *The Proceedings of the English Colonie in Virginia, 1606–1612* (Oxford, 1612), reprinted in *Travels and Works of Captain John Smith*, ed. E. Arber and A. G. Bradley, vol. 1 (Edinburgh, 1910).

23 Ibid.

24 J. C. Pearson, "The Fish and Fisheries of Colonial Virginia," *William and Mary College Quarterly Historical Magazine* 2nd ser., 22, no. 4 (1942): 353–60.

25 R. Beverley, *The History of Virginia in Four Parts* (Richmond, Va.: J. W. Randolph, 1855), p. 119.

26 *A Map of Virginia, with a Description of the Country, The Commodities, People, Government and Religion, written by Captain Smith, sometime Governor of the Colony* (1612); available at Virtual Jamestown Web site, http://www.virtualjamestown.org/firsthand.html.

27 A. Burnaby, quoted in C. Roberts, *The Unnatural History of the Sea: The Past and Future of Humanity and Fishing* (London: Gaia Thinking, 2007).

28 A. van der Donck, "A Description of the New Netherlands," in *Collections of the New York Historical Society*, pp. 125–242 (New York, printed for the society, 1841); facsimile available at www.americanjourneys.org/aj-096/.

29 *New Englands Rarities discovered by John Josselyn* (1672; reprint, Bedford: Applewood Books, 1986).

30 Quoted in F. Mowat, *Sea of Slaughter* (Shelborne: Chapters Publishing, 1996).

31 F. Tilp, *This Was Potomac River*, (Alexandria: Frederick Tilip, 1978).

32 D. J. Grettler, "The Nature of Capitalism: Environmental Change and Conflict over Commercial Fishing in Nineteenth-Century Delaware," *Environmental History* 6 (2001): 451–73.

33 G. B. Goode and A. H. Clark, *The Fisheries and Fishing Industry of the United States* (Washington, D.C.: Government Printing Office, 1887).

34 W. Wood, *New England's Prospect* (London, 1674; reprint, Amherst: University of Massachusetts Press, 1977), p. 55.

35 Mowat, *Sea of Slaughter*.

36 *National Coalition for Marine Conservation Bulletin*, Fall 2003.

37 R. Ellis, *The Empty Ocean* (Washington, D.C.: Island Press, 2003).

38 D. H. Secor and E. J. Niklitschek, "Hypoxia and Sturgeons" (report to the Chesapeake Bay Program Dissolved Oxygen Criteria Team, Tech Report Series No. TS-314-01-CBL, 2001).

39 T. J. Pitcher, "Fisheries Managed to Rebuild Ecosystems: Reconstructing the Past to Salvage the Future," *Ecological Applications* 11(2001):601–17.

CHAPTER 6: ANGELS FROM THE NORTH

1 E. T. Ben–Ari, "A New Wrinkle in Wildlife Management BioScience," *Flooding: Natural and Managed* 48, no. 9 (1998): 667–73.

2 J. Lawson, *A New Voyage to Carolina; Containing the Exact Description and Natural History of That Country* (1709), p. 147; available at http://docsouth.unc.edu/nc/lawson/menu.html.

3 W. Wood, *New England's Prospect* (1634), ed. A. T. Vaughan (Amherst: University of Massachusetts Press, 1977), p. 52.

4 *A Map of Virginia, with a Description of the Country, The Commodities, People, Government and Religion, written by Captain Smith, sometime Governor of the Colony*; available at Virtual Jamestown Web site, www.virtualjamestown.org/firsthand.html.

5 J. Danckaerts (1680), quoted in J. R. Wennersten, *The Chesapeake: An Environmental Biography* (Baltimore: Maryland Historical Society, 2001).

6 R. Beverley, *The History of Virginia in Four Parts* (1720; reprint, Richmond: J. W. Randolph, 1855).

7 D. G. Krementz, "American Black Duck (*Anas rubripes*)," in *Habitat Requirements of Chesapeake Bay Living Resources*, ed. S. L. Funderburk, S. J. Jordan, J. A. Mihursky, and D. Riley, pp. 16-1–16-7 (Annapolis: Maryland Department of Natural Resources, 1991).

8 J. J. Audubon, *Birds of America* (1840–44); facsimile available at www.audobon.org/bird/boa_index.

9   L. Turner (1884), quoted in F. Mowat, *Sea of Slaughter* (Shelborne: Chapters Publishing, 1996).

10 "The Eskimo Curlew," Birds of America, Cornell University and American Ornithologists Union; available at http://bna.birds.cornell.edu/bna.

11 J. B. Gollop, T. W. Barry, and E. H. Iversen, "Eskimo Curlew: A Vanishing Species?" (Saskatchewan Natural History Society Special Publication No. 17, 1986).

12 Quoted in Mowat, *Sea of Slaughter.*

13 Quoted in ibid.

CHAPTER 7: EARTHLY PARADISE OR EARTHLY HADES?

1   *Voyage of John de Verazzano, along the Coast of North America, from Carolina to Newfoundland, A.D.* (1524); facsimile available at www.americanjourneys.org/aj-094/.

2   J. Lawson, *A Description of North Carolina* (1709), quoting the earlier 1632 expedition of Capt. Anthony Long, William Hilton, and Peter Fabian. A. Hilton, *A Relation of a Discovery Lately Made on the Coast of Florida* (1664), p. 45; facsimile available at http://docusouth.unc.edu/nc/lawson.html.

3   W. Bartram, *Travels Through North and South Carolina, Georgia, East and West Florida* (1791; reprint, London: Dover Publications, 1928).

4   *Voyage of John de Verazzano, along the Coast of North America, from Carolina to Newfoundland, A.D.*

5   T. Hariot, *A Brief and True Report of the New Found Land of Virginia;* facsimile available at http://digitalcommons.unl.edu/etas/20.

6   T. R. McCabe and R. E. McCabe, "Recounting Whitetails Past," in *The Science of Overabundance: Deer Ecology and Population Management* (Washington, D.C.: Smithsonian Books, 1997).

7   W. Talbot, *The Discoveries of John Lederer in three several marches from Virgina to the west of Carolina* (1672); reproduced by the University of North Carolina at http://rla.unc.edu/Archives/accounts/Lederer/LedererText.html.

8   W. Wood, *New England's Prospect* (1634), p. 43.

9   Ibid.

10 J. Josselyn, *New England's Rarities Discovered* (1672; reprint, Bedford: Applewood Books, 1986), p. 19.

11 Ibid., p. 20.

12 G. A. Feldhamer et al., eds., *Wild Mammals of North America: Biology Management and Conservation* (Baltimore: Johns Hopkins Press, 2003).

13 P. D. McLoughlin et al., "Declines in Populations of Woodland Caribou," *Journal of Wildlife Management* 67(2003):755–61.

14 D. Boone, quoted in F. Mowat, *Sea of Slaughter* (Shelborne: Chapters Publishing, 1984).

15 T. Walker, *Journal* (1750), quoted in W. H. Goetzmann and G. Williams, *The Atlas of North American Exploration.* (Norman: University of Oklahoma Press, 1998).

16 T. H. Ward, "The Bull in the North Carolina Buffalo," *Southern Indian Studies* 39 (1990):19–30.

17 F. G. Roe, *The North American Buffalo* (Toronto: University of Toronto Press, 1970).

18 H. Hudson, quoted in B. Lawrence, *The Early American Wilderness.* (New York: Paragon House, 1991), p. 141.

19 Quoted in ibid.

20 W. E. Doolittle, "Permanent vs. Shifting Cultivation in the Eastern Woodlands of North America prior to European Contact," *Agriculture and Human Values* 21(2004): 181–89.

21 J. Adair (1775), quoted in T. W. Neumann, "The Role of Prehistoric Peoples in Shaping Ecosystems," in *Wilderness and Political Ecology: Aboriginal Influences on the Original State of Nature,* ed. C. E. Kay and R. T. Simmons, (Salt Lake City: University of Utah Press, 2002), p. 164.

22 Neumann, "The Role of Prehistoric Peoples in Shaping Ecosystems."

23 Quoted in J. R. Wennersten, *The Chesapeake: An Environmental History* (Baltimore: Maryland Historical Society).

24 *Voyage of John de Verazzano, along the Coast of North America, from Carolina to Newfoundland, A.D.,* p. 43.

25 Ibid., p. 48.

26 *The Complete Works of John Smith;* available at Virtual Jamestown Web site, www .virtualjamestown.org/firsthand.html.

27 A. E. Cowdrey, *This Land, This South: An Environmental History* (Lexington: University Press of Kentucky, 1983), p. 15.

28 W. Wood, *New England's Prospect,* p. 38.

29 R. Williams, quoted in G. G. Whitney, *From Coastal Wilderness to Fruited Plain* (New York: Cambridge University Press, 1994), p. 109.

30 C. E. Olmsted, "Vegetation of Certain Plains of Connecticut," *Botanical Gazette* 99 (1937):209–300.

31 *Observations by Master George Percy* (1607); facsimile available at www.american journeys.org/aj-073/.

32 W. Wood, *New England's Prospect.*

33 T. Hariot, *A Brief and True Report of the New Found Land of Virginia;* facsimile available at http://docsouth.unc.edu/nc/hariot/hariot.html.

34 Summarized in C. Mann, *1491: New Revelations of the Americas Before Columbus* (New York: Knopf, 2005).

35 Quoted in B. Hampton, *The Great American Wolf* (New York: Henry Holt & Co., 1997):67.

36 J. Lawson, *A Journey of a Thousand Miles* (1709); facsimile available at http://docu south.unc.edu/nc/lawson.html.

37 Wood, *New England's Prospect,* p. 42.

38 W. Byrd, *The History of the Dividing Line betwixt Virginia and North Carolina* (1733), p. 56; facsimile available at http://docsouth.unc.edu/nc/byrd/byrd.html.

39 Quoted in C. Bolgiano and J. Roberts, eds., *The Eastern Cougar* (Mechanicsburg, Pa.: Stackpole Books, 2005).

40 T. Wright, quoted in Mowat, *Sea of Slaughter,* p. 118.

41 P. Radisson, quoted in Lawrence, *The Early American Wilderness.*

42 S. Krech, *The Ecological Indian* (New York: W. W. Norton and Co., 1999).

43 J. Smith, quoted in Cowdrey, *This Land, This South: An Environmental History.*

44 Summarized in Mann, *1491: New Revelations of the Americas Before Columbus.*

45 Virtual Jamestown Web site, www.virtualjamestown.org/firsthand.html.

46 Cowdrey, *This Land, This South: An Environmental History.*

47 Wood, *New England's Prospect,* p. 69.

48 N. Denys, quoted in C. Martin, "The European Impact on the Culture of a North-eastern Algonquian Tribe: An Ecological Interpretation," *William and Mary Quarterly,* 3rd ser., 31(1974):4–26, quote on p. 11.

49 Lawson, *A Description of North Carolina,* p. 210.

50 South Carolina Archives; available at www.state.sc.us/scdah/guide/rg0171.htm.

51 H. Fairfield Osbourne, quoted in T. Flannery, *The Eternal Frontier* (London: Heinemann, 2001).

52 Quoted in R. M. C. Peck, *Land of the Eagle* (London: BBC Books, 1990), p. 49.

53 W. Cronon, *Changes in the Land: Indians, Colonists, and the Ecology of New England* (New York: Hill and Wang, 1983).

54 T. Dwight, quoted in ibid., p. 112.

55 B. Donahue, *The Great Meadow: Farmers and the Land in Colonial Concord* (New Haven, Conn.: Yale University Press, 2004).

56 Quoted in Cowdrey, *This Land, This South: An Environmental History.*

57 G. Pinchot, *The Fight for Conservation* (New York: Doubleday, 1910), p. 48.

58 D. S. Wilcove, *The Condor's Shadow* (New York: Anchor Books, 2000).

59 W. J. McShea and J. H. Rappole, "Herbivores and the Ecology of Forest Understory Birds," in *The Science of Overabundance: Deer Ecology and Population Management* (Washington, D.C.: Smithsonian Books, 1997).

CHAPTER 8: POLL, BEN, AND MARTHA

1 J. Parton, *The Life of Thomas Jefferson* (1874), p. 165.

2 R. A. Askins, *Restoring North America's Birds: Lessons from Landscape Ecology* (New Haven, Conn.: Yale University Press, 2002).

3 J. J. Audubon, *Ornithological Biography* (1831), quoted in ibid.

4 Askins, *Restoring North America's Birds: Lessons from Landscape Ecology.*

5 J. Ross (1812), quoted in T. F. Belue, *The Long Hunt: Death of the Buffalo East of the Mississippi* (Mechanicsburg, Pa.: Stackpole Books, 1996), p. 14.

6 G. G. Whitney, *From Coastal Wilderness to Fruited Plain* (New York: Cambridge University Press, 1994).

7 T. M. Brewer, *Wilson's American Ornithology with Notes by Jardine* (New York: T. L. Maganos & Co., 1854), pp. 246–53.

8 J. J. Audubon, *The Birds of North America*, vol, 4; facsimile available at www.abirds home.com/Audubon/VolIV/00454.html.

9 B. Barton (1799), quoted in N. F. R. Snyder, *The Carolina Parakeet, Glimpses of a Vanished Bird* (Princeton, N.J.: Princeton University Press, 2004).

10 Snyder, *The Carolina Parakeet, Glimpses of a Vanished Bird.*

11 Quoted in ibid.

12 Ibid.

13 Brewer, *Wilson's American Ornithology with Notes by Jardine.*

14 Audubon, *The Birds of North America*, vol. 4.

15 Ibid.

16 Alexander Wilson, *American Ornithology*, vol. 4; facsimile avaiable at http://xroads .virginia.edu/~public/wilson/29.html.

17 J. A. Jackson, *In Search of the Ivory-Billed Woodpecker* (Washington, D.C.: Smithsonian Books, 2004).

18 W. L. Dawson, *The Birds of California* (San Francisco: South Multon Co., 1923).

19 C. C. Abbott, *The Birds about Us* (1894), quoted in Jackson, *In Search of the Ivory-Billed Woodpecker*, p. 57.

20 Jackson, *In Search of the Ivory-Billed Woodpecker.*

21 J. T. Tanner, "The Ivory-billed Woodpecker" (Ph.D. thesis; published as Research Report No. 1 of the National Audubon Society, 1942; reprint, New York: Dover, 2003).

22 J. M. Swart, "Rediscovering Tanner's Woodpecker: Reflections of the Survival of the Ivorybill" (2006); available at http://staff.utia.cas.cz/swart/IBWO.pdf.

23 D. A. Sibley et al., Comment on "Ivory-billed Woodpecker (*Campephilus principalis*) Persists in Continental North America," *Science* 311(2006):1555a.

24 G. E. Hill et al., "Evidence Suggesting That Ivory-Billed Woodpeckers (*Campephilus principalis*) Exist in Florida," *Avian Conservation and Ecology* 1, no. 3 (2006): 2.

25 Snyder, *The Carolina Parakeet, Glimpses of a Vanished Bird.*

26 Audubon, *The Birds of North America*, vol. 5; facsimile available at www.abirdshome .com/Audubon/VolV/00505.html.

27 J. M. Wheaton, quoted in E. Fuller, *Extinct Birds* (Oxford: Oxford University Press, 2000), p. 190.

28 Wilson, *American Ornithology*, vol. 5.

29 S. Pokagon, "The Wild Pigeon of North America," *Chautauquan* 22(1895):202–6.

30 D. E. Blockstein, "Passenger Pigeon (*Ectopistes migratorius*)," in *The Birds of North America*, No. 611, ed. A. Poole and F. Gill (Philadelphia: Birds of North America, 2002).

31 E. H. Bucher, "The Causes of the Extinction of the Passenger Pigeon," in *Current Ornithology*, ed. D. M. Power (Plenum, 1992), 9:1–36.

32 Blockstein, "Passenger Pigeon (*Ectopistes migratorius*)."

33 A.W. Schorger, *The Passenger Pigeon: Its Natural History and Extinction* (Madison: University of Wisconsin Press, 1955).

34 Audubon, *The Birds of North America*, vol 5.

35 P. A. Stephens and W. J. Sutherland, "Consequences of the Allee Effect for Behaviour, Ecology and Conservation," *Trends in Ecology and Evolution* 14(1999):401–5.

36 Blockstein, "Passenger Pigeon (*Ectopistes migratorius*)."

37 W. Brewster, "The Heath Hen of Massachusetts," *The Auk* 2(1885):80–84.

38 A. O. Gross, "Banding the Last Heath Hen," *Bird Banding* 2(1931):99–105.

39 Ibid.

40 C. Cokinos, *Hope Is the Thing with Feathers* (New York: Putnam, 2000).

CHAPTER 9: SOULS AND FURS

1 David Thompson's narrative of his explorations in North America (1784–1812), quoted in C. Martin, *Keepers of the Game* (Berkeley: University of California Press, 1978), p. 106.

2 F. Rosell et al., "Ecological Impact of Beavers *Castor fiber* and *Castor canadensis* and Their Ability to Modify Ecoysytems," *Mammal Review* 35(2005):248–76.

3 D. Muller-Schwarze and L. Sun, *The Beaver: Natural History of a Wetlands Engineer* (Ithaca, N.Y.: Cornell University Press, 2003).

4 M. C. McKinstry et al., "The Importance of Beaver to Wetlands Habitats and Waterfowl in Wyoming," *Journal of the American Water Resources Association* 37(2001): 1571–77.

5 W. McNeel, "Beaver Cuttings in Aspen Indirectly Detrimental to White Pine," *Journal of Wild Life Management* 28(1964):861–63.

6 G. D. Martinsen, E. M. Driebe, and T. G. Whitman, "Indirect Interactions Mediated by Changing Plant Chemistry: Beaver Browsing Benefits Beetles," *Ecology* 79 (1998):192–200.

7 Rosell et al., "Ecological Impact of Beavers *Castor fiber* and *Castor canadensis* and Their Ability to Modify Ecoysytems."

8 A. I. Hollowell, *Culture and Experience* (Philadelphia: University of Pennsylvania Press, 1955).

9   "The First Relation of Jacques Cartier of S. Malo" (1534), in *Early English and French Voyages, Chiefly from Hakluyt, 1534–1608*, ed. H. S. Burrage , pp. 3–31 (New York: Charles Scribner's Sons, 1906); facsimile available at www.americanjourneys.org/aj-026/.

10 "Shorte and Briefe Narration (Cartier's Second Voyage), 1535–1536," in ibid., pp. 35–88; facsimile available at www.americanjourneys.org/aj-027/.

11 "The First Relation of Jacques Cartier of S. Malo."

12 P.-E. Radisson, "Radisson's Account of His Third Journey, 1658–1660," in *Early Narratives of the Northwest, 1634–1699*, ed. C. P. Kellog, pp. 29–65 (New York: Charles Scribner's Sons, 1917), p. 41; facsimile available at www.americanjourneys.org/aj-045.

13 A. Parkhurst (ca. 1578), quoted in F. Mowat, *Sea of Slaughter* (Shelborne: Chapters Publishing, 1996), p. 123.

14 Quoted in Mowat, *Sea of Slaughter*, p. 130.

15 J. H. Waters and C. W. Mack, "Second Find of Sea Mink in Southeastern Massachusetts, *Journal of Mammalogy* 43(1962):429–30.

16 Muller-Schwarze and Sun, *The Beaver: Natural History of a Wetlands Engineer.*

17 Quoted in Martin, *Keepers of the Game*, p. 101.

18 D. Thompson, quoted in ibid., p. 106

19 A. Henry the Elder, quoted in ibid., p. 107.

20 A. M. Carlos and D. L. Lewis, "Economic History of the Fur Trade (1670–1870)"; available at http://eh.net/encyclopedia/article/carlos.lewis.furtrade.

21 A. Henry the Younger, quoted in Martin, *Keepers of the Game*, p. 102.

22 D. Cameron, quoted in ibid.

23 Carlos and Lewis, "Economic History of the Fur Trade (1670–1870)."

24 Facsimile available at http://puffin.creighton.edu/jesuit/relations/.

25 S. Houston et al., *Eighteenth Century Naturalists of Hudson's Bay* (Montreal: McGill-Queen's University Press, 2003).

26 Carlos and Lewis, "Economic History of the Fur Trade (1670–1870)."

27 Houston et al., *Eighteenth Century Naturalists of Hudson's Bay.*

28 P. Fidler, Report of District (from Fort Dauphin) (1820), Document 6; available at www.mcgill.ca/mcqupress/homepa/eighteenth-centurynaturalists/fidler.html.

29 E. T. Seton, quoted in Houston et al., *Eighteenth Century Naturalists of Hudson's Bay*, p. 179.

30 D. K. Woodward et al., "Economic and Environmental Impacts of Beavers in North Carolina" (in Proceedings of the Second Eastern Wildlife Damage Control Conference, North Carolina State University, Raleigh, 1985).

CHAPTER 10: GATHERING OF WATERS

1 G. de la Vega, *The Florida of the Inca*, ed. J. G. Varner and J. J. Varner (Austin: University of Texas, 1951).

2 M. Twain, *Life on the Mississippi* (Montreal: Dawson Brothers, 1883), p. 23.

3 H. H. Tanner, ed., *Atlas of Great Lakes Indian History* (Norman: University of Oklahoma Press, 1987).

4 Quoted in M. B. Bogue, *Fishing the Great Lakes, An Environmental History, 1783–1933* (Madison: University of Wisconsin Press, 2000).

5 Quoted in ibid.

6 C. Dablon, quoted in O. Fowl, *Sault Ste. Marie and Its Great Waterway* (New York: Putnam, 1925), p. 100.

7 Louis Armand de Lom d'Arce, baron de Lahontan, *New Voyages to North America* (1703).

8 Quoted in Bogue, *Fishing the Great Lakes*, p. 21.

9 Ibid., p. 25.

10 G. T. O. LeBreton, F. W. H. Beamish, and R. Scott McKinley, eds., *Sturgeons and Paddlefish of North America* (Dordrecht: Kluwer, 2004).

11 Quoted in Bogue, *Fishing the Great Lakes*, p. 155.

12 Quoted in A. E. Jenks, "The Wild Rice Gatherers of the Upper Lakes," *Annual Report of the Bureau of American Ethnology to the Secretary of the Smithsonian Institution* 19, no. 2 (1900).

13 Quoted in ibid.

14 P.-E. Radisson, "Radisson's Account of His Third Journey, 1658–1660," in *Early Narratives of the Northwest, 1634–1699*, ed. C. P. Kellog, pp. 29–65 (New York: Charles Scribner's Sons, 1917), p. 47; facsimile available at www.americanjourneys.org/aj-045.

15 J. Carver, *Jonathon Carver's Travels through America, 1766–1768*, ed. N. Gelb (New York: John Wiley and Sons, 1993), p. 72.

16 Ibid.

17 J. Marquette, "The Mississippi Voyage of Jolliet and Marquette," in *Early Narratives of the Northwest, 1634–1699*, ed. L. P. Kellogg, pp. 223–57 (New York: Charles Scribner's Sons, 1917), p. 236; facsimile available at www.americanjourneys.org/aj-051/.

18 Ibid., p. 231.

19 Twain, *Life on the Mississippi*, p. 27.

20 D. A. Etnier and W. C. Starnes, *Fishes of Tennessee* (Knoxville: University of Tennessee Press, 1993).

21 C. S. Rafinesque, *Ichthyologia Ohiensis, or Natural History of the Fishes Inhabiting the*

River Ohio and Its Tributary Streams (Lexington, Ky.: W. G. Hunt, 1820; reprinted, New York: Arno Press, 1970).

22 Marquette, *The Mississippi Voyage of Jolliet and Marquette*, p. 237.

23 *Relation of the Discoveries and Voyages of Cavelier de La Salle from 1679 to 1681: The Official Narrative*, trans. M. B. Anderson, p. 79 (Chicago: Caxton Club, 1901); facsimile available at www.americanjourneys.org/aj-122/.

24 H. de Tonti, *Memoir on La Salle's Discoveries, 1678–1690*, reproduced in *Early Narratives of the Northwest, 1634–1699*, p. 298; facsimile available at www.american journeys.org/aj-053/.

25 W. C. Foster, *The La Salle Expedition on the Mississippi River: A Lost Manuscript of Nicholas de La Salle, 1682*, trans. J. S. Warren (Austin: Texas State Historical Association, 2003), p. 115.

26 Ibid.

27 Ibid.

28 Summarized in C. Mann, *1491: New Revelations of the Americas before Columbus* (New York: Knopf, 2006).

29 De Tonti, *Memoir on La Salle's Discoveries, 1678–1690*, p. 302.

30 G. T. Watters, "North American Freshwater Mussels"; available at http://www .conchologistsofamerica.org/articles/y1994/9406_watters.asp.

31 C. E. Kay and R. T. Simmons, eds., *Wilderness and Political Ecology; Aboriginal Influences on the Original State of Nature* (Salt Lake City: University of Utah Press, 2002).

32 E. Peacock, "Future Directions in the Analysis of Freshwater Bivalves in Archaeology"; available at http://www.assemblage.group.shef.ac.uk/1/peacock.html.

33 Etnier and Starens, *Fishes of Tennessee*.

34 G. W. Benz and D. E. Collins, eds. *Aquatic Fauna in Peril: The Southeastern Perspective*, Special Publication No. 1 (Chattanooga, Tenn.: Southeastern Aquatic Research Institute, 1997).

35 P. W. Parmalee and A. E. Bogan, *The Freshwater Mussels of Tennessee* (Knoxville: University of Tennessee Press, 1998).

36 R. J. Neves et al., "Status of Aquatic Mollusks in the Southeastern United States; A Downward Spiral of Diversity," in *Aquatic Fauna in Peril: The Southeastern Perspective*.

37 Quoted in S. Petersen, "Congress and Charismatic Megafauna: A Legislative History of the Endangered Species Act," *Environmental Law* 29 (1999):463–91, p 463.

38 Quoted in ibid. p. 486.

39 Parmalee and Bogan, *The Freshwater Mussels of Tennessee*.

40 C. Fremling, *The Immortal River: The Upper Mississippi in Ancient and Modern Times* (Madison: University of Wisconsin Press, 2005).

41 M. N. Charlton, "Did Zebra Mussels Clean Up Lake Erie?" *Great Lakes Review* 5, no. 2 (2001): 11–15.

42 P. L. Klerks, P. C. Fraleigh, and J. E. Lawniczak, "Effects of Zebra Mussels (*Dreissena polymorpha*) on Seston Levels and Sediment Deposition in Western Lake Erie," *Canadian Journal of Fishery and Aquatic Science* 49(1996):416–22.

43 D. J. Jude, "Round Gobies: Cyberfish of the Third Millennium," *Great Lakes Research Review* 3, no. 1 (1997); available at www.eng.buffalo.edu/glp/articles/glrrv3n1_1997.html.

44 Bogue, *Fishing the Great Lakes, An Environmental History, 1783–1933.*

45 S. Wilmot, quoted in ibid.

46 F. C. Cornelius, "New York's Lake Erie Fisheries: Response to Change," *Great Lakes Research Review* 5, no. 1 (2000): 1–12.

47 M. J. Hansen et al., "Lake Trout Populations in Lake Superior and Their Restoration in 1959–1983," *Journal of Great Lakes Research* 21 (1995):152–75.

48 "A Review of the Current Status of Lake Ontario's Pelagic Fish Community," Report of the 1996 Lake Ontario Technical Panel, *Great Lakes Research Review* 2, no. 2 (1996): 4–10.

49 S. S. Crawford, *Salmonine Introductions to the Laurentian Great Lakes: An Historical Review and Evaluation of Ecological Effects,* Canadian Special Publication of Fisheries and Aquatic Sciences No. 132 (National Research Council Canada, 2001).

50 Ibid.

51 Z. M. Pike, *An Account of Expeditions to the Sources of the Mississippi, and Through the Western Parts of Louisiana, to the Sources of the Arkansaw, Kans, La Platte, and Pierre Jaun, Rivers* (1805–7); facsimile available at www.americanjourneys.org/aj_143/.

52 Twain, *Life on the Mississippi.*

53 Fremling, *The Immortal River: The Upper Mississippi in Ancient and Modern Times.*

54 L. W. Larson, "The Great Midwest Flood of 1993" (Natural Disaster Survey Report, National Weather Service, Kansas City, Mo., 1993).

55 E. C. Masteller and E. C. Obert, "Excitement along the Shores of Lake Erie — Hexagenia — Echoes from the Past," *Great Lakes Research Review* 5, no. 1 (2000): 25–36.

56 Ibid.

57 A. Ricciardi and J. B. Rasmussen, "Extinction Rates of North American Freshwater Fauna," *Conservation Biology* 13(1999):1220.

CHAPTER 11: A SEA OF ISLANDS

1 J. B. C. Jackson, "Reefs since Columbus," *Coral Reefs* 16(1997):S23–S32.

2 *First Letter of Christopher Columbus circa 1493,* quoted in *The Islands and the Sea,* ed. J. A. Murray (New York: Oxford University Press, 1991), p. 29.

3 Ibid.

4   R. H. Fuson, *The Log of Christopher Columbus* (Camden, Maine: International Marine Publishing, 1987), p. 89.

5   Ibid., p. 84.

6   R. M. Timm, R. M. Salazar, and A. Townsend Peterson, "Historical Distribution of the Extinct Tropical Seal, *Monachus tropicalis* (Carnivora: Phocidae)," *Conservation Biology* 11 (April 1997): 549.

7   "Ghost of a Monk Seal," *Animals*, November/December 1997.

8   History of Marine Animal Populations Annual Report (2004); available at http://hmap.ruc.dk/documents/HMAP%20Summary%20Report%202004%20final%20January.pdf.

9   "Ghost of a Monk Seal."

10 J. E. Reynolds, III, and D. K. Odell, "Manatees and Dugongs," *Facts on File* (New York, 1991).

11 Quoted in R. McC. Peck, *Land of the Eagles* (London: BBC Books, 1990), p. 92.

12 W. Dampier, *A New Voyage around the World* (London, 1697; reprint, New York: Dover, 1968).

13 Ibid.

14 Reynolds and Odell, "Manatees and Dugongs."

15 Jackson, "Reefs since Columbus."

16 Quoted in ibid.

17 Peck, *Land of the Eagle*, p. 92.

18 E. Long (1774), writing of the late 1600s, quoted in Jackson, "Reefs since Columbus," p. 527.

19 R. Ellis, *The Empty Ocean* (Washington, D.C.: Island Press, 2003).

20 P. Martyr, *The Decades of the Newe Worlde* (1555), quoted in *The Islands and the Sea*, p. 55.

21 K. A. Bjorndal and A. B. Bolten, "From Ghosts to Key Species: Restoring Sea Turtle Populations to Fulfil Their Ecological Roles," *Marine Turtle Newsletter* 100 (2003):16–21.

22 J. Wyneken and M. Salmon, "Frenzy and Postfrenzy Swimming Activity in Loggerhead, Green, and Leatherback Hatchling Sea Turtles," *Copeia* 1992, no. 2 (1992): 478–84.

23 K. J. Lohman et al., "Long Distance Navigation in Sea Turtles," *Ethology Ecology and Evolution* 11(1999):1–23.

24 F. Pierce, "Green Turtle Demise Greatly Exaggerated," *New Scientist*, February 4, 2006.

25 R. Marquez et al., "Results of the Kemp's Ridley Nesting Beach Conservation Efforts in México," *Marine Turtle Newsletter* 85(1999):2–4.

26 R. Witham, "Headstarting Revisited," *Marine Turtle Newsletter* 67(1994):24–26.

27 D. J. Shaver et al., "Record 42 Kemp's Ridley Nests Found in Texas in 2004," *Marine Turtle Newsletter* 108(2005):1–3.

28 A. Carr, *The Windward Road* (New York: Alfred A. Knopf, 1955), p. 241.

29 Quoted in Murray, ed., *The Islands and the Sea*, p. 50.

30 C. Roberts, *The Unnatural History of the Sea: The Past and Future of Humanity and Fishing* (London: Gaia Thinking, 2007).

31 A. Alberts, "West Indian Iguanas: Status, Survey and Conservation Action Plan," IUCN/SSC West Indian Iguana Specialist Group, Gland, Switzerland; available at www.iucn-isg.org/actionplan.

32 D. A. MacMahon and W. H. Marquardt, *The Calusa and Their Legacy* (Gainesville: University Press of Florida, 2004), p. 105.

33 H. Fontenada, "Fontenada's Memoir," trans B. Smith (1854); facsimile available at www.keyshistory.org/fontendada.html.

34 Quoted in J. E. S. Thompson, "Canoes and Navigation of the Maya and Their Neighbours," *Journal of the Royal Anthropological Institute of Great Britain and Ireland* 79(1949):69–78, 69.

35 A. P. Andrews, "America's Ancient Mariners," *Natural History*, October 1999, pp. 72–75.

36 E. S. Wing, "The Sustainability of Resources Used by Native Americans on Four Caribbean Islands," *International Journal of Osteoarchaeology* 11(2001):112–26.

37 Jackson, "Reefs since Columbus."

38 Executive summary of NOAA workshop; available at www.nmfs.noaa.gov/habitat/ead/Acropora%20Workshop/AcroporaWrkspExecSummary.pdf.

39 J. W. Porter and K. G. Porter, *The Everglades, Florida Bay, and Coral Reefs of the Florida Keys* (Boca Raton, Fla.: CRC Press, 2002).

40 J. M. Pandolfi et al., "Are U.S. Coral Reefs on the Slippery Slope to Slime?" *Science* 307(2005):1725–26.

CHAPTER 12: ISLANDS IN THE SEA

1 C. Columbus, *Journals and Other Documents on the Life and Voyages of Christopher Columbus*, trans. Samuel Eliot Morison (New York: Heritage Press, 1963).

2 A. Crosby, *The Columbian Exchange: Biological and Cultural Consequences of 1492* (Westport, Conn.: Greenwood Press, 1972).

3 J. Acosta, quoted in *The Islands and the Sea*, ed. J. A. Murray (New York: Oxford University Press, 1991), p. 71.

4 Ibid.

5 Crosby, *The Columbian Exchange: Biological and Cultural Consequences of 1492*.

6 Quoted in ibid., p. 67.

7 Oviedo, quoted in ibid., p. 68.

8   Quoted in ibid., p. 64.

9   D. G. Campbell, *The Ephemeral Islands: A Natural History of the Bahamas* (London: MacMillan Educational Ltd., 1978).

10 R. H. Fuson, *The Log of Christopher Columbus* (translation based on Las Casas's abstract of the log with additions from his Historia and Fernando Columbus's Historie) (Camden, Maine: International Marine Publishing, 1992), p. 88.

11 *The Letter of Doctor Chanca on the Second Columbus Voyage*, in *The Northmen, Columbus and Cabot, 985–1503: The Voyages of the Northmen; The Voyages of Columbus and of John Cabot*, ed. J. E. Olson and E. G. Bourne, pp. 281–313 (New York: Charles Scribner's Sons, 1906); facsimile available at www.americanjourneys.org/aj-065/.

12 D. Watts, *The West Indies: Patterns of Development, Culture and Environmental Change since 1492*, Cambridge Studies in Historical Geography No. 8 (Cambridge: Cambridge Univesity Press, 1987).

13 A. Alberts, "West Indian Iguanas: Status, Survey and Conservation Action Plan," IUCN/SSC West Indian Iguana Specialist Group, Gland, Switzerland; available at www.iucn-isg.org/actionplan.

14 *The Letter of Doctor Chanca on the Second Columbus Voyage*.

15 E. S. Wing, "The Sustainability of Resources Used by Native Americans on Four Caribbean Islands," *International Journal of Osteoarchaeology* 11(2001):112–26.

16 *The Letter of Doctor Chanca on the Second Columbus Voyage*.

17 Wing, "The Sustainability of Resources Used by Native Americans on Four Caribbean Islands."

18 D. G. Campbell et al., "The Effect of Introduced Hutias (*Geocapromys ingrahami*) on the Woody Vegetation of Little Wax Cay, Bahamas," *Conservation Biology* 5 (1991):536–41.

19 Crosby, *The Columbian Exchange: Biological and Cultural Consequences of 1492*.

20 K. Deagan, "After Columbus: The Sixteenth-Century Spanish-Caribbean Frontier," in *Puerto Real: The Archaeology of a Sixteenth-Century Spanish Town in Hispaniola*, ed. K. Deagan (Gainesville: University Press of Florida, 1995).

21 E. O. Wilson, "Early Ant Plagues in the New World," *Nature* 433(2005):32.

22 Ibid.

23 Fuson, *The Log of Christopher Columbus*, p. 89.

24 *The Letter of Doctor Chanca on the Second Columbus Voyage*.

25 B. de las Casas, quoted in S. L. Olson, "Refutation of the Historical Evidence for a Hispaniolan Macaw," *Caribbean Journal of Science* 41(2005):319–23.

26 T. Juniper and M. Parr, *Parrots: A Guide to the Parrots of the World* (Robertsbridge: Pica Press, 1998).

27 W. T. Hornaday, *Our Vanishing Wildlife: Its Extermination and Preservation* (New York: Charles Scribner's Sons, 1913).

28 A. H. Clark, "Notes on the Guadeloupe Macaw," *The Auk* 51(1934):377.

29 Ibid.

30 Olson, "Refutation of the Historical Evidence for a Hispaniolan Macaw."

31 N. Snyder et al., *The Parrots of Luquillo: Natural History and Conservation of the Puerto Rican Parrot* (Los Angeles: Western Foundation of Vertebrate Zoology, 1987).

32 E. A. Schreiber and D. S. Lee, "West Indian Seabirds: A Disappearing Natural Resource"; available at http://sxm.birds.free.fr/CaribbeanSeabirdsFrame.htm.

33 D. Steadman et al., "Fossil Vertebrates from Antigua, Lesser Antilles: Evidence for late Holocene Human-Caused Extinctions in the West Indies," *Proceedings of the National Academy of Sciences* 81(1984):4448–51.

34 Schreiber and Lee, "West Indian Seabirds."

35 J. J. Audubon, *The Birds of North America.* vol. 7; facsimile available at www .abirdshome.com/Audubon/VolVII/00717.html.

36 Ibid.

37 Ibid.

38 E. A. Schreiber, C. J. Feare, B. A. Harrington, B. G. Murray, Jr., W. B. Robertson, Jr., M. J. Robertson, and G. E. Woolfenden. "Sooty Tern (*Sterna fuscata*)," in *The Birds of North America*, No. 665, ed. A. Poole and F. Gill (Philadelphia: Birds of North America, 2002).

39 S. Purchas, *Purchas His Pilgrimes*, vol. 19 (reprint, New York: MacMillan, 1906).

40 J. Madeiros, "Bermuda's Remarkable Cahow," *World Birdwatch*, December 2002.

41 S. Purchas, *Purchas His Pilgrimes*, vol. 19.

42 J. Smith, *Historie of Bermudas, or Summer Ilands*, quoted in *The Islands and the Sea.*

43 S. Purchas, *Purchas His Pilgrimes*, vol. 19.

44 Du Tertre (1654), quoted in Schreiber and Lee, "West Indian Seabirds."

45 Labat (1724), quoted in ibid.

46 R. Hakluyt, *Hakluyt's Voyages*, ed. R. David (London: Chatto and Windus, 1981).

47 A. von Humboldt, *The Island of Cuba* (New York: Derby and Jackson, 1856).

CHAPTER 13: LA FLORIDA

1 C. T. Simpson, quoted in M. Grunwald, *The Swamp: The Everglades, Florida and the Politics of Paradise* (New York: Simon and Schuster, 2006), p. 13.

2 S. de R. Diettrich, "Florida's Climatic Extremes: Cold Spells and Freezes," *Economic Geography* 25(1949):68–74.

3 C. T. Simpson, quoted in Grunwald, *The Swamp: The Everglades, Florida and the Politics of Paradise*, p. 11.

4 J. K. Small, "A Botanical Excursion to Big Cypress," *Natural History* 20(1920):488– 500.

5 Quoted in Grunwald, *The Swamp: The Everglades, Florida and the Politics of Power*, p. 12.

6 Soldier in Col. W. S. Handy's command, quoted in T. Levin, *Liquid Land: A Natural History of the Everglades* (Athens: University of Georgia Press, 2003), p. xvi.

7 J. K. Small, quoted in E. O. Rothra, *Florida's Pioneer Naturalist: The Life of Charles Torrey Simpson* (Gainesville: University Press of Florida, 1995), p. 130.

8 Quoted in Grunwald, *The Swamp: The Everglades, Florida and the Politics of Power*.

9 Quoted in D. T. Frederick, "History of Juan Ponce de Leon's Voyages to Florida: Source Records," *Florida Historical Society Quarterly* 14(1935):3–70, p. 60; facsimile available at www.americanjourneys.org/aj-095/.

10 H. Fontenada, "Fontenada's Memoir," trans B. Smith (1854); facsimile available at www.keyshistory.org/fontendada.html.

11 J. E. Chance, *My Life in the Old Army: The Reminiscences of Abner Doubleday* (Fort Worth: Texas Christian University Press, 1998), p. 198.

12 J. J. Audubon, quoted in Grunwald, *The Swamp: The Everglades, Florida and the Politics of Paradise*.

13 J. J. Audubon, *Birds of North America*, vol. 5; facsimile available at www.abirdshome .com/Audubon/VolV/00592.html.

14 W. B. Robertson, Jr., and J. A. Kushlan, *The Southern Florida Avifauna*, Memoir 2 (Coral Gables, Fla.: Miami Geological Society, 1974).

15 P. C. Frohring, D. P. Voorhees, and J. A. Kushlan, "History of Wading Bird Populations in the Florida Everglades: A Lesson in the Use of Historical Information," *Colonial Waterbirds* 11, no. 2 (1988): 328–35.

16 Audubon, *Birds of North America*, vol. 6; facsimile available at www.abirdshome .com/Audubon/VolVI/00630.html.

17 Quoted in exhibit on Cuthbert Lake, America Museum of Natural History, New York.

18 Small, "A Botanical Excursion to Big Cypress."

19 Quoted in R. Mc. C. Peck, *Land of the Eagle* (London: BBC Books, 1990), p. 115.

20 Small, "A Botanical Excursion to Big Cypress."

21 F. H. Sklar et al., "The Ecological-Societal Underpinnings of Everglades Restoration," *Frontiers in Ecology and the Environment* 3(2005):161–69.

22 P. R. Wetzel et al., "Maintaining Tree Islands in the Florida Everglades: Nutrient Redistribution Is the Key," *Frontiers in Ecology and the Environment* 3(2005): 370–76.

23 Sklar et al., "The Ecological-Societal Underpinnings of Everglades Restoration."

CHAPTER 14: . . . TO SHINING SEA

1   C. F. Carter, "Duhaut-Cilly's Account of California in the Years 1827–1828," *Quarterly Journal of the California Historical Society* 8(1929):131–66, 214–50, 306–36, p. 157; facsimile available at www.americanjourneys.org/aj-098.

2   G. R. De Montalvo, *Las Sergas de Esplandián* (1510).

3   H. R. Wagner, "Pearl Fishing Enterprises in the Gulf of California," *Hispanic American Historical Review* 10(1930):188–203.

4   J. Arvizu-Martinez, Fisheries Activities in the Gulf of Mexico, Fisheries in the Gulf of Mexico (California Cooperative Oceanic Fisheries Investigations Annual Report vol. 28, 1987).

5   V. Coules, *The Trade* (Edinburgh: Birlinn Press, 2007).

6   C. L. Mackenzie, "A History of the Pearl Oyster Fishery in the Archipelago de las Perlas, Panama," *Marine Fisheries Review* 61(1999):51–65.

7   E. Bryant, *What I Saw in California* (1849); facsimile available at http://infomotions .com/etexts/gutenberg/dirs/1/7/0/0/13002.htm.

8   A. Sáenz-Arroyo et al., "The Value of Evidence about Past Abundance: Marine Fauna of the Gulf of California through the Eyes of 16th to 19th Century Travellers," *Fish and Fisheries* 7(2006):128–46.

9   Quoted in ibid., p. 135.

10   Quoted in ibid.

11   R. Cannon, quoted in C. Roberts, *The Unnatural Sea: The Past and Future of Humanity and Fishing* (London: Gaia Thinking, 2007), p. 261.

12   "Diary of Sebastian Vizcaino, 1602–1603," in *Spanish Exploration of the Southwest, 1542–1706*, pp. 43–103 (New York: Charles Scribner's Sons, 1916), p. 56; facsimile available at www.americanjourneys.org/aj-002/.

13   Quoted in Sáenz-Arroyo et al., "The Value of Evidence about Past Abundance: Marine Fauna of the Gulf of California through the Eyes of 16th to 19th Century Travellers," p. 135.

14   Ibid.

15   Arvizu-Martinez, "Fisheries Activities in the Gulf of California."

16   G. Kira, "Unique Ensenada Fish Breeding Lab Struggles for Funding," *Western Outdoor News*, July 14, 2003.

17   J. Steinbeck and E. F. Ricketts, *The Log of the Sea of Cortez*, Penguin Great Books of the Twentieth Century (New York: Penguin, 2008).

18   R. Sáenz-Arroyo et al., "Rapidly Shifting Baselines among Fishers of the Gulf of California," *Proceedings of the Royal Society B* 272(2005):1957–62.

19   Quoted in Sáenz-Arroyo et al., "The Value of Evidence about Past Abundance: Marine Fauna of the Gulf of California through the Eyes of 16th to 19th Century Travellers."

20 S. Richardson, "Washington State Status Report for the Olive Ridley" (Washington Department of Fish and Wildlife, Olympia, 1997).

21 D. Mack, "Worldwide Trade in Wild Sea Turtle Products: An Update," *Marine Turtle Newsletter* 24(1983):10–15.

22 National Marine Fisheries Service and U.S. Fish and Wildlife Service, "Recovery Plan of US Pacific Populations of the Olive Ridley Turtle (*Lepidochelys olivacea*)" (1998).

23 R. A. Valverde, "Letter to the Editors: On the Ostional Affair," *Marine Turtle Newsletter* 86(1999):6–8.

24 S. Honarvar et al., "Density-Dependent Effects on Hatching Success in Olive Ridley Sea Turtles" (paper presented at Society for Integrative and Comparative Biology meeting, January 3–7, 2007, Phoenix).

25 L. L. Campbell, "Use Them or Lose Them: Conservation and the Consumptive Use of Marine Turtle Eggs at Ostional, Costa Rica," *Environmental Conservation* 25(1998):305–19.

26 R. H. Horwich and J. Lyon, "Community Conservation: Practitioners Answers to Critics," *Oryx* 41(2007)376–85.

27 "Diary of Sebastian Vizcaino."

28 J.-F. de Galaup de La Perouse, *The Journal of Jean-Francois de la Perouse 1785–1788*, 2 vols., trans. and ed. John Dunmore (London: Hakluyt Society, 1994).

29 R. H. Dana, Jr., *Two Years before the Mast* (reprint, New York: New American Library, 1964).

30 Quoted in Sáenz-Arroyo et al., "The Value of Evidence about Past Abundance: Marine Fauna of the Gulf of California through the Eyes of 16th to 19th Century Travellers," p. 132.

31 C. M. Scammon, *The Marine Mammals of the North-western Coast of North America* (1874; reprint, New York: Dover Publications, 1968), p. 11.

32 Ibid., p. 32.

33 "NOAA Reports Significant Increase in 2006 Gray Whale Calf Numbers" (NOAA 2006-R114, National Oceanic and Atmospheric Administration Press Report, Washington, D.C., 2006).

34 S. E. Alter, E. Rynes, and S. R. Palumbi, "DNA Evidence for Historic Population Size and Past Ecosystem Impacts of Gray Whales," *Proceedings of the National Academy of Sciences* 104, no. 38 (2007): 15162–67.

35 S. T. Turvey et al., "First Human-Caused Extinction of a Cetacean Species," *Biology Letters* 3(2007); available at http://journals.royalsociety.org/content/15782wq 480207749.

36 L. Rojas-Bracho et al., "Conservation of the Vaquita *Phocoena sinus*," *Mammal Review* 36(2006):179–216.

37 A. Jaramillo-Legorreta et al., "Saving the Vaquita: Immediate Action Not More Data," *Conservation Biology*; available at http://www.vaquita.org/PDF%20Files/Jaramillo_et_al_2007_Conservation_Biology%5B1%5D.pdf.

38 A. Leopold, *A Sand County Almanac and Sketches Here and There* (New York: Oxford University Press, 1989), p. 142.

39 R. C. Bueno, "Co-Management of the Hookah Diving Fisheries," *CEDO News* 9 (1999):12–13.

40 *The Voyage of Francisco de Ulloa* (1539), in *Spanish Voyages to the Northwest Coast of America in the Sixteenth Century*. ed. H. R. Wagner, pp. 11–50 (San Francisco: California Historical Society, 1929); facsimile available at www.americanjourneys .org/aj-113/.

41 Quoted in Sáenz-Arroyo et al., "The Value of Evidence about Past Abundance: Marine Fauna of the Gulf of California through the Eyes of 16th to 19th Century Travellers."

42 O. W. Frost, ed., *Journal of a Voyage with Bering, 1741–1742: Georg Wilhelm Steller* (Stanford, Calif.: Stanford University Press, 1988).

43 Ibid., p. 78.

44 Ibid., p. 114.

45 Ibid., p. 128.

46 Ibid., p. 162.

47 Ibid., p. 134.

48 Scammon, *The Marine Mammals of the North-western Coast of North America*, p. 135.

49 R. H. Colten and J. E. Arnold, "Prehistoric Marine Mammal Hunting on California's Northern Channel Islands," *American Antiquity* 63(1998):679–701.

50 C. E. Kay and R. T. Simmons, *Wilderness and Political Ecology: Aboriginal Influences and the Original State of Nature* (Salt Lake City: University of Utah Press, 2002).

51 R. L. Merrick, "Current and Historical Roles of Apex Predators in the Bering Sea Ecosystem," *Journal of Northwest Atlantic Fishery Science* 22(1997):343–55.

52 A. W. Trites and C. P. Donnelly, "The Decline of Steller Sea Lions *Eumetopias jubatus* in Alaska: A Review of the Nutritional Stress Hypothesis," *Mammal Review* 33(2003):3–28.

53 R. Ellis, *The Empty Ocean* (Washington, D.C.: Island Press, 2003).

54 Quoted in R. McC. Peck, *Land of the Eagle* (London: BBC Books, 1990).

55 Frost, *Journal of a Voyage with Bering, 1741–1742: Georg Wilhelm Steller*.

56 Scammon, *The Marine Mammals of the North-western Coast of North America*, p. 174.

57 Ibid.

58 Carter, "Duhaut-Cilly's Account of California in the Years 1827–1828."

59 C. A. Simenstad et al., "Aluets, Sea Otters, and Alternate Stable-State Communities," *Science* 200(1978):403–11.

60 Roberts, *The Unnatural History of the Sea: The Past and Future of Humanity and Fishing.*

61 T. M. Williams et al., "Killer Appetites: Assessing the Role of Predators in Ecological Communities," *Ecology* 85(2004):3373–84.

62 J. M. Erlandson et al., "Sea Otters, Shellfish and Humans: 10,000 Years of Ecological Interaction on San Miguel Island, California" (Proceedings of the 6th California Islands Symposium, 2005).

CHAPTER 15: BLESSINGS FIT FOR THE USE OF MAN

1 E. Bakker, *An Island Called California: An Ecological Introduction to Its Natural Communities* (Berkeley: University of California Press, 1984).

2 P. Steinhart, *California's Wild Heritage: Threatened and Endangered Animals in the Golden State* (San Francisco: Sierra Club Books, 1990).

3 M. K. Anderson, *Tending the Wild: Native American Knowledge and the Management of California's Natural Resources* (Berkeley: University of California Press, 2005).

4 Quoted in J. Bakeless, *The Eyes of Discovery* (New York: Dover Press, 1950).

5 Quoted in ibid.

6 Quoted in Anderson, *Tending the Wild: Native American Knowledge and the Management of California's Natural Resources.*

7 P. Munoz, *The Gabriel Moraga Expedition of 1806: The Diary of Fr. Pedro Munoz,* ed. R. G. Cleland (Whitefish, Mont.: Kessinger, 2007).

8 Ibid.

9 Quoted in Bakeless, *The Eyes of Discovery.*

10 F. Drake, in *Early English and French Voyages, Chiefly from Hakluty, 1534–1608,* pp. 151–73 (New York: Charles Scribner's Sons, 1906), p. 171; facsimile available at www .americanjourneys.org/aj-032/.

11 J. M. Broughton, "Pre-Columbian Human Impact on California Vertebrates," in *Wilderness and Political Ecology,* ed. C. E. Kay and R. T. Simmons (Salt Lake City: University of Utah Press, 2002).

12 D. R. McCullough, *The Tule Elk: Its History, Behavior and Ecology* (Berkeley: University of California Press, 1969).

13 G. A. Feldhamer et al., *Wild Mammals of North America: Biology, Management and Conservation* (Baltimore: Johns Hopkins University Press, 2003.)

14 V. Geist, *Deer of the World: Their Evolution, Behaviour and Ecology* (Mechanicsburg, Pa.: Stackpole Books, 1998).

15 Broughton, "Pre-Columbian Human Impact on California Vertebrates," p. 44.

16 Quoted in Bakeless, *The Eyes of Discovery.*

17 Quoted in Anderson, *Tending the Wild: Native American Knowledge and the Management of California's Natural Resources.*

18 P. Browning, ed., *The Discovery of San Francisco Bay: The Portola Expedition of 1769–1770* (Lafayette, Calif.: Great West Books, 1992).

19 Broughton, "Pre-Columbian Human Impact on California Vertebrates.," p. 44.

20 Ibid.

21 Translation of a letter, dated July 3, 1769, from Junipero Serra to his biographer, Father Palu.

22 Anderson, *Tending the Wild: Native American Knowledge and the Management of California's Natural Resources*.

23 T. L. Jones et al., "The Protracted Holocene Extinction of California's Flightless Sea Duck (*Chendytes lawi*) and Its Implications for the Pleistocene Overkill Hypothesis," *Proceedings of the National Academy of Science* 105(2008):4105–8.

24 Anderson, *Tending the Wild: Native American Knowledge and the Management of California's Natural Resources*.

25 Browning, ed., *The Discovery of San Francisco Bay: The Portola Expedition of 1769–1770*, p. 63.

26 W. Preston, "Post Columbian Wildlife Irruptions in California: Implications for Cultural and Environmental Understanding," in *Wilderness and Political Ecology*.

27 P. M. Daggett and D. R. Henning, "The Jaguar in North America," *American Antiquity* 39(1974):465–69.

28 T. I. Storer and L. P. Trevis, Jr., *California Grizzly* (1955; reprint, Berkeley: University of California Press, 1996).

29 Anderson, *Tending the Wild: Native American Knowledge and the Management of California's Natural Resources*.

30 Storer and Trevis, *California Grizzly*.

31 Ibid.

32 J. Miller, *True Bear Stories* (New York: Rand McNally & Co., 1900; reprint, Santa Barbara, Calif.: Capra Press, 1987).

33 Browning, ed., *The Discovery of San Francisco Bay: The Portola Expedition of 1769–1770*.

34 Ibid., p.119.

35 Ibid., p. 95.

36 Quoted in Anderson, *Tending the Wild: Native American Knowledge and the Management of California's Natural Resources*.

37 J. P. Ryder and R. T. Alisauskas, "Ross's Goose (*Chen rossii*)," in *The Birds of North America Online*, ed. A. Poole (Ithaca, N.Y.: Cornell Lab of Ornithology, 1995); available at http://bna.birds.cornell.edu/bna/species/162 doi:10.2173/bna.162.

38 W. H. Thomes, *On Land and Sea or California in the Years 1843, '44 and '45* (Boston: DeWolfe, Fiske and Co., 1884).

CHAPTER 16: RIVERS OF FISH

1   R. J. Behnke, *Trout and Salmon of North America* (New York: Free Press, 2002).

2   C. T. Dairmont, T. E. Reimchen, and P. C. Paquet, "Foraging Behaviour by Gray Wolves on Salmon Streams in Coastal British Columbia," *Canadian Journal of Zoology* 81(2003):349–53.

3   T. Reimchen, "Salmon Nutrients, Nitrogen Isotopes and Coastal Forests," *Ecoforestry*, Fall 2001, pp. 13–16.

4   D. R. Montgomery, *King of Fish: The Thousand Year Run of Salmon* (Boulder, Colo.: Westview Press, 2003), p. 126.

5   J. A. Lichatowich, *Salmon without Rivers: A History of the Pacific Salmon Crisis* (Washington, D.C.: Island Press, 1999).

6   S. L. Swezey and R. F. Heizer, "Ritual Management of Salmonid Fish Resources in California," in *Before the Wilderness: Environmental Management by Native Californians*, ed. T. C. Blackburn and K. Anderson, pp. 299–327 (Menlo Park, Calif.: Ballena Press, 1993).

7   A. F. McEvoy, *The Fisherman's Problem: Ecology and Law in the California Fisheries, 1850–1980* (New York: Cambridge University Press, 1986).

8   Quoted in Montgomery, *King of Fish: The Thousand Year Run of Salmon*, p. 127.

9   Quoted in ibid.

10 C. T. Meengs and R. T. Lackey, "Estimating the Size of Historical Oregon Salmon Runs," *Fisheries Science* 13(2005):51–66.

11 R. S. Waples, "Pacific Salmon (*Oncorhynchus spp.*) and the Definition of 'Species' under the Endangered Species Act," *Marine Fish Review* 53(1991):11–22.

12 B. McMillan, "Historic Steelhead Abundance: Washington NW Coast and Puget Sound," Briefing Document for the Wild Salmon Center; available at http://www.wildsalmoncenter.org/pdf/mcmillan_gayeski_report/part_3_conclusions_and_reference.pdf.

13 Ibid.

14 M. H. Ruckelshaus et al., "The Pacific Salmon Wars: What Science Brings to the Challenge of Recovering Species," *Annual Review of Ecology and Systematics* 33(2002): 665–706.

15 T. P. Poe et al., "Ecological Consequences of Introduced Piscivorous Fishes in the Lower Columbia and Snake Rivers," in *Theory and Application in Fish Feeding Ecology*, ed. D. J. Stouder et al. (Columbia: University of South Carolina Press, 1994).

16 Ruckelshaus et al., "The Pacific Salmon Wars: What Science Brings to the Challenge of Recovering Species."

17 R. T. Lackey, "Salmon Recovery: Learning from Successes and Failures," *Northwest Science* 76(2002):356–60.

18 Ruckelshaus et al., "The Pacific Salmon Wars: What Science Brings to the Challenge of Recovering Species."

CHAPTER 17: WILDERNESS CATHEDRAL

1   J. Muir, quoted in T. P. Duane, *Shaping the Sierra: Nature, Culture and Conflict in the Changing West* (Berkeley: University of California Press, 2000), p. 8.

2   D. Beesley, *Crow's Range: An Environmental History of the Sierra Nevada* (Reno: University of Nevada Press, 2004), p. 15.

3   M. Austin, *The Land of Little Rain* (1903; reprint, New York: Dover, 1996).

4   Mono Basin Clearinghouse; available at http://www.monobasinresearch.org/timelines/waterfowl.htm.

5   W. Brewer, *Up and Down California in 1860–1864: The Journal of William H. Brewer* (Berkeley: University of California Press, 1975), bk. 4.

6   J. Muir, *My First Summer in the Sierra* (1911; reprint, New York: Penguin Nature Classics, 1997).

7   Ibid.

8   H. Lewis, *Patterns of Burning in California: Ecology and Ethnohistory*, Ballena Press Anthropological Papers 1 (Menlo Park, Calif.: Ballena Press, 1973).

9   J. L. Lowry, "Caching In: The Landscaping Ideas of Jays," *Bay Nature*, October–December 2005.

10 Quoted in Beesley, *Crow's Range: An Environmental History of the Sierra Nevada*.

11 Quoted in ibid.

12 Ibid.

13 P. White, *The Farallon Islands: Sentinels of the Golden Gate* (San Francisco: Scottwall Associates, 1995).

14 W. J. Sydeman, "Population Change of Common Murres: Perspectives from the Farallon Islands"; available at http://montereybay.noaa.gov/educate/newsletters/ecosystem2000/birdpopulations.html.

15 Quoted in K. T. Anderson, *Tending the Wild: Native American Knowledge and the Management of California's Natural Resources* (Berkeley: University of California Press, 2005), p. 20.

16 Quoted in ibid., p. 95.

17 Quoted in ibid.

18 J. Grinnell, quoted in ibid., p. 94.

19 J. M. Linsdale, "Facts Concerning the Use of Thallium in California to Poison Rodents—Its Destructiveness to Game-Birds, Song-Birds and Other Valuable Wildlife," *The Condor* 23(1931):92–106.

20 Ibid.

21 D. F. Williams, "Distribution and Population Status of the San Joaquin Antelope Squirrel and Giant Kangaroo Rat" (California Department of Fish and Game, Sacramento, Nongame Wildlife Investigations, Final Report E-W-R, IV-10.0).

22 D. Dennis, "John Muir and the Origin of Yosemite Valley," *Annals of Science* 48 (1991):453–85.

23 Quoted in Anderson, *Tending the Wild: Native American Knowledge and the Management of California's Natural Resources*.

24 Quoted in ibid.

25 Quoted in F. P. Farquhar, *History of the Sierra Nevada* (Berkeley: University of California Press, 1965).

26 Quoted in ibid.

27 M. Reisner, *Cadillac Desert: The American West and Its Disappearing Water*, rev. ed. (New York: Penguin, 1993).

CHAPTER 18: THE GREAT STILLNESS

1 Quoted in J. Bakeless, *The Eyes of Discovery: America as Seen by Its First Explorers* (New York: Dover Publications, 1961), p. 314.

2 Quoted in R. McC. Peck, *Land of the Eagle* (London: BBC Books, 1990), p. 126.

3 R. Baird, *View of the Valley of the Mississippi* (Philadelphia, 1832).

4 T. Jefferson letter to Lewis and Clark; facsimile available at www.lewisandclark trail.com/legacy/letter.htm.

5 J. Bakeless, ed., *The Journals of Lewis and Clark* (New York: Mentor, 1964), p. 61.

6 E. T. Seton, *Lives of Game Animals* (New York: Doubleday, Doran and Co., 1929).

7 R. Manes, "Does the Prairie Dog Merit Protection Via the Endangered Species Act?" in *Conservation of the Black-Tailed Prairie Dog: Saving North America's Western Grasslands*, ed. John L. Hoogland (Washington, D.C.: Island Press, 2006).

8 L. T. Vermeire et al., "The Prairie Dog Story: Do We Have It Right?" *Bioscience* 54(2004):689–95.

9 S. Forrest, "Getting the Story Right: A Response to Vermeire and Colleagues," *Bioscience* 55(2005):526–30.

10 P. A. Johnsgard, *Great Wildlife of the Great Plains* (Lawrence: University Press of Kansas, 2003).

11 N. B. Kotliar et al., "The Prairie Dog as a Keystone Species," in *Conservation of the Black-Tailed Prairie Dog: Saving North America's Western Grasslands*.

12 N. B. Kotliar et al., "A Critical Review of Assumptions about the Prairie Dog as a Keystone Species," *Environmental Management* 24(1999):177–92.

13 Kotliar et al., "The Prairie Dog as a Keystone Species."

14 A. G. Feldhamer et al., *Wild Mammals of North America: Biology Management and Conservation*, 2nd ed. (Baltimore: Johns Hopkins University Press, 2003).

15 Kotliar et al., "The Prairie Dog as a Keystone Species."

16 Bakeless, ed., *The Journals of Lewis and Clark*, p. 61.

17 W. D. Street, quoted in D. A. Dary, *The Buffalo Book* (Athens: Swallow Press/Ohio University Press, 1990), p. 26.

18 D. F. Lott, *American Bison: A Natural History* (Berkeley: University of California Press, 2002).

19 P. S. Martin and C. R. Szuter, "War Zones and Game Sinks in Lewis and Clark's West," *Conservation Biology* 13(1999):36–45.

20 R. D. Guthrie, *Frozen Fauna of the Mammoth Steppe: The Story of Blue Babe* (Chicago: University of Chicago Press, 1989).

21 T. Flannery, *The Eternal Frontier: An Ecological History of North America and Its Peoples* (London: Vintage, 2002).

22 P. A. Johnsgard, "Where Have All the Curlews Gone?" *Natural History* 89(1980): 30–33.

23 J. B. Gollop, T. W. Barry, and E. H. Iversen, "Eskimo curlew, a Vanishing Species?" (Saskatchewan Natural History Society Special Publication No. 17, Regina, Saskatchewan, 1986).

24 R. E. Gill, Jr., p. Canevari, and E. H. Iversen, "Eskimo Curlew (*Numenius borealis*)," in *The Birds of North America*, No. 347, ed. A. Poole and F. Gill (Philadelphia: Birds of North America, 1998).

25 D. Flores, *The Natural West: Environmental History in the Great Plains and Rocky Mountains* (Norman: University of Oklahoma Press, 2001).

26 R. V. Hine and M. F. Faracher, *The American West: A New Interpretive History* (New Haven, Conn.: Yale University Press, 2000).

27 Lott, *American Bison: A Natural History.*

28 Quoted in Peck, *Land of the Eagle*, p. 143.

29 Lott, *American Bison: A Natural History,* p. 182.

30 C. Delano, Annual Report of the Department of the Interior (1873); available at www.buffalofieldcampaign.org/aboutbuffalo/bisonslaughterhistory.htm.

31 G. Catlin, *North American Indians*, ed. P. Matthiessen (New York: Penguin, 2004), p. 260.

32 P. Norris, *Annual Report of the Superintendent of the Yellowstone National Park to the Secretary of the Interior, 1880* (Washington, D.C.: Government Printing Office, 1881).

CHAPTER 19: DEVILS IN PARADISE

1 E. O. Wilson, quoted in E. Callenback, *Bring Back the Buffalo: A Sustainable Future for America's Great Plains* (Berkeley: University of California Press, 2000), p. 7.

2 Quoted in J. T. Coleman, *Vicious: Wolves and Men in America* (New Haven, Conn.: Yale University Press, 2004).

3 B. Hampton, *The Great American Wolf* (New York: Henry Holt and Co., 1997).

4 T. Jefferson, Letter to James Madison (1787), Papers 12, p. 442; available at http:// etext.virginia.edu/jefferson/quotations/jeff1320.htm.

5 H. E. Evans, *The Natural History of the Long Expedition to the Rocky Mountains, 1819– 1820* (New York: Oxford University Press, 1997).

6 Ibid.

7 R. Manning, *Grassland: The History, Politics and Promise of the American Prairie* (New York: Penguin, 1995).

8 W. G. Hartley, "Mormons, Crickets and Gulls: A New Look at the Old Story," *Utah Historical Quarterly* 38(1970):224–39.

9 Quoted in ibid.

10 S. V. Romney, "An Overview of the Mormon Cricket Infestation in Northeastern Utah," *Proceedings of the Utah Mosquito Abatement Association* 38–39(1985):17–19.

11 S. J. Simpson, G. A. Sword, P. D. Lorch, and I. D. Couzin, "Cannibal Crickets on a Forced March for Protein and Salt," *Proceedings of the National Academy of Science USA* 103(2006):4152–56.

12 J. A. Lockwood, *Locust: The Devastating Rise and Mysterious Disappearance of the Insect That Shaped the American Frontier* (New York: Basic Books, 2004).

13 R. V. Hine and J. M. Faragher, *The American West: A New Interpretive History* (New Haven, Conn.: Yale University Press, 2000).

14 J. E. Weaver and F. W. Albertson, *Grasslands of the Great Plains: Their Nature and Use* (Lincoln, Neb.: Johnsen Publishing Co., 1956).

15 Quoted in D. Worster, *Under Western Skies: Nature and History in the American West* (New York: Oxford University Press, 1992).

16 Ibid.

17 Quoted in Hampton, *The Great American Wolf*, p. 6.

18 E. T. Seton, *Wild Animals I Have Known* (1899); available at www.fullbooks.com/ Wild-Animals-I-Have-Known1.html.

19 A. Leopold, *A Sand County Almanac* (New York: Oxford University Press, 1949).

20 A. Leopold, quoted in Hampton, *The Great American Wolf*, p. 151.

21 H. Axtell, quoted in ibid., p. 225.

22 T. Wilkinson, *Wildlife Conservation*, April 2007.

23 A. Leopold, "The Ecological Conscience," *Bulletin of the Garden Club of North America*, September 1947.

CHAPTER 20: A NEW WORLD?

1 D. H. Rumsfeld, U.S. Department of Defense news briefing, February 12, 2002,

2 W. Laurance, "Expect the Unexpected," *New Scientist*, April 12, 2008, p. 17.

3   Quoted in S. Petersen, Congress and Charismatic Megafauna: A Legislative History of the Endangered Species Act," *Environmental Law* 29(1999):463–91, p. 486.

4   P. Hawken, *The Ecology of Commerce: How Business Can Save the Planet* (London: Wiedenfeld and Nicolson, 1994).

5   J. Porritt, *Capitalism as if the World Matters* (Sterling, Va.: Earthscan, 2005).

6   N. Myers, "Lifting the Veil on Perverse Subsidies," *Nature* 392 (March 26, 1998).

7   J. Alexander et al., "Balancing the Earth's Accounts," *Nature* 401 (September 23, 1999).

8   A. Sen, *Development as Freedom* (Oxford: Oxford University Press, 1999).

9   C. Hamilton, *The Growth Fetish* (Crows Nest: Allen and Unwin, 2003).

Index

abalone, 332. *See also* black abalone; green abalone; pink abalone; red abalone; white abalone
Abbott, Charles Conrad, 157
Abundant Wildlife Society of North America, 448
Acadie, 71
Acansa, 202, 203
acorn, 175, 355, 377, 378
acorn woodpecker, 156, 377
Acosta, José de, 253, 254
Act Agaynst the Killinge of Ouer Young Tortoyses, An, 239
Adams, John, 39
Age of Enlightenment, 143, 174, 401, 429
agrarian democracy, 428, 429, 437
Alabama, 139, 158, 208
Alabama River, 211
Alaska, 96, 112, 326, 361, 414, 445
Albany, 151
Albemarle Sound, 71, 73
Alberta, 114
alcatraz (bird), 272, 382
Alcatraz (California), 351, 382
Aleut, 326, 329–31
Aleutian Islands, 319, 324, 326, 333
alewife, 27, 87, 88, 117, 217, 218
Alexandria, 87
Alfred P. Sloane Foundation, 65
Algonquian, 75
alkaline lake, 375, 393
Allard, Charles, 424
Allee, Warder C., 166
Allee effect, 166, 167
Alleghenies, 113, 139–41

alligator, 277, 283
alligator gar, 201
Allyón, Lucas Vasquez de, 70
alpaca, 253
Amazon, 122, 455
Amazonian manatee, 235
Amazon parrot, 262, 263
American basswood, 108
American beech, 108, 110, 161
American Bottom, 206
American cheetah, 412
American chestnut, 121
American eel, 195, 196
American Fur Company, 421
American golden plover, 103, 104
American mink, 177, 187
American Museum of Natural History, 288
American Ornithologists' Union, 152, 167, 288
American Ornithology, 146
American paddlefish, 202
American River, the, 358, 359, 379
American shad, 87, 90
Amerike, Richard, 23
Amtrak, 191
Anderson, Kat, 346, 347
anchovy, 304
anhinga, 204, 277
Anhinga Trail, 275, 277
Ano Nuevo (California), 328, 329
Anticosti Island, 126
Anti-Debris Association of the Sacramento Valley, 384
Antigua, 265

Antilocapridae, 345, 409
ant plague, 261
Anza, Juan Bautista de, 352, 355
aporath. *See* great auk
Appalachian Mountains, 106, 108, 110, 111, 113, 114, 131, 139–41, 148, 193
apple snail, 278
apponatz. *See* great auk
Arapaho, 419
Arawak, 228, 235, 245, 260
Arcadia, 71
Archaic culture, 208
arctic fox, 187, 322, 323
arctic tern, 36, 64
Argentina, 68, 76, 164
Aristotle, 252
Arizona, 392
Arkansas, 158, 159, 353
Arkansas River, 202, 410, 428
Armada, the, 49, 341
Army Corps of Engineers, 221, 222, 295
arribada, 242, 309, 310
arsenic, 383
Ascension Island, 236, 237, 241, 266, 267
Asheville (North Carolina), 106, 114, 139
Askins, Robert, 148, 149
aspen, 172
Astor, John Jacob, 421
Atlantic menhaden. *See* menhaden
Atlantic salmon, 9, 88, 117; decline in England, 14; decline in North America, 15, 16; different genetic stocks, 17, 18, 36; European market for, 15, 16; farmed salmon, 16–19; in Great Lakes, 195–97, 218; historic abundance, 13, 14, 86; historic distribution, 13; life cycle, 12; Norse description, 10; timing of migration, 18
Atlantic Seal Hunt Management Plan, 59

Atlantic sturgeon, 85, 86, 91
Audubon, Jean, 147
Audubon, John James, 102, 144, 146–48, 406, 427; on bobolinks, 148; on Carolina parakeets, 151, 153, 154; on Dry Tortugas, 266; on egret plumes, 288; on Florida Keys, 287; on heron rookeries, 291; on ivory-billed woodpeckers, 156, 157; on passenger pigeons, 161–66
Audubon Plumage Bill, 291
Audubon Society. *See* National Audubon Society
Axtell, Horace, 446, 449
Aztec, 70, 299, 316

baccallaos, 27
Bachman's warbler, 158
Back to the Future project, 66
Baffin Island, 96
Bahamas, the, 49, 227, 228, 231, 261
baidarka, 326, 330
baiji, 313
Bailey Wildlife Foundation Wolf Compensation Trust, 446
Baja California, 50, 300–302, 304, 310, 324, 344
Baker, Senator Howard, 212, 213
Bakker, Elna, 336
Balboa, Vasco Nuñez de, 70, 299, 300
bald cypress. *See* swamp cypress
baleen, 48, 52
balsam poplar, 107
Baltic, the, 40
Baltimore, 79, 102
banana, 255
banana republic, 255
Banks, Joseph, 177
Barbados, 229, 261

Bardot, Brigitte, 59
Bartholin, Thomas, 50, 51
Bartram, John, 145, 430
Bartram, William, 121, 122, 145–47, 276, 285; on size of trees, 110
Basque: fishermen, 29; whalers, 48, 49, 51, 52
Battle of Horseshoe Bend, 286
Bay of Biscay, 48
Bay of Fundy, endangered salmon, 16
Bay of Pigs, 232
bean, 118, 120
bear, 113, 126–29, 135, 165, 199, 360. *See also* black bear; grizzly bear, Californian; polar bear; short-faced bear
beaver, 121, 452; dams, 114; decline, 184; fur trade, 114, 115, 132, 174, 178–80, 183, 184, 187, 378, 379, 421; historical abundance, 177, 187, 199, 220; in Indian philosophy, 182, 183; meadows, 130, 149, 173; ponds, 171, 172; recovery 190, 191
Beaver War, 179, 180
bee hummingbird, 229
bee swarm orchid. *See* cigar orchid
Behnke, Robert, 13
Belize, 249, 251, 272
Belize Barrier Reef, 226, 227
Bella Coola, 396
beluga, 46, 53, 54
Beothuk Indians, 31
Bering, Vitus, 319, 322
Bering Island, 322, 329, 330
Bering Sea, 327
Bering Straits, 62
Berkeley, 339
Bermuda, 103, 238, 239, 246, 247, 251, 267–71

Bermuda petrel. *See* cahow
Bermudez, Juan de, 268
big bluestem, 426
Big Cypress Swamp, 279
bighorn sheep, 345, 382, 423
Big Pine Key, 283
big-tooth aspen, 107
Big Woods (Arkansas), 158
biofuel, 455
biophilia, 385
Bird Cay (Belize), 272
bird effigy mound, 205
Bird Rocks, 33
Birdseye, Clarence, 39
Birds of California, 344, 352
bison, 200, 203, 207, 427, 439, 451, 454; decline, 420–22; in eastern forests, 113, 114, 125, 129, 133, 142, 151; evolutionary history, 412–14; on Great Plains, 398, 401, 405, 418, 419; hide and tongue trade, 421, 422; historic abundance on plains, 410, 411; long-horned bison, 414; and prairie dogs, 406; recovery, 423, 424; wood bison, 114
black abalone, 334
black band disease, 251
black bear, 122, 126, 129, 173, 187
black-capped petrel, 271
black duck, 98, 105, 172
Black Elk, 94
black-footed ferret, 406, 407
Black Hills, 410
black murex snail, 315
black oak, 110, 377
Black Robe, 180, 181
black-tailed deer, 343
black vulture, 277
blasting, 53
Blue Babe, 414

blueback herring, 87
blue catfish, 200, 201
blue crab, 74
blue dicks, 374
blue jay, 320
blue land crab, 204
Blue Licks (Kentucky), 113
blue pike, 195, 216
Blue Ridge, 113
Blue Ridge Parkway, 106
Bluff Head (Newfoundland), 27
bobcat, 122, 125
Bob Marshall Wilderness, 445
bobolink, 148, 399
Bodmer, Karl, 417, 418
Boepple, John F., 213
Bogue, Margaret, 216
Bolanos, Francisco de, 300
Bombay Hook National Wildlife Refuge, 93–95
Bonaparte, Napoleon, 297
Bond, James, 264
booby, 267, 272. See also red-footed booby
Book of Mormon, The, 431
Booming Ben, 168, 169
booming ground, 168
Boone, Daniel, 99, 109, 127; on bison, 113
Boone and Crockett Club, 99, 100, 140
boreal forest, 107, 108, 186
Boston, 46, 102
bottomland forest, 157, 158, 170, 192, 206, 222, 223
bounty: absence on Carolina parakeets, 154; on seals, 57; on wolves, 123
bowhead whale, 52, 53, 65
Bradford, William, 118; on New England, 116
Bradley, Guy, 289, 291

Brasil, 24
Brazil, 235, 236
Breton fishermen, 29
Brewer, William, 376; on elk, 382
Bridalveil Falls, 373, 388
Brief and True Report of the New Found Land of Virginia, A, 70
Brief Discourse on the New Found Land, A, 28
Brief History of the Destruction of the Indies, A, 245, 246
brine fly, 374–76
brine shrimp, 375
Bristol: discoveries from, 24; merchants, 23, 24
British Columbia, 113, 361, 368, 396
British Virgin Islands, 244
Broderick, Annette, 241
brook trout, 172
Broward, Napoleon Bonaparte, 293
Browne, J. Ross, 380
brown pelican, 205, 283, 286, 290, 291, 382
brown trout, 217
Brule, Etienne, 177
Bryant, Edwin, 302
buccaneer, 260
buckaroo, 439
buffalo. See bison
Buffalo Gap National Grasslands, 407
Buffalo Cross Roads (Pennsylvania), 133
Buffon, Comte de, 144
bull shark, 306
Bureau of Biological Survey, 279, 441
Burmeister's porpoise, 314
bur oak, 108
Burroughs, John, 443
burrowing owl, 293
Bushyhead, Eddy, 131

butterfly, 377. *See also* California tortoiseshell; monarch
Butz, Earl, 438

Cabo San Lucas Bay (Baja), 303, 308
Cabot, John, 24
Cabot, Sebastian, 27
Cabrillo, Juan Rodriguez, 316, 341, 346
Cabrillo Beach, 304
Cabrillo Marine Aquarium, 304
Cabrillo National Monument, 316
Cacafuego, the, 342
Cache River National Wildlife Refuge, 158, 159
cactus, 430
Cadillac, Antoine, 195
Cadillac Desert, 392
Cahokia, 205–7
cahow, 268–71
Cahuilla, 348
Calaveras Grove, 388
California, 156
California condor, 338
California Current, 317
California Department of Fish and Game, 305
California Geological Survey, 376
California gold rush, 372, 379–81, 384, 385
California gull, 375, 393, 432, 433
California poppy, 338
California quail, 344, 382
California sea lion, 318
California Swamp (Florida), 157
California tortoiseshell, 340
calliope hummingbird, 338
Caloosahatchee River (Florida), 279
Calusa, 230, 247–49, 282–85
Camino Real, 355, 378

Camp River Dubois, 402
Canada goose, 172, 414
Canadian Department of Fisheries and Oceans, 41, 53
canebrake, 158
canine distemper, 407
cannery, 365
Cannery Row, 307
canning, 365
canvasback, 98
Cape Breton, 36, 71
Cape Cod, 45, 46, 116, 117, 176; sturgeon, 85
Cape Fear, 71, 120
Cape Hatteras, 22, 71
capelin, 22, 27–29, 64
Cape Mendocino, 317
Cape Royall. *See* Bluff Head (Newfoundland)
Cape Sable, 112, 287
capitalism, 137, 451, 456, 457; Christian, 81; origins, 6
Capitalism as if the World Matters, 457
Carib, 245, 263
caribou, 112, 113
Carolina parakeet, 150–55, 157, 160, 169
Carr, Archie, 239, 242–45
Carson, Rachel, 65
Carter, Jimmy, 213
Cartier, Jacques, 29, 30, 32, 176, 179; on New France, 175; on seals, 55; on whales, 46
Cartwright, George: background, 13; on great auks, 31, 35, 36; on salmon, 14
Cartwright, Labrador, 13, 14
Carver, Jonathon, on Fox River, 199
Cascades, 337
Castle Island (Bermuda), 270
cat, 259, 266, 267, 270

Catawba, 131
caterpillar, 339, 376
Catesby, Mark, 144, 320; on wolves, 123
Cathedral Range, 377
Cat Island, 227
Catlin, George, 418, 419, 421–23
catlinite, 221
Catoctin Mountain Park, 141
cattail, 295
cattle: in California, 356, 387; in
    Caribbean, 259, 260; in east, 130, 136,
    137, 142; on Great Plains, 405, 408,
    436, 440; on Greenland, 10. *See also*
    shorthorn; Texas longhorn
cattle baron, 439
caviar, 89
Cayman Islands, 238, 271
Central and Southern Florida Project,
    295
Central Hatchery, 367
Central Valley, 337, 353, 373, 378, 379, 383,
    384
Chafee, Senator John, 212, 455, 456
Chain of Lakes (Florida), 279
Champlain, Samuel de, 176–79
changing baseline syndrome, definition,
    2, 65, 241, 308
channel catfish, 370
Channel Islands, 318, 324, 325, 335
Chapman, Frank, 288–90
char, 197
Charles II of England, 43, 185
Charlevoix, Pierre de, 27, 37
Chendytes lawi, 347
Cherokee, 131–33, 142, 175, 286, 420
Chesapeake Bay, 71, 75, 91, 215;
    agriculture, 119, 138; fisheries, 89, 90;
    forests, 120, 134, 137; legislation, 88;
    oysters, 77, 79, 82, 83; swans, 96–98

chestnut oak, 109
chestnut-sided warbler, 148
Cheyenne, 419
Chicago, 177, 215
Chicago Mill and Lumber Company,
    158, 170
Chickasaw, 420
Chickasaw Bluffs (Tennessee), 192
Chickasaw plum, 122
Child, Albert, 433, 434
China, 452
Chinatown, 392
Chinook (tribe), 361
Chinook salmon, 217, 218, 361, 362, 365,
    366, 369, 370
Chippewa, 220
Choctaw, 131, 420
Choctawhatchee River (Florida), 159
Chokoloskee, 247
Choptank River, 90
Choynumni, 347
Christianity, 180, 252, 253, 432, 458
Chrysomela confluens, 172
Chukchansi, 347
Chumash, 326, 334, 335
chum salmon, 362
Churchill, 186, 187
Churchill, Winston, 452
cigar orchid, 280
Cincinnati Zoo, 152, 167, 170
ciscoe, 195, 218
Civil War, the, 139, 165
Clark, Galen, 387
Clark, William, 141, 220, 345, 397, 398,
    402, 403, 409, 416–18, 428; on bison,
    410; on decline of fur-bearers, 421; on
    inter-tribal warfare, 413; on Pacific
    salmon, 360; on prairie dogs, 408; on
    pronghorn, 409, 410

Clayton, John, 125
Clean Water Act, 215, 219
climate change, 60, 64
Clough, Garrett, 258
Clover, Katherine, 376
Coastal Range, 337, 350
coat beaver, 179
Cobo, Bernabé, 255
cocklebur, 153, 154
cod, 21–23, 33, 43 117; collapse, 40–42, 59, 60, 63, 81; dried and salted, 22, 23, 37, 39; fishing, 36–38; historic abundance, 25–28, 62
coho salmon, 217, 362, 365, 366, 369
Colnett, James, 311
Colorado River, 313, 314, 430
Columbian Exchange, 252
Columbia River, 360, 365, 367–70
Columbus, 4, 24, 70, 232, 245, 254, 255, 259, 260; on birds, 261; on Caribbean islands, 228, 229, 252, 256, 257; discovery of Bahamas, 227; on manatees, 233; on marine life, 230; on sighting birds at sea, 103, 104; on turtles, 236
Comanche, 419
Commander Islands, 321
common tern, 64
Comprehensive Everglades Restoration Plan, 297
computer model: cod, 41, 63; harp seal, 59–61; shark, 62
conch, 247–49
Concord, 135–37
Condor, The, 383
Coney Island, 115
conglutinate, 210
Connecticut, 121
Connecticut River: abundance of salmon, 13; river herring, 87, 89

Conservation and Protection Branch (Canadian govt.), 57
Conservation International, 229
Convention on International Trade in Endangered Species of Wild Fauna and Flora (CITES), 58
Cook, Captain James, 341, 342, 397
Coosa River, 211
coral die-off, 227, 250, 251
coral reef, 226, 227, 242, 250, 251
Cordona Company, 301, 302
corn, 118, 120, 136, 137, 440
Cornell Laboratory of Ornithology, 158, 159
Corn Tassel, 142
Corps of Discovery, 397, 403
Cortes, Hernan, 230, 299–301, 316
Corua, 205
Costa Rica, 239, 240, 309, 310, 334
cottontail, 343
cottonwood, 172, 173
cougar, 122, 127, 135, 431. *See also* eastern cougar; Florida panther
coureur de bois, 177, 180
Courtemanche, Sieur de: on seal abundance, 55; on whale abundance, 47, 48
Cousteau, Jacques, 32
cowbird, 93
cowboy, 439, 440
cow-nosed ray, 83
coyote, 383, 393, 399, 405, 426, 442
Coyote Creek (California), 359
Crabb, Henry, 384
crane, 70, 97
Crassostrea gigas, 83
Crassostrea virginica. See eastern oyster
crayfish, 210, 211, 222; Shasta crayfish, 359
Cree, 182, 183

Creek, 131, 284
Creek wars, 286
Crisfield (Maryland), 79
Croatoan, 74
Crockett, Davy, 99
crop, European, 254, 255
crowberry, 102
Crystal River, 232, 233
Cuba, 158, 228, 229, 235, 238, 258, 262, 266, 284
Culture and Experience, 175
Cumberland Gap, 113
Cumberland River, 210
Cusabo Indians, 72
Cushing, Frank, 247, 282, 283
Custer, George, 410
Custer State Park, 411
Custer Wolf, 441, 442
Custis, Peter, 417, 419, 429
Cuthbert Lake (Florida), 289
cycle of abundance, 188, 250
Cypress Island Preserve, 205
Cyrtopodium punctatum, 280

Dalles, The, 362
Daly, Herman, 61
dam, 211–13, 221, 222, 314, 368, 369, 391, 392; splash, 381
Dampier, William, 234, 235
Dana, Richard Henry, 311
Dances with Wolves, 411
Darien Mountains, 70
darter (fish), 210. *See also* snail darter
Darwin, Charles, 37, 226, 254
Dasmann, Raymond, 383
Davidson, Captain Hunter S., 80, 81
Davies, Brian, 58
Davis Strait, 21
Dawson, William, 344, 352, 377

Day, John, 24
Death Valley, 337, 338, 374
Declaration of Independence, 143
deer, 110, 113, 120, 121, 123, 128, 129, 134, 165, 199, 203, 343, 345, 347, 351, 441. *See also* black-tailed deer; caribou; elk; mule deer; white-tailed deer
Deere, John, 429
Defenders of Wildlife, 446, 447
Delano, Columbus, 423
Delaware, 93, 101; legislation, 88; whaling, 51
Delaware Bay, 67–69, 71, 93, 354
Delaware River, 89, 145
Delmarva Peninsula, 93
demersal, 61
democracy, 139, 452, 453. *See also* agrarian democracy
Denys, Nicolas, 13, 36, 37, 55; on Indian hunting, 132
dermo, 82
desert locust, 434
Des Groseilliers, Médard Chouart, 185, 186
de Soto, Hernando, 192–94
Destruction of California, The, 383
Detroit, 224
Development as Freedom, 458
diablotin. *See* black-capped petrel
Diadema antillarum, 250
Diamond, Jared, 5
diamondback terrapin, 74
dickcissel, 148
Diporeia, 215, 219
dire wolf, 412
Discovery, 76
disease: in birds, 154; in coral, 227; in Europeans, 78; in Indians, 114, 127, 128, 132, 157, 165, 181, 182, 207, 246, 260, 325,

346, 363, 451; old world origins, 6; in
 salmon, 369
DNA analysis: Atlantic salmon, 18;
 cougar, 125; mitochondrial, 47; Pacific
 gray whale, 313; salmon eggs, 19
Dodge, Colonel Richard, 410, 411
dodo, 2
dog, 259
dolphin, 54
domestic animal, 130, 131, 387. *See also*
 cattle; horse; pig; sheep
Dominica, 256
Dominican Republic, 228, 229
Donahue, Brian, 135, 137
Donck, Adriaen van der, on waterfowl,
 95, 96
Doolittle, William, 118
Douglas, Majory Stoneman, 279, 294–96
Douglas fir, 337, 338
Drake, Francis, 74, 341, 383; on Pacific
 coast, 342
Drake's Bay, 316, 354
Dred, 289
Dry Tortugas, 237, 238, 264, 265
duck, 70, 72, 96, 145, 199, 222, 286, 344
duck stamp, 100
Ducks Unlimited, 100, 105
Dudley, Paul, 50
dugong, 234
Duhaut-Cilly, Auguste, 298, 382
Dust Bowl, 438
Duyck, Bill, 106, 108, 148
Dwight, Timothy, 135

eared dove, 164
eared grebe, 375
eastern cougar, 124, 125, 283
eastern elk, 111–13, 121, 125, 133, 141, 173,
 343

eastern forest, 107
eastern hemlock, 107–9, 141
eastern meadowlark, 148
eastern oyster, 76, 215; conflicts over, 80,
 81; decline, 81; disease, 82; ecology, 82;
 fishery, 80; as food, 78, 79; predation
 on, 83
Eastern Shore (Maryland), 79, 80
ecological extinction: green turtle, 241;
 manatee, 235
Ecology of Commerce, The, 457
economic growth, origins of philosophy, 6
economics, of fishing, 38
ecosystem-based fisheries policy, 91
ecosystem engineer, 172
Ecuador, 309
Efford, John, 60
Egg War, 382
egret, 72
eider duck, 21
Eldey (Iceland), 30
El Dorado, 171, 192
elephant seal, 324, 328, 329
Elizabeth I of England, 49, 341, 342
elk: in California, 343–45, 347, 356, 382;
 in eastern forest, 111–13, 121, 125, 133,
 141, 173; on Great Plains, 398, 441,
 448; in north, 187. *See also* eastern elk;
 Merriam elk; Rocky Mountain elk;
 Roosevelt elk; tule elk
elkhorn coral, 250
Elkhorn Plains, 384
Elkhorn Slough, 329
Elk Lake, 220
Ellesmere Island, 445
elm decline, 208
El Niño Southern Oscillation, 325, 363,
 382

Elton, Charles, 188, 189
Emerson, Ralph Waldo, 386
encomienda, 260, 355
Endangered Species Act (1973), 125, 169,
   212, 213, 250, 334, 367, 369, 370, 404,
   407, 408, 440, 445–48, 455
Enlightenment. *See* Age of
   Enlightenment
Environmental Protection Agency, 296
epidemic, 6
Epioblasma spp., 208
Ericsson, Leif, 13, 21; discoveries, 10, 11
Erik the Red, history, 9, 10
Eskimo curlew, 102–5, 415, 416
Eternal Frontier, The, 413
Etnier, David, 201, 212, 213
Eurasia, spread of agriculture, 5
European beaver, 178
European Community, 59
Everglades, 274–97
Everglades Agricultural Area, 295, 296
Everglades Forever Act, 296, 297
Everglades National Park, 275, 294, 297
Evolutionary Significant Unit, 367
exclusive economic zone, 40
external cost, 456
Exuma Cyas, 258

factory ships, 39, 40
Faeroes, escapes from fish farms, 17
Fairtry, The, 39
Faragher, John, 438
Farallon Islands, 319, 328, 381, 382
feathers: great auk, 35; egrets, 288–90
Felis concolor couguar. See eastern cougar
Ferdinand VII of Spain, 357
fibropappiloma, 240
fiddler crab, 203, 204
Fidler, Peter, 188

finerayed pigtoe, 209
fin whale, 47
fir, 173
fire: California, 386, 387; eastern forest,
   108; on Great Plains, 400
First Salmon Ceremony, 364, 365
Fish and Wildlife Service, 100, 101, 273,
   404, 408, 444, 446
fisher, 114, 178
Fisherman's Problem, The, 366
Fishes of Tennessee, The, 201
fish hatchery, 367, 368
fish trap: in California, 364; on
   Chesapeake Bay, 84, 87, 88; for eels,
   196
Flagler, Henry, 292
Flannery, Tim, 2, 423
flood, 223
Florida, 70–72, 153, 156, 157, 190, 228, 230,
   232, 233, 247, 274–96
Florida Keys, 249, 282, 283
Florida panther, 283
Fontenada, Hernando, 230, 283, 284; on
   Calusa food, 248
Food and Drug Administration, 88
Forbes, Stephen, 210
forbs, 406
Forest and Stream, 424
forest reserve, 140, 390
Forest Reserve Act, 140
Forest Service, 106, 139
Fort Caroline, 72
Fort Dusquesne, 189
Fort Pierce, 204
Fort Prince George, 189
Fort Ross, 331
forty-niners, 359, 380, 381
Fountain Hills (Arizona), 392
Fourth Cavalry, 389, 390

fox, 405, 431
Fox River, 198–200
Franklin, Benjamin, 138
Fraser River, 368
free market economy, 38, 41, 59, 81, 99, 137, 422, 423, 438, 451, 452, 456; origins, 6
French and Indian War, 219
French and Iroquois War, 179
freshwater mussel, 208–11, 454
Friends of the Everglades, 295
frigatebird, 267. *See also* magnificent frigatebird
Frontenac, Comte de, 180, 194
frozen food, 39
Funk Island, 29, 30, 31, 35, 36
fur seal, 317, 318, 451. *See also* Galapagos fur seal; Guadalupe fur seal; Juan Fernandez fur seal; northern fur seal; South American fur seal
Fur Seal Act, 327
Fur Seal Commission, 327
Fur Seal Convention (1911), 332
fur trade, 115, 171, 173, 174, 176, 178–82, 184, 185, 189–91, 202, 396, 421

Gadidae, 22
Gadus morhua. See cod
Galapagos fur seal, 318
Gallagher, Tom, 158, 159
Gallivan, James, 43
gannet, colonies, 8, 33
Gardeur, Augustin le. *See* Courtemanche, Sieur de
Garn, Senator Jake, 212
Gavin, Angus, 353
gene pool, Atlantic salmon, 18
General Sherman (tree), 389
genetic drift, definition, 17

genetic engineering, 19
Georges Bank, 62
Georgia, 70, 114, 152, 285
giant armadillo, 412
Giant Forest, 388, 399
giant kangaroo rat, 384
Giants in the Earth, 399
Giant sloth, 401, 412
Gilded Age, 423
gill-netting, 38
glacier, 386
Glacier National park, 445
globalization, 452, 454
glochidia, 210
glycoside, 172
God Committee, 213
godetz, 33
Godspeed, 76
gold, 43, 54, 300, 319, 342, 358, 359, 365, 366, 379–81, 385, 410, 436
goldfield, 338
goliath grouper, 305
goose, 70, 145, 344, 352. *See also* Canada goose; Ross's goose; snow goose
Gordon-Cummings, Constance, 387
Gosse, Philip Henry, 262
Gould's petrel, 271
granary tree, 156
Grand Banks, the, 27, 31, 35, 40; description, 25; fishery, 40, 62; spawning capelin, 28
Grand Village (of the Natchez), 207
Grant, Ulysses, S., 423
grape, wild, 11, 12, 72, 77, 117, 175
grasshopper, 339, 415, 432. *See also* desert locust; migratory locust; Mormon cricket; Rocky Mountain locust
grassland: in California, 337; in east, 149. *See also* Great Plains, the; prairie

Gray, Captain Robert, 360
gray seal, 40, 55–59
gray whale: Atlantic, 49–53, 64, 65, 312; Pacific, 50, 51, 310–13, 333
Great American Desert, 430
great auk, 2, 30, 31–36, 50
Great Basin, 373
Great Bay of Shells, 76, 83
Greater Antilles, 228, 245, 257, 271
Great Depression, the, 57
Greater Yellowstone Ecosystem, 440
Great Lakes, the, 108, 171, 174, 177, 189, 194–98, 202, 203, 215–19, 452, 454
Great Plains, the, 113, 337, 345, 346, 398–425, 439
Great Plains low level jet, 434
Great Plow Up, 438
Great Salt Lake, 375, 432, 434
Great Slaughter, 423
Great Smoky Mountain National Park, 109, 125, 141
Great Spirit, 183
Great Sun, the, 207
great white egret, 288
great white heron, 278
Great Wildlife of the Great Plains, 405
Greeley, Horace, 385, 437
green abalone, 334
Green Bay, 198, 199
Green Farm (Martha's Vineyard), 168
green heron, 277
green iguana, 259
Greenland, 21–23, 25; Viking colony, 9; trade, 10
Greenpeace, 59
Green River (Kentucky), 162, 163
green turtle, 73, 236–42, 308, 454; exploitation, 238; historic abundance, 236

Griffon, the, 202, 203
Grinnell, George Bird, 242
Grinnell, Joseph, 377, 383
grizzly bear, Californian, 347–50
ground squirrel, 342, 383. *See also* San Joaquin antelope squirrel
grunion, 304, 305
Guadaloupe, 263
Guadalupe, 324, 328
Guadalupe fur seal, 318, 323, 324, 328
Guadalupe Victoria, 357
guanaco, 253
guano, 272, 273
Guano Islands Act, 273
Guiana, 235
guillemot, 33
guinea pig, 258
Gulf grouper, 305
Gulf of California, 300, 301, 306–8, 313, 314
Gulf of Mexico, 105, 228, 243, 244
Gulf of St. Lawrence, 174, 175; abundance of fish, 27; harp seals, 60; historic bird abundance, 32, 64; historic seal abundance, 56; historic walrus abundance, 55; historic whale abundance, 46, 48, 53; oyster distribution, 76
Gulf Stream, the, 8, 25, 72
Gunnbiorn, 9
Guns, Germs and Steel, 5
Guthrie, Dale, 414

haddock, 62
Haiti, 228, 273
Hakluyt, Richard, 75
Half Dome, 373
halibut, 21
Hall, Minna, 289

Hallowell, Alfred, 175
hammerhead, 306
hammock (tree island), 275, 280, 295
Hanson, Stanley, 279
harbor porpoise, 313
harbor seal, 55, 57–59, 196
Hardin, Garrett, 81, 82, 315
Hariot, Thomas, 69, 71, 73; on deer, 110;
  on walnuts, 122
harp seal, 40, 55, 56; hunting, 58–60, 63
Harrison, Benjamin, 98
Harrison, Bobby, 158, 159
Harvard University, 47
Haudenosaunee, 179, 180
Hawaii, 375
Hawken, Paul, 457
Hawkins, John: on seabirds, 271, 272; on
  turtles, 238
hawksbill, 74, 242, 244, 308
hay meadow, 130, 134, 136
Hearne, Samuel, 186–88
heath hen, 167–69
Hehaka Sapa. *See* Black Elk
Heights of Abraham, 190
Helluland, 10
Hemenway, Harriot, 289
Hempstead Plain, 149
Henry, Alexander, the Elder, 182
Henry VII of England, 24
Herjolffson, Bjarni, 10
heron, 72, 97, 286, 288
Herrera, Andrés, 242, 243
herring, 22, 28, 64, 73, 327, 328. *See also*
  blueback herring; lake herring; river
  herring
Hetch Hetchy, 391, 392, 394
Hewitt, Goldsmith, 139
Hexagenia, 224, 225
hickory shad, 87, 90

Hidalgo, Miguel, 357
hierarchical ecology, 454–56
high grading, 39
Hill, Geoff, 159
Hine Robert, 438
Hispaniola, 70, 228, 230, 254, 259–62
Historia Natural y General de las Indias, 255
Historia Natural y Moral de las Indias, 253
Historias de las Indias, 249
History of Marine Animal Populations
  project, 65, 231
Hochelaga, 175–77
hog. *See* pig
Holyoke Dam, 89, 90
Homestead Act, 437, 438
Homosassa Springs, 232
honeybee, 154
hooded merganser, 172
hooded seal, 40, 55; in Caribbean, 232
Hopkinsville (Kentucky), 149
Hornaday, William, 443
horse, 259, 260, 356, 387, 418, 419
horsefly, 430
horseshoe crab, 67–69; eggs, 69, 73
hotspot, 229
Hudson, Henry, 115, 178, 185, 186
Hudson Bay, 95, 186, 187
Hudson River, 91, 165
Hudson's Bay Company, 186–88, 190,
  353, 379, 403, 421
Hudson Valley, 95
Humboldt, Alexander von, on
  frigatebirds, 272
Humboldt Current, 273
humpback whale, 45, 47, 53, 65, 311
Huron, 174, 177, 179–81
Hurricane Katrina, 223
hutia, 257–59
Huxley, Thomas, 37, 38, 63

hvalross. See walrus
hydraulic mining, 380, 384

Iceland, 23–25, 30, 50
Ichthyologia Ohiensis, 201
Idaho, 368, 445, 446
Idaho Anti-Wolf Coalition, 447
Ignatius of Loyola, 253
Iguana delicatissima, 257
Illinois River, 202, 203, 215
Inca, 70
Incas, 152
India, 452
Indian: and bison, 413, 414; burning,
   120, 121, 149, 157; causing extinctions,
   264, 265; competition with wild
   animals, 128, 164, 165; conflicts and
   wars, 189, 190, 345–46; deer skin trade,
   131, 132; diversity in California, 338;
   ecology around Great Lakes, 195–98;
   ecology in north east, 117–19, 128, 129;
   farming in east, 118; fur trade, 184, 189;
   harvesting insects, 376–77; horses,
   418, 419; hunting, 234, 235, 325; land
   management, 450; market economy,
   174, 221; mission, 356, 357; overhunting,
   420; philosophy of hunting, 180–83;
   population in California, 345, 346;
   population in Caribbean, 246; salmon
   fishing, 363, 364, 366; wild rice harvest,
   198. *See also* disease: in Indians
Indian Removal Act, 285, 286, 420
Ingstad, Helge, 11
International Center for the Study of
   Deserts and Oceans, 315
International Fisheries Exhibition
   (1883), 37
International Fund for Animal Welfare
   (IFAW), 59, 60

International Union for the
   Conservation of Nature, 232, 241
International Whaling Commission, 64
introduced animal, 454; California, 336,
   356; Caribbean, 259
introduced plant, 336
Inuit, 39, 102
Inyo Mountains, 337
Iowa, 213, 415
Irish elk, 112
Iroquois Confederacy, 119, 179. *See also*
   Haudenosaunee
isinglass, 89
Isla de Cedros (Baja), 324
Island Called California, An, 336
Island of Birds, 29
Island of Cuba, The, 272
Isles de Madeleine, 54, 55
Isthmus of Panama, 299
ivory, 54
ivory-billed woodpecker, 155–60, 166,
   169, 170

jack rabbit, 343
Jackson, Andrew, 285, 286
Jackson, Jeremy, 62, 63, 251
jaguar, 253, 348
Jamaica, 238, 239, 258, 271
Jamaica petrel, 271
James, Edwin, 429, 430
James I of England, 138
James River, 77
Jamestown, 77, 78, 80, 84, 86, 89, 96, 115,
   138, 177, 451
Jefferson, Thomas, 143, 144, 146, 219, 360,
   396, 397, 401, 428–31, 437, 439
Jeffersonian grid, 428, 429
Jesuit, 75, 180, 181, 184, 186, 194, 195, 197,
   202, 252, 301, 356

Jesuit Relations, 180, 181, 185, 195
jet stream, 438
Jimenez, Fortún, 300, 301
Johnsgard, Paul, 405
Johnson, Lyndon Baines, Wilderness Act, 4
Johnson, Paul, 209, 210
Johnson, Robert Underwood, 387
joint stock company, 451
Jolliet, Louis, 194, 198, 201–3
Joslyn Art Gallery, 417
Josselyn, John, 86, 107, 109; on moose, 112
Joyce Kilmer Memorial Forest, 108
Juan Fernandez fur seal, 318, 323
Juan Fernandez Islands, 318
Judeo-Christian, view of nature, 34
Jukes, Professor, J. B., 56
Junaluska, 286

Kamchatka, 319–21, 329, 330
Kansas, 410, 415
Karlsefni, Thorfinn, 21
Kato, 349
Kaweah Cooperation Colony, 388, 389
Kayak Island, 320
keepers of the game, 175, 181
Keepers of the Game, 182
kelp forest, 332, 333
Kemp's ridley turtle, 242–44, 308
Kentucky, 113, 146, 147, 149, 161, 162, 164
key deer, 282, 283
Key Deer National Wildlife Refuge, 283
Key Marco, 247, 282, 283
Key Marco cat, 283
keystone species, 172, 191, 404, 405, 407
killer whale, 333
Kilmer, Joyce, 109
Kissimmee River, 279, 286, 292
Kitchi Manitou, 183

Klamath (tribe), 364
Klamath River, 360, 364, 369
Knife Point Glacier, 436
Kodiak Island, 363
kokanee, 217
Kolosky, Stanley, on Carolina parakeets, 152
Kumeyaay, 357
Kurile Islands, 329, 331
Kushlan, James, 287, 288

Labrador, 39, 47; coast, 8, 10; Eskimo curlews, 102, 104, 415, 416; historic salmon numbers, 12; seal numbers, 56; whale numbers, 46, 51
Labrador Current, 25
Labrador duck, 101, 102
Lacey Act, 290, 291
Lahontan, Louis-Armand, Baron de, 196
Lake Erie, 202, 216, 217, 224
lake herring, 195, 216
Lake Huron, 176, 195
Lake Itasca, 191, 220, 221
Lake Michigan, 177, 195, 198, 214, 215
Lake Nipigon, 184
Lake Nippising, 177
Lake Okeechobee, 279–81, 292, 294, 296
Lake Ontario, 176, 196, 217–19
Lake Pepin, 215
Lake Shasta, 367
lake sturgeon, 197, 202, 216
Lake Superior, 185, 217
Lake Tahoe, 373
lake trout, 195, 197, 215–19
lake whitefish, 195, 215, 216, 219
Lake Winnebago, 199
Lake Winnipeg, 183
Lakota, 94
Lamanite, 431

lamprey, 359. See also sea lamprey
Lane, John, Jr., 429
l'Anse aux Meadows, 11, 21
La Paz (Baja), 301, 302
La Perouse, Comte de, 310
la Salle, Rene–Robert, Sieur de, 202–8, 221
las Casas, Bartolomé de, 245, 246, 249, 262, 302
laughing gull, 68
Laurance, William, 455
Laurentian Highlands, 175
Lawson, John: on Indian beliefs, 132, 182; on predators, 123; on snow geese, 95
Laysan teal, 375
leather, from beluga, 53
leatherback turtle, 242, 244
LeClerc, George. See Buffon, Comte de
Lederer, John, 111
Leech Lake, 220
lek, 168
Leonard, Zenas, 379
Leopold, Aldo, 3, 158; on Colorado River delta, 314; on wolves, 443, 444, 449
Leptotyphlops bilineata, 229
Lesser Antilles, 228, 245, 256, 257, 265, 271
Lewis, Merriwether, 146, 220, 345, 360, 397, 398, 401–3, 408, 409, 414, 416, 417, 428
Leyden (Holland), 116
Life Histories of Northern Animals, 443
limpkin, 278, 286
Lincoln, Abraham, 437
Lindquist, Ole, 50
Linsdale, Jean, 383
liquidamber, 110
little blue heron, 291
little curlew, 415
Little Ice Age, 46

Little Rock, 158
Little Tennessee River, 212
Lives of Game Animals, The, 443
Lobo, 442, 443
Lockwood, Jeffrey, 434–36
loggerhead, 74, 242, 308
Log of the Sea of Cortez, The, 307
Lonesome Larry, 369
Long, Major Stephen, 429, 430
Long, William, 124
longhorn beetle, 156
Long Island, 79, 101, 149, 168
longleaf pine, 107, 108
long-lining, 38
Look, 274
Los Angeles, 392, 393
Los Angeles Aqueduct, 394
Los Angeles Department of Water and Power, 394
Los Osos (California), 347–49
Lost Colony, the, 74
Louis XIV, 194, 202, 205
Louisiana, 157, 158, 190, 193, 205, 219, 353, 397, 418, 429
Louisville, 146, 161, 164
Lower Columbia River Fisheries Development Program, 368
lumpsucker, 31
Luquillo Mountains (Puerto Rico), 263
Lynn (Massachusetts), 85
lynx, 110, 122, 187, 188

macaw: Cuban, 262; Guadaloupe, 263; Hispaniolan, 263; hyacinth, 262; Jamaican red, 262; St Croix, 263
Machias Seal Island, 64
Mackenzie, Alexander, 396, 416
Mackenzie River Valley, 188
mackerel, 27

Madison, James, 428

Magdalena Bay, 310

Magdelen Islands. *See* Isles de Madeleine

Magellan, Ferdinand, 70

magnificent frigatebird, 272

Maguire, Jean-Jacques, 42

Maidu, 346, 349, 379

Maine, 69; endangered salmon, 16; heath hen, 167; waterfowl, 172; whaling, 51

mallard, 100, 172

Maltby, Caleb, 79

mammoth, 149, 412

manatee. *See* Amazonian manatee; dugong; West Indian manatee

mangrove, 280

Manifest Destiny, 396

Manila galleon, 316, 317, 342

manitou, 175, 181

Mannahata, 115

Manteo, 75

Manuel F. Correllus State Forest, 168

manure: from cattle, 136; fish as, 87

margaulx. *See* gannet, colonies

Marine Mammals of the Northwestern Coast of North America, the, 311

Mariposa (California), 339–41

Mark-land, 10

marlin, 62

Marquette, Jacques, 194, 198, 203; on American paddlefish, 201, 202; on Fox River, 199; on Mississippi River, 200; on prairies, 200

Marshall, James, 358, 379

Martin, Calvin, 182, 183

Martinique, 229

marten, 114, 115

Martha, 167, 170

Martha's Vineyard, 167, 168

Martyr, Peter, on turtles, 238

Maryland, 79–81, 97, 101, 133, 138, 139, 141

Maryland Department of Natural Resources, 90, 101

Mason, John, 27

Massachusetts, 89, 104, 127, 133, 135, 168, 177

Massachusetts Audubon Society, 289, 290

Massachusetts Bay, 112

mast, 162, 164, 166, 167

mastodon, 412

Mather, Cotton, 125

Matthew, the, 24, 25, 27, 29

Maya, 249

Mayflower, the, 46, 116

mayfly, 224, 225

McCartney, Paul, 59

McCloud River (California), 367

McMillan, Bill, 368

Mech, David, 445

Meeker, Ezra, 365

Meeteetse (Wyoming), 407

megafauna, 149, 412, 413, 418

Memphis, 192

Menendez de Avilés, Pedro, 72, 284

menhaden, 87–90

Menominee, 174, 197, 198, 200

Merced River, 385, 391

mercury, 381

Merriam, C. Hart, 378, 404, 405

Merriam elk, 343

Mersey River, return of salmon, 15

Métis, 421, 422

Mexico, 300, 309, 321, 340, 344, 376, 401; independence, 357, 358; monarch groves, 436, 437

Miantonomo, 134

Miccosukee, 285, 297

Michel, Franis Louis, 76
Michigan, 112, 151, 163, 194
Michilimackinac, 195, 198
midden: Aleut, 333; California, 325, 335, 345; Caribbean, 230, 258; English, 22; Mississippi, 208
Middle Ages, 6
Middlesbrough, 14
Migratory Bird Conservation Act, 100
Migratory Bird Conservation Fund, 100
Migratory Bird Hunting Stamp Act, 100
Migratory Bird Treaty Act, 64, 101, 291
migratory locust, 435
Miller, Joaquin, 349
Mill Grove (Pennsylvania), 147
minke whale, 47
Minnesota, 113, 191, 221, 441
Miq'mac, 174, 176, 179, 182
Miracle of the Gulls, 432
Miskito, 234
mission, 355–57, 378
missionary, 180
mission fig, 336
Mission San Diego, 357
Mississippi, 201
Mississippian culture, 205–9
Mississippi River, 114, 154, 157, 185, 192–94, 202–7, 214, 215, 219–25, 401, 402, 454
Mississippi Valley, 201
Missouri River, 193, 201, 220, 223, 402, 414, 421, 430
mitochondrion, 47
Miwok, 373, 378, 379, 385–87, 391, 392
mixed grass prairie, 400, 404, 415
Mojave (tribe), 357
monarch, 340, 341; groves in Mexico, 436, 437
mongoose, 259, 267

monk seal: Hawaiian, 230; Mediterranean, 230; West Indian, 230–32, 238
Mono Lake, 373–77, 393, 394
Montana, 114, 439, 445
Monterey Bay, 310, 316, 317, 329, 344, 345, 350–52, 354
Montreal, 53, 176, 177, 185
Moon Lake (Mississippi), 201
moose, 112, 117, 132, 144, 173, 423
moose sickness, 113
Moraga, Gabriel, 339–41
Moravian, 137
Mormon, 431, 432, 437
Mormon cricket, 432, 433
Mormon War in Illinois, 431
Morton, Thomas, 127
mosquito, 278
mound-building, 205, 247, 248
mountain man, 378
Mount McKinley, 445
Mount Vernon, 87
Mount Whitney, 338, 373
Mount Wollaston, 127
Mowat, Farley, 27, 33, 48, 57, 127, 178
Mrazek Pond, 277
MSX, 82, 83
Muir, John, 372, 376, 386–88, 390–92
mule deer, 343
mullet, 27, 73
Mullholland, William, 394
Muñoz, Pedro, 339, 340
Murie, Adolph, 445
murre, common, 32, 381, 382
Muscatine (Iowa), 213, 214
Muscle Shoals (Alabama), 208, 210, 211
Museum of Koblenz, 417
Museum of Vertebrate Zoology (Berkeley), 383

muskrat, 211
mussel, marine, 76, 102. *See also* freshwater mussel; quagga mussel; zebra mussel
mute swan, 97, 98, 101, 105
mycobacteriosis, 90, 91
Myers, Norman, 229
Myers, Ransom, 37, 43

Nahai, David, 394
Nancite (Costa Rica), 309
Nantucket Island, 104
Napa Valley, 345
Narraganset, 134
Narraganset Bay, 71, 110, 120
Narvaez, Panfilo, 282
Nash, Reverend Daniel, 127
Nashville, 150
Nassau grouper, 249
Natchez, 205–7
National Audubon Society, 158, 290, 291, 292
National Bison Range, 424, 425
National Bison Society, 424
national forest, 140, 390
National Forest Service, 390
National Ocean and Atmospheric Administration, 312
National Park Service, 275, 445
National Wildlife Refuge System, 100, 291
Natural History of Florida and the Bahamas, 320
natural selection, 427, 456
Nauvoo, 431
Navassa Island (Haiti), 273
Navidad, La, 254
Neamathla, 285
Nebraska, 409, 415, 433

Nelson, Dee Jay, 152
Neumann, Thomas, 119, 128, 129
Nevada Falls, 385, 388
New England, 38, 71, 86, 112, 113, 115, 134, 135; bears, 126; beavers, 184; cod fishery, 43; environmental laws, 88; Eskimo curlews, 104, 416; European farming, 136; forests, 109; Indian agriculture, 119; menhaden fishery, 88; oyster fishery, 79; sturgeon, 85; use of salmon, 15; whaling, 49, 51; wolves, 124
New England's Prospect, 4, 86; description of land, 3
New England's Rarities Discovered, 112
Newfoundland, 27, 37, 48, 71; coast, 8, 10, 29, 35; crab fishery, 61; Eskimo curlews, 102, 104; great auks, 31; seal hunt, 58; spawning capelin, 28; whale abundance, 46, 51
Newfoundland House of Assembly, 60
New France, 180, 185, 189, 190, 199
New Hampshire, 27, 113
New Jersey, 69, 96
New Mexico, 353, 357
New Netherlands, 96, 115
New Orleans, 223, 397
New York, 86, 90, 113, 126, 151, 165
New York Botanical Garden, 279
New York City, 54, 93, 101, 165
New York Harbor, 71, 115
New York Tribune, 437
New York Zoological Society, 133
Nez Perce, 446
Nicollet, Jean, 177
night heron, 286
Niña, 227
nine-foot channel project (Mississippi), 222

nitrogen isotope analysis, 363
Nixon, Richard, 296, 438
noble savage, 174, 449
noddy tern, 265, 266
Nonsuch, the, 185
Nonsuch Island (Bermuda), 270
Nonsuch Living Museum, 270
Norris, Philetus, 423
Norse sagas, 8–12
North Carolina, 22, 69, 71, 86, 96, 106, 113, 120, 122, 123, 131, 139, 152, 155
northern fur seal, 318, 323, 325, 328
northern goshawk, 168, 188
northern hardwood forest, 108
North Pacific Fur Seal Convention, 326
North West Company, 190, 403, 421
Northwood, Richard, 269
Norumbega, 115
Norway: nonnative salmon in rivers, 17; trade with England, 22
no-take reserve, 42, 315
Notch Brook (New Jersey), 214
Notes on the State of Virginia, 401
Nova Albion, 342
Nova Scotia, 36, 40, 54

oak, 121, 175, 377, 386
Oakwood College (Alabama), 158
Ohio, 113, 147, 214
Ohio River, 147, 150, 157, 189, 201, 208, 209
Ohio Valley, 113, 189, 190, 398
oil: from great auk, 34, 35; elephant seal, 324, 328; fish, 87, 88; seal, 56–58, 60; train, 35; walrus, 54; whale, 48, 51–53, 60
Ojibwa, 174, 175, 182, 198–200
Okefenokee Swamp, 152
Oklahoma, 405, 415
Old Baldy (Nebraska), 409

Old Lefty, 442
olive ridley turtle, 242, 308–10
Omega Protein Corporation, 88, 90
Oncorhynchus spp., 361, 368
Onondaga, 119
Ontario, 164, 196
Operation Green Turtle, 239, 240, 243, 244
optimal foraging, 38
Oregon, 361
Oregon Trail, 365
Origin of Species, The, 254
Osbourne, Henry, on destruction of wildlife in east, 133
Osceola, 286
Ostional (Costa Rica), 309, 310
Ostreidae, 301
Ottawa (city), 185
Ottawa (tribe), 174
otter, 114, 115; historical abundance, 177; skins, 132
Outer Banks, the, 69, 71, 120
ovenbird, 141
Oviedo, Gonzalo de, 255, 259, 269
Owens Lake, 374, 393, 394
Owens River, 374, 392, 394
Owens Valley, 374, 392–94
owl's clover, 338
oyster, 73, 76, 130, 300–302. *See also* eastern oyster; pearl oyster; suminoe oyster
Ozawindib, 220

Pablo, Michael, 424
Pacific Decadal Oscillation, 363
Pacific Egg Company, 381, 382
Pacific Fur Company, 365
Pacific salmon, 359–71; decline, 366; historic abundance, 363–65

Pacific Salmon Treaty, 366
Padre Island National Seashore, 243, 244
Pa-Hay-Okee, 278, 286
Paiute, 374, 380, 392
pallid sturgeon, 202
Pamlico Sound, 71, 75
Panama, 70
Panamint Mountains, 337
Pando Grove, 389
paper birch, 107
Paradise Key, 276, 293
Parkman, Francis, 423
parr, Atlantic salmon, 18, 19
parrot, 97, 261, 262. *See also* Amazon parrot; macaw; Puerto Rican parrot
Parton, James, 143
Pascua Florida, 281
passenger pigeon, 102, 151, 160–67, 169, 451, 452
Patagonia, 102
Patuxent River, 90
Patuxet, 128
Pauly, Daniel, 61, 65
Peale, Titian, 430
pearl: cultured, 214; freshwater, 214; marine, 300–302
pearl button, 213, 214
pearl oyster, 300–302
pecan, 121
peccary, 130
Peck, Robert, 398
pelagic, 61, 63
pelagic sealing, 326
Pelican Island National Wildlife Refuge, 290, 291
penguin, 32; emperor, 32; island of, 34; king, 30; meaning great auk, 26, 30, 35
Pennsylvania, 101, 113, 124, 133, 147

Percy, George, 76, 77; on strawberries, 121
peregrine falcon, 93
Perry River, 353
Petersen, Roger Tory, 152
Petoskey (Michigan), 164
petrel. *See* black-capped petrel; cahow; Gould's petrel; Jamaica petrel; Wilson's petrel
Phantom, 442
Pheidole megacephala, 261
Philadelphia, 101, 145, 146
Philadelphia Academy of Natural Sciences, 398
Phoenix, 392
phosphorus, 295, 296
Phragmites, 222
phytoplankton, 41, 61
Pickwick Landing Dam, 211
pig, 87, 130, 134, 142, 167, 259, 260, 269, 356, 387
Pigou, Arthur, 456
Pike, Zebulon, 220
pike minnow, 369, 370
Pikes Peak, 298
pileated woodpecker, 159
Pilgrim Fathers, the, 49, 85, 115–17, 120, 127, 128, 180
Pinchot, Gifford, 140, 279, 290, 386, 390, 391
Pinctada mazatlanica, 301
Pine Cay, 259
pink abalone, 334
Pinta, 227
Pismo Beach (California), 340
Pitillo, Dan, 108
Pit River, 359
Pittsburgh, 189
Pizarro, Francisco, 192

plaice, 73

Plana Cays, 258

Platte River, 430

Pleistocene, 409, 413, 418

plow, 429

plume trade. *See* feathers

Plymouth, 85, 115, 118

Pocahontas, 78

pocket gopher, 343, 383

Pokagon, Chief Simon, 163

polar bear, 187

Poll, 150, 151, 155

Pomo, 349

Ponce de Leon, Juan, 237, 238, 281

Pontiac Rebellion, 190

porpoise, 54, 73

Porritt, Jonathon, 6, 457

Portola, Gaspar de, 344, 346, 347, 350, 351, 354, 355

Port Royal (South Carolina), 72

Portuguese fishermen, 29

possum, 129

Potawatomi, 163

Poverty Point, 205

powdawe, 49

Powell, John Wesley, 430

Powhatan, 78

prairie, 199, 399, 400, 430, 438; California coastal, 337, 356; Central Valley, 383; palouse, 424; Texas coastal, 415. *See also* mixed grass prairie; short-grass prairie; tallgrass prairie

prairie chicken, 167–69

prairie dog: black-tailed, 403–9, 425; Mexican, 404; Utah, 404

precautionary principle, 60, 170, 370

Pribilof, Gavril, 323

Pribilof Island, 323, 326, 327

Prince Rupert, 185, 186

Pristine Myth, the, 5

promyshleniki, 330

pronghorn, 345, 354, 409, 410, 423

Protect the Birds, 290

Provincetown (Massachusetts), 45, 46

ptarmigan, 322

Pteria sterna, 301

Pteriidae, 301

Puerto Rican parakeet, 264

Puerto Rican parrot, 263, 264

Puerto Rico, 228, 263, 281

puffin, 32, 33

Puget Sound, 360

punt gun, 98

Puritans, the, 85, 116, 123

purple-clawed hermit crab, 246, 247

purple-fringed orchid, 141

Quadrupeds of North America, The, 406

quagga mussel, 216

quaking aspen, 107

Qualla Boundary Reservation, 131

Quebec City, 55, 56, 177, 179, 185, 196; fall of, 190

Quechan, 357

Queen Anne's War, 284

Queen Isabella of Spain, 24

Quileute, 365

quota, 42, 60

rabbit, 343, 344, 347. *See also* cottontail; jack rabbit; snowshoe hare

raccoon, 128, 129, 165, 253

Raddison, Pierre-Esprit, 177, 185, 199

Rafinesque, Constantine, 201, 209

rainbow smelt, 217, 218

rainbow trout, 217

Raker Act, 392

Raleigh, Sir Walter, 69, 70, 74, 75, 451

Rancho la Brea, 298, 299
Rancho Nuevo, 242–44
Range of Light, 372
rapid wasting disease, 251
Rappahannock River, 91
rat, 259, 267, 269, 270
Ray, John, 124
razorbill, 32, 33
red abalone, 332, 334, 335
red-backed vole, 173, 188
Red Bay (Labrador), 52
red deer. *See* elk
reddish egret, 204
Redfish Lake (Idaho), 368, 369
red-footed booby, 273
red knot, 68, 69, 102
red land crab, 204
red oak, 108
Red River, 419
Red River (of the north), 421
Red River Expedition, 417, 429
red-tail hawk, 399
redwing blackbird, 93
redwood, 337, 338, 350, 351, 379, 382, 384
Reed, Sherry, 204
Reisner, Marc, 392
remora, 235
Republican Party, 437
Restigouche River (New Brunswick), 87
rhesus monkey, 267
Rhode Island, 71, 110, 120
Ribault, Jean, 72
rice rat, 257
Richmond, 138
Ricketts, Ed, 307
right whale, 48, 49, 51, 52, 64, 65
ringed seal, 187
river herring, 87, 89
River of Grass, The, 279, 294

Roanoke, 69–71, 73, 74, 78, 451
Roanoke River, 86
Robinson, Andrew, 38
rock fight, 86
Rockies, 193, 373, 400, 419, 436
rock iguana, 257–59, 261; Bahamas, 259
Rocky Mountain elk, 343
Rocky Mountain locust, 433–37
Rolfe, John, 138
Roosevelt, Theodore, 98–100, 105, 140, 290, 387, 424, 443
Roosevelt elk, 343
Rose, George, 41
roseate spoonbill, 204, 205, 277, 278, 286
Ross, Alexander, 421
Ross's goose, 352, 353
Rothschild, Walter, 262
round goby, 219
Rousseau, Jean-Jacques, 174
Rowan, John, 16, 27
Royal Entomological Society of London, 339
royal palm, 275, 276
Royal Palm Hammock, 276, 277
Royal Palm State Park, 293, 294
Royal Society, 186
Rozier, Ferdinand, 147
Rumsfeld, Donald, 455
Rupert's Land, 186, 190
Russian American Company, 323

saber-toothed cat, 412
Sable Island, 54, 57
Sacramento, 379
Sacramento River, 337, 360, 365, 370
Sacramento Valley, 349, 384
Saga of Eirik the Red, The, 2, 9
Saga of the Greenlanders, The, 9–11
Sagard, Gabriel, 195

salamander, 210
Salem, 137
Salmo, 361
salmon farms: Atlantic salmon, 16–19;
    escaped fish, 17
Salt Lake City, 432
Samana Cay, 227
Sampson's pearlymussel, 211
San Carlos de Borromeo de Monterey
    (California), 351
sand eel, 64
Sandfly Island (Florida), 248
sandhill crane, 352
San Diego, 316, 344, 345, 355
San Diego Bay, 341
sandlaegja. See gray whale
Sand Lake (South Dakota), 353, 354
sand spur, 153, 154
San Francisco, 339, 359, 381, 382;
    earthquake, 391
San Francisco Bay, 337, 351, 382
San Joaquin antelope squirrel, 383
San Joaquin River, 337
San Joaquin Valley, 384
San Luis Obispo, 347
San Miguel de la Gualdape, 70
San Miguel Island, 316, 318, 335
San Nicolas Island, 324, 331
San Pedro Bay, 346
San Salvador (Bahamas), 104, 227, 228
Santa Maria, 227, 254
Santee River, 152
sardine, 304, 310
Savannah River, 70
sawgrass, 280, 294, 295
Sawyer Decision, 384
Say, Thomas, 430
Scammon, Charles, 311, 312; on sea otters,
    331, 332

scarlet macaw, 221
Schoolcraft, Henry, 220
schooner, 38
Schutze, Bill, 354
Schwarzenegger, Arnold, 395
Scioto pigtoe, 210
Sclater, Philip, 253, 254
Scotian Shelf, The, 40, 54
Scotland, 144
Scott, Peter, 274
scrag whale. *See* gray whale
Scribner's Magazine, 443
sculpin, 31, 218
Sea Around Us, The, 65
sea bass, 27
sea grass, 235, 239, 250
sea lamprey, 217
sea lion, 317, 318. *See also* California sea
    lion; Steller sea lion
sea mink, 177, 178
Sea of Cortez, 301, 306, 307, 313–16, 334
Sea of Slaughter, 57
sea otter, 329–35
Sea Shepherd Conservation Society, 59
sea urchin, 250, 332, 334
Sea Venture, 268, 269
seekanauk, 69, 73
Selkirk, Alexander, 318
Selway-Bitterroot Wilderness Area, 445,
    446
Seminole, 278, 279, 285, 286, 420
Seminole War: First, 285; Second, 286,
    292
Sen, Amartya, 458
sequoia, 337, 338, 379, 384, 389
Sequoia National Park, 350, 389
Seranilla Bank, 231
Serra, Father, 346, 351
Serratia marescens, 251

Seton, Ernest Thompson, 110, 403, 405, 411, 442, 443

sewage: clean up in Great Britain, 16; in Mississippi, 223, 224

shad, 27, 88. *See also* American shad; hickory shad

shaman, 181

shark, 43, 62, 306, 314. *See also* bull shark; hammerhead

Shark Slough, 280

sharp-tailed grouse, 149

sheep, 387, 388–90

sheephead, 333

Sheridan, General Philip, 423

Shirley Basin, 407

short-faced bear, 412

short-grass prairie, 400, 404, 412, 430

shorthorn, 439, 440

short-nosed sturgeon, 85, 90, 91

Shoshone, 419

shovelnose sturgeon, 202

shrimping boat, 243, 314

Sibley, David, 159

Sierra Club, 389, 391, 392

Sierra Madre Mountains, 340

Sierra Nevada, 339, 350, 358, 372–95

Silent Spring, The, 65

silver, 43

silver maple, 223

Simpson, Charles Torrey, 276, 280; on Everglades, 278, 293

Singer Tract, 157–59, 169

Sioux, 419, 422

sirenian, 321

siscowet, 197

six-foot channel project (Mississippi), 222

Six Nations, 179

Skiagunsta, 133

Small, John Kunkel, 279, 280; on Everglades, 293

smallmouth bass, 222, 370

smartweed, 222

smelt, 27, 28, 117. *See also* rainbow smelt

smelting, 87

Smith, Adam, 43

Smith, Jeddediah, 378

Smith, John, 78, 83, 84, 96, 114, 116, 119, 178; on Bermuda rat plague, 269; on forests, 120; on Indian hunting, 129

Smith, Joseph, 431

Smithsonian Institution, 204, 247, 328

Smithsonian Tropical Research Institute, 455

smolt, Atlantic salmon, 18

Smyrna (Delaware), 93

snail darter, 212, 213, 455

Snake Hammock, 280

snow crab, 61

Snowdrift, 442

snow goose: greater, 94–96, 352; lesser, 94, 95, 352–54, 414, 415

snowshoe hare, 188

snowy egret, 204, 277, 292

snuffbox, 209

Snyder, Noel, 151, 153, 160

Society for the Preservation of National Parks, 392

Society of Jesus. *See* Jesuit

Sockeye salmon, 362, 365, 368, 369

Solenopsis geminate, 261

Somers, George, 268

Soncino, Raimondo de, 24

sooty tern, 265–67

South American fur seal, 318

South Carolina, 70–72, 86, 91, 95, 130, 152

South Dakota, 353, 407, 411, 422, 441, 448

Southern Pine Association, 139

Soviet Union, 456
soya, 455
Sparke, John, 281
Sparling, Gene, 158
sparrow: clay-colored, 399; Henslow's,
  399; vesper, 399
Species at Risk Act (2002), 169
spectacled cormorant, 321
sperm whale, 311
spiny lobster, 333
Spitsbergen, 49
spruce, 107, 109
Squanto, 118, 128
squash, 118
Stadacona, 176, 177, 179
stag, 110, 119. *See also* elk
stagshorn coral, 250
St. Agustín. *See* St. Augustine
Stamping Ground (Kentucky), 113
Stannard, David, 127
starving time, 78, 79, 81
State Oyster Police Force, 80
St. Augustine, 73
Steedman, J. G. W., Dr., 200
steelhead trout, 218, 360, 362, 370; red-
  band steelhead, 362
Steinbeck, John, 307
Steller, Georg, 319–23, 329, 330, 361
Steller sea lion, 318, 327, 328, 333
Steller's jay, 320, 378
Steller's sea cow, 321, 333
Stewart, George, 388, 389
Stewart, Granville, 439, 440
Stingray Point, 84
St. Johns River, 72, 276
St. Kilda, 31
St. Lawrence River, 94, 171, 176, 185, 189,
  196
St. Louis, 193

St. Lucia, 229, 296
St Lucie River (Florida), 279, 294
stockfish, 24
Stone, Livingston, 367
stool pigeon, 164
Storer, Tracy, 348
Stowe, Harriot Beecher, 289, 290
St. Peter, the, 319–21, 329, 330
Strachey, William, 268, 269
Straits of Anian, 300, 342, 360
Straits of Belle Isle, 51
strawberry, 121
striped bass, 86, 87, 89; decline, 90, 91
Structure and Function of Coral Reefs, The,
  226
strychnine, 356
sturgeon, 73, 117, 201, 202, 341;
  exploitation, 85, 89; historic size
  and abundance, 84–86, 195; threats,
  91. *See also* Atlantic sturgeon; lake
  sturgeon; pallid sturgeon; short-nosed
  sturgeon; shovelnose sturgeon
subsidies, 39, 41, 451, 457; farming, 439;
  seal hunt, 60
sugar cane, 255, 261
sugar maple, 108
sugar plantation: Caribbean, 87; Florida,
  294–96
Suidae, 130
suminoe oyster, 83
Susan Constant, 76
Susquehanna River, 90
sustainable growth, 457
Sutter, John, 379, 380
swamp cypress, 151, 275
Swampland Act, 292
swidden agriculture, 118
Swift, the, 145
swim frenzy, 240

swordfish, 62
sycamore, 109, 151, 152
sylvatic plague, 407

Tadoussac (Quebec), 176
Taensa, 205, 206
Taino, 228, 245, 247, 256, 260, 281
Talleyrand, 397
tallgrass prairie, 149, 400, 415, 426, 429
Tallgrass Prairie Preserve, 426
Tamiami Trail, 293, 294
Tanner, James, 158
Tayassidae, 130
Taylor Slough, 277, 280
teal, 96, 97
Tees, River, 14; return of salmon, 15
Teesdale, 14
Tehachapi Mountains, 337
Tellico Dam, 212, 213
Tenaya, Chief, 387
Tending the Wild, 346
Tennessee, 141, 192, 212
Tennessee Aquarium, 209
Tennessee riffleshell, 210
Tennessee River, 208, 210, 213
Tennessee Valley Authority, 212, 213
Tensas Swamp National Park, 158
Texas, 357, 404
Texas longhorn, 439, 440
thallium, 383
Thomes, William, 353
Thompson, David, 182, 183
Thoreau, David Henry, 3, 4, 65, 386
Three Toes, 442
thrush, 70
thylacine, 2
Tierra del Fuego, 68
Tieve, Diego de, 25
tipping point, 42, 454, 458

Tisquantum. See Squanto
tobacco, 138, 139, 239, 255
Tohono O'Odam, 392
Toledo, 224
tortoise, 256, 257
Tortugeuro, 239–41
total allowable catch, 59
totoaba, 306, 307, 314, 315
Townsend, Charles, 328
tragedy of the commons, the, 81, 88, 315, 335, 364, 453
Trail of Tears, 285, 286, 420
transition forest, 108
trayne. See oil
Treaty of Guadalupe Hidalgo, 357
Treaty of Paris, 190
Trevis, Lloyd, 348
tricolored heron, 291
trophic cascade, 61, 91
trout, 72
True Bear Stories, 349
True Repertory of the Wrecke, A., 268
trumpeter swan, 172
trunk (turtle), 244
tube-nosed goby, 219
Tulare Lake, 337
tule elk, 343–45
tulip poplar, 109, 110
tulotoma snail, 211
tuna, 43, 62
tundra swan, 96, 97, 100, 101
Tuolumne Meadows, 373, 377, 387, 391
turgid blossom, 209
turkey, 72, 109, 113, 120, 128, 134, 165; domestic, 168
turkey vulture, 277
Turner, Lucien, 102; on Eskimo curlews, 103
Turner, Steve, 458

turtle. *See* green turtle; hawksbill;
  Kemp's ridley turtle; leatherback
  turtle; loggerhead; olive ridley turtle
turtle excluder device, 243
Tuscarora, 179
Twain, Mark, 193, 194, 221, 293

Ulloa, Francisco de, 300, 303, 311, 317
Umatilla, 364
Uncle Tom's Cabin, 289, 290
United Fruit Company, 255
Up and Down California in 1860–1864, 376
uppewoc, 138
urchin barrens, 333, 334
U.S. Department of Agriculture, 447
U.S. Exploring Expedition, 362
U.S. Food Administration, 217
Utah, 431–33
Ute, 419
Uvarov, Boris, 435

Valley Forge (Pennsylvania), 147
Valparaiso, 342
vaquero, 439
vaquita, 313–15
Vermont, 113, 191
Verrazano, Giovanni de, 71, 72, 74; on
  fields, 119; on fire, 120; on forests, 107,
  110, 120
Vespucci, Amerigo, 23
Vikings: New World settlements, 11, 22,
  227; spread, 9
Villaraigosa, Mayor Antonio, 394
vine. *See* grape, wild
Vinland, 11, 21
Virginia, 69, 78, 80, 101, 119, 131, 133, 138,
  139, 167
Virginia Mountains, 380
Visalia Delta, 388

Vitis riparia, 12. *See also* grape, wild
Vizcaino, Sebastian, 301, 304, 316, 317;
  on abundance of California, 344;
  on Indian hunting, 326; on whales, 310
von Wied, Maximilian, 417
Voyages from Montreal, 396

Wacissa River (Florida), 157
Walden, 4
Walden Pond, 3
Walker, Thomas, 113
Walking Coyote, Samuel, 424
Wallace, Alfred Russel, 37, 254
walleye, 216, 222, 370
walleye pollock, 327, 328
walnut, 121
walrus, 54, 55
Walters, Carl, 42
Wampanoag, 119
wampum, 174
Wanchese, 75
wapiti, 112
Washington, George, 87, 189
Washington Consensus, 451
Washington DC, 438
Washington State, 337, 361
wasting disease. *See* mycobacteriosis
waterfowl, 117, 191, 382, 393; historical
  abundance, 96, 199, 203, 376;
  hunting, 98
Watlings Island, 227
Waymouth, George, on whaling, 49, 50
Wealth of Nations, The, 43
Weaver Bottoms (Minnesota), 222
Weldon (North Carolina), 86
Welland Ship Canal, 217
western scrub jay, 377
West Indian manatee, 232–35
West Indian top shell, 246, 249

West Tisbury (Martha's Vineyard), 168

West Virginia, 113

whalebone, 48

whale: baleen, 48; historic abundance in Atlantic, 46–49; historic abundance in Gulf of California, 310–16; Hudson Bay, 62, 187; toothed, 48. *See also* bowhead whale; gray whale; humpback whale; right whale; sperm whale

What I saw in California, 302

Wheaton, John Maynard, on passenger pigeons, 162

Wheeler Dam, 211

whelk. *See* West Indian top shell

whimbrel, 415

White, John, 69, 73, 74

white abalone, 334

whitecoat, 59

white ibis, 287, 291

white oak, 108

white pine, 107–9, 135, 172, 220

white pine weevil, 172

white pox disease, 251

white sturgeon, 197, 201

white-tailed deer, 110, 113, 128, 172, 282, 283; historical abundance, 111; modern abundance, 141; skin trade, 131–33, 182. *See also* key deer

Whitewater Falls, 148

Whitney, J. D., 386

Wild Animals I Have Known, 443

Wilderness Act, 390, 391; misconceptions, 5, 391; wording, 4

Wilderness Society, 390

Wilderness Trail, 113

Wild Fish Conservancy, 368

wild rice, 195, 198

Wild Salmon Center, 368

Wilkes, Charles, on salmon fishing, 362

Williams, Harry Percival, 441, 442

Williamsburg, 138

Wilmington, 155

Wilmot, Samuel, 216

Wilmot's Creek (Ontario), 196

Wilson, Alexander, 145–48, 150; on Carolina parakeets, 150, 151, 153, 155; on ivory-billed woodpeckers, 155, 156; on passenger pigeons, 164

Wilson Dam, 211

Wilson, Edward, 261, 385, 427

Wilson's petrel, 269

Wilson's phalarope, 375

Windward Road, The, 244

Wingate, David, 270

Wingfield, Edward Maria, 77

Winnebago (tribe), 199

Wintu, 367

Wisconsin, 163, 166

Wisconsin River, 200

Wiyot, 348

wolf, 458; in east, 122, 123, 127, 134, 141, 173; eating salmon, 360, 361; last wolves, 441–44; on plains, 420, 426–29, 431–32, 440; reintroduction, 444–49

Wolf, The, 445

Wood, Captain Abram Epperson, 389, 390

Woodland culture, 208

woodpecker, 172. *See also* acorn woodpecker; ivory-billed woodpecker

Woodruff vs. North Bloomfield Mining Company, 384

Wood, William, 3; on berries, 121; on cougars, 124; on domestic animals, 131; on Indian burning, 120; on moose, 112; on striped bass, 89; on sturgeon, 85; on waterfowl, 96

wood stork, 277, 287, 291
World War I, 139, 217, 438
World War II, 158, 327, 332
Worster, Donald, 3, 440; America as
    Paradise, 6
Wright, Thomas, on black bears, 126
Wyoming, 407

Yaqui, 302
yellow-bellied marmot, 345
yellow perch, 218
Yellowstone, 387, 389, 424, 448
Yellowstone, the, 421, 423
Yellowstone National Park, 423, 445, 446

yellow-tail flounder, 62
yeoman farmer, 137
Yokut, 339
York Factory, 187
York River, 91
Yosemite, 373, 379, 385, 387–89
Yosemite Falls, 388
Yount, George, 345, 348, 352
Yucatan Peninsula, 69, 228, 232

Zahniser, Howard, 390
zebra mussel, 214–16, 219
zooplankton, 42, 61